CAMBRIDGE
Idioms Dictionary

CAMBRIDGE UNIVERSITY PRESS
Cambridge, New York, Melbourne, Madrid, Cape Town, Singapore, São Paulo

Cambridge University Press
The Edinburgh Building, Cambridge CB2 2RU, UK

www.cambridge.org
Information on this title: www.cambridge.org/9780521677691

First published 1998
This edition published 2006

Printed in Italy by LegoPrint S.p.A

A catalogue record for this publication is available from the British Library

Library of Congress Cataloging-in-Publication Data
Cambridge idioms dictionary. – 2nd ed.
p. cm.
Rev. ed. of: English international dictionary of idioms. 1998.
ISBN 0-521-86037-7 – ISBN 0-521-67769-6
1. English language – Idioms – Dictionaries. 2. English language – Conversation and phrase books. I. Cambridge University Press. II. Cambridge international dictionary of idioms. III. Title: Idioms dictionary.

PE1460.C25 2006
423'.13–dc22
2006013124

ISBN-13 978-0-521-86037-6 hardback
ISBN-10 0-521-86037-7 hardback

ISBN-13 978-0-521-67769-1 paperback
ISBN-10 0-521-67769-6 paperback

Cambridge Idioms Dictionary

Academic Consultant
Professor Michael McCarthy

Senior Commissioning Editor
Elizabeth Walter

Theme pages and exercises
Julie Moore

Editorial Contributors
Virginia Klein, Mairi MacDonald, Melissa Good

Illustrations
David Shenton

Previous edition:
Project manager
Glennis Pye

Lexicographers
Stephen Curtis, Alice Grandison, Kerry Maxwell, Clea McEnery, Elaine McGregor, Sandra Pyne, Susannah Wintersgill, Kate Woodford

American English Consultants
Carol-June Cassidy, Sabina Sahni

Australian English Consultants
Barbara Gassman, Sue Bremner

Editorial Contributors
Annetta Butterworth, Dominic Gurney, Emma Malfoy, Geraldine Mark

Contents

Introduction

Idioms are a colourful and fascinating aspect of English. They are commonly used in all types of language, informal and formal, spoken and written. Your language skills will increase rapidly if you can understand idioms and use them confidently and correctly. One of the main problems students have with idioms is that it is often impossible to guess the meaning of an idiom from the words it contains. In addition, idioms often have a stronger meaning than non-idiomatic phrases. For example, *look daggers at someone* has more emphasis than *look angrily at someone*, but they mean the same thing. Idioms may also suggest a particular attitude of the person using them, for example disapproval, humour, exasperation or admiration, so you must use them carefully.

The *Cambridge Idioms Dictionary* explains the meaning and use of around 7,000 idioms in a clear and helpful way. It is a truly international dictionary: it covers current British, American and Australian idioms.

It includes:

- traditional idioms (e.g. turn a blind eye to sth, throw the baby out with the bathwater)
- idiomatic compounds (e.g. fall guy, turkey shoot)
- similes and comparisons (e.g. as dull as ditchwater, swear like a trooper)
- exclamations and sayings (e.g. Bully for you!, Over my dead body!)
- clichés (e.g. all part of life's rich tapestry, There's many a true word spoken in jest.)

The definitions are clear and precise. They have been written using a carefully controlled defining vocabulary of under 2,000 words. Every idiom is illustrated with examples based on sentences from the *Cambridge International Corpus*. This means that all of the examples reflect natural written and spoken English. Information about grammar is shown clearly, without complicated grammar codes. The origins of idioms are explained, where appropriate, to help understanding.

At the back of the book is a section with groups of idioms organised by topics such as 'agreeing and disagreeing' and 'explaining and understanding'. There are also photocopiable worksheets for use either in class or for studying alone.

We hope you enjoy using the *Cambridge Idioms Dictionary*. You can contact us or look at our other dictionaries on our website at: dictionary.cambridge.org.

How to use this dictionary

Finding an idiom

In general, idioms are found at their first important word. This is usually a verb, noun or adjective.

E.g.: **a house of cards** is at **house**
eat sb **out of house and home** is at **eat**

If the first word has more than one alternative, the idiom is at the first fixed word.

E.g.: **ask/cry for the moon** is at **moon**

However, if you look this idiom up at **ask** or **cry**, you will find a cross reference that looks like this:

See also: ask/cry for the **moon**

Idioms are not listed at the following verbs because there are so many of them: **come, get, give, go, have, make, put, take**.

If there is no noun, verb, or adjective in an idiom, it is found at the first word (excluding 'be').

E.g.: **on and off** is at **on**
be all in is at **all**

The form of the idiom

This is the basic form of the idiom.

paint the town red *informal*
to go out and enjoy yourself in the evening, often drinking a lot of alcohol and dancing • *Jack finished his exams today so he's gone off to paint the town red with his friends.*

Many idioms have different possible forms. When the difference is just one word, it is shown like this.

put/stick the knife in *British & Australian, informal*
to do or say something unpleasant to someone in an unkind way • *'No one in the office likes you, you know, Tim,' she said, putting the knife in.* • *The reviewer from The Times really stuck the knife in, calling it the worst play he'd seen in years.*

When the difference is more than one word, the alternative forms are shown on different lines.

raise (sb's) **hackles**
make (sb's) **hackles rise**
to annoy someone ✍ Hackles are the hairs on the back of a dog's neck which stand up when it is angry. • *The politician's frank interview may have raised hackles in his party.* • *The movie's pro-war message made many people's hackles rise.*

Words in brackets can be omitted, and the meaning will be the same.

have had it (up to here) *informal*
to be so angry about something that you do not want to continue with it or even think about it any more • *I've had it! From now on they can clear up their own mess.* • (often + **with**) *I've had it up to here with lawyers!*

'sb' means 'somebody'. It can be replaced by a person's name or by 'him/her/you/them/me/us'.

give sb **the push**
1 *British & Australian, informal* to end someone's employment • *After twenty years' loyal service, they gave her the push.*

'sth' means 'something'. It can be replaced by a non-human object.

let sth **ride**
to not take action to change something wrong or unpleasant • *Don't panic about low sales. Let it ride for a while till we see if business picks up.*

'your' can be replaced by 'his/her/their/our/my'.

mind your **own business** *informal*
something that you say in order to tell someone not to ask questions or show too much interest in other people's lives • *'How much did that dress cost you?' 'Mind your own business!'* • *I wish he'd mind his own business and stop telling me how to do my job!*

'swh' means 'somewhere'. It can be replaced by the name of a place.

be fresh from swh *British*
be fresh out of swh *American & Australian*
to have just finished education or training in a particular school or college and not have much experience • *Our course is taught by a young professor fresh out of law school.*

Other forms of the idioms

Some idioms have a basic form but are often found in slightly different constructions. If they are common, these different constructions are shown in sub-entries.

have your **head in the clouds**
to not know what is really happening around you because you are paying too much attention to your own ideas • *He's an academic. They've all got their heads in the clouds.*
with your **head in the clouds** • *He was walking along with his head in the clouds as usual when he tripped over a paving stone.*

Sometimes different parts of speech can be formed from the basic idiom. In this case, the main form is a verb phrase and the sub-entry is an adjective.

catch sb's **eye**
1 to be noticed by someone because you are looking at them • *She lit a cigarette while he tried to catch the waiter's eye.*
2 to be attractive or different enough to be noticed by people • *There were lots of dresses to choose from, but none of them really caught my eye.*
eye-catching • *There is an eye-catching mural in the hall.*

Opposites are shown as sub-entries.

strike a blow for sth/sb
to do something to support an idea or to change a situation to something which you believe is good • *He claims to be striking a blow for gender equality by employing an equal number of men and women.* • *This latest agreement will strike a blow for free trade within the EU.*
OPPOSITE strike a blow against/at sth/sb • *The court's decision strikes a blow against minority rights.*

Grammar

The basic grammatical structure of an idiom is shown in its entry. This idiom is followed by an infinitive.

be man enough to do sth
to be brave enough to do something • *He was man enough to admit he had made a mistake.*

This idiom is followed by an –ing form.

be on the brink of doing sth
to be likely to do something very soon • *The club's manager dismissed reports that he was on the brink of buying Peter Beardsley.*

This idiom is always reflexive.

tie yourself **(up) in knots**
to become very confused or worried when you are trying to make a decision or solve a problem

Idioms which are whole sentences start with a capital letter and end with a full stop or other punctuation.

Act your **age!**
something that you say to someone who is being silly to tell them to behave in a more serious way • *Oh, act your age, Chris! You can't expect to have your own way all the time.*

This idiom is always used in negative sentences.

not **look a gift horse in the mouth**
if someone tells you not to look a gift horse in the mouth, they mean that you should not criticize or feel doubt about something good that has been offered to you • *Okay, it's not the job of your dreams but it pays good money. I'd be inclined not to look a gift horse in the mouth if I were you.*

Common grammatical features are labelled at examples which demonstrate them. This idiom is often followed by the preposition 'of'.

a rich seam *formal*
a subject which provides a lot of opportunities for people to discuss, write about or make jokes about • (often + **of**) *Both wars have provided a rich seam of drama for playwrights and novelists alike.*

Examples

Examples show how idioms are used in natural speech and writing.

Very common collocations are shown in dark type.

put a bomb under sth/sb *British & Australian*
if you want to put a bomb under a person or an organization, you want to make them do things faster • *I'd like to put a bomb under those solicitors.*

slip through your **fingers**
1 if something you hope to achieve slips through your fingers, you do not manage to achieve it • *He has seen the world championship slip through his fingers twice.* • *This is my big chance to make a career in journalism. I can't **let it slip through my fingers**.*
2 if someone slips through your fingers they manage to escape from you • *We've got men guarding all the exits and more men on the roof. He won't slip through our fingers this time.*

Other things you need to know about idioms

Idioms with different forms in British, American or Australian are shown on separate lines.

blow a raspberry *British & Australian, informal*
give a raspberry *American, informal*
to make a rude noise by putting your tongue between your lips and blowing • (often + **at**) *A boy of no more than six appeared, blew a raspberry at me and then ran away.*

If an idiom is formal, informal, old-fashioned, etc. this is shown with a label.

be/go (out) on the razzle *British, informal, old-fashioned*
to enjoy yourself by doing things like going to parties or dances • *We're going out on the razzle on New Year's Eve – do you fancy coming?*

The history of idioms is explained when this helps to understand the meaning of the idiom.

be in the doldrums
1 if a business, an economy or a person's job is in the doldrums, it is not very successful and nothing new is happening in it ✍ The doldrums was the name for an area of sea where ships were not able to move because there was no wind.

Idioms on blue boxes are very common and useful to learn.

not **have a clue** *informal*
to have no knowledge of or no information about something • *'How much do houses cost in Yorkshire?' 'I haven't got a clue.'* • *(often +* **about***) Internet researchers in the 1980s didn't have a clue about the exciting online landscapes of the future.*

Regional labels

British	this idiom is only used in British English
American	this idiom is only used in American English
Australian	this idiom is only used in Australian English
mainly British	this idiom is mainly used in British English
mainly American	this idiom is mainly used in American English

Register labels

informal	idioms which are used with friends and family or people you know in relaxed situations
formal	idioms which are used in a serious or polite way, for example in business documents, serious newspapers and books, lectures, news broadcasts, etc.
very informal	idioms which are used in a very informal or not very polite way, often between members of a particular social group
old-fashioned	idioms which are still used but sound old-fashioned
taboo	idioms which are likely to offend people and are not used in formal situations
humorous	idioms which are intended to make people laugh
literary	idioms which are mainly used in literature

A

from A to Z
including all the facts about a subject • *This book tells the story of Diana's life from A to Z.*

get/go from A to B
to travel from one place to another place • *When I'm travelling, I try to work out the quickest way of getting from A to B.*

about

▶ See: About **time** too!

about-face

an about-face *mainly American*
a sudden and complete change of someone's ideas, plans, or actions • *In an about-face on the morning of his trial, the accused changed his plea to guilty.* • *Both papers* ***did an about-face*** *and published a condemnation of his actions.*

above

above and beyond sth
more than • *The support given to us by the police was above and beyond what we could have expected.* • *She doesn't receive any extra money, above and beyond what she's paid by the council.* • *The number of hours she puts into her job is definitely* ***above and beyond the call of duty****.* (= more than is expected of her)

▶ See also: be above **board**

absence

Absence makes the heart grow fonder.
something that you say which means being apart from someone that you love makes you love them even more • *'My boyfriend's going to South America and I won't see him for six months.' 'Ah well, absence makes the heart grow fonder.'*

accept

▶ See: accept/take sth as **gospel** (truth)

accident

an accident waiting to happen
a very dangerous situation in which an accident is very likely • *The speed that people drive along this road, it's an accident waiting to happen.*

(whether) by accident or design
whether intended to be this way or not • *The system, whether by accident or design, benefits people who live in the cities more than people who live in the country.*

more by accident than (by) design
because of luck and not because of skill • *I kicked the ball and, more by accident than design, it found its way into the net.*

accidentally

accidentally on purpose *humorous*
if you do something accidentally on purpose, you intend to do it but you pretend that it was an accident • *If I, accidentally on purpose, forget to bring her address with us, we won't be able to visit her after all.*

accidents

accidents will happen
something that you say in order to make someone feel less guilty when they have just damaged something that does not belong to them • *Oh well, accidents will happen. I can always buy another bowl.*

accord

of your **own accord**
if you do something of your own accord, you do it without being asked to do it • *She left of her own accord. I didn't tell her to go.*

account

be brought/called to account *formal*
to be forced to explain something you did wrong, and usually to be punished • *What concerns us most is that the people responsible for the violence should be brought to account.*

on sb's **account**
if you do something on someone's account, you do it because of that person • *Don't cook anything special on my account. I'm not even very hungry.*

on no account must/should sb do sth *formal*
if you tell someone that on no account must they do something, you mean that they must never, for any reason do that thing • *On no account must the contents of this document be shown to any other person.*

on your **own account**
if you do something on your own account, you do it by yourself or for yourself • *I decided to ask a few questions about the accident on my own account.*

take sth/sb **into account**
take account of sth/sb
to think about something or someone when you are making a decision or a judgement • *I hope they'll take her age into account when they're judging her work.* • (often + **that**) *They took into account that he'd never been in trouble before.* • *Her book* ***takes no account of*** (= does not consider) *recent research carried out in America.*

accounting

There's no accounting for taste!
something that you say when you cannot understand why someone likes something or someone • *'I love having a cold shower before breakfast.' 'Well, there's no accounting for taste!'*

ace

an ace in the hole *American*
an advantage that you have that other people do not know about • *The local team has an ace in the hole with their new player.*

come within an ace of sth/doing sth
to almost achieve something • *Linford Christie came within an ace of the world indoor record for the 100m last night.*
be within an ace of sth/doing sth
• *Her ambition to star in a musical is within an ace of being* (= is almost) *fulfilled following talks with a West End producer.*

have an ace up your **sleeve**
to have an advantage that other people do not know about • *The new game show has an ace up its sleeve. It will allow viewers to play from home and win prizes.*

play your **ace**
to do the thing that you know will bring you success • *The prosecutor played her ace, the results of the DNA tests on samples taken from the victim's clothing.*

aces

have/hold all the aces
to be in a strong position when you are competing with someone else, because you have all the advantages • *In the battle between road builders and environmentalists, the road builders seem to hold all the aces.*

Achilles

an Achilles' heel
a small fault in a person or system which might cause them to fail ✍Achilles was a man in Greek mythology (= an ancient set of stories) who was killed when he was injured on the heel. This was the only part of his body where he could be harmed. • *As a team they're strong on attack but they have a weak defence that might prove to be their Achilles' heel.* • *Vanity was his Achilles' heel.*

acid

an acid test
a test which will really prove the value, quality, or truth of something • *The new show was well received but viewing figures for the next episode will be the real acid test.* • *The acid test for the product will be whether people actually buy it.*

across

► See: across the **board**

act

Act your **age!**
something that you say to someone who is being silly to tell them to behave in a more serious way • *Oh, act your age, Chris! You can't expect to have your own way all the time.* • *I always want to tell middle-aged men in sports cars to act their age.*

a balancing/juggling act

a balancing/juggling act
a difficult situation in which you try to achieve several different things at the same time • *It's so exhausting having to perform the balancing act between work and family.* • *Keeping both sides in the dispute happy was a difficult juggling act which required an extraordinary degree of diplomacy.*

be a hard/tough act to follow
to be so good it is not likely that anyone or anything else that comes after will be as good • *Last year's thrilling Super Bowl, when the New York Giants beat the Buffalo Bills 20-19 will be a hard act to follow.* • *The new Chairman knows his predecessor is a tough act to follow.*

get your **act together** *informal*
to organize your activities so that you do things in an effective way • *If these people could ever get their act together, they could produce unbeatable wines.* • *You'd better get your act together and start looking for a job.*

get in on the act
to become involved in something successful that someone else has started so that you can become successful yourself • *We ran a successful local delivery business until other local companies started trying to get in on the act.*

▶ See also: **catch** sb in the act
clean up your act,
act/play the **fool**
act/play the **goat**

action

be out of action
1 if a machine or vehicle is out of action, it is not working or cannot be used • *I'm afraid the TV's out of action.*
put sth **out of action** • *The freezing weather has put many trains out of action.*
2 if someone who plays sport is out of action, they are injured and cannot play • *Towers is out of action with a broken wrist.*
put sb **out of action** • *A bad fall put him out of action for 2 months.*

a piece/slice of the action *informal*
being involved in something successful that someone else started • *Now research has proved that the new drug is effective, everyone wants a piece of the action.*

actions

Actions speak louder than words.
something that you say which means that what you do is more important than what you say • *Of course the government have made all sorts of promises but as we all know, actions speak louder than words.*

actress

as the actress said to the bishop *humorous*
used to show that someone has said something that could have another meaning connected to sex • *It slides right in the hole, as the actress said to the bishop.*

Adam

▶ See: not **know** sb from Adam

add

add fuel to the fire/flames
to make an argument or a bad situation worse • *His mild words only added fuel to the fire. Isabelle was furious.*

add insult to injury
to make a bad situation even worse for someone by doing something else to upset them • *First of all he arrived an hour late and then, to add insult to injury, he proceeded to complain about my choice of restaurant.*

ad hoc

ad hoc

an ad hoc organization or process is not planned but is formed or arranged when it is necessary for a particular purpose • *An ad hoc group of 75 parents is leading the protest to demand the resignation of the headteacher.* • *He doesn't charge a set amount for his work but negotiates fees on an ad hoc basis.*

ad infinitum

ad infinitum

if something happens or continues ad infinitum, it happens again and again in the same way, or it continues forever • *The TV station just shows repeats of old comedy programmes ad infinitum.* • *Her list of complaints went on and on ad infinitum.*

ad nauseam

ad nauseam

if someone discusses something ad nauseam, they talk about it so much that it becomes very boring • *She talks ad nauseam about how brilliant her children are.*

ado

much ado about nothing

a lot of trouble and excitement about something which is not important ✍*Much Ado about Nothing* is the title of a famous play by Shakespeare. • *People have been getting very upset about the seating arrangements for the Christmas dinner, but as far as I'm concerned it's all much ado about nothing.*

without further/more ado

without any delay • *And so, without further ado, let me introduce you to tonight's speaker.*

afraid

be afraid of your **own shadow**

to be extremely nervous and easily frightened • *She's always having panic attacks, she's the kind of person who's afraid of her own shadow.*

after

▶ See: after a **fashion**

against

▶ See: against your **better** judgement
go against the **grain**
against (all) the **odds**

age

come of age *slightly formal*

1 to reach the age when you are an adult and are legally responsible for your behaviour • *So what of all the fifty-thousand youngsters who come of age this spring? Who will they be voting for?*

2 something or someone that has come of age has reached full, successful, development • *After years of sophisticated mimicry, Japanese design has come of age.*

▶ See also: **act** your age!

agenda

at the top of the/sb's **agenda**
high on the/sb's **agenda**

if a subject or plan is at the top of someone's agenda, it is the most important thing they want to discuss or deal with • *The government has put education at the top of its agenda.* • *When the schoolteachers meet, classroom violence will be high on the agenda.* (= one of the most important subjects to discuss)

on the/sb's **agenda**

if a subject, plan, or activity is on the agenda, people are willing to talk about it, or to try to make it happen • *He made it clear that strike action was not on the agenda*

OPPOSITE **off the/**sb's **agenda** • *Foreign travel is off the agenda* (= not going to happen) *until we've got some money together.*

▶ See also: a **hidden** agenda
set the agenda

agony

▶ See: **pile** on the agony

ahead

▶ See: be ahead of the **game**
be ahead of the **pack**

aid

What's sth **in aid of?** *British & Australian informal*

something that you say when you want to know why someone has done something • *I heard the shouting from the other side of the building. What was that in aid of?* • *A present! What's this in aid of?*

aide-mémoire

an aide-mémoire *formal*
a piece of writing or a picture that helps you to remember something • *I write notes to myself and put them on the board. It serves as an aide-mémoire.*

ain't

▶ See: If it ain't **broke**, don't fix it.

air

be floating/walking on air
to be very happy and excited because something very pleasant has happened to you • *When the doctor told me I was going to have a baby, I was walking on air.*

be in the air
1 if a feeling, especially excitement, is in the air, everyone is feeling it at the same time • *There was excitement in the air as people gathered in the main square to hear the proclamation.*
2 to be going to happen very soon • *The daffodils are in flower and spring is definitely in the air.* • *I get the feeling that change is in the air.*

be up in the air
if a matter is up in the air, no decision has been made, often because other matters have to be decided first • *I may be moving to New Zealand, but it's still up in the air.*

▶ See also: **clear** the air
air your **dirty** laundry/linen in public
pluck sth out of the air

airs

airs and graces
false ways of behaving that are intended to make other people feel that you are important and belong to a high social class • *The other children started calling her 'princess' because of her airs and graces.* • *It's no good* ***putting on airs and graces*** *with me. I knew you when you were working in a shop!* • *Look at you* ***giving*** *yourself* ***airs and graces*** *– think you're better than us, do you?*

airy-fairy

airy-fairy *British informal*
not practical or not useful in real situations • *She's talking about selling her house and buying an old castle in Ireland. It all sounds a bit airy-fairy to me.*

aisles

▶ See: have sb **rolling** in the aisles

à la carte

à la carte
if you eat à la carte, you choose each dish from a separate list instead of eating a fixed combination of dishes at a fixed price • *I don't know whether to have the set-menu or go à la carte.*
à la carte • *I'm just going to pick a starter and a main course from the à la carte menu.*

Aladdin

an Aladdin's cave *British*
a place that contains many interesting or valuable objects • (often + **of**) *We found a shop that was a real Aladdin's cave of beautiful antiques.*

à la mode

à la mode
fashionable • *Velvet trousers are à la mode this season.*

alarm

set (the) alarm bells ringing
if something sets alarm bells ringing, it makes you feel worried because it is a sign that there may be a problem • *Symptoms which should set alarm bells ringing are often ignored by doctors.*
ring/sound alarm bells • *The huge vote for fascist candidates should ring alarm bells* (= cause people to worry) *across Europe.*
alarm bells start to ring • *Alarm bells started to ring* (= I became worried) *when I found out that he still lived with his mother.*

albatross

albatross around/round your **neck**
literary
something that you have done or are connected with that keeps causing you problems and stops you from being successful ✍An albatross is a large white bird. In the poem *The Rime of the Ancient Mariner*, by Samuel Taylor Coleridge, a man on a ship kills an albatross which is then hung round his neck to show that he has brought bad

luck. • *The company that he founded in 1983 is now an albatross around his neck, making losses of several hundreds of thousands a year.*

alert

be on full/red alert

if soldiers are on full alert, they know that a situation is dangerous and are prepared to act immediately if necessary • *The British flagship in the area went to battle stations and remained on full alert for twenty minutes.*

be put on full/red alert • *The army was put on red alert as the peace talks began to break down.*

al fresco

al fresco

outside • *We ate al fresco under the olive trees.* • *An al fresco performance of The Tempest was the highlight of our visit.*

alive

be alive and kicking

to continue to live or exist and be full of energy • *She said she'd seen him last week and he was alive and kicking.* • *Theatre in Madrid is alive and kicking.*

be alive and well

to continue to be popular or successful • *Despite rumours to the contrary, feminism is alive and well.* • (often + **and** doing sth) *Quadrophonic sound is alive and well and making money for its inventor.*

be alive with sth

to be covered with or full of something that is moving • *Don't sit there – the grass is alive with ants.*

▶ See also: **eat** sb alive
skin sb alive

all

all in all

thinking about all parts of a situation together • *All in all, I think we can say the visit was a success.*

all or nothing

completely or not at all • *If she can't be the best she won't even compete.* ***It's all or nothing*** *with her.* • *Tom has an all or nothing approach to relationships.*

all told

in total • *There were 550 people there, all told.*

be all in *old-fashioned*

to be very tired and unable to do any more • *I've had six children to look after today and I'm all in.*

be all over sb

to touch and kiss someone sexually again and again in a public situation • *He was all over her at the party last night.* • *(humorous) It was disgusting, he was* ***all over her like a rash****.*

be all over the shop *British informal*
be all over the lot *American informal*

1 to be scattered in a lot of different places • *What have you been doing with your clothes? They're all over the shop!*

2 to be confused and badly organized • *I've been so unimpressed by their campaign. They're all over the shop.* • *How can I tell what's the best deal when lending rates are all over the lot?*

not **be all there** *informal*

to be slightly crazy • *Some of the things she said made me think she's not quite all there.*

be all very well
be all well and good

if you say that something is all very well, you mean that although it is good in some ways, it is bad in some ways too • (usually + **but**) *Electric heating is all very well, but what happens if there's a power cut?*

be as [fast/hot/thin etc.] as all get out *American & Australian informal*

to be extremely fast, hot, thin etc. • *He's a terrific runner – as fast as all get out.*

be [faster/hotter/thinner etc.] than all get out • *It's hotter than all get out* (= extremely hot) *in here.*

give your **all**

to do everything you can in order to achieve something • *You've really got to give your all in the championships.*

give it your **all**

to do everything you can in order to achieve something • *I want the job badly and I'm prepared to give it my all.*

go all out

to use all your effort and energy to

achieve something • (often + to do sth) *They went all out to make the party a success.* • (often + **for**) *The team is going all out for victory.*

all-out • (always before noun) *We made an all-out effort to finish decorating the hall by the end of the weekend.*

it's all (that) sb **can do** to do sth

if it's all someone can do to do something, they just manage to do it although it is difficult • *It was all I could do to stop myself screaming with pain.*

It's all the same to me. *British, American & Australian*

It's all one to me. *Australian*

something that you say when it is not important to you what happens • *'Would you prefer to go out for a meal or eat in?' 'It's all the same to me.'*

That's sb **all over!** *informal*

something that you say when you are talking about something bad that someone has done and you want to say that it is typical of their character • *She's always complaining. That's Claire all over.*

to cap/crown/top it all

something that you say when you want to tell someone the worst event in a series of bad events that has happened to you • *He spilled red wine on the carpet, insulted my mother, and to cap it all, broke my favourite vase.*

► See also: for all sb **cares**
be all in a **day**'s work
I've never [felt/heard/seen etc.] sth in all my (born) **days**!
be all **ears**
if all **else** fails
all **eyes** are on sb/sth
be all **eyes**
be all **fur** coat and no knickers
It's all **go**.
All in **good** time.
It's all **Greek** to me.
be all **heart**
at all **hours** (of the day and night)
at all **hours** (of the night)
to all **intents** and purposes
and all that **jazz**
for all sb **knows**
be all in the/your **mind**
in all **modesty**
not be all **moonlight** and roses
be all **mouth**
in all but **name**
That's all you **need**!
be all **smiles**
be all **sweetness** and light
all **systems** go
be all **talk** (and no action)
would not do sth for all the **tea** in China
be all **things** to all men
be all fingers and **thumbs**
go all the **way**
be all **wet**
All **work** and no play (makes Jack a dull boy).
That's all she **wrote**!

alley

be (right) up sb's **alley** *informal*

be (right) down sb's **alley** *American & Australian informal*

if something is right up someone's alley, it is exactly the type of thing that they know about or like to do • *The job should be right up Steve's alley – working with computers, software and stuff.*

allow

► See: allow/give sb (a) **free** rein
allow/give sth (a) **free** rein
allow/give sth **full** play

all-rounder

an all-rounder *British & Australian*

someone who is good at many different things, especially in sport • *The most recent member of the England team is a good all-rounder.*

all-singing

all-singing, all-dancing *humorous*

very modern and technically advanced • *She showed us the new all-singing, all-dancing graphics software she'd bought for her computer.*

alma mater

the alma mater *American*

the official song of a school, college or university • *We ended our class reunion by singing the alma mater.*

your **alma mater** *formal*

the school, college, or university where you studied • *She has been offered the position of professor of international economic policy at Princeton, her alma mater.*

alone

go it alone

to do something by yourself and without help from other people • *Honda has chosen to go it alone rather than set up a joint venture with an American partner.*

leave/let well alone *British, American & Australian*

leave/let well enough alone *American*

to leave something the way it is, because trying to improve it might make it worse • *In cases of back trouble, it's difficult to know whether to operate or leave well alone.* • *I'm not doing any more on that painting – it's time to let well enough alone.*

along

▶ See: somewhere along the **line**
along the **lines** of sth
along the **way**

altogether

in the altogether *humorous*

naked • *He was just standing there in the altogether.*

always

▶ See: always the **bridesmaid**, never the bride

amber

an amber gambler *British informal*

someone who drives very fast past the lights that control traffic when the signal is about to tell them to stop • *She's an impatient driver – a bit of an amber gambler.*

ambulance

an ambulance chaser *informal*

a lawyer who finds work by persuading people who have been hurt in accidents to ask for money from the person who injured them • *He was a notorious ambulance chaser. He made millions out of other people's misfortunes.*

amen

Amen to that.

said to show that you agree strongly with something that someone has just said • *'Thank goodness we didn't go.' 'Amen to that!'*

American

be as American as apple pie

to be typically American • *Country and western music is as American as apple pie.*

amiss

not **go amiss** *British, American & Australian informal*

not **come amiss** *British & Australian informal*

if something would not go amiss, it would be useful and might help to improve a situation • (usually in conditional tenses) *A word of apology would not go amiss.* • *Some extra helpers never come amiss.*

amour propre

amour propre *formal*

the good feelings and respect you have for yourself • *The critics' negative reaction to his first novel wounded his amour propre.*

another

▶ See: be another/a different **kettle** of fish
live to fight another day
another **nail** in the coffin
but that's another **story**
another **string** to your bow
be in another **world**

answer

answer the call of nature *humorous*

to urinate (= pass liquid from the body) • *I had to go into the woods to answer the call of nature.*

sb's **answer to** sb/sth

someone or something that is just as good as a more famous person or thing in the place where it comes from • *The Kennedy clan was America's answer to the royal families of Europe.*

the answer to sb's **prayers**

someone or something that someone has needed very much for a long time • *A new supermarket delivery service was the answer to my prayers.*

not **take no for an answer**

if someone will not take no for an answer, they continue asking for something although their request has already been refused • *I've told her again and again that you're too busy to see her, but she won't take no for an answer.*

▶ See also: have a **lot** to answer for

ants

raise/up the ante

to increase your demands or to increase the risks in a situation, in order to achieve a better result ✍The ante is an amount of money that must be paid in card games before each part of the game can continue. • *The government has upped the ante by refusing to negotiate until a ceasefire has been agreed.*

ants

have ants in your **pants** *humorous*

to not be able to keep still because you are very excited or worried about something • *She's got ants in her pants because she's going to a party tonight.*

any

▶ See: Any **port** in a storm.
at any **price**
(in) any **way**, shape, or form
no one will be any the **wiser**

anybody

anybody who is anybody *humorous*

if anybody who is anybody is doing something, all the most famous and important people are doing that thing • *Anybody who is anybody will be at the Queen's birthday celebrations.*

be anybody's guess

if a piece of information is anybody's guess, no one knows it • *Why Becky left is anybody's guess.* • *'So what's going to happen now?' '**That's anybody's guess.**'*

ape

go ape *informal*
go apeshit *taboo*

to become very angry • *Vicky'll go ape when she sees this mess.*

apology

be an apology for sth *humorous*

to be a very bad example of something • *That old thing is an apology for a car.*

appearances

▶ See: **keep** up appearances

appetite

▶ See: **whet** sb's appetite

apple

An apple a day keeps the doctor away. *old-fashioned*

something that you say which means eating an apple every day will keep you healthy • *If 'an apple a day keeps the doctor away,' then why have I got this terrible cold?*

the apple of sb's **eye**

the person who someone loves most and is very proud of • *His youngest son was the apple of his eye.*

a bad/rotten apple

one bad person in a group of people who are good • *You'll find the occasional rotten apple in every organization.*

applecart

▶ See: **upset** the applecart

apple-pie

be in apple-pie order

to be very tidy and in good order • *Wendy kept all her belongings in apple-pie order.*

apples

apples and oranges *American*

if two people or things are apples and oranges, they are completely different • *You can't compare inner city schools and schools in the suburbs – they're apples and oranges.*

She'll be apples. *Australian informal*
She's apples. *Australian informal*

something that you say in order to tell someone that they do not need to worry and that everything will happen as it should • *'What if it rains for the wedding?' 'Don't worry, she'll be apples.'*

▶ See also: How do you **like** them apples!

aprés-ski

aprés-ski

the social activities that take place in the evening at hotels and restaurants in towns where people go to ski • *If it's aprés-ski you're after, this town with its hundred or so bars is the resort for you.* • *Bars and dancing are among the aprés-ski activities for the adults.*

a priori

a priori *formal*
accepted without being thought about or questioned • *The existence of God is a priori for most people with a religious faith.* • *In a court of law, a priori assumptions about guilt and innocence can be dangerous.*

argue

argue the toss *British & Australian informal*
to disagree with a decision or statement • *Are you prepared to argue the toss when you might have to go to court to prove it?*

argy-bargy

argy-bargy *British informal*
loud arguments • *Did you hear all that argy-bargy outside the Kingston Arms last night?*

ark

be out of the ark *British & Australian*
to be very old-fashioned • *My granny's hat was straight out of the ark.*

went/had gone out with the ark *British & Australian humorous*
if an object or method went out with the ark, it is not used any more • *These old manual printing presses went out with the ark – everything's computerized these days.*

arm

hold/keep sb **at arm's length**
to not allow someone to become too friendly with you • *I always had the feeling she was keeping me at arm's length.*

put the arm on sb *American informal*
to try to force someone to do something • *If he won't pay up, we'll get Rick to put the arm on him.*

▶ See also: could do sth with one arm/hand tied behind their **back**
chance your arm
cost (sb) an arm and a leg
twist sb's arm

armed

be armed to the teeth
if a person or a country is armed to the teeth, they have many weapons • *We walked past a group of soldiers, armed to the teeth.*

armpit

be the armpit of the world/universe *humorous*
to be a very unpleasant and often dirty place • *For some people it's an exciting, big city – for others it's the armpit of the universe.*

arms

be up in arms
to be very angry • (often + **about**) *The students are up in arms about the standard of teaching at the college.* • (often + **over**) *Local traders are up in arms over the effect of the new parking regulations on their businesses.*

around

have been around (a bit) *informal*
if someone has been around, they have had a lot of experience of life and know a lot of things • *She's been around a bit – she should know how to look after herself.*

arse

arse about face *British & Australian very informal*
if something is arse about face, it is placed or arranged the opposite way to the way it should be • *No wonder it doesn't look right, mate, you've got the whole frame in arse about face.*

arse over tip *British very informal*
arse over tit *British & Australian very informal*
if you go arse over tip, you turn upside down with your feet above your head • *He put on the front brake too hard and went arse over tip over the handlebars.*

be (right) up sb's **arse** *British very informal*
to be driving too close to the car in front of you • *That police car's been up my arse since we left London.*

In the following phrases, **arse** is used in British and Australian English, and **ass** in American English.

can't tell your **arse from** your **elbow** *very informal*
not **know** your **arse from** your **elbow** *very informal*
if you can't tell your arse from your elbow, you are stupid and become confused about simple things • *It's no*

good asking him to organize anything – he can't tell his arse from his elbow.

get your **arse in gear** *very informal*
to force yourself to start working or to hurry • *If she doesn't get her arse in gear she'll be late again.*

get off your **arse** *very informal*
to stop being lazy and start doing something • *Tell that lazy sod to get off his arse and get some work done!*

kiss/lick sb's **arse** *taboo*
to try too hard to please someone and to agree with everything they say, in a way which other people find unpleasant • *I'm not interested in promotion if you have to lick the boss's arse to get it.*
arse-licker/kisser *taboo* • *He surrounded himself with arse-lickers.*

Move/Shift your **arse!** *very informal*
something that you say to tell someone to hurry or to get out of your way • *Shift your arse! We're late.*

My arse! *very informal*
something that you say after repeating something someone has just said, in order to show that you do not believe it • *'She's offering good money.' 'Good money, my arse! I can't feed my kids on that!'*

Shove/Stick sth **up your arse!** *taboo*
something that you say in order to tell someone in a very angry way that you do not want or need something they could give you • *Tell Mr Peabody he can take his job and shove it up his arse!*

► See also: **Kiss** my arse!
Lick my arse!
sit on your arse
talk out of your arse
work your arse/backside off

arsed

can't be arsed *British taboo*
if you can't be arsed, you will not make the necessary effort to do something • (often + to do sth) *I can't be arsed to go to the party. It's too far away.*

article

an article of faith
something that someone believes very strongly without thinking about whether it could be wrong • *It was an article of faith with Mona that everything she used should be recycled.*

arty-farty

arty-farty *British informal*
artsy-fartsy *American informal*
something or someone that is arty-farty tries too hard to seem connected with serious art, and is silly or boring because of this • *Rob's friends were a couple of arty-farty types who talked endlessly about the decline of the modern American novel.*

as

as is
exactly as something is without any changes or improvements made to it • *I'll have to hand this report in as is – there's no time to update it.*

ashes

► See: **rake** over the ashes

ask

ask for it
if you say that someone who gets hurt or punished was asking for it, you mean that they deserved what happened to them • *Picking a fight with those hooligans was really asking for it.* • *Fired? Well, she asked for it, didn't she?*

Don't ask me. *informal*
something that you say when you do not know the answer to a question • *'Who's in charge round here?' 'Don't ask me. I'm as confused as you.'* • (often + question word) *She's decided to dye her hair bright green, don't ask me why.*

I ask you! *informal*
something that you say in order to show your surprise or anger at something someone has done • *They stayed for a month and left without even saying thank you! Well, I ask you!*

You may well ask! *humorous*
Well may you ask! *humorous, formal*
something that you say when someone asks you about something which you think is strange, funny, or annoying • *'Why is Timothy sitting in the kitchen with a saucepan balanced on top of his head?' 'You may well ask!'* • *'What happened to the money you gave Sharon to buy food?' 'Well may you ask! She says she lost it.'*

▶ See also: ask/cry for the **moon**

asking

be asking for trouble
to behave stupidly in a way that is likely to cause problems for you • *Drinking and driving is just asking for trouble.*

be sb's **for the asking**
if something is someone's for the asking, they only have to ask for it and it will be given to them • *The contract was Ron's for the asking.*

asleep

be asleep at the switch *American*
if someone is asleep at the switch, they are not ready to act quickly to avoid problems and do their job well • *Let's face it, if employees were stealing all that money, then management was asleep at the switch.*
fall asleep at the switch • *The Party was simply too confident of victory and fell asleep at the switch.*

aspersions

▶ See: **cast** aspersions on sb/sth

ass

sb's **ass is on the line** *American very informal*
if someone's ass is on the line, they are in a situation where they will be blamed if things go wrong • *I hope this conference is a success – my ass is on the line here.*

ass over teacup/teakettle *American very informal*
if you go ass over teacup, you turn upside down with your feet above your head • *She slipped and fell ass over teakettle down the hill.*

be on sb's **ass**
1 *American very informal* to annoy someone by always watching what they are doing and criticizing them • *She was on my ass all morning telling me the things I was doing wrong.*
2 *American very informal* to be driving too close to the car in front of you • *There's a Mercedes on my ass and he's making me nervous.*

get sb's **ass** *American very informal*
to find someone and punish them for something they have done • *Don't worry – the cops'll get that maniac's ass.*

make an ass of yourself
to behave in a silly way • *Simon drank too much and made a complete ass of himself at the party.*

▶ See also: **bust** your ass
chew sb's ass (out)
cover your ass
haul ass
kick (sb's) ass
kiss (sb's) ass
work your arse/backside off

astray

▶ See: **lead** sb astray

at

be at it
1 *informal* if two people are at it, they are having sex • *They're **at it the whole time**!*
2 *informal* if two or more people are at it, they are talking too much in a way that annoys other people • *I wish they'd shut up – they've been at it all morning.*

atmosphere

▶ See: you could **cut** the atmosphere with a knife

au courant

au courant
1 *formal* if you are au courant, you have the most recent information about something or someone • (usually + **with**) *I bought a copy of Hello magazine in an attempt to be au courant with the lives of the rich and famous.*
2 *mainly American* modern and fashionable • *If you want to keep your au courant status this winter, you won't be wearing black.*

au fait

be au fait with sth
to know a lot about a subject • *Are you au fait with the latest developments in computer technology?*

au naturel

au naturel *formal*
1 without clothes or without make-up (= substances that women put on their faces to improve their appearance) • *I thought I'd leave off the lipstick for a couple of days and go au-naturel.*
2 without having been cooked, or cooked in

a very simple way with nothing added • *You can stew these berries briefly with a little sugar or you can eat them au naturel.*

automatic

on automatic pilot *informal*
on autopilot *informal*

if you are on automatic pilot, or do something on automatic pilot, you do something without thinking about what you are doing, usually because you have done it many times before • *By the second week of the election campaign she was making all her speeches on automatic pilot.*

autumn

autumn years *literary*

the later years of a person's life, especially after they have stopped working • *He spent his autumn years surrounded by family and friends.*

avant-garde

the avant-garde

the artists, writers, musicians etc. of any period whose work is very modern and very different to what has been done before • *Since 1948, the exhibition has been a major showcase for the avant-garde.*

avant-garde • *They are currently exhibiting a collection of postwar avant-garde art from Japan.*

avoid

avoid sb/sth **like the plague**

to try very hard to avoid someone or something that you do not like ✍A plague is a serious disease which kills many people. • *I'm not a fan of parties – in fact I avoid them like the plague.*

away

▶ See: be away with the **fairies**

awkward

an awkward customer

a person, group, or thing that causes problems, usually because they will not behave in the way you want or expect them to • *There's usually at least one awkward customer who insists on doing everything according to the rule book.*

axe

get the axe
be given the axe

1 if a person gets the axe, they lose their job • *Senior staff are more likely to get the axe because the company can't afford their high salaries.*

2 if a plan or a service gets the axe, it is stopped • *My research project was the first thing to be given the ax when the new boss took over.*

have an axe to grind

to have a strong opinion about something, which you are often trying to persuade other people is correct • *As a novelist, he has no political axe to grind.*

Bb

babe

a babe in the woods *American & Australian*
someone who has not had much experience of life and trusts other people too easily • *When it comes to dealing with men, she's a babe in the woods.*

baby

the baby blues
a feeling of sadness that some women experience after they have given birth to a baby • *According to this article, as many as 60% of women suffer from the baby blues.*

a baby boomer *mainly American*
someone who was born between 1945 and 1965, a period in which a lot of babies were born • *Clinton was the first baby boomer in the White House.* • *The ads are supposed to appeal to the* ***baby boomer generation****.*

► See also: **cry** like a baby
throw the baby out with the bath water
wet the baby's head

back

at the back of your **mind**
if a thought that worries you is at the back of your mind, it is always in your mind although you do not spend time thinking about it • *It's always at the back of my mind that the illness could reccur.*

at/in the back of beyond
in a place which is far away from other towns and difficult to get to • *He lives in some tiny, remote village in the back of beyond.*

back and forth
if someone or something moves back and forth between two places, they move from one place to the other place again and again • *Nurses went back and forth among the wounded, bringing food and medicine.*

back the wrong horse
to support a person or thing that fails • *It was only after we'd invested all the money that we discovered we'd been backing the wrong horse.*

back-to-back *mainly American*
back-to-back events happen one after the other • *He appeared in three back-to-back interviews on television last night.* • *His idea of a good time is to go to three French movies back-to-back.*

be fed up/sick to the back teeth *British & Australian informal*
to be bored or angry because a bad situation has continued for too long or a subject has been discussed too much • (often + **with**) *He's been treating me badly for two years and, basically, I'm fed up to the back teeth with it.* • (often + **of**) *You're probably sick to the back teeth of hearing about my problems!*

be on sb's **back** *informal*
to keep asking someone to do something, or to keep criticizing someone in a way that annoys them • *He's still on my back about those end of term reports.*

be on the back burner
if a plan is on the back burner, no one is dealing with it at present, but it has not been completely forgotten • *For the moment, strike action is on the back burner.*
put sth **on the back burner** • *Plans for a new sports complex have been put on the back burner.*

behind sb's **back**
if you do something behind someone's back, you do it without them knowing, in a way which is unfair • *I don't want to talk about it behind his back.* • *She was accused of* ***going behind*** *her colleagues'* ***backs*** *to talk to management.*

by/through the back door
not in a direct, official, or honest way • *He accused the government of privatizing the health service through the back door.*
back-door • *The minister dismissed suggestions that the move was a back-door attempt to introduce national identity cards.*

could do sth **with one arm/hand tied behind** their **back** *informal*
if someone could do something with one hand tied behind their back, they can do it very easily • *Her part in the film wasn't very demanding – she could have played it with one hand tied behind her back.*

fit/write sth **on the back of a postage stamp**
if you say you could write what you know about a subject on the back of a postage stamp, you mean you know very little about that subject • *What I know about car maintenance could be written on the back of a postage stamp.*

get sb **off** your **back** *informal*
to stop someone trying to force you to do something, or to stop someone criticizing you • *I had to sell my house to get the creditors off my back.*
get off sb's **back** *informal* • *Can't you just get off his back and let him rest for a while?*

get/put sb's **back up** *informal*
to do or say something which annoys someone ✍When a cat feels angry it raises its back. • *She put my back up immediately by interrupting everything I said.*

have your **back against/to the wall**
to have very serious problems which limit the ways in which you can act • *With rising labour costs, industry has its back to the wall.* • *When **his back was against the wall** he became very aggressive.*

off the back of a lorry *British humorous*
off the back of a truck *Australian humorous*
if you say that you got something off the back of a lorry, you mean that it was probably stolen • *I don't know where he gets this stuff – probably off the back of a lorry.* • *There's a new stereo too which, I suspect, **fell off the back of a lorry**.*

put your **back into** sth
to use a lot of physical effort to try to do something • *You could dig this plot in an afternoon if you put your back into it.*

take a back seat
1 if an activity takes a back seat, you spend less time doing that than other things • *He's been putting all his energies into house-hunting recently so his studies have had to take a back seat.* • (sometimes + **to**) *In my early twenties, politics very much took a back seat to sport and socializing.*
2 to let other people take a more active and responsible part in an organization or a situation • *I was content to take a back seat and let the rest of my family deal with the crisis.*

turn your **back on** sb
to refuse to help someone • *These people are appealing to our government to help them. We can't just turn our backs on them.*

when/while sb's **back is turned**
while someone is somewhere else or unable to notice what is happening • *When my mother's back was turned, my grandmother would give me chocolates.*
the minute sb's **back is turned** • *The minute the teacher's back is turned* (= as soon as she cannot see them)*, they start messing around and throwing things at each other.*

▶ See also: **break** your back
break the back of sth
cover your back
know sth like the back of your hand
be back on the **rails**
ride on the back of sth
You **scratch** my back and I'll **scratch** yours.
be [glad/happy/pleased etc.] to **see** the back of sb/sth
stab sb in the back
talk out of the back of your head
turn your back on sth
watch your back

backed

be backed into a corner
to be forced into a difficult situation which you have little control over • *I feel I've been backed into a corner and I have no choice but to sign the contract.*

back-handed

▶ See: a back-handed **compliment**

backing

backing and filling *American*
continuously changing or delaying a decision • *After much backing and filling she finally agreed to hand over the company's books.*

backroom

a backroom boy *informal*
someone who does a lot of work in the type of job where they are not often seen by the public • (often plural) *Editors are very much the backroom boys of the film world.*

backs

▶ See: **live** off the backs of sb

backseat

a backseat driver
1 a passenger in a car who continuously tells the driver how they should drive • *Mike's a real backseat driver and I find it so irritating.*
2 *mainly American* someone who expects to control things although it is not their responsibility to do this • *Tell her you're in charge now. It's time she stopped being a backseat driver.*

backside

get off your **backside** *British & Australian very informal*
to stop being lazy and start doing something • *It's time the government got off its backside and did something about improving the railways.*

sit (around) on your **backside** *British & Australian very informal*
to do nothing, especially when other people are busy or need your help • *How do people expect things to change if they just sit on their backsides and don't bother to vote?*

▶ See also: **work** your arse/backside off

backward

not **be backward in coming forward** *British & Australian humorous*
to be confident and always ready to express an opinion • *If he doesn't like it, he'll tell you. He's not exactly backward in coming forward.*

without a backward glance
if you leave without a backward glance, you are completely happy to leave and have no sad feelings about it • *She left the city she had lived in all her life without a backward glance.*

backwards

bend/lean over backwards to do sth *British, American & Australian*
fall over backwards to do sth *Australian*
to try very hard to do something, especially to help or please someone else • *Banks are bending over backwards to help those in difficulties.*

▶ See also: **know** sth backwards

bacon

▶ See: **save** sb's bacon

bad

bad blood
feelings of hate between people because of arguments in the past • (often + **between**) *Police say the arson attack may have been the result of bad blood between the two families.*

a bad egg *mainly American informal*
someone who behaves in a bad or dishonest way • *He's a bad egg – don't believe anything he says.*

A bad workman blames his tools.
something that you say when someone blames the objects they are using for their own mistakes • *'This oven burns everything.' 'You know what they say, a bad workman blames his tools.'*

be bad news
to be unpleasant and to have a bad effect on other people or situations • *I've worked with her in the past and I'm telling you she's bad news.* • (often + **for**) *The government's failure to be firm on air quality is bad news for the environment.*

be in a bad way *British & Australian*
to be ill, unhappy, or in a bad state • *She was thin and tired-looking and generally in a bad way.* • *After 17 years of Conservative government, the country was in a bad way.*

be in bad odour with sb *British & Australian old-fashioned*
be in bad odor with sb *American old-fashioned*
if you are in bad odour with someone, they are angry with you because of something you have done • (often + **with**) *He's in bad odour with his business partners for having pulled out of the deal*

at the last minute.

give sth/sb **a bad name**

to cause people to lose respect for something or someone • *A few badly behaved football fans give all football supporters a bad name.*

have a bad name • *Foreign aid has a bad name because it often fails to help the people most in need.*

give sth **up as a bad job**

to stop doing something because you do not feel it is worth continuing • *After three attempts to explain the joke I gave it up as a bad job.*

go from bad to worse

if a situation goes from bad to worse, it gets worse than it already was • *The troubles started when John lost his job last March and things have gone from bad to worse ever since.*

have a bad hair day

1 *humorous* to not feel attractive or happy all day because you cannot make your hair look nice • *I'm having a bad hair day today – I just couldn't do a thing with it this morning.*

2 *humorous* if a machine has a bad hair day, it does not work as it should all day • *My computer's having a bad hair day.*

have got it bad *informal, humorous*

to be very much in love • *He missed the football game to see her – he must have got it bad!*

take the bad with the good

to accept the unpleasant parts of a situation as well as the pleasant parts • *Bringing up children certainly has its problems, but you learn to take the bad with the good.*

► See also: a bad/rotten **apple**
leave a bad taste in your mouth
turn up like a bad penny

bad-mouth

bad-mouth sb/sth

to say unpleasant things about someone or something, especially in order to spoil other people's opinions of them • *She's always bad-mouthing her colleagues.* • *Bad-mouthing the police is hardly an original occupation.*

bag

bag and baggage *slightly formal*

with all the things that you own • *We were told we'd have to be out of the house, bag and baggage, in a week's time.*

a bag lady

a woman who has no home and carries everything she owns around with her in plastic bags • *Did you see that bag lady looking through the rubbish at the side of the road?*

a bag of bones *informal*

a person or animal that is extremely thin • *All the plumpness she'd acquired in middle age had gone. She was a bag of bones.*

sb's **bag of tricks**

all the clever methods by which someone achieves something • *It remains to be seen what this side will pull out of their bag of tricks for the semi-final.*

not **be** your **bag** *informal*

to not be something that you are interested in • *Country music isn't really my bag.*

in the bag *informal*

if something is in the bag, you are certain to get it or to achieve it ✍Someone who hunts puts what they have killed in a bag. • *Once we'd scored the third goal, the match was pretty much in the bag.* • *Nobody knows who'll get the job, despite rumours that Keating* ***has it in the bag****.*

► See also: be a bag of **nerves**
pull something out of the bag

bags

► See: **pack** your bags

bait

swallow/take the bait

to accept something that is only being offered to you so that you will do something • *The offer of a free radio with every television proved very popular, and hundreds of shoppers swallowed the bait.*

► See also: **rise** to the bait

baker

a baker's dozen *old-fashioned*

thirteen • *The judges selected a baker's dozen of promising entries from the hundreds they received.*

balance

be/hang in the balance

if something hangs in the balance, no one knows whether it will continue to exist in the future or what will happen to it • *Judd's career hung in the balance last night after his team lost their sixth successive game.* • *The financial situation is by no means resolved and the club's future is still very much in the balance.*

on balance

after thinking about all the different facts or opinions • *On balance, I would say that it hasn't been a bad year.* • *The report found that, on balance, most people would prefer a female doctor to a male one.*

swing/tip the balance

to make something more likely to happen, or to make someone more likely to succeed • *They were both well-qualified for the job but Ian had more experience and that tipped the balance.* • *The success of this film could* ***tip the balance in favour of*** *other British films in the future.*

► See also: **throw** sb off balance

balancing

► See: a balancing/juggling **act**

bald

be as bald as a coot *humorous*

to be completely bald (= having no hair on your head) ✍A coot is a small, dark grey bird with a circle of white feathers on its head. • *Then he took off his hat and he was as bald as a coot.*

ball

a ball and chain

something which limits your freedom ✍A ball and chain was a heavy metal ball that was fastened to a prisoner's leg by a chain, used to stop them moving. • *The house had become a ball and chain – we couldn't sell it and neither could we rent it out.*

a ball-breaker *British & Australian very informal*

a woman who does not like men and is unpleasant towards them • *I don't think you're going to like your new flat mate – she's a bit of a ball-breaker.*

the ball is in sb's court

if the ball is in someone's court, they have to do something before any progress can be made in a situation ✍In a game of tennis, if the ball is in your court then it is your turn to hit the ball. • *I've told him he can have his job back if he apologizes. The ball's in his court now.*

put the ball in sb's **court** • *This pay offer has put the ball firmly in the court of the union.*

be no ball of fire *American & Australian informal*

to lack energy and interest • *It's a little ironic that he criticizes Bill for not being dynamic. He's no ball of fire himself.*

be on the ball *informal*

to be quick to understand and to react to things • *I rely on my co-driver to be on the ball.* • *I didn't sleep well last night and I'm not really on the ball today.*

have a ball *old-fashioned*

to enjoy yourself very much • *'So how was the party last night?' 'It was wonderful - we had a ball!'*

pick up/take the ball and run (with it) *mainly American*

to take an idea or plan and develop it further • *This is a good proposal. I think we should pick up the ball and run with it.*

set/start the ball rolling

to do something which starts an activity, or to start doing something in order to encourage other people to do the same • *I've started the ball rolling by setting up a series of meetings.* • *The hospital appeal received a gift for $1 million to set the ball rolling.*

keep the ball rolling • *The product has been a great success, and we hope this advertising campaign will keep the ball rolling.*

a whole new ball game
a totally different ball game

a completely different situation, often one which is difficult or which you know very little about • *We'd done a lot of climbing in Scotland, but the Himalayas were a whole new ball game.*

► See also: **carry** the ball
drop the ball
play ball
the **whole** ball of wax

ballistic

go ballistic *informal*
to become very angry and start shouting or behaving violently • *Apparently, he told Sandra that he'd been out for a drink with his ex-girlfriend and she went ballistic.*

balloon

the balloon goes up
if the balloon goes up, a situation suddenly becomes very serious or unpleasant • *The balloon went up last Friday when the scandal became public.*

ballpark

a ballpark estimate/figure
a number which is only approximate, but which should be near to the correct number • *We're expecting sales of the book to generate around $10,000 dollars, although obviously that's just a ballpark figure.*

be in the same ballpark
to be of a similar amount or cost • *Jamie makes over two hundred thousand dollars and I don't know exactly how much Tom makes but I guess it's in the same ballpark.*
be in the (right) ballpark • *'And do you think the projected sales figures are realistic?' 'They're in the right ballpark.'* (= they are close to the right amount)

balls

have sb **by the balls** *very informal*
to have someone in a situation where you have complete power over them • *I owe them £5,000. They've got me by the balls.*

balls-up

a balls-up *British & Australian very informal*
a situation in which everything goes wrong • *The trip was a complete balls-up from beginning to end.*

banana

a banana republic *informal*
a small, poor country with a weak or dishonest government • *People fear that the country will become a banana republic if the economy doesn't pick up.*

a banana skin *British*
something which causes or is very likely to cause embarrassing problems • *The new tax has proved to be a banana skin for the government.*

bananas

go bananas *informal*
to become very angry • *She'll go bananas if she sees the room in this state.*

band-aid

a Band-Aid *American*
a temporary solution to a problem, or something that seems to be a solution but has no real effect ✍Band-Aid is a trademark for a thin piece of sticky material used to cover small cuts on the body. • *A few food and medical supplies were delivered to the region but it was little more than a Band-Aid.*
Band-Aid *American* • *He criticized what he called 'the government's Band-Aid approach' to serious environmental issues.*

bandwagon

get/jump/leap on the bandwagon
to become involved in an activity which is successful so that you can get the advantages of it yourself • *The success of the product led many companies to jump on the bandwagon.* • *Publishers are rushing to get on the CD-ROM bandwagon.*
the bandwagon effect • *The bandwagon effect accounts for the increasing number of girl groups on the pop scene.*

bane

the bane of your **life**
someone or something that is always causing problems for you and upsetting you • *I have a sister who's always getting into trouble and expecting me to sort her out. She's the bane of my life.*

bang

Bang goes sth**!** *informal*
something that you say when you have just lost the opportunity to do something • *I've just been told I'm working late this evening. Oh well, bang goes the cinema!*

a bang up job *American informal*
a very successful piece of work • *You've done a bang up job clearing out the garage.*

be bang on *informal*
to be exactly correct • *You said she'd be in*

her early forties, didn't you? You were bang on.

go with a bang *British & Australian informal*

go over with a bang *American informal*

if an event, especially a party, goes with a bang, it is very exciting and successful • *A karaoke machine? That should help your party go with a bang!*

[more/a bigger etc.] bang for your **buck** *American informal*

if something that you buy gives you more bang for your buck, you get more value for your money by buying this product than from buying any other ✍'Buck', in American English, is an informal way of saying 'dollar' (= a unit of money in America). • *If all you want is death-benefit cover, this type of insurance policy will give you more bang for your buck.*

not **with a bang but with a whimper** *literary*

if something ends not with a bang but with a whimper, it ends in a disappointing way • *The concert ended not with a bang but with a whimper, the rain forcing the performance to stop fifteen minutes early.*

► See also: bang/beat the **drum**
catch/have sb bang to **rights**

banging

► See: be banging/hitting your **head** against a brick wall

bank

► See: not **break** the bank

banner

under the banner of sth

if you do something under the banner of a belief or idea, you say that you are doing it in order to support that belief or idea • *The pro-lifers are campaigning under the banner of traditional family values.*

baptism

a baptism by/of fire

a very difficult first experience of something • *I was given a million-dollar project to manage in my first month. It was a real baptism by fire.*

bar

► See: It's all over bar the **shouting**.

bare

the bare bones

the most basic parts of something, without any detail • *We believe we have the bare bones of an agreement.* • *Reduced to its bare bones, the theory states that animals adapt to suit their surroundings.*

bare-bones • (always before noun) *Even from this bare-bones plot summary, we can deduce that the story is highly implausible.*

bare your **heart/soul**

to tell someone your secret thoughts and feelings • (often + **to**) *We don't know each other that well. I certainly wouldn't bare my heart to her.*

with your **bare hands**

without using any type of tool or weapon • *The court heard how Roberts strangled the woman with his bare hands.*

► See also: **lay** bare sth

bargain

into the bargain *British, American & Australian*

in the bargain *American*

in addition to the other facts previously talked about • *Caffeine is a brain-stimulant, does not have any beneficial effects on health and is mildly addictive into the bargain.*

bargaining

a bargaining chip *British, American & Australian*

a bargaining counter *British*

something that you can use to make someone do what you want • *The workers' strongest bargaining chip in the negotiations is the threat of strike action.* • *Hostages were used as a bargaining counter during the seige.*

barge

► See: I wouldn't **touch** sb/sth with a barge pole.

bark

sb's **bark is worse than** their **bite**

if someone's bark is worse than their bite, they are not as unpleasant as they seem, and their actions are not as bad as their threats • *I wouldn't be scared of her if I were you. Her bark's a lot worse than her bite.*

barking

be barking mad *British & Australian old-fashioned*
to be crazy • *You went swimming in the sea in the middle of winter? You must be barking mad!*

be barking up the wrong tree *informal*
to be wrong about the reason for something or the way to achieve something • *New evidence suggests that we have been barking up the wrong tree in our search for a cure.*

barrel

not **be a barrel of laughs** *informal*
to not be enjoyable • *'He's a bit serious, isn't he?' 'Yeah, not exactly a barrel of laughs.'*

be more fun than a barrel of monkeys *American*
be as funny as a barrel of monkeys *American*
to be very funny or enjoyable • *Their show was one of the funniest I've ever seen – more fun than a barrel of monkeys!*

have sb **over a barrel**
to put someone in a very difficult situation in which they have no choice about what to do • *She knows I need the work, so she's got me over a barrel in terms of what she pays me.*

▶ See also: **scrape** the barrel

barrels

with both barrels
if you criticize someone with both barrels, you do it in a forceful and angry way • *The manager blasted his players with both barrels at half time.*

bars

behind bars *informal*
in prison • *He spent ten years behind bars after being convicted for armed robbery.*

base

be off base *American & Australian*
to be wrong • *The company chairman dismissed the experts' report as completely off base.*

▶ See also: **touch** base

bases

cover all the bases *American & Australian*
touch all the bases *American*
to deal with every part of a situation or activity • *It's a pretty full report. I think we've covered all the bases.*

bash

have a bash *British & Australian informal*
to try to do something, or to try an activity that you have not tried before • (often + **at**) *I thought I'd have a bash at fixing the washing machine tonight.* • *I've never programmed a video before but I'll have a bash if you want.*

basket

a basket case
1 *informal* someone who is crazy and unable to organize their life • *She'll never get a job. She's a basket case.*
2 a very poor country which needs economic help from other countries, or a business that is in a very bad financial situation • *Twenty years ago the country was an economic basket case.*

bat

(right) off the bat *American & Australian*
immediately • *I could tell right off the bat there was something different about this man.*

not **bat an eye/eyelash/eyelid**
to not show any shock or surprise • *'So what did she say when you told her you were leaving?' 'She didn't bat an eyelid.'*

bat for the other side *British humorous*
if someone bats for the other side, they are homosexual (= sexually attracted to people of the same sex) • *What about you, Justin? Do you think he bats for the other side?*

go to bat for sb *American & Australian*
to give help and support to someone who is in trouble, often by talking to someone else for them • *Give me some decent evidence and I'll go to bat for you.*

like a bat out of hell
if you go somewhere like a bat out of hell, you go very fast • *He ran out of the building like a bat out of hell.*

off your own bat *British & Australian*
if you do something off your own bat, you do it without anyone else telling you or asking you to do it • *He chose to talk to the press off his own bat.*

bated

with bated breath
if you wait for something with bated breath, you feel very excited or anxious while you are waiting • *'His name wasn't by any chance, Max Peters?' Helena asked with bated breath.* • *We were* ***waiting with baited breath*** *for the prizes to be announced.*

bath

take a bath *mainly American*
to suffer a bad financial loss • *Several banks took a bath when the industry collapsed.*

baton

hand over/pass the baton
to give responsibility for something important to another person ✍If someone running in a race passes the baton, they give a stick to the next person to run. • (often + **to**) *Dougal resigns as head of the treasury this month, passing the baton to one of his closest associates.*
pick up/take the baton • *He is a great dancer, but there are plenty of youngsters waiting to pick up the baton when he retires.*

bats

have bats in the belfry *old-fashioned*
to be crazy • *Don't tell anyone else I said that or they'll think I've got bats in the belfry.*

batten

batten down the hatches
to prepare yourself for a difficult period by protecting yourself in every possible way ✍When there is a storm, ships batten down the hatches (= close the doors to the outside) as protection against bad weather. • *When you're coming down with a cold, all you can do is batten down the hatches and wait for the body to fight it off.*

batteries

▶ See: **recharge** your batteries

batting

be batting a thousand *American*
to do something extremely well and better than you had hoped to do it • *Gloria felt she was batting a thousand. She'd got everything she asked for when she saw her boss.*

▶ See also: be (batting) on a **sticky** wicket

battle

the battle lines are drawn
something that you say when two arguing groups have discovered exactly what they disagree about, and are ready to fight each other • *The battle lines are drawn for the leadership contest.*

the battle of the sexes
the disagreements and fight for power that exist between men and women • *So has equality brought an end to the battle of the sexes?*

a battle of wills
a situation in which there are two competing people or groups, and both sides are equally determined to get what they want • *I'm sure there was some point to the original dispute but it's become a battle of wills over the months.*

a battle of wits
a situation in which two people or groups try to defeat each other by using their intelligence • (often + **between**) *It appears that the battle of wits between the two negotiating teams is set to continue for some time.*

▶ See also: a battle/war of **nerves**

bay

▶ See: **keep** sth/sb at bay

baying

be baying for blood *British*
if a group of people are baying for blood, they want someone to be hurt or punished • *Families of the victims were baying for blood during the trial.*

be

be that as it may *formal*
something that you say which means although you accept a piece of information as a fact, it does not make you think differently about the subject that you are discussing • *He certainly was*

under pressure at the time. Be that as it may, he was still wrong to react in the way that he did.

▶ See also: Be my **guest**.

bead

draw/take a bead on sb/sth *American*

to aim a gun at someone or something • *He drew a bead on the last truck in line and fired at the fuel tank.*

beady

have your **beady eye on** sth/sb *humorous*

to watch someone or something very carefully • *We'd better not talk – Miss Stricket's got her beady eye on us.*

be-all

the be-all and end-all

the most important thing ✍This phrase comes from the play *Macbeth* by William Shakespeare. • (often + **of**) *It would be wrong to see Manhattan as the be-all and end-all of the financial world.* • *We all agreed that winning was not the be-all and end-all.*

beam

be off beam *British & Australian*

to be wrong • *Overall the article was well-written although one or two points that she made were a little off beam.* • *I'm afraid your calculations are **way off beam**.*

bean

a bean counter *informal*

an impolite way of describing someone who is responsible for the financial decisions within a company • *When decisions that affect people's lives are in the hands of bean counters, it's bad news.*

not **have a bean** *British & Australian*

to have no money • *Most people in the area are unemployed and don't have a bean to spend.*

beans

▶ See: not **know** beans about sth
spill the beans

bear

be like a bear with a sore head *British & Australian humorous*

to be in a bad mood which causes you to treat other people badly and complain a lot • *If his newspaper doesn't arrive by breakfast time he's like a bear with a sore head.*

bear a grudge

to continue to feel angry or not friendly towards someone who has done something to upset you in the past • *She got the job I applied for, but I'm not one to bear a grudge.* • (sometimes + **against**) *He still bears a grudge against her because she refused to go out with him years ago.*

bear fruit

if something someone does bears fruit, it produces successful results • *The work he began did not bear fruit until after his death.*

a bear hug

an action in which you put your arms tightly around someone and hold them close to you in order to show them affection • *Her cousin gave her an affectionate bear hug which almost took her breath away.*

bear testimony/witness to sth *formal*

if something bears testimony to a fact, it proves that it is true • *The numerous awards on his walls bear witness to his great success.*

▶ See also: **bring** sth to bear
bear/take the **brunt** of sth

beard

beard sb **in** their **den**
beard the lion in their **den**

to visit an important person in the place where they work, in order to tell or ask them something unpleasant • *A group of journalists bearded the director in his den to ask how he was going to deal with the crisis.* • *Who's going to beard the lion in her den and explain what's gone wrong?*

bears

Do bears shit in the woods? *humorous taboo*

used to say that the answer to a question you have just been asked is obviously 'yes' • *Would the children like to go to Disneyland? Do bears shit in the woods?*

beast

a beast of burden *literary*

a large animal, such as a donkey (= an

animal like a small horse with long ears), which is used for pulling vehicles or carrying heavy loads • *Huskies are traditionally used in the Arctic as beasts of burden.*

beat

beat a path to sb's **door**
to be very eager to speak to someone and do business with them • *Put that ad in the paper and you'll have half the town beating a path to your door.*

beat a retreat
to leave a place because it is dangerous or unpleasant • *When the cold grows overwhelming, visitors can beat a retreat to Joe Mulligan's warm saloon.* • *When we saw the police arriving we* ***beat a hasty retreat****.*

beat about/around the bush
to avoid talking about a difficult or embarrassing subject because you are worried about upsetting the person you are talking to • (usually negative) *Don't beat around the bush. Just tell me where my brother is.* • *There is no point in beating about the bush. I'm leaving you.*

beat your **brains out**
to spend a lot of time worrying about a problem and thinking about how to deal with it • (often + doing sth) *I've been beating my brains out trying to think of a way of getting the money to her in time.*

beat your **breast**
to publicly pretend that you feel sad or guilty • *Managers are beating their breasts about the loss of 50 jobs, but staff suspect more redundancies are on the way.*
breast-beating • *No amount of breast-beating will bring back those who died in the crash.*

beat sb **hollow** *British & Australian*
to defeat someone easily and by a large amount • *We played my brother's school at football and beat them hollow.*

Beat it! *mainly American informal*
a rude way of telling someone to go away • *OK you kids, beat it!*

beat the bushes *American*
to try very hard to get or achieve something • *She's not out there beating the bushes for a job – she's just as happy not working.*

beat the rap *American informal*
to escape being punished • *There's no way he can beat the rap now. No lawyer can save him.*

beat sb **to a pulp** *informal*
to hit someone hard until they are seriously injured • *He was beaten to a pulp in a back street and left to die.*

beat sb **to it** *informal*
to do something before someone else does it • *I was just about to open some wine but I see you've beaten me to it.*

beat sb **to the punch** *American*
to do something before someone else does it • *I was thinking of applying for that job but Carol beat me to the punch.*

beat sb **to within an inch of** their **life**
to attack someone so violently that they almost die • *She was beaten to within an inch of her life on a back street in London.*

If you can't beat 'em, (join 'em)! *informal*
something that you say when you decide to do something bad because other people are getting an advantage from doing it and you cannot stop them. • *If everyone else is making a bit of money out of it I will too. If you can't beat 'em, join 'em, is what I say.*

► See also: beat/knock the (living) **daylights** out of sb
beat a **dead** horse
beat sth to **death**
bang/beat the **drum**
without **missing** a beat
beat/turn **swords** into ploughshares
beat/knock the **tar** out of sb

beaten

be off the beaten track *British, American & Australian*
be off the beaten path *American*
if a place is off the beaten track, not many people go there • *Unfortunately, because the gallery's a bit off the beaten track, it doesn't get many visitors.*

beating

take a beating
to be defeated or to lose a lot of money • *The Knicks really took a beating in last night's game.* • *The company took a beating last year, losing $50 million in profits.*

beats

(it) beats me *informal*
something that you say when you cannot understand something • (often + question word) *It beats me how he managed to survive for three weeks alone in the mountains.*
what beats me *informal* • *What beats me is how he persuaded Pam to lend him the money.*

That beats everything! *British, American & Australian informal*
That beats all! *American informal*
something that you say when something has surprised you, or you find something hard to believe • *I can't believe he expected you to drive all that way in the middle of the night. That beats everything!*

beau monde

the beau monde *formal*
rich and fashionable people • *She took no interest in the glittering beau monde that she had married into.*

beauty

Beauty is in the eye of the beholder.
something that you say which means that each person has their own opinion about what or who is beautiful • *Personally, I can't understand why she finds him attractive, but they do say beauty is in the eye of the beholder.*

Beauty is only skin deep.
something that you say which means a person's character is more important than their appearance • *She may not be conventionally pretty but you know what they say, beauty's only skin deep.*

sb's **beauty sleep** *humorous*
the sleep that someone needs in order to feel healthy and look attractive • *If you don't mind, I'm going to bed now. I have to get my beauty sleep.*

beck

be at sb's **beck and call**
to be always willing and able to do what someone asks you to do • *She had a dozen servants at her beck and call.* • *TV companies should not be at the beck and call of government ministers.*

bed

be a bed of nails
if a situation, especially a job, is a bed of nails, it is difficult or unpleasant • *He resigned last week, describing the post as a bed of nails.*

be in bed with sb
to work with a person or organization, or to be involved with them, in a way which causes other people not to trust you • *They were accused of being in bed with the communists.*
climb/get/hop into bed with sb • *Rather than hopping into bed with a leading merchant bank, it chose to remain an independent partnership.*

be no bed of roses
not **be a bed of roses**
if a situation is no bed of roses, it is difficult or unpleasant • *It's no bed of roses, raising two kids on one salary, that's for sure.* • *Life isn't a bed of roses, you know.*

get out of bed on the wrong side *British, American & Australian*
get up on the wrong side of the bed *American*
if someone got out of bed on the wrong side, they are in a bad mood and are easily annoyed all day • *What's the matter with you? Did you get out of bed on the wrong side or something?*

go to bed with sb
to have sex with someone • *I can't believe she went to bed with him on their first date!*
get sb **into bed** to persuade someone to have sex with you • *It took 3 months before she finally got him into bed.*

put sth **to bed**
if you put something that is printed, for example a book or magazine, to bed, you finish writing it • *We put the first edition to bed an hour before the deadline.*

You've made your bed (and you'll have to lie in it).
You made your bed (now lie in it).
something that you say in order to tell someone that they must accept that they will suffer as a result of something bad that they have done • *Don't come crying to me if it all goes wrong. You've made your bed and you'll have to lie in it.*

bedfellows

make odd/strange bedfellows

If two people or groups make strange bedfellows, they are connected in a particular activity though they are very different and would not usually have the same opinions or be seen together. • *Priests and pop stars make strange bedfellows, but on this issue they agree.*

bedpost

▶ See: **between** you, me and the bedpost

bedroom

bedroom eyes

if someone has bedroom eyes, they look as if they are interested in sex • *He told me I had bedroom eyes.*

bee

be the bee's knees *British & Australian informal*

to be extremely good • *Have you tried this double chocolate-chip ice cream? It's the bee's knees, it really is.*

have a bee in your **bonnet**

to keep talking about something again and again because you think it is important, especially something that other people do not think is important • (often + **about**) *She's got a real bee in her bonnet about people keeping their dogs under control.*

beef

Where's the beef? *American informal*

something that you say when you think someone does not have enough ideas to make their plans work • *Where's the beef? The Senator has no new political initiatives or ideas.*

beeline

make a beeline for sb/sth

to move quickly and directly towards a particular person or thing • *Phil arrived at about nine and made a beeline for the champagne.*

beer

not **be all beer and skittles** *British & Australian old-fashioned*

if a situation or activity is not all beer and skittles, it has unpleasant parts as well as pleasant ones • *It's not all beer and skittles, this job. It's hard work.*

beeswax

none of your **beeswax** *American & Australian informal*

an impolite way of saying that you do not want someone to know about your private life • *'So where the heck have you been?' 'None of your beeswax!'*

beet

go beet red *American*

go as red as a beet *American*

to become very red in the face, usually because you are embarrassed ✍ A beet is a small, round vegetable that is a very dark red/purple colour. • *I only had to smile at him and he went beet red.*

beetroot

go beetroot (red) *British & Australian*

go as red as a beetroot *British & Australian*

to become very red in the face, usually because you are embarrassed ✍ A beetroot is a small, round vegetable that is a very dark red/purple colour. • *Whenever the kids asked him about his girlfriend he'd go beetroot.*

before

▶ See: be before your **time**

beg

beg the question

1 if a statement or situation begs the question, it causes you to ask a particular question • *It's all very well talking about extra staff but it rather begs the question of how we're going to pay for them.*

2 *formal* if something that someone says begs the question, it suggests that something is true which might in fact be false • *We're assuming, are we, that Anthony will still be in charge this time next year? That rather begs the question, doesn't it?*

I beg to differ/disagree *formal*

a polite way of saying that you disagree with something that someone has said • *I beg to differ with Mr Stahl's final assertion.*

beggars

Beggars can't be choosers.

something that you say which means when you cannot have exactly what you want, you must accept whatever you can get • *I would have preferred a house of my own rather than sharing but I suppose beggars can't be choosers.*

begging

be going begging

if something is going begging, it is available to be taken because no one else wants it • *There's a big box of apples going begging.*

beginning

the beginning of the end

the time at which it becomes clear that a situation or process will end, although it does not end immediately • (often + **for**) *The ban on tobacco advertising may be the beginning of the end for the cigarette companies.*

behind

▶ See: behind sb's **back**
behind **bars**
be behind the **eight** ball
behind the **scenes**
be behind the **times**

believe

not **believe a word of it**

to not believe that something is true • *Have you heard what they're saying about Andrew? I don't believe a word of it.*

can't believe your **ears**

if you can't believe your ears, you are very surprised at something that someone tells you • (usually in past tenses) *She couldn't believe her ears when they told her Jim had been arrested.*

couldn't believe your **eyes**

if you say that you couldn't believe your eyes when you saw something, you mean that you were very surprised by it • *She couldn't believe her eyes when she saw him drive up in his new car.* • *I could hardly believe my eyes. They'd made so many changes, it looked like a completely different house.*

I'll believe it when I see it.

something that you say to show that you do not think something will happen, and you will not believe it until it does happen • *He says he's going to decorate the house, but I'll believe it when I see it.*

If you believe that, you'll believe anything! *informal*

something that you say to emphasize that something is obviously not true • *He said the car in front backed into him, and if you believe that, you'll believe anything!*

make believe

imaginary or invented • *I had to explain to Sam that it was only make believe and that they weren't real monsters.*

▶ See also: You('d) **better** believe it!

bell

give sb **a bell**

give sb **a bell** *British & Australian informal*

to telephone someone • *Give me a bell when you get home so I know you're OK.*

▶ See also: **ring** a bell,

bells

bells and whistles

the things that something, especially a device or machine, has or does that are not necessary but that make it more exciting or interesting • *Your computer software may have all the latest bells and whistles, but is it good value for money?*

with bells on

1 *British humorous* if you describe something as a particular thing with bells on, you mean that it has similar qualities to that thing but they are more extreme • *This latest series is melodrama with bells on.*

2 *American & Australian humorous* if you go somewhere or do something with bells

on, you do it with a lot of interest and energy • *I'll be at the party with bells on.*

belly

a belly laugh

a loud laugh which cannot be controlled • *It's not often you hear the kind of jokes that give you a real belly laugh.*

go belly up *informal*

if a business goes belly up, it fails • *Factories and farms went belly up because of the debt crisis.*

bellyful

have had a bellyful of sth *informal*

if you have had a bellyful of an unpleasant situation or someone's bad behaviour, you have had much too much of it and it has made you angry • *He's probably had a bellyful of your moaning.*

below

▶ See: be below the **belt**

belt

be below the belt

if something someone says is below the belt, it is cruel and unfair ✍In a boxing match it is wrong to hit the person you are fighting against below the belt. • *It was below the belt to mention his brother's criminal record.*

aim/hit below the belt • *In the run-up to the election, politicians won't hesitate to aim below the belt.*

belt and braces

using more than one method to make sure that something is safe or sure to happen • *Our staff have identity cards and number codes to open doors – that's part of our **belt and braces approach** to security.*

under your **belt**

if you have an experience or a qualification under your belt, you have completed it successfully, and it may be useful to you in the future • *She was a capable individual, with fourteen years as managing director under her belt.* • *He has several major drama awards under his belt.*

▶ See also: **tighten** your belt

bend

bend sb's **ear** *informal*

to talk to someone for a long time, usually about something boring • (often + **about**) *Don't let her bend your ear about how overworked she is.*

drive/send sb **round the bend** *informal*

to make someone very angry, especially by continuing to do something annoying • *You're driving me round the bend with your constant complaining.*

round the bend *informal*

crazy • *Tell me frankly: do you think my father's round the bend?* • *I was sure I'd locked that door. I must be **going round the bend**.*

▶ See also: bend/lean over **backwards** to do sth

bend/stretch the **rules**

bended

on bended knee/knees *humorous*

if you ask for something on bended knee, you ask very politely or with a lot of emotion for something that you want very much • *I had to **go down on bended knee** and beg my Dad to let me have the party.* • *He begged me on bended knee to marry him.*

benefit

give sb **the benefit of the doubt**

to believe something good about someone, rather than something bad, when you have the possibility of doing either • *After hearing his explanation, I was prepared to give him the benefit of the doubt.*

bent

get bent out of shape *American informal*

to become very angry or upset • *It's ok, don't worry about returning the books. I don't get bent out of shape about things like that.*

beside

be beside yourself

to feel an emotion that is so strong it is impossible to control • *He was beside himself when she didn't come home last night.* • (often + **with**) *We were beside ourselves with excitement as we watched the race.*

▶ See also: be beside the **point**

best

as best you **can** *British & Australian*
as best as you **can** *American*
if you do something that is difficult as best you can, you do it as well as you are able to do it • *If one of us loses our job we'll just have to cope as best we can.* • *Just clean up the mess as best as you can.*

at the best of times
even with the best possible conditions or in the best possible situation • *Journalism is a highly competitive profession at the best of times.* • *Even at the best of times, this region is hard to farm.*

be for the best
if an action is for the best, it seems unpleasant now but it will improve a situation in the future • *I know it's hard to end a long-term relationship, but in this case it's for the best.*

be on your **best behaviour** *British & Australian*
be on your **best behavior** *American & Australian*
to behave very well, usually because you are in an important or formal situation • *Now children, I want you all to be on your best behaviour when grandma arrives.*

be the best of a bad bunch/lot *British & Australian*
to be slightly less bad than other bad people or things in a group • *This picture isn't exactly what I would have chosen, but it was the best of a bad lot.*

sb's **best bet**
the thing someone should do which is most likely to achieve the result they want • *If you want a cheap jacket, your best best is to try the second-hand shops.* • *I told him his best bet would be to get a bus as there are no direct trains.*

your **best bib and tucker** *old-fashioned, humorous*
the best or most formal clothes that you own • *We were all dressed in our best bib and tucker for my aunt's wedding.*

the best of both worlds
if you get the best of both worlds, you get the advantages of two different things at the same time • *She works in the city and lives in the country, so she gets the best of both worlds.* • *With these delicious but healthy recipes you can have the best of both worlds.*
OPPOSITE **the worst of both worlds**
• *Farmers have the worst of both worlds: low prices for their products, and no guarantee they'll be able to sell them.*

the best of British (luck) *British informal*
used to wish someone luck, especially when you do not think they have much chance of success or happiness • *You're going to ask her father for money? Best of British, mate!*

give it your **best shot**
to do something as well as you possibly can, although you are not sure whether you will be able to succeed • *Greg will be a tough opponent to beat, but I'll give it my best shot.*

make the best of sth *British, American & Australian*
make the best of a bad job *British & Australian*
to try to think and act in a positive way when you have to accept a situation which you do not like but cannot change • *The room they've given us is too small really, but we'll just have to* ***make the best of it***. • *It was a difficult speech to give, but I think she made the best of a bad job.*

May the best man win.
something that you say just before a competition starts to say that you hope the person who deserves to win will win • *Is everyone ready? Then may the best man win.*

put your **best foot forward**
1 to do something as well as you can • *Make sure you put your best foot forward for tonight's performance.*
2 to start to walk more quickly • *You'll have to put your best foot forward if you want to be there by nine.*

with the best will in the world
if something cannot be done with the best will in the world, it is impossible, although you would make it possible if you could • *With the best will in the world, if you don't have a passport you can't go.*

▶ See also: the best/greatest **thing** since sliced bread

bet

bet the farm/ranch *American*
to spend almost all the money you have on something that you think might bring you success • (often + **on**) *TV networks are obviously willing to bet the ranch on special sports events – they paid millions to broadcast the Olympics.*

Don't bet on it. *informal*
I wouldn't bet on it. *informal*
something that you say when you do not think that something is likely to happen or to be true • *'Do you think the builders will finish by Friday?' 'I wouldn't bet on it.'*

a safe bet *British, American & Australian*
a sure bet *American*
1 something that you are certain will happen • *It's a safe bet that those two will settle down and have children.* • *Wheeler is a sure bet for a place on the team.*
2 someone or something that you are certain will win or succeed • *She is still a safe bet for re-election.* • *Simplicity of design is a sure bet in the fashion world.*

You bet your (sweet) ass! *American very informal*
something that you say in order to emphasize what you have said • *You bet your ass I feel bad about her leaving.* • *You can bet your sweet ass he's guilty!*

you can bet your life/your bottom dollar
if you say you can bet your life that something will happen or is true, you mean you are completely certain • *You can bet your life she won't apologize.*

▶ See also: How much do you **want** to bet?

bête noire

sb's **bête noire**
someone or something that you really hate or that really annoys you • *People who use jargon are his particular bête noire.*

bets

▶ See: **hedge** your bets

better

against your **better judgement**
if you do something against your better judgement, you do it although you think it is wrong • *I lent him the money against my better judgement.*

Better (to be) safe than sorry.
something that you say which means it is best not to take risks even if it seems boring or hard work to be careful • *I'll hold the ladder while you climb up. Better safe than sorry.*

Better late than never.
something that you say which means it is better for someone or something to be late than never to arrive or to happen • *'Karen's card arrived 2 weeks after my birthday.' 'Oh well, better late than never.'*

better than sex *informal*
extremely enjoyable or exciting • *To me, nothing compares with the thrill of surfing – it's better than sex.*

for better or (for) worse
for better, for worse
if a situation exists or happens for better or for worse, it exists or happens whether its results are good or bad ✍This phrase is used in a traditional marriage ceremony in which the man and woman promise to stay together whether their life is good or bad. • *France has a new government, for better or for worse.* • *We cannot deny that our childhood experiences affect us, for better, for worse.*

get the better of sb
if a feeling gets the better of you, it becomes too strong to control • *Finally curiosity got the better of her and she opened the letter.* • *Try to remain calm – don't let your anger get the better of you.*

You('d) better believe it! *informal*
something that you say to emphasize that something strange or shocking is true • *'Does he really know the President?' 'You better believe it!'*

▶ See also: better the **devil** you know (than the **devil** you don't)
sb's better/other **half**
have **seen** better days
think better of sth
for **want** of a better word

between

between you and me *British, American & Australian*
between you, me and the bedpost/gatepost *British & Australian humorous*
something that you say when you are going to tell someone something you do not want them to tell anyone else • *Just between you and me, I don't think his work is quite up to standard.* • *Between you, me and the gatepost, I'm thinking of leaving.*

► See also: between the **devil** and the deep blue sea
between a **rock** and a hard place

beyond

► See: get/go beyond a **joke**
be beyond sb's **ken**
be beyond the **pale**
beyond your **wildest** dreams

Bible

a Bible-basher *British & Australian informal*
a Bible-thumper *mainly American informal*
an insulting way of describing someone who tries very hard to persuade other people to believe in Christianity • *I have nothing against religion, but I hate Bible-bashers.*

the Bible Belt
the southern and central area of the United States, where many people have very strong traditional Christian beliefs • *Country music is very popular in the Bible Belt.*

biblical

but not in the biblical sense *humorous*
if you say you know someone but not in the biblical sense, you mean you have not had sex with them ✍In the Bible, 'to know' someone meant to have sex with them. • *'Did you know her then?' 'Yes, but not in the biblical sense.'*

bidding

do sb's **bidding** *old-fashioned*
to do what someone tells or asks you to do • *In some societies, men still assume their wives are there to do their bidding.*

bide

bide your **time**
to wait patiently for a good opportunity to do something • *She was biding her time until she could get her revenge.*

big

be big of you
if an action is big of you, it is kind, good, or helpful ✍This phrase is usually used humorously or angrily to mean the opposite. • *It was big of him to admit that these problems are really his fault.* • *You can spare me an hour next week? That's really big of you!*

be big on sth
to be very interested in something and think that it is important • *The magazine is big on research into what their readers want.* • *He's not big on self-analysis – it's no good asking him why he left her.*

a big ask
a request to someone to do something for you that you know will be difficult for them • *It's a big ask but could you feed our cats for the two weeks we're away?*

Big Brother
a government or a large organization which tries to control every part of people's lives and to know everything about them ✍In the book 1984 by George Orwell, Big Brother is the very powerful ruler. • *Many people are concerned about Big Brother having computer files on them to which they do not have access.*
Big Brother • (always before noun) *Employees have complained because of the 'Big Brother' approach of the new security measures.*

a big cheese *humorous*
an important or powerful person in a group or organization • *Apparently her father is a big cheese in one of the major banks.*

the big daddy *American & Australian*
the biggest or most important person, animal or thing in a group • *It's the largest electronics company in the world – the big daddy of them all* • *Shamu the killer whale is the big daddy of the aquarium.*

a big deal
a subject, situation, or event which

people think is important • *I don't know why this issue has become such a big deal.* • *Losing the match was* ***no big deal.*** • *All I said was, I'm going to have a baby –* ***what's the big deal?*** • *Yes, it's his birthday today, but he doesn't want to* ***make a big deal of it.*** (= make people notice it by having a special celebration)

Big deal! *informal*
something that you say to show that you do not think that something is either important or interesting • *'Did I tell you Ann got a new car?' 'Big deal!'*

a big fish *informal*
an important or powerful person in a group or organization • *Mrs Coughlin is one of the directors – a big fish.*

a big fish in a small pond
one of the most important people in a small group or organization, who would have much less power and importance if they were part of a larger group or organization • *As the manager of a local company, he enjoys being a big fish in a small pond.*

a big girl's blouse *British & Australian humorous*
a man or a boy who behaves in a way which other men think is how a woman would behave, especially if they show they are frightened of something • *Come on you big girl's blouse, drink up and I'll get you another pint.*

a big gun/noise *informal*
an important or powerful person in a group or organization • *She's a big gun in city politics.*

a big mouth *informal*
if you have a big mouth, you talk too much, especially about things that should be secret • *Helen's got such a big mouth – the news'll be all over the town by tonight.* • *I knew I shouldn't have mentioned the letter. Oh dear, me and my big mouth!*
a big-mouth • *Dave's a real big-mouth, so don't tell him anything.*

the big picture
the most important facts about a situation and the effects of that situation on other things • *In my political work I try to concentrate on the big picture and not be distracted by details.*

a big shot/wheel *American & Australian informal*
an important or powerful person in a group or organization • *Mr Madison is a big shot in the world of finance.*

big ticket *American & Australian*
very expensive • (always before noun) *It's a good time to buy a* ***big ticket item*** *like a car or household appliance, as prices have fallen.*

big time *informal*
very much • *He really owes her big time for everything she has done for him.* • *The school was into discipline big time.*

the big time *informal*
the time when someone is famous or successful • *Miss Lee* ***hit the big time*** (= became famous) *after winning a talent contest.* • *The band is hoping to return to the big time.*
big-time • *He played the saxophone with big-time swing bands.* • *It's a film about drug dealers and big-time gangsters.*

have big ears *Australian informal*
to listen to other people's private conversations • *Don't talk so loudly unless you want everyone to know. Bill has big ears you know.*

make a big thing (out) of sth
to behave as if something is very important • *He always makes a big thing out of helping me cook.* • *I want some sort of party, but I don't want to make a big thing of it.*

make it big *informal*
to become very successful or famous • *After years of trying, he finally made it big in America.*

too big for your **boots** *British, American & Australian informal*
too big for your **britches** *American informal*
someone who is too big for their boots behaves as if they are more important or more clever than they really are • *Since he was made team captain, he's been ordering us all around and generally* ***getting*** *much* ***too big for his boots.***

What's the big idea? *informal*
something that you say when you want to know why someone has done something that annoys you • *What's the big idea?*

That's my lunch you're eating.

▶ See also: as big as **life**
make (a) big **play** of sth
think big

bigger

The bigger they are, the harder they fall.
something that you say which means the more power or success a person has, the harder it is for them to accept losing it • *She's very bitter about losing the directorship. The bigger they are, the harder they fall.*

▶ See also: have bigger/other **fish** to fry
be bigger than **life**

big-head

a big-head *British & Australian*
someone who believes that they are very clever or very good at an activity and who thinks that other people should admire them • *Dan's such a big-head, always reminding us what fantastic results he got in his exams.*
big-headed *British, American & Australian* • *Mary's got so big-headed since she won the geography prize.*

bike

get on your bike *British*
to go out to look for work • *There are plenty of jobs in the area – he just needs to get on his bike.*

On yer bike! *British & Australian very informal*
an impolite way of telling someone to go away • *'Can you lend me some money?' 'On yer bike, mate!'*

bill

bill and coo *old-fashioned*
if you bill and coo with someone you love, you talk quietly to them and kiss them ✍If birds bill and coo, they touch beaks and make noises to each other. • (often in continuous tenses) *I don't know why they bother to come out if they're going to spend all their time billing and cooing.*

fit the bill *British, American & Australian*
fill the bill *American & Australian*
to have the qualities or experience which are needed • *I'm looking for someone with several years of publishing experience and you seem to fit the bill.* • *The city needs a strong leader, and the new mayor just doesn't fill the bill.*

▶ See also: **foot** the bill
pick up the bill/tab
sell sb a bill of goods

billet-doux

a billet-doux *humorous*
a love letter • *They've been exchanging billets-doux, but I don't know how serious it is.*

bird

The bird has flown.
something that you say which means that someone has escaped or disappeared • *It's no use searching any more. The bird has flown.*

A bird in the hand (is worth two in the bush).
something that you say which means it is better to keep what you have than to risk losing it by trying to get something better • *If I were you I'd accept the money they're offering. After all, a bird in the hand...*

a bird's eye view
a view from a very high place which allows you to see a large area • *We had a bird's eye view of the old town from the top of the city walls.*

flip/give sb **the bird** *American & Australian very informal*
to make a very impolite sign by raising your middle finger towards someone in order to show that you are angry with them • *If he'd shouted at me like that I'd have flipped him the bird.*

▶ See also: **eat** like a bird

bird-brain

a bird-brain *informal*
a stupid person • *He's just a bird-brain – he can't get anything right.*
bird-brained *informal* very stupid • (always before noun) *I'm not listening to her bird-brained schemes any longer.*

birds

be (strictly) for the birds *American & Australian informal*
if you think something is for the birds, you think it is stupid and has no use • *Gambling, games of chance – that sort of thing is strictly for the birds.*

the birds and the bees *humorous*
if you tell someone, especially a child, about the birds and the bees, you tell them about sex • *My parents never actually sat down and told me about the birds and the bees.*

Birds of a feather flock together.
something that you say which means people who have similar characters or similar interests will often choose to spend time together • *I saw the boy who stole my bag with that gang of trouble makers last night – well, birds of a feather flock together, they say.*
birds of a feather people who are similar • *The survey reports that people who are 'birds of a feather' make better marriages than those who are opposites.*

birth

▶ See: **strangle** sth at birth

birthday

in your **birthday suit** *humorous*
not wearing any clothes ✍Babies are naked at the time of their birth. • *He walked out of the bathroom in his birthday suit – obviously not expecting to find anyone in the flat.*

biscuit

▶ See: **take** the biscuit

bit

be a bit much
if you say something is a bit much, you think that it is not fair or that it is more than you can deal with • *I think it's a bit much to expect her to play 3 matches in one day.*
get a bit much • *It gets a bit much sometimes having to listen to other people's problems all the time.*

be champing/chomping at the bit
be chafing at the bit
to be very keen to start an activity or to go somewhere • *By the time he arrived to pick us up we were champing at the bit with impatience.* • *I'm not sure if he's ready for extra responsibility yet, but he's chafing at the bit.*

a bit of all right *British very informal*
if you describe someone as a bit of all right, you mean that they are sexually attractive • *Cor! She's a bit of all right.*

a bit of fluff/skirt *British & Australian old-fashioned, very informal*
a sexually attractive woman • *Who was that nice bit of skirt I saw you with last night?*

a bit of how's your father *British & Australian humorous*
sexual activity • *Apparently he came home and discovered them having a bit of how's your father in the kitchen.*

a bit of rough *British humorous*
someone, usually a man, from a lower social class than their sexual partner • *Jenny's chatting up the barman again. She likes a bit of rough.*

a bit on the side *British & Australian*
if someone has a bit on the side, they are involved in a sexual relationship with someone who is not their usual partner • *He had a bit on the side for years until his wife found out.* • *I knew she'd never leave her husband for me. I was just her bit on the side.*

get/take the bit between your **teeth** *British, American & Australian*
take the bit in your **teeth** *American*
to start doing something in a very keen way • *When the team really gets the bit between their teeth, they are almost impossible to beat.*
have the bit between your **teeth** *British, American & Australian* • *Caroline had the bit between her teeth and nothing would stop her from finding out the truth.*

It's/That's a bit steep! *British & Australian*
something that you say when you think something is not fair • *Keith, calling me boring? That's a bit steep!*

the whole bit *American informal*
the whole of something, including everything that is connected with it • *And what a night it was – moonlight, wine, good food, soft music – the whole bit.*

bite

Bite me! *American very informal*
used to say to someone that they have made you feel angry or embarrassed • *'You're looking a bit rough today.' 'Oh, bite me!'*

a bite of the cherry *British & Australian*
a part of something good, especially when there is not enough for everyone who wants it • *Job-sharing would give twice as many people a bite of the cherry.*

another bite at the cherry *British*
another opportunity to achieve something or to get something you want • *He just missed a gold medal in the 100 metres, but got another bite at the cherry in the 400 metres.* • *She failed the exam but she will get a second bite at the cherry next year.*

bite off more than you **can chew** *informal*
to try to do more than you are able to do • *Don't bite off more than you can chew. Let someone else organize the party.*

bite the bullet
to make yourself do something or accept something difficult or unpleasant ✍When army doctors performed painful operations without drugs, they gave patients a bullet to put between their teeth. • *They decided to bite the bullet and pay the extra for the house they really wanted.* • *Car drivers are biting the bullet after another rise in petrol prices.*

bite the dust
1 *informal* to fail or to stop existing • *Three hundred more people lost their jobs in the same region when another firm bit the dust.* • *She can't make it on Saturday? Oh, well, another good idea bites the dust!*
2 *humorous* to die • *Two Hollywood stars of the thirties have recently bitten the dust.*

bite the hand that feeds you
to treat someone badly who has helped you in some way, often someone who has provided you with money • *Leaving the company after they've spent three years training you up – it's a bit like biting the hand that feeds you.*

bite your **tongue**
to stop yourself from saying something because it would be better not to, even if you would like to say it • *I really wanted to tell her what I thought of him but I had to bite my tongue.*

come back to bite you
If something will come back to bite you, it will cause problems for you in the future. • *Her unpleasant remarks may well come back to bite her later.*

put the bite on sb *American informal*
to ask someone for something that you want, especially money • (often + **for**) *She put the bite on her sister for $20.*

sb/sth **won't bite** *humorous*
something that you say in order to tell someone not to be frightened of someone or something • *I think you should talk to your uncle about this. Go on, he won't bite.*

▸ See also: bite/snap sb's **head** off

biter

the biter (is) bit *British old-fashioned*
someone who has caused harm to other people in the past has now been hurt • *It's **a case of the biter bit**. After years of breaking girls' hearts, he finally fell for someone who didn't love him.*

biting

What's biting sb? *informal*
something that you say in order to ask why someone is in a bad mood • *What's biting her? She hasn't said a word all morning.*

bits

bits and pieces *British, American & Australian*
bits and bobs *British*
small things of different types • *Can you tidy away all your bits and pieces before you go to bed?* • *I put all the bits and bobs I can't find a home for in this drawer.*

▸ See also: **love** sb/sth to bits

bitten

▸ See: **once** bitten, twice shy.

bitter

be bitter and twisted
to be angry and unhappy, usually because you are unable to forget bad things which have happened to you in the past • *I had a difficult childhood, but there's no point getting all bitter and twisted about it.*

the bitter fruits *literary*
the unpleasant results of something • *Disease and malnutrition are the bitter fruits of an inefficient social healthcare policy.*

a bitter pill (to swallow)
bitter medicine

a situation that is unpleasant but must be accepted • *Losing the championship to a younger player was a bitter pill to swallow.* • *Cuts in salaries are a dose of bitter medicine that may help the company to survive.*

to the bitter end

if you do something to the bitter end, you continue it until it is finished, although it is difficult and takes a long time • *Many climbers gave up before they reached the summit, but I was determined to stick it out to the bitter end.*

black

not **be as black as** you **are/it is painted**

if people or situations are not as black as they are painted, they are not as bad as people say they are • *I've met him a few times. He's not as black as he's painted.*

be in the black

If a bank account is in the black, it contains some money, and if a person or business is in the black, they have money in the bank and are not in debt. • *Incredibly, we're still in the black after our holiday.*

black and blue

if a person or part of their body is black and blue, their skin is covered with bruises (= black marks caused by being hit) • *He was* ***beaten black and blue*** *at boarding school.*

black and white

if you think facts or situations are black and white, you have a simple and very certain opinion about them, often when other people think they are really more complicated • *The issue of nuclear weapons isn't as black and white as it used to be.*

a black day

a day when something very unpleasant or sad happens • (usually + **for**) *A bomb went off early this morning. This is a black day for the peace process.*

a black mark

if you get a black mark, people think that something you have done is bad and they will remember it in future • *This administrative error will be a black mark on his record.* • (often + **against**) *If I'm late for work it'll be another black mark against me.*

the black sheep (of the family)

someone who is thought to be a bad person by the rest of their family • *My father was the black sheep – he ran away at 16 to become an actor and his parents never forgave him.*

in black and white

written down • *I wouldn't have believed him capable of fraud, but there it was, in black and white.*

pretend/say that black is white

to say the opposite of what is really true • *She'll say that black is white if she thinks it's to her advantage.*

blank

a blank cheque

as much money to spend as is wanted or needed • (not used with *the*) *We are not giving the redevelopment project a blank cheque. The organizers will be working within a strictly limited budget.*

draw a blank

to be unable to get information, think of something, or achieve something • *Ask them about the car's performance and you'll draw a blank.* • *We've asked 2000 schools to join the campaign, but so far we've drawn a blank.* (= none of them agreed)

blanks

fire/shoot blanks *humorous*

if a man is firing blanks, there is no sperm (= the cells which combine with the female's egg to start life) in his semen ✍ (= the liquid produced in the male sexual organs) • (usually in continuous tenses) *They had a series of fertility tests done and found out that basically Tony was firing blanks.*

blast

a blast from the past *informal*

something that suddenly and strongly makes you remember a previous time in your life • *Hearing that record again was a real blast from the past.*

▶ See also: blast/blow sb/sth to **kingdom** come

blaze

blaze a trail

to do something that no-one has done before, especially something which will be important for other people • *The hospital has blazed a trail in developing new techniques for treating infertility.*

a trail-blazer someone who is the first person to do something • *He will be remembered as a trail-blazer in cancer research.*

trail-blazing • (always before noun) *We'll be discussing the latest book from trail-blazing American feminist Gloria Steinem.*

blazes

[What/Why/Who etc.] the (blue) blazes *old-fashioned, informal*

if you start a question with what/who/why etc. the blazes, you show that you are very surprised or angry about the thing you are asking about • *What the blazes are they doing up on the roof?*

Go to blazes! *old-fashioned, informal*

a rude and angry way of telling someone to go away and that you do not care what happens to them • *Just go to blazes! I'm sick of your rudeness!* • *If he's going to start making demands, he can go to blazes.*

bleed

bleed sb **dry**

to take someone's money until most or all of it has gone • *Repayments on the new furniture were bleeding me dry.*

bleeding

a bleeding heart

someone who shows too much sympathy for everyone • *The anti-hunting campaigners are just a bunch of bleeding hearts who don't understand the countryside.*

bless

Bless her/his **cotton socks.** *British & Australian humorous*

something that you say when you want to express affection for someone • *My little niece – bless her cotton socks – won the school poetry prize this year.*

blessing

be a blessing in disguise

to be something which has a good effect, although at first it seemed that it would be bad or not lucky • *Losing my job turned out to be a blessing in disguise because it forced me to think carefully about my future.*

blessings

▶ See: **count** your blessings

blind

be as blind as a bat *humorous*

to be completely blind • *I'm as blind as a bat without my glasses.*

a blind alley

a method of thinking or acting which is not effective because it does not produce any results • *The latest evolutionary theory may turn out to be a blind alley.*

a blind date

an arranged meeting for two people who have never met each other before, in order to try to start a romantic relationship • *I agreed to go on a blind date with one of Savita's ex-boyfriends.*

the blind leading the blind

a situation where someone is trying to show someone else how to do something which they do not know how to do themselves • *I tried to explain how the software works, but it was* ***a case of the blind leading the blind****, really.*

a blind spot

something that you do not understand at all, often because you are not willing to try • *He had a complete blind spot where public relations were concerned, so his political career was doomed from the start.* • *Languages are my blind spot – I was always terrible at French.*

blind sb **with science** *British & Australian*

if you blind someone with science, you confuse them by using technical language that they are not likely to understand • *I think he decided to blind us with science because he didn't want us asking any difficult questions.*

not **take a blind bit of notice** *British & Australian informal*

to not give someone or something any

attention at all • *Protesters were shouting and waving banners outside the embassy, but no-one took a blind bit of notice.* • (often + **of**) *They didn't take a blind bit of notice of our objections.*

► See also: **fly** blind
swear blind
turn a blind eye

blinder

► See: **play** a blinder

blink

be on the blink *informal*
if a machine is on the blink, it is not working as it should • *I think the photocopier's on the blink.*

before sb **could blink**
very quickly or suddenly • *Before you could blink, he'd grabbed the purse and was halfway down the street.*

in the blink of an eye
extremely quickly • *In the blink of an eye the handsome prince was transformed into an ugly frog.*

block

have been around the block
1 to have had a lot of experience of a particular situation • *His lawyer has been around the block a few times and knows what to expect.*
2 to have had a lot of experience of life, especially difficult or unpleasant experience • *His girlfriend looks like she's been around the block a bit.*

on the block *American*
if something is on the block, it is for sale, especially at an auction (= a sale where the person who offers most money for something can buy it) • *The best pieces of furniture from the old mansion are going on the block next month.* • *The Seattle radio station has been on the block for a year with no offers to buy it.*

put your **head/neck on the block**
to risk doing something which will make other people lose their good opinion of you if it fails ✍In the past, the block was a large piece of wood on which criminals had their heads cut off. • *He put his head on the block by promising his team wouldn't lose any more matches this year.* • *I'm not going to put my head on the block for you – it could cost me my promotion.*

► See also: **knock** sb's block off

blocks

be off the (starting) blocks
be out of the (starting) blocks
to have started an activity • *Rival telephone companies were* ***quick off the blocks*** *with their reduced price offers.* • *The project for rebuilding the theatre is now off the starting blocks.*
on the/your **(starting) blocks** to be ready and waiting to start an activity • *The management is on its starting blocks, prepared for a flood of orders.*

blood

be after sb's **blood**
to want to catch someone in order to hurt them or punish them • *He'd cheated them and now they were after his blood.*

be in the/your **blood**
if an ability or a skill is in someone's blood, they have it naturally, usually because it already exists in their family or is a tradition of their social group • *She's a wonderful dancer just like her mother. It must be in her blood.*

be out for blood
if you are out for blood, you are determined to find someone to attack or blame for something • *These people are out for blood and if they find out you're involved you're in serious trouble.*

blood and guts *informal*
violence shown on television, film, or in the theatre, where people are seen being injured or killed • *It was all blood and guts. I came out feeling quite ill.*

blood and thunder
a speech or performance that is loud and full of emotion, especially anger • *We sat through 2 hours of blood and thunder and came out feeling exhausted.*

a blood brother
a man who has promised to treat another man as his brother, often in a ceremony in which they cut themselves and mix their blood together • *We were blood brothers – I was ready to die for him.*

Blood is thicker than water.
something that you say which means family relationships are stronger and

more important than other kinds of relationships, such as being friends • *They say blood is thicker than water, so how come so many families hate each other?*

sb's blood is up

if someone's blood is up, they are very angry or excited about something and may act in a violent way • *Now Tom's blood was up – he ran at Bob waving his fists.*

blood, sweat and tears

a lot of effort and suffering • *This house is the result of 3 years' blood, sweat and tears.*

burst/bust a blood vessel *informal*

1 to use a lot of effort doing something • *I'd like the designs as soon as possible, but don't bust a blood vessel!*

2 to become very angry and start shouting • *He nearly burst a blood vessel when he heard what they'd done to his car.*

get blood out of a stone

if making someone give or tell you something is like getting blood out of a stone, it is very difficult • *Collecting the rent money from him each month is* ***like getting blood out of a stone.*** • *I tried to talk to her, but I may as well have tried to get blood out of a stone.*

have blood on your hands
have sb's blood on your hands

to be responsible for someone's death • *The leaders of this war have the blood of many thousands of people on their hands.*

make sb's blood boil

to make someone very angry • *When I saw the rude way she talked to him it made my blood boil.*

sb's blood boils • *His blood boiled when he thought about how unfairly he'd been treated.*

make sb's blood run cold
make sb's blood curdle

if something makes someone's blood run cold, it makes them very frightened • *I heard a scream which made my blood run cold.*

sb's blood runs cold • *Steph's blood ran cold as she heard someone move in the shadows.*

smell/taste blood

to recognise an opportunity to be more successful, especially by taking advantage or someone who is in a difficult situation • *Environmental groups smell blood, and are increasing their campaign against the airport.*

► See also: be **baying** for blood
draw blood
scent blood
spit blood
sweat blood

bloodied

bloodied but unbowed *literary*

harmed but not defeated by an unpleasant situation or competition • *I emerged bloodied but unbowed from my oral exam.*

bloody

bloody minded *British & Australian informal*

someone who is bloody minded makes difficulties for other people, usually by arguing against their actions or ideas without a good reason • *There's no reason why we shouldn't do aerobics in the squash court – the sports committee are just being bloody minded.*

give sb a bloody nose

to defeat or damage someone, but not permanently or seriously • *The pro-Europeans gave their opponents a bloody nose in the debate.*

get a bloody nose • *They got a bloody nose when their new satellite channel failed due to lack of funding.*

► See also: **scream** bloody murder

blot

blot your copybook *British & Australian*

to do something which spoils someone's opinion of you • *She blotted her copybook by arriving late to a meeting.*

a blot on the landscape

something which looks unpleasant and spoils a pleasant view • *That new chemical factory is a real blot on the landscape.*

blow

blow a fuse/gasket *informal*

to become very angry and shout or

behave in a violent way • *Jim'll blow a fuse if he finds you here.* • *When her husband realised how much she'd spent he blew a gasket.*

blow a hole in sth
if you blow a hole in someone's opinions or arguments, you show that they are not true or right • *Bloodstains on the sheets blew a hole in the defence's argument.*

blow away the cobwebs *British & Australian*
to do something which makes you feel less tired or bored, especially to spend time outside in the fresh air ✍Cobwebs are made by spiders (= small insects with 8 legs) and are usually found in rooms or places that no one uses very much. • *A stroll along the cliffs will blow away the cobwebs.*

blow sb's **brains out**
to kill someone by shooting them in the head • *After two unsuccessful suicide attempts, she finally blew her brains out.*

blow-by-blow
a blow-by-blow description of an event gives every detail of how it happened • *She gave me a* ***blow-by-blow account*** *of her car crash.*

blow sb's **cover**
to let people know secret information about who someone is or what someone is doing • *Someone recognised him and phoned the newspapers, which blew his cover.*

blow hot and cold
to sometimes like or be interested in something or someone and sometimes not, so people are confused about how you really feel • *It's impossible to have a relationship with someone who blows hot and cold all the time.* • (often + **about**) *Sophie kept blowing hot and cold about the idea of working abroad.*

blow it *informal*
to spoil your chance of achieving something you want because of something you do or say • *She was hoping for promotion but she blew it when she got pregnant.* • *They want to publish his autobiography so let's hope he doesn't blow it by arguing with the publishers.*

a blow job *taboo*
the sexual activity of touching a man's penis with your mouth and tongue to give him pleasure • *She gave him a blow job.*

blow your **mind** *informal*
if something blows your mind, you find it extremely surprising and exciting • *The first time I heard this band, they completely blew my mind and I've been a fan ever since.*
mind-blowing *informal* • *The special effects in this film are mind-blowing.*

blow sth **out of (all) proportion**
to behave as if something that has happened is much worse than it really is • *They had a minor argument in a restaurant but the press have blown it out of all proportion, speculating about divorce.*

blow sth/sb **out of the water**
to destroy or defeat something or someone completely • *They came to court with fresh evidence that would, they said, blow the prosecution's case completely out of the water.*

blow sth **sky-high**
to make something that someone is trying to achieve fail completely, often by telling people something which should have been a secret • *He blew the whole deal sky-high by telling the newspapers about it.*

blow smoke *American*
to say things that are not true in order to make yourself or something you are involved with seem better than it is • *The team put on an unbelievable performance. I'm not just blowing smoke – they were great.*

blow your **stack/top** *informal*
to suddenly become very angry • *My mother blew her top when she saw the mess we'd made in the kitchen.*

blow the gaff *British old-fashioned, informal*
to cause trouble for someone by letting other people know something that they were trying to keep secret • (often + **on**) *They killed Green because he was about to blow the gaff on their drug dealing.*

blow the whistle on sb/sth
to tell someone in authority about

something bad that is happening so that it can be stopped • *He was dismissed when he tried to blow the whistle on the safety problems at the factory.* • *The kids are encouraged to blow the whistle on any of their friends who are using drugs.*

a whistle-blower • *Every organization needs a whistle-blower, someone who can stand up and say, 'Hey, you can't do that!'*

blow sth **wide open**

1 to make it impossible to guess who will win a competition • *She was the favourite to win, so her withdrawal has blown the election wide open.*

2 to make something that someone is trying to achieve fail completely, often by telling people something which should have been a secret • *He's threatening to blow the whole operation wide open if we don't give him a bigger share of the profits.*

cushion/soften the blow

to make a difficult experience less unpleasant • *Free street parking is to be abolished, but residents are being offered reduced price parking permits in an attempt to cushion the blow.*

▶ See also: blow up/explode in sb's **face**
blow/make a **hole** in sth
blast/blow sb/sth to **kingdom** come
blow/take the **lid** off sth
blow your **own** trumpet
blow a **raspberry**
blow/knock your **socks** off
blow off **steam**
strike a blow for sth/sb

blows

come to blows

to have a fight or a serious argument with someone • *Demonstrators nearly came to blows with the police during the march.* • (often + **over**) *It seems increasingly unlikely that the two countries will come to blows over this latest territorial dispute*

blue

blue blood

someone who has blue blood is from a family of the highest social class • *He has a fair bit of blue blood coursing through his veins.*

blue-blooded • *He comes from the blue-blooded section of the ruling classes.*

into the wide/wild blue yonder *literary*

if you go into the wide blue yonder, you go somewhere far away that seems exciting because it is not known • *I have a sudden desire to escape, to head off into the wide blue yonder and never return.*

like blue blazes *American & Australian old-fashioned*

if someone or something does something like blue blazes, they do it a lot • *This sweater itches like blue blazes.*

out of the blue *British, American & Australian*

out of a clear (blue) sky *American & Australian*

if something happens out of the blue, it happens suddenly and you are not expecting it • *Then one day, completely out of the blue, I had a letter from her.* • *The invasion came out of a clear blue sky and caught everyone off guard.*

until you **are blue in the face**

if you say something until you are blue in the face, you keep saying the same thing again and again but no one listens to you • *I can tell him to tidy his room until I'm blue in the face, but it's always a mess.*

▶ See also: **once** in a blue moon
scream blue murder
talk a blue streak

blue-arsed

[run around/rush around etc.] like a blue-arsed fly *British & Australian informal*

to move around quickly trying to finish your work when you are very busy • *I've been running around like a blue-arsed fly trying to get everything organized before I go on holiday.*

blue-collar

blue-collar

a blue-collar worker is someone who does physical work, often in a factory • (always before noun) *Blue collar workers in the factories and shipyards were demanding wage increases.* • *They are hoping the new factory will create many more blue collar jobs.* (= jobs for blue collar workers)

blue-eyed

▶ See: a blue-eyed **boy**

bluff

▶ See: **call** sb's bluff

blushes

save/spare sb's **blushes** *British & Australian*
to do something to prevent someone feeling embarrassed • *Granger saved the team's blushes by scoring the only goal in the last five minutes of the game.* • *The audience's blushes were spared because the censors had removed all the explicit sex scenes from the film.*

board

across the board
if something is done, happens, or exists across the board, it is done, happens, or exists in every part or area of something • *The company is proposing to cut spending* ***right across the board****.* • *Even as late as September, there are still course vacancies across the board, although the majority are in sciences.*

be above board
to be honest and legal • *The deal was completely above board.*

go by the board *British, American & Australian*
go by the boards *American*
if something that has been planned or arranged goes by the board, it does not happen, and if something that exists goes by the board, it ends • *All our careful arrangements went by the board when the trip was cancelled at the last minute.* • *When modern machinery was introduced, old-fashioned printing methods went by the board.*

on board
if someone is on board, they are working with an organization or group of people • *A new financial director has been* ***brought on board*** *to help us assess the cost of the project.* • *We hope to* ***have*** *a new doctor* ***on board*** *by the end of the month.*

take on board sth
to understand and accept ideas and opinions which may change the way you behave in the future • *Banks need to take on board the views of their customers.* • *It seems that young people are finally taking on board the message that it's not cool to smoke.*

▶ See also: **sweep** the board

boards

▶ See: **tread** the boards

boat

▶ See: **miss** the boat
push the boat out
rock the boat

Bob

Bob's your uncle! *British & Australian informal*
something that you say after you have explained how to do something, to emphasize that it will be simple and successful • *You simply put on the stain remover, leave it for an hour and Bob's your uncle, the stain's gone.*

bodice-ripper

a bodice-ripper *humorous*
a romantic book, usually where the story happens a long time ago, in which the characters show very strong emotions • *She's written a serious novel, not some sort of bodice-ripper.*

body

body and soul
if you do something or believe something body and soul, you do it or believe it completely • *She dedicated herself to her research, body and soul.*

a body blow *mainly British*
something that causes serious difficulty or disappointment • *Losing the court case was a body blow to animal rights campaigners.* • *Her hopes of competing in the Olympics were* ***dealt a body blow*** *when she fell and injured her back.*

▶ See also: **keep** body and soul together

bog

bog standard *British informal*
completely ordinary • *I just want a completely bog standard washing machine.*

boil

can't boil an egg *humorous*
if someone can't boil an egg, they are not able to cook ✍This phrase comes from the idea that boiling an egg is a very easy thing to do. • *Don't expect a dinner*

invitation from Laura – she can't boil an egg.

go off the boil

1 *British & Australian* to become less successful • *After winning their first two matches this season, the French team seem to have gone off the boil.*

2 *British* if a situation or feeling goes off the boil, it becomes less urgent or less strong • *The housing issue has gone off the boil recently, despite attempts to revive public interest.* • *Our affair went off the boil when I discovered he was married.*

on the boil *British*

if a situation or feeling is on the boil, it is very strong or active • *The corruption scandal is being kept on the boil by a series of new revelations.*

boiling

► See: **reach** boiling point

bold

as bold as brass

with too much confidence • *He walked up to me bold as brass and asked if I had any spare change.*

bolt

a bolt from the blue
a bolt out of the blue

something that you do not expect to happen and that surprises you very much • *The news that they had got married was a bolt from the blue.* • *He seemed to be very happy in his job, so his resignation* ***came as a bolt out of the blue.***

bolt upright

in a position where you are sitting up with your back very straight • *He woke to see her sitting bolt upright beside him and wondered what was the matter.*

► See also: **shoot** your bolt

bomb

go (like) a bomb *British & Australian informal*

to be very successful • *Judging from the noise they're making, the party must be going like a bomb.*

go like a bomb *British & Australian informal*

if a vehicle goes like a bomb, it can move very fast • *Henry's new sportscar goes like an absolute bomb.*

put a bomb under sth/sb *British & Australian*

if you want to put a bomb under someone, you want to make them do things faster • *I'd like to put a bomb under those solicitors.*

► See also: **cost** a bomb
drop a bomb

bombshell

► See: **drop** a bombshell

bona fide

bona fide

if someone or something is bona fide, they are what they seem to be and they are not trying to deceive you • *The new immigration policy is so severe it risks rejecting bona fide political refugees.*

bone

be bone dry
be as dry as a bone

to be completely dry • *The ground was bone dry after 3 weeks without rain.*

be bone idle *British*

to be very lazy • *She's bone idle – she just sits around the house all day watching TV.*

be close to the bone
be near the bone

if something you say or write is close to the bone, it is close to the truth in a way that may offend someone • *He said he was only joking, but his comments were a bit close to the bone.* • *Your remark about people who've been in trouble with the police was very near the bone.*

a bone of contention

something that people argue about for a long time • *The main bone of contention was deciding who would take care of the children after the divorce.*

have a bone to pick with sb

something that you say when you want to talk to someone about something they have done that has annoyed you • *I have a bone to pick with you. Did you eat that chocolate mousse I was saving for my tea?*

he/she doesn't have a [jealous, mean, unkind etc.] bone in his/her body

something that you say in order to emphasize that someone is not jealous, mean, unkind etc. • *He'd never deliberately hurt someone's feelings – he doesn't have a mean bone in his body.*

there isn't a [mean, jealous, unkind etc.] bone in sb's **body** • *She wasn't the possessive type, and there wasn't a jealous bone in her body.*

▶ See also: **chill** sb to the bone/marrow
be **chilled** to the bone/marrow
be **cut** to the bone

bones

make no bones about sth

to say clearly what you think or feel although you may embarrass or offend someone • *He made no bones about his dissatisfaction with the service in the hotel.* • *She makes no bones about wanting John to leave.*

▶ See also: I (can) **feel** it in my bones.

bon mot

a bon mot

a funny or clever remark • *Wilde's bons mots are legendary.*

bon viveur

a bon viveur *mainly British*

someone who enjoys good food and wine • *A noted bon viveur, he had a passion for French cuisine.*

boo

▶ See: not **say** boo
wouldn't **say** boo to a goose

book

go by the book
do sth **by the book**

to do something exactly as the rules tell you • *My lawyer always goes strictly by the book.* • *This is a private deal – we don't have to do everything by the book.*

in my book *informal*

in my opinion • *She's never lied to me, and in my book that counts for a lot.*

read sb **like a book**

if you can read someone like a book, you know exactly what they are feeling or thinking without having to ask • *You're bored, aren't you? I can read you like a book.*

▶ See also: **bring** sb to book
crack a book
You can't **judge** a book by its cover.
throw the book at sb

books

be in sb's **good books** *informal*

if you are in someone's good books, they are pleased with you • *I cleaned the bathroom yesterday so I'm in Mum's good books.*

OPPOSITE **be in** sb's **bad books** *informal*

• *He's in Melanie's bad books because he arrived 2 hours late.*

That's/There's one for the books. *British, American & Australian informal*
That's/There's a turn-up for the books. *British & Australian informal*

something that you say when something strange or surprising happens • *My sister stayed in on a Saturday night! There's one for the books.* • *That's a turn-up for the books – a Frenchman who loves English food.*

▶ See also: **cook** the books
hit the books

boom

▶ See: **lower** the boom

boot

give sb **the boot**

1 *informal* to stop employing someone • *They gave him the boot for swearing at his manager.*

get the boot *informal* • *Did she tell you why she got the boot?*

2 *informal* to end a romantic relationship with someone • *She gave him the boot because he wouldn't stop talking about his ex-girlfriends.*

put the boot in *British informal*

1 to make a bad situation worse • *He lost his job and then his wife put the boot in by announcing she was leaving him.*

2 to attack someone by kicking them again and again, usually when they are lying on the ground • *Four lads pushed him down and then put the boot in.*

▶ See also: the boot is on the other **foot**

boots

► See: **die** with your boots on
hang up your boots
lick sb's boots
be **quaking** in your boots
be **shaking** in your boots/shoes

bootstraps

haul/pull yourself **up by** your **bootstraps**
to improve your situation by your own efforts without any help from other people • *My father pulled himself up by his bootstraps to become one of the richest men in the country.*

bore

bore the arse off sb *British & Australian very informal*
bore the ass off sb *American very informal*
to make someone very bored • *These wildlife programmes bore the arse off me.*

bored

be bored to death/tears *informal*
be bored stiff *informal*
to be very bored • *The speeches went on for an hour. I was bored to death.*
bore sb **to death/tears** • *That film bored me to tears.*

born

be born with a silver spoon in your **mouth**
to be the son or daughter of a very rich family • *His complete lack of concern about money is natural of someone who was born with a silver spoon in their mouth.*

born and bred
if you were born and bred in a place, you were born and grew up in that place and have the typical character of someone who lives there • (often + **in**) *She was born and bred in Jamaica but now lives in France.* • *He's a Londoner born and bred.*

I/he/she wasn't born yesterday!
something that you say in order to tell someone that a person is not stupid and cannot be easily deceived • *You'd better think of a better excuse about the dent in my car. I wasn't born yesterday, you know!* • *You can't expect your mother to believe that – she wasn't born yesterday!*

► See also: There's **one** born every minute.

bosom

in the bosom of sb *literary*
if you are in the bosom of a group of people, especially your family, you are with people who love you and make you feel safe • *She was glad to be home again, back in the bosom of her family.*

bossy

a bossy boots *British & Australian informal*
an impolite way of describing someone who always tells other people what to do • *Karen's such a bossy boots – ordering us around all the time.*

both

► See: the **best** of both worlds
cut both/two ways
jump in with both feet
keep your/both feet on the ground
swing both ways

bottle

► See: **hit** the bottle

bottom

at the bottom of the heap/pile
in a worse situation than anyone else in a group of people • *Those at the bottom of the heap feel that society has failed them.* • *The homeless are at the bottom of the pile with little hope of improving their situation.*

be/lie at the bottom of sth
to be the real reason for something unpleasant • *I don't know for certain why she dislikes you, but I suspect jealousy* ***is at the bottom of it****.*

sb's **bottom drawer**
the things a young woman collects to use in her home after she is married • *I've given her some silver cutlery for her bottom drawer.*

the bottom drops/falls out of the market
if the bottom drops out of the market of a product, people stop buying it • *The bottom fell out of the art market and dealers were left with hundreds of unsaleable paintings.*

sb's **bottom line**
the lowest amount of money that

someone is willing to give or receive in payment for something • *My bottom line on this job is $5000 – I can't do it for less.*

the bottom line

1 the most important fact in a situation • *The bottom line is that people's health is at risk if they smoke.*

2 the total amount of money that a business makes or loses • *The bottom line is what counts in most companies these days.*

from the bottom of your **heart**

with sincere feeling • *We would like to thank you from the bottom of our hearts for all your help.*

get to the bottom of sth

to discover the truth about a situation • (often + question word) *The family finally got to the bottom of why their boy was killed.* • *How will investigators get to the bottom of the affair with so little evidence?*

▶ See also: you can **bet** your life/your bottom dollar
be **bumping** along the bottom
knock the bottom out of sth

bottomless

a bottomless pit

someone or something that always needs or wants more of whatever they are given, especially money • *It's a poor country with a bottomless pit of debt.* • *Seb'll eat any food that's left over. He's a bottomless pit!*

bouncing

be bouncing off the walls *informal*

to be excited and full of nervous energy • *We need to get out for a walk. The children are bouncing off the walls.*

bound

be bound and determined *American*

to have a strong wish to do something and to not allow anything to stop you from doing it • (often + to do sth) *She's bound and determined to make her career in medical research.*

bounds

be out of bounds

1 if an area is out of bounds, you are not allowed to go there • *All military sites are totally out of bounds.*

2 if an activity or object is out of bounds, it is not approved of or not allowed • *High fat foods are out of bounds on this diet.*

▶ See also: **know** no bounds

bow

bow and scrape

to try too hard to please someone in a position of authority • (often in continuous tenses) *It's embarrassing to see staff bowing and scraping to the new Prime Minister.*

bowl

▶ See: **life** is just a bowl of cherries.

box

box clever *British*

to behave in a clever and sometimes slightly dishonest way to try to achieve a result you want ✍A good boxer (= man who fights as a sport) is a person who uses skill as well as strength to win fights. • *Obviously he would have to box clever in the witness stand to avoid implicating himself.*

box sb's **ears** *old-fashioned*

to hit someone, usually as a punishment • *I'll box your ears, young man, if you come home late again!*

▶ See also: **think** outside the box

boy

a blue-eyed boy *British & Australian*
a fair-haired boy *American & Australian*

a man who is liked and admired by someone in authority • *He was very much the blue-eyed boy in the office.*

a mummy's/mother's boy *British & Australian*
a mama's boy *American*

a boy or man who allows his mother to have too much influence on him • *Derek's a bit of a mummy's boy. He finished with his last girlfriend because his mother disapproved.* • *He was often depicted as a weak-willed mama's boy with a domineering mother.*

▶ See also: the boy/girl **next** door

boys

the boys in blue *British & Australian*

the police • *The boys in blue were round again last night, asking questions.*

Boys will be boys.
something that you say which means it is not surprising when boys or men behave in a noisy, rude, or unpleasant way • *He goes drinking on a Friday night and always ends up in a fight. Boys will be boys.*

brain

be brain dead *humorous*
if someone is brain dead, their mind is not working effectively, usually because they are very tired or very bored • *By the time I leave work I'm completely brain dead.*

be out of your **brain** *British very informal*
to be very drunk • *By the time I arrived at the party he was out of his brain.*

a brain box *British & Australian informal*
a very intelligent person • *Come on brain box, what's the answer?*

a brain drain
the movement of people with education and skills from their own country to another country where they are paid more for their work • *There is a brain drain of British mathematicians to the United States.*

a brain trust *American & Australian*
a group of people with special knowledge or skills who give advice to someone in a position of authority • *He joined the President's brain trust for the election campaign.*

get your **brain in gear** *informal*
to make yourself start thinking clearly and effectively • *I've got to get my brain in gear for the meeting this afternoon.*

have sth **on the brain** *informal*
to not be able to stop thinking or talking about one particular thing • *You've got cars on the brain. Can't we talk about something else for a change?*

▶ See also: **rack** your brain/brains

brains

be the brains behind sth
to be the person who plans and organizes something, especially something successful • *He was the brains behind many of the best movies ever made.*

▶ See also: **beat** your brains out
blow sb's brains out
pick sb's brains
rack your brain/brains

brakes

put the brakes on
to stop an activity • *The government has put the brakes on any further spending.*

brass

brass monkey weather *British very informal*
extremely cold weather • *It's brass monkey weather today, isn't it!*
be cold enough to freeze the balls off a brass monkey *British very informal* • *We were in Moscow, and it was cold enough to freeze the balls off a brass monkey.*

the brass ring *American*
success or a reward that you try to achieve, often by competing against other people • *Our aim is to have the best team in the league – the brass ring is there guys, go and get it.*

get down to brass tacks
to start talking about the most important or basic facts of a situation ✍Brass tacks is Cockney rhyming slang (= an informal kind of language said to be used in parts of London) for facts. • *Let's get down to brass tacks. Who's paying for all of this?*

have the brass (neck) to do sth *British informal*
have the brass (balls) to do sth *American & Australian very informal*
to have the confidence to do something that is rude or shows a lack of respect, without caring whether people approve • *How does she have the brass to ask for a day off during our busiest period?* • *He had the brass balls to announce his engagement to Sally in front of his ex-wife.*

▶ See also: with (brass) **knobs** on

brave

put a brave face/front on sth
to behave in a way that makes people think you are happy when you are not • *They've had some bad luck, but they've put a brave face on their problems.* • *She's very ill but she's* ***putting a brave front on it.*** (= making people believe her ill-

ness does not worry her)

put on a brave face/front • *He doesn't seem upset about losing. Do you think he's just putting on a brave face?*

brawn

be all brawn and no brains

to be physically strong but not very intelligent • *I agree he's got a good body, but he's all brawn and no brains.*

breach

▶ See: **step** into the breach

bread

sb's **bread and butter** *informal*

a job or activity that provides you with the money you need to live • *Teaching at the local college is his bread and butter.*

bread and butter a bread and butter subject or problem is about things that people need in order to live, such as money and jobs • *Unemployment and taxes are the bread and butter issues of this campaign.*

bread and circuses

activities that are intended to keep people happy so that they do not complain about problems • *Tax cuts are just bread and circuses designed to distract attention from the underlying economic crisis.*

breadline

be/live on the breadline *British & Australian*

to be very poor ✍In America, breadlines were very poor people standing in a line waiting for free food provided by the government. • *Most families of the unemployed are on the breadline.* • *How many elderly people in Britain are living on the breadline?*

be/live below the breadline • *There are immigrant families living below the breadline in some areas.*

break

Break a leg!

something that you say to wish someone good luck, especially before they perform in the theatre ✍Some people believe that if you say the words 'good luck' to an actor, you will bring them bad luck. • (usually an order) *'Tonight's the first night of the play.' 'Is it? Well, break a leg!'*

break your **back** *informal*

to put a lot of effort into doing something • (often + doing sth) *I'm not going to break my back working for £120 a week!*

break even

if a person or a business breaks even, they do not make or lose any money from their business • *After a bad year in 1995, the company just about broke even in 1996.*

break faith with sth/sb *formal*

to stop supporting an idea or person, especially by not doing what you promised to do • *She claims that the government has broken faith with teachers by failing to give additional funds to education.*

break sb's **heart**

1 to make someone who loves you very sad, especially by telling them you do not love them any more • *He broke my heart, but I'll never forget him.*

2 if an unpleasant situation or event breaks your heart, it makes you feel very sad • (often + to do sth) ***It breaks my heart** to think about all those poor stray dogs.*

break new ground

to do something that is different to anything that has been done before • *We're breaking new ground in television comedy. You'll never have seen anything like this before.*

ground-breaking • (always before noun) *It was with her ground-breaking, all-women production of Hamlet that she really established herself.*

to discover new information about a subject • *So are scientists breaking new ground in their quest to discover what causes the disease?*

ground-breaking • (always before noun) *This company has produced some ground-breaking research.*

break ranks

to publicly show that you disagree with a group of which you are a member • (often + **with**) *Junior officers were said to be prepared to break ranks with the leadership.*

break the back of sth

1 to defeat an enemy or to deal with an unpleasant situation • *There is evidence that government troops have broken the back of the resistance.*

2 *British* to complete the worst or biggest part of the job • *We managed to break the back of the building work before the weather changed.*

not **break the bank**

to not be too expensive • *And at £12.99 a bottle, this is a champagne that won't break the bank.*

break the ice

to make people who have not met before feel more relaxed with each other • *We played a couple of party games to break the ice.*

an ice-breaker • *We usually start the session with an ice-breaker in the form of a game.*

break the mould

to do something differently, after it has been done in the same way for a long time • *She broke the mould by insisting on becoming a doctor instead of a nurse.* • (often + **of**) *A new TV show is about to be launched which aims to break the mold of the usual daytime programs.*

break wind

to allow gas to escape from your bottom, especially loudly • *At a wedding that I attended last summer, one of the guests broke wind very loudly during the groom's speech.*

give sb **a break** *informal*

to stop criticizing or behaving in an unpleasant way to someone • *Give her a break – she's only a child and she didn't mean any harm.*

Give me/us a break! *American & Australian informal*

something that you say when you do not believe what someone has just said • *'You're going to run a marathon? Give me a break!'*

Why break the habit of a lifetime? *British & Australian humorous*

something that you say which means that you do not believe that someone will stop doing something bad that they have done all their lives • *'I must stop writing my essays the night before the deadline.' 'Why break the habit of a lifetime?'*

► See also: **make** or break sth

breakfast

► See: **eat** sb for breakfast

breaking

It's/You're breaking my heart! *humorous*

something that you say in order to tell someone you do not feel sad about an event or situation • *'Things are so bad right now she's had to sell one of her houses.' 'You're breaking my heart!'*

breast

► See: **beat** your breast

breath

a breath of fresh air

someone or something that is new and different and makes everything seem more exciting • *Angela's like a breath of fresh air when she comes to stay.* • *After all the criticism, his positive comments came as a breath of fresh air.*

take your **breath away**

if something takes your breath away, you feel surprise and admiration because it is very beautiful, good, or exciting • *The beauty of the Taj Mahal took my breath away.*

under your **breath**

if you say something under your breath, you say it very quietly so that people cannot hear the exact words • *'I don't believe you.' she muttered under her breath.*

► See also: **catch** your breath
Don't **hold** your breath.
waste your breath

breathe

breathe (new) life into sth

to make something that was boring seem interesting again • *Breathe new life into a tired old bathroom with a coat of brightly coloured paint in this season's exciting colours.*

not **breathe a word**

to not tell people a secret • *Please tell me what happened. I promise I won't breathe a word.*

breathe down sb's **neck**
to pay very close attention to what someone does in a way that annoys or worries them • *It's awful having to work with a boss who's breathing down your neck the whole time.*

breathe fire
to be very angry about something • (sometimes + **over**) *The bishop was breathing fire over the press release made a few days ago.*

breed

breed like rabbits *informal*
if people breed like rabbits, they produce too many babies very quickly • *It's like I was saying to Derek, they all intermarry and they breed like rabbits.*

breeze

▶ See: **shoot** the breeze/bull

brick

be/come up against a brick wall
to not be able to continue an activity or do something you want to do • *I've tried everywhere I can think of for funding but I've come up against a brick wall.* • *My brother wants to leave home but he can't find a job. He's up against a brick wall.*

▶ See also: be **built** like a brick shithouse
hit a/the (brick) wall
shit a brick
be like **talking** to a brick wall

bricks

You can't make bricks without straw.
something that you say which means you cannot do something correctly without the necessary materials • *I need an electric drill to put these shelves up. You can't make bricks without straw.*

bridesmaid

always the bridesmaid, never the bride
used to talk about someone who is never the most important person in a situation • *Huw worked with a host of great actors, but somehow was always the bridesmaid, never the bride.*

bridge

▶ See: I'll/We'll **cross** that bridge when I/we come to it.

bridges

▶ See: **build** bridges

bright

be as bright as a button *British & Australian*
to be intelligent and able to think quickly • *She was bright as a button – always asking questions and quick to help.*

be bright and breezy
to be happy and confident • *I get a bit depressed at times, whereas Gill's always bright and breezy.*

bright and early
very early in the morning • *You're up bright and early.*

the bright lights
exciting and attractive people and places in big cities • *I went in search of the bright lights, but all I found was poverty and loneliness.*

a bright spark *British & Australian*
an intelligent person ✍This phrase is often used humorously to mean the opposite. • *Some bright spark was clearing up and threw my invitation away.*

a bright spot
a pleasant or successful event or period of time when most other things are unpleasant or not successful • (often + **in**) *The only bright spot in Liverpool's disastrous performance was a stunning goal in the second half.*

▶ See also: **look** on the bright side

bright-eyed

be bright-eyed and bushy-tailed *humorous*
to be full of energy and eager to do things • *She was bright-eyed and bushy-tailed the next morning, despite having been up half the night.*

bring

bring a lump to your **throat**
if something someone says or does brings a lump to your throat, it makes you feel such strong emotions that you want to cry • *I thought it was a very moving*

speech. It almost brought a lump to my throat.

bring sb **down a peg or two**
to do something to show someone that they are not as good as they thought they were • *He's one of these super-confident types who really needs to be brought down a peg or two.*

bring home the bacon *informal*
1 to earn money to live on • *If Jo's going to be at home looking after the kids, someone needs to bring home the bacon.*
2 to do something successfully, especially to win a game or race • *Racegoers crowded the stand to see him bring home the bacon.* (= win the race)

bring sth **home to** sb
to make someone understand something much more clearly than they did before, especially something unpleasant • *These photographs finally brought home to us the terrible realities of war.* • *It took an international crisis to bring it home to British politicians that they desperately needed allies in Europe.*
come home to sb if something comes home to someone, they understand it clearly • *It suddenly came home to me that I had made the most awful mistake.*

bring sth **into play**
to begin to involve or use something in order to help you do something • *Even bringing into play all the resources available would not resolve the immediate shortfall in production.*

bring out the best in sb
to make someone show or use the good qualities they have • *Stressful situations don't usually bring out the best in people.*
OPPOSITE **bring out the worst in** sb • *I can't stop criticizing her – she just brings out the worst in me.*

bring the house down
if someone or something brings the house down during a play or show, they make the people watching it laugh or clap very loudly • *The clown sang a duet with the talking horse, which brought the house down every night.*

bring sth **to bear** *formal*
to use influence, arguments, or threats in order to change a situation • (often + **on**) *Pressure should be brought to bear on the illegal regime and support given to the resistance.*

bring sb **to book** *British & Australian*
to punish someone • (usually passive) *A crime has been committed and whoever is responsible must be brought to book.*

bring sb/sth **to** their **knees**
to destroy or defeat someone or something • *Sanctions were imposed in an attempt to bring the country to its knees.* • *The strikes brought the economy to its knees.*

bring sth **to light**
to discover facts, often about something bad or illegal • (usually passive) *When their accounts were examined, several errors were brought to light.*

come to light
• *Several other problems came to light during the course of the investigation.*

bring sth/sb **to mind**
to cause you to think of someone or something • *Something about his face brings to mind an old friend of mine.*

bring sb **to the [bargaining/peace etc.] table**
to persuade a person or a country to join discussions in order to find a solution to a problem • *We hope to be able to bring the warring factions to the negotiating table to try to end this conflict.*
come to the [bargaining/peace etc.] table • *You have to be prepared to make concessions when you come to the bargaining table.*

bring sth **to the party**
to have something useful that you can offer in a particular situation • *The company was doing well, but Hodge brought some much-needed marketing skills to the party.*

bring up the rear
to be at the back of a group of people who are walking or running • *Ceri was in the lead. Bringing up the rear, a mile or so down the road, was Simon.*

▶ See also: bring/call sb to **heel**
bring/pull sb up with a **start**

brink

be on the brink of doing sth
to be likely to do something very soon • *The club's manager dismissed reports*

that he was on the brink of buying Peter Beardsley.

on the brink of sth

if someone or something is on the brink of a situation, that situation is likely to happen soon • *The country is on the brink of civil war.* • *We are* ***teetering on the brink of*** *bankruptcy.* • *She is on the brink of international stardom.*

broad

be broad in the beam *old-fashioned*

to have a large bottom • *Tess has always been rather broad in the beam, despite all those diets.*

broad (brush) strokes

if you describe a situation with broad strokes, you describe it in a very general way without giving any details • *The novel's historical background is filled in with broad brush strokes.* • *In a few broad strokes he summed up his beliefs.*

a broad church *British*

an organization that includes many different types of people with different opinions • *The Congress remains a broad church with members from a diversity of backgrounds.*

have a broad back

not be easily hurt by criticism • *It helps to have a broad back in showbusiness.*

to be able to help other people with their problems without becoming tired or upset • *Why don't you tell me what's wrong? I've got a broad back.*

in broad daylight

if a crime is committed in broad daylight, it happens during the day when it could easily have been seen and prevented • *The man was shot at close range in broad daylight in front of his house.*

broaden

▶ See: broaden/widen sb's **horizons**

broke

go for broke *informal*

to risk everything in order to achieve the result you want • *She decided to go for broke and pursue her acting career full-time.*

If it ain't broke, don't fix it.

something that you say which means if a system or method works well there is no reason to change it • *We're happy with our exam system in Scotland, and as they say, if it ain't broke, don't fix it.*

They broke the mould when they made sb/sth.

something that you say which means someone or something is very special and that there is not another person or thing like them • *They broke the mold when they made Elvis. There's never been a star to match him.*

Bronx

a Bronx cheer *American informal*

a rude sound you make by holding your tongue between your lips and blowing • *Cindy turned around and blew a Bronx cheer at the kids who'd been teasing her.*

brother

▶ See: not be your brother's **keeper**

brought

▶ See: be brought/called to **account**

brown

be as brown as a berry *British & Australian*

if someone is as brown as a berry their skin has become much darker because of the effects of the sun • *She's as brown as a berry after a month in Greece.*

brown-bagging

brown-bagging *American informal*

taking your own food, usually in a brown paper bag, to eat in the middle of the day when you are not at home • *We've stopped brown-bagging – it's too cold now to eat in the park.*

brown-bag • (always before noun) *We had our meeting over a brown-bag lunch.*

brownie

earn/get brownie points *informal*

to get praise or approval for something you have done • *I thought I might get some brownie points by helping to organize the party.*

brown-nose

brown-nose *informal*

to try too hard to please someone, especially someone in a position of authority, in a way that other people find unpleasant • *The rest of the class were sick of watching him brown-nose.*

brows

▶ See: **knit** your brows

brunt

bear/take the brunt of sth

to receive the worst part of something unpleasant or harmful, such as an attack • *The oldest parts of the town bore the brunt of the missile attacks.*

bubble

the bubble bursts

a very happy or successful period of time suddenly ends • (usually in past tenses) *The economy was booming, then the bubble burst with the stockmarket crash of October 1987.*

burst the bubble • *Their first argument burst the bubble.*

buck

buck naked *American & Australian informal*

completely naked • *I got a shock when I saw her sitting buck naked, drink in hand, watching TV.*

The buck stops here.

something that you say in order to tell someone that you will take responsibility for a situation or problem • *We carry out all the safety tests in this department, so the buck stops here.*

The buck stops with sb. • *The police authorized the raid and they must accept that the buck stops with them.*

buck the trend

to be noticeably different from the way that a situation is developing generally, especially in connection with financial matters • *Spending is down this season, but the tourist industry is managing to buck the trend, with thousands more holidays sold.*

make a fast/quick buck *American & Australian informal*

to earn money quickly and often in a way that is not honest ✍A buck is an informal word for a dollar (= a unit of money in America). • *Times are hard – you have to make a fast buck wherever and however you can.*

▶ See also: **pass** the buck

bucket

▶ See: **kick** the bucket

buckets

▶ See: **sweat** buckets

bucks

a bucks party *Australian*

a party for a man who is going to get married to which only his male friends are invited • *I got a bit drunk at Pete's bucks party and disgraced myself.*

bud

▶ See: **nip** sth in the bud

budge

▶ See: not budge/give an **inch**

buff

in the buff *old-fashioned*

naked • *He came out of the bedroom in the buff.*

buffers

▶ See: **hit** the buffers

build

build bridges

to improve relationships between people who are very different or do not like each other • (often + **between**) *A local charity is working to build bridges between different ethnic groups in the area.*

▶ See also: build/get/work up a **head** of steam

built

be built like a brick shithouse *British & Australian very informal*

if someone is built like a brick shithouse, they are very strong and very big • *I wasn't going to argue with him – he was built like a brick shithouse.*

be built like a tank

if a person or a vehicle is built like a tank, they are very strong and very big • *These cars are built like tanks.* • *I should imagine he's pretty strong – he's built like a tank.*

be built on sand

if something is built on sand, it is not firmly established and is likely to fail • *They seem quite happy now but I have a feeling that this marriage is built on sand.*

bulging

▶ See: be bulging/bursting at the **seams**

bull

be like a bull in a china shop

to often drop or break things because you move awkwardly or roughly • *Rob's like a bull in a china shop – don't let him near those plants.* • *She's like a bull in a china shop when it comes to dealing with people's feelings.* (= behaves in a way that offends people)

like a bull at a gate

if you do something like a bull at a gate, you do it very quickly • *Al wants to finish the shelves today so he's **going at them like a bull at a gate**.*

take the bull by the horns

to do something difficult in a determined and confident way • *Why don't you take the bull by the horns and tell him to leave?*

▶ See also: **shoot** the breeze/bull

bullet

▶ See: **bite** the bullet

bullets

▶ See: **sweat** bullets

bull-headed

bull-headed

someone who is bull-headed is determined to do exactly what they want to do, and does not think about what other people want • *He's completely bull-headed. I asked him not to throw out that old table, but he did it anyway.*

bully

Bully for you! *informal*

something that you say when you do not think what someone has done deserves praise or admiration, although they think it does • *'I cleaned the whole house yesterday.' 'Bully for you!'*

a bully pulpit *American*

an important job or position that someone can use to persuade other people to accept their ideas • *The presidency is a wonderful bully pulpit to convince the country of the need for a balanced budget.*

bum

a bum rap *American informal*

blame or punishment that is not fair • *Teachers are getting a bum rap from people who say they don't work hard enough.* • *She was sent up to the penitentiary on a bum rap.*

a bum steer *American & Australian informal*

information that is not correct or not helpful • *The bus driver gave us a bum steer and we ended up miles from where we wanted to go.* • *Her suggestion to eat at that little Italian restaurant was a bum steer.* (= a bad suggestion)

the bum's rush *American informal*

the action of getting rid of someone who is not wanted • *The photographer was given the bum's rush by two policemen guarding the office.* • *Why do I feel I'm getting the bum's rush? Where are you off to?*

bump

like a bump on a log *American informal*

if someone sits or stands somewhere like a bump on a log, they do not react in a useful or helpful way to the activities happening around them • *Don't just sit there like a bump on a log, come and help us!*

bumper

bumper to bumper

bumper to bumper

vehicles that are bumper to bumper are in a line one after another and are moving very slowly or stopped • *Cars were lined up bumper to bumper along the whole length of the road.*

bumper-to-bumper • (always before noun) *We were caught in bumper-to-bumper traffic for over an hour.*

bumping

be bumping along the bottom *British*

if an economic system is bumping along the bottom, it is working very slowly • *With the economy bumping along the bottom, it seems unlikely any new jobs will be created.*

bumpy

▶ See: a bumpy/rough **ride**

bums

▶ See: bums on **seats**

bun

have a bun in the oven *British & Australian humorous*

to be pregnant • *I hear Wendy's got a bun in the oven.*

bundle

not **be a bundle of laughs** *informal*

to not be entertaining or enjoyable • *She's not a bundle of laughs, your cousin.* • *The funeral wasn't exactly a bundle of laughs.*

a bundle of joy *informal*

a baby • *Three days after the birth, Sandra took home her little bundle of joy.*

not **go a bundle on** sth *British informal*

to not like something • *I don't go a bundle on Anne's new haircut.*

▶ See also: be a bundle of **nerves**

bunnies

▶ See: **fuck** like bunnies

burn

burn your **boats** *British & Australian*

burn your **bridges** *British, American & Australian*

to do something that makes it impossible for you to change your plans and go back to the situation you were in before • *She didn't want to burn her boats by asking for a divorce, so she suggested a trial separation instead.* • *I'd already burned my bridges with my previous employer by publicly criticizing their products.*

burn the candle at both ends

to get little sleep or rest because you are busy until late every night and you get up early every morning • (usually in continuous tenses) *She'd been burning the candle at both ends studying for her exams and made herself ill.*

burn the midnight oil

to work very late into the night • *I've got to get this report finished by tomorrow so I guess I'll be burning the midnight oil tonight.*

▶ See also: burn your **fingers**

burned

▶ See: be burned to a **crisp**

burning

have sth **burning a hole in** your **pocket** *humorous*

if someone has money burning a hole in their pocket, they want to spend it as soon as possible • *I had a fifty dollar bill that was burning a hole in my pocket, so I figured I'd go out and have a really good time.*

burnt

▶ See: be burnt to a **crisp**

burst

▶ See: burst/bust a **blood** vessel

bursting

▶ See: be bulging/bursting at the **seams**

burton

gone for a burton *British old-fashioned*

to be broken, spoiled or dead • *There's our quiet evening gone for a burton!*

bury

bury your **head in the sand**

to refuse to think about an unpleasant situation, hoping that it will improve so that you will not have to deal with it • *Parents said bullying was being ignored, and accused the headmaster of burying his head in the sand.*

bury the hatchet

to forget about arguments and disagreements with someone and to become friends with them again • *It had been over a year since the incident and I thought it was time we buried the hatchet.*

bush

bush league *American informal*
not done to the usual or accepted standards • *His article was a bush league stunt to discredit the company, and he has apologized.*

the bush telegraph *British & Australian*
the way in which people quickly pass important information to other people, especially by talking • *News of the redundancies spread immediately on the bush telegraph.*

▶ See also: **beat** about/around the bush

bushes

▶ See: **beat** the bushes

business

be in business *informal*
to be able to start doing something because you have everything you need to do it • *As soon as I find my map and my keys we're in business.*

business as usual
a situation that has returned to its usual state again after an unpleasant or surprising event • *It was business as usual at the school yesterday only a month after the fire.*

the business end *informal*
the business end of a weapon or tool is the end which does the damage or work • *She screamed when she found herself facing the business end of his gun.*

business is business
something that you say which means the purpose of business is to make a profit, and that other things, such as personal feelings, must not be allowed to prevent this • *Business is business, and if your friend can't produce the work on time, I'll have to find someone else.*

do the business *British & Australian informal*
1 to achieve what is wanted or needed in a situation • *As long as he does the business on the football field, the club is happy with him.*
2 to have sex • *So he went home with her. Do you think they did the business?*

not **in the business of** doing sth
if you are not in the business of doing something, you do not do it, usually because you think it is wrong • *I'm not in the business of causing trouble.*

▶ See also: **mean** business
mix business with pleasure

busman

a busman's holiday
time away from work that is spent doing something that is similar to your usual job • *Going to the beach is too much of a busman's holiday for him – he's a lifeguard!*

bust

bust a gut *informal*
to work very hard or to make a big effort to achieve something • *I really bust a gut to get that report finished on time.*

bust a gut (laughing) *informal*
to laugh a lot • *I bust a gut laughing at his imitation of the Queen.*

bust your **ass** *American very informal*
to work very hard • *He'll just have to bust his ass to make sure the job is finished on time.*

bust your **ass/balls** *American very informal*
bust your **arse** *Australian very informal*
to use a lot of effort to do something • *I busted my balls getting him that ticket, and now he's changed his mind!* • *He bust his arse for ten years in that job and got no thanks for it.*

▶ See also: burst/bust a **blood** vessel

busy

be as busy as a bee *old-fashioned*
be a busy bee *old-fashioned*
to be very busy or very active • *She's as busy as a bee, always going to meetings and organizing parties.*

butt

sb's **butt is on the line** *American & Australian very informal*
if someone's butt is on the line, they are in a situation where they will be blamed if things go wrong • *It's my butt on the line if we don't make this delivery today, so get moving guys.*

▶ See also: **kick** (sb's) butt
work your butt off

butter

butter wouldn't melt in sb's **mouth**

if butter wouldn't melt in someone's mouth, they look as if they would never do anything wrong although you think they would • *She looks as though butter wouldn't melt in her mouth but I've seen her fighting with the younger kids.*

butterflies

have butterflies (in your **stomach)**

to feel very nervous, usually about something you are going to do • *She had butterflies in her stomach as she walked out onto the stage.*

button

(right) on the button *mainly American informal*

if a remark is on the button, it is exactly right • *Your remarks about Tim were right on the button. He's arrogant, rude and selfish.*

Button it! *informal*

an impolite way of telling someone that you want them to stop talking • *Button it, OK! I'm trying to think.*

on the button *mainly American informal*

if something happens at a particular time or is a particular amount on the button, it happens at exactly that time or is exactly that amount • *We always sit down to eat at 6.00 on the button.*

buzz

a buzz word

a word or phrase that people in a particular group start to use a lot because they think it is important • *Minimalism is the latest buzz word in modern architecture.*

give sb **a buzz**

1 *informal* to telephone someone • *Give me a buzz when you get home.*

2 if something gives you a buzz, it makes you feel excited • *Watching live bands really gives me a buzz.*

get a buzz from sth/doing sth *informal* • *I get a real buzz from seeing my name in print.*

bygones

► See: **let** bygones be bygones.

by-your-leave

without so much as a by-your-leave *old-fashioned*

if you say that someone does something without so much as a by-your-leave, you mean you are angry because they did not ask your permission to do it • *That's twice now he's just marched in here without so much as a by-your-leave and picked a book off my shelf!*

Cc

caboodle

the whole (kit and) caboodle *informal*
the whole of something, including everything that is connected with it • *I like everything about Christmas – the presents, the food, the carols – the whole caboodle.*

cack-handed

cack-handed
1 *British & Australian informal* lacking skill with your hands • *Rob made a cack-handed attempt to fix the door and now it won't close at all.* • *She doesn't strike me as the practical sort – she's a bit cack-handed.*
2 *British & Australian informal* lacking skill in the way that you deal with people • *What struck me was the cack-handed way that he dealt with the whole situation.*

cage

▶ See: **rattle** sb's cage

cahoots

be in cahoots
to be secretly planning something together, especially something dishonest • (usually + **with**) *There are theories that someone in the government was in cahoots with the assassin.*

Cain

▶ See: **raise** Cain

cake

have your **cake and eat it (too)**
to have or do two good things that it is usually impossible to have or do at the same time • *He wants to have his cake and eat it. He wants the security of marriage and the excitement of affairs.* • *You* ***can't have your cake and eat it****. If you want better local services, you have to pay more tax.*

▶ See also: the **icing** on the cake
take the cake

call

call a spade a spade
to tell the truth about something, even if it is not polite or pleasant • *You know me, I call a spade a spade and when I see someone behaving like an idiot, I tell them.*

call sb's **bluff**
to make someone prove that what they are saying is true, or to make someone prove that they will really do what they say they will do, because you do not believe them ✍If you are playing a card game and you call someone's bluff, you force them to show you the cards they have. • *Alice called his bluff and dared him to tell everyone what he knew about her.*

a call girl
a woman who has sex with men for money, especially one who arranges her meetings by telephone • *His ex-wife claimed that call girls had visited his apartment each week.*

call sth **into question** *formal*
to cause a feeling of doubt about something • *The report's findings call into question the safety and effectiveness of all such drugs.*

call it a day *informal*
to stop doing something, especially working • *After playing together for 20 years the band have finally decided to call it a day.* • *It's almost midnight – I think it's time to call it a day.*

call it quits
1 *informal* to stop doing something • *The relationship had been going from bad to worse and we just decided it was time to call it quits.*
2 *informal* to agree with someone that a debt has been paid and that no one owes money to anyone • *You paid for the theatre tickets so if I pay for dinner we can call it quits.*

call sb **names**
to use impolite or unpleasant words to describe someone • *I was afraid that if I wore glasses to school, the other kids would call me names.* • *It's a good thing he didn't hear me earlier – I was* ***calling*** *him* ***all the names under the***

sun. (= using a lot of impolite words to describe him)

name-calling • *If you think about all that name-calling that goes on in school playgrounds, kids can be very cruel.*

call off the dogs

to stop attacking or criticizing someone • *The bank has agreed to call off the dogs until we can get the business up and running again.*

call the shots/tune

to be the person who makes all the important decisions and who has the most power in a situation • *She was used to calling the shots, to being in charge.*

▶ See also: **answer** the call of nature
call/cash in your **chips**
bring/call sb to **heel**

called

▶ See: be brought/called to **account**

calling

a calling card

1 something that shows a person or animal has been in a place • *The beetles leave behind their calling cards: little white balls on the outside of the trees.*

2 *mainly American* a quality or achievement that gives someone an advantage • *This performance acted as the calling card that landed Taylor her first major film role.*

calm

the calm before the storm

a peaceful and quiet period before a period of activity or trouble • *The family are arriving this afternoon so I'm just sitting down with a cup of coffee, enjoying the calm before the storm.*

camp

a camp follower

someone who strongly supports a person or group although they are not a member of an official organization • *The campaign for real ale had gathered quite a number of camp followers.*

can

be in the can

if a film is in the can, it has been completed and is now ready to be shown • *We started filming in April so the final sequence should be in the can at the end of the month.*

a can of worms *informal*

a situation which causes a lot of trouble for you when you start to deal with it • *Quite what we do with all the waste generated by this industry is another can of worms.* • *Once you start making concessions to individual members of staff, you really* ***open up a can of worms***. (= cause a lot of trouble for yourself)

▶ See also: **carry** the can
piss or get off the can/pot!

candle

▶ See: **burn** the candle at both ends
can't **hold** a candle to sb/sth

can-do

can-do

willing to try different ways to solve problems and confident that you will succeed • (always before noun) *Her can-do attitude is the reason we chose her for the job.*

candy

eye/mind candy *mainly American*

something that is intended to be pleasant to look at but has no real meaning • *A lot of these books are little more than eye candy: cute photos with one-line captions and that's about all.*

▶ See also: be like **taking** candy from a baby

cannon

cannon fodder

soldiers who are not believed to be important and who are sent to fight in the most dangerous places where they are likely to die • *Inexperienced troops were used as cannon fodder.*

canoe

▶ See: **paddle** your own canoe

can't

▶ See: You can't make an **omelette** without breaking eggs.

cap

to cap it all

if you have been describing bad things which happened and then say that to cap it all something else happened, you mean that the final thing was even worse • *He spilled red wine on the carpet, insulted my mother, and, to cap it all, he broke my favourite vase.*

▶ See also: to cap/crown/top it **all**
If the cap **fits** (wear it).
come/go cap in **hand**

capital

with a capital [A/B/C etc.]

1 something that you say in order to emphasize a particular quality • *You're trouble with a capital T, you are!*

2 if you talk about a subject with a capital A/B/C etc., you mean the most formal and often limited understanding of that subject • *The Academy has been criticized for being too traditional and only supporting Art with a capital A.*

carbon

a carbon copy

someone or something that is extremely similar to someone or something else • (usually + **of**) *He's a carbon copy of his father.*

card

be one card/several cards short of a full deck *humorous*

if someone is one card short of a full deck, they are stupid or crazy • *Do you think your cousin might be one card short of a full deck?*

have a card up your **sleeve**

to have an advantage that other people do not know about • *I still had a card up my sleeve in the form of a letter from his father.*

cardboard

cardboard city

an area of a large city where many people without a home sleep outside ✍Cardboard is a type of thick, stiff paper used to make the type of boxes that people living outside sometimes sleep in to keep warm. • *Young people come to the capital full of hope and end up in cardboard city.*

card-carrying

▶ See: be a fully paid-up **member** of sth

cards

be on the cards *British, American & Australian*
be in the cards *American & Australian*

to be likely to happen ✍Tarot cards are a special set of cards with pictures on them, which some people believe can be used to find out what is going to happen in the future. • *'Do you think there'll be an election next year?' 'I think it's on the cards'.* • (often + **for**) *There are some big changes in the cards for next year.*

the cards are stacked against sb

if the cards are stacked against someone, they are not at all likely to succeed in a particular situation because they have a lot of problems • *He fought a brilliant campaign, but the cards were stacked against him from the start.*

have/hold all the cards

to be in a strong position when you are competing with someone else, because you have all the advantages • *There isn't much hope of him getting custody of the children – as far as the law goes, she holds all the cards.*

keep/play your **cards close to** your **chest**

to not tell anyone what you plan to do • *I never know what Martin's next move will be. He plays his cards close to his chest.*

lay/put your **cards on the table**

to tell someone honestly what you think or what you plan to do • *I'll put my cards on the table: I don't like the way you've been behaving.* • *She thought it was time to put her cards on the table and tell him that she had no intention of marrying him.*

▶ See also: (if you) **play** your cards right

care

not **have a care in the world**

to be completely happy and not have any worries • *I was sixteen years old and didn't have a care in the world.* • *He was walking along the street whistling,* ***looking as if*** *he* ***didn't have a care in the world.***

without a care in the world • *This time last week I was lying on a sunny beach without a care in the world.*

▶ See also: not care/give a **fig**
not care/give a **hoot**

not care/give a **toss**
not care/give **tuppence**

cares

for all sb **cares** *informal*
if you say that someone can do something unpleasant for all you care, you mean that you do not care about what happens to them • *She can go to hell for all I care.*

▶ See also: have the cares/weight of the **world** on your shoulders

carpet

on the carpet *American*
to be in trouble with someone in authority • *He's going to be on the carpet for his rudeness.*

▶ See also: **sweep** sth under the carpet

carried

be carried out feet first
if someone will not leave a place until they are carried out feet first, they will not leave until they are dead • *James would never leave his home to go to a retirement village – he'd be carried out feet first!*

carrot-and-stick

carrot-and-stick
if you use a carrot-and-stick method to make someone do something, you both offer rewards and threaten punishments • (always before noun) *I've had to take the* ***carrot-and-stick approach*** *to disciplining my kids. The harder they work, the more money they get.*

carrot-top

a carrot-top *informal*
a person with hair that is an orange colour • *Joe's blond and Rosie's a carrot-top.*

carry

carry a torch for sb *old-fashioned*
to secretly love someone who does not love you • *Graeme's been carrying a torch for Linda for years.*

carry the ball *American*
to take control of an activity and do what is needed to get a piece of work done • *The people who carried the ball for his campaign were mainly volunteers.*

carry the can *British & Australian*
to take the blame or responsibility for something that is wrong or has not succeeded • (often + **for**) *She suspected that she'd be left to carry the can for her boss's mistakes.*

carry the day
1 to win a war or a fight • *At the beginning of the American Civil War, many southerners believed their soldiers and statesmen would carry the day.*
2 if you carry the day, you persuade people to support your ideas or opinions, or if a particular idea carries the day, it is accepted by a group of people • *The Republicans carried the day in the dispute over the new jet fighter.* • *Her argument in favour of pay increases eventually carried the day.*

carry weight
if what you do or say carries weight with someone, it seems important to them and will influence what they do or think • (often + **with**) *Her opinion carries a lot of weight with the boss.*

▶ See also: carry/take **coals** to Newcastle

cart

put the cart before the horse
to do things in the wrong order • *Deciding what to wear before you've even been invited to the party is rather putting the cart before the horse, isn't it?*

carte blanche

give sb **carte blanche** *slightly formal*
to let someone do whatever they want in a particular situation • (usually + to do sth) *She gave her interior decorator carte blanche to do up her apartment.*
get/have carte blanche *slightly formal* • *He had carte blanche when it came to choosing which actors he wanted to work with.*

carved

▶ See: be carved/set in **stone**

case

be on the case
to be doing what needs to be done in a particular situation • *'We need to book a flight before it's too late.' 'Don't worry, I'm on the case, just leave it to me.'*

a case in point
an example which shows that what you are saying is true or helps to explain why you are saying it • *Lack of communication causes relationships to fail. Your parents' marriage is a case in point.*

get on sb's **case** *informal*
to criticize someone in an annoying way for something that they have done • *I just don't want him getting on my case for being late for work.*
be on sb's **case** *informal* • *Some feminists decided that my remarks were sexist and they've been on my case ever since.*
get off sb's **case** *informal* • *I told him very straightforwardly that the problem had already been dealt with and he was to get off my case.* (= stop criticizing me)

make (out) a case for sth/doing sth
to give good reasons why something should be done • *You've certainly made out a case for us buying a dishwasher.*

► See also: I **rest** my case.

cash

a cash cow
a business or a part of a business that always makes a lot of profit • *The British newspapers are the group's biggest cash cow, earning nearly 40% of group profits.*

cash on the barrelhead *American*
money that is paid immediately when something is bought • *She's asking $6000 for the car – cash on the barrelhead.*

hard cash *British, American & Australian*
cold cash *American & Australian*
money in the form of coins or notes (= paper money) • *We gave him half the money in hard cash and wrote a cheque for the rest.*

► See also: call/cash in your **chips**

cast

be cast in the same mould
if two people are cast in the same mould, they have the same type of character • *Jack is cast in the same mould as his father – intelligent, kind, but stubborn.*
OPPOSITE **be cast in a different mould** • *She's cast in a very different mould from her sister. You'd never know they were from the same family.*

cast a pall on/over sth
if an unpleasant event or piece of news casts a pall on something, it spoils it • *News of her sudden death cast a pall on the awards ceremony.*

cast aspersions on sb/sth *formal*
to criticize someone or someone's character • *His opponents cast aspersions on his patriotism.*

cast your **mind back**
to try to remember something • (usually + **to**) *Cast your mind back to the first time we met Tony. Can you remember who he was with?*

cast your **net wide/wider**
to think about a large number of things or people when choosing the thing or person that you want • *If we don't get many interesting candidates this time round we may have to cast our net a little wider.*

► See also: cast/run your/an **eye** over sth
cast in your **lot** with sb

casting

the casting couch *humorous*
a situation in which an actor, usually a woman actor, agrees to have sex with someone in order to get a part in a film or play • *Thankfully, the casting couch is no longer the only route to success for aspiring young actresses.*

cast-iron

cast-iron
a cast-iron promise or arrangement is one that can be trusted completely • (always before noun) *No new business comes with a cast-iron guarantee of success.*

castles

castles in the air
plans or hopes that have very little chance of happening • *She tells me she's planned out her whole career, but as far as I can see it's all just castles in the air.* • *Before you start* ***building castles in the air****, just think how much all this is likely to cost.*

cat

be like a cat on a hot tin roof
to be nervous and unable to keep still • *What's the matter with her? She's like a cat on a hot tin roof this morning.*

be the cat's whiskers *British & Australian*
to be better than everyone else • *I thought I was the cat's whiskers in my new dress.*

fight like cat and dog *British & Australian*
fight like cats and dogs *British & American*
to argue violently all the time • *We get on very well as adults but as kids we fought like cat and dog.*

Has the cat got your **tongue?**
something that you say to someone when you are annoyed because they will not speak • *Well, has the cat got your tongue? I'm waiting for an explanation.*

not **have a cat in hell's chance** *British*
to have no chance at all of achieving something • (usually + **of** + doing sth) *Thay haven't a cat in hell's chance of getting over the mountain in weather like this.*

like the cat that got the cream *British & Australian*
like the cat that ate the canary *American*
if someone looks like the cat that got the cream, they annoy other people by looking very pleased with themselves because of something good that they have done • *Of course Mark got a glowing report so he was sitting there grinning like the cat that got the cream.*

put/set the cat among the pigeons *British & Australian*
to do or say something that causes trouble and makes a lot of people angry or worried • *Tell them all they've got to work on Saturday. That should set the cat among the pigeons.*

When/While the cat's away (the mice will play).
something that you say which means when the person in authority is absent, people will not do what they should do • *Do you think it's wise to leave the children alone for so long? You know, while the cat's away...*

► See also: **let** the cat out of the bag
look like something the cat brought/dragged in
look what the cat's dragged in!
play cat and mouse

catbird

be (sitting) in the catbird seat *American old-fashioned*
to be in a position of power and importance • *He'll be sitting in the catbird seat when the boss retires.*

catch

Catch 22
a Catch 22 situation
a situation where one thing must happen in order to cause another thing to happen, but because the first thing does not happen the second thing cannot happen ✍*Catch 22* is the title of a book by Joseph Heller about the experiences of an American pilot. • *If you don't have a place to stay, you can't get a job and with no job, you can't get an apartment. It's a Catch 22 situation.*

catch your **breath**
1 to stop breathing for a moment because something surprises or frightens you • *I caught my breath when I saw the scar on her face.*
2 to rest for a moment after doing physical exercise and wait until you can breath regularly again • *She stopped to catch her breath at the top of the hill.*

catch sb **cold** *American*
informal to surprise someone with an event, a question, or a piece of news they are not expecting • *You caught me cold with this news – I didn't know anything about it.*

You'll **catch** your **death (of cold)!** *informal*
something that you say to warn someone that they will become ill if they go outside while they are wet or wearing too few clothes • *You can't go out dressed like that in this weather – you'll catch your death of cold!*

catch sb's **eye**
1 to be noticed by someone because you are looking at them • *She lit a cigarette while he tried to catch the waiter's eye.*
2 to be attractive or different enough to be noticed by people • *There were lots of dresses to choose from, but none of them really caught my eye.*
eye-catching • *There is an eye-catching mural in the hall.*

catch sb **in the act**
to discover someone doing something wrong • *I was trying to clear up the mess on the carpet before anyone noticed it, but Isobel came in and caught me in the act.*

you'll **catch it** *British informal*
something that you say in order to tell someone they will be punished for something bad they have done • *You'll catch it if dad sees you smoking.*

catch sb **on the hop**
if you catch someone on the hop, you do something when they are not ready for it and may not be able to deal with it well • *I'm afraid you've caught me on the hop – I wasn't expecting your call until this afternoon.* • *If we attack at the very start of the game, we may just catch their defenders on the hop.*

catch sb **red-handed**
to discover someone doing something illegal or wrong • (often + doing sth) *I caught him red-handed trying to break into my car.*

catch some rays

catch some rays *informal*
catch a few rays *informal*
to lie or sit outside in the sun • *I thought I'd take my lunch outside and catch a few rays.*

catch the wave *American & Australian*
to try to get an advantage for yourself by becoming involved with something that is becoming popular or fashionable • *Older Spanish restaurants are expanding to try to catch the tapas wave.*

► See also: get sb's/the **drift**
catch/take sb off **guard**
catch/get **hell**
catch/have sb dead to **rights**

catch-as-catch-can

catch-as-catch-can *American*
achieved any way that is possible and not in a planned way • *We were working round the clock to finish the project so food and sleep were catch-as-catch-can.*

catches

► See: when sb/sth sneezes, sb/sth catches a **cold**

cattle

► See: a cattle **market**

catty-corner

catty-corner *American*
catty-cornered *American*
in a direction from one corner of a square to the opposite, far corner • (often + **to**) *Catty-corner to the theatre, there's a drugstore.*

caught

be caught in the crossfire
to be badly affected by a situation where two people or groups are arguing with each other • (often + **of**) *Unhappy children are often caught in the crossfire of arguing parents.* • (often + **between**) *She became caught in the crossfire between two bosses with different ideas about what her job involved.*

be caught in the middle
to be in a difficult situation because two people who you know well are arguing and both of them criticize each other to you • *My mother and sister are always arguing and I find myself caught in the middle.*

be caught napping
to not be ready to deal with something at the time when it happens • *Arsenal's defence was caught napping as Andrews chipped in a goal from the right.*

be caught short
1 *British & Australian informal* to have a sudden urgent need to go to the toilet • *You should go to the toilet before you leave. You don't want to be caught short on the journey.*

2 *American & Australian informal* to suddenly find you are not prepared for a situation, especially to be without money when you need it • *I'm caught short. Can you you lend me some money so I can pay for my lunch?*

be caught with your **pants/trousers down**

1 to be suddenly discovered doing something that you did not want other people to know about, especially having sex • *Apparently he was caught with his pants down. His wife came home to find him in bed with the neighbour.*

2 to be asked to do or say something that you are not prepared for • *He asked me where I'd been the previous evening and I was caught with my trousers down.*

▶ See also: wouldn't be caught/seen **dead**
be caught between **two** stools

cause

▶ See: cause/create a **stir**

cause célêbre

a cause célêbre

a famous event or legal case which people discuss a lot because it is so interesting or shocking • *The relationship between Edward Prince of Wales and Wallis Simpson became an international cause célêbre in the 1930s.*

caution

▶ See: **throw** caution to the wind(s)

ceiling

▶ See: **hit** the ceiling/roof

centre

be/take centre stage *British*
be/take center stage *American*

to be the most important thing or person at an event or in a situation, or to be the thing or person that people notice most • *A new range of electric cars will be centre stage at next month's exhibition.*

cents

▶ See: for **two** cents

certain

sb **of a certain age** *humorous*

used to avoid saying that a person, usually a woman, is no longer young but is not yet old • *It's a clothes boutique which caters for women of a certain age.*

c'est la vie

C'est la vie.

something that you say when something happens that you do not like but which you have to accept because you cannot change it • *I've got so much work that I can't go away this weekend. Oh well, c'est la vie.*

chafing

▶ See: be chafing at the **bit**

chain

pull/yank sb's **chain** *American & Australian informal*

to say or do something that upsets another person, especially because you enjoy upsetting them • *Boy, she really knows how to pull your chain!*

chalk

be (like) chalk and cheese *British & Australian*
be as different as chalk and cheese *British & Australian*

if two people are like chalk and cheese, they are completely different from each other • *I don't have anything in common with my brother. We're like chalk and cheese.*

▶ See also: put sth down to **experience**

chalkface

at the chalkface

a teacher who is at the chalkface is teaching students, and is not working in any other kind of job connected with education • *The media give a picture of falling standards in schools, but there is optimism at the chalkface.*

champing

▶ See: be champing/chomping at the **bit**

chance

chance your **arm** *British & Australian informal*

to take a risk in order to get something that you want • *Aren't you chancing your arm a bit giving up a secure job to start a business?*

Chance would be a fine thing! *British informal*

something that you say which means that

you would very much like something to happen but there is no possibility that it will • *He said I could do it in my spare time. Spare time? Chance would be a fine thing!*

▶ See also: not have a chance/hope in **hell**
stand a chance

change

change hands

to be sold by someone and bought by another person • *The hotel has changed hands twice since 1982.*

a change of heart

if someone has a change of heart, they change their opinion or the way they feel about something • *The revised legislation follows a change of heart by the government.* • *She was going to sell the house but **had a change of heart** at the last minute.*

the change of life

the time in a woman's life when she is no longer young and stops having a monthly flow of blood • *For the last ten years she's been blaming all her health problems on the change of life.*

change your tune

to change your opinion completely, especially because you know it will bring you an advantage • *He was against the idea to start with, but he **soon changed** his **tune** when I told him how much money he'd get out of it.*

get no change out of sb *British & Australian informal*

if you say that someone will get no change out of another person, you mean that person will not help them • *You'll get no change out of Chris. He'll just say it's not his problem.*

▶ See also: change **tack**
change/keep up/move with the **times**
change/mend your **ways**

changes

▶ See: **ring** the changes

chapter

be a chapter of accidents *British & Australian formal*

to be a series of unpleasant events • *The whole trip was a chapter of accidents.*

give/quote (sb) chapter and verse

to give exact information about something, especially something in a book • *The strength of the book is that when it makes accusations it gives chapter and verse, often backed up by photographic evidence.* • *I can't quote you chapter and verse, but I'm pretty sure it's a line from 'Macbeth'.*

charity

Charity begins at home.

something that you say which means you should try to help your family and friends before you help other people • *You ought to stay in and look after your father. Charity begins at home.*

charley

a charley horse *American informal*

a sudden, painful tightening of a muscle in your arm or leg • *She got a charley horse in her leg and had to stop dancing.*

charm

▶ See: **work** like a charm

charmed

have/lead/live a charmed life

to always be lucky and safe from danger • *After her miraculous escape from the fire we've decided she leads a charmed life.*

chase

chase rainbows

to waste your time trying to get or achieve something impossible • (usually in continuous tenses) *I don't think my parents ever believed I'd make it as an actor. I think they thought I was just chasing rainbows.*

chase the dragon

to take heroin (= a powerful drug which is taken illegally for pleasure) by smoking it • *The drug can be smoked, which is known as chasing the dragon.*

▶ See also: **cut** to the chase

chasing

be chasing your tail

to be very busy doing a lot of things, but achieving very little • *I've been chasing my tail all morning trying to fix a day when everyone can attend.*

chattering

the chattering classes *British humorous*
educated people who like to discuss and give their opinions about political and social matters • *Football has recently become a trendy topic among the chattering classes.*

cheap

cheap and cheerful *British informal*
costing little money but attractive, pleasant, or enjoyable • *They specialize in cheap and cheerful package holidays to Spain and Portugal.*

cheap and nasty *British & Australian*
costing little money and of bad quality • *You know the sort of cheap and nasty clothes that are sold on market stalls.*

Cheap at half the price! *British & Australian humorous*
something that you say when something is very expensive • *'That'll be £5.20 please.' 'What? For one bottle of beer! Cheap at half the price.'*

a cheap shot
a criticism of someone that is not fair • *She dismissed his comments as a 'cheap shot', saying that he was only concerned to defend himself.* • *Federal bureaucracy is the target for every* ***cheap shot artist*** (= someone who likes criticizing other people) *in America.*

on the cheap
if you buy or do something on the cheap, you buy or do it for very little money, often with the result that it is of bad quality • *The buildings would have been a whole lot better if they hadn't been built on the cheap.*

check

hold/keep sth/sb **in check**
to keep something or someone under control, usually to stop them becoming too large or too powerful • *The natural order of things is that the predators of an animal keep the population in check.* • *The central bank's action seemed at the time to be holding the dollar in check.*

checks

checks and balances
rules intended to prevent one person or group from having too much power within an organization • *A system of checks and balances exists to ensure that our government is truly democratic.*

cheddar

Hard/Tough cheddar! *British & Australian informal*
Stiff cheddar! *Australian informal*
something that you say to or about someone to whom something bad has happened in order to show that you have no sympathy for them • *It's about time Richard realized that he can't have everything his own way – tough cheddar, that's what I say!*

cheek

cheek by jowl
very close together ✍Jowl is a word for the loose flesh by the lower jaw, which is very close to the cheek. • *The poor lived cheek by jowl in industrial mining towns in Victorian England.*

cheer

cheer sb **to the echo** *British old-fashioned*
to shout and clap a lot in order to support someone • *The team captain was cheered to the echo when he was presented with the cup.*

cheese

Hard/Tough cheese! *British & Australian informal*
Stiff cheese! *Australian informal*
something that you say to or about someone to whom something bad has happened in order to show that you have no sympathy for them • *So he's fed up because he's got to get up early one morning in seven, is he? Well hard cheese!*

► See also: **say** cheese!

cheese-paring

cheese-paring *British*
actions that show you are not willing to spend or give money • *I'm fed up with all this cheese-paring. You've got to spend money if you want to make money.*

chef d'oeuvre

a chef d'oeuvre *formal*
an artist's or writer's best piece of work • *The Decameron is widely regarded as Boccaccio's chef d'oeuvre.*

cherry-pick

cherry-pick sb/sth
to choose only the best people or things in a way that is not fair • (usually in continuous tenses) *Isn't there a danger that the state schools might start cherry-picking the pupils with the best exam results?*
cherry-picking • *I suspect there's some cherry-picking going on, with lawyers only taking on the sort of cases that they're likely to win.*

chest

get it off your **chest**
to tell someone about something that has been worrying you or making you feel guilty for a long time, in order to make you feel better • *It was something that had been bothering me for some time and it felt good to get it off my chest.*

chew

chew sb's **ass (out)** *American very informal*
to speak or shout angrily at someone because they have done something wrong • *His boss will chew his ass if he doesn't finish the report on time.*

chew the cud *informal*
to think about something carefully and for a long time • *He sat chewing the cud all morning.*

chew the fat *British informal*
chew the rag *American informal*
to have a long friendly conversation with someone • *We spent the evening watching the TV and chewing the fat.*

chicken

a chicken and egg situation
a situation in which it is impossible to say which of two things existed first and which caused the other • *It's a chicken and egg situation – I don't know whether I was bad at the sciences because I wasn't interested in them or not interested in them and therefore not good at them.*

chicken feed
a very small amount of money, especially money that is paid for doing a job • *He pays his labourers chicken feed.*

like a headless chicken *British*
like a chicken with its head cut off *American*
if you do something like a headless chicken, you do it very quickly and without thinking carefully about what you are doing • (usually in continuous tenses) *I've got so much work to do – I've been* ***running around like a headless chicken*** *all week.* • *He was racing around like a chicken with its head cut off trying to do the work of two people.*

chicken-hearted

chicken-hearted *American*
not brave • *These chicken-hearted bosses always seem to give in at the first sign of a strike.*

chickens

chickens come home to roost
if you say that chickens are coming home to roost, you mean that bad or silly things done in the past are beginning to cause problems • *There was too much greed in the past, and now the chickens are coming home to roost with crime and corruption soaring.*
come home to roost • *The city's budget problems are coming home to roost and everybody is paying with higher taxes.*

► See also: Don't **count** your chickens (before they're hatched).

chief

be chief cook and bottle washer *humorous*
to be the person who is responsible for cooking meals and washing the pans and dishes • *It's my birthday party, so Alan is chief cook and bottle washer tonight.*

chiefs

too many chiefs (and not enough Indians)
too many bosses, and not enough people to do the work • *I can't find anyone to do the photocopying. There are too many chiefs and not enough Indians in this company.*

child

be child's play
to be very easy • *Using this new computer is child's play.*

be like a child in a sweetshop *British*
to be very happy and excited about the things around you, and often to react to them in a way which is silly and not controlled • *Give him a room full of old books and he's like a child in a sweetshop.*

be with child *old-fashioned*
to be pregnant • *Emily was unable to make the journey, being heavy with child.*

children

Children should be seen and not heard.
something that you say which means that children should be quiet • *I can't stand all that shouting. Children should be seen and not heard, in my opinion.*

chill

chill sb **to the bone/marrow**
to make someone feel very frightened • *The sound of scraping at the window chilled me to the bone.*

chilled

be chilled to the bone/marrow
to be very cold • *After an hour standing at the bus stop I was chilled to the bone.*

chills

send chills down/up sb's **spine**

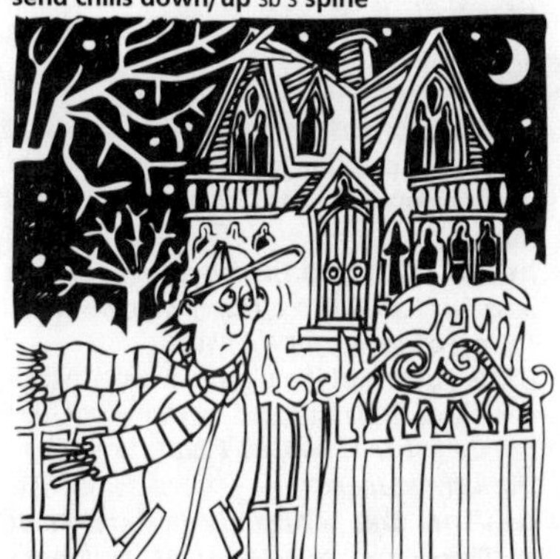

send chills down/up sb's **spine**
to make someone feel very frightened • *Just thinking about walking back through the dark streets sent chills down her spine.*

chin

Chin up! *old-fashioned*
something that you say to someone in a difficult situation in order to encourage them to be brave and to try not to be sad • *Chin up, you'll feel better after a few days' rest.*
keep your **chin up** • *We're pleased to hear that you're keeping your chin up despite all your difficulties.*

take it on the chin
1 to be brave and not to complain when bad things happen to you or people criticize you • *Atkinson took it all on the chin, though some members of his team were very upset by the criticism they received.*
2 to have a lot of bad things happen to you or to be criticized a lot • *The company has been taking it on the chin in recent months, but the future looks much brighter now and their sales are picking up.*

▶ See also: be **up** to your chin in sth

chink

a chink in sb's **armour** *British & Australian*
a chink in sb's **armor** *American & Australian*
if someone or something which seems to be strong has a chink in their armour, they have a small fault which may cause them problems • *She's a brilliant businesswoman, but her lack of political awareness may be the chink in her armour.*

chinless

a chinless wonder *British & Australian humorous*
an English man from a high social class, who thinks he is intelligent and important, but who other people think is weak and stupid • *He's just another chinless wonder doing a job that his Daddy got for him.*

chip

a chip off the old block
if someone is a chip off the old block, they are very similar in character to one of their parents or to another older member of their family • (not used with **the**) *Look at her bossing everyone around – she's a*

real chip off the old block!

have a chip on your **shoulder**

to blame other people for something bad which has happened to you and to continue to be angry about it so that it affects the way you behave • (often + **about**) *Even though he went to university, he's always had a chip on his shoulder about his poor upbringing.*

chips

be in the chips *American informal*

if someone is in the chips, they have suddenly got a lot of money • *Apparently his uncle's left him everything, so he's really in the chips.*

call/cash in your **chips**

1 *humorous* to die • *He cashed in his chips shortly before his ninetieth birthday.*

2 to sell things that you own, especially shares (= parts of a business), because you need some money ✍Chips are the round pieces of plastic that are used in some games played for money. • *I think it's time to cash in our chips. It's the only way we can pay the bill.*

have had your **chips**

1 *British informal* if you have had your chips, something bad is going to happen to you, usually a punishment for something bad you have done • *When the police knocked on his door early in the morning, he knew he'd had his chips.*

2 *British informal* to miss an opportunity to achieve something you want • *John's had his chips. I gave him the chance of a promotion and he threw it away.*

have had its chips *informal*

something that has had its chips is going to end because it is not wanted or needed any more • *It looks as though the mainframe computer has had its chips.*

when the chips are down

when you are in a difficult or dangerous situation, especially one which tests whether you can trust people or which shows people's true opinions • *When the chips are down, you need people around you that you can depend on.* • *When the chips were down, she found she didn't really love him as much as she thought.*

▶ See also: **let** the chips fall where they may

spit chips

chocolate

chocolate box

a chocolate box place or thing is very attractive in a way that does not seem real • (always before noun) *We drove through a series of chocolate box villages on our way down to Brighton.*

choice

be spoilt for choice *mainly British*

be spoiled for choice *mainly American*

to have so many good possible choices that it is difficult to make a decision • *With 51 flavours of ice-cream to choose from you are spoiled for choice.*

chomping

▶ See: be champing/chomping at the **bit**

chop

chop and change *British & Australian*

to keep changing what you do or what you plan to do, often in a way that is confusing and annoying for other people • *After six months of chopping and changing, we've decided to go back to our old system.*

Chop chop! *British & Australian informal*

something that you say in order to tell someone to hurry • *Come on, chop chop, up to bed!*

get the chop

be given the chop

1 *British informal* if a person gets the chop, they lose their job • *Anyone who argued with the foreman was liable to be given the chop.*

be for the chop *British informal* • *The boss has asked to see Henry this morning. I've a feeling he's for the chop.*

2 *British informal* if a plan or a service gets the chop, it is stopped • *Our local bus service got the chop, so I have to walk to work or use the car.*

be for the chop *British informal* • *There are rumours that children's hearing tests may be for the chop.*

chord

strike/touch a chord

if something strikes a chord with someone, they are interested in it and like it because it is connected with their own lives or opinions • *Clearly the book has struck a chord, as we can see from the hundreds of letters we have received from readers.* • (often + **with**) *Her ideas on social reform will strike a chord with poor people everywhere.*

▶ See also: **strike** a chord

chosen

the chosen few

a small group of people who are treated differently or better than other people, often when they do not deserve it • *There's a special entrance with revolving doors for the chosen few in the company.*

chump

be off your **chump** *British old-fashioned*

to be crazy • *Don't listen to him. He's off his chump.*

circle

▶ See: **square** the circle

circles

go around/round in circles

if you go round in circles when you are discussing something or trying to achieve something, you do not make any progress because you keep going back to the same subjects or the same problems. • *I need some more data to work on, otherwise I'm just going round in circles.* • *We can't go round in circles all day – someone will have to make a decision.*

go around/round in circles
run around/round in circles

to use a lot of time and effort trying to do something, without making any progress • *We spent the whole day running around in circles looking for a document which everyone thought was lost but which wasn't.*

circulation

out of circulation

if someone is out of circulation they are no longer taking part in social activities • *Work on my latest book has kept me out of circulation for the past few months.*

back in circulation • *I hear she's back in circulation again after her accident.*

civil

▶ See: **keep** a civil tongue in your head

claim

sb's **claim to fame**

a reason for a person or place to be well known or famous • *The town's main claim to fame is that the President was born here.* • *(humorous) His only claim to fame is that he nearly met Princess Diana.*

▶ See also: **stake** a/your claim

clam

▶ See: **shut** up like a clam

clanger

▶ See: **drop** a clanger

clap

▶ See: clap **eyes** on sb/sth

Clapham

the man/woman on the Clapham omnibus *British*

an imaginary person whose opinions and behaviour are thought to be typical of ordinary British people • (usually singular) *The man on the Clapham omnibus probably knows nothing about Rwanda.*

clapped-out

clapped-out *British & Australian informal*

if something, especially a car, is clapped-out, it is in a very bad condition because it is old or has been used a lot • *He still drives a clapped-out Mini which he bought when he was at college.*

clappers

like the clappers *British informal*

very quickly • *He works like the clappers – he'll have it finished in no time!* • *They ran like the clappers when the policeman came round the corner.*

clarion

a clarion call *literary*

a strong and clear request for people to do something • (often + **for**) *The charity commission's clarion call for more donations has produced an immediate response.* • (often + **to**) *Her unification speech was seen as a clarion call to party members.*

claw

claw your way back from sth

if you claw your way back from a bad situation, you succeed in improving your situation again by making a big effort • *They clawed their way back from almost certain defeat to win by a single point.*

claws

get your **claws into** sb *informal*

to find a way of influencing or controlling someone • *If the loan company gets its claws into you, you'll still be paying off this debt when you're 50.*

get her claws into sb *informal*

if a woman gets her claws into a man, she manages to start a relationship with him, often because she wants to control him or get something from him • *If she gets her claws into that young man she'll ruin his political career.*

clean

be as clean as a whistle

if someone is as clean as a whistle, they are not involved in anything illegal • *He hasn't got a criminal record – he's clean as a whistle.*

be as clean as a whistle
be as clean as a new pin

to be very clean • *The café's as clean as a whistle, and the food's excellent.*

a clean bill of health

if you give someone or something a clean bill of health, you examine them and state that they are healthy, in good condition, or legal • *John will have to stay at home until the doctors give him a clean bill of health.* • *Of 30 countries inspected for airline safety only 17 received a clean bill of health.*

a clean break

if you make a clean break from someone or something, you leave them quickly and completely, and are not involved with them at all in the future • (often + **with**) *Sometimes we need to* ***make a clean break*** *with the past.* • (often + **from**) *The Japanese are planning a clean break from the old television technologies.*

a clean sheet

1 *mainly British* if you are given a clean sheet, you can start something again, and all the problems caused by you or other people in the past will be forgotten • *I want us to forget all the arguing of the past, and* ***start*** *the New Year* ***with a clean sheet.***

2 *British* if a football team or a goalkeeper (= the player who stands in the goal) has a clean sheet, they do not allow the other team to score any goals • *United kept a clean sheet in an away match for the first time this season.*

a clean slate

if you are given a clean slate, you can start something again, and all of the problems caused by you or other people in the past will be forgotten • *The company's debts have been paid so that the new manager can* ***start with a clean slate.***

wipe the slate clean to make it possible to start something again, without any of the mistakes or problems of the past • *The time he spent in prison should have wiped the slate clean.*

a clean sweep

if you make a clean sweep, you win a competition or an election very easily or you win all the prizes in a competition • *China's women divers achieved a clean sweep in yesterday's competitions.* • *Analysts are predicting a clean sweep for the ruling party in the forthcoming elections.*

clean up your **act** *informal*

to stop doing things that other people do not approve of and start to behave in a more acceptable way • *There's a very strong anti-press feeling at the moment. A lot of people think it's time they cleaned up their act.*

come clean

to tell the truth, often about something bad that you have been trying to keep a secret • *I felt it was time to come clean and tell her what the doctor had told me.* • (often + **about**) *It's time for the Chancellor to come clean about the proposed tax rises.*

make a clean breast of it

to tell the truth about something, especially something bad or illegal that you have done, so that you do not have to feel guilty any more • *After months of lying about the money, I decided to make a clean breast of it and tell the truth.*

show sb **a clean pair of heels** *British*
to go faster than someone else in a race • *Butler showed them all a clean pair of heels as he raced for the finishing line.*

cleaner

take sb **to the cleaner's**
1 *informal* to get a lot of money from someone, usually by cheating them • *He got into a game of poker with two professional gamblers and, of course, they took him to the cleaner's.*
2 *informal* to defeat someone by a very large amount • *They don't like playing us because we took them to the cleaner's last year and the year before.*

cleanliness

Cleanliness is next to Godliness. *old-fashioned*
something that you say which means that except for worshipping God, the most important thing in life is to be clean • *Could you try to wash behind your ears occasionally? Cleanliness is next to Godliness, you know.*

clear

be as clear as crystal
to be very easy to see or understand • *'Are the instructions easy to understand?' 'Yes, clear as crystal.'*
crystal clear • *She made it crystal clear that she was only helping us because she had to.*

be as clear as mud *humorous*
to be impossible to understand • *'Does that make sense?' 'Yes, it's as clear as mud.'*

be in the clear
to not be guilty of a crime, or not be responsible for a mistake • *Video evidence proved that the boys were in the clear.*

clear sb's **name**
to prove that someone is not guilty of something • *He was convicted of drug-smuggling four years ago and has been trying to clear his name ever since.*

clear the air
if an argument or discussion clears the air, it causes bad feelings between people to disappear • *The meeting didn't solve anything, but at least it cleared the air.*

clear the decks *informal*
to finish dealing with what you are doing so that you can start to do something more important ✍If navy officers clear the decks they prepare a ship for war. • *His company is clearing the decks for major new investment in the Far East.*

▶ See also: out of a clear **blue** sky
be as clear/plain as **day**
steer clear of sth/sb

clear-cut

clear-cut
clear and certain, so that there is no doubt about something • *She has clear-cut evidence that the company cheated her.* • *The link between alcohol and crime is clear-cut.*

clear-eyed

clear-eyed *mainly American*
a clear-eyed understanding of a situation is correct • (always before noun) *John's clear-eyed assessment of the company's problems saved it from bankruptcy.*

cleft

in a cleft stick *British & Australian old-fashioned*
if someone is in a cleft stick, they have a problem which is very difficult to solve • *I'm in a real cleft stick because I can't sell my house.* • *Because of new employment laws, these companies are* ***caught in a cleft stick.***

clever

be too clever by half *British*
to be too confident of your own intelligence in a way that annoys other people • *At school he had a reputation for arrogance. 'Too clever by half' was how one former teacher described him.*

a clever clogs *British & Australian humorous*
a clever boots *Australian humorous*
if you call someone a clever clogs, you mean that they are very clever • *I bet old clever clogs here knows the answer.*

a clever dick *British & Australian*
someone who tries too hard to show that they are clever, in a way which annoys other people • *He's such a clever dick, talking loudly on the phone in lots of different languages.*

▶ See also: **box** clever

climb

▶ See: climb into **bed** with sb
climb/get on your **high** horse

climbing

be climbing the walls *informal*
to be extremely nervous, worried, bored, or annoyed • *I was practically climbing the walls at her stupidity.*

cling

▶ See: cling on/hang on by your **fingernails**
cling on/hang on by your **fingertips**

clip

clip sb's **wings**
to limit someone's freedom ✍Birds who have had their wings clipped (= cut) cannot fly. • *She never had kids. I guess she thought motherhood would clip her wings.*

cloak-and-dagger

cloak-and-dagger
cloak-and-dagger behaviour is when people behave in a very secret way, often when it is not really necessary ✍A cloak is a type of long, loose coat and a dagger is a small sharp knife used as a weapon. In 17th century Spanish theatre, cloak-and-dagger was worn by a dishonest character in the play. • (always before noun) *Is all this cloak-and-dagger stuff necessary? Why can't we just meet in a café like everyone else?*

clock

around/round the clock
all day and all night • *Doctors and nurses worked around the clock to help the people injured in the train crash.* • *This station broadcasts news round the clock.*
around-the-clock • (always before noun) *The police are mounting an around-the-clock guard on the embassy.*

put/turn the clock back
to make things the same as they were at an earlier time • *The court's decision has put the clock back a hundred years.* • (often + **to**) *Let's turn back the clock to 1963 and listen to the Beatles singing 'Love, love me do'.*

run out the clock *American & Australian*
kill the clock *American*
to keep the ball away from the team competing against you at the end of a game so that they cannot score any points • *The Pistons thought they were running out the clock but lost the ball and the game in the last nine seconds.*

▶ See also: **race** against the clock
watch the clock
work against the clock

clockwork

go/run/work like clockwork
if an event or a system goes like clockwork, it happens exactly as it was planned, without any problems • *The whole ceremony went like clockwork.* • *The Swiss railways run like clockwork.*

like clockwork
if something happens like clockwork, it happens at regular times • *He arrived at 7 every evening, like clockwork.*

clogs

▶ See: **pop** your clogs

close

be close to home
if a subject is close to home, it affects you in a personal way, and it can upset you if someone says something unpleasant about it • *His comments about working mothers were a bit close to home for me.*

be too close for comfort
to make people worried or frightened by being too close in distance or too similar in amount • *Those lions were much too close for comfort.* • *The party will have to work hard to improve its image – the last election result was too close for comfort.*

a close call
1 a situation where something very unpleasant or dangerous nearly happened • *We managed to get out of the car before it caught fire, but we had a very close call.* • *The business survived, but it was a close call.*
2 if a competition or an election is going to be a close call, more than one person has a good chance of winning • *It's going to be a close call. The vote could go either way.*

be too close to call if a competition or an election is too close to call, it is impossible to guess who will win • *The election result is still too close to call.*

close ranks

if members of a group close ranks, they publicly show that they support each other, especially when people outside of the group are criticizing them ✍If soldiers close ranks, they move closer together so that it is more difficult to go past them. • *In the past, the party would have closed ranks around its leader and defended him loyally against his critics.*

a close shave

a situation where something unpleasant or dangerous nearly happened • *I had a close shave when a tree fell just where I had been standing.*

Close your eyes and think of England. *mainly British humorous*

if you close your eyes and think of England when you have sex with someone, you do not enjoy it, but do it because you think you should • *Just close your eyes and think of England. He'll never notice.*

Close, but no cigar. *American & Australian humorous*

something that you say to someone if what they tell you or what they do is nearly correct but not completely ✍A cigar (= a type of thick cigarette) was sometimes used as a prize in games and competitions people paid to play. • *'Is his name Howard?' 'Close, but no cigar. It's Harold.'*

► See also: be close to the **bone**
close/shut the **door** on sth
close/shut your **eyes** to sth
close/near at **hand**
close/dear to sb's **heart**
be close to the **mark**
sail close to the wind
close up **shop**

closed

be a closed book

to be something that you know or understand nothing about • (usually + **to**) *I'm afraid physics will always be a closed book to me.*

behind closed doors

if something is done behind closed doors, it is done in private • *The United Nations Security Council met behind closed doors in New York.*

closed-door a closed-door event is one that is secret and not open to the public • (always before noun) *At a special closed-door session of the UN, the ambassador confirmed the withdrawal of his country's troops.*

closet

come out of the closet

1 to talk in public about something which you kept secret in the past because you were embarrassed about it • *It's time hairy women came out of the closet. It's a problem that affects all women to a greater or lesser degree.*

2 to tell people that you are homosexual (= sexually attracted to people of the same sex as you) so that it is no longer a secret • *He finally decided to come out of the closet so his mother would stop asking him why he wasn't married.*

OPPOSITE **in the closet** • *You can't live your life in the closet. At some stage you've got to come out and admit you're gay.*

closing

► See: closing/shutting the **stable** door after the horse has bolted

cloth

cloth ears *British old-fashioned, humorous*

something you call someone who has not heard something you said • *Hey, cloth ears, I asked if you wanted a drink.*

take the cloth *formal*

to become a priest • *He took the cloth in 1945.*

► See also: **cut** your coat according to your cloth

cloud

be on cloud nine *informal*

to be very happy • *For a few days after I heard I'd got the job, I was on cloud nine.*

be under a cloud

if someone or something is under a cloud, they are not trusted or not popular because people think they have done something bad • *The bishop's brother resigned from his job under a cloud.* • *The hotel business is under a cloud at the moment after newspapers revealed that many tourists were being systematically overcharged.*

a cloud on the horizon
a problem or difficulty which you expect to happen in the future • *The only cloud on the horizon is the physics exam in June – I'm sure I'll do fine in all the others.*

Every cloud has a silver lining.
something that you say which means that there is something good even in an unpleasant situation • *As the trip's been cancelled I'll be able to go to the match this Saturday. Every cloud has a silver lining.*

cloud-cuckoo

▶ See: **live** in cloud-cuckoo land

clover

be in clover
to be in a very pleasant situation, especially because you have a lot of money • *With the income from the family estate, she's in clover*

club

be in the club *British old-fashioned*
to be pregnant • *Is Tina in the club? She's looking quite large around the tummy.*

Join the club! *British, American & Australian*
Welcome to the club! *American & Australian*
something that you say to someone who has just told you about an experience or problem that they have had in order to show that you have had the same experience or problem too • *'I can't stop eating chocolate.' 'Join the club!'* • *'We can't afford a vacation this year.' 'Welcome to the club!'*

clue

not **have a clue** *informal*
to have no knowledge of or no information about something • *'How much do houses cost in Yorkshire?' 'I haven't got a clue.'* • (often + **about**) *Internet researchers in the 1980s didn't have a clue about the exciting online landscapes of the future.*

clutch

▶ See: clutch/grasp at **straws**

clutches

▶ See: **fall** into sb's clutches

C-note

a C-note *American informal*
a piece of paper American money that is worth 100 dollars • *Joe took a wad of bills out of his pocket, peeled off a C-note and handed it over.*

coach

▶ See: **drive** a coach and horses through sth

coalface

at the coalface *British & Australian*
someone who is at the coalface is doing the work involved in a job, not talking about it, planning it, or controlling it • *You sit in your office looking at consultants' reports, but it's the men and women at the coalface who really understand the business.*

coals

carry/take coals to Newcastle *British*
to take something to a place or a person that has a lot of that thing already ✍Newcastle is a town in Northern England which is in an area where a lot of coal was produced. • *Exporting pine to Scandinavia is a bit like carrying coals to Newcastle.*

drag/haul sb **over the coals**
to speak angrily to someone because they have done something wrong • *If I make a spelling mistake, I get hauled over the coals by my boss.* • (often + **for**) *They dragged her over the coals for being late with her assignment.*

▶ See also: **rake** over the coals

coast

(from) coast to coast
from one side of a country to the other • *We travelled across America coast to coast.*
coast-to-coast • *It was the first fully paved coast-to-coast US highway, between New York and San Francisco.*

the coast is clear
if the coast is clear, you can do something or go somewhere because there is no one near who might see or hear you • *You can come out now, the coast is clear.* • *I waited*

outside the house until the coast was clear, then softly tapped on the window.

coat-tails

on sb's **coat-tails**

if you achieve something on someone's coat-tails, you only achieve it because of their help or influence • *She'd risen to fame on the coat-tails of her half-sister.*

cobwebs

▶ See: **blow** away the cobwebs

cock

cock a snook *British old-fashioned*

to show that you do not respect something or someone by doing something that insults them • (usually + **at**) *In the end he refused to accept his award, cocking a snook at the film industry for which he had such contempt.*

the cock of the walk *British old-fashioned*

a man who acts as if he is more fashionable or important than other people • *He acts like the cock of the walk around the office.*

cock-and-bull

a cock-and-bull story *informal*

a story or explanation which is obviously not true • *She told me some cock-and-bull story about her car breaking down.*

cockles

▶ See: **warm** the cockles of your heart

coffee

a coffee table book

a large, expensive book with a lot of pictures, that is often kept on a table for people to look at • *A glossy coffee table book of his art work will be published next year.*

▶ See also: **wake** up and smell the coffee!

cog

a cog in the machine/wheel

one part of a large system or organization • *He was just a small cog in the large wheel of organised crime.* • *This warehouse is an important cog in our distribution machine.*

coin

to coin a phrase

something that you say before you use a phrase which sounds slightly silly • *He was, to coin a phrase, as sick as a parrot.*

coining

be coining it *British & Australian informal*

be coining money *American & Australian informal*

to be earning a lot of money quickly • *The magazine has been coining it since the new editor took over.*

cold

be as cold as ice

to be very cold • *Come in and get warm, your hands are as cold as ice.*

be cold comfort

if something someone tells you to make you feel better about a bad situation is cold comfort, it does not make you feel better • (usually + **to**) *The doctor said only his legs are paralysed, not his whole body, but I think that will be cold comfort to him.*

a cold fish

a person who does not seem very friendly and does not show their emotions • *He isn't very demonstrative, but his mother was a cold fish so he probably gets it from her.*

a cold snap

a sudden and short period of cold weather • *The recent cold snap has led to higher food prices.*

cold turkey

the unpleasant physical and mental effects someone suffers when they suddenly stop taking drugs • *The addict himself must make the decision that he wants to* ***go cold turkey****.* • *The nurses are there to encourage patients through cold turkey.*

cold-turkey • (always before noun) *Cold-turkey treatment of addicts will always produce withdrawal symptoms.*

come in from the cold

if someone comes in from the cold, they become part of a group or an activity which they were not allowed to join before • *Turkey is now keen to come in*

from the cold and join the European community. • *After four years away from the fashion scene, Jasper has come in from the cold with his new 1997 designer collection.*
bring sb **in from the cold** • (usually passive) *South African cricket has finally been brought in from the cold after years of exclusion from the international cricket scene.*

get cold feet
to suddenly become too frightened to do something you had planned to do, especially something important like getting married • *We're getting married next Saturday – that's if Trevor doesn't get cold feet!* • *I'm worried she may be getting cold feet about our trip to Patagonia.*

give sb **the cold shoulder**
to behave towards someone in a way that is not at all friendly, sometimes for reasons that this person does not understand • *What have I done to him? He gave me the cold shoulder the whole evening at the party.*
cold-shoulder sb • *After their argument, Peter cold-shouldered Jonathan for the rest of the week.*

in cold blood
if you do something, especially kill someone, in cold blood, you do it in a way which is cruel because you plan it and do it without emotion • *Four men were charged with the killing, in cold blood, of a French tourist last summer.* • *An unarmed boy was shot in cold blood outside his home yesterday.*

in the cold light of day
if you think about something in the cold light of day, you think about it clearly and calmly, without the emotions you had at the time it happened, and you often feel sorry or ashamed about it • *The next morning, in the cold light of day, Sarah realized what a complete idiot she had been.*

pour/throw cold water on sth *informal*
if you pour cold water on opinions or ideas, you criticize them and stop people believing them or being excited about them • *Margaret Thatcher poured cold water on the idea of a European central bank.*

take a cold shower *humorous*
if you tell someone to take a cold shower, you mean they should do something to stop themselves thinking about sex • *She's clearly not interested, so why don't you just take a cold shower?*

when sb/sth **sneezes,** sb/sth **catches a cold** *mainly British*
if sb/sth **catches a cold,** sb/sth **gets pneumonia** *mainly British*
when one person or organization has a problem, this problem has a much worse effect on another person or organization • *When New York sneezes, I'm afraid London catches a cold – that is just the way the stock markets operate now.* • *If the country's economy catches a cold, local businesses get pneumonia.*

▶ See also: cold **cash**
catch sb cold
leave sb cold
leave sb out in the cold
in a (cold) **sweat**

collision

be on a collision course
if two people or groups are on a collision course, they are doing or saying things which are certain to cause a serious disagreement or a fight between them • *All attempts at diplomacy have broken down and the two states now appear to be on a collision course.* • (often + **with**) *The British government is on a collision course with the American administration over trade tariffs.*
put/set sb **on a collision course** • (usually + **with**) *Her statements to the press have put her on a collision course with the party leadership.*

colonel

a Colonel Blimp *British old-fashioned*
an old man who has old-fashioned ideas and believes he is very important • *He's very much a Colonel Blimp with his comments about foreign influences dividing our society.*

colour

see the colour of sb's **money** *British & Australian*
see the color of sb's **money** *American & Australian*
to make sure that someone can pay for something before you let them have it • *I want to see the colour of his money before I say the car's his.*

colours

nail your **colours to the mast** *British & Australian*
nail your **colors to the mast** *American & Australian*
to publicly state your opinions about a subject • *Nobody knows which way he's going to vote because he has so far refused to nail his colours to the mast.*

▶ See also: nail your **colours** to the mast
show sb in their true colours

come

be as [crazy/rich etc.] as they come
to be very rich, crazy etc. • *Jenny's as crazy as they come.*

Come again? *informal*
something that you say when you want someone to repeat what they have just said because you did not hear or understand it • *'What's amazing is that Pauline's half sister's son is the father of her cousin's child.' 'Come again?'*

come out fighting *British, American & Australian*
come out swinging *mainly American*
if someone comes out fighting, they defend themselves or something they believe in, in a very determined way • *They were criticized from all sides but they came out fighting.* • *The candidates came out swinging in the first few minutes of the debate.*

come what may
whatever happens • *I shall be there tonight come what may.* • *It's always good to know that, come what may, your job is safe.*

▶ See also: come of **age**
not come **amiss**
come back to **bite** you
come to **blows**
come **clean**
come a **cropper**
come **face** to **face** with sb
come **face** to **face** with sth
come under **fire**
come through/pass with **flying** colours
come to a **full** stop
come/go/turn **full** circle
come on like **gangbusters**
come up with the **goods**
come to **grief**
come/get to **grips** with sth
come a **gutser**
come/go under the **hammer**
come/go cap in **hand**
come to a **head**
come to **heel**
come **hell** or high water
come within an **inch** of doing sth
have come a **long** way
come/spring to **mind**
come **one**, come all
come into your/its **own**
come down the **pike**
come the **raw** prawn
come/go along for the **ride**
come to your **senses**
come out of your **shell**
come out/up **smelling** of roses
come on **strong**
come to **terms** with sth
come/go with the **territory**
come up/turn up **trumps**
come **unglued**
come **unstuck**
come out in the **wash**
come/crawl out of the **woodwork**
come/go down in the **world**

comes

as it comes *British & Australian*
if someone asks you how they should prepare your drink and you say as it comes, you mean that any way they prepare it will be acceptable • *'How do you like your coffee?' 'Oh, as it comes, please – I'm not fussy.'*

comeuppance

get your **comeuppance**
if you get your comeuppance, something bad happens to you as a result of something bad that you have done to someone else • *He'll get his comeuppance, you'll see. You can't treat people the way he does and not go unpunished in this world.*

coming

had it coming *informal*

if someone had it coming, something bad happened to them which they deserved • (often + **to**) *I wasn't at all surprised to hear he'd been fired. With all that unexplained time off he had it coming to him.*

have sth **coming out of** your **ears** *informal*

to have more of something than you want or need • *He's going to have money coming out of his ears if this deal comes off.*

▶ See also: be coming/falling apart at the **seams**

comings

the comings and goings

the movements of people arriving at places and leaving places • *One of our neighbours is always at her window watching the comings and goings of everyone in the street.*

commando

go commando *informal*

to wear trousers with no underpants • *There isn't time to dress properly – we'll have to go commando.*

comme il faut

be comme il faut *formal*

behaviour that is comme il faut is correct because it follows the formal rules of social behaviour • *It's not exactly comme il faut to be seen making jokes at a funeral.*

commit

commit sth **to memory**

to make yourself remember something • *I haven't got a pen to write down your phone number – I'll just have to commit it to memory.*

common

as common as muck *British & Australian informal*

an impolite way of describing someone who is from a low social class • *You can tell from the way she talks she's as common as muck.*

common ground

shared opinions between two people or groups of people who disagree about most other subjects • *It seems increasingly unlikely that the two sides will find any common ground.*

the common touch

the ability of a rich or important person to communicate well with and understand ordinary people • *It was always said of the princess that she **had the common touch** and that's why she was so loved by the people.* • *He was a dedicated and brilliant leader but he lacked the common touch.*

make common cause with sb *formal*

if one group of people makes common cause with another group, they work together in order to achieve something that both groups want • *Environment protesters have made common cause with local people to stop the motorway from being built.*

common-or-garden

common-or-garden *British*

very ordinary • (always before noun) *I just want a common-or-garden bike – it doesn't have to have special wheels or lots of gears or anything like that.*

compare

compare notes

if two people compare notes, they tell each other what they think about something that they have both done • *We'd had the same boyfriend at different times in our life so it was quite interesting to compare notes.*

comparison

▶ See: **pale** by/in comparison

compliment

a back-handed compliment *British, American & Australian*

a left-handed compliment *American*

a remark which seems approving but which is also negative • *He gave me that classic back-handed compliment. He said I played football very well 'for a woman'.*

▶ See also: **return** the compliment

compliments

▶ See: **fish** for compliments

compos mentis

be compos mentis *humorous*

if someone is compos mentis, they are

able to think clearly and are responsible for their actions • *My mother was quite old at the time but she was perfectly compos mentis.*

conclusions

▶ See: **jump** to conclusions

concrete

▶ See: be **set** in concrete

conniption

have a conniption fit *American old-fashioned*

to be very angry or upset • *My mother would have a conniption fit if she could see me now.*

conscience

▶ See: **prick** sb's conscience

conspicuous

be conspicuous by your **absence** *humorous*

if someone is conspicuous by their absence, people notice that they are not present in a place where they are expected to be • *Helen was conspicuous by her absence at the meeting yesterday.*

contemplate

▶ See: gaze at/contemplate your **navel**

contradiction

a contradiction in terms

a phrase that is confusing because it contains words that seem to have opposite meanings • *A British summer is a bit of a contradiction in terms.* • *Euro Disney always seems to me a contradiction in terms because Disney is so typically American.*

contrary

contrary to popular belief/opinion

something that you say before you make a statement that is the opposite of what most people believe • *Contrary to popular belief, bottled water is not always better than tap water.*

conventional

▶ See: the conventional/received **wisdom**

conversation

a conversation piece

a strange or interesting object that people talk about • *Charlotte's collection of Victorian cards were a good conversation piece.*

converted

▶ See: **preach** to the converted

cook

cook sb's **goose** *informal*

if you cook someone's goose, you do something that spoils their plans and prevents them from succeeding • *Disgruntled employees cooked Blackledge's goose by leaking private documents to the press.*

cook the books *informal*

to record false information in the accounts of an organization, especially in order to steal money • (usually in continuous tenses) *One of the directors had been cooking the books and the firm had been losing money for years.*

cooked

▶ See: be cooked/done to a **turn**

cookie-cutter

cookie-cutter *American*

a cookie-cutter building or plan is exactly similar to many others of the same type • (always before noun) *The architects were determined that it wouldn't be just another cookie-cutter mall.* • *Management too often uses a cookie-cutter approach to solving problems.*

cooking

be cooking on gas *British informal*

be cooking with gas *American informal*

to be making good progress and to be likely to succeed • *We're cooking on gas. Keep the work coming in like this and we'll meet the deadline.*

What's cooking? *American old-fashioned*

something that you say in order to ask someone what is happening • *Hey, you guys, what's cooking? Are we going out for a drink or not?*

cooks

Too many cooks (spoil the broth).

something that you say which means that if too many people try to work on the same piece of work, they will spoil it • *There were so many people working on the same project, no one knew what anyone else was doing. I think it was a case of too many cooks.*

cool

be as cool as a cucumber *humorous*
to be very calm and relaxed, especially in a difficult situation • *I expected him to be all nervous before his interview but he was as cool as a cucumber.*

a cool customer *informal*
someone who stays calm and does not show their emotions, even in a difficult situation • *I can imagine Pete being good at negotiating. He's a pretty cool customer.*

a cool head
the ability to stay calm and think clearly in a difficult situation • *These are high pressure situations and you have to **keep a cool head**.*

cool your **heels**
if someone leaves you to cool your heels, they force you to wait, often until you become calmer • *The youths were **left to cool their heels** overnight in a police cell.*

Cool it! *informal*
something that you say in order to tell someone to stop arguing or fighting • *Hey, cool it, you guys, fighting's not going to solve anything.*

▶ See also: **keep** your cool
lose your cool
play it cool

coop

▶ See: **fly** the coop

cop

not **be much cop** *British informal*
to not be very good • *These scissors aren't much cop – do you have any sharper ones?*

cop a feel *American very informal*
to touch someone's body without their permission in order to get sexual excitement • *He saw she was drunk and tried to cop a feel.*

cop a plea *American informal*
to admit that you are guilty of a crime in order to try to get a less severe punishment • *The police hoped the men would cop a plea and testify against the ringleaders in return for reduced sentences.*

cop it sweet *Australian informal*
to be lucky in a way that you did not expect • *We copped it sweet this afternoon – the boss went home early.*

copper-bottomed

copper-bottomed
a copper-bottomed plan, agreement, or financial arrangement is completely safe • (always before noun) *She has a copper-bottomed contract with a very successful company.*

copybook

▶ See: **blot** your copybook

cord

▶ See: **cut** the (umbilical) cord

cordon bleu

cordon bleu
cordon bleu cooking is food which is prepared to the highest standard and a cordon bleu cook is someone who cooks to a very high standard • (always before noun) *She spent five years working as a cordon bleu chef before opening her own restaurant.*

core

to the core
in every part ✍The core is the central part of something, for example an apple or the earth. • *He's convinced that the army is **rotten to the core**.* • *I'd never heard anything like it. I was shocked to the core.* (= extremely shocked)

corner

around the corner
going to happen very soon • *With the end of the century **just around the corner**, major celebrations were being planned.*

corner the market
to become so successful at selling or making a particular product that almost no one else sells or makes it • *They've more or less cornered the fast-food market – they're in every big city in the country.*

have sb **in** your **corner**
to have the support or help of someone • *We're lucky we've got James in our corner. No one can beat him in a debate.*

▶ See also: be **backed** into a corner
fight your corner

paint yourself into a corner
turn the corner

corners

▶ See: **cut** corners

corners

corridors

the corridors of power
the highest level of government where the most important decisions are made • *His laziness became a legend in the corridors of power.*

cost

cost a bomb *informal*
to be very expensive • *Strawberries cost a bomb at this time of year.*

cost (sb) **a pretty penny**
to be very expensive • *That diamond ring must have cost him a pretty penny.*

cost (sb) **an arm and a leg** *informal*
to be very expensive • *These opera tickets cost us an arm and a leg!*

cost sb **dear**
if something that someone does, especially something stupid, costs them dear, it causes them a lot of problems • *Later that year he attacked a photographer, an incident that cost him dear.*

▶ See also: **count** the cost
and **hang** the cost/expense

costs

at all costs
if something must be done or avoided at all costs, it must be done or avoided whatever happens • *The only other option is working on Saturdays which is something I want to avoid at all costs.* • *He appears to have decided that he must stay in power at all costs.*

cotton

▶ See: **bless** her/his cotton socks.
wrap sb up in cotton wool

cotton-picking

cotton-picking *American & Australian informal*
something that you say before a noun to express anger • *Get your cotton-picking feet off my chair!*

couch

a couch potato

a couch potato *informal*
a person who does not like physical activity and prefers to sit down, usually to watch television ✍A couch is a piece of furniture that people sit on. • *The remote control television was invented for couch potatoes.*

could

▶ See: You could have **heard** a pin drop.

counsel

▶ See: **keep** your own counsel

count

be out for the count
to be sleeping deeply ✍When boxers (= men who fight as a sport) are still not conscious after ten seconds have been counted they are described as 'out for the count'. • *I was out for the count so I didn't hear any of it going on.*

can count sth **on the fingers of one hand**
if you say that you can count things on the fingers of one hand, you are emphasizing that they are very rare • *I can count on the fingers of one hand the number of times she's actually offered to buy me a drink.*

count your **blessings**
to think about the good things in your life, often to stop yourself becoming too unhappy about the bad things • *School children today should count their blessings. At least they're not beaten for talking*

in class as we were.

count the cost

to start to understand how badly something has affected you • *I didn't read the contract fully before I signed it but I'm counting the cost now.*

Don't count your **chickens (before they're hatched).**

something that you say in order to warn someone to wait until a good thing they are expecting has really happened before they make any plans about it • *You might be able to get a loan from the bank, but don't count your chickens.*

counter

over the counter

if a type of medicine is available over the counter, you can buy it without the permission of a doctor • *You can't buy antibiotics over the counter – they're a prescription drug.*

over-the-counter • (always before noun) *Many over-the-counter painkillers contain paracetamol.*

under the counter

if something is bought or sold under the counter it is bought or sold secretly or in a way that is not legal • *Many of his books are banned and only available under the counter.*

country

go to the country *British & Australian slightly formal*

if a government or the leader of a government goes to the country, they have an election • *The Prime Minister has decided to go to the country next spring.*

coup de grâce

a coup de grâce *formal*

an action or event which ends or destroys something that is gradually becoming worse • *Jane's affair delivered the coup de grâce to her failing marriage.*

couple

▶ See: a couple of **sandwiches** short of a picnic
a couple of **shakes**

courage

have the courage of your **convictions**

to have the confidence to do or say what you think is right even when other people disagree • *Have the courage of your convictions – don't go out to work if you feel your children need you at home.*

▶ See also: **screw** up your courage

course

be on course for sth
be on course to do sth

to be very likely to succeed at something • *If he keeps playing like this, Henman is on course for his third victory.*

▶ See also: **run** its course
stay the course

court

▶ See: **hold** court
laugh sth/sb out of court

Coventry

▶ See: **send** sb to Coventry

cover

cover your **back** *British, American & Australian*
cover your **ass** *American & Australian very informal*

to make sure that you cannot be blamed or criticized later for something you have done • *The race organizers cover their backs by saying they can't take responsibility for any injuries.* • *I'm gonna cover my ass and get written permission before I go.*

cover the waterfront *American*

to talk about every part of a subject, or to deal with every part of a job • *It was a mistake to try and cover the waterfront in her talk – one or two points would have been enough.* • *It's obvious one salesman can't cover the waterfront. We'll need a whole team for this area.*

cover your **tracks**

to hide or destroy the things that show where you have been or what you have been doing • *Roberts covered his tracks by throwing the knife in the river and burying his wife's body.*

▶ See also: cover all the **bases**
blow sb's cover
cover/hide a **multitude** of sins

cow

have a cow *American*

to be very worried, upset, or angry about

something • *I thought he was going to have a cow when I told him I'd lost his key.*

cows

until the cows come home

for a very long time • *We could talk about this problem until the cows come home, but it wouldn't solve anything.*

crack

at the crack of dawn

very early in the morning • *We had an early flight so we were up at the crack of dawn.*

crack a book *American informal*

to open a book in order to study • (usually negative) *I haven't seen her crack a book and the French test is tomorrow.*

crack a smile *informal*

to smile, especially when you do not feel like smiling • (usually negative) *The man barely cracked a smile at his friend's joke.*

crack the whip

to use your authority to make someone work harder, usually by threatening or punishing them ✍A whip is a piece of leather or rope fastened to a stick which you hit a horse with in order to make it go faster. • *We were already three months behind schedule so I thought it was time to crack the whip.*

have/take a crack at sth

to try to do something although you are not certain that you will succeed • *He didn't win the tennis championships, but he plans to have another crack at it next year.*

get a crack at sth • *Don't worry, you'll all get a crack at using the camera.*

cracked

not **be all it's cracked up to be**

if something is not all it's cracked up to be, it is not as good as people say it is • *Her latest book isn't all it's cracked up to be. I wouldn't bother reading it if I were you.* • *It's a good restaurant, but* ***it's not all it's cracked up to be.***

cracking

Get cracking! *informal*

something that you say in order to tell someone to hurry • *Get cracking! We're leaving in 5 minutes.*

cracks

fall/slip through the cracks

to get lost or be forgotten, especially within a system • *It seems that important information given to the police may have fallen through the cracks.*

cradle

from the cradle to the grave

during the whole of your life • *Free medical care might not be with us from the cradle to the grave, as we once hoped.*

cradle-robber

a cradle-robber *American humorous*

someone who has a romantic or sexual relationship with a much younger partner • *He's a cradle-robber. He married a 16 year-old and he's nearly 30!*

rob the cradle *American humorous* • *People are always telling her she's robbing the cradle. She's ten years older than Joe.*

cradle-snatcher

a cradle-snatcher *British & Australian humorous*

someone who has a romantic or sexual relationship with a much younger partner • *He's three years younger than you? You cradle-snatcher!*

cradle-snatching *British & Australian humorous* • *Pete's new girlfriend's only 15. I'd call that cradle-snatching.*

cramp

cramp sb's **style**

to prevent someone from enjoying themselves as much as they would like, especially by going somewhere with them • *Are you sure you don't mind your old mother coming along with you? I'd hate to cramp your style.*

crap

► See: **cut** the crap!

crash

crash and burn *American & Australian informal*

to fail suddenly and completely • *While the big companies merge, the small companies crash and burn.*

craw

▶ See: **stick** in your craw

crawl

▶ See: come/crawl out of the **woodwork**

crazy

like crazy *informal*

if you do something like crazy, you do it a lot or very quickly • *We'll have to work like crazy to finish the decorating by the weekend.*

cream

the cream of the crop

the best of a particular group • *These artists are the best of this year's graduates – the cream of the crop.*

create

▶ See: cause/create a **stir**

creature

creature comforts

things that make life more comfortable and pleasant, such as hot water and good food • *I hate camping. I can't do without my creature comforts.*

credibility

a credibility gap

a difference between what someone says about a situation and what you know or see is true • *There's a credibility gap developing between me and my builders. This is the third week they've told me they'll finish by Friday.*

creek

be up the creek (without a paddle) *informal*

be up shit creek (without a paddle) *very informal*

to be in a very difficult situation that you are not able to improve • *If the car breaks down we're really up the creek.* • *He'll be up shit creek unless he finds the money to pay off his loan.*

creeps

▶ See: **give** sb the creeps/willies

crême de la crême

the crême de la crême

the best people or things in a group or of a particular type • (often + **of**) *The crême de la crême of young designers will be showing their collections at London Fashion Week.*

crest

be on the crest of a wave

to be very successful so that many good things happen to you very quickly • *The band are currently on the crest of a wave, with a new album and a concert tour planned for next year.*

ride the crest of a wave • (usually in continuous tenses) *Our local team are riding the crest of a wave with their third win this season.*

cricket

It's/That's (just) not cricket! *British & Australian humorous*

something that you say when you think something someone has said or done is not right or not fair • *You can't make me do the washing up after I did all the cooking – it's just not cricket!*

crime

Crime doesn't pay.

something that you say which means if you do something illegal, you will probably be caught and punished • *Police arrests are being given maximum publicity as a reminder that crime doesn't pay.*

crisp

be burnt to a crisp *mainly British*

be burned to a crisp *mainly American*

to be very burnt • *By the time I remembered the pizza was in the oven, it was burnt to a crisp.*

crock

be a crock of shit *American & Australian taboo*

to be stupid or not true • *He says he's not to blame? What a crock of shit.*

crocodile

shed/weep crocodile tears

to show sadness that is not sincere ✍Some stories say that crocodiles cry while they are eating what they have attacked. • *Political leaders shed crocodile tears while allowing the war to continue.*

cropper

come a cropper

1 *British informal* to fall to the ground

• *Supermodel Naomi Campbell came a cropper last week on the catwalk of a Paris fashion show.*

2 *British informal* to make a mistake or to have something bad happen to you which makes you less successful than before • *The leading actor came a cropper when he forgot his lines halfway through the second act.*

cross

a cross (sb **has) to bear** *British & Australian*
a cross (sb **has) to carry** *American & Australian*

an unpleasant situation or responsibility that you must accept because you cannot change it ✍In the past, criminals were made to carry crosses as a form of punishment. • *Someone has to look after mother and because I live the closest it's a cross I have to bear.*

Everyone has their cross to bear.
• *I hate my red hair and pale skin, but everyone has their cross to bear.*

cross your **mind**

if an idea or thought crosses your mind, you think about it for a short time • (often + **that**) *The thought did cross my mind that she might be taking drugs.* • (often negative) *The idea of failure never crossed his mind.*

Cross my heart (and hope to die).
something that you say in order to emphasize that something is true • *I want to go to the party with you, not Sarah – cross my heart!*

cross sb's **path**
to meet someone, especially by accident • *If he ever crosses my path again, I'll kill him.*

cross swords with sb
to argue with someone • *We don't always agree, in fact I've crossed swords with her several times at committee meetings.*

cross the line
if someone crosses the line they start behaving in a way that is not socially acceptable • *Players had crossed the line by attacking fans on the pitch.*

cross the Rubicon *formal*
to do something which will have very important results, which cannot be changed later ✍Julius Caesar started a war by crossing the river Rubicon in Italy. • *International pressure may be able to prevent the country crossing the Rubicon to authoritarian rule.*

I'll/We'll cross that bridge when I/we come to it.

something that you say in order to tell someone that you will not worry about a possible problem but will deal with it if it happens • *'What if the flight is delayed?' 'I'll cross that bridge when I come to it.'*

▶ See also: cross your **fingers**

crossed

get your **lines/wires crossed**
if two people get their lines crossed, they do not understand each other correctly ✍When telephone lines get crossed, a mistake is made and you are connected to the wrong person. • *Somehow we got our lines crossed because I'd got the 23rd written down in my diary and Jenny had the 16th.*

crossfire

▶ See: be **caught** in the crossfire

cross-purposes

at cross-purposes

if two people are at cross-purposes, they do not understand each other because they are trying to do or say different things but they do not know this • *I think we're talking at cross-purposes here. You mean the old building, but I was talking about the new one.*

crossroads

be at a crossroads
to be at a stage in your life when you have to make a very important decision or do something that will affect your life a lot • *She's at a crossroads in her career, and the way she performs in this race could decide her future.*

come to/reach a crossroads • *He had reached a crossroads in his life and needed to decide whether or not to continue in medicine.*

crow

as the crow flies
if the distance between two places is measured as the crow flies, it is measured

as a straight line between the two places • *'How far is it from Cambridge to London?' 'About 50 miles as the crow flies.'* • *Our farm is only five miles from town as the crow flies, but the winding roads mean we have to drive nearly eight miles to get there.*

► See also: **eat** crow

crowd-puller

a crowd-puller *British & Australian*
something or someone that many people are keen to go and see • *This year's final will be a major crowd-puller – Manchester United and Liverpool are two of the country's most popular teams and are also fierce rivals.*

crown

► See: to cap/crown/top it **all**

crows

► See: **stone** the crows!
be **up** with the crow

cruel

You have to be cruel to be kind.
something that you say when you do something to someone that will upset them now because you think it will help them in the future • *I told her she's just not good enough to be a professional dancer – sometimes you have to be cruel to be kind.* • *I know you have to be cruel to be kind, Sam, but telling Amy that she looked fat in her party dress was a bit harsh.*

crunch

if/when it comes to the crunch
if you talk about what someone will do if it comes to the crunch, you mean what they will do if a situation becomes serious or they have to make an important decision • *If it comes to the crunch, will she play well enough to win?* • *Don't worry, Ben will be right there with us when it comes to the crunch.*

cry

cry your **eyes out** *informal*
to cry a lot and for a long time • *I cried my eyes out when my cat died.* • *Don't just sit there crying your eyes out, Meg – get out there and find a new boyfriend!*

cry like a baby

cry like a baby
to cry a lot • *When I heard that she was safe, I cried like a baby.*

cry wolf
to ask for help when you do not need it, with the result that no one believes you when help is necessary • *She had repeatedly rung the police for trivial reasons and perhaps she had cried wolf too often.*

► See also: cry/sob your **heart** out
ask/cry for the **moon**

cry-baby

a cry-baby *informal*
someone, usually a child, who cries too easily and too often • *Don't be such a cry-baby – I hardly touched you.*

crying

For crying out loud! *informal*
something that you say when you are annoyed • *For crying out loud! Can't you leave me alone even for a minute!*

It's a crying shame!
something that you say when you think a situation is wrong • (often + **that**) *It's a crying shame that she only gets one month's maternity leave.*

It's no good/use crying over spilt milk.
There's no point crying over spilt milk.
something that you say which means you should not get upset about something bad that has happened that you cannot change • *Sometimes I regret not taking*

that job in London. Oh well, there's no point crying over spilt milk.

cuckoo

a cuckoo in the nest
someone who is part of a group of people but different from them and not liked by them • *For Peter, his new father was a cuckoo in the nest.*

cud

▶ See: **chew** the cud

cudgels

take up the cudgels for sb/sth *British & Australian*
take up the cudgels on behalf of sb/sth *British & Australian*
to argue strongly in support of someone or something ✍A cudgel is a short, heavy stick which is used as a weapon. • *Relatives have taken up the cudgels for two British women accused of murder.*
OPPOSITE **take up the cudgels against** sb/sth *British & Australian* • *Environmental groups have taken up the cudgels against multinational companies.*

culture

a culture shock
feelings of being confused or surprised that you have when you are in a country or social group that is very different from your own • *The first time she went to Japan, Isabel got a huge culture shock.*

a culture vulture *humorous*
someone who is very keen to see and experience art, theatre, literature, music etc. • *She's a bit of a culture vulture. She'll only visit places that have at least one art gallery.*

cup

not **be** sb's **cup of tea**
if someone or something is not your cup of tea, you do not like them or you are not interested in them • *If Yeats isn't your cup of tea, why not try some of the more contemporary Irish poets?*

cupboard

cupboard love *British & Australian*
love that you give in order to get something from someone • *I suspected all along it was just cupboard love, and what she really liked about him was his car.*

cups

be in your **cups** *old-fashioned*
to be very drunk • *When he was in his cups he would recite lines of poetry in a loud voice.*

curate

a curate's egg *British*
something which has both good and bad parts ✍A curate is a priest. There is a joke about a curate who was given a bad egg and said that parts of the egg were good because he did not want to offend the person who gave it to him. • *Queen's College is something of a curate's egg, with elegant Victorian buildings alongside some of the ugliest modern architecture.*

curiosity

Curiosity killed the cat.
something that you say in order to warn someone not to ask too many questions about something • *'Why are you going away so suddenly?' 'Curiosity killed the cat.'*

curl

curl your **lip** *literary*
to lift one side of your mouth in an expression which shows that you do not like or respect something or someone • *Don't you curl your lip at me, young miss!*

▶ See also: curl sb's **hair**
make sb's **toes** curl
want to curl up and die

curry

curry favour
to try to make someone like you or support you by doing things to please them • (usually + **with**) *The government has promised lower taxes in an attempt to curry favour with the voters.*

curtain

the curtain comes down on sth
the curtain falls on sth
if the curtain comes down on something, especially a period of time, it ends ✍In a theatre the large curtains above the stage are brought down at the end of a performance. • *Last night, the curtain came down on 14 years of Tory rule.*

curtains

it's curtains *informal*
something that you say when you believe something will end or someone will have to stop doing something • (usually + **for**) *If audience figures don't improve, it's curtains for DJ Mike Hamilton.*

curve

▶ See: **throw** (sb) a curve (ball)

cushion

▶ See: cushion/soften the **blow**

cut

be a cut above sth/sb
to be better than other things or people • *This dark chocolate contains 70% cocoa solids. It's a cut above ordinary chocolate.* • *Our new luxury apartments are* ***a cut above the rest****.*

be cut from the same cloth
to be very similar • *Despite differences in age and in experience, these two great writers are cut from the same cloth.*

be cut to the bone
if a service or an amount of money is cut to the bone, it is reduced as much as possible • *How can we create quality programmes when our funding has been cut to the bone?*

can't cut the mustard *British, American & Australian*
can't cut it *British*
if you can't cut the mustard, you cannot deal with problems or difficulties • *If she can't cut the mustard, we'll have to find someone else to do the job.*

cut a deal *American*
to make an agreement or an arrangement with someone, especially in business or politics • *The property developer tried to cut a deal with us to get us out of the building.*

cut a fine figure *British, American & Australian old-fashioned*
cut a dash *British old-fashioned*
if someone cuts a fine figure, people admire their appearance, usually because they are wearing attractive clothes • *Giles cut a fine figure in his black velvet suit.* • *Lucy cut a dash in her purple satin ballgown.*

cut a rug *old-fashioned*
to dance • *Twenty disco classics on one CD. Now there's music to cut a rug to.*

cut a swath/swathe through sth
to cause a lot of destruction, death, or harm in a particular place or among a particular group of people • *Violent electrical storms cut a swath through parts of the South yesterday.* • *The AIDS epidemic has already cut a swath through the fashion industry.*

cut an [interesting/ridiculous/unusual etc.] figure
if someone cuts an interesting, ridiculous, unusual etc. figure, they seem interesting, ridiculous, unusual etc. • *My Russian uncle cut an unusual figure among the very British audience.*

cut and run
to avoid a difficult situation by leaving suddenly • *When his business started to fail, he decided to cut and run, rather than face financial ruin.*

the cut and thrust of sth
lively discussion or activity • *James enjoys the cut and thrust of debating.*

cut both/two ways
to have two different effects at the same time, usually one good and one bad • (never in continuous tenses) *Censorship cuts both ways; it prevents people from being corrupted, but it often also prevents them from knowing what is really going on.*

cut your **coat according to** your **cloth**
cut your **cloth according to** your **means**
to only buy what you have enough money to pay for • *Of course we'd love a huge expensive house, but you have to cut your coat according to your cloth.*

cut corners
to do something in the easiest, quickest, or cheapest way, often harming the quality of your work • *We've had to cut corners to make a film on such a small budget.* • *Companies are having to cut corners in order to remain competitive in the market.*

cut sb **dead**
to ignore someone when you see them or when they speak to you because you are

angry with them or do not like them • *I asked her about it in the meeting and she just cut me dead.*

cut sb **down to size**
to criticize someone who you think is too confident in order to make them feel less confident or less proud • *When he started he thought he knew everything, but we soon cut him down to size.*

cut it/things fine
to only leave yourself just enough time to do something • *Only allowing half an hour to get from the station to the airport is cutting it fine, isn't it?*

cut loose
1 if a person or organization cuts loose, they separate themselves from another person or organization • (usually + **from**) *She cut loose from her sponsors and decided to try to fund herself instead.*
cut loose sb/sth to get rid of someone or something that you control or own • *We're cutting loose only those teachers whose work is below standard.*
2 to behave in a way that is free and relaxed, especially when you are enjoying yourself • *After a few glasses of wine everyone just cut loose and started dancing.*

cut your **losses**
to stop doing something that is already failing in order to reduce the amount of time or money that is being wasted on it • *I wasn't benefiting from the course and it was costing so much that I thought I'd better cut my losses.*

cut no ice with sb
if something cuts no ice with someone, it does not cause them to change their opinion or decision • *I've heard her excuses and they cut no ice with me.*

cut off your **nose to spite** your **face**
to do something because you are angry, even if it will cause trouble for you • *'The next time he treats me like that, I'm just going to quit my job.' 'Isn't that a bit like cutting off your nose to spite your face?'*

cut your **own throat**
to do something because you are angry, even if it will cause trouble for you • *If she won't take the job out of pride, she's cutting her own throat.*

cut sb **some slack** *American & Australian informal*
to allow someone to do something that is not usually allowed, or to treat someone less severely than is usual • *Officials have asked the Environmental Protection Agency to cut Utah some slack in enforcing the Clean Air Act.*

cut your **teeth** *British, American & Australian*
cut your **eye teeth** *American*
to get your first experience of a particular type of work and learn the basic skills • (often + **on**) *She cut her teeth on a local newspaper before landing a job on a national daily.*

cut the (umbilical) cord
to stop needing someone else to look after you and start acting independently ✍An umbilical cord is a long narrow tube of flesh which connects a baby to its mother when it is growing inside her. • *In order to achieve true independence, smaller nations must cut the cord and stop depending on the United States for financial aid.*

Cut the crap! *very informal*
an impolite way of telling someone to stop saying things that are not true or not important • *Just cut the crap, will you, and tell me what really happened last night.*

cut the ground from under sb/sb's **feet**
to make someone or their ideas seem less good, especially by doing something before them or better than them • *The opposition claimed today's speech was an attempt to cut the ground from under their feet.*

cut to the chase *informal*
to talk about or deal with the important parts of a subject and not waste time with things that are not important • *I didn't have long to talk to him so I cut to the chase and asked whether he was still married.*

cut sb **to the quick** *old-fashioned*
to upset someone by criticizing them • (usually passive) *I was cut to the quick by her harsh remarks.*

cut up rough *British old-fashioned*
to become very angry • (often + **about**)

Dad cut up rough about me staying out all night.

you could cut the atmosphere with a knife

something that you say to describe a situation in which everyone is feeling very angry or nervous and you feel that something unpleasant could soon happen • *There was a lot of tension between Diane and Carol; you could cut the atmosphere in that room with a knife.*

► See also: **fish** or cut bait.
cut/go through sth like a (hot) **knife** through butter
to cut a **long** story short

cut-and-dried

cut-and-dried

1 if a decision or agreement is cut-and-dried, it is final and will not be changed • *Although a deal has been agreed, it is not yet cut-and-dried.*

2 if a subject, situation, or idea is cut-and-dried, it is clear and easy to understand • *The human rights issue is by no means cut-and-dried.*

cute

be as cute as a button *American & Australian*

to be very attractive • *At 14, she was as cute as a button and the boys were starting to notice her.*

cutting

at/on the cutting edge

in the area of a subject or activity where the most recent changes and developments are happening • (often + **of**) *New, young, Italian designers are at the cutting edge of fashion.*

dab

be a dab hand *British & Australian*
to be very good at an activity • (often + **at**) *You should get Ann to have a look at that. She's a dab hand at getting stains out of clothes.* • (often + **with**) *I hear you're a dab hand with the paintbrush.* (= you are good at painting)

daft

be as daft as a brush *British informal*
if someone is as daft as a brush, they behave in a very silly way • *I remember him as a kid and he was as daft as a brush then.*

daggers

be at daggers drawn *British & Australian*
if two people or groups are at daggers drawn, they are angry and ready to fight or argue with each other ✍A dagger is a sharp pointed knife that was used in the past as a weapon. • (often + **with**) *Local residents are at daggers drawn with the council over rubbish collection.* • (often + **over**) *The two countries have several times been at daggers drawn over the future of the island.*

▶ See also: **look** daggers at sb

damage

What's the damage? *informal, humorous*
used to ask how much you have to pay for something • *'We've mended your car.' 'Great. What's the damage?'*

damn

damn sb/sth **with faint praise**
to praise something or someone in such a weak way that it is obvious you do not really admire them • *She damned Reynolds with faint praise, calling him one of the best imitators in the world.*

not **give a damn** *informal*
to not be interested in or worried about something or someone • *He can think what he likes. I don't give a damn.* • (often + **about**) *Most companies don't give a damn about the environment.* • (often + question word) *I've made my decision and I don't give a damn what they think.*

damned

be damned if you **do and damned if** you **don't**
if you say that someone is damned if they do and damned if they don't, you mean they will be criticized whatever they do • *When it comes to removing children from parents suspected of abuse, social workers are damned if they do and damned if they don't.*

damp

a damp squib *British & Australian*
an event which people think will be exciting but which is disappointing when it happens ✍A squib is a type of firework (= a small container filled with chemicals which explodes to produce bright lights and loud noises) and if it becomes wet, it will not explode. • *The party turned out to be a bit of a damp squib. Half the people who'd been invited didn't turn up.*

damper

put a damper/dampener on sth
to stop an occasion from being enjoyable ✍A damper is a device used on piano strings to make the sound less loud. • *Steve lost his wallet so that rather put a damper on the evening.* • *We were both ill while we were in Boston, which put a bit of a dampener on things.*

dance

dance to sb's **tune**
to always do what someone tells you to do, whether you agree with it or not • *Powerful local residents seem to have the council dancing to their tune.*

▶ See also: **lead** sb a (merry) dance

dangerous

on dangerous ground
if you are on dangerous ground, you are

talking about a subject which might upset or offend people • *The author is on dangerous ground when he starts criticizing modern women's literature.* • *She sensed she was* ***treading on dangerous ground*** *when her father began to look rather annoyed.*
OPPOSITE **on safe ground** • *You'll be on safe ground if you ask him about his childhood.*

dark

a dark horse
1 *British & Australian humorous* a person who does not tell other people about their ideas or skills and who surprises people by doing something that they do not expect • *I didn't know Linda had written a novel. She's a bit of a dark horse, isn't she?*
2 a person who wins a race or competition although no one expected them to • (sometimes + **for**) *17-year-old Karen Pickering could also be a dark horse for* (= she could win) *a medal in the European Championships.*
dark-horse *American* • (always before noun) *She's* ***a dark-horse candidate*** *for the position of company director.*

be in the dark
to not know about something that other people know about • *I'm totally in the dark. I don't know what's going on.* • (often + **about**) *We're still in the dark about whether any jobs are going to be cut.*
keep/leave sb **in the dark** to not tell someone about something • *She claims she knew nothing about the deal and was deliberately kept in the dark.*

keep sth **dark**
to keep something secret • *If he did know that Anna was leaving, he certainly kept it dark.*

darken

never darken your **door again** *old-fashioned*
if you tell someone never to darken your door again, you mean you never want to see them again • *Did her father really tell you never to darken his door again? How melodramatic.*

darkest

The darkest hour is just before the dawn.
something that you say which means a bad situation often seems worse just before it improves • *There's still a chance she might recover. The darkest hour is just before the dawn.*

dash

► See: **cut** a dash

Davy Jones

Davy Jones's locker *humorous*
the bottom of the sea • *No one knows how many wrecked ships there are in Davy Jones's locker.*

day

be all in a day's work
if something difficult or strange is all in a day's work for someone, it is a usual part of their job • (often + **for**) *Drinking champagne with Hollywood stars is all in a day's work for top celebrity reporter Gloria Evans.* • *We worked in blizzard conditions to restore all the power lines, but it's all in a day's work.*

be as clear/plain as day
to be obvious or easy to see • *She's in love with him – it's as plain as day.*

day in, day out
day in and day out
if you do something day in, day out, you do it every day over a long period, often causing it to become boring • *Life can become very tedious if you do the same work day in, day out.* • *Dave wore the same tie day in and day out.*

the day of reckoning
the time when an unpleasant situation has to be dealt with, or the time when you are punished or criticized for the things you have done wrong ✍In the Bible, the day of reckoning is the day at the end of the world when God will judge everyone. • *Taking out a further loan to cover your debts will only postpone the day of reckoning.*

Don't give up the day job! *humorous*
something that you say to someone who is performing in order to tell them that you do not think they are very good at it • *'What did you think of my singing, then?'*

'Er, don't give up the day job!'

get/have your **day in court** *American & Australian*
to get an opportunity to give your opinion on something or to explain your actions after they have been criticized • *She was fiercely determined to get her day in court and the TV interview would give it to her.*

have had its/your **day**
to be much less popular than before • *The general view in the country is that socialism has had its day.* • *She was a best-selling author in the 1950s and 60s, but I think she's had her day.*

in this day and age
in modern times • *She said she was appalled that so much injustice could exist in this day and age.*

make sb's **day**
to make someone very happy • *Go on, tell him you like his jacket. It'll make his day!* • *I was so pleased to hear from Peter. It really made my day.*

take each day as it comes
take it one day at a time
to deal with things as they happen, and not to make plans or to worry about the future • *I've lived through a lot of changes recently, but I've learnt to take each day as it comes.*

That'll be the day!
something that you say in order to show you think an event or action is not likely to happen • *A pay rise? That'll be the day!*

▶ See also: **call** it a day
carry the day
name the day
save the day
seize the day
win the day

daylights

beat/knock the (living) daylights out of sb
to hit someone very hard many times • *I'll knock the living daylights out of him if I catch him doing it again!*

frighten/scare the (living) daylights out of sb
to frighten someone very much • *Don't come up behind me like that. You scared the living daylights out of me!*

days

sb's/sth's **days are numbered**
if someone's or something's days are numbered, they will not exist for much longer • *As our local cinema struggles to survive, it seems clear that its days are numbered.*

I've never [felt/heard/seen etc.] sth **in all my (born) days!** *old-fashioned*
something that you say when you are shocked or very surprised by something • *There were two men kissing in the street. I've never seen anything like it in all my born days!*

Those were the days!
something that you say which means life was better at the time in the past that you are talking about • *We had no money but we were young and madly in love. Oh, those were the days!*

day-to-day

day-to-day
a day-to-day activity is one of the things that you have to do every day, usually as a part of your work • (always before noun) *It's Sheila who's responsible for the day-to-day running of the school.*

dead

be a dead cert *British & Australian informal*
to be certain to happen or to be certain to achieve something • (often + **for**) *He's a dead cert for an Oscar nomination.*

be a dead loss
1 *informal* if something or someone is a dead loss, they disappoint you because they are of bad quality or because they are not able to do what you want them to do • *The meeting was a dead loss. We didn't come to a single decision.* • *He may have been a great poet, but he was a dead loss as a husband.*
2 *informal* to be very bad at a particular activity or subject • (sometimes + **at**) *I was an absolute dead loss at sport when I was at school.*

be a dead ringer for sb/sth
to look very similar to someone or something • *He's a dead ringer for Bono from U2 – people often come up to him in the street and ask for his autograph.*

be as dead as a dodo *informal*
if something is as dead as a dodo, it is not important or popular any more ✍The dodo was a large bird which could not fly and which does not exist any more. • *Who cares about socialism any more? Socialism's as dead as a dodo.* • *Any hopes she had of becoming a professional gymnast are now as dead as a dodo.*

be as dead as a doornail *informal*
to be dead • *I found the fish, dead as a doornail, floating on the surface of the water.* • *At first I thought Jake was as dead as a doornail, but he was only fast asleep.*

be dead and buried
to be ended completely • *As far as I'm concerned the matter's dead and buried.* • *I won't rest until fascism is dead and buried in this country.*

be dead from the neck up *humorous*
if a person is dead from the neck up, they are very stupid • *Her last boyfriend was dead from the neck up.* • *I can't believe he's failed the test twice – he must be dead from the neck up!*

be dead from the waist down *humorous*
if someone is dead from the waist down, they do not experience sexual excitement • *It's no good flirting with him – he's dead from the waist down.* • *You don't think he's gorgeous? You must be dead from the waist down!*

be dead in the water
if something is dead in the water, it has failed, and it seems impossible that it will be successful in the future • *So how does a government revive an economy that is dead in the water?* • *As soon as Mum finds out that you'll be away overnight, your plan's going to be dead in the water.*

be dead meat *American & Australian informal*
if you say that someone is dead meat, you mean that they will be punished severely for something they have done • *You touch any of my things again and you're dead meat!* • *If her parents find out that she's been sneaking out to see Glenn, she'll be dead meat and so will he.*

be dead on your feet

be dead on your **feet**
to be very tired • *I've spent the whole day cleaning the house and I'm dead on my feet.*

be dead to the world
to be sleeping very deeply • *Guy was curled up on the sofa, dead to the world.*

be the dead spit of sb *British*
to look very much like someone else • *He's the dead spit of this bloke I used to know.*

come back from the dead
rise from the dead
to become successful or popular again after a period of not being successful or popular • *This was a company that had risen from the dead under the new direction of Tom Wiles.*

a dead duck
1 *informal* something or someone that is not successful or useful • *The project was a dead duck from the start due to a lack of funding.* • *My first agent turned out to be a bit of a dead duck and he failed to find me any work.*
2 *American & Australian informal* someone who is going to be punished severely for something they have done • *If Dad finds out you used the car, you'll be a dead duck.*

a dead end
a situation in which no progress can be made ✍A dead end is also a road which is closed at one end and does not lead anywhere. • *Negotiators have reached a dead end in their attempts to find a peaceful solution to the crisis.*

dead-end • (always before noun) *He found himself stuck in a low-paid, **dead-end job**.* • *She moved to London to escape from a dead-end relationship.*

the dead hand of sth

something that stops progress from being made • *Economic development has been held back by the dead hand of bureaucracy.*

a dead letter

an agreement or a law which still exists but which people do not obey or which is not effective any more • *The ceasefire agreement was a dead letter as soon as it was signed since neither side had any intention of keeping to it.*

Dead men tell no tales.

something that you say which means people who are dead cannot tell secrets • *I suspect they killed him because he knew too much. Dead men tell no tales.*

a dead weight

1 if someone is a dead weight, they are very heavy and difficult to carry, often because they are not conscious • *Tom was a dead weight and her muscles ached as she carried him upstairs.*

2 something or someone who prevents other people from making progress • *We must free ourselves from **the dead weight of** history.* • *She's just a dead weight on the business at the moment.*

dead wood

people in a group or organization who are not useful any more and who need to be removed • *There's a lot of dead wood in the team which needs to be cleared out.*

flog a dead horse *British, American & Australian*

beat a dead horse *American*

to waste time trying to do something that will not succeed • (usually in continuous tenses) *You're flogging a dead horse trying to persuade Simon to come to Spain with us – he hates going abroad.* • *Do you think it's worth sending my manuscript to other publishers or I am just beating a dead horse?*

in the dead of night/winter

in the middle of the night or in the middle of winter • *The fire broke out in the dead of night.*

over my dead body

if you say that something will happen over your dead body, you mean that you will do everything you can to prevent it • *'Josh says he's going to buy a motorbike.' 'Over my dead body!'* • *If they cut down those trees, they'll do it over my dead body.*

wouldn't be caught/seen dead *informal*

if someone wouldn't be seen dead in a particular place or doing a particular thing, they would never do it, usually because it would be too embarrassing • (often + *adv/prep*) *John's dad won't go to the christening, he wouldn't be seen dead in a church.* • (often + doing sth) *Chris wouldn't be seen dead driving a Lada.*

▶ See also: **cut** sb dead
drop dead!
knock them/'em dead

deaf

be as deaf as a post *British, American & Australian informal*

be as deaf as a doorknob/doornail *Australian*

to be completely deaf • *She's 89 and as deaf as a post.*

▶ See also: **fall** on deaf ears
turn a deaf ear

deal

What's the deal? *informal*

something that you say in order to ask someone to explain what they have been doing or what they are planning to do • *'You haven't been at work all week – what's the deal?'* • *So, what's the deal – are we going out to dinner?*

▶ See also: **cut** a deal

dear

a Dear John letter *humorous*

a letter that you send to a man telling him you want to end a romantic relationship with him • *I've always thought Dear John letters a cowardly way of ending a relationship.*

hang/hold on (to sth/sb**) for dear life**

to hold something or someone as tightly as you can in order to avoid falling • *I sat behind Gary on the bike and hung on for dear life as we sped off.* • *A rope was passed down and she held on to it for dear life as she was pulled to safety.*

▶ See also: **cost** sb dear
close/dear to sb's **heart**

death

be at death's door *informal*
to be nearly dead • *Don't exaggerate, it was only flu – you were hardly at death's door.*

be done to death *informal*
if a particular style or subject is done to death, it is used or discussed so many times that it is not interesting any more • *The military look was done to death in last season's fashion shows.*

a death blow
an action or an event which causes something to end or fail • (usually + **to**) *This renewed outbreak of fighting has been seen as a death blow to any chance for peace.* • *The scandal* ***dealt a death blow to*** (= ended) *his political ambitions.*

a death trap
a building, road, or vehicle which is very dangerous and which could cause people to die • *The whole house was a death trap with faulty gas fires, broken stairs, and bad wiring.* • *The road becomes a death trap in icy weather.*

flog sth **to death** *British, American & Australian informal*
beat sth **to death** *American*
to use a particular style or to discuss a particular subject so many times that it is not interesting any more • *He basically takes one theme and flogs it to death for three hundred and fifty pages.* • *No sporting event is beaten to death more than the Sugar Bowl – it is analyzed again and again by the commentators.*

frighten/scare sb **to death**
to make someone feel very frightened • *David suddenly appeared in the doorway and scared me to death.*
be frightened/scared to death • *I'm scared to death she's going to tell him.* • (often + **of**) *She's frightened to death of dogs.*

like death (warmed up) *British & Australian*
like death (warmed over) *American*
if you feel or look like death warmed up, you feel or look very ill • *I wish I'd got to bed earlier last night – I feel like death warmed up.* • *The poor guy looked like death warmed over.*

to death
if someone is worried or bored to death, they are very worried or bored • *Why didn't you ring and say you were going to be late? I was worried to death.* • *You must be bored to death, sitting here all day with nothing to do.*

▶ See also: You'll **catch** your death (of cold)!
dice with death
die a death
sign your own death warrant

deck

on deck
1 *American & Australian* if someone is on deck, they are present and ready to do something • *Bill's batting next – tell him to get on deck.* • *Ann, if you can be on deck at 9.00 I'll give you a lift to the meeting.*
2 *Australian informal* alive • *Don't tell me old Bill's still on deck. I thought he died years ago.*

▶ See also: **hit** the deck/dirt
stack the deck

deckchairs

▶ See: be like **rearranging** the deckchairs on the Titanic

decks

▶ See: **clear** the decks

deep

be in deep water
to be in a difficult situation which is hard to deal with • *We're going to be in deep water if the bank refuses to authorize a bigger loan.*
get into deep water to become involved in a difficult situation • *I think we're getting into deep water here talking about gender issues.*

be in too deep *informal*
to be so involved in a situation or relationship that you are unable to stop

being involved • *I knew I should leave him but I was in too deep.*

deep down

if you know or feel something deep down, you are certain that it is true or you feel it strongly although you do not admit it or show it • *Deep down, she knew that what she was doing was wrong.* • *He tried to convince himself that he was enjoying his job, but deep down he was really miserable.*

deep pockets

if an organization or a person has deep pockets, they have a lot of money • *Anyone who tries to help that company will need deep pockets – it is nearly bankrupt.*

go off the deep end *informal*

to suddenly become very angry or upset and start shouting at someone • *One minute we were having a perfectly reasonable discussion and the next minute you just went off the deep end!*

go/run deep

if a feeling or a problem goes deep, it is very strong or serious and has existed for a long time • *Feelings of anger went deep on both sides.* • *Underlying problems in the company run deep and it is unlikely that a new director will be able to solve them.*

throw sb **in at the deep end**

to make someone do something difficult, especially a job, without preparing them for it or giving them any help • *I had to deal with a strike threat on my first day – talk about being thrown in at the deep end!*

jump in at the deep end to start a new job or activity without being prepared for it • *Philips is jumping in at the deep end, acting as captain in his first match with the team.*

▶ See also: **dig** deep
be in deep/the **shit**

deep-six

deep-six sb/sth *American informal*

to get rid of someone or something • *They want to deep-six the project because it's costing too much money.*

deer

▶ See: be like a deer/rabbit caught in the **headlights**

de facto

de facto *formal*

a de facto situation is one which exists or is true although it has not been officially accepted or agreed • (always before noun) *Edwards has established himself as the de facto leader of the group.*

de facto *formal* • *The United Nations has recognized de facto the country as independent.*

déjà vu

déjà vu

the strange feeling that you have already seen or experienced something • *As I walked into the house, I had a strange sense of déjà vu.*

deliver

▶ See: deliver the **goods**

delusions

delusions of grandeur

the belief that you are much more important or powerful than you really are • *Young bands sometimes get delusions of grandeur after their first number one hit.*

demon

the demon drink *humorous*

a way of referring to alcohol when you are talking about the unpleasant effects it can have • *My grandfather used to lecture us about the dangers of the demon drink.*

den

▶ See: **beard** sb in their den

dent

make a dent in sth *British, American & Australian*

put a dent in sth *American*

to reduce the amount or level of something • *The roof repairs made quite a dent in our savings.* • (often negative) *Police efforts have hardly put a dent in the level of drug trafficking on the streets.*

depart

depart this life *formal*

to die • *Here lies Henry Stanford, who*

departed this life January 13th 1867.

department

not **be** sb's **department** *informal*

if something is not your department, you are not responsible for dealing with it or you do not know much about it • *As regards getting your computer fixed, you'll have to ask someone else – I'm afraid it's not my department.* • *In general doctors don't know much about nutrition: that's not their department.*

OPPOSITE **be** sb's **department** *informal* • *I've chosen the paint and wallpaper, but the actual job of decorating is Neil's department.*

depth

be out of your **depth**

to not have the knowledge, experience, or skills to deal with a particular subject or situation • *When Ruth started talking about the differences between the databases, I knew I was out of my depth.* • *By half-time, England was losing 4-0 and the English players were looking hopelessly out of their depth.*

depths

▶ See: **plumb** the depths
sink to such depths

de rigeur

de rigeur *formal*

if something is de rigeur, it is necessary if you want to be thought fashionable or if you want to follow a custom • *Leather jackets and jeans are still de rigeur for hard rock fans.*

deserve

deserve a medal *humorous*

if you say that someone deserves a medal, you mean that you admire them for dealing with such a difficult situation or person for so long • (never in continuous tenses; often + **for**) *She deserves a medal for putting up with that husband of hers.*

designated

a designated driver *American*

one person in a group who agrees not to drink alcohol in order to drive the other people to and from a place where they will drink alcohol • *Tom said he'd be the designated driver when we go out tonight.*

designs

have designs on sb

to want to have a sexual relationship with someone • *She suspected that Helen had designs on her husband.*

have designs on sth

to want to have something and to plan to get it • *I knew that David had designs on my half of the business.*

de trop

de trop *formal*

more than is needed or wanted • (always after verb) *I thought his comments at the meeting were a little de trop.*

deus ex machina

a deus ex machina *formal*

a way of ending a play or event that seems false and that involves problems being dealt with too easily • *Shakespeare produces a very unsatisfying deus ex machina in 'The Winter's Tale' when a statue of the queen comes to life.*

devil

(let) the devil take the hindmost *old-fashioned*

something that you say to mean that you should only think about yourself and your own success and not care about other people • *You've got to be tough to survive in this business – grab what you can and let the devil take the hindmost.*

better the devil you know (than the devil you don't)

something that you say to mean it is better to deal with a person or thing you know, even if you do not like them, than to deal with a new person or thing who could be even worse • *I know Mike can be difficult to work with sometimes, but better the devil you know.*

between the devil and the deep blue sea

if you are between the devil and the deep blue sea, you must choose between two equally unpleasant situations • *For most people a visit to the dentist is the result of a choice between the devil and the deep blue sea – if you go you suffer, and if you don't go you suffer.*

The devil finds work for idle hands.

something that you say which means

people who have no work or activity are more likely to do things they should not do, such as commit crimes • *There's plenty more tidying to do if you've finished the bedroom. The devil finds work for idle hands.*

Go to the devil! *old-fashioned*
an impolite way of telling someone to go away because you are annoyed with them • *I told him that if he wasn't prepared to change his ideas he could go to the devil!*

have the devil's own job doing sth/to do sth *old-fashioned*
to spend a long time trying to do something difficult • *I had the devil's own job to find a parking space near here.*

have the devil's own luck *old-fashioned*
to be very lucky • *He found a job and an apartment within a week – he really has the devil's own luck, that man.*

speak/talk of the devil *humorous*
something that you say when a person you are talking about arrives and you are not expecting them • *Apparently, Lisa went there and wasn't very impressed – oh, talk of the devil, here she is.*

▶ See also: give the devil his **due**
play devil's advocate

devil-may-care

devil-may-care *old-fashioned*
relaxed and not worried about the results of your actions • *He had a rather devil-may-care attitude towards money which impressed me at the time.*

diamond

▶ See: a **rough** diamond

dibs

have dibs on sth *American informal*
to make it clear that something belongs to you or that you should be the next person to use something • *I have dibs on the Sunday paper.*

dice

the dice are loaded against sb
if the dice are loaded against someone, they are not likely to succeed • *When I realized I was the only male applicant I knew that the dice were loaded against me.*

dice with death
to do something very dangerous • (often in continuous tenses) *You're dicing with death driving at that sort of speed on icy roads.*

▶ See also: **no** dice

diddly-squat

diddly-squat *American informal*
nothing at all • *What does he know about the South? Diddly-squat!* • *The lyrics in his songs aren't worth diddly-squat – it's the melodies that make you feel good.*

die

die a death *British*
die a natural death *American & Australian*
to fail and end • *The principle of free health care for everyone is likely to die a death in the next ten years.* • *The play, like so many others, died a natural death after only one week.*

die hard
if a habit, custom, or belief, dies hard, it takes a long time to change or end it • (usually in present tenses) *After a successful 30-year career, he no longer has any need to work – but* ***old habits die hard.*** • *These ancient traditions die hard in the isolated communities of rural China.*
die-hard • (always before noun) *Die-hard* (= refusing to change) *communists have regrouped to form the Communist Refoundation.*

the die is cast
something that you say when a decision has been made or something has happened which will cause a situation to develop in a particular way ✍A die is a small block of wood or plastic with different numbers of spots on each side, used in games, and 'cast' means to throw. • *From the moment the first shot was fired, the die was cast and war became inevitable.*

die with your **boots on**
to die while you are still actively involved in your work • *I never want to retire – I'd rather die with my boots on.*

to die for *informal*
if something is to die for, it is extremely good • *The weather's fantastic, the people*

are warm and friendly and the food is to die for. • *She's a beautiful-looking girl with a voice to die for.*

► See also: die on the **vine**

difference

make all the difference

if something makes all the difference, it has a very good effect on a thing or a situation • *It's that little bit of salt that you add to the dressing – it makes all the difference.* • (often + **to**) *Working with a nice bunch of people can make all the difference to your job.*

different

(It's) different strokes for different folks. *mainly American*

something that you say which means that different people like or need different things • *I've never enjoyed winter sports, but different strokes for different folks.*

► See also: a totally different **ball** game
be as different as **chalk** and cheese
be another/a different **kettle** of fish
march to a different drummer
be different **sides** of the same coin

dig

dig deep

to use a lot of your own money to pay for something • *Church members* ***dug deep into their pockets*** *to pay for a new roof.* • *The city will have to dig deep if it wants to host the next Olympics.*

dig your heels in

to refuse to do what other people are trying to persuade you to do, especially to refuse to change your opinions or plans • *We suggested it would be quicker to fly, but she dug her heels in and insisted on taking the train.*

dig your own grave

to do something stupid that will cause problems for you in the future • *He's dug his own grave really. If he'd been a bit more cooperative in the first place they might still employ him.*

dig the dirt
dig up dirt

to try to find out bad things about someone in order to stop other people admiring them • (often + **on**) *No effort is being spared to dig up dirt on the enemy.*

► See also: dig/dip into your **pocket**
dig yourself into a **hole**

dignity

► See: **stand** on your dignity

dime

be a dime a dozen *American & Australian informal*

to be common and not have much value • *Romantic novels like these are a dime a dozen.*

not be worth a dime *American informal*

to have little or no value • *It turns out her precious painting isn't worth a dime – it's a fake.*

on a dime *American informal*

if a vehicle or its driver turns or stops on a dime, they turn or stop in a very small space • *His car is great for parking – it can turn on a dime.*

dinner

be done like a (dog's) dinner *Australian informal*

to be completely defeated • *Whatever possessed her to play tennis against Sue? She was done like a dinner.*

dip

► See: dig/dip into your **pocket**

dire

be in dire straits

to be in a very difficult or dangerous situation • *The earthquake and the war will leave the country in dire straits for a long time.* • *They are in dire financial straits.*

dirt

dirt cheap *informal*

extremely cheap • *This may seem like a great deal of money but in advertising terms it is dirt cheap.*

dirt-poor *informal*

extremely poor • *Most of the population in this undeveloped area were dirt-poor and jobless.*

do sb dirt *American informal*

to behave unfairly or badly towards someone, often without them knowing • *Mack really did me dirt – he stopped me from getting my promotion.*

► See also: **dig** the dirt

dish the dirt
hit the deck/dirt
treat sb like dirt

dirty

dirty your **hands**
to become involved in bad activities that might spoil other people's opinions of you • (usually negative) *The royal family don't usually dirty their hands with politics.*

a dirty old man *informal*
an older man who shows a strong and unpleasant interest in sex • *On the top shelf they've got all those horrible magazines for dirty old men.*

a dirty trick
a dishonest action • *He resigned after allegations of dirty tricks during the election campaign.* • *Telling her you needed the money for a friend was a dirty trick.*

a dirty weekend *British & Australian humorous*
a weekend when two people who are not married go away somewhere to have sex • *At first I thought he was asking me to go away for a dirty weekend.*

a dirty word
if something is a dirty word, people do not generally approve of it • *For the environmentally conscious, 'disposable' has become a dirty word.*

do sb's **dirty work**
to do something unpleasant or difficult for someone else because they do not want to do it themselves • *Well next time, Kevin can do his own dirty work.* • (often + **for**) *Tell her yourself – I'm not going to do your dirty work for you!*

do the dirty on sb *British & Australian informal*
to behave unfairly or very badly towards someone, often without them knowing • *And then he did the dirty on her and went and had an affair with her best friend.*

give/shoot sb **a dirty look**
to look at someone in an angry way • *I didn't know what I'd said that was so offensive but she gave me a really dirty look.*

wash your **dirty laundry/linen in public** *British & Australian*
air your **dirty laundry/linen in public** *American & Australian*
to talk to other people about personal things that you should keep private • *I was brought up to believe that it was wrong to wash your dirty linen in public.*

► See also: **play** dirty
talk dirty

disappear

► See: disappear/vanish off the **face** of the earth

disaster

a disaster area
1 if a place is a disaster area, it is very untidy ✍A disaster area is also a place where an event like a storm or a flood causes serious damage and the government gives help for the emergency. • *The kitchen was a disaster area, with greasy plates piled high in the sink.*
2 if a subject, a piece of work, or an organization is a disaster area, it causes many problems, often because it is badly organized • *Government housing policy is a complete disaster area.*

discretion

Discretion is the better part of valour. *British & Australian literary*
Discretion is the better part of valor. *American & Australian literary*
something that you say which means that it is better to be careful and think before you act than it is to be brave and take risks • *She decided not to voice her opposition to the Chairman's remarks. Perhaps discretion was the better part of valour.*

dish

dish the dirt *informal*
to tell people unpleasant or shocking personal information about someone • (often + **on**) *Shauna agreed to dish the dirt on her millionaire ex-lover for a fee of £5,000.* • *Some journalists just enjoy dishing the dirt.*

distance

go the (full) distance
to continue to do something until it is successfully completed • *It's a really*

tough course – I'm just worried that I won't be able to go the distance.

in/within spitting distance
in/within striking distance

very close to something or someone • (often + **of**) *The great thing about the house is that it's within spitting distance of the sea.* • *The move to Ascot put us within striking distance of London.*

distraction

▶ See: **drive** sb to distraction

divide

divide and conquer/rule

a way of keeping yourself in a position of power by making the people under you disagree with each other so that they are unable to join together and remove you from your position • *A small minority have continued to govern by a policy of divide and conquer.*

divide-and-conquer/rule • (always before noun) *They used divide-and-rule tactics to isolate their opponents.*

dividends

▶ See: **pay** dividends

do

It's do or die.

something that you say when you are in a situation in which you must take a big risk in order to avoid failure • *It's now or never – do or die – risk everything or regret it for the rest of your life.*

do-or-die • (always before noun) *It was a do-or-die save by the goalkeeper that won the game.*

▶ See also: it's **all** (that) sb can do to do sth
do the **business**
do yourself a **favour**
Do me a **favour**!
do me/us a **favour**
not do sb any **favours**
not do anything/things by **halves**
do sb's **head** in
do your **homework**
Do you **mind**!
do yourself a **mischief**
do a **number** on sb
do your **nut**
do your **own** thing
do sb **proud**
do the **rounds**
do your **stuff**
do **time**
do the **trick**

doctor

be just what the doctor ordered

humorous

to be exactly what is wanted or needed • *'Andy's making us some lunch.' 'Great, just what the doctor ordered.'* • *A night out on their own was just what the doctor ordered.*

dog

be like a dog with a bone *British*

to refuse to stop thinking about or talking about a subject • *On the subject of fathers' rights, he's like a dog with a bone.*

be like a dog with two tails

to be very happy • *Ben's team won the match. Their manager was like a dog with two tails.*

a dog and pony show *American*

a show or other event that has been organized in order to get people's support or to persuade them to buy something • *The film is part of the dog and pony show the company puts on for the benefit of foreign journalists.*

the dog days

the hottest days of the summer ✍Some people believe there is a star called the dog star which can only be seen during a hot period in the summer. • (usually + **of**) *At times, during the dog days of summer, the stream dries up completely.*

dog eat dog

if a situation is dog eat dog, people will do anything to be successful, even if what they do harms other people • *In showbusiness it's dog eat dog – one day you're a star, the next you've been replaced by younger talent.*

dog-eat-dog • *It's a dog-eat-dog world out there so you've got to know who your real friends are.*

a dog in the manger

someone who keeps something that they do not really want in order to prevent anyone else from having it • *Stop being such a dog in the manger and let your sister ride your bike if you're not using it.*

dog-in-the-manger • (always before noun) *The British have a dog-in-the-*

manger attitude to the island, no longer needing it themselves, but wanting to deny it to others.

a dog's breakfast/dinner *British & Australian informal*
something that has been done very badly • *She tried to cut her hair and* ***made a*** *real* ***dog's breakfast*** *of it.* • *You should have seen the ceiling after he'd finished painting it. It was a complete dog's breakfast.*

done up/dressed up like a dog's dinner *British & Australian*
wearing clothes which make you look silly when you have tried to dress for a formal occasion • *There she was, all dressed up like a dog's dinner, in a ridiculous frilly shirt and a skirt that was far too short.*

Every dog has its day.
something that you say which means that everyone is successful during some period in their life • *He'll get that promotion eventually. Every dog has its day.*

Give a dog a bad name. *old-fashioned*
used to say that when someone has been accused of behaving badly in the past, people often expect them to behave like that in the future • *People were quick to blame local youths for the fire. Give a dog a bad name.*

not **have a dog's chance** *informal*
to not have any chance of doing something that you want to do • (usually + **of** + doing sth) *He hasn't a dog's chance of getting that job.*

It's a dog's life.
something that you say which means that life is hard and unpleasant • *I've got to go to the supermarket, then cook a meal, then pick Dave up from the station – it's a dog's life!*

► See also: be done like a (dog's) **dinner**
Why **keep** a dog and bark yourself?
put on the dog
work like a dog/trojan

doggo

► See: **lie** doggo

doghouse

be in the doghouse *informal*
if someone is in the doghouse, another person is annoyed with them because of something they have done • *I forgot to turn the oven off and the dinner's ruined, so I'm really in the doghouse.*

dogs

go to the dogs
if a country or an organization is going to the dogs, it is becoming less successful than it was in the past • (usually in continuous tenses) *They sat in the bar the night before the election, moaning that the country was going to the dogs.*

► See also: **call** off the dogs
throw sb to the dogs

dog-tired

dog-tired *informal*
extremely tired • *He usually got home at around seven o'clock, dog-tired after a long day in the office.*

doldrums

be in the doldrums
1 if a business, an economy or a person's job is in the doldrums, it is not very successful and nothing new is happening in it ✍The doldrums was the name for an area of sea where ships were not able to move because there was no wind. • *High-street spending remains in the doldrums and retailers do not expect an imminent recovery.*
OPPOSITE **out of the doldrums** • *A cut in interest rates will be needed to lift the property market out of the doldrums.*
2 to feel sad and to lack the energy to do anything • *He's been in the doldrums these past couple of weeks and nothing I do seems to cheer him up.*

dollars

dollar signs in sb's **eyes** *American & Australian*
if someone has dollar signs in their eyes, they are thinking about the money they could get • *Local taxi drivers approached us with dollar signs in their eyes.*

dollars to donuts/doughnuts *American informal*
if you say that something will happen, dollars to donuts, you mean you are sure

it will happen • *Dollars to donuts the company is going to fold.* • *I'll* ***bet you dollars to doughnuts*** *she won't come to the party.*

dollars-and-cents

dollars-and-cents *American & Australian*
if something is discussed or thought about in a dollars-and-cents way, the exact amounts of money involved are thought about • (always before noun) *The dollars-and-cents details of the new budget will be presented tomorrow by the government.*

domino

a domino effect
the effect which a situation or event has on a series of other situations or events ✍Dominoes are a set of small, rectangle-shaped pieces of wood or plastic, marked with spots on one side. If dominoes are placed standing next to each other, each one will knock the next one over. • *Young people can't afford even the small houses, so the people in those houses can't move on to the bigger houses. It's the domino effect.*

done

be done in *British, American & Australian informal*
be all done in *American*
to be too tired to do any more • *She was done in by the time she had cleared up after the party.* • *I'm all done in – sorry, but I can't walk any further without a rest.*

done and dusted *British old-fashioned*
successfully completed • *We expect the deal to be done and dusted before the end of next week.*

a done deal *mainly American*
a final decision or agreement • (often negative) *It's not a done deal – we're still talking about who to hire for the job.*

▶ See also: be done to **death**
be done like a (dog's) **dinner**
done up/dressed up like a **dog**'s dinner
the done **thing**
be cooked/done to a **turn**

don Juan

a Don Juan
a man who has had sex with a lot of women • *At 47 he detests his image as a Don Juan.*

donkey

donkey's years *informal*
a very long time • *I've been doing this job for donkey's years.*

▶ See also: donkey **work**

don't

Don't even go there. *informal*
used to say that you do not want to think or talk about something because it is too difficult or unpleasant • *She's very old-fashioned, and as for the subject of single mothers – don't even go there!*

▶ See also: Don't **ask** me.
Don't give up the **day** job!
Don't **give** me that!
Don't get **mad**, get even.
Don't **sweat** it!
Don't take any **wooden** nickels.

doom

doom and gloom
the feeling that a situation is bad and is not likely to improve • *Come on, it's not all doom and gloom, if we make a real effort we could still win.*

door

close/shut the door on sth
to make it impossible for something to happen, especially a plan or a solution to a problem • *There are fears that this latest move might have closed the door on a peaceful solution.*

get a/your **foot in the door** *British, American & Australian*
get a leg in the door *Australian*
to start working at a low level for an organization because you want a better job in the same organization in the future • *I know it's not the job you'd hoped for, but at least you can use it to get your foot in the door.*

give sb **a foot in the door** • *The freelance work I did gave me a foot in the door.*

▶ See also: never **darken** your door again
lay sth at sb's door
open the door to sth
show sb the door

doors

▶ See: **open** (new) doors

doorstep

on sb's **doorstep**

very near to where someone lives • *The great thing is we've got all the local amenities right on our doorstep.*

dos

dos and don'ts

rules about what you must do and what you must not do in a particular situation • *In the back of the guide there's a list of the dos and don'ts of local etiquette.*

dose

go through sb/sth **like a dose of salts** *old-fashioned*

if something you eat goes through your body like a dose of salts, it goes through you very quickly • *Those beans went through me like a dose of salts.*

▶ See also: give sb a dose/taste of their own **medicine**

dot

dot the/your **i's and cross the/**your **t's** *informal*

to do something very carefully and in a lot of detail • *She writes highly accurate reports – she always dots her i's and crosses her t's.*

on the dot

if something happens at a particular time on the dot, it happens at exactly that time • *Shops in this part of the city shut at 5.30 pm on the dot.* • (sometimes + **of**) *The first customers arrived on the dot of 9 am.*

dotted

▶ See: **sign** on the dotted line

double

at the double *British & Australian*
on the double *American & Australian*

if you go somewhere or do something at the double, you go there or do it very quickly • *Two surgeons arrived in the emergency room at the double.*

do a double take

to look at something or someone twice because you are so surprised at what you have seen • *He walked past her and she did a double take. Without his beard he was quite transformed.*

a double bind

a situation in which you cannot succeed because whatever you decide to do, there will be bad results • *Women find themselves* ***in a double bind****. If they stay at home with their kids they're regarded as non-achievers and if they go out to work, people say they're neglecting their family.*

double Dutch *British & Australian*

speech or writing that is nonsense and cannot be understood • *He came out with a load of sophisticated grammatical codes and it all sounded like double Dutch.*

a double-edged sword

something that causes both advantages and problems • *His great intelligence was a real double-edged sword because he never felt he could communicate with ordinary people.*

a double whammy *informal*

a situation where two bad things happen at the same time • *Critics claim that the cuts in public spending coupled with a pay freeze is a double whammy which will affect low-paid workers badly.*

double-dipping

double-dipping *American*

the activity of receiving money from two different places or two different jobs, often when it is not honest or legal • *The government has introduced tighter rules on employees' pensions to discourage double-dipping.*

double-dip *American* • *It is tempting for physicians to double-dip by sending their patients to labs they have a financial interest in.*

double entendre

a double entendre

a word or phrase which has two different meanings, one of which is sexual or rude • *His speech at the dinner was full of bad jokes and double entendres.*

double-talk

double-talk *British, American & Australian*
double-speak *mainly American*

a way of speaking that confuses people in order to avoid telling them the truth • *He said the new train service would run fewer trains, but would provide a better service – sheer double-talk.*

doubting

a doubting Thomas

a person who refuses to believe anything until they are given proof ✍In the Bible, Thomas would not believe that Jesus had come back from the dead until he saw him. • *He's a real doubting Thomas – he simply wouldn't believe I'd won the car until he saw it with his own eyes.*

down

down-and-dirty

1 *American informal* down-and-dirty behaviour is not pleasant or honest • *He ran a down-and-dirty political campaign.*

2 *American informal* something that is down-and-dirty is shocking, often because it is connected with sex • *He likes his films down-and-dirty.*

a down and out *British & Australian*
a down-and-outer *American*

someone who has no home, no job and no money • *I just assumed he was a down and out, begging on the street corner.* • *She was one of the many down-and-outers waiting for the soup kitchen to open.* **down-and-out** • (always before noun) *His next film was about two down-and-out drifters who met in New York.*

down the drain *British, American & Australian informal*
down the gurgler *Australian informal*

if work or money goes down the drain, it is wasted • *Then our funding was withdrawn and two years' work* ***went down the drain****.* • *Say he gives up his training, that's four thousand pounds down the gurgler.*

down the toilet *British, American & Australian informal*
down the pan *British informal*

if something goes down the toilet, it is wasted or spoiled • *After the drug scandal, his career went down the toilet.* • *If the factory closes, that'll be a million pounds' worth of investment down the pan.*

down tools *British & Australian*

to refuse to work, especially because you are not satisfied with your pay or working conditions • *Thousands of Krakow steelworkers downed tools to demand more pay.*

Down Under *informal*

Australia and New Zealand, or in or to Australia and New Zealand • *The British rugby team are going on a tour Down Under later this year.* • *I think she's from down under judging by her accent.*

▶ See also: have sth down to a **fine** art
Down the **hatch**!
be down on your **luck**
be down in the **mouth**

down-at-heel

down-at-heel *British, American & Australian*
down-at-the-heel *American*

badly dressed or in a bad condition because of a lack of money • *When I first met her she was down-at-heel but still respectable.* • *The play was set in a down-at-heel hotel in post-war Germany.*

downer

have a downer on sb *British & Australian informal*

to not like someone • *I didn't realise she felt like that about Julian. She's got a real downer on him.*

downhill

go downhill

to gradually become worse • *The area has started to go downhill economically in the last ten years.* • *We started to argue soon after we got married, and things went downhill from there.*

down-home

down-home *American*

down-home things are simple and typical of life in the countryside • (always before noun) *It's a diner with down-home American cooking where you can take all the family.* • *He's a folksy, down-home sort of guy.*

down-to-earth

down-to-earth

down-to-earth people or ideas are practical and work well • *David's very arty and a bit of a dreamer – Ruth's much more down-to-earth.* • *I like her down-to-earth approach to problem-solving.*

dozen

by the dozen

if something is being produced by the dozen, large numbers of that thing are being produced • *The government is producing new policies by the dozen.*

nineteen/ten to the dozen *British & Australian informal*

if someone is talking nineteen to the dozen, they are talking very fast, without stopping • *Gaby was chatting away nineteen to the dozen behind me and I couldn't concentrate.*

drag

drag your **feet/heels**

to deal with something slowly because you do not really want to do it • (often + **on**) *He was asked why the government had dragged its feet on the question of a single European currency.* • (often + **over**) *We don't want to look as if we're dragging our heels over promoting women to senior positions.*

drag sb's **name through the mire/mud**

to tell people about something bad that someone has done so that people will have a bad opinion of them • *Her name was dragged through the mud after she admitted offering money in return for votes.*

► See also: drag/haul sb over the **coals**

dragon

► See: **chase** the dragon

drain

► See: **laugh** like a drain

drape

► See: drape/wrap yourself in the **flag**

draw

be quick on the draw

to be fast at understanding or reacting to a situation • *He was quick on the draw answering the reporter's questions.*

OPPOSITE **be slow on the draw** *mainly American* • *You're a bit slow on the draw aren't you? Can't you see the joke?*

draw a line under sth

if you draw a line under something, it is finished and you do not think about it again • *Let's draw a line under the whole episode and try to continue our work in a more positive frame of mind.*

draw a veil over sth

if you draw a veil over a subject, you do not talk about it any more because it could cause trouble or make someone embarrassed • *I think we should draw a veil over this conversation and pretend it never happened.*

draw blood

to make someone very angry or upset • *He always draws blood with his film reviews.*

draw (sb's) **fire** *mainly American*

if something or someone draws fire, they are criticized • (often + **from**) *The advertisements have drawn fire from anti-smoking campaigners* • *His radical approach is expected to draw fire.*

draw the line

to think of or treat one thing as different from another • (often + **between**) *It all depends on your concept of fiction and where you draw the line between fact and fiction.* • *So at what point do we consider the foetus a baby? We've got to draw the line somewhere.*

draw the line at sth

if someone says that they draw the line at a particular way of behaving, they mean that they do not do it because they think it is wrong or too extreme • *I know I swear a lot but I do draw the line at certain words.* • *I like a beer or two as you know but even I draw the line at sitting in a pub on my own and drinking.*

draw the short straw *informal*

to be the member of a group who has to do an unpleasant job • *Sorry, Jim, you drew the short straw. You're on toilet-cleaning duty.*

► See also: draw/take a **bead** on sb/sth
draw a **blank**
draw/pull in your **horns**

drawing

back to the drawing board

if you go back to the drawing board, you have to start planning a piece of work again because the previous plan failed • *If the education reform is too expensive to implement, it's back to the drawing board for the committee.* • *Our proposal might not be accepted, in which case we'll have to* ***go back to the drawing board****.*

a drawing card *American & Australian*
a famous person who attracts a lot of people to a public event • *Babe Ruth was the outstanding player of his time – the real drawing card for Yankee Stadium.*

dread

▶ See: I dread/shudder to **think**

dreaded

the dreaded lurgy *British & Australian humorous*
an illness that is not serious but passes easily from person to person • *My throat is sore and my head hurts. I think I've caught the dreaded lurgy.*

dream

be/live in a dream world
to have ideas or hopes which are not practical and are not likely to be successful • (usually in continuous tenses) *If she thinks he's suddenly going to turn into the perfect boyfriend, she's living in a dream world.*

Dream on! *humorous*
something that you say to someone who has just told you about something they are hoping for, in order to show that you do not believe it will happen • *'I've a feeling I'll win something on the lottery this week.' 'Dream on!'*

a dream ticket
two politicians who have joined together to try to win an election and who are likely to succeed because together they have the support of many different groups of people • *Clinton and Gore transformed themselves into a dream ticket in the last American election.*

like a dream
if something or someone does something like a dream, they do it very well • *Everything had happened as it was meant to. Oscar's plan had worked like a dream.* • *Our new car goes like a dream.*

wouldn't dream of doing sth
if someone wouldn't dream of doing something, they would never do it because they think it is wrong or silly • *I wouldn't dream of asking my father for money.*

dreams

In your dreams! *humorous*
something that you say to someone who has just told you about something they are hoping for, in order to show that you do not believe it will happen • *Dave, buy you a car? In your dreams!*

the man/woman/sth **of** your **dreams**
the person or thing that you would like more than any other • *I'm not sure I'll ever meet the man of my dreams, or if he even exists.* • *At last, we'd found it, the house of our dreams.*

dressed

be all dressed up and/with nowhere to go
to be dressed and ready to go somewhere nice, but not have anywhere to go • *Rob rang up and said he had to work late, so there I was, all dressed up with nowhere to go.*

be dressed to kill
to be wearing clothes which are intended to make people sexually attracted to you • *Rosie emerged from the house, dressed to kill and clutching a bottle of champagne.*

be dressed up to the nines *informal*
to be wearing very fashionable or formal clothes for a special occasion • *They must have been on their way to a wedding or something. They were dressed up to the nines.*

▶ See also: done up/dressed up like a **dog**'s dinner

dribs

in dribs and drabs
in small amounts or a few at a time • *We could only afford to pay the builder in dribs and drabs.* • *The hostages have been released in dribs and drabs.*

drift

drift with the tide
to agree with other people without thinking about things for yourself and making your own decisions • *We are looking for someone with the ability to lead rather than just drift with the tide.*

get sb's**/the drift** *informal*
catch sb's**/the drift** *informal*
to understand what someone is saying • *Can you explain that again? I don't quite*

get your drift. • *I didn't understand everything he was saying but I think I caught the drift.*

if you catch/get my drift *informal*
something that you say to suggest that you have left out information or your opinion from what you have just told someone • *She always has to be the centre of attention, if you catch my drift.*

drink

drink like a fish *informal*
to regularly drink a lot of alcohol • *Harriet had two bottles of wine with her meal – that girl drinks like a fish!*

drink sb **under the table** *informal*
if you can drink someone under the table, you can drink a lot more alcohol than they can • *I like a few beers but Mel can drink me under the table.*

▶ See also: **drive** sb to drink
can't **hold** their drink/liquor

drive

drive a coach and horses through sth *British*
if someone drives a coach and horses through a rule, an opinion, a plan, or a tradition, they destroy it by doing something against it which it is too weak to prevent • *His company drove a coach and horses through employment legislation.* • *She produced statistics which drove a coach and horses through the chairman's argument.*

drive a hard bargain
to demand a lot or refuse to give much when making an agreement with someone • *I'm impressed that you got £2000 for that car. You certainly drive a hard bargain.*

drive a wedge between sb
if you drive a wedge between two people or two groups of people, you do something which spoils their relationship • *She thinks Samantha's jealous and is trying to drive a wedge between her and her boyfriend.* • *This is a clear attempt to drive a wedge between the USA and its western allies.*

drive sb **to distraction**
to make someone very angry or very bored • *Looking after six children every day is enough to drive you to distraction.* • *There's a constant buzzing noise and it's driving me to distraction.*

drive sb **to drink** *humorous*
to make someone extremely anxious and unhappy • *I just couldn't live with someone like Malcolm. It would drive me to drink.*

drive sb **up the wall** *informal*
to make someone very angry or very bored • *I was being driven up the wall by their silly chatter.* • *Working in a factory would have driven me up the wall.*

▶ See also: drive/send sb round the **bend**
push/drive sb over the **edge**
drive/run/work yourself into the **ground**
drive/hammer sth **home**
drive/send sb round the **twist**

driver

▶ See: be in the driver's **seat**

driving

▶ See: be in the driving **seat**

drop

at the drop of a hat
if you do something at the drop of a hat, you do it suddenly and easily, often without any preparation • *I can't go rushing off to Florida at the drop of a hat.* • *We now have a situation where laws may be changed at the drop of a hat.*

drop a bombshell *British, American & Australian*
drop a bomb *American*
to suddenly tell someone a piece of news that upsets them very much • *My sister dropped a bombshell by announcing she was leaving her job.* • *Her husband dropped a bomb over dinner. 'I'm seeing another woman,' he said.*

drop a clanger *British & Australian informal*
to say something by accident that embarrasses or upsets someone • *I dropped a clanger by asking John how his dog was when it's been dead three months.*

drop sb **a line** *slightly informal*
to write a short letter to someone • *If you've got a few minutes to spare you could always drop her a line.*

Drop dead! *very informal*
a rude way of telling someone that you

are very angry at something they have just said or done • *A guy started hassling me while I was ordering drinks at the bar, so I told him to drop dead.*

drop everything

if you drop everything, you suddenly stop what you are doing in order to do something else instead • *I **can't just drop everything** and go into town with you. I have to finish this letter.*

a drop in the ocean *British, American & Australian*

a drop in the bucket *American*

a very small amount in comparison to the amount that is needed • *A hundred thousand may seem a lot but it's a drop in the ocean compared to the millions that need to be spent.*

drop sb/sth **like a hot brick/potato** *informal*

to suddenly get rid of someone or something that you have been involved with because you do not want them any more or you are worried they may cause problems • *The government dropped the plan like a hot brick when they realized the bad feeling it was causing.*

drop the ball *American informal*

to make a mistake, especially by doing something in a stupid or careless way • *For god's sake don't drop the ball – we're relying on you.*

fit/ready to drop

extremely tired • *I'd just walked 10 miles and I was ready to drop.*

▶ See also: drop/lower your **guard**
drop/fall into your **lap**

drop-dead

drop-dead *informal*

a drop-dead person or piece of clothing is very beautiful • (always before noun) *Her exquisite figure was shown off to the full in a drop-dead black dress.* • *He turned up to the concert with a **drop-dead gorgeous** woman on his arm.*

dropping

be dropping like flies

if people are dropping like flies, large numbers of them are dying or becoming ill or injured within a short period of time • *The heat was overwhelming and people were dropping like flies.*

drown

drown your **sorrows**

to drink a lot of alcohol because you want to stop feeling sad • *I've got a bottle of whiskey here – shall we stay in and drown our sorrows?*

drowned

▶ See: **look** like a drowned rat

drum

bang/beat the drum

to speak eagerly about something that you support • (often + **for**) *Once again she was banging the drum for pre-school nurseries.* • *The opposition parties are always beating the environmental drum.*

drunk

as drunk as a lord/skunk

very drunk • *He rolled out of the club into a taxi, drunk as a lord.* • *We'd get drunk as a skunk at lunch and sleep all afternoon.*

dry

be as dry as a bone

to be extremely dry • *I don't think he's been watering these plants – the soil's as dry as a bone.*

There wasn't a dry eye in the house.

something that you say which means that all the people in a particular place were very sad about what they had seen or heard and many of them were crying • *She began to talk about her son who had died and by the end of her speech there wasn't a dry eye in the house.*

▶ See also: **bleed** sb dry
be **bone** dry
hang sb out to dry
a dry **run**

duck

be duck soup *American informal*

to be very easy to do • *Winning your case in court ought to be duck soup.*

take to sth **like a duck to water**

to learn how to do something very quickly and to enjoy doing it • *Sue just took to motherhood like a duck to water.* • *He's taken to his new school like a duck to water.*

▶ See also: If it **looks** like a duck and

walks/quack/flies, etc. like a duck, it is a duck.

ducking

ducking and diving *informal*

if you spend your time ducking and diving, you are involved in many different activities, especially ones which are not honest • *'What do you do for a living?' 'This and that, ducking and diving.'*

ducks

get your **ducks in a row** *American informal*

to organize things well • *The government talks about tax changes but they won't fix a date or an amount – they just can't get their ducks in a row.*

due

give sb their **due**

give the devil his due

something that you say when you want to describe someone's good qualities after they have done something wrong or after you have criticized them • *She might be bad at writing letters but I'll give her her due, she always phones me at the end of the month.* • *Geoff usually forgets my birthday, but give the devil his due, he always buys me a lovely Christmas present.*

in due course *slightly formal*

if you say that something will happen in due course, you mean that it will happen at a suitable time in the future • *You will receive notification of the results in due course.*

dues

▶ See: **pay** your dues

duff

be up the duff *British & Australian informal*

to be pregnant • *Oh, don't tell me Kylie's up the duff again!*

dull

be as dull as dishwater/ditchwater *informal*

to be very boring • *He loved the book but I thought it was as dull as ditchwater.*

dummy

▶ See: a dummy **run**

dumps

be down in the dumps *informal*

to be unhappy • *Things hadn't been going so well for her at work and she was feeling a bit down in the dumps.*

dust

the dust settles

if the dust settles after an argument, a problem, or an event which has caused a lot of changes, the situation becomes calmer • *We decided to* ***let the dust settle*** *before trying to deal with any other problems.* • *You'd better* ***wait until the dust settles*** *before you mention anything else.*

▶ See also: **bite** the dust
gather dust
not **see** sb for dust
turn to dust

Dutch

Dutch courage *humorous*

the confidence that you get by drinking alcohol before you do something that you are frightened of doing • *He had another drink to give him Dutch courage for what he might find at home.*

a Dutch treat

a Dutch treat

an occasion when two or more people agree to share the cost of something, especially a meal • *She and Callahan often met for lunch. It was always a Dutch treat.*

go Dutch

to share the cost of something, especially

a meal • *'Will you let me take you out tonight?' 'As long as we go Dutch.'*

duty

be duty bound to do sth

if you are duty bound to do something, you have to do it because it is your duty • *The government is duty bound to compensate those who lost money.* • *I've been given a certain amount of training so I feel duty bound to stay in the job for at least a year.*

do (double) duty as/for sth *American & Australian*

to also have another purpose • *They make an electronic identity card that will do duty for a credit card and pocket calculator.* • *She's really the secretary but she does double duty as the receptionist during Katrina's lunch hour.*

dyed-in-the-wool

dyed-in-the-wool

if you describe someone as dyed-in-the-wool, you mean they have very strong opinions and will not change • (always before noun) *He's a dyed-in-the-wool traditionalist where cooking is concerned – he won't have any modern gadgets in the kitchen.*

Ee

each

each to his/her **own**
to each his/her **own**
something that you say which means that it is acceptable for people to like or believe in different things • *I find it hard to believe that anyone enjoys gardening. Ah well, each to his own.*

▶ See also: take each **day** as it comes
live in each other's pockets

eager

an eager beaver
someone who works very hard and is very eager to do things ✍A beaver is a small animal which people traditionally believe to be hard-working. • *Who's the eager beaver who came in at the weekend to finish this work off?*

eagle

watch sb/sth **with an eagle eye**
watch sb/sth **with eagle eyes**
to watch someone or something very closely and carefully ✍An eagle is a large bird which can see very well. • *The teacher was watching the children with an eagle eye, making sure they behaved themselves.*
an eagle eye if someone has an eagle eye, they are good at noticing small details because they watch things very carefully • *Nothing escapes his eagle eye.*
eagle-eyed • *This article is full of printer's errors, which an eagle-eyed proofreader would have spotted.*

ear

be out on your **ear** *informal*
to be forced to leave your job because you have done something wrong, or because your work is not good enough • *You'll be out on your ear if you don't start doing some work around here.*

can do sth **on** their **ear** *Australian informal*
if someone can do something on their ear, they can do it very easily • *Ask Jane to make it, she can bake a soufflé on her ear.*

grin/smile from ear to ear
to look extremely happy • (usually in continuous tenses) *We've had a fantastic response,' he said, grinning from ear to ear.*

have an ear for sth
if someone has an ear for music, poetry, or languages, they are good at hearing, repeating, or understanding these sounds • (often negative) *She's never had much of an ear for languages.*

have sb's **ear**
if someone has the ear of an important and powerful person, that person is willing to listen to their ideas • *He's a powerful industrialist who has the President's ear.*

▶ See also: **bend** sb's ear
keep an/your ear to the ground
lend an ear
go in **one** ear and out the other
play it by ear

earful

give sb **an earful** *informal*
to tell someone how angry you are with them • *You can just imagine the earful he gave her when they got home.*

early

an early bath *British & Australian informal*
if you take an early bath, you are forced to stop doing an activity sooner than you intended to ✍This phrase is often used about sports such as football. • *The spokesman **took an early bath** after a series of embarrassing and incorrect statements.* • *And that's his second yellow card so it looks like an early bath for Taylor.*

an early bird
someone who gets up early in the morning • *Ellen's the early bird in this house, not me.*

The early bird catches the worm.
something that you say in order to tell someone that if they want to be successful they should do something

immediately • *If you see a job that interests you, apply as soon as possible. The early bird catches the worm.*

it's early days (yet) *British & Australian*
something that you say which means that it is too soon to make a judgement about something • *Both teams are near the bottom of the league, but it's early days yet.*

earn

earn your **stripes**
to do something to show that you deserve a particular rank or position and have the skills needed for it • *She earned her stripes as a junior reporter before becoming education correspondent.*

► See also: earn/get **brownie** points
earn/win your **spurs**

ears

about/around sb's **ears**
if something falls, or is brought about someone's ears, it suddenly fails completely and destroys someone's hopes and plans • *His business folded and collapsed about his ears.* • *Her entire world seemed to have come crashing around her ears when he died.*

be all ears

be all ears *informal*
to be very eager to hear what someone is going to say • *'Do you want to hear what happened at the party last night?' 'Oh yes, I'm all ears'.*

(sb's) **ears are flapping** *informal*
something that you say when you think that someone is listening to your private conversation • *I can't talk now. Ears are flapping.*

your **ears must be burning**
something that you say to someone who is being talked about • *All that talk about William – his ears must have been burning.* **Were** your **ears burning?** • *Were your ears burning? We were just talking about you.*

have nothing between the/your **ears** *informal*
to be stupid • *He's very good-looking but has absolutely nothing between the ears, I'm afraid.*

► See also: can't **believe** your ears
box sb's ears
pin back your ears
prick your ears up
be **up** to your ears/eyeballs/eyes in sth

earth

an earth mother
a woman who has children and who has a natural ability as a mother • *My older sister's a real earth mother. She has four kids and she's completely happy to stay at home all day with them.*

come (back) down to earth (with a bang/bump/jolt)
to have to start dealing with the unpleasant or boring things that happen every day after a period of excitement and enjoyment • *We came down to earth with a bump when we got back from our holidays to find we had a burst pipe.* **bring** sb **(back) down to earth** • *I had a huge pile of work waiting for me on my desk so that brought me back down to earth.*

the earth moved *humorous*
something that you say to describe how good a sexual experience was • *'How was it for you?' 'Ooh, the earth moved!'* • *Did the earth move for you?*

go to earth *British & Australian*
to go away somewhere where people will not be able to find you • *I'll go to earth in my uncle's holiday cottage until all the publicity has died down.*

► See also: **promise** (sb) the earth
run sb to earth

earth-shattering

[hardly/scarcely etc.] earth-shattering
not very surprising or shocking • *We were all expecting the announcement. It wasn't exactly earth-shattering news.*

easier

easier said than done
something that you say when something seems like a good idea but it would be difficult to do • *The doctor says I should stop smoking but that's easier said than done.*

easy

be as easy as abc
to be very easy • *You won't have any problems assembling your new bed – it's as easy as abc.*

be as easy as falling off a log *British, American & Australian*
be as easy as rolling off a log *American*
to be very easy • *She said writing stories was as easy as falling off a log for her.*

be as easy as pie
to be very easy • *Oh, come on! Even a child could do that, it's as easy as pie.*

be easy meat *British & Australian informal*
be an easy mark *American*
someone or something that is easy meat is easy to beat, criticize, or trick • *United were easy meat in the semifinal on Wednesday.* • *The elderly living alone are an easy mark for con-men.*

make easy meat of sth/sb *British & Australian informal* • *Our team made easy meat of them in the final.*

be easy on the ear
if music is easy on the ear, it has a pleasant and relaxing sound • *When I'm driving, I like to listen to music that's easy on the ear and not too demanding.*

be easy on the eye
to have an attractive appearance • *It's not a painting which is easy on the eye, but it attracts your attention for other reasons.*

easy come, easy go *informal*
something that you say in order to describe someone who thinks that everything is easy to achieve, especially earning money, and who therefore does not worry about anything • *Les could certainly spend money. Easy come, easy go it was with him.*

Easy does it! *informal*
something that you say in order to tell someone to do something carefully • *'Easy does it!' Bob shouted, as I steered the boat into the dock.*

easy money
money that you earn with very little work or effort • *It must be easy money writing for one of those magazines.*

go easy *informal*
to not take or use too much of something • (often + **on**) *Avoid fried foods and go easy on the snacks.* • *Go easy! There's not much left!*

go easy on sb *informal*
to treat someone in a gentle way and not punish them severely if they have done something wrong • *They'll probably go easy on him since he hasn't been in trouble before.*

It's easy to be wise after the event. *British, American & Australian*
It's easy to be smart after the fact. *American*
something that you say which means that it is easy to understand what you could have done to prevent something bad from happening after it has happened • *In retrospect I suppose we should have realised that she was in trouble and tried to help her, but then I suppose it's easy to be wise after the event.* • *People often tell me they'd never have taken out a loan if they'd thought about it more carefully – but it's easy to be smart after the fact.*

take it easy
to relax and not use up too much energy • *You'd better take it easy for a while – you don't want to get ill again.*

Take it easy!
something that you say in order to tell someone to be calm and not to get too angry or excited • *Take it easy! I didn't mean any offence.*

▶ See also: be as easy as **taking** candy from a baby
be an easy/soft **touch**

eat

sb**, eat your heart out!** *humorous*
something that you say which means that you or someone you know can do something better than a person who is famous for doing that thing • *I'm taking singing lessons. Celine Dion, eat your heart out!*

eat sb **alive**
to criticize someone very angrily • *If we get our facts wrong we'll be eaten alive by the press.*

eat sb **for breakfast**
to speak angrily to someone, or to criticize someone • *My boss would eat me for breakfast if I asked for more money.*

eat humble pie *British, American & Australian*
eat crow *American*
to be forced to admit that you are wrong and to say you are sorry • *The producers of the advert had to eat humble pie and apologize for misrepresenting the facts.*

eat like a bird
to eat very little • *We went out for a meal, but she ate like a bird and hardly said a word.*

eat like a horse
if you eat like a horse, you always eat a lot of food • *She eats like a horse, so I don't know how she manages to stay so thin.*

eat like a pig *informal*
to eat a lot, or to eat noisily and unpleasantly • *Christine is one of those lucky people who can eat like a pig and still stay thin.*

eat sb **out of house and home** *humorous*
to eat most of the food that someone has in their house • *The boys have only been back two days and they've already eaten me out of house and home.*

have to eat your **words**
to be forced to admit that something you said before was wrong • *She told me I'd never be able to give up smoking, but she had to eat her words.*
make sb **eat** their **words** • *She made him eat his words about women not having the physical strength to become boxers.*

I could eat a horse.
something that you say when you are very hungry • *I've had nothing but a sandwich all day – I could eat a horse.*

I'll eat my hat *old-fashioned*
if you say you will eat your hat if something happens or does not happen, you mean you will be very surprised if it happens or does not happen • *If we can't beat a second-rate team like Sheffield, I'll eat my hat.*

eating

what's eating sb**?** *informal*
something that you ask when someone is angry and you want to know why • *He suddenly noticed I wasn't joining in the conversation. 'What's eating you tonight?' he asked.*

ebb

the ebb and flow
the way in which the level of something frequently becomes higher or lower in a situation • (often + **of**) *The government did nothing about the recession, hoping it was just part of the ebb and flow of the economy.*

echo

▶ See: **cheer** sb to the echo

eclipse

be in eclipse *literary*
if something is in eclipse, it is less successful than it was before • *His career was in eclipse until he made a comeback in this surprise hit film.*

economical

be economical with the truth *humorous*
to not be completely honest about something • *He was economical with the truth – he gave her a censored account of what was discussed.*

edge

be on edge
to be nervous or worried about something • *The players were all a little on edge before the big game.*
put sb **on edge** • *Knowing that I might be called on to answer a question at any point always puts me on edge.*

have the edge on/over sb/sth
to be slightly better than someone or something else • *He's got the edge over other teachers because he's so much more experienced.* • *The new Renault has the edge on other similar models – it's larger and cheaper.*

keep sb **on the edge of** their **seat** *British, American & Australian*
keep sb **on the edge of** their **chair** *American*
if a story keeps you on the edge of your seat, it is very exciting and you want to know what is going to happen next • *You must rent this video. It keeps you on the edge of your seat right up to the end.*

live on the edge
to have a type of life in which you are often involved in exciting or dangerous activities • *If you were always living on the edge like that I'm sure you wouldn't live past the age of sixty.*

push/drive sb **over the edge** *informal*
if an unpleasant event pushes someone over the edge, it makes them start to behave in a crazy way • *She had been driven over the edge by the separation from her husband.*

take the edge off sth
to make something unpleasant have less of an effect on someone • *Have an apple. It'll take the edge off your hunger for a while.* • *His apology took the edge off her anger.*

▶ See also: **lose** your edge

edges

▶ See: **fray** around/at the edges

educated

an educated guess
a guess that is likely to be correct because you have enough knowledge about a particular subject • *Scientists can do no more than make educated guesses about future climate changes.*

effing

effing and blinding *British & Australian informal*
swearing angrily ✍Effing here represents the letter 'F' as a way of avoiding saying 'fuck' or 'fucking'. Blinding comes from an old-fashioned phrase 'Blind me!' • *I could hear Bill effing and blinding as he tried to repair the washing machine.*

egg

have egg on your **face** *informal*
to seem stupid because of something you have done • *You'll be the one who has egg on your face if it goes wrong.*

▶ See also: can't **boil** an egg
lay an egg

eggs

put all your **eggs in one basket**
to risk losing everything by putting all your efforts or all your money into one plan or one course of action • *If you're going to invest the money, my advice would be don't put all your eggs in one basket.*

eggshells

be walking/treading on eggshells
if you are walking on eggshells, you are trying very hard not to upset someone ✍An eggshell is the hard outside covering of an egg which breaks very easily. • *It was like walking on eggshells with my father. The smallest thing would make him angry.*

ego

an ego trip
something that you do in order to make yourself feel important • *Running the university Film Society is a big ego trip for her.*

eight

be behind the eight ball *American & Australian informal*
to be in a difficult situation and unable to make progress ✍In a game of pool (= a game in which you hit numbered balls into holes around a table), if you are behind the black, number eight ball you are in a difficult position to take your next turn. • *The police are very much behind the eight ball – they've had no more leads on these burglaries.*

elbow

at sb's **elbow**
near someone, often in order to help them • *She hovered constantly at Charles's*

elbow to make sure he had everything he wanted.

elbow grease *humorous*
hard work, especially when you are cleaning something • *With determination and elbow grease we soon transformed the filthy kitchen.*

elbow room
1 space which allows you to move around • *There's no elbow room at all in this kitchen.*
2 the freedom to do what you want to do • *The President should be given as much elbow room as he needs to solve these international problems.*

give sb **the elbow** *British informal*
to end a romantic relationship with someone • *They went out together for a month and then she gave him the elbow.*

elbows

▶ See: **rub** elbows with sb

elders

your **elders and betters** *old-fashioned*
people who are older than you and who should be treated with respect • *When we were children, we were always taught to respect our elders and betters.*

element

be in your **element**
to feel happy and relaxed because you are doing something that you like doing and are good at • *You should have seen her when they asked her to sing, she was in her element.*

OPPOSITE **be out of** your **element**
to feel unhappy or strange because you are in a situation that you are not familiar with • *He felt out of his element at such a formal occasion.*

elevator

elevator music *American*
pleasant but boring recorded music that is played in public places • *You can't get away from elevator music in some shopping malls.*

eleventh

at the eleventh hour
almost too late • *Negotiators reached agreement at the eleventh hour, just in time to avoid a strike.*

eleventh-hour • (always before noun) *The accused was saved from execution by an eleventh-hour confession from her father.*

else

if all else fails
if you decide that you will do something if all else fails, you decide that that is what you will do if none of your ideas or plans succeed • *Well, if all else fails you'll just have to get a part-time job to earn a bit of extra money.*

embarrassment

an embarrassment of riches *formal*
if you have an embarrassment of riches, you have more of something than you need and this makes it difficult for you to make a choice • *This club has an embarrassment of riches. All their players are good, so who do they pick for their side?*

éminence grise

an éminence grise *formal*
someone who has a lot of power and influence but no official position • *Although he never became a minister, he was the party's éminence grise for 15 years.*

empty

empty nest syndrome
the sad feelings which parents have when their children grow up and leave home • *The last of her children had recently moved out and she was suffering from empty nest syndrome.*

Empty vessels make (the) most noise/sound.
something that you say which means that people who talk a lot and frequently express their opinions are often stupid • *David talks as if he's an expert on everything, but empty vessels make most noise.*

enchilada

the whole enchilada *mainly American informal*
the whole of something, including everything that is connected with it • *We had the flowers, the speeches, the presents – the whole enchilada.*

end

[days/months/weeks etc.] on end
if something happens or continues for days, months etc. on end, it continues for several days, months, or weeks without stopping • *We sometimes don't see each other for months on end, but we're still good friends.*

an end in itself
if an activity or action is an end in itself, it is important to you not because it will help you to achieve something else, but because you enjoy doing it or think that it is important • *Education should be an end in itself.*

at the end of the day *informal*
something that you say before you say what you believe to be the most important fact of a situation • *Sure we missed our best player but at the end of the day, John, we just didn't play well enough to win the game.* • *At the end of the day, what matters is that you're safe.*

be at the end of your **tether** *British, American & Australian*
be at the end of your **rope** *American*
to be so tired, worried, or annoyed by something that you feel unable to deal with it any more ✍An animal which is tied up by a rope cannot reach the grass which is further away than the end of the rope and becomes hungry and unhappy. • *After a day with four screaming kids I'm at the end of my tether.* • *He's out of work, hanging around the house all day and at the end of his rope.*
reach the end of your **tether** *British, American & Australian*
• *She finally reached the end of her tether and told him exactly what she thought of his behaviour.*

be the end of the line/road
to be the end of a situation or process • *After losing his title in last night's fight, the former heavyweight champion knows that this is the end of the road.* • (often + **for**) *When she found out that Jim had been seeing another woman, it was the end of the line for their marriage.*
reach the end of the line/road • *I think our friendship has reached the end of the road – you've lied to me once too often.*

not **be the end of the world**
if you say that if something happens it won't be the end of the world, you mean it will not cause very serious problems • *If I don't get the job, it won't be the end of the world.*

can't see beyond/past the end of your **nose**
if you can't see beyond the end of your nose, you think so much about yourself and what affects you that you do not see what is really important • *These people are so busy making money, they can't see beyond the end of their nose.*

end it all *informal*
to kill yourself • *After his wife died, he was so depressed he decided to end it all.*

The end justifies the means.
something that you say which means that in order to achieve an important aim, it is acceptable to do something bad • *Unfortunately, we'll have to cut down the forest to make space for the golf course, but I feel the end justifies the means.*

End of story. *informal*
something that you say when you think that the opinion you have just expressed about something is correct and that there is no other possible way of thinking about it • *If you don't have the money, you don't spend it. End of story.*

get/have your **end away** *British very informal*
if a man gets his end away, he has sex • *Did you get your end away last night, then?*

hold/keep your **end up** *British informal*
to do what you are expected to do • *After my maternity leave, I made sure I kept my end up at work. I didn't want to give my boss an excuse to complain about working mothers.*

It'll (all) end in tears.
something that you say which means something will end badly and the people involved will be upset • *She only met him in May and they were married by July. It'll end in tears, you'll see.*

You'll **never hear the end of it.** *informal*
something that you say which means that someone will continue to talk about something they have achieved for a long time and in an annoying way • *If she wins you know we'll never hear the end of it.*

▶ See also: **no** end

ends

go to the ends of the earth
to do everything possible in order to achieve something • (often + to do sth) *Some journalists would go to the ends of the earth to get a story.*

make (both) ends meet
to have just enough money to pay for the things that you need • *My wages were so low that I had to take a second job just to make ends meet.*

play both ends against the middle *American informal*
to try to make two people or groups compete with each other in order to get an advantage for yourself • *He's playing both ends against the middle – telling two prospective employers that the other has offered a higher salary.*

enfant terrible

an enfant terrible
a famous or successful person who likes to shock people by behaving badly • (usually + **of**) *Jean Paul Gaultier, the enfant terrible of French fashion, arrived at the show wearing a mini kilt.*

Englishman

An Englishman's home is his castle. *British old-fashioned*
something that you say which means that British people believe they should be able to control what happens in their own homes, and that no one else should tell them what to do there • *An Englishman's home is his castle. The government has no right to interfere in our private lives!*

enough

Enough is as good as a feast. *British old-fashioned*
something that you say which means you should not have more of something than you need • *No, thank you, nothing more to drink for me. Enough is as good as a feast.*

enough is enough
something that you say in order to tell someone that you think what is happening should stop • *Look, enough is enough. He's borrowed £300 already.*

Enough said.
something that you say in order to tell someone that you have clearly understood what they have just said and do not need any more explanation • *'His father's a duke.' 'Enough said.'*

▶ See also: have a lot/enough on your **plate**
give sb enough **rope** (to hang themselves)

en route

en route
if you are en route to a place, you are on your way there • (usually + **to**) *They were en route to Geneva when they heard the news.*

enter

▶ See: enter/join the **fray**
enter/get into the **spirit** of sth

equal

▶ See: (all) other **things** being equal

err

err on the side of caution
if you err on the side of caution when you are deciding what to do, you do the thing that is safe instead of taking a risk • *I decided to err on the side of caution and spend less than my full allowance.*

To err is human, (to forgive, divine). *formal*
something that you say which means it is natural to make mistakes and it is important to forgive people when they do • *You'd think he could find it in his heart to forgive her. To err is human and all that.*

error

see the error of your **ways**
to understand that you have been behaving badly and to decide to improve your behaviour • *It's the story of a corrupt policeman who finally sees the error of his ways.*

esprit de corps

esprit de corps *formal*
feelings of pride and loyalty that are

shared by members of a group • *Companies that involve their employees in planning have the best esprit de corps.*

essence

be of the essence

to be the most important thing for achieving success • ***Time is of the essence*** *because the building must be completed by June.* • *For successful military strategy, secrecy is of the essence.*

et al.

et al.

something that you say after a name or list of names to refer to other people in the group • *This issue is discussed in more detail in the article by Cooper et al.*

even

even stevens *British informal*
even steven *American & Australian informal*

if two or more people are even stevens, they have the same amount of something or are at the same level • *Give me £20 and we're even stevens – I'm not worried about a few pence.*

get an even break *American & Australian*

if someone gets an even break, they get the same opportunity to improve their situation as other people • *This guy has the talent. He just needs to get an even break and he could be up there with the best of them.*

give sb **an even break** *American & Australian* • *Until now no one had given her an even break to prove what she could do.*

get even *informal*

if you get even with someone who has done something bad to you, you do something bad to them • *Vinnie's a spiteful kind of guy. Who knows what he might think up to get even.* • (often + **with**) *He swore he'd get even with Lee for humiliating him.*

on an even keel

calm and not likely to change suddenly • *My main priority is to keep my life on an even keel for the sake of my two boys.*

▶ See also: **break** even
don't even go there.

every

every man jack (of us/them) *old-fashioned*
every last man (of us/them) *old-fashioned*

every single person • *If you sack me the others will walk out too, every man jack of them.* • *Every last man of us is ready to fight for their country.*

every now and again/then
every so often

sometimes • *Every now and then I go to town and spend loads of money.*

every other

happening or existing regularly on every second one of the things you are counting • *Our discussion group meets every other Friday at eight o'clock.* • *Every other shelf on the bookcase was full of books.*

every which way *American & Australian informal*

in many different directions • *The documents lay scattered every which way on his desk.*

▶ See also: Every **cloud** has a silver lining.
Every **dog** has its day.
be every **inch** sth
It's every **man** for himself.
every **time** sb turns around/round
every **trick** in the book
at every **turn**

everyone

everyone and his brother *American*

a very large number of people • *We couldn't get in to see the movie – everyone and his brother had decided to go.*

▶ See also: be on everyone's **lips**

everything

Everything's coming up roses.

something that you say when a situation is successful in every way • *Everything's coming up roses for George at the moment – he's been promoted at work and he's just got engaged.*

▶ See also: Everything in the **garden** is rosy.
everything but the **kitchen** sink

evidence

▶ See also: **turn** king's/queen's evidence
turn state's evidence

evil

give sb the evil eye

give sb **the evil eye**
to look at someone in an angry or unpleasant way • *I arrived late for the meeting and Steve Thomson gave me the evil eye.*

ex cathedra

ex cathedra *formal*
if someone speaks ex cathedra or makes an ex cathedra statement, they say something in an official way as if it must be obeyed or accepted • *His policy pronouncements made ex cathedra angered many of his colleagues.*

exception

be the exception that proves the rule
if you say something is the exception that proves the rule, you mean that although it does not support the statement you have made, the statement is usually true • *This woman is the exception that proves the rule that it is impossible to be a warmonger and a feminist at the same time.*

ex gratia

ex gratia
an ex gratia payment is one which someone makes in order to show that they are kind and not because it is legally necessary • (always before noun) *The company has refused to admit it acted unlawfully but it has offered the victims an ex gratia payment of £5,000 each.*

exhibition

make an exhibition of yourself
to do something that makes you look stupid and attracts other people's attention • *If he keeps on drinking he's going to end up making an exhibition of himself!*

expense

no expense is spared
if no expense is spared in arranging something, a lot of money is spent to make it extremely good • *No expense was spared in making the guests feel comfortable.*
no expense spared • *It was only the best for his daughter's wedding, no expense spared.*

▶ See also: and **hang** the cost/expense

experience

put sth **down to experience** *British, American & Australian*
chalk sth **up to experience** *American & Australian*
to decide that instead of being upset about something bad that you have done or that has happened, you will learn from it • *'I'm so ashamed. I let him take advantage of me.' 'Don't be so hard on yourself. Just put it down to experience.'*

explode

▶ See: blow up/explode in sb's **face**

extoll

extoll the virtues of sb/sth *formal*
to praise the good qualities of someone or something • *He wrote several magazine articles extolling the virtues of country life.*

extra

go the extra mile
to make more effort than is expected of you • (often + **for**) *He's a nice guy, always ready to go the extra mile for his friends.*

extracurricular

extracurricular activity *humorous*
sexual activity, especially when it is secret ✍Extracurricular activities can also mean things that you do which are not part of your school or college course. • *You're looking very tired these days, Ron. Been indulging in too much extracurricular activity?*

eye

An eye for an eye (and a tooth for a tooth).

something that you say which means if someone does something wrong, they should be punished by having the same thing done to them ✍This phrase comes from the Bible. • *If you murder someone you deserve to die. An eye for an eye.*

be in the eye of the storm

to be very much involved in an argument or problem that affects a lot of people • *International aid agencies were in the eye of the storm when war broke out in the country.*

cast/run your/**an eye over** sth

to look at something quickly without looking at the details • *Would you mind casting an eye over my essay and giving me your comments?*

get your **eye in** *British & Australian*

to become very good at a sport or other activity by practising it • *It'll take me a while to get my eye in. I haven't played for years.*

keep your **eye in** *British & Australian* • *I try to play regularly to keep my eye in.*

give your **eye teeth for** sth *informal*
give your **eye teeth** to do sth *informal*

if you would give your eye teeth for something, you would very much like to have or be that thing • *I'd give my eye teeth for a house like that.* • *Most women would give their eye teeth to be tall and thin like you.*

have an eye for sth

to be good at noticing a particular type of thing • *She* ***has an eye for detail.*** • *He had an eye for the unusual and the exotic which made him a very good shopping companion.*

have an eye for/on the main chance *British & Australian*

if someone has an eye for the main chance, they are always looking for opportunities to make money and to improve their situation • *She was someone who had an eye on the main chance and who never missed an opportunity to exploit others.*

have your **eye on** sth

to have seen something that you want and that you intend to get • *I've got my eye on a really nice sofa – I just hope we can afford it.*

keep your **eye on the ball**

to give your attention to what you are doing all the time • *You have to keep your eye on the ball in business.*

OPPOSITE **take** your **eye off the ball** • *If you're a manager, you can't afford to take your eye off the ball for one minute.*

There is more to sth/sb **than meets the eye.**

something that you say when you think that something or someone is less simple than they seem to be at first • *There's more to this than meets the eye. I suspect Tom's not telling the truth.* • *There must be more to him than meets the eye, or else why would she be interested in him?*

with an eye to sth

if you do something with an eye to something else, you do it for that reason • *With an eye to the upcoming election the President has hired a new speechwriter.* • *A lot of costume drama is produced with an eye to American sales.*

▶ See also: not **bat** an eye/eyelash/eyelid
eye/mind **candy**
catch sb's eye
cut your eye teeth
keep your/an eye on sth/sb
keep an eye out for sb/sth
look sb in the eye/eyes
be **one** in the eye for sb
have/keep **one** eye on sth/sb
see eye to eye

eyeball

eyeball to eyeball

if you are eyeball to eyeball with an enemy or someone that you are arguing with, you deal with them in a direct way • *Troops on the ground are likely to remain eyeball to eyeball for a while yet.*

eyeball-to-eyeball • (always before noun) *The public wants to see an eyeball-to-eyeball confrontation between the two party leaders.*

eyeballs

▶ See: be **up** to your ears/eyeballs/eyes in sth

eyebrows

▶ See: **raise** (a few) eyebrows

eyeful

get an eyeful *informal*

to clearly see someone or something that is surprising • *Ed got an eyeful on the beach when a woman took her top off right in front of him.* • (often an order) ***Get an eyeful of this!*** (= Look at this) *I bet you've never seen so much money in one place before.*

eyelash

▶ See: not **bat** an eye/eyelash/eyelid

eyelid

▶ See: not **bat** an eye/eyelash/eyelid

eyes

all eyes are on sb/sth

if all eyes are on someone or something, everyone is watching that person or thing and waiting to see what will happen • *All eyes are on the Prime Minister to see how he will respond to the challenge to his leadership.*

be all eyes

to watch something or someone with a lot of interest • *We were all eyes as the prince and princess emerged from the palace.*

can't take/keep your **eyes off** sb/sth

if you can't take your eyes off someone or something, you are unable to stop looking at them because they are so attractive or interesting • *I thought he was so beautiful - I couldn't take my eyes off him.* • *I couldn't keep my eyes off her amazing hairdo.*

close/shut your **eyes to** sth

to pretend that something bad does not exist because you do not want to deal with it • *She was besotted with him and closed her eyes to his character defects.* • *You can't just shut your eyes to your problems and hope that they'll go away.*

OPPOSITE **open** your **eyes to** sth • *He's finally opened his eyes to what has been going on behind his back.*

sb **could** do sth **with** their **eyes closed/shut**

if someone could do something with their eyes shut, they can do it very easily, usually because they have done it so many times before • *I've driven along this route so often, I could do it with my eyes shut.*

sb's **eyes are bigger than** their **belly/stomach** *humorous*

something that you say when someone has taken more food than they can eat • *I can't finish this piece of cake. I'm afraid my eyes were bigger than my stomach as usual.*

sb's **eyes are out on stalks** *informal*

sb's **eyes are popping out of** their **head** *informal*

if someone's eyes are out on stalks, they are looking at someone or something in a way that shows that they think that person or thing is extremely surprising or attractive ✍In funny drawings, people and animals are often drawn with their eyes coming out of their head to show that they are very surprised. • *You should have seen Pete when Bec turned up in her short skirt. His eyes were out on stalks.*

have eyes in the back of your **head** *informal*

to know everything that is happening around you • *Parents of young children have to have eyes in the back of their heads.*

have eyes like a hawk

if someone has eyes like a hawk, they notice everything • *The supervisor has eyes like a hawk, so be careful she doesn't catch you eating at your desk.*

in sb's **eyes**

in someone's opinion • *And although she was probably just an ordinary-looking kid, in my eyes she was the most beautiful child in the world.*

lay/set eyes on sb/sth *British, American & Australian*

clap eyes on sb/sth *British & Australian*

to see someone or something for the first time • *I've loved him ever since I first set eyes on him.* • *I wish I'd never clapped eyes on that money.*

make eyes at sb

to look at someone in a way that shows them that you think they are sexually attractive • (usually in continuous tenses) *Sally spent the whole evening making eyes at Stephen.*

only have eyes for sb

to be interested in or attracted to only one person • *You've no need to be jealous. I only have eyes for you.*

with your **eyes open**
knowing about all the problems there could be with something that you want to do • *'You want to get married? But you're only 18!' 'I'm doing this with my eyes open, so don't worry about me.'* • *It was difficult to succeed in the acting profession but I went into it with my eyes open.*

► See also: couldn't **believe** your eyes
Close your eyes and think of England.
cry your eyes out
feast your eyes on sth
hit sb (right) between the eyes
keep your eyes peeled/skinned
open sb's eyes to sth
be **up** to your ears/eyeballs/eyes in sth

face

be in your **face** *American informal*
if someone is in your face, they criticize you all the time • *One of the managers is always in my face.*

be in your face *informal*
to be shocking or annoying in a way that is difficult to ignore • *It's pop music that's sexy, colourful and in your face.*
in-your-face • (always before noun) *We ran an in-your-face poster campaign to promote the magazine.*

blow up/explode in sb's **face**
if a plan or situation blows up in your face, it has a bad effect on you instead of the result you expected • *The government's attempts at reform have blown up in its face, with demonstrations taking place all over the country.*

come face to face with sb
to suddenly meet someone by chance • *As I was going into the restaurant, I came face to face with my ex-husband who was just leaving.*

come face to face with sth
to see or experience a problem for the first time • *It was only after I started working for the charity that I came face to face with poverty.*
bring sb **face to face with** sth • *They were brought face to face with the fact that their son was a drug addict when he took an overdose.*

disappear/vanish off the face of the earth *British, American & Australian*
fall off the face of the earth *American*
to disappear completely • *We lost contact with Ed after he left college – he just disappeared off the face of the earth.*

sb's **face doesn't fit**
if someone's face doesn't fit, their appearance or personality are not suitable for a particular job or activity • *He'd always wanted to star in action movies but his face just didn't fit.*

sb's **face is a picture**
if someone's face is a picture, their face shows that they are very surprised or angry • *Her face was a picture when I told her the news.*

face the music
to accept criticism or punishment for something that you have done • *When the missing money was noticed, he chose to disappear rather than face the music.*

face to face
if two people meet or talk face to face, they meet or talk when they are both together in the same place • *I'd prefer to sort this problem out face to face rather than over the phone.* • *She's been writing to her cousin in Australia for years but they've never met face to face.*
face-to-face • (always before noun) *He's refused a face-to-face interview but he's agreed to answer our questions in a letter.*

Get out of my face! *very informal*
something that you say in order to tell someone to stop annoying you • *Just get out of my face and leave me alone!*

have a face like a wet weekend *British informal*
have a face as long as a wet week *Australian*
to look very unhappy • *He's had a face like a wet weekend all day.*

make/pull a face
to show that you do not like something or someone by making an unpleasant expression • *'I hate pepperoni pizza!' he said, making a face.*

on the face of it
something that you say when you are describing the way a fact or situation seems in order to show that you think it may really be completely different • *On the face of it, the trip seems quite cheap, but there could be extra expenses we don't know about yet.*

take sth **at face value**
to accept something because of the way it first looks or seems, without thinking about what else it could mean ✍The face value of a note or a coin is the number written on it. • (often negative) *These results should not be taken at face*

value – careful analysis is required to assess their full implications.

to sb's **face**

if you say something unpleasant to someone's face, you say it to them directly, without worrying whether they will be upset or angry • *Everyone refers to him as 'Junior' but no one would dare call him that to his face.*

what's his/her face *informal*

a way of talking about someone whose name you have forgotten • *Have you seen the new Bond film with Pierce Brosnan and what's her face, that model?*

► See also: **fly** in the face of sth
laugh in sb's face
look sb in the face
lose face
save face
set your face against sth/doing sth
show your face
shut your face/gob/mouth/trap!
be **staring** sb in the face
stuff your face
throw sth back in sb's face
have a face like **thunder**

faces

make (funny) faces

to make silly expressions with your face in order to make people laugh • (usually in continuous tenses) *Karl was making faces at me across the library and I couldn't stop giggling.*

fact

a fact of life

an unpleasant fact or situation which people accept because they cannot change it • (not used with *the*) *She grew up in Northern Ireland during the 1970s when violence had become a fact of life.*

factory

factory farming

a system for producing eggs, meat, and milk quickly and cheaply by keeping animals in small closed areas and giving them food which makes them grow quickly • *They've launched a campaign against the abuses of factory farming.*

a factory farm • *The use of antibiotics in some factory farms has been linked to the recent increase in food poisoning.*

factory-farmed *mainly British* • *Factory-farmed chickens contain a lot of fat because they're kept indoors and don't get any exercise.*

on the factory floor

1 if someone works on the factory floor, they are one of the ordinary people who work in a factory • *He spent five years on the factory floor before being promoted to supervisor.*

the factory floor • *She's worked her way up from the factory floor to a top job in the union.*

2 in the part of a factory where goods are produced • *The problem was only discovered when the system was tested on the factory floor.*

the factory floor • *The new computer system ensures that orders reach the factory floor in less than 24 hours.*

facts

the facts of life

if you tell someone, especially a child, the facts of life, you tell them about sex and how babies are born • *Parents are often embarrassed about telling their children the facts of life.*

fade

► See: fade/pale into **insignificance**

fag

a fag hag *very informal*

an impolite way of referring to a woman with a lot of male friends who are homosexual (= sexually attracted to other men) ✍'Fag' is an offensive word for a homosexual man, and 'hag' is an offensive word for an old woman. • *Have you been out clubbing with Mark and Jim again? You're turning into a real fag hag!*

fag-end

the fag-end of sth *British & Australian informal*

the last part of a period of time, usually the least interesting or least exciting part • *We went away at the fag-end of summer when all the shops and restaurants were starting to close.*

fail

without fail

1 if something happens without fail, it

always happens • *Every Tuesday afternoon, without fail, Helga went to visit her father.*

2 something that you say in order to emphasize that something will be done or will happen • *'You will meet me at the airport, won't you?' 'Don't worry, I'll be there without fail.'*

faint

▶ See: **damn** sb/sth with faint praise

faintest

not have the faintest (idea)

to have no knowledge of or no information about something • *'Do you know where Anna is?' 'I haven't the faintest.'* • (often + question word) *I haven't the faintest idea what you're talking about.*

faint-hearted

not be for the faint-hearted

if something is not for the faint-hearted, it is not suitable for people who become frightened easily • *The drive along the winding coast road is not for the faint-hearted, particularly when it's foggy.*

fair

All's fair in love and war.

something that you say which means behaviour that is unpleasant or not fair is acceptable during an argument or competition • *We weren't cheating, we were just playing to win. Anyway, all's fair in love and war.*

be fair game

to be easy to criticize, or to deserve criticism • *Members of the Royal family are considered fair game by journalists.*

by fair means or foul

if you try to achieve something by fair means or foul, you use any method you can to achieve it, even if it is not honest or fair • *He was determined to become senator, by fair means or foul.*

fair and square

1 in an honest way and without any doubt • *We won the match fair and square.*

2 if you hit someone fair and square on a particular part of their body, you hit them hard exactly on that part • *She hit me fair and square on the nose.*

fair dinkum *Australian informal*

true or honest • *I didn't believe her at first but she swore the story was fair dinkum.* • *He's a fair dinkum sort of guy – he wouldn't lie to you.*

Fair do's *British informal*

something that you say in order to tell someone that you think something is fair • *Fair do's, Josh. You've been on the computer for hours – let your sister use it for a while!*

fair enough

something that you say in order to show that you understand why someone has said or done something • *'I don't feel like going out tonight – I've got a bit of a headache.' 'Fair enough.'* • *Having health warnings on cigarette packets is fair enough but I do think alcohol should carry warnings too.*

fair play

1 if there is fair play in a game or competition, people obey the rules and do not cheat • *The World Cup organizers are keen to promote the idea of fair play.*

2 a way of treating people that is fair and equal • *Ministers are demanding fair play and more access to European markets for British companies.* • *The committee's decision offended her* ***sense of fair play***. (= she believed their decision was not fair)

a fair shake *American informal*

a way of treating someone that is fair • *They want a lawyer who will make sure they get a fair shake in the courts.*

fair to middling *informal*

neither very good nor very bad • *'What's your French like?' 'Oh, fair to middling.'*

Fair's fair. *informal*

something that you say in order to tell someone that a particular type of behaviour is fair • *Fair's fair, Chris. You chose where to eat last time so it's my turn this time.*

the fair/fairer sex *old-fashioned*

women ✍Some women think this phrase is offensive. • *My father hated the idea of me joining the army. He always said it wasn't a suitable occupation for the fair sex.*

give sb **a fair crack of the whip** *British & Australian informal*
to give someone an opportunity to do something • *Will you make sure all the speakers are given a fair crack of the whip in the debate?*
get/have a fair crack of the whip • *We'll take turns to host the conference. That way we'll all get a fair crack of the whip.*

have had more than your **fair share of** sth
to have had more of something unpleasant than other people when you do not deserve it • *Jane's had more than her fair share of bad luck recently, what with losing her job and getting divorced.*

It's a fair cop. *British & Australian very informal*
something that you say in order to admit that someone has caught you doing something wrong • *It's a fair cop. I was driving way too fast.*

with your **own fair hands** *humorous*
if you do something with your own fair hands, you do it yourself without any help • *'Did you buy this cake?' 'No, I made it with my own fair hands.'*

fair-haired

▶ See: a fair-haired **boy**

fairer

▶ See: I/You can't **say** fairer than that.

fairies

be away with the fairies *humorous*
to be slightly mad • *It's no good asking her to look after the children – she's away with the fairies most of the time.*

fair-weather

a fair-weather friend
someone who is only your friend when you are happy and successful • *I had a lot of money and I knew a lot of people, but most of them turned out to be fair-weather friends.*

fairy

a fairy godmother
someone who helps you solve your problems, usually by giving you money ✍In children's stories, a fairy godmother is a woman with magic powers who helps someone who is in trouble. • *A local company acted as fairy godmother to the theatre by giving a big donation.*

fait accompli

a fait accompli
a decision or action which has already been made or done and which cannot be changed • *The sudden change in policy was presented to the party as a fait accompli, without any consultation.*

faith

▶ See: **break** faith with sth/sb
in **good** faith
keep faith with sth/sb

fall

be heading/riding for a fall
be headed for a fall
to be behaving in a way that is likely to cause problems for you • *Greg's riding for a fall – he gets to work late and spends hours talking to his friends on the phone.*

fall by the wayside
1 if someone falls by the wayside, they fail to finish an activity • *A lot of students fall by the wayside during their first year at university.*
2 if something falls by the wayside, people stop doing it, making it, or using it • *Many new drugs fall by the wayside in the laboratory.*

fall down on the job
to fail to do something that you should do • *The armed forces will take over if the local authorities fall down on the job.*

fall flat
1 if an entertainment or a joke falls flat, people do not enjoy it and do not think it is funny • *Several attempts at humour during his speech fell flat.*
2 if an attempt to influence people's behaviour or opinions falls flat, it fails • *The advertising campaign which had worked so well in the US fell flat in China.*

fall for sb **hook, line and sinker**
to fall very much in love with someone • *I'd never seen such a good-looking bloke – I just fell for him hook, line and sinker.*

fall for sth **hook, line and sinker**
to completely believe something someone tells you which is not true • *I told him I needed the money for my baby, and he fell*

for it hook, line and sinker.

fall foul of sb

to upset someone, so that they do not like you and try to harm you • *Officials who fall foul of the mayor find themselves exiled to the most boring departments.*

fall foul of sth *slightly formal*

to break a law or a rule, and often be punished • *If their market share grows too large, they will fall foul of anti-monopoly laws.*

fall from grace

to do something bad which makes people in authority stop liking you or admiring you • *When a celebrity falls from grace, they can find it very difficult to get work in television.*

a fall from grace • *He used to be one of the president's closest advisers before his fall from grace.*

a fall guy *mainly American informal*

someone who is blamed for another person's mistake or crime • *The book claims Lee Harvey Oswald didn't kill President Kennedy – he was just the fall guy.*

fall in a heap *Australian informal*

to lose control of your feelings and start to cry • *The case collapsed when the main witness fell in a heap and was escorted from the court.*

fall in/into line

to start to accept the rules of a company or other organization • (often + **with**) *Employees were expected to fall into line with the company's new practices or face dismissal.*

fall into sb's **clutches**

to become influenced or controlled by someone who is likely to use their power in a bad way • *He fell into the clutches of a nationalist terrorist group.* • *There were fears that the weapons might fall into the enemy's clutches.*

be in sb's **clutches** • *She couldn't bear to think of her precious daughter being in the clutches of a religious fanatic.*

fall into sb's **hands**

if something falls into the hands of a dangerous person or an enemy, the dangerous person or enemy starts to own or control it • *There were concerns that the weapons might fall into the hands of terrorists.*

fall into place

1 if something that happens makes everything fall into place, it makes you understand something that you did not understand before • *Once I discovered that the woman I had seen him with was his daughter, everything fell into place,*

2 if things fall into place in a situation, they happen in a satisfactory way, without problems • *If a project is well-planned, everything should fall into place.*

fall into the trap of doing sth

to do something which is not wise although it seemed to be a good idea when you decided to do it • *Don't fall into the trap of buying the extra insurance.*

fall into the wrong hands

if something falls into the wrong hands, a dangerous person or an enemy starts to own or control it • *There are fears that weapons might fall into the wrong hands.* • *If this sort of information fell into the wrong hands, we could be in serious trouble.*

fall off your **perch** *British old-fashioned, humorous*

to die • *By the time I fall off my perch, Britain may well be a republic.*

fall off the wagon

to start drinking alcohol again, especially too much alcohol, after a period when you have not drunk any • *Six months later he fell off the wagon in spectacular fashion with a three-day drinking spree.*

fall on deaf ears

if a request or advice falls on deaf ears, people ignore it • *Appeals to release the hostages fell on deaf ears.* • *Warnings that sunbathing can lead to skin cancer have largely fallen on deaf ears in Britain.*

fall on hard times

to have difficulties because you suddenly do not have any money • *Millions of workers fell on hard times during the great depression of the 1930s.*

fall on stony ground

if a request, a warning, or advice falls on stony ground, people ignore it ✍This phrase comes from the Bible. • *Repeated requests to stop the fighting have fallen on stony ground.* • *Warnings about the disastrous effect on the environment fell on stony ground.*

fall over yourself to do sth *British, American & Australian*
fall all over yourself to do sth *American*
to be very eager to do something • (usually in continuous tenses) *They were falling over themselves to be helpful.*

fall short of sth
if something falls short of a particular level or standard, it does not reach it • *Sales for the first half of the year fell short of the target.*

nearly fall off your **chair**
to be very surprised about something • *When my mother told me she was getting remarried I nearly fell off my chair.*

take the fall for sb/sth *mainly American informal*
to accept the blame for something bad or not legal that another person has done • *Bob'll take the fall for the director – he'd do anything to save his boss.*

▶ See also: fall over **backwards** to do sth
fall/slip through the **cracks**
fall off the **face** of the earth
fall on your **feet**
fall/go through the **floor**
drop/fall into your **lap**
go down/fall like **ninepins**
go/fall to **pieces**
fall off/drop off the **radar**
fall between **two** stools

fallen

a fallen angel
a company or sports team that was successful in the past but is not successful now • (usually plural) *Derby County were this season's fallen angels, being sent into the Second Division after losing all their matches.*

a fallen idol
a person who was admired in the past but who is not admired any more • *Highly respected during his lifetime, he became a fallen idol after his death when his research was found to be full of errors.*

a fallen woman *old-fashioned*
a woman who is not respected any more because she had sex without being married • *Many fallen women were forced to work as prostitutes, some were shut away in asylums.*

falling

▶ See: be coming/falling apart at the **seams**

false

a false alarm
a situation when you think that something bad or dangerous is going to happen but you discover you were wrong • *Someone called to say there was a bomb inside the building, but it turned out to be a false alarm.*

a false dawn
something which seems to show that a successful period is beginning or that a situation is improving when it is not ✍False dawn is the light which appears in the sky just before the sun rises in the morning. • *His victory in the French Open proved to be a false dawn after he failed to win another title for the next five years.*

a false economy
something that you think will save you money but which means you will have to spend a lot more money later • *She told me that buying a cheap washing machine was a false economy because it was more likely to break down.*

a false start
a failed attempt to begin an activity or event ✍In a race, a false start is when one person starts before the signal has been given. • *After a false start when he left his first job after only a week, he was offered some modelling work.*

lull sb **into a false sense of security**
give sb **a false sense of security**
to make someone feel safe when they are not • *Wearing suntan lotion can lull people into a false sense of security and make them spend longer in the sun than they should.*

under false pretences
if you do something under false pretences, you do it when you have lied about who you are or what you are doing • *The police charged him with obtaining money under false pretences.*

▶ See also: **sail** under false colours

familiar

have a familiar ring (to it)

if something has a familiar ring, you believe that you have heard it before • *I thought that name had a familiar ring. I went to school with that girl.*

familiarity

Familiarity breeds contempt.

something that you say which means if you know someone very well or experience something a lot, you stop respecting them • *You two are going to find it difficult living and working together. Familiarity breeds contempt, you know.*

family

a family man

a man who likes to spend a lot of time with his wife and children • *He was known as a devoted family man who was closely involved in community life.*

in the family way *old-fashioned*

pregnant • *Have you heard that Jean's in the family way?*

▶ See also: **run** in the family

famous

Famous last words. *humorous*

something that you say in order to emphasize that what someone said is wrong or is very likely to be wrong • *James assured me it was always sunny in Italy in June. Famous last words. It rained every day of our trip.*

fan

fan the flames

to cause anger or other bad feelings to increase • (usually + **of**) *His speeches fanned the flames of racial tension.*

fancy

take/tickle sb's **fancy** *informal*

if something takes someone's fancy, they suddenly think it seems interesting • *She's got enough money to buy whatever takes her fancy.*

fancy-pants

fancy-pants *American & Australian informal*

trying to seem too attractive or too clever in a way that is false • (always before noun) *We liked the restaurant's food but not the fancy-pants decor.* • *I don't know what she sees in that fancy-pants college professor of hers.*

fannies

▶ See: fannies in the **seats**

far

be a far cry from sth

to be very different from something • *His new luxury mansion is a far cry from the one-bedroom cottage he lived in as a child.*

be far and away the [best/greatest/worst etc.]

to be much better or much worse or to have much more of a particular quality than anyone or anything else • *He's far and away the best tennis player I've ever seen.*

far be it from me to do sth

something that you say when you are giving advice or criticizing someone and you want to seem polite • *Far be it from me to tell you what to do, but don't you think you should apologize?*

Far from it.

something that you say in order to tell someone that something is not true • *'I thought Jeff spoke fluent French.' 'Far from it – all he can say is "bonjour"!'*

So far so good.

something that you say which means an activity is continuing successfully, especially when you think something may go wrong • *The first round of talks went well. So far so good. The next stage will involve much tougher negotiation.*

farm

▶ See: **bet** the farm/ranch

fashion

after a fashion

1 if you do something after a fashion, you manage to do it although not very well • *I can paint after a fashion, but I'm certainly not as good as you.*

2 almost, but not completely • *'A vegetarian diet is much healthier.' 'That's true after a fashion, although I don't believe all meat is bad for you.'*

a fashion victim *humorous*
an impolite way of referring to someone who buys too many fashionable clothes • *She's a complete fashion victim! Why else would she pay £100 for a pair of jeans?*

like it's going out of fashion *informal*
if you use something like it's going out of fashion, you use large amounts of it very quickly • *Emma spends money like it's going out of fashion.*

fast

fast and furious
if an activity is fast and furious, it is done quickly and with a lot of energy • *The first half of the game was fast and furious with both teams scoring three goals each.*

a fast talker *American & Australian informal*
someone who can talk in a clever way in order to persuade people to do or believe something, often something that is not honest or not true • *Don't trust him Sal, he's a fast talker who's always out for his own good.*

a fast track
a very quick way of achieving something or dealing with something • (often + **to**) *Management training offers a fast track to the top of the company.* • *The government has announced that the reforms will be* ***put on the fast track***. (= dealt with very quickly)
fast-track • (always before noun) *We are introducing a fast-track procedure for dealing with applications.*

play fast and loose with sth/sb
to treat something or someone without enough care • *Like many film-makers, he plays fast and loose with the facts to tell his own version of the story.*

pull a fast one *informal*
to successfully deceive someone • (often + **on**) *I paid him for six bottles of champagne, but he pulled a fast one on me and gave me six bottles of cheap wine.*

▶ See also: make a fast/quick **buck**

fat

a fat cat *informal*
an impolite way of referring to someone who is very rich and powerful • *He's just another fat cat – a corporate tycoon from Boston.*
fat-cat *informal* • (always before noun) *There's a lot of resentment against fat-cat lawyers who've made huge amounts from the case.*

Fat chance! *informal*
something that you say which means something is not very likely to happen • *'D'you think your Dad'll drive us to the disco?' 'Fat chance!'*

the fat is in the fire *old-fashioned*
something that you say which means there will soon be problems because of something that has happened • *Susie knows you've been seeing her boyfriend, so the fat's in the fire.*

a fat lot of good/use *informal*
not helpful or useful • *She can't lift anything heavy, so she's a fat lot of use!* • *'I'm going to tell him exactly what I think of him.' 'A fat lot of good that'll do you!'*

It's not over until the fat lady sings. *informal*
something that you say when someone is losing a game or competition but you think there is still a chance they might win • *Tony's only two games behind. And as they say, it's not over until the fat lady sings.*

▶ See also: **chew** the fat
live off the fat of the land

fate

be a fate worse than death *humorous*
to be the worst thing that can happen to you • *When you're 16, an evening at home with your parents is a fate worse than death.*

▶ See also: **seal** sb's fate
tempt fate/providence

fatted

▶ See: **kill** the fatted calf

fault

to a fault
if someone is generous or has another good quality to a fault, they are very generous or have more of that good quality than other people • *Nigel was generous to a fault, taking me out to*

dinner and buying me flowers and chocolates.

faux pas

a faux pas

an embarrassing mistake made in public • *I realized I'd made a real faux pas by eating my soup with my dessert spoon.*

favour

do yourself **a favour** *British & Australian*

do yourself **a favor** *American & Australian*

something that you say when you are advising someone to do something which will have a good effect or will give them an advantage • (often + **and** + do sth) *You're looking really tired. Why don't you do yourself a favour and take a break?*

Do me a favour! *British & Australian informal*

Do me a favor! *American & Australian*

something that you say in order to tell someone that what they have just said is stupid • *'Why don't you go out with Brian?' 'Oh, do me a favour! He's almost 50, and he still lives with his mother!'*

do me/us a favour *British & Australian informal*

do me/us a favor *American & Australian informal*

if you tell someone to do you a favour, you are telling them to stop doing something that is making you angry • (often + **and** + do sth) *Why don't you do us all a favor and keep your opinions to yourself!*

▶ See also: **curry** favour

favourite

a favourite son *British & Australian*

a favorite son *American & Australian*

a famous person, especially a politician, who is supported and praised by people in the area they come from • *Let me introduce to you the favorite son of Russell, Kansas: Bob Dole.*

favours

not **do** sb **any favours** *British, American & Australian*

not **do** sb **any favor** *American*

to do something that is likely to have a bad effect on you or on another person • (often reflexive) *You're not well, and you're not doing yourself any favours by taking on extra work.* • (usually in continuous tenses; often + **by** + doing sth) *The government isn't doing the families of the victims any favor by hiding the truth about what really happened.*

fear

put the fear of God into sb

to frighten someone very much • *What were you doing up on the roof? You put the fear of God into me!*

▶ See also: **No** fear!

feast

feast your **eyes on** sth

to look at something with a lot of pleasure • *Just feast your eyes on this fabulous painting.*

feast or famine

something that you say which means that you either have too much of something or you have too little • *It's either feast or famine on television; last week there was nothing I wanted to see and this week there are three good films on at the same time.*

the ghost/spectre at the feast *British literary*

something or someone that spoils your enjoyment by making you remember something unpleasant • *John was the spectre at the feast, always reminding her of her broken promise.*

feather

a feather in sb's **cap** *old-fashioned*

something very good that someone has done • *A new television series will be another feather in his cap.*

feather your **own nest**

to dishonestly use your position at work to get a lot of money for yourself • *What angers him most of all is the implication that he has been feathering his own nest.*

▶ See also: You could have **knocked** me down/over with a feather!

feathers

the feathers fly *American*

if the feathers fly, people fight or argue a lot • *The feathers'll fly if he finds out you've borrowed his car.*

▶ See also: **ruffle** sb's feathers

federal

make a federal case (out) of sth
American
to make something seem more important or serious than it really is • (usually negative) *He only swore at you – there's no need to make a federal case out of it!*

fed up

▶ See: be fed up/sick to the **back** teeth

feed

feed sb **a line** *informal*
to tell someone something which may not be completely true, often as an excuse • *She fed me a line about not having budgeted for pay increases this year.*

▶ See also: feed/throw sb to the **lions**

fed up

▶ See: be fed up/sick to the **back** teeth

feeding

a feeding frenzy
a situation where people try to get as much information as possible about an event, or to make as much profit as they can from it, especially in an unpleasant way ✍If hungry animals have a feeding frenzy, they become very excited by the smell of food and fight each other to get a share of it. • *Her sudden tragic death sparked off a feeding frenzy in the media.*

It's feeding time at the zoo!
humorous
something that you say when a group of people are eating together in a way that is not controlled or organized • *I see it's feeding time at the zoo. I'd better help myself to some food before it's all gone.*

feel

feel hard done-by
if you feel hard done-by, you feel you have been treated unfairly • *I'm feeling hard done-by because I've been looking after the kids all week while Steve's been out every night.*

feel the pinch
to have problems with money because you are earning less than before • *When my father lost his job and we had to live on my mother's earnings, we really started to feel the pinch.*

I (can) feel it in my bones.
something that you say when you are certain something is true or will happen, although you have no proof • *Something terrible is going to happen. I feel it in my bones.*

make sb **feel small**
to say something which makes someone feel not important or stupid • *As a manager you have to be able to criticize people but you don't want to make them feel small.*

▶ See also: **cop** a feel
feel/go **hot** and cold (all over)
look/feel (like) a **million** dollars
be/feel under the **weather**

feelers

put out feelers
to try to discover what people think about something that you might do ✍An insect's feelers are the two long stick parts on its head which it uses to touch things and discover what is around it. • *I've been putting out a few feelers and it seems that most people are against changing the way we elect the committee.*

feet

be run/rushed off your **feet**
to have to work very hard or very fast • *There's only one secretary working for the whole accounts department and the poor woman is run off her feet.* • *We weren't exactly rushed off our feet – there was only one visitor all afternoon.*

be under your **feet**
if someone is under your feet, they annoy you because they are always near you in a way that makes it difficult for you to do something • *The children have been under my feet all morning so I haven't been able to get any work done.*
get under sb's **feet** • *Why don't you ask Kelly to sit in the other room for a while? That way she won't keep getting under my feet.*

feet of clay
if you say that someone you admire has feet of clay, you mean they have hidden faults • *Some of the greatest geniuses in history had feet of clay.*

get your **feet under the table** *British*
to become familiar with and confident in

a new job or situation • *It's better to wait until you've got your feet firmly under the table before you make any big changes.*

get your **feet wet** *mainly American*
to experience something for the first time, especially something that involves taking a risk • *Investors are encouraged to get their feet wet by buying just a few shares to begin with.*

in (your) **stocking/stockinged feet**
wearing socks or a similar covering on your feet, but not wearing shoes • *She crept upstairs in stocking feet so as not to wake the baby.* • *He **stood** five feet five **in his stockinged feet**.* (= his height was five feet five, without shoes)

land on your **feet** *British, American & Australian*
fall on your **feet** *British & Australian*
to be lucky or successful after you have been in a difficult situation • *She really landed on her feet – she found an apartment right in the middle of San Francisco.* • *Richard takes the most awful risks, but he always seems to fall on his feet.*

put your **feet up**
to relax, especially by sitting with your feet supported above the ground • *I'm going to make myself a cup of coffee and put my feet up for half an hour.*

▶ See also: **drag** your feet/heels
find your feet
jump in with both feet
keep your/both feet on the ground
sweep sb off their feet
think on your feet
vote with your feet

fell

at/in one fell swoop
if you do something at one fell swoop, you do everything you have to do at the same time • *I'd prefer to do the paperwork in one fell swoop. At least then we know it's finished with.*

femme fatale

a femme fatale
a woman who is sexually attractive but who is likely to cause trouble for men who are attracted to her • *She plays a Russian femme fatale in the latest Bond film.*

fence

▶ See: **sit** on the fence

fences

▶ See: **mend** (your) fences

fender

a fender bender *American informal*
a car accident in which a car is slightly damaged • *We got into a fender bender just as we were leaving the parking lot at the mall.*

fever

fever pitch
if you say that a feeling or a situation has reached fever pitch, you mean that people's emotions have become so strong that they can only just control themselves • *By the time the princess appeared on the balcony, excitement among the crowd was **at fever pitch**.* • *Tension reached fever pitch as reports came in of further bomb attacks in the north.*

few

be few and far between
to be very few • *There are plenty of houses for sale, but buyers are few and far between.*

▶ See also: **hoist** a few

fiddle

be on the fiddle *British & Australian informal*
to get money in a way that is not honest or not legal • *If he's not on the fiddle, how did he afford that huge car?*

fiddle while Rome burns
to spend time enjoying yourself or doing things that are not important when you should be dealing with a serious problem
✍This phrase comes from a story about the Roman emperor Nero, who fiddled (= played the violin) while the city of Rome was burning. • *Environmentalists claim that the government is fiddling while Rome burns.*

field

have a field day
to have an opportunity to do a lot of something you want to do, especially to criticize someone • *The newspapers would have a field day if their affair ever*

became public knowledge.

▶ See also: **lead** the field
leave the field clear for sb
play the field

fifth

I take/plead the Fifth (Amendment) *American humorous*
something that you say in order to tell someone you are not going to answer a question ✍The Fifth Amendment is the part of American law that says someone does not have to answer questions about themselves in a law court. • (sometimes + **on**) *'So who do you like best, Jenny or Kim?' 'Sorry, I take the Fifth on that.'*

▶ See also: a fifth/third **wheel**

fifty-fifty

fifty-fifty
if something is divided fifty-fifty, it is divided equally between two people • *We decided to split the money fifty-fifty.* • *Let's **go fifty-fifty** on the expenses for our trip.*

a fifty-fifty chance
if there is a fifty-fifty chance of something happening, it is equally likely to happen or not to happen • (usually + **of** + doing sth) *I'd say he's got a fifty-fifty chance of winning the race.*

fig

not **care/give a fig** *old-fashioned*
if you say that you don't care a fig, you mean that something or someone is not important to you at all • *They can say what they like, I don't give a fig.*

a fig leaf
something that you use to try to hide an embarrassing fact or problem ✍In the Bible, Adam and Eve used fig leaves to cover their sexual organs when they discovered they were naked. • *Are the peace talks simply providing a fig leaf for the continuing aggression between the two countries?*

▶ See also: not be **worth** a fig

fight

fight a losing battle
to try hard to do something when there is no chance that you will succeed • (usually in continuous tenses) *We try our best to cope with the workload but we're fighting a losing battle.*

fight a rearguard action
to try very hard to prevent something from happening when it is probably too late to prevent it • (often + **against**) *The unions were fighting a rearguard action against the government's attempt to strip them of their powers.*

fight your **corner** *British*
to defend something that you believe in by arguing • *You'll have to be ready to fight your corner if you want them to extend the project.*

fight fire with fire
to attack someone with a lot of force because they are attacking you with force • *In the face of stiff competition from rival firms we had to fight fire with fire and slash our prices.*

fight shy of sth/doing sth
to try to avoid something • *He fought shy of entering his poems in the competition, although everyone said he should.* • *Ellen fights shy of parties – she hates crowds.*

fight tooth and claw/nail
to fight very hard to achieve something • (often + to do sth) *We fought tooth and nail to retain our share of the business.*

▶ See also: fight like **cat** and dog

fighting

be fighting fit
to be very healthy • *She was fighting fit after 10 weeks of intense physical training.*

be fighting for your **life**
1 to be so ill or injured that you might die • *One of the passengers was fighting for her life last night after receiving multiple injuries in the collision.*
a fight for life • *Throughout Christopher's fight for life, his parents never left his bedside.*
2 if an organization or system is fighting for its life, people are trying very hard to prevent it from being defeated or destroyed • *With debts of over $2 million dollars, the corporation is fighting for its life.*

be fighting mad *American & Australian informal*
to be very angry • *When Dad finds out you've crashed the car, he'll be fighting mad.*

be in fighting trim *mainly American*
ready to deal with a situation, especially because you are in good physical condition • *It was a challenging performance, but the dancers were in fighting trim.*

a fighting chance
a small but real possibility that you might do or achieve something • (often + **of** + doing sth) *If we can raise another thousand pounds we'll* ***have a fighting chance*** *of saving the theatre.* • *A good education will ensure that even the most disadvantaged children are* ***given a fighting chance****.*

▶ See also: **come** out fighting

figment

be a figment of your/**the imagination**
if something is a figment of your imagination, it seems real although it is not • *I thought I saw someone standing in the shadows, but it was just a figment of my imagination.*

figure

a figure of fun
someone who people laugh at because they seem silly or stupid • *She's fed up with being treated as a figure of fun and insists that her ideas deserve serious attention.*

Go figure! *American*
used when you tell someone a fact and you want them to say that the fact is surprising or strange or stupid • *It's a terrible movie and it made $200 million. Go figure!*

▶ See also: **cut** an [interesting/ridiculous/unusual etc.] figure

fill

have had your **fill**
to have had enough to eat or drink • *No more pudding thanks, I've had my fill.*

have had your **fill of** sth
if you have had your fill of an unpleasant situation, you will not accept it any longer • *People have had their fill of empty promises and want action.*

▶ See also: fill the **bill**
fill sb's **shoes**
fill a/the **void**

filthy

▶ See: filthy/stinking **rich**

final

the final curtain
the end of something, usually something that has lasted for a long time • *As the final curtain fell on the longest match in tennis history, Agassi emerged victorious.*

in the final analysis
something that you say when you are talking about what is most important or true in a situation • *In the final analysis, the only people who will benefit are property owners.*

▶ See also: the final **nail** in the coffin
the final/last **straw**
have the final/last **word**

find

find your **feet**
to become familiar with a new place or situation • *It's important to give new students a chance to find their feet.*

find your **tongue**
to begin to speak after being silent because you felt nervous or frightened • *Amy took a step forward and finally found her tongue. 'I'm Rhoda's friend,' she said.*

▶ See also: find out/see how the **land** lies

finders

Finders keepers (losers weepers).
something that you say when you find something that belongs to someone else and decide you are going to keep it • *'Finders keepers,' he said, putting the money away in his pocket.*

fin de siècle

fin de siècle
typical of or existing at the end of a century, especially the 19th century • *The fin de siècle despair increased in the last few years of the century.* • *Tanya chose a course in fin de siècle literature.*

fine

be a fine figure of a man/woman
old-fashioned
to be someone who is big and strong with an attractive body • *She's a fine figure of a woman – not like all these skinny models.*

be in fine fettle
to be very healthy or working well • *She was in fine fettle when she came back from her trip to the States.* • *The business is in fine fettle and we're even planning to expand.*

have sth **down to a fine art** *British, American & Australian*
have sth **off to a fine art** *British & Australian*
to be able to do something very well, usually because you have been doing it for a long time • *He's got sandwich making down to a fine art.*

not **to put too fine a point on it**
something that you say when you are going to say exactly what you mean, even if other people may not like it • *Well, not to put too fine a point on it, it's entirely your fault.*

You're a fine one to talk! *informal*
something that you say when someone criticizes another person for doing something that they do themselves • *'He's always complaining.' 'You're a fine one to talk!'*

► See also: **cut** a fine figure
cut it/things fine
a fine/pretty **kettle** of fish
a fine/thin **line**
the fine/small **print**

fine-tooth

with a fine-tooth comb
if you examine something with a fine-tooth comb, you examine every part of it very carefully • *I'd advise you to examine your insurance policy with a fine-tooth comb to make sure you're covered if you take your car abroad.*

finger

get/pull your **finger out** *British & Australian very informal*
if you tell someone to get their finger out, you mean they should start working hard • *You'd better pull your finger out, you should have finished this job hours ago.*

give sb **the finger** *American very informal*
to make an offensive sign at someone by raising your middle finger towards them • *When the kids were told to leave the store, they gave the manager the finger and ran off.*

have a finger in every pie
to be involved in and have influence over many different activities, often in a way that other people do not approve of • *You can't make a decision on any kind of funding without consulting him – he has a finger in every pie.*
have a finger in the pie to be involved in a particular activity • *When it comes to trade in the underdeveloped parts of the world, most Western countries want to have a finger in the pie.*

have a/your **finger on the button**
to be the person who controls the nuclear weapons (= weapons that use power made by dividing atoms) that a country has and decides whether to fire them • *If Europe has its own nuclear deterrent, whose finger would be on the button?*

have your **finger on the pulse**
to be familiar with the most recent developments • *Whoever designed the new model obviously had their finger on the pulse – it's precisely the sort of computer everyone's been waiting for.*
keep your **finger on the pulse** • *As editor of a fashion magazine, she keeps her finger firmly on the pulse of the London scene.*

put your **finger on** sth
to discover the exact reason why a situation is the way it is, especially when something is wrong • (often negative) *I know there's something wrong, but I can't put my finger on exactly what it is.* • *I think you've just put your finger on the biggest problem facing the Conservative party in this election.*

put the finger on sb *very informal*
to tell someone in authority, especially the police, that someone has committed a crime • *If Big Joe finds out you put the finger on him, you won't live long enough to spend the reward money.*

► See also: **lay** a finger on sb/sth
not **lift** a finger
point the finger at sb

fingernails

cling on/hang on by your **fingernails**
if you are clinging on by your fingernails,

you are only just managing to avoid danger or failure • (usually in continuous tenses) *We're hanging on by our fingernails and hoping that it rains before we lose our entire crop.*

fingers

burn your **fingers**
have/get your **fingers burned/burnt**
to suffer unpleasant results of an action, especially loss of money, so you are not keen to try the same thing again • *Many investors burn their fingers when they are tempted by get-rich-quick schemes.* • *Several art dealers got their fingers burned on old master paintings that later turned out to be fakes.*

cross your **fingers**
keep your **fingers crossed**
to hope that things will happen in the way you want them to ✍People often cross their middle finger over their first finger as a sign that they are hoping for luck. • *We're crossing our fingers and hoping that the weather stays fine.* • (often an order) *Keep your fingers crossed, everyone, Jane's only got to answer one more question.*
fingers crossed something that you say to show that you hope that what you have just said will happen or be true • *Fingers crossed, we'll get the job done in time, but there's still an awful lot to do.*

wear/work your **fingers to the bone**
to work very hard for a very long time • *I've been working my fingers to the bone to get the dress ready in time for the wedding.*

▶ See also: can **count** sth on the fingers of one hand
slip through your fingers
be all fingers and **thumbs**
have your fingers/hand in the **till**

fingertips

at your **fingertips**
if you have information at your fingertips, you are able to get it very easily • *Every fact and figure he needed was at his fingertips.*

be an [artist/patriot/professional/ etc.] to your **fingertips**
if you say that someone is an artist, patriot, professional etc. to their fingertips, you mean that they behave in a way which is completely typical of such a person, and it is the most important part of their character • *Mark, a professional to his fingertips, insisted that we should make proper joints, not simply nail the pieces of wood together.*

cling on/hang on by your fingertips
if you are clinging on by your fingertips, you are only just managing to avoid danger or failure • (usually in continuous tenses) *We were clinging on by our fingertips, desperately trying to stop them scoring another goal.*

fire

come under fire
to be criticized • (often + **from**) *Last night's announcement quickly came under fire from the trade unions.* • (sometimes + **for**) *Mr Johnson has since come under fire for being sarcastic and dismissive of his clients.*

fire a shot across sb's/**the bows**
slightly formal
if you fire a shot across someone's bows, you do something in order to warn them that you will take strong action if they do not change their behaviour • *Airline staff have* ***fired a warning shot across*** *the company's* ***bows*** *by threatening strike action if higher pay increases are not offered.*

fire in your/**the belly**
if you have fire in your belly, you are ready to fight with energy and determination for what you believe is right • *He will approach the committee with plenty of fire in his belly.*

go through fire and water
old-fashioned
to experience many difficulties or dangers in order to achieve something • (often + to do sth) *They went through fire and water to ensure the prince's safety.*

hang/hold fire
to delay doing something, especially making a decision, because you are waiting to see what will happen • *It would have been good to settle the matter now, but I think we should hang fire until the general situation becomes clearer.* • (often + **on**) *The chancellor has said he*

will continue to hold fire on a further reduction in interest rates.

▶ See also: fire/shoot **blanks**
breathe fire
draw (sb's) fire
fight fire with fire
light a fire under sb
light your fire
play with fire

firing

be firing on all cylinders
to be operating as powerfully and effectively as possible • *Dawson will be firing on all cylinders after 2 months of fitness training.*

be in the firing line *British, American & Australian*
be on the firing line *American & Australian*
if someone or something is in the firing line, they are likely to be criticized, attacked, or got rid of • *The judge found himself in the firing line from women's groups after his controversial comments about sexual assault.* • *Recent cuts in council budgets mean that concessionary fares were next on the firing line.*
OPPOSITE **out of the firing line** • *As the president's wife, there was little hope of her staying out of the firing line during the election campaign.*

firm

▶ See: a firm/steady **hand** on the tiller

first

at first blush *mainly American*
when you first start to think about something • *His decision isn't as odd as it may seem at first blush.*

at first glance/sight
if something or someone seems a particular way at first glance, they seem that way when you first look at them • *The system is more complicated than it appears at first glance.*

be first among equals
to officially be on the same level as other members in a group, but in fact have slightly more responsibility or be slightly more important • *The chairman of the joint chiefs of staff was always considered first among equals.*

be first past the post *British & Australian*
if someone is first past the post in a competition, they are the first to achieve something • *The Russian team were first past the post in the race to complete the expedition.*
first-past-the-post in a first-past-the-post system of voting, a person is elected if they get the most votes in a particular area, even if their political party did not get most votes in the whole country • (always before noun) *Many people think the British first-past-the-post system is unfair.*

be in the first flush of sth
if someone is in the first flush of something, they are at the start of it • *You're no longer **in the first flush of youth**, you know, Dad!*

first and foremost
more than anything else • *He remains first and foremost a businessman, not a politician.* • *In order to be successful a film has to be, first and foremost, a good story.*

First come, first served.
something that you say which means that the people who ask for something first will be the ones who get it, when there is not enough for everyone • *We've got ten cheap computers on offer. It's first come, first served.*
first-come, first-served • *Tickets for the show are limited and we operate **on a first-come, first-served basis**.*

first hand
if you experience something first hand, you experience it yourself • *Many reporters based in the capital are experiencing the war first hand.* • *It is difficult to appreciate the scale of the problem without seeing the effects of the famine **at first hand**.*
first-hand • (always before noun) *I've been a teacher for a long time, and have first-hand experience of the way these students behave.*

First in, best dressed. *Australian*
something that you say which means that the first people to do something will get something first or will have an advantage • *I've got ten free tickets to the movies to hand out, so it's first in, best dressed.*

the first string *American informal*
the group of people who are regularly chosen to play in the best sports team, or to do the most important work in a job • *He didn't make first string on the football team until his senior year at college.*
first-string *American informal* • *She's a first-string reporter on the paper.*

First things first.
something that you say in order to tell someone that more important things should be done before less important things • *I know you want to talk about my trip, but first things first, how have you been while I was away?*

get to first base
1 *American & Australian informal* to begin to have success with something that you want to do ✍First base is the first place a player must run to after they hit the ball in a game of baseball. • *They won't even get to first base with the directors with a proposal like that.*
2 *mainly American humorous* to get to the first stage of a sexual relationship, where partners kiss and touch each other • *Jimmy hasn't even gotten to first base yet with his girlfriend.*

give sb **(the right of/to) first refusal**
to offer to sell someone something before you offer it to anyone else • (often + **on**) *I have given my existing publishers first refusal on my next book.*
have (the right of/to) first refusal • *Manfield has the right of first refusal on any surplus stock.*

have first call on sth
to have the right to use something first • *John has first call on the car as he needs it for work.*

If at first you don't succeed, (try, try, and try again).
something that you say in order to tell someone they must keep trying in order to achieve something • *My novel has been rejected by three publishers already. Still, if at first you don't succeed ...*

in the first place
in the beginning • *We should never have agreed to this in the first place.* • *We only had four of these glasses in the first place, and now I've broken two of them.*

of the first water *literary*
of the best or most extreme kind • *He is an artist of the first water* • *Her husband is a bully of the first water.*

▶ See also: not **know** the first thing about sth

fish

be like a fish out of water
to feel awkward because you are not familiar with a situation or because you are very different from the people around you • *All the other children in the school had rich, middle-class parents, and she was beginning to feel like a fish out of water.*

be neither fish nor fowl
if something is neither fish nor fowl, it is difficult to describe or understand because it is like one thing in some ways but like another thing in other ways • *The hovercraft has always suffered from the fact that it is neither fish nor fowl.*

fish for compliments
to try to make someone praise you, often by criticizing yourself to them • (usually in continuous tenses) *Emma, you know you don't look fat in that dress. Are you fishing for compliments?*

Fish or cut bait. *American*
something that you say to someone when you want them to make a decision and take action without any more delay • *Your relationship's going nowhere. It's time to fish or cut bait.*

have bigger/other fish to fry
to have something more important or more interesting to do • *I couldn't waste my time trying to reach an agreement with them, I had other fish to fry.*

there are plenty more fish in the sea
used to say that there are many other people or possibilities, especially when one person or thing has been unsuitable or unsuccessful • *Don't cry over Pierre – there are plenty more fish in the sea.*

▶ See also: **drink** like a fish

fishing

a fishing expedition *mainly American*
an attempt to discover the facts about something by collecting a lot of

information, often secretly • *The investigators' request for the company's accounts is simply a fishing expedition - they have no real evidence of wrongdoing.*

fishy

▶ See: **smell** fishy

fist

▶ See: make a **good** fist of sth/doing sth

fit

be as fit as a fiddle *British, American & Australian*
be as fit as a flea *British & Australian*
to be very healthy • *My Dad's nearly eighty now but he's as fit as a fiddle.*

be fit to be tied *American*
to be very angry or upset • *She was fit to be tied when she discovered she'd left her purse on the train.*

fit (sb) **like a glove**
if a piece of clothing fits someone like a glove, it fits their body perfectly • *My new jeans contain Lycra so they fit like a glove.*

have/throw a fit
to be very angry • *My mother threw a fit when she saw the mess we'd made.*

▶ See also: fit/write sth on the **back** of a postage stamp
fit the **bill**
fit/ready to **drop**

fits

If the cap fits (wear it). *British, American & Australian*
If the hat/shoe fits (wear it). *American*
something that you say to tell someone that if they are guilty of something bad, they should accept criticism • *Look, I didn't say who was to blame for this mess – but if the cap fits, wear it.*

in fits and starts
if something happens in fits and starts, it often stops and then starts again • *Replies are arriving in fits and starts.*

five

Give me five! *mainly American informal*
something that you say when you want someone to hit your open hand with theirs, in order to greet them or to show how pleased you are • *Hi there little buddy, give me five!*

Give me a high five! *American informal*
something that you say when you want someone to hit your open hand with theirs, at a level above your shoulder • *Yo, Bob! Give me a high five!*

Take five! *American informal*
something that you say in order to tell other people to take a short rest from work or exercise • *'OK everybody, take five.'*

fix

be in a fix
to be in a difficult situation • *I'm in a real fix, the tyre's flat and I haven't got a spare.*

flag

drape/wrap yourself **in the flag**
to pretend to do something for your country when you are really doing it for your own advantage • *Companies in the UK are finding it useful to wrap themselves in the British flag.*

fly/show/wave the flag
to support or to represent your country • (often + **for**) *In the absence of any other Italian film directors, Mr Infascelli bravely flew the flag for his country.*

flagpole

▶ See: **run** sth up the flagpole

flags

Put the flags out! *British humorous*
something that you say when you are pleased and surprised that something has happened • *John's done the washing up. Put the flags out!*

flak

get/take (the) flak *informal*
to receive strong criticism • (often + **from**) *Channel 4 took the flak from angry viewers protesting about the show.* • (often + **for**) *She got a lot of flak for deserting her children.*

flames

go up in flames
to fail or come to an end suddenly and completely • *Final hopes of a pay settlement went up in flames yesterday after talks broke down.*

▶ See also: **fan** the flames
shoot sth/sb down in flames

flash

a flash in the pan
something that happens only once or for a short time and will not be repeated • *We're hoping that this is a long-term opportunity, and not just a flash in the pan.*

flat

be as flat as a pancake
to be very flat • *My cake hasn't risen – it's as flat as a pancake!*

be flat broke

be flat broke *informal*
to have no money at all • *I can't even pay the rent this month. I'm flat broke.*

fall flat on your/**its face**
to fail or make a mistake in an embarrassing way • *The new scheme fell flat on its face in spite of all the financial support that was given.* • *It's always amusing to see a newscaster fall flat on his face.*

flat out
1 if a person or a machine is doing something flat out, they are doing it as fast and with as much energy as they can • (often + to do sth) *The decorators have been working flat out to get the job finished.* • *My car only does 60 mph, even when it's going flat out.*
2 *American* if someone says something flat out, they say it in a very clear and direct way, even if it might upset people • *He called up and flat out asked if I was having an affair with Bob.*

▶ See also: **fall** flat

flattery

Flattery will get you **nowhere.** *humorous*
something that you say to someone in order to tell them that their praise will not persuade you to do anything that you do not want to do • *Well, I'm glad you liked the meal, but flattery will get you nowhere!*

flaunt

If you've got it, flaunt it! *informal*
something that you say which means if you have something you are proud of, such as beauty or wealth, you should make it obvious • *If I had legs like yours I'd wear really short dresses. If you've got it, flaunt it!*

flavour

the flavour of the month *British & Australian*
the flavor of the month *American & Australian*
someone or something that has suddenly become very popular, but may not remain popular for long • *Role-playing games are suddenly the flavour of the month.*

flea

▶ See: **send** sb away with a flea in their ear

flesh

be sb's **(own) flesh and blood**
to be someone's relative • *How can you be so cruel to him when he's your own flesh and blood?*

flesh and blood
1 human • *Many of the cartoon characters are more popular than their flesh and blood counterparts.*
2 if you say that someone is flesh and blood, you mean that they have feelings or faults that are natural because they are human • *I may be a priest, but I'm not immune to pretty women. I'm* ***only flesh and blood****, after all.*

make sb's **flesh crawl/creep**
if someone or something makes your flesh creep, you think they are extremely unpleasant or frightening • (often in present tenses) *Spiders and insects really make my flesh crawl.* • *I hate that guy in accounts, he makes my flesh creep.*

meet/see sb **in the flesh**
to meet or see someone yourself, instead of watching them in a film or on television, etc. • *I knew his face so well from the photographs that it felt a bit strange when I finally saw him in the flesh.*

put flesh on (the bones of) sth
to add more detail to something in order to make it more interesting or easier to understand • *We need some real figures and evidence to put flesh on the theory.* • *It would be wise to put flesh on the bones of your basic proposal before you ask them to consider it.*

▶ See also: **press** the flesh

flex

flex your **muscles**
if a person or an organization flexes their muscles, they take some action to let people know how powerful they are • *The latest bomb scare was just the terrorists flexing their muscles – showing us they haven't gone away.*

flies

There are no flies on sb.
something that you say which means that someone is intelligent and able to think quickly • *The minute she heard the business was for sale she was on the phone making an offer. There are no flies on her.*

flight

a flight of fancy/fantasy/imagination
an idea which shows a lot of imagination but which is not practical or useful in real situations • *You were talking about cycling across the US, or was that just another flight of fancy?*

flip

flip your **lid**
1 *humorous* to become crazy • *I thought he'd finally flipped his lid when he bought that old helicopter.*
2 *informal* to suddenly become very angry • *She'll flip her lid when she finds out what's been going on.*

▶ See also: flip/give sb the **bird**

flip-flop

a flip-flop *American*
a complete change, especially from one decision or opinion to another • *The government has made a policy flip-flop over arms sales.*
flip-flop *American* • (often + **on**) *The Senator wouldn't dare flip-flop on the abortion issue – he'd lose too many votes.*

float

not float sb's **boat** *informal*
If something does not float your boat, you do not enjoy it or want it. • *The idea of crawling through an underground cave doesn't really float my boat.*

floating

▶ See: be floating/walking on **air**

flog

▶ See: flog a **dead** horse
flog sth to **death**

floodgates

▶ See: **open** the floodgates

floor

fall/go through the floor
if the price or value of something falls through the floor, it becomes very low • *House prices have gone through the floor this year.*

floor it *American informal*
to drive a car as fast as it will go • *He likes to take his sports car out on the road and floor it.*

wipe the floor with sb *British, American & Australian*
mop the floor with sb *American*
to defeat someone easily • *Alex is always really good in a debate, she'll wipe the floor with them.*

flotsam

flotsam and jetsam
people or things which are not wanted or have no value ✍Flotsam and jetsam are the pieces of broken wood and other waste material found on the beach or floating on the sea. • *Drug addicts, the homeless, all are viewed as the flotsam and jetsam of today's society.*

flow

go with the flow
to do what other people are doing or to agree with other people because it is the easiest thing to do • *I wasn't very keen on*

the decision but it was easier just to go with the flow.

OPPOSITE **go against the flow** • *I decided to go against the flow and try something different from the rest of them.*

fly

fly a kite

1 to suggest a possible explanation for something • *I'm just flying a kite, but I suspect he was in love with her.*

2 to make a suggestion in order to see what other people think about your idea • *I'm just flying a kite, really, but do you think there would be any demand for a course on European art?*

fly blind

to try to do something new without any help or instructions • (usually in continuous tenses) *We've never dealt with Eastern Europe before, so we're flying blind.*

fly by the seat of your **pants** *informal*

to do something difficult without the necessary experience or ability • (often in continuous tenses) *None of us had ever worked on a magazine before so we were flying by the seat of our pants.*

by the seat of your **pants** if you do something by the seat of your pants, you do it using your own experience and ability, without help from anyone else • *We found our way by the seat of our pants, but if I ever did another jungle trek I'd take a guide.*

fly in the face of sth *slightly formal*

to be the opposite of what is usual or accepted • *These recommendations fly in the face of previous advice on safe limits for alcohol consumption.*

a fly in the ointment

someone or something that spoils a situation which could have been successful or pleasant • *The only fly in the ointment was my mother, who insisted on whispering through the first half of the show.*

fly off the handle *informal*

to react in a very angry way to something someone says or does • *He really flew off the handle when I suggested selling the house.*

a fly on the wall

if you say you would like to be a fly on the wall in a certain situation, you mean that you would like to be there secretly to see and hear what happens • *I'd give anything to be a fly on the wall when she tells him.*

fly-on-the-wall

a fly-on-the-wall film or television programme is one where the people involved forget or do not know that they are being filmed • (always before noun) *The five-part fly-on-the-wall documentary series focusses on the lives of three student nurses.*

fly the coop *mainly American*

to leave somewhere, especially to leave your home for the first time in order to live away from the family ✍A coop is a place where chickens are kept. • *The last of our kids has finally flown the coop so we have the whole house to ourselves.*

Go fly a kite! *mainly American informal*

something that you say in order to tell someone who is annoying you to go away • *Go fly a kite! It's just not funny any more.*

It'll never fly. *American*

something that you say when you think an idea will not be successful • *He sent me a movie script but it'll never fly – it's just too unbelievable.*

on the fly *American*

if someone does something on the fly, they do it quickly and without thinking carefully before they do it • *She was the sort of person who would make decisions on the fly rather than allowing herself time to think.*

wouldn't harm/hurt a fly

if you say that someone wouldn't hurt a fly, you mean that they are a gentle person and that they would not do anything to injure or upset anyone • *Damian just isn't the violent type. He wouldn't hurt a fly.*

► See also: fly/show/wave the **flag**
let fly (sth)
fly/leave the **nest**

fly-by-night

fly-by-night

a fly-by-night person or organization

cannot be trusted because they have not been established long, and could leave or close at any time • (always before noun) *They've opened one of those cheap and nasty fly-by-night stores on the High Street.* • *I'm serious about representing my constituents. I'm not a fly-by-night politician.*

flying

be flying high

1 if a person or a company is flying high, they are very successful • *The company was flying high as a maker of personal computers.*

2 *American informal* to be very excited or happy, often because of the effect of drugs • *The guy was on drugs – flying high and scaring everyone around him.* • *When the winter Olympics came to Canada, the whole country was flying high.*

come through/pass with flying colours *British & Australian*
come through/pass with flying colors *American & Australian*
to pass an examination with a very high score or to complete a difficult activity very successfully • *She took her university entrance exam in December and passed with flying colours.* • *The officer training was gruelling, but he came through with flying colours.*

get off to a flying start
to begin an activity very successfully • *Maria got off to a flying start in her new job.* • *With several customers on the books already, Tim's new business had got off to a flying start.*

foaming

foaming at the mouth
very angry • *The court's decision has left bloodsport enthusiasts foaming at the mouth.*

foggiest

not **have the foggiest (idea/notion)** *informal*
to not know the answer to a question • *'Do you know where Kate's gone?' 'I haven't the foggiest.'* • (often + question word) *The photocopier's broken down again, and nobody has the foggiest idea how to fix it.*

follow

follow in sb's **footsteps**
to do the same job or the same things in your life as someone else, especially a member of your family • *He followed in his father's footsteps and went into the army.*

follow your **nose**

1 to make decisions by thinking of how you feel about someone or something instead of finding out information about them • *As far as recruitment is concerned, I tend to follow my nose. I meet someone for an informal interview and see if I like them.*

2 *informal* if someone tells you to follow your nose when they are explaining how to go to a place, they are telling you to continue in the same direction • *Take the first on your right and follow your nose.*

follow suit
to do the same as someone else has just done ✍ If you follow suit when you are playing a card game, you put down a card with the same type of symbol on it as the card put down by the person before you. • *If other companies lower their prices, we shall have to follow suit.*

food

give sb **food for thought**
to make someone think seriously about something • *What you've suggested has certainly given me food for thought.*

fool

act/play the fool
to behave in a silly way, often in order to make people laugh • *Come on guys, stop acting the fool and pay attention.*

be no/nobody's fool
to be intelligent • *John's no fool. He's never going to believe that excuse.*

A fool and his money are soon parted.
something that you say which means that stupid people spend money without thinking about it enough • *Gianni relishes his extravagant lifestyle – but then a fool and his money are soon parted.*

a fool's errand
an attempt to do something that has no chance of success • *Billions of dollars have been spent on long-range weather*

forecasting, but it's a fool's errand.

make a fool of yourself
to do something which makes you seem stupid • *He's always getting drunk and making a fool of himself at parties.*

More fool you! *British, American & Australian*
The more fool you! *American*
something that you say in order to show that you think someone has done something stupid • *You lent her sixty pounds and expected it back? More fool you!* • *'He's volunteered to work late.' 'The more fool him, then.'*

▶ See also: **live** in a fool's paradise
play sb for a fool

fooled

You could've fooled me. *informal*
something that you say when you do not believe what someone says about something that you saw or experienced yourself • *'No, I wasn't angry, I was just a little surprised.' 'Really? You could've fooled me.'*

fools

Fools rush in (where angels fear to tread).
something that you say which means that stupid people do things without thinking about them enough • *Alan volunteered to be chairman and now he regrets it. Fools rush in, is all I can say.*

▶ See also: not **suffer** fools gladly

foot

the boot is on the other foot *British & Australian*
the shoe is on the other foot *American*
if you say that the boot is on the other foot, you mean that a situation is now the opposite of what it was before, often because a person who was in a weak position is now in a strong position • *In the past, we had great influence over their economy, but the boot is on the other foot now.*

foot the bill

foot the bill
to pay for something • (often + **for**) *Who's going to foot the bill for all the repairs?*

get off/start off on the wrong foot
1 if you get off on the wrong foot with someone you have just met, your relationship starts badly, often with an argument • (usually in past tenses) *I don't really know why, but somehow Clare and I got off on the wrong foot.*
OPPOSITE **get off/start off on the right foot** • (usually in past tenses) *I got off on the right foot by telling her how impressed I was with her work.*
2 to start an activity badly • *If I get off on the wrong foot with one of my paintings, I know it will never be right.*
OPPOSITE **get off/start off on the right foot** • *The commission has started off on the right foot by consulting local people.*

have/keep a foot in both camps
to be involved with two groups of people who often have very different aims and opinions • *He has moved from fringe to mainstream theatre, but he still keeps a foot in both camps.*

My foot! *old-fashioned*
something that you say after repeating something someone has just said, in order to show that you do not believe it • *A fluent French speaker my foot! He knows a few words at the most.*

not **put a foot wrong** *British & Australian*
to not make any mistakes • *Angie has*

always been good at her job, she never puts a foot wrong.

can't put a foot wrong *British & Australian* if someone can't put a foot wrong, people like them so much that they think everything they do is perfect • *As far as Charles is concerned, she can't put a foot wrong.*

put your **foot down**

1 to tell someone in a strong way that they must do something or that they must stop doing something • *You can't just let him do what he wants, you'll have to put your foot down.* • *When Anna came home drunk one afternoon I decided it was time to put my foot down.*

2 *mainly British informal* to suddenly increase your speed when you are driving • *The road ahead was clear, so I put my foot down and tried to overtake the car in front.*

put your **foot in it** *British, American & Australian informal*
put your **foot in** your **mouth** *American*
to say something by accident which embarrasses or upsets someone • *I really put my foot in it with Julie. I didn't realise she was a vegetarian.*

put your **foot to the floor** *American*
to suddenly increase your speed when you are driving • *I put my foot to the floor and reached the apartment in less than an hour.*

► See also: get a/your foot in the **door**
have **one** foot in the grave
shoot yourself in the foot

footloose

be footloose and fancy-free *old-fashioned*
if someone is footloose and fancy-free, they can do what they want because they are not married or do not have many responsibilities • *Jane's planning to go to parties and clubs every night now that she's footloose and fancy-free.*

footsie

► See: **play** footsie
play footsie with sb

footsteps

► See: **follow** in sb's footsteps

forbidden

forbidden fruit
something that you want very much but are not allowed to have, especially a sexual relationship ✍In the Bible, the forbidden fruit was an apple which God told Adam and Eve they could not eat. • *He'd spent many years lusting after his brother's wife – the forbidden fruit.*

force

be a force to be reckoned with
if an organization or person is a force to be reckoned with, they are very powerful • *The Scottish team's performance last month shows that they are once again a force to be reckoned with.*

be out in force
to be present in large numbers • *The Prince's young supporters were out in force.*

force sb's **hand**
to make someone do something or to make someone do something sooner than they want to • *I'm sure they don't want to reduce the price but if you threaten to pull out of the sale that might force their hand.*

force of habit
if someone does something from force of habit, they do it without thinking because they have done it so often before • *Even though he's gone she still keeps laying the table for two – force of habit, I guess.*

foregone

a foregone conclusion
a result that is obvious to everyone even before it happens • (not used with *the*) *It seems like this year's election results are a foregone conclusion.* • (often + **that**) *It's certainly not a foregone conclusion that we'll win.*

forelock-tugging

forelock-tugging *British*
showing too much respect towards someone who is in a high position • *As the General marched in, the collective forelock-tugging began.*

forest

► See: can't **see** the forest for the trees

forewarned

Forewarned is forearmed.

something that you say which means that if you know about something before it happens, you can be prepared for it • *Apparently Simon has some criticisms of my book. Still, forewarned is forearmed.*

forked

▶ See: **speak** with (a) forked tongue

form

▶ See: **true** to form/type

fort

▶ See: **hold** the fort

Forth Bridge

▶ See: be like **painting** the Forth Bridge

Fort Knox

be like Fort Knox *humorous*

if a building or an area is like Fort Knox, it is very difficult to enter or leave it because it is so well protected ✍Fort Knox is the building where the United States keeps its supplies of gold. • *Our house is like Fort Knox with all these extra security locks.*

forty

forty winks *informal*

a short sleep during the day • *She just had time to put her feet up and **catch forty winks** before dinner.*

foul

foul play

1 actions which are not fair or honest • *A virus wiped out all our computer-held records. We suspect foul play on the part of an ex-employee.*

2 murder • *It's not clear why the man drowned, but the police haven't ruled out foul play.*

▶ See also: **fall** foul of sb
fall foul of sth

foul-mouthed

foul-mouthed

someone who is foul-mouthed swears a lot • *He was foul-mouthed and violent.*

foundations

rock/shake sth **to its foundations**
rock/shake the foundations of sth

to damage or change an organization or a person's beliefs very much • *Allegations of scandal and abuse have rocked the party to its foundations.* • *The ideas seemed to make sense, but shook the foundations of her own Christian beliefs.*

four

the four corners of the earth/world

every part of the world • *Wedding guests arrived from the four corners of the world.*

four-letter

a four-letter word

a short word that is extremely rude • *The player was suspended after using a variety of four-letter words in front of the umpire.*

frame

be in the frame *British & Australian*

to be likely to achieve something or to be chosen for a job or an activity • (often + **for**) *Anderson was in the frame for the job in sales, but decided not to take it.* • (sometimes + to do sth) *Only Ferrari are in the frame to win the championship.*

a frame of mind

the way someone feels at a particular time • *A few hours later he was **in a** much more positive **frame of mind**.* • *Whether or not you enjoy the film may depend on your frame of mind.*

Frankenstein

a Frankenstein's monster

something that cannot be controlled and that attacks or destroys the person who invented it ✍This phrase comes from the book *Frankenstein* by Mary Shelley. • *Giving extra powers to the army turned it into a Frankenstein's monster that is now threatening to overthrow the ruling party.*

fray

enter/join the fray

to become involved in an argument or a fight • *Members of the royal family rarely enter the political fray.*

fray around/at the edges

to start to become less effective or successful • *This songwriting partnership began to fray at the edges after both partners got married.*

frazzle

▶ See: **wear** sb to a frazzle

free

allow/give sb **(a) free rein**

to allow someone to do what they want or go where they want to • (often + to do sth) *The older kids were given free rein to do whatever they wanted.* • *We shut the kitten out of the bedroom but allowed her free rein in the rest of the apartment.*

allow/give sth **(a) free rein**

if you give ideas or emotions free rein, you allow them to develop and do not try to control them • *With all these materials available, we can give our creativity free rein.*

as free as a bird

completely free to do what you want and without any worries • *She'd been travelling alone round the Greek islands for a year – free as a bird.*

feel free

something that you say in order to tell someone that they are allowed to do something • (often + to do sth) *The restaurant doesn't sell alcohol, so feel free to bring your own beer and wine.* • *If you want to use my computer for your report, feel free.*

a free agent

someone whose actions are not limited or controlled by anyone else • *Once the divorce has come through you'll be a free agent again.*

free and easy

relaxed and informal • *The atmosphere in our office is always free and easy.*

a free ride

an opportunity or advantage that someone gets without having done anything to deserve it • *Just because he was the boss's son didn't mean Tim got a free ride.*

a free spirit

someone who does what they want and does not feel limited by the usual rules of social behaviour • *His brothers describe Nick as something of a free spirit, unconventional and adventurous.*

give sb **a free hand**

to allow someone to do whatever they think is necessary in a particular situation • (often + to do sth) *His manager had given him a free hand to make whatever changes he felt necessary.*

have a free hand • (sometimes + **in** + doing sth) *The editor said I could have a free hand in designing the cover page.*

It's a free country!

something that you say which means that you have the right to do something even if someone else has criticized you for it • *I'll shout if I want to – it's a free country!*

make free with sth

to use something a lot, even when it does not belong to you • *I won't have him in my house, making free with my whiskey.*

freefall

go into freefall

1 If prices or the value of something go into freefall, they lose value very quickly. • *Problems with TV deals have sent football finances into freefall.*

2 If someone's career, life, or ability goes into freefall, it gets bad and out of control very quickly. • *When he was diagnosed with cancer, his life went into freefall.*

free-for-all

a free-for-all

a situation that is not controlled, and where everyone does what they want or fights for what they want to get • *This is supposed to be a sensible debate, don't let it degenerate into a free-for-all.* • *In the economic free-for-all of the final years of communism, he was able to amass a sizeable fortune.*

French

French leave *old-fashioned, humorous*

a period when you are absent from work without asking for permission ✍In the 18th century in France, it was the custom to leave an official event or party without saying goodbye to the person who had invited you. • *Is Ray really ill again, or is he just taking French leave?*

a French letter *informal, old-fashioned*

a thin rubber covering that a man can wear on his penis during sex to stop a woman becoming pregnant or to protect him or his partner against infectious diseases • *In those days, French letters were the only form of contraceptive we had.*

▶ See also: **pardon** my French!

fresh

be as fresh as a daisy
to be full of energy and enthusiasm • *It's been a long drive but give me a cup of tea and I'll soon feel fresh as a daisy.*

be fresh from swh *British*
be fresh out of swh *American & Australian*
to have just finished education or training in a particular school or college and not have much experience • *Our course is taught by a young professor fresh out of law school.*

be fresh out of sth *mainly American & Australian*
to have just finished or sold a supply of something, and have no more left • *Sorry, we're fresh out of bread this morning.*

get fresh
to show by your actions or words that you want to have sex with someone • (usually + **with**) *If he tries to get fresh with you, tell him to keep his hands to himself.*

get fresh with sb *American & Australian*
to talk to someone in an impolite way or behave in a way which shows you do not respect them • *Don't you get fresh with me, young lady!*

Friday

a girl/man/person Friday
a person who does many different types of usually not very interesting work in an office ✍Man Friday is the name of the servant in the book *Robinson Crusoe* by Daniel Defoe. • *The ad said, 'Person Friday required for general office duties'.*

friend

A friend in need (is a friend indeed).
something that you say which means that someone who gives you help when you need it is a really good friend • *She looked after my dogs while I was in hospital. A friend in need is a friend indeed.*

friends

have friends in high places
to know important people who can help you get what you want • *He has plenty of friends in high places willing to support his political career.*

With friends like that, who needs enemies? *humorous*
something that you say when someone you thought was your friend treats you in an unpleasant way • *He told my girlfriend I was boring. With friends like that, who needs enemies!*

frighten

▶ See: frighten/scare the (living) **daylights** out of sb
frighten/scare sb to **death**
frighten/scare the **hell** out of sb
frighten/scare the **life** out of sb
frighten/scare sb out of their **wits**

frighteners

put the frighteners on sb *British old-fashioned, informal*
to threaten someone • *He said he wouldn't pay up so I sent my brothers round to put the frighteners on him.*

fritz

be on the fritz *American informal*
if a piece of equipment or machinery is on the fritz, it does not work as it should • *It will be a long, hot summer – our air conditioning is on the fritz.*

frog

have a frog in your **throat** *informal*
to be unable to speak clearly until you give a slight cough • *Excuse me, I've got a bit of a frog in my throat.*

from

▶ See: from **time** to **time**

front

be in the front line
to be in an important position where you have influence, but where you are likely to be criticized or attacked • (often + **of**) *Many social workers are in the front line of racial tension.*

the front office *American*
the managers of a company • *The front*

office has decided to cut back on technical staff.

front-office *American* • (always before noun) *She's one of the key front-office advisers.*

put on/up a front

to pretend to feel a certain way • *He hasn't shown any signs of grief over his father's death, but I'm sure he's just putting up a front.*

up front

if you give someone an amount of money up front, you pay them before they start a job • *Did you pay up front or are you waiting till they've finished the job?*

frozen

▶ See: be chilled/frozen to the **marrow**

fruit

the fruit of your **loins** *humorous*

your children • *The fruit of my loins you may be, but that doesn't mean I have to look after you all my life!*

▶ See also: **bear** fruit

frying

▶ See: **jump** out of the frying pan (and) into the fire

fuck

fuck like bunnies *American taboo*

if people fuck like bunnies they produce too many babies very quickly • *Ten kids! Those people fuck like bunnies.*

fuddy-duddy

a fuddy-duddy *informal*

someone who has old-fashioned ideas and dresses in an old-fashioned way • *You don't want to take any notice of her, she's just a pompous old fuddy-duddy!*

fuddy-duddy *informal* • *His ideas were irrelevant, boring and fuddy-duddy.*

fuel

▶ See: **add** fuel to the fire/flames

full

(at) full pelt/steam/tilt *informal*

as fast as possible • *He was going full pelt down the motorway but he still didn't make it to the airport in time.*

(at) full throttle

if a person or a machine is at full throttle, they are doing something as well and with as much energy as they can • *By the end of May, the assembly line will be working at full throttle.*

allow/give sth **full play**

if something is given full play, it is used or developed as much as possible • *The themes of love and bereavement are given full play in Oliver's new novel.* • *He urges that market forces should be allowed full play in the villages.*

come into full play • *Here, his genius for networking came into full play.*

at full stretch *British*

if someone or something is at full stretch, they are working as hard as possible • *The emergency services are working at full stretch to cope with the accident.* • *When the plant is operating at full stretch it can employ 800 people.*

be as full as a boot/tick *Australian informal*

to be very drunk • *Old Clive was as full as a boot when he left the hotel last night.*

be full of yourself

to think that you are very important in a way that annoys other people • *I'm not sure I like Sarah, she's so full of herself all the time.*

be full of beans

to have a lot of energy and enthusiasm • *I've never met anyone so full of beans before breakfast.*

be full of crap/shit *British, American & Australian taboo*

be full of bull *American very informal*

to often say stupid or wrong things • *I wouldn't listen to what Jeremy says, he's always full of shit.*

be full of holes

if an idea or plan is full of holes, it is not complete or has many faults • *His theory is full of holes so we should have no problem convincing people that he's wrong.*

be full of piss and vinegar *American very informal*

to have a lot of energy • *He's full of piss and vinegar this morning.*

be full of the joys of spring *British & Australian humorous*

to be very happy • *He bounced into the*

office, full of the joys of spring.

be in full cry *British & Australian*
to criticize someone or something in a noisy and eager way • *The opposition was in full cry over the changes to the education bill.*

be in full flow/spate *British & Australian*
if an activity is in full flow, it is happening fast and with energy • *He had this annoying habit of interrupting her when she was in full spate.* • *The royal wedding preparations were now in full flow.*

be in full swing
if an event is in full swing, it has already been happening for a period of time and there is a lot of activity • *When we got to Vicki's place the party was in full swing.*

not **be the full quid** *Australian informal*
to be slightly crazy or stupid • *He's a bit odd – I don't think he's the full quid.*

come to a full stop
to end, especially because of a problem or difficulty • *After a series of health problems his career came to a full stop.*

come/go/turn full circle
if something or someone has come full circle after changing a lot, they are now the same as they were at the beginning • *My career has come full circle and I am back at the school where I started out as a teacher thirty years ago.* • *In the meantime her opinions have gone full circle and she has decided to rejoin the party.*
bring sb **full circle** • *The poem brings us full circle, and leaves us with an image of the daffodils still dancing by the lake.*

The wheel has come/turned full circle. something that you say which means a situation is the same now as it was before things started to change • *The wheel had finally come full circle; we were together as a family again.*

the full monty *mainly British humorous*
if something is the full monty, it is as complete as possible • *Their wedding was magnificent, with a champagne reception, three-course dinner and a band – the full monty.*

full steam ahead
with all possible energy and enthusiasm • *We're going full steam ahead to expand the business.* • *Now we've solved a few problems* ***it's full steam ahead.***

in full force
if a group of people are at a place in full force, all of them are there • *Heidi's side of the family were there in full force but Bill's brother was the only one to show up.*

► See also: be on full/red **alert**
have your **plate** full

full-court

a full-court press *American*
a big effort to achieve something • *The Mayor has urged a full-court press for civil rights and fair housing in the city.*

fullness

in the fullness of time
if you say that something will happen in the fullness of time, you mean that it will happen if you wait long enough • *Everything will become clear in the fullness of time.*

fun

not **be all fun and games**
if an activity is not all fun and games, parts of it are difficult or unpleasant • *Being a tour representative isn't all fun and games, I can tell you.*

have fun and games *humorous*
to have difficulty doing something or dealing with someone • (often + doing sth) *We had fun and games trying to give the dog a bath.* • (often + **with**) *She's had fun and games with the tax office.*

It was fun while it lasted.
something that you say when something good has ended but you are not sorry • *I wouldn't have wanted more than 3 years at university, but it was fun while it lasted.*

make fun of sb/sth
poke fun at sb/sth
to make a joke about someone or something in an unkind way • *At first the kids made fun of her because she spoke with a Dutch accent.*

► See also: be more fun than a **barrel** of monkeys

funeral

it's your **funeral**
something that you say in order to tell

someone that if they suffer bad results from their actions it will be their own fault • *'I'm not coming to the meeting, I can't afford the time.' 'Okay, it's your funeral.'*

funk

be in a (blue) funk

to be very worried or unhappy about something • *He's been in a real funk since she left him.*

funny

funny business *informal*

dishonest or unpleasant actions • *If you try any funny business you'll be sorry.*

a funny farm *humorous*

a hospital for people who are mentally ill ✍This expression may be offensive in some situations. • *If things get much worse they'll be carrying me off to the funny farm.*

funny money

money that has been printed by criminals, or which has come from dishonest activities • *He was caught passing funny money through the business.*

▶ See also: be as funny as a **barrel** of monkeys

fur

be all fur coat and no knickers *humorous*

to look attractive but not really be very interesting or of good quality • *When he took over as chairman we discovered he was all fur coat and no knickers.*

the fur flies

the fur flies

if the fur flies, people have a bad argument • *The fur was really flying during that meeting.*

set the fur flying to cause a bad argument • *She set the fur flying by demanding to see the letters.*

furrow

▶ See: **plough** a lone/lonely furrow

fuse

▶ See: **blow** a fuse/gasket

fuss

▶ See: **kick** up a fuss/row/stink

gaff

▶ See: **blow** the gaff

gain

gain ground
if a political party or a belief gains ground, it becomes more popular or accepted • (often in continuous tenses) *The Republicans are gaining ground in the Southern states.*
OPPOSITE **lose ground** • (often + **to**) *Recent polls suggest that the government is fast losing ground to the opposition.*

▶ See also: have the **upper** hand

gallery

▶ See: **play** to the gallery

gallows

gallows humour *British & Australian*
gallows humor *American & Australian*
humour that makes unpleasant things, such as death, seem funny ✍The gallows are a wooden frame used in the past for killing criminals by hanging them from a rope tied around their neck. • *Many of the patients I worked with knew they were dying. There was a lot of gallows humour.*

game

be ahead of the game
to know more about the most recent developments in a particular subject or activity than the people or companies with whom you are competing • *A very extensive research and development programme ensures that we're ahead of the game.*
stay ahead of the game • *Staying ahead of the game in these days of rapid technological advancements is no easy task.*

be on the game *informal*
if someone, especially a woman, is on the game, they regularly have sex with men for payment • *Her older sister was on the game by the time she was sixteen.*
go on the game *informal* • *A lot of these girls find they can't even pay the rent so they go on the game.*

a game plan
a plan for achieving success, especially in business or politics • *Part of the firm's game plan is to expand into Eastern Europe.*

The game's up! *informal*
something that you say to tell someone that their secret plans or tricks have been discovered and they cannot continue • *Okay, you two, the game's up! Give me the cigarettes – this time I'm telling your parents.*

give the game away
to spoil a surprise or a joke by letting someone know something that should have been kept secret • *We were trying to pretend we didn't know it was her birthday but Sam gave the game away.*

What's sb's **game?** *informal*
something that you say when you want to know the real reason for someone's behaviour • *You're being exceptionally nice today. What's your game?*

▶ See also: **play** the game
raise your game

games

▶ See: **play** games

gangbusters

come on like gangbusters *American informal*
to start doing something eagerly and with a lot of energy, especially performing or talking to people ✍*Gangbusters* was a radio program in the US about police who went after criminals with much energy and success. • *In one of his most renowned performances, Cagney comes on like gangbusters as hoodlum Tom Powers.*

like gangbusters *American informal*
very successfully • *Both books have been selling like gangbusters.*

garbage

Garbage in, garbage out. *mainly American*
something you say which means that something produced from materials of low quality will also be of low quality • *The meals are pretty poor but then they never use fresh ingredients – garbage in, garbage out.*

garden

Everything in the garden is rosy.
something that you say which means that there are no problems in a situation • (often negative) *But not everything in the garden is rosy. Sales may look good but they're actually 10% down on last year.*

▶ See also: **lead** sb up the garden path

garden-variety

garden-variety *American & Australian*
very ordinary • (always before noun) *It's just a garden-variety shopping mall, large but not special in any way.*

gas

a gas guzzler

a gas guzzler *American informal*
a car that uses a lot of fuel • *I want to sell this huge gas guzzler and buy something that's cheaper to run.*

▶ See also: **run** out of gas
step on the gas!

gasket

▶ See: **blow** a fuse/gasket

gatepost

▶ See: **between** you, me and the bedpost/gatepost

gather

gather dust
to not be used for a long time • (often in continuous tenses) *If these books are going to sit around gathering dust in the garage you might as well give them to Frank.*

gather your **wits** *literary*
to make an effort to become calm and think more clearly • *Sitting down in one of the chairs I attempted to gather my wits and decide what I should do.*

gauntlet

▶ See: **run** the gauntlet
throw down the gauntlet

gay

just gay enough *informal*
A man who is just gay enough is not gay but has some of the qualities typical of gay men that many women like, such as an interest in clothes or being able to talk about emotions. • *Her new husband is wonderful – tall and handsome, and just gay enough.*

gaze

▶ See: gaze at/contemplate your **navel**

gear

get in/into gear
to start to work effectively and with energy • *After a few days out of the office it always takes me a while to get into gear when I come back.*

move/step up a gear
to start to work or play more effectively or quickly than before • *With just five lengths to go, the German swimmer stepped up a gear and edged ahead to win the race.*

generation

a generation gap
the lack of understanding between older and younger people that is caused by their different experiences, opinions and behaviour • *It is unusual for a singer to* ***bridge the generation gap*** *and appeal to both young and old alike.* • *There's a big*

age difference between us but we've never been troubled by a generation gap.

genie

▶ See: **let** the genie out of the bottle

gentle

be as gentle as a lamb

to be very calm and kind • *I thought she was gentle as a lamb until I heard her shouting at Richard.*

a gentle giant

a man who is very tall and strong, but has a very quiet, gentle character that does not match his appearance • *As placid and amiable as he was tall, he became known as the gentle giant of the squad.*

get

Get away with you! *British & Australian old-fashioned*

something that you say when someone says something that is silly, surprising or not true • *'Be honest with me, do I look fat in these trousers?' 'Get away with you!'*

▶ See also: get your **act** together
get in on the **act**
get sb's **ass**
get/put sb's **back** up
get/jump/leap on the **bandwagon**
get into **bed** with sb
get/take the **bit** between your teeth
Get out of my **face**!
get your **feet** under the table
get/pull your **finger** out
get to **first** base
get off to a **flying** start
get in/into **gear**
get your **goat**
get a **grip** (on yourself)
come/get to **grips** with sth
get (sth) off the **ground**
get a **handle** on sth
get your **hands** dirty
get your **hands** on sb
get/lay your **hands** on sth
get the **hang** of sth
build/get/work up a **head** of steam
get your **head** around sth
get your **head** down
get/put your **head** down
catch/get **hell**
get the **hell** out
climb/get on your **high** horse
get/let sb off the **hook**
get your **hooks** into sth/sb
get on like a **house** on fire
get/put your own **house** in order
get the **hump**
get your **knickers** in a twist
Get **knotted**!
Get a **life**!
Get **lost**!
get the **message**
get your **mind** around sth
get a **move** on
get/grate on sb's **nerves**
get up sb's **nose**
get your **oats**
get/put **one** over on sb
get your **own** back
get your **own** way
get with the **program**
I'll get a **rain** check
Get **real**!
get **religion**
get your **rocks** off
get the **sack**
get the **shaft**
get **shot** of sb/sth
Get your **skates** on!
enter/get into the **spirit** of sth
get into your **stride**
get into the **swing** of it/things
get it out of your **system**
get off your **tail**
get/sink your **teeth** into sth
get it **together**
get your **tongue** around/round sth
get on sb's **wick**
get **wind** of sth
get/put the **wind** up sb

get-up-and-go

get-up-and-go

if someone has get-up-and-go, they have energy and enthusiasm • *You need a bit of get-up-and-go if you're going to work in sales.*

ghost

not a ghost of a chance

if someone does not have a ghost of a chance, they are not at all likely to succeed • (sometimes + **of** + doing sth) *Against competition like that, they didn't have the ghost of a chance of winning.*

give up the ghost

1 to stop trying to do something because

you know that you will not succeed • *She'd been trying to break into acting for ten years without success and was just about to give up the ghost.*

2 *humorous* if a machine gives up the ghost, it stops working • *We've had the same television for fifteen years and I think it's finally about to give up the ghost.*

▶ See also: the ghost/spectre at the **feast**
lay the ghost of sth/sb (to rest)

gift

the gift of the gab *British, American & Australian*
the gift of gab *American*
an ability to speak easily and confidently and to persuade people to do what you want • *An Irishman, he **had the gift of the gab**. You might hate what he said but you had to listen.*

▶ See also: not **look** a gift horse in the mouth

gild

gild the lily
to spoil something by trying to improve or decorate it when it is already perfect ✍To gild something is to cover it with a thin layer of gold. A lily is a beautiful white flower. To gild a lily would not be necessary. • *Should I add a scarf to this jacket or would it be gilding the lily?*

ginger

a ginger group *British & Australian*
a small group within a larger political party or organization that tries to persuade the other members to accept their beliefs and ideas • *He was soon won over to the left wing as a member of a marginal ginger group called the New Beginning.*

gird

gird (up) your **loins** *humorous*
to prepare yourself mentally to do something difficult ✍This phrase comes from the Bible, where girding up your loins meant to tie up long, loose clothes so that they were more practical when you were working or travelling. • *Both sides are presently girding their loins for the legal battles that lie ahead.*

girl

▶ See: a girl/man/person **Friday**

give

Don't give me that! *informal*
something that you say when you do not believe an explanation that someone has given you • *Don't give me that! I saw you with him, Karen – I drove right past you!*

give it a shot/whirl *informal*
to attempt to do something • *I've never danced salsa before but I'll give it a shot.*

give sb **the creeps/willies** *informal*
to make you feel frightened and anxious, especially when there is no real reason for this • *This old house gives me the creeps.* • *I've never liked spiders – they give me the willies.*

I'll give you **what for!** *informal*
something that you say when you are very angry with someone and intend to punish them • *I'll give you what for, young lady, coming home at 2 o'clock in the morning!*

▶ See also: give your **all**
give it your **all**
give sth up as a **bad** job
flip/give sb the **bird**
give sb a **break**
Give me/us a **break**!
not give a **damn**
give your **eye** teeth for sth
not care/give a **fig**
give sb the **finger**
give sb (the right of/to) **first** refusal
Give me **five**!
give sb **food** for thought
allow/give sb (a) **free** rein
allow/give sth (a) **free** rein
give sb a **free** hand
allow/give sth **full** play
give the **game** away
give up the **ghost**
give sb the **glad** eye
give as **good** as you get
give sb/sth the **green** light
give sb **grief**
give **ground**
give sb a **hand**
give sb a **hard** time
give sb their **head**
give sb the (old) **heave** ho
give sb **hell**

Give them **hell**!
not care/give a **hoot**
not give sth/sb **house** room
not budge/give an **inch**
Give sb an **inch** and they'll take a mile.
give your **life**
give sth a **miss**
not give a **monkey**'s
give sb the **nod**
give/hand sth to sb on a **plate**
give/hand sth to sb on a (silver) **platter**
give a **raspberry**
Give it a **rest**!
would give their **right** arm
give sb a **rocket**
give sb enough **rope** (to hang themselves)
give sb the **runaround**
would give you the **shirt** off their back
not give a **shit**
give sb/sth **short** shrift
give sb the **slip**
Give it to me **straight**.
not give sb the **time** of day
not care/give a **toss**
not care/give **tuppence**
give sb/sth a **wide** berth

give-and-take

a give-and-take *American*
a conversation in which people give their opinions and listen to those of other people • *The candidates entered into a lively give-and-take.*

give-and-take
a situation in which two people or groups allow each other to have or do some of the things that they want • *You can't always insist on your own way – there has to be some give-and-take.*
give and take
• *Partners need to give and take, to make allowances, to find compromises.*

given

▶ See: given **half** a/the chance

glad

give sb **the glad eye** *British & Australian old-fashioned*
to look at someone in a way that makes it obvious that you are sexually attracted to them • *I think you have an admirer. That man in the corner is giving you the glad eye.*

your **glad rags** *old-fashioned*
the clothes that you wear when you are going somewhere special • *Put your glad rags on, we're going to a party.*

glamour

a glamour girl/puss *British & Australian*
a glamor girl/puss *American & Australian*
a sexually attractive woman who is very interested in her clothes and appearance • *His name was always linked to some glamor girl.* • *I think she sees herself as a bit of a glamour puss with her high heels and her blonde hair.*

glass

a glass ceiling
the opinions of people in a company which prevent women from getting such important positions as men • *The problem for women in broadcasting is the glass ceiling. Women rise but not to the top.*

glistens

▶ See: All that glistens/glitters is not **gold**.

glitters

▶ See: All that glistens/glitters is not **gold**.

glory

sb's/sth's **glory days**
a time in the past when someone or something was very successful • *The book focusses on the glory days of the jazz scene in the early 1940's and 1950's.*

glove

▶ See: **fit** (sb) like a glove

gloves

the gloves are off *informal*
if the gloves are off in an argument or competition, the people involved have started to argue or compete in a more determined or unpleasant way • *She gave a second interview later that year but this time the gloves were off. Her ex-boss, she said, was 'a tyrant and a fraud'.*

glued

▶ See: glued/rooted to the **spot**

glutton

a glutton for punishment *humorous*
someone who seems to like working hard or doing things that most people would find unpleasant • *So as well as a full-time job and a family to look after, she's started taking an evening class. She's a glutton for punishment, that woman.*

gnashing

gnashing of teeth *humorous*
angry complaining • *There was much gnashing of teeth over his omission from the England squad.*

go

be on the go *informal*
to be very busy and active • *I've been on the go all morning and I'm exhausted.*

have a go at sb
1 *British & Australian informal* to criticize someone angrily • *She had a go at me over breakfast this morning – she said I wasn't doing my share of the housework.*
2 *British & Australian informal* to attack someone physically • *A couple of kids had a go at him as he was leaving school.*

have sth **on the go** *British & Australian*
if you have something on the go, it is happening or being produced now • *She's got two films on the go, but still finds time to spend every weekend with her family.*

It's all go. *British & Australian*
something that you say when you are very busy or when lots of things are happening around you • *I've got an hour to do the shopping before I pick the children up from school. It's all go, I tell you.* • *It was all go in the office this morning, the phone never stopped ringing.*

make a go of sth
1 *informal* if two people who are in a romantic relationship make a go of it, they try to make that relationship succeed • *We decided to try and **make a go of it** for the sake of the children.*
2 *informal* to try to make something succeed, usually by working hard • *He's determined to make a go of the bookshop.*

▶ See also: go **all** out
go it **alone**
not go **amiss**
go **ape**
go **ballistic**
Go to **blazes**!
go for **broke**
go off the **deep** end
Go to the **devil**!
go to the **dogs**
go **dutch**
go the **extra** mile
go through **fire** and water
go up in **flames**
fall/go through the **floor**
go with the **flow**
come/go/turn **full** circle
be/go at it **hammer** and tongs
come/go under the **hammer**
come/go cap in **hand**
go **hand** in **hand**
go **haywire**
go **head** to **head**
go over sb's **head**
go to sb's **head**
go **hell** for leather
go through **hell**
go to **hell** in a handbasket/handcart
Go to **hell**!
go/jump through **hoops**
feel/go **hot** and cold (all over)
go/sell like **hot** cakes
go (all) round the **houses**
go for the **jugular**
go (in) for the **kill**
go down like a **lead** balloon
go **mental**
go through the **mill**
go through the **motions**
go down/fall like **ninepins**
no go
go **overboard**
go into **overdrive**
go/fall to **pieces**
go down the **plughole**
go **postal**
go to **pot**
go into **raptures**
go on **record**
come/go along for the **ride**
go down that **road**
go like a **rocket**
go through the **roof**
go/run to **seed**
go to **show** (sth)
go up in **smoke**
go **spare**
go **stag**
go to the **stake**
go with a **swing**

go off on a **tangent**
come/go with the **territory**
go/swim against the **tide**
go down a **treat**
go to the **wall**
go **west**
come/go down in the **world**

goal

► See: **move** the goal

goalposts

► See: **move** the goalposts

goat

act/play the goat *informal*
to behave in a silly way, sometimes in order to make people laugh • *Insecure and lonely, he resorted to acting the goat to get people's attention.*

get your **goat** *British, American & Australian informal*
get on your **goat** *Australian informal*
to annoy you • *It really gets my goat when people push past without saying 'Excuse me'.* • *The kid never stops whingeing – he really gets on my goat.*

gob

► See: **Shut** your face/gob/mouth/trap!

God

God rest her/his soul. *old-fashioned*
something that you say when you are talking about someone who is dead, to show that you respect them • *My old father – God rest his soul – now he could drink a pint or two.*

► See also: God/Heaven **help** sb
play God
think you are God's gift to women

God-given

a God-given right
if someone thinks they have a God-given right to do something, they think they should be allowed to do it even if other people do not like it • (often + to do sth) *He seems to think he has a God-given right to tell us all what to do.*

goes

► See: It goes without **saying**.
what goes around comes around

go-getter

a go-getter
someone who has a lot of energy and confidence and wants to succeed • *I remember him as a real go-getter – someone who you knew would reach the top of whatever profession he chose.*

goggle-box

the goggle-box *British & Australian old-fashioned*
the television • *There are plenty of good shows on the goggle box at the moment.*

going

have something going with sb *informal*
have a thing going with sb *informal*
if you have something going with someone, you are having a sexual relationship with them • *She had something going with a guy on the staff.* • *Larry's obviously had a thing going with her for several months now.*

when the going gets rough/tough
when a situation becomes difficult or unpleasant • *I run the farm on my own, but a local boy helps me out when the going gets tough.*
if the going gets rough/tough • *I'm spending Christmas with my family, but if the going gets tough I might escape back to London.*

while the going is good *informal*
if you do something while the going is good, you do it while it is still easy to do • *If you are unsure about marrying him,* ***get out*** *now* ***while the going is good****.*

► See also: be going **begging**
like it's going out of **fashion**
be going **great** guns
have a **lot** going for you
be going **spare**

gold

All that glistens/glitters is not gold. *British, American & Australian*
All that glisters is not gold. *British literary*
something that you say to warn someone that sometimes people or things that appear attractive have no real value • *This film has an all-star cast, but all*

that glisters is not gold. It fails because of its weak story.

a gold digger *old-fashioned*

a woman who has relationships with rich men so that they will give her money • *I'm not saying she's a gold digger, but how come all her boyfriends have been rich?*

like gold dust *British & Australian*
like gold *American*

if things or people are like gold dust, they are difficult to get because a lot of people want them • *Tickets for the Coldplay concert were like gold dust. We were really lucky to get them.* • *Skilled workers are like gold in the engineering industry.*

▶ See also: **strike** gold

golden

a golden boy/girl

someone who is successful and admired • (often + **of**) *Henman is the golden boy of British tennis this season.*

golden handcuffs

financial arrangements given by a company to an important employee in order to influence them to stay with the company • *Share options are offered to top executives as golden handcuffs.*

a golden handshake

a large sum of money which is given to someone when they leave a company, especially if they are forced to leave • *The manager got early retirement and a £600,000 golden handshake when the company was restructured.*

a golden oldie

a record that was very popular in the past and that people still know and like today • *I listen to the Sunday morning show when they play all the golden oldies.*

a golden parachute

if an important manager in a company has a golden parachute, the company agrees to give them a very large sum of money if they lose their job • *He insisted on a substantial golden parachute as part of the package before taking up the post.*

gone

be gone on sb *informal*

to be very attracted to someone • *Sue's really gone on this new boyfriend of hers.*

▶ See also: gone for a **burton**

good

All in good time.

something that you say to tell someone to be patient because the thing they are eager for will happen when the time is right • *'Can we open our presents now?' 'All in good time. Let's wait till Daddy comes.'*

be as good as gold

if a child is as good as gold, they behave very well • *The children were as good as gold today.*

be as good as new

if something is as good as new, it has either been kept in the same good condition as when it was new, or repaired so that it is as good as it was then • *The exterior of the building has been restored and it now looks as good as new.*

be as good as your **word**

to keep a promise • *Jack said he would call and he was as good as his word.*

be in good company

to have done or experienced something bad which someone who people admire has also done or experienced • *Don't worry, Einstein did badly at school, so you're in good company.*

be on good terms with sb

to be friendly with someone • *We were always on good terms with our neighbours.*

OPPOSITE **be on bad terms with** sb • *It doesn't help matters if you're on bad terms with your doctor.*

be on to a good thing *informal*

to be in a pleasant or successful situation • *'My wife does all the housework and cooking.' 'You're on to a good thing there!'* • (often + **with**) *He's on to a good thing with this chauffeur service he runs.*

be too good to be true

if something is too good to be true, you do not believe it can really be as good as it seems • *The job turned out to be really boring. I knew it was too good to be true.*

be up to no good *informal*

if someone is up to no good, they are doing something bad • *She thinks her husband has been up to no good because she found long blonde hairs on his jacket.*

for good *British, American & Australian informal*
for good and all *American informal*
forever • *I'm leaving for good this time.*

for good measure
if you do something or add something for good measure, you do it or add it in addition to something else • *In today's programme we have a full report on today's top football matches, with some cricket and athletics* ***thrown in for good measure****.* • *I swept the floor and polished the table, and then, for good measure, I cleaned the windows.*

give as good as you **get** *informal*
to be strong and confident enough to treat people in the same way that they treat you, especially in an argument or a fight • *When you are a woman working with a lot of men, you have to be able to give as good as you get.*

good and proper *informal*
if someone does something good and proper, they do it completely and with a lot of force • *He warned me off good and proper after I kissed his girlfriend.*

a good egg *old-fashioned, humorous*
a person with good qualities such as kindness • *He's a good egg, your brother – he visited me every day while I was ill.*

the good old days
if you talk about the good old days, you mean a time in the past when you believe life was better • *I wish my grandma would stop going on about the good old days.* • ***In the good old days****, we used to tell stories round the fire.*

Good riddance (to bad rubbish)! *informal*
an impolite way of saying that you are pleased someone has left • *Good riddance! I hope she never comes back.*

a good Samaritan
someone who tries to help people who have problems ✍This phrase comes from a story in the Bible where a Samaritan man helped someone who was injured even though others would not help him. • *He's such a good Samaritan. He used to go shopping for my gran when she was ill.*

have a good head on your **shoulders**
to be clever • *You can trust Laura with the money – she's got a good head on her shoulders.*

have a good mind to do sth *informal*
if you say you have a good mind to do something, especially to punish someone, you mean that you would like to do it, and might do it, although you probably will not • *I have a good mind to report you to the headmaster for playing truant.*

have a good run for your **money**
to have a long period of success or enjoyment • *I've achieved a lot in my life and I feel I've had a good run for my money.*

have had a good innings *British & Australian*
to have had a long and active life or a long and successful period of time in a job ✍In cricket, the innings is the time when one team or player is batting (= hitting the ball). • *I've had a good innings but my old heart is very weak now.* • *He's had a good innings as club president.*

have it on good authority
to believe that a piece of information is true because you trust the person who told you • (often + **that**) *I have it on good authority that we're about to be given a pay increase.*

in good faith
if you act in good faith, you believe that what you are doing is right and legal • *His defence was that he had acted in good faith. He did not know when he bought the car that it had been stolen.*
OPPOSITE **in bad faith** if you do something in bad faith, you know that it is not honest or legal • *The court ruled that the sellers had acted in bad faith.*

make (it) good *American & Australian*
to become successful or to achieve something you want • *The film's main character is a poor Mexican boy who made it good in Chicago.* • *He'll make good, you'll see. He works hard and knows what he's after.*

make a good fist of sth/doing sth *British & Australian old-fashioned*
to do something well • *He made a good fist of explaining why we need to improve our*

public transport system. • *He built the house himself and made a surprisingly good fist of it.*

OPPOSITE **make a bad/poor fist of** sth/doing sth *British & Australian old-fashioned* • *Our lawyer made a poor fist of advising us.*

make good on sth *American & Australian informal*
to give back money that you owe someone, or to keep a promise to do something • *I want to make good on that loan I got from Joan.* • *Tom made good on his promise to paint the living room.*

put in a good word for sb *informal*
to try to help someone achieve something by saying good things about them to someone with influence • (sometimes + **with**) *I'm applying for a job in your office. Could you put in a good word for me with your boss?*

take sth **in good part** *British*
if you take criticism or jokes in good part, you are not upset or annoyed by them • *His friends used to call him 'Big Ears' but he* ***took it all in good part****.*

too much of a good thing
if you have too much of a good thing, something pleasant becomes unpleasant because you have too much of it • *I felt sick after I'd eaten all those chocolates. You* ***can have too much of a good thing****.* • *All this attention she's getting could prove to be too much of a good thing.*

turn/use sth **to good account** *formal*
to use something to produce good results • *She turned her natural curiosity to good account by becoming a detective.*

▶ See also: be in sb's good **books**
It's no good/use **crying** over spilt milk.
while the **going** is good
What's good for the **goose** (is good for the gander).
hold good
You can't **keep** a good man/woman down.
if sb **knows** what's good for them
be no good/use to **man** or beast
One good turn deserves another.
good/right and **proper**
stand sb in good stead
throw good money after bad

goodbye

kiss/say/wave goodbye to sth
if you say goodbye to something, you accept that you will not have it any more or that you will not get it • *You can say goodbye to your £10. Tom never repays his debts.*

good-for-nothing

a good-for-nothing
a person, usually a man, who is lazy and does not do anything useful • *That man is a crook and a good-for-nothing.*
good-for-nothing • *Where's that good-for-nothing husband of mine?*

goods

deliver the goods *informal*
come up with the goods *informal*
if someone or something delivers the goods, they do what people hope they will do • *So far the team's new player has failed to deliver the goods. He hasn't scored in his first five games.*

your **goods and chattels** *formal*
all the things that belong to you ✍This is an old legal phrase. • *Jim arrived at the flat with all his goods and chattels packed into two shopping bags.*

goody-goody

a goody-goody
someone who tries too hard to please people in authority, especially teachers or parents • *Sandra's a real goody-goody – always doing extra homework and arriving early to lessons.*

goose

What's sauce for the goose (is sauce for the gander). *British, American & Australian old-fashioned*
What's good for the goose (is good for the gander). *American & Australian old-fashioned*
something that you say to suggest that if a particular type of behaviour is acceptable for one person, it should also be acceptable for another person • *If your husband can go out with his friends, then surely you can go out with yours. What's sauce for the goose is sauce for the gander.*

▶ See also: **cook** sb's goose
kill the goose that lays the golden egg

gooseberry

► See: **play** gooseberry

Gordian

a Gordian knot *formal*

a difficult problem ✍In an old story, King Gordius of Phrygia tied a complicated knot which no one could make loose, until Alexander the Great cut it with his sword. • *Homelessness in the inner cities has become a real Gordian knot.*

cut the Gordian knot to deal with a difficult problem in a strong, simple and effective way • *There was so much fighting between staff, she decided to cut the Gordian knot and sack them all.*

Gordon Bennett

Gordon Bennett! *British old-fashioned*

something that you say when you are surprised, shocked, or angry ✍This phrase was originally said in order to avoid saying 'God'. • *Gordon Bennett! The mortgage rate's gone up again!*

gory

the gory details *humorous*

the interesting details about an event • *I hear you went away with Stuart. I want to hear* ***all the gory details.***

gospel

accept/take sth **as gospel (truth)**

to believe that something is completely true • *You shouldn't accept as gospel everything you read in the newspapers.*

the gospel truth

the complete truth • *I didn't touch your stereo, and that's the gospel truth.*

got

► See: If you've got it, **flaunt** it!
Got it in **one**!

grab

a grab bag *American & Australian*

a mixture of different types of things • (often + **of**) *Airlines are offering a grab bag of discounts, air miles and car rentals to attract customers.*

grabs

up for grabs *informal*

if something is up for grabs, it is available to anyone who wants to compete for it • *We've got $1000 up for grabs in our new quiz. All you have to do is call this number.*

grace

There but for the grace of God (go I).

something that you say which means something bad that has happened to someone else could have happened to you • *When you hear about all these people who've lost all this money, you can't help thinking there but for the grace of God go I.*

► See also: **fall** from grace

grade

make the grade

to succeed at something, usually because your skills are good enough • (often negative) *He wanted to get into medical school but he failed to make the grade.*

grain

go against the grain

if something that you say or do goes against the grain, you do not like saying or doing it and it is not what you would usually say or do • *It goes against the grain for William to admit that he's wrong.* • *I don't think she likes to praise men. It goes against the grain.*

a grain of truth

a small amount of truth • *There's a grain of truth in what she says but it's greatly exaggerated.*

► See also: take sth with a grain of **salt**

grand

the grand old man of sth *humorous*

a man who has been involved in a particular activity for a long time and is known and respected by a lot of people • *It was in this play that he formed a double act with that other grand old man of the Berlin theatre, Bernhard Minetti.*

► See also: in the grand/great **scheme** of things

grandmother

► See: **teach** your grandmother to suck eggs

granted

take sb **for granted**

to not show that you are grateful to

someone for helping you or that you are happy they are with you, often because they have helped you or been with you so often • *One of the problems with relationships is that after a while you begin to take each other for granted.*

take sth **for granted**

to expect something to be available all the time and forget that you are lucky to have it • *We take so many things for granted in this country – like having hot water whenever we need it.*

take it for granted

to believe that something is true without first thinking about it or making sure that it is true • (usually + **that**) *I'd always seen them together and just took it for granted that they were married.*

grapevine

▶ See: **hear** sth on/through the grapevine

grasp

grasp the nettle *British & Australian*

to take action immediately in order to deal with an unpleasant situation ✍A nettle is a plant which can sting if you touch it. • *I've been putting off tackling the problem for too long and I think it's time to grasp the nettle.*

▶ See also: clutch/grasp at **straws**

grass

The grass is always greener (on the other side of the fence).

something that you say which means that other people always seem to be in a better situation than you, although they may not be • *And when I haven't been out for a while I start to envy Miriam with her great social life. Oh well, the grass is always greener.*

the grass roots

the ordinary people in a society or political organization and not the leaders • (often + **of**) *The feeling among the grass roots of the party is that the leaders aren't radical enough.*

grass-roots • (always before noun) *He's popular enough within the leadership but he doesn't have much grass-roots support.*

a grass widow *humorous*

a woman who spends a lot of time apart from her husband, often because he is working in another place • *'I hear Steve's in Florida again.' 'Yes, I've become a grass widow ever since he's had this new job.'*

▶ See also: not **let** the grass grow under your feet
be like **watching** grass grow

grate

▶ See: get/grate on sb's **nerves**

grateful

▶ See: be grateful/thankful for **small** mercies

grave

▶ See: **dig** your own grave
turn in your grave

graveyard

the graveyard shift

a period of time late at night, when people have to work, often in hospitals or factories • *I'm working the graveyard shift this week.*

gravy

the gravy train

an activity from which people make a lot of money very quickly and easily • *A lot of people thought they'd get on the gravy train in the eighties and make some money out of property.*

grease

grease sb's **palm**

to give money to someone in authority in order to persuade them to do something for you, especially something wrong • *Drug barons were greasing the palm of the chief of police.*

greased

like greased lightning *old-fashioned*

if someone does something like greased lightning, they do it very quickly • *I mentioned work and he was out of the room like greased lightning.*

greasy

the greasy pole *British & Australian*

the attempt to improve your position at work • *His ascent up the greasy pole of academic advancement was remarkably quick.*

a greasy spoon *informal*

a small, cheap restaurant which mainly

serves fried food of a low quality • *There's a greasy spoon on the corner of his street where he usually has breakfast.*

great

be going great guns

to be doing something very successfully and quickly • *I know he had a little difficulty at the start of the course but he's going great guns now.*

be no great shakes *informal*

to not be very good at doing something • *He was a very creative chef but no great shakes on the management side of business.*

go to great lengths to do sth

to try very hard to achieve something • *I went to great lengths to explain the situation to him but he still didn't seem to understand.*

go to any lengths to do sth

• *Some men will go to any lengths* (= try any method) *to disguise the fact that they're going bald.*

the great and the good *humorous*

important people • *The move toward a more democratic state will not be universally welcomed by the great and the good.*

Great minds (think alike). *humorous*

something that you say when someone else has the same idea as you or makes the same suggestion • *'Why don't we take a walk before dinner?' 'I was just going to say the same thing.' 'Ah, great minds think alike.'*

► See also: Great/Mighty **oaks** from little acorns grow.
make (a) great **play** of sth
in the grand/great **scheme** of things

greatest

► See: the best/greatest **thing** since sliced bread

Greek

It's all Greek to me. *informal*

something that you say when you do not understand something that is written or said ✍This phrase comes from Shakespeare's play, *Julius Caesar*. • *I've tried reading the manual but it's all Greek to me.*

green

be green about/around the gills *humorous*

to look ill, as if you are going to vomit • *He was out drinking last night, was he? I thought he looked a bit green about the gills this morning.*

be green with envy

to wish very much that you had something that another person has • *Sharon's going off to the south of France for three weeks and we're all green with envy.*

give sb/sth **the green light**

to give permission for someone to do something or for something to happen • (often + to do sth) *They've just been given the green light to build two new supermarkets in the region.* • (often + **to**) *The local prefect has given the green light to the dam at Serre de la Fare.*

get the green light • (often + **from**) *As soon as we get the green light from the council we'll start building.*

have green fingers

have green fingers *British & Australian*
have a green thumb *American*

to be good at keeping plants healthy and making them grow • *I'm afraid I don't have green fingers. I've killed every plant I've ever owned.* • *I was just admiring your beautiful plants, Helen. You must have a green thumb.*

green-fingered *British & Australian* • *There's plenty of rainfall from winter through to early spring, which makes it popular with green-fingered gardeners.*

greener

greener pastures
a better or more exciting job or place • *A lot of scientists are seeking greener pastures abroad because of the scarcity of opportunities at home.*

green-eyed

the green-eyed monster *humorous*
the feeling of being jealous • *Do you think his criticisms of Jack are valid or is it just a case of the green-eyed monster?*

greet

▶ See: greet/welcome sb/sth with **open** arms

grey

a grey area *British & Australian*
a gray area *American*
a subject or problem that people do not know how to deal with because there are no clear rules • *The legal difference between negligence and recklessness is a bit of a grey area.*

grey matter *British & Australian humorous*
gray matter *American humorous*
your intelligence • *It's an entertaining film but it doesn't exactly stimulate the old grey matter.*

grief

come to grief
to suddenly fail in what you are doing, often because you have an accident • *The Italian champion was in second position when he came to grief on the third lap.*

give sb **grief** *informal*
to criticize someone angrily • *Don't give me any grief – I've done all I can!*
get grief *informal* • *I've been getting a load of grief off Julie because I came home late last night.*

grim

the Grim Reaper *literary*
death ✍Death is sometimes thought of as an old man with a large curved tool for cutting crops. • *When the Grim Reaper comes for you, there's no escaping.*

hang/hold on like grim death *British & Australian informal*
to hold something very tightly, usually because you are frightened that you will fall • *Darren always drives the bike and I sit behind him, hanging on like grim death.*

grin

grin and bear it
to accept an unpleasant or difficult situation because there is nothing you can do to improve it • *I don't want to spend the whole weekend working but I guess I'll just* ***have to grin and bear it****.*

a grin like a Cheshire cat
a very wide smile ✍The Cheshire cat is a character in Lewis Carroll's book *Alice in Wonderland* and is famous for its big smile. • *I just presumed he'd got the job because he walked in here with a grin like a Cheshire cat.*
grin like a Cheshire cat • (usually in continuous tenses) *What have you got to look so happy about, walking round here grinning like a Cheshire cat?*

▶ See also: grin/smile from **ear** to **ear**

grind

grind to a halt/standstill
if an organization, system, or process grinds to a halt, it stops working, usually because of a problem • *If the computer network crashed, the whole office would grind to a halt.*

grip

be in the grip of sth
to be experiencing something unpleasant that you have no control over • *The country is currently in the grip of the worst recession for twenty years.*

get a grip (on yourself**)**
to make an effort to control your emotions and behave more calmly • *Come on, get a grip, we've got an important meeting in five minutes.* • *I just think he ought to get a grip on himself – he's behaving like a child.*
keep a grip on yourself • *I was so angry I could have hit him – I really had to keep a grip on myself.*

have a grip on sth
to have control over something • *Certainly in the first half England didn't seem to have a grip on the game.*

▶ See also: **lose** your grip

grips

come/get to grips with sth

to make an effort to understand and deal with a problem or situation • *It's further proof of the government's failure to get to grips with two of the most important social issues of our time.*

grist

(all) grist to the mill *British, American & Australian*

grist for your **mill** *American*

something that you can use in order to help you to succeed • *As an actor, all experience is grist to the mill.*

grit

grit your **teeth**

to accept a difficult situation and deal with it in a determined way • *I can't do anything to change the situation so I'll just have to grit my teeth and put up with it.*

groove

be (stuck) in a groove

to feel bored because you are doing the same things that you have done for a long time • *We never do anything exciting any more – we seem to be stuck in a groove.*

be in the groove

to be having a very successful period • *The early nineties were difficult for Carlton but he's back in the groove again with a new hit series.*

ground

be thin on the ground *British & Australian*

if things or people are thin on the ground, there are not many of them • *Bears are getting rather thin on the ground in European forests.* • *I get the impression work is a bit thin on the ground at the moment.*

OPPOSITE **be thick on the ground** *British & Australian* • *Traditional English pubs are thick on the ground in this area.*

drive/run/work yourself **into the ground**

to work so hard that you become very tired or ill • *He'll run himself into the ground if he doesn't take some time off.*

get in on the ground floor

to become involved in something from the beginning • *It is potentially a very lucrative market and those who get in on the ground floor might well make a fortune.*

get (sth) **off the ground**

if a plan or activity gets off the ground or you get it off the ground, it starts or succeeds • *The scheme should get off the ground towards the end of this year.* • *A lot more public spending will be required to get this project off the ground.*

give ground

to change your opinions or your demands in a discussion or argument so that it becomes easier to make an agreement • *The dispute is set to continue for some time as neither side seems willing to give ground.*

go to ground

to hide • (usually + *adv/prep*) *She found the constant media attention intolerable and went to ground in France for a few months.*

hold/stand your **ground**

1 to refuse to change your opinions or behaviour, even if other people try to force you to do this • *The union stood its ground in negotiations despite pressure by management to accept a pay cut.*

2 to refuse to move backwards, especially when you are being attacked • *The small, poorly armed band of guerrillas stood their ground against an overwhelming attacking force.*

run into the ground *British & Australian*

if something such as an activity or a plan runs into the ground, it fails • *The talks ran into the ground because the ceasefire was broken.*

sb's **stamping/stomping ground**

a place where you regularly spend a lot of time • *I spent an afternoon in Camden, my **old stomping ground**.*

► See also: **cut** the ground from under sb/sb's feet
gain ground
hit the ground running
prepare the ground
run sth into the ground
run sb to ground
shift your ground
suit sb down to the ground

wish the ground would swallow you up

groves

the groves of academe *formal*
universities or education • *After a year's travelling in South America, Jack returned to the groves of academe to teach Spanish at Cambridge.*

grow

grow like Topsy
to grow very fast • *The government must decide how to allocate health-care resources in the face of demand that is growing like Topsy.*

growing

growing pains
the problems or difficulties of a new organization or activity • *Even highly successful businesses will have experienced growing pains in the early days.*

grudge

► See: **bear** a grudge

grunt

grunt work *American informal*
hard work that is not very interesting • *Her job was nothing glamorous – a lot of grunt work drafting agreements for others to sign.*

► See also: donkey **work**

guard

be on (your) **guard**
to be careful to avoid being tricked or getting into a dangerous situation • *I feel I have to be on my guard with her because she's always trying to get information out of me.* • (often + **against**) *Shop assistants must always be on guard against shoplifters.*

catch/take sb **off guard**
to surprise someone by doing or saying something they were not expecting • *One of the larger airlines caught its rivals off guard yesterday by suddenly announcing a cut in fares.* • *When they asked me to babysit, I was taken off guard and found myself agreeing to it.*

drop/lower your **guard**
to stop being careful to avoid danger or difficulty • *Once he knew I wasn't a journalist, he dropped his guard and even let me take a photograph of him.*

guess

Your guess is as good as mine. *informal*
something that you say when you do not know the answer to a question • *'How long do you think this job will take?' 'Your guess is as good as mine.'*

► See also: be **anybody**'s guess

guessing

► See: **keep** sb guessing

guest

Be my guest.
something that you say in order to give someone permission to do something • *'Can I use your toilet, please?' 'Be my guest.'*

guiding

a guiding light/spirit
someone who influences a person or group and shows them how to do something successfully • *She was the founder of the company, and for forty years its guiding light.*

guilt

a guilt trip *informal*
a strong feeling of guilt • *I'm **on a guilt trip** about not visiting my parents often enough.*

send sb **on a guilt trip** *British informal*
lay/put a guilt trip on sb *American informal*
to make someone feel very guilty • *I'm tired of environmentalists who put a guilt trip on the rest of us for causing pollution with our life styles.* • *She's sent me on a guilt trip about my treatment of Steven.*

guinea

a guinea pig
if someone is used as a guinea pig, new ideas or products are tested on them • *They're looking for volunteers to act as guinea pigs for a new AIDS vaccine.*

gullet

► See: **stick** in your gullet/throat

gum

gum up the works
to prevent a machine or system from

operating correctly • *In bad weather, twice as many people use their cars on the road, which really gums up the works.*

▶ See also: be up a gum **tree**

gun

be under the gun *mainly American*
to feel anxious because you have to do something by a particular time or in a particular way • *Al's under the gun to decide by the end of the month whether to move with his company.*

hold/put a gun to sb's **head**
to use threats to force someone to do what you want • *Management are holding a gun to our heads. If we don't behave we'll lose our jobs.*

▶ See also: **jump** the gun

gunboat

gunboat diplomacy
if a country uses gunboat diplomacy, it uses the threat of military force to make another country obey it • *Gunboat diplomacy is a dangerous option in the age of nuclear weapons.*

gung-ho

gung-ho *informal*
too eager to do something, often without thinking about the risks involved in a situation • *Our new salesman is rather gung-ho.* • *I'm not sure I approve of my bank's gung-ho approach to lending.*

be gung-ho about/for sth *American informal* very interested in or excited by something • *He's been gung-ho for football ever since he played in high school.*

gunning

be gunning for sb
1 *informal* to try to harm or defeat someone • *The coach has been gunning for me from the day I joined the team.*
2 *informal* to support someone • *Which side will you be gunning for in the elections?*

guns

stick to your **guns** *British, American & Australian informal*
stand by your **guns** *American informal*
to refuse to change your ideas although other people try to make you change them ✍If a soldier sticks to his guns he continues to shoot at the enemy. • *David's family were against him becoming an actor but he stuck to his guns.* • *Stand by your guns and don't let them talk you into working full time if you don't want to.*

with (your) **guns blazing**
all guns blazing
if you do something, especially argue, with guns blazing, you do it with a lot of force and energy • *The boy's mother arrived at the school, all guns blazing, furious that her son had been suspended.*

▶ See also: **spike** sb's guns

gunwales

to the gunwales *old-fashioned*
if something is filled to the gunwales, it is very full ✍A gunwale is the top part of the side of a boat. • *The room was packed to the gunwales with food and crates of wine.*

gut

a gut feeling
a feeling that you are certain is right, even if you cannot explain why • *My gut feeling was that she was lying.*

a gut reaction
a reaction that is based on your immediate feelings about someone or something • *When a tragedy like this happens, I think people's gut reaction is anger and a desire to find someone to blame.*

▶ See also: **bust** a gut
bust a gut (laughing)

gut-bucket

a gut-bucket *informal*
someone who is very fat • *She introduced me to her son who was a real gut-bucket with tattoos all over his arms.*

guts

have your **guts for garters** *British informal*
if you say that you will have someone's guts for garters, you mean that you intend to punish them very severely • *If I catch you smoking again I'll have your guts for garters.*

slog/sweat/work your **guts out** *informal*
to work very hard or to use a lot of

effort to do something • *You've got this wonderful man slogging his guts out for you, and all you do is criticize him!* • *After working his guts out at the gym, he spoilt it all by going straight to the pub.*

▶ See also: **hate** sb's guts
spill your guts

gutser

come a gutser

1 *Australian informal* to fall while you are walking or running • *I was in a rush, tripped and came a gutser on the step.*

2 *Australian informal* to fail at something • *Paul's too confident for his own good. I hope he doesn't come a gutser.*

habit

▶ See: Why **break** the habit of a lifetime? **kick** the habit

hackles

raise (sb's) **hackles**
make (sb's) **hackles rise**

to annoy someone ✍Hackles are the hairs on the back of a dog's neck which stand up when it is angry. • *The politician's frank interview may have raised hackles in his party.* • *The movie's pro-war message made many people's hackles rise.*

sb's **hackles rise** • *She spoke to me as if I was about thirteen and I **felt my hackles rise**.*

had

have had it *informal*

1 if you say that if something happens, someone has had it, you mean that they will die or they will fail in what they are trying to do • *When they run out of ammunition, they've had it.* • *The course is hard, and if you can't face that fact, you've had it.*

2 to be tired or bored with what you are doing and decide to stop it • *I've had it for today. Let's go home.*

3 if something has had it, it is so damaged it cannot be repaired • *I think this washing machine's had it.*

have had it (up to here) *informal*

to be so angry about something that you do not want to continue with it or even think about it any more • *I've had it! From now on they can clear up their own mess.* • (often + **with**) *I've had it up to here with lawyers!*

hail-fellow-well-met

hail-fellow-well-met *old-fashioned*

a man who is hail-fellow-well-met is very friendly and pleasant, often in a way that you do not trust • *He was a hail-fellow-well-met sort of a man who'd greet you with a big slap on the back.*

hair

curl sb's **hair** *American*
make sb's **hair curl** *American*

to frighten or shock someone • *The scene where the guy follows her into the apartment curled my hair.*

get in sb's **hair** *informal*

to annoy someone, especially by being near them for a long period • *Harry usually keeps the kids occupied so they don't get in my hair while I'm cooking.*

OPPOSITE **out of** sb's **hair** • *I don't care where she is now. She's out of my hair and that's all that matters.* • *I was hoping James would take the kids to the park for a couple of hours just to **get them out of my hair**.* (= stop them annoying me by taking them away)

the hair of the dog (that bit you)

an alcoholic drink that you drink to cure the pain in your head that was caused by drinking too much alcohol the night before ✍In the past people believed that if you were bitten by a crazy dog, the injury could be made better by putting hairs from the dog's tail on it. • *It was early in the morning and Catherine reached for her glass. 'Hair of the dog?' asked Lee with a smile.*

not **a hair out of place**

if someone does not have a hair out of place, their appearance is very tidy • *She was immaculate as ever, not a hair out of place.*

a hair shirt

if someone wears a hair shirt, they choose to make their life unpleasant by not having or experiencing anything that gives them pleasure • *I don't think you have to put on a hair shirt in order to be a socialist.*

a hair's breadth

a very small distance or amount • *Enemy forces are **within a hair's breadth of** the city.* • *We were a hair's breadth away from getting caught.* (= we were almost caught)

make sb's **hair stand on end**

to make someone feel very frightened • *The thought of jumping out of an aeroplane makes my hair stand on end.*

pull/tear your **hair out**

to be very anxious about something • (often in continuous tenses) *I've been tearing my hair out trying to get the job finished on time.*

put hair(s) on your **chest** *humorous*

if you say that food or drink will put hair on someone's chest, you mean that the food will make them strong and healthy or that the drink is very alcoholic • *Here, have a swig of this. That should put hair on your chest!*

▶ See also: **harm** a hair on sb's head
Keep your hair on!
let your hair down
not **turn** a hair

hair-raising

hair-raising

very frightening • *Driving through the mountains was a hair-raising experience.*

hairs

▶ See: **split** hairs

halcyon

the halcyon days *literary*

a very happy or successful period in the past ✍Halcyon days are two weeks of good weather during the winter when the days are the shortest in the year. • (often + **of**) *She recalled the halcyon days of childhood.* • *That was in the halcyon days of the 1980's when the economy was booming.*

hale

hale and hearty

an old person who is hale and hearty is still very healthy and strong • *At 77 he is hale and hearty, getting up at six every morning to walk three miles.*

half

not **be half bad** *informal*

if something is not half bad, it is good, often better than you thought it would be • *Actually, we had dinner there and it wasn't half bad.*

be half the [dancer/writer etc.] you **used to be**

if you are half the dancer, writer etc. you used to be, you are much less good at doing something than you used to be • *She's half the tennis-player she used to be.*

be half the battle (won)

to be the most difficult part of a process so that once you have completed this part, you have almost succeeded • *When you're training a dog, getting it to trust you is half the battle.*

sb's **better/other half** *old-fashioned*

someone's husband or wife or the person with whom they have a romantic relationship • *I should think 3.30 on Wednesday will be fine but I'd better check with my other half.*

given half a/the chance *informal*

if someone would do something given half a chance, they would certainly do it if they had the opportunity • *He'd steal from his own grandmother, given half the chance.* • *Given half a chance I'd leave this job today.*

not **half** *British & Australian informal*

something that you say in order to emphasize an opinion or a statement • *He didn't half eat a lot.* • *She isn't half brave, your sister.*

Half a loaf is better than none.

something that you say which means it is better to take what you are offered, even if it is less than you wanted, because it is better than nothing • *I only got half the salary rise I asked for, but I took it anyway on the grounds that half a loaf is better than none.*

have half a mind to do sth

something that you say to a child who you are threatening with punishment • *It's the second time this month I've caught you smoking. I've half a mind to report you to your parents!*

if you have half a mind to tell someone something unpleasant, you are very seriously thinking about telling them • ***I've half a mind to tell** her to rewrite the whole report it's so bad.*

have half an ear on sth

to listen to something without giving it all your attention • *I had half an ear on the radio as he was talking to me.*

listen with half an ear • *I listened with half an ear as she explained what she'd been doing.*

have/keep half an eye on sth/sb
to watch something or someone without giving them all your attention • *I had half an eye on the TV while I was writing my letter.* • *She kept half an eye on the kids all through our conversation.*
with half an eye on sth/sb • *I ate my lunch with half an eye on the clock to make sure I didn't miss my train.*

how the other half lives
how people who are much richer than you live their lives • *As the popularity of such magazines testify, people are always curious to* ***see how the other half lives****.* • *'They spend two or three months of the summer on a luxury yacht in the south of France.' 'How the other half lives!'*

not **know the half of it** *informal*
Have not **heard the half of it!** *informal*
if someone does not know the half of it, they know that a situation is bad but they do not know how bad it is • *Tom's not happy with the situation and he doesn't even know the half of it!* • *'I hear you're having a few problems with the new guy'. 'A few problems? You haven't heard the half of it!'*

Not half! *British & Australian informal*
something that you say when you agree strongly with something that has just been said or you are keen to accept an offer • *'Do you fancy a drink, then?' 'Not half!'* • *'He's a nice-looking bloke, isn't he?' 'Not half!'*

That was a [game/meal/walk etc.] and a half! *informal*
something that you say about something that was very surprising, very good, or took a lot of time • *That was a walk and a half! I'm exhausted.*

► See also: Half/Just a **mo**.

half-arsed

half-arsed *British very informal*
half-assed *American very informal*
a half-arsed attempt to do something lacks energy and enthusiasm • *I made a half-arsed attempt to write the introduction and then went back to bed.*

half-baked

half-baked *informal*
not thought about or planned carefully • *It was just another half-baked scheme of his – it was never going to work.*

half-cock

go off at half-cock *old-fashioned*
go off half-cocked *old-fashioned*
to suddenly give your opinion without preparing what you are saying or understanding the subject you are talking about, often because you are angry • *You don't listen. You just go off at half-cock without even hearing the end of my sentence.*

half-cut

be half-cut *British & Australian old-fashioned*
to be drunk • *He was half-cut before he even got to the party.*

half-dead

be half-dead *informal*
to be very tired • *We've been walking all day and I'm half-dead.*

half-hearted

half-hearted
a half-hearted attempt to do something lacks effort and enthusiasm • *I made a half-hearted attempt to start a conversation with him and then gave up.*
half-heartedly • *A few people at the back applauded half-heartedly.*

half-mast

be at half-mast *British humorous*
if someone's trousers are at half-mast, they are too short • *His hair was dirty and his trousers at half-mast.*

halfway

a halfway house
something which combines the qualities of two different things, often something which is not as good as either of those things on their own • (often + **between**) *It's sort of a halfway house between classical music and pop.*

► See also: **meet** sb halfway

half-wit

a half-wit *informal*
a stupid person • *Some half-wit had filled the kettle too full and water spilt out everywhere.*
half-witted • *I hope she's not bringing*

that half-witted brother of hers.

halt

▶ See: **grind** to a halt/standstill

halves

not **do anything/things by halves**

if you do not do things by halves, you always make a lot of effort and do things very well • *'I didn't realise you were decorating the whole house!' 'Oh, we don't do things by halves round here.'*

ham-fisted

ham-fisted British
ham-handed American

lacking skill with the hands • *I hoped you weren't watching my ham-fisted attempts to get the cake out of the tin.*

lacking skill in the way that you deal with people • *The report criticizes the ham-fisted way in which complaints are dealt with.*

hammer

be/go at it hammer and tongs informal

to do something, especially to argue, with a lot of energy or violence • *You should have heard last night's argument – they were at it hammer and tongs till four o'clock this morning.*

come/go under the hammer

to be sold at an auction (= a public sale where objects are bought by the people who offer the most money) • *Both collections will come under the hammer and are expected to make £1m at Phillips' in London next month.*

▶ See also: drive/hammer sth **home**

hand

be in hand

if a plan or a situation is in hand, it is being dealt with • *The arrangements for the party are all in hand so we don't need to worry about that.*

have sth **in hand** • *After days of rioting, the troops now have the situation in hand.* (= are dealing with the situation)

take sb/sth **in hand** to start to deal with someone or something that is causing problems • *Their youngest child needs taking in hand, if you ask me.*

be on hand

to be near and ready if needed • *Extra supplies will be on hand, should they be needed.*

have sb/sth **on hand** • (often + to do sth) *The new store has extra staff on hand to help customers pack their shopping.*

close/near at hand

very near • *To have a few basic shops and services near at hand is a great thing.*

come/go cap in hand British, American & Australian
come/go hat in hand American

to ask someone for money or help in a way which makes you feel ashamed • (often + **to**) *I had to go cap in hand to my parents again to ask for some money.*

a firm/steady hand on the tiller

if someone has a firm hand on the tiller, they have a lot of control over a situation ✍A tiller is a long handle which is used to control the direction a boat travels. • *What people want is a president with a firm hand on the tiller.*

get out of hand

if a situation gets out of hand, it cannot be controlled any more • *Things got a little out of hand at the party and three windows were broken.* • *In my first year at college my drinking got a bit out of hand.*

give sb **a hand**

to help someone do something, especially something that involves physical effort • (often + **with**) *Could you give me a hand with these boxes, Mike?* • *Let me know when you're moving and I'll give you a hand.*

go hand in hand

if two things go hand in hand, they exist together and are connected with each other • (often + **with**) *Crime usually goes hand in hand with poor economic conditions.*

hand in glove British, American & Australian
hand and glove American

if one person or organization is working hand in glove with another, they are working together, often to do something dishonest • *It was rumoured at the time that some of the gangs were working hand in glove with the police.*

hand over fist

if you make or lose money hand over fist, you make or lose large amounts of it very quickly • *Business was good and we were making money hand over fist.*

hand over the reins

to allow someone else to control something you controlled previously, especially an organization or a country • *Company chiefs are often reluctant to* ***hand over the reins of power*** *to younger people.* • (often + **to**) *I built up the business, but I handed over the reins to my daughter last year.*

The hand that rocks the cradle (rules the world).

something that you say which means women are very powerful because they have most influence over the way in which children develop into adults • *The article claimed that most of the world's dictators had very domineering mothers. You know what they say, the hand that rocks the cradle.*

have a hand in sth

to be involved in something • *The party was basically Kim's idea but I think Lisa had a hand in it too.*

I/You have to hand it to sb

something that you say which means that you admire someone's achievement or you admire a quality in someone, even if you do not admire everything about that person • *I don't especially like the man, but you've got to hand it to him, he's brave.*

out of hand

if you refuse something out of hand, you refuse it completely without thinking about it or discussing it • *Moving to London is certainly a possibility. I wouldn't dismiss it out of hand.*

put your **hand in** your **pocket**

to give money to charity (= organizations that collect money to give to poor people, ill people etc.) • *People are more inclined to put their hands in their pockets to help children.*

put your **hand on** your **heart**

if you can put your hand on your heart and say something, you can say it knowing that it is the truth • *I couldn't put my hand on my heart and say I'd never looked at another man.*

hand on heart • *Are you telling me, hand on heart, that you have never read anyone's private mail?*

▶ See also: could do sth with one arm/hand tied behind their **back**
hand over/pass the **baton**
bite the hand that feeds you
force sb's hand
hold sb's hand
keep your hand in
lay a hand on sb
lend (sb) a hand
live (from) hand to mouth
on the **one** hand...on the other hand
overplay your hand
give/hand sth to sb on a **plate**
give/hand sth to sb on a (silver) **platter**
raise your hand against/to sb
show your hand
throw in your hand
have your fingers/hand in the **till**
tip your hand
try your hand at sth
turn your hand to sth
wait on sb hand and foot

handle

get a handle on sth *informal*

to find a way to understand a situation in order to control it • *We need to get a better handle on the effects of climate change.*

▶ See also: **fly** off the handle
handle/treat sb with **kid** gloves

hand-me-down

a hand-me-down

a piece of clothing that used to belong to an older brother or sister and is now worn by a younger brother or sister • (usually plural) *As a child I was always dressed in my sister's hand-me-downs and I longed for something new to wear.*

hands

all hands on deck
all hands to the pumps

something that you say when everyone's help is needed, especially to do a lot of work in a short amount of time • *We've got to get all this cleared up before they arrive so it's all hands on deck.*

be in sb's **hands**

to be dealt with or controlled by someone

• *The arrangements for the party are now in Tim's hands.*

leave sth **in** sb's **hands** • *So, Sue, regarding the hotel bookings and so on, can I leave all that in your hands?*

be out of sb's **hands**

if a problem or decision is out of someone's hands, they are not responsible for it any more • *The court will decide how much money you get – the decision is out of our hands.*

can't keep your **hands off** sb *informal*

if you can't keep your hands off someone you are having a sexual relationship with, you touch them very often because you feel very attracted to them • *They can't keep their hands off each other. It's embarrassing to be in their company.*

get your **hands dirty** *informal*

to involve yourself in all parts of a job, including the parts that are unpleasant, or involve hard, practical work • *Unlike other bosses, he's not afraid to get his hands dirty and the men like that in him.*

get your **hands on** sb *informal*

if you say you will kill someone when you get your hands on them, you mean you will be very angry with them • *You wait till I get my hands on her – I'll kill her!*

get/lay your **hands on** sth

to succeed in obtaining something • *As a kid I read anything I could lay my hands on.* • *If you ever get your hands on a copy, I'd love to have a look.*

sb's **hands are tied**

if someone's hands are tied, they are not free to behave in the way that they would like • *I'd like to raise people's salaries but my hands are tied.*

have your **hands full**

to be so busy that you do not have time to do anything else • (often + doing sth) *It's no use asking Alice for help, she's got her hands full looking after the kids.* • (often + **with**) *Right now I've got my hands full with preparations for the conference.*

have sth **on** your **hands**

if you have a difficult situation on your hands, you have to deal with it • *If the police carry on like this, they'll have a riot on their hands before long.* • *With four kids I suspect she's got enough on her hands.*

off sb's **hands**

if someone or something is off someone's hands, they are not responsible for them any more • *I've got a lot of freedom now the kids are off my hands.*

take sb/sth **off** sb's **hands** • *I'm willing to take the kids off your hands for a few hours, if you need me to.*

▶ See also: **change** hands
dirty your hands
fall into sb's hands
keep your hands clean
play into sb's hands
sit on your hands
wash your hands of sb/sth
win (sth) hands down
wring your hands

handwriting

▶ See: the handwriting is on the **wall**

hang

and hang the cost/expense

if you say that you will do or have something and hang the cost, you mean that you will spend whatever is necessary • *I thought for once in our lives let's treat ourselves really well and hang the cost.*

get the hang of sth *informal*

to succeed in learning how to do something after practising it • *After three weeks of using this computer I think I've finally got the hang of it.*

hang (on) in there *informal*

to continue to try to do something although it is very difficult • *All relationships go through rough times. You just have to hang in there.* • *Just hang on in there. The physical training is tough but it's worth it.*

hang a left/right *American informal*

if you tell the driver of a car to hang a left/right, you mean turn left/right • *You hang a left at the gas station and then drive straight ahead for two miles.*

hang by a thread

if something hangs by a thread, it is likely to fail in the near future • *Peace and democracy hang by a thread in this troubled country.*

hang your **head (in shame)**
to be ashamed • *Athletes caught taking drugs should hang their heads in shame.*

Hang loose! *American old-fashioned*
something that you say in order to tell someone to stay calm and relaxed • *Hang loose, guys! The rest of us will be there to back you up.*

hang out your **shingle** *American*
to start your own business, especially as a doctor or a lawyer • *He hung out his shingle in Brandon many years ago, and has been a lawyer there ever since.*

hang sb **out to dry**
to get someone into trouble, especially by making them take the blame for a bad situation • *When the department got into difficulties, his bosses simply hung him out to dry.*

hang tough *American informal*
to not change your actions or opinions although other people try to make you do this • *The President is hanging tough on the hostage crisis.*

hang up your **boots**
to permanently stop playing a sport • *After a disastrous season it is rumoured that Gregory may hang up his boots once and for all.*

hang up your hat
to leave your job for ever • *When I stop enjoying my work, that'll be the time to hang up my hat.*

▶ See also: be/hang in the **balance**
hang/hold on (to sth/sb) for **dear** life
cling on/hang on by your **fingernails**
cling on/hang on by your **fingertips**
hang/hold **fire**
hang/hold on like **grim** death
let it all hang out
Hang on a **mo**.

hanged

▶ See: I might as well be hanged/hung for a **sheep** as a lamb.

hanger-on

a hanger-on
a person who spends time with rich or important people, hoping to get an advantage • (usually plural) *Wherever there is royalty, there will always be hangers-on.*

hanging

be hanging over you
be hanging over your **head**
if something is hanging over you, it is causing you to worry all the time • *He's got financial worries hanging over him too which can't make life any easier.*

▶ See also: be **left** hanging (in the air/in midair)

hangs

Thereby/Therein hangs a tale. *British & Australian humorous*
something that you say when you have been asked about something that needs a long explanation • *'So what were you doing in Nick's garage at three o'clock in the morning?' 'Ah, thereby hangs a tale.'*

hang-up

a hang-up
a feeling of shame or worry about something in your appearance, your behaviour, or your past, especially one that other people do not understand • (often + **about**) *I think Melanie**'s got** a bit of **a hang-up** about her lack of education.* • *The English are notorious for their sexual hang-ups.*
be hung-up • (often + **about**) *Why are so many women hung-up about their bodies?*

hanky-panky

hanky-panky *old-fashioned*
sexual activity, especially when it is secret • *It was alleged that all kinds of hanky-panky went on in the president's office.*

happy

not **be a happy camper** *British & American humorous*
not **be a happy bunny** *British humorous*
to be annoyed about a situation • *Her computer crashed an hour ago and she's lost a morning's work – she's not a happy camper.*

be as happy as Larry/a sandboy *British & Australian*
be as happy as a clam *American*
to be very happy and to have no worries • *We married nine days after we met, and three years on we're happy as Larry.*

• *Since he's been at college he's as happy as a clam.*

a happy accident

a pleasant situation or event that is not planned or intended • *We never planned to have a third child – it was a happy accident.*

the happy event *humorous*

the birth of a child • *So when are they expecting the happy event?*

a happy hunting ground

a place where you can find exactly what you want ✍The happy hunting ground was a Native American way of referring to heaven, or where they went when they died. • *Flea markets are a happy hunting ground for people looking for antiques at good prices.*

a happy medium

a way of doing something which is good because it avoids being extreme • (often + **between**) *What you want from a holiday is a happy medium between activity and relaxation.* • *I'm either exercising all the time or I'm doing nothing but I can't seem to* ***find a happy medium****.*

happy-go-lucky

happy-go-lucky

a happy-go-lucky person is happy all of the time and does not worry about anything • *He struck me as a happy-go-lucky kind of guy.*

hard

be as hard as nails

to have no feelings or sympathy for other people • *She'll be good in business – she's as hard as nails.*

be hard pressed *British, American & Australian informal*

be hard pushed *British*

to be having difficulty doing something, especially because there is not enough time or money • (usually + to do sth) *I'll be hard pressed to get this report done by Friday.* • *You'd be hard pushed to find a good car for under £1,000.* • *With cuts in government funding, hospitals are hard pressed at the moment.*

be hard put to do sth

if you are hard put to do something, it is not likely that you will be able to do it • *You'd be hard put to find a better school for your kids.* • *She'll be hard put to buy her own home on what she earns.*

be hard up *informal*

to have too little money • *We're a bit hard up at the moment so I can't really afford a new coat.*

give sb **a hard time**

1 *informal* to criticize someone and make them feel guilty about something that they have done • (often + **about**) *I came home late one night last week and she's been giving me a hard time about it ever since.*

2 to treat someone severely or to cause difficulties for them • *She'd always wanted to be a teacher, but those kids gave her a really hard time.*

have a hard time (of it) • *He had a hard time last year. He lost his job and was unemployed for 6 months.*

hard feelings

anger towards a person that you have argued with • (usually negative) *It's very rare that couples break up and there are no hard feelings on either side.* • *So we're friends again, are we?* ***No hard feelings?***

hard going

difficult to do or understand • *It was a good course but I* ***found it hard going*** *in parts.*

Hard lines. *British & Australian informal*

something that you say in order to express sympathy for someone • *'I failed my driving test again.' 'Hard lines.'*

the hard sell

a method of trying very hard to persuade someone to buy something even if they do not want to • *All I did was ask for a price list and a carpet salesman started giving me the hard sell.*

OPPOSITE **the soft sell** • *We prefer to use the soft sell on our customers. We simply explain the insurance packages and leave them to decide for themselves.*

the hard stuff *humorous*

alcoholic drink • *He likes* ***a drop of the hard stuff****.*

hard to swallow

if something that someone says is hard to

swallow, it is difficult to believe • *I found her story rather hard to swallow.*

make hard work of sth/doing sth

to do something in a way which makes it more difficult than it should be • *He's really making hard work of that ironing.*

no hard and fast rules

if there are no hard and fast rules, there are no clear rules which you must obey • *There are no hard and fast rules about how much weight you can safely gain in pregnancy.*

▶ See also: be a hard/tough **act** to follow
hard **cash**
Hard/Tough **cheddar**!
Hard/Tough **cheese**!
die hard
drive a hard bargain
fall on hard times
feel hard done-by
hard/hot on sb's **heels**
hard/hot on the **heels** of sth
hit sth hard
a hard/tough **nut**
a hard/tough **nut** to crack
play hard to get
a hard/tough **row** to hoe

hardball

▶ See: **play** hardball

hard-boiled

hard-boiled *informal*

a hard-boiled person behaves as if they have no emotions • (always before noun) *Bogart plays the hard-boiled detective that women find irresistibly attractive.*

harden

harden your **heart** *slightly formal*

to make yourself stop feeling kind or friendly towards someone • *You've just got to harden your heart and tell him to leave.*

hard-nosed

hard-nosed

practical and determined • *Keaton has a reputation as a hard-nosed businessman who always gets what he wants.* • *The new hard-nosed management style is unpopular amongst employees.*

hard-on

a hard-on *taboo*

a hardening of the penis caused by sexual excitement • *I can't wait to see you – **I've got a hard-on** just thinking about it.*

hare

▶ See: **run** with the hare and hunt with the hounds

harm

harm a hair on sb's **head**

to hurt someone • (often negative) *He adores the girl – he wouldn't harm a hair on her head.* • *If he so much as harms a hair on her head, I won't be responsible for my actions.*

▶ See also: wouldn't harm/hurt a **fly**

harness

be back in harness *mainly British*

to have returned to work again after not working for a period of time • *How does it feel to be back in harness after 8 months?*

in harness

if two or more people work in harness, they work together to achieve something • *French and British police are working in harness to solve the problem.*

harvest

▶ See: **reap** a/the harvest of sth

has-been

a has-been

someone who was popular and famous in the past but is now forgotten • *I forget who the third guest was – some old has-been whose name I didn't even know.*

haste

▶ See: **Marry** in haste, repent at leisure.

hat

be wearing your **[teacher's/lawyer's etc.] hat**

have your **[teacher's/lawyer's etc.] hat on**

to be acting as you do when you are working as a teacher, lawyer etc., which may be different from the way you act in other situations • *I was wearing my teacher's hat at the meeting.*

with your **[teacher's/lawyer's etc.] hat on** • *I'd like to talk to you with your lawyer's hat on.*

I take my hat off to sb *British, American & Australian*
I tip my hat to sb *American*
something that you say which means that you admire and respect someone for something they have done • *I take my hat off to people who do voluntary work in their spare time.* • *I tip my hat to our teachers who've raised standards in the school with very few resources.*

throw/toss your **hat in the ring** *American & Australian*
to do something that makes it clear you want to compete with other people, especially to compete for a political position • *She's seriously considering throwing her hat in the ring and declaring herself a candidate for the election.*

▶ See also: I'll **eat** my hat
If the hat/shoe **fits** (wear it).
come/go hat in **hand**
hang up your hat
keep sth under your hat
pass the hat around/round
be **talking** through your hat

hatch

Down the hatch! *informal*
something that you say before drinking an alcoholic drink, especially when you are going to drink it all without stopping • *And a whisky for you. Down the hatch, as they say.*

hatches

▶ See: **batten** down the hatches

hatchet

a hatchet job *informal*
strong and unfair criticism of someone or something, especially on television or in a newspaper • *She **did a** real **hatchet job on** his latest novel in one of the Sunday papers.*

a hatchet man *informal*
someone who is employed by an organization to make changes that people do not like • *The hatchet man is called in whenever a company needs to reduce its staff.*

▶ See also: **bury** the hatchet

hate

hate sb's **guts** *informal*
to hate someone • *I hate his guts for treating my sister so badly.*

hats

hats off to sb
something that you say when you want to express your admiration for someone • *Hats off to her – it takes a lot of courage to go travelling on your own at that age.*

haul

haul ass *American very informal*
to move very quickly, especially in order to escape • *When the shooting started we hauled ass out of there.*

▶ See also: haul/pull yourself up by your **bootstraps**
drag/haul sb over the **coals**

have

have it away *British very informal*
have it off *British & Australian very informal*
to have sex with someone • (often + **with**) *She was having it away with her best friend's husband.*

have it in for sb *informal*
to be determined to harm or criticize someone • *Zoe's really got it in for me. She went and told my mother I'd been smoking.*

have it out with sb
to talk to someone about something they have done which makes you angry, in order to try to solve the problem • *She's late for work every morning – I'm going to have to have it out with her.*

▶ See also: have/hold all the **aces**
have a **ball**
have your **cake** and eat it (too)
have/hold all the **cards**
not have the **faintest** (idea)
have a **field** day
have a **finger** in every pie
have your **finger** on the pulse
have/throw a **fit**
not have the **foggiest** (idea/notion)
have/keep a **foot** in both camps
have a **go** at sb
have it on **good** authority
have your **guts** for garters
have a **hand** in sth
I/You have to **hand** it to sb
have your **hands** full
have sth on your **hands**

to have the **hots** for sb
have the **measure** of sb/sth
have your **nose** in a book
catch/have sb dead to **rights**
Have sth will **travel**!
have/keep your **wits** about you
have **words**

haw

hum and haw *mainly British*
hem and haw *American & Australian*
to take a long time to say something and speak in a way that is not clear, in order to avoid giving an answer • *He hemmed and hawed and finally admitted taking the money.*
humming and hawing *mainly British* • *After much hemming and hawing and throat-clearing, she announced that she was leaving.*

hawk

▶ See: **watch** sb like a hawk

hay

make hay while the sun shines
to do something while the situation or conditions are right • *I've got a few hours to finish the housework before the kids come home so I might as well make hay while the sun shines.*

▶ See also: **hit** the hay

haywire

go haywire *informal*
if a system or machine goes haywire, it stops working as it should and starts working in a way that is completely wrong • *My CD player goes haywire every time my neighbour uses his cordless phone.*

head

[laugh/scream/shout etc.] your head off
to laugh/scream/shout etc. very much and very loudly • *He laughed his head off when he read the letter.*

an old head on young shoulders
a wise head on young shoulders
a child or young person who thinks and talks like an older person who has more experience of life • *My little nephew said people who dislike other people don't like themselves very much. That's an old head on young shoulders.*

be banging/hitting your **head against a brick wall**
to keep asking someone to do something which they never do • *I've been trying to get the rules changed for years now but I'm hitting my head against a brick wall.* • *He never listens to me – sometimes I feel like I'm banging my head against a brick wall.*

be head over heels (in love)
to be in love with someone very much, especially at the beginning of a relationship • *It's obvious that they're head over heels in love with each other.*
fall head over heels (in love) • *As soon as we met we fell head over heels in love.* • *I fell head over heels in love with Simon on our first date.*

be in over your **head**
to be involved in a situation that is too difficult for you to deal with • *I'm in over my head with all these exhibition arrangements.*

be out of your **head** *British, American & Australian informal*
be off your **head** *British & Australian informal*
1 to be crazy • *He took the car out in this weather – he must be off his head!*
2 to not be in control of your behaviour because of the effects of alcohol or drugs • *She's completely off her head, she is – what's she been drinking?*

bite/snap sb's **head off** *informal*
to answer someone angrily • *I only asked if I could borrow your bike. There's no need to bite my head off!* • *She snaps his head off every time he opens his mouth.*

build/get/work up a head of steam
to get enough energy, support, or enthusiasm to do something effectively ✍A head of steam is the pressure that is needed in the engine of an old-fashioned steam train to make it start moving. • *In the last three months the campaign has built up a good head of steam.*

can't make head nor/or tail of sth
to not be able to understand something at all • *We couldn't make head or tail of the film.* • *'What does his message say?' 'I*

don't know – I can't make head or tail of it.'

come to a head

if a problem or a disagreement comes to a head, it becomes so bad that you have to start dealing with it • *Things hadn't been good between them for a while but it all came to a head last week when Phil failed to come home one night.*

bring sth **to a head** • *The row over the project has brought to a head a more fundamental disagreement over funding.*

do sb's **head in** *British & Australian informal*

to make someone feel confused and unhappy • *Getting up at 4 o'clock every morning is doing my head in.* • *I've been trying to make sense of all these figures and it's doing my head in.*

get your head around sth

get your **head around** sth *informal*

to be able to understand something • (usually negative) *He's tried to explain the rules of the game dozens of times but I just can't get my head around them.*

get your **head down** *British & Australian*

to work hard at something that involves reading or writing • *I'm sure I can finish the article – I just need to get my head down this afternoon.*

get/put your **head down**

to sleep for a short while • *I'm just going to put my head down for an hour – I feel so tired.*

give sb their **head**

to allow someone the freedom to do what they want • *He's got some great ideas. Why not give him his head and see what kind of campaign he comes up with.*

go head to head

to compete with someone directly • (often + **with**) *The tobacco industry's best lawyers will go head to head with the government in court tomorrow.*

go over sb's **head**

1 to talk to or deal with someone's boss without talking to them first • *I really don't want to go over her head but if she won't listen to me I have no choice.*

2 if a piece of information goes over someone's head, they do not understand it • *The bit about tax went straight over my head – was it important?*

go to sb's **head**

1 if an alcoholic drink goes to someone's head, it makes them feel drunk very quickly • *That glass of wine I had before supper went straight to my head.*

2 if success goes to someone's head, it makes them believe they are more important than they are • *Just because you won the poetry prize, you won't let it go to your head now, will you?*

have a head start

to have an advantage that makes you more likely to be successful • (often + **on**) *Bigger companies have a head start on us.*

give sb **a head start** • (often + **over**) *Bamforth's natural popularity gave him a head start over the other leadership contenders.*

have your **head (stuck) up** your **arse** *British & Australian taboo*

to spend so much time thinking about yourself that you have no time to think about other more important things • *'What does Charles think about it?' 'Who knows? He's got his head stuck so far up his arse he probably isn't even aware that there's a problem.'*

have your **head in the clouds**

to not know what is really happening around you because you are paying too much attention to your own ideas • *He's an academic. They've all got their heads in the clouds.*

with your **head in the clouds** • *He was walking along with his head in the clouds as usual when he tripped over a paving stone.*

have your **head screwed on (the right way)** *informal*
if someone has their head screwed on the right way, they do not do stupid things • *Don't worry about Sal, she'll be all right – she's got her head screwed on the right way.*

head and shoulders above [the others/the rest etc.]
much better than other similar people or things • *He's a head and shoulders above the other actors in the film.* • *When you think back on the other writers of this period, James* ***stands head and shoulders*** *above them all.*

the head honcho *mainly American informal*
the most important person in an organization • *You'll have to ask Alan, he's the head honcho in our department.*

sb's **head on a plate/platter**
if you want someone's head on a plate you are very angry with them and want them to be punished • *The director was furious at what had happened and wanted Watt's head on a platter.*

on sb's **(own) head be it** *slightly formal*
something that you say in order to tell someone what they intend to do is silly and they must accept the blame or responsibility if it goes wrong • *If you don't want to take out any insurance, ok, but on your head be it.*

put/stick your **head above the parapet**
to be brave enough to state an opinion that might upset people • *Kearton was one of the very few to put his head above the corporate parapet and speak his mind in public.*

raise/rear its (ugly) head
if something unpleasant raises its ugly head, it becomes a problem that people have to deal with • *All over Europe, racism is rearing its ugly head once more.*

stand/turn sth **on its head**
to make an idea or belief the opposite of what it was before • *The first feminists simply took the accepted view that men were superior to women and turned it on its head.*

take it into your **head** to do sth
to decide to do something, often something that seems silly or surprising • *He's taken it into his head to become really jealous.*

▶ See also: put your head/neck on the **block**
bury your head in the sand
hang your head (in shame)
hold your head up high
keep your head
keep your head above water
keep your head down
knock sth on the head
lose your head
need your head examined/examining

heading

▶ See: be heading/riding for a **fall**

headless

▶ See: like a headless **chicken**

headlights

be like a deer/rabbit caught in the headlights
to be so frightened or surprised that you cannot move or think • *Each time they asked him a question he was like a deer caught in the headlights.*

headlines

hit/make the headlines
to become important news and be reported in the newspapers and on the television and radio • *The latest scandal to hit the headlines is about a minister's son arrested for drug-dealing.*

heads

heads will roll
something that you say which means people will lose their jobs as punishment for making serious mistakes • *If the accident was caused by company negligence, then heads will roll.*

put their **heads together**
if a group of people put their heads together, they think about something in order to get ideas or to solve a problem • *If we put our heads together I know we*

can come up with a design that really works.

▶ See also: **turn** heads

headway

make headway

to make progress • (often negative) *Talks between the two countries are making very little headway.*

heap

▶ See: **fall** in a heap

hear

can't hear yourself **think**
can barely/hardly hear yourself **think**

if you can't hear yourself think, there is so much noise around you that it is impossible to hear anything • *The music was so loud I could hardly hear myself think.*

hear sth **on/through the grapevine**

to hear news from someone who heard the news from someone else • (usually + **that**) *I heard on the grapevine that she was pregnant, but I don't know anything more.*

won't hear a word (said) against sb/sth

if you won't hear a word said against someone or something, you refuse to believe anything bad about them • *He's completely infatuated with the woman and won't hear a word said against her.*

heard

You could have heard a pin drop.

something that you say in order to describe a situation where there was complete silence, especially because people were very interested or very surprised by what was happening • *Margaret's ex-husband turned up at the wedding. Honestly, you could have heard a pin drop.*

▶ See also: have not heard the **half** of it
have heard/seen the **last** of sb/sth

heart

be all heart

to be very kind and generous ✍This phrase is often used humorously to mean the opposite. • *Ellie can't bear to see anyone upset – she's all heart.* • *'I'm sorry they're splitting up, but at least she gets to keep the car.' 'You're all heart!'*

close/dear to sb's **heart**

if something is dear to someone's heart, it is very important to them • *Animal rights is an issue very close to my heart.*

cry/sob your **heart out** *informal*

to cry a lot • *Poor little love, her cat died and she's been crying her heart out all afternoon.*

have a heart of gold

to be extremely kind and helpful • *She'll do anything for anyone – she's got a heart of gold.*

have a heart of stone

to be cruel and have no sympathy for people • *He wouldn't help his own mother if she needed it – he's got a heart of stone.*

Have a heart! *humorous*

something that you say in order to ask someone to be kinder to you • *Have a heart! I can't walk another step!*

your **heart bleeds**

if your heart bleeds for someone who is in trouble, you feel sadness and sympathy for them ✍This phrase is often used humorously to mean the opposite. • (often + **for**) *My heart bleeds for the poor children caught up in the fighting.* • *Brenda can't afford another diamond necklace? My heart bleeds!*

your **heart goes out to** sb

if your heart goes out to someone who is in trouble, you feel sympathy for them • *Our hearts go out to the families of the victims of this terrible tragedy.*

sb's **heart is in** their **boots**

if someone's heart is in their boots, they feel sad or worried • *His heart was in his boots as he waited for news of the accident.*

sb's **heart is in** their **mouth**

if someone's heart is in their mouth, they feel extremely nervous • *My heart was in my mouth as I walked onto the stage.*

sb's **heart is in the right place**

if someone's heart is in the right place, they are a good and kind person even if they do not always seem to be • *Jerry's a bit annoying sometimes but his heart's in the right place.*

sb's **heart isn't in** sth

if someone's heart is not in something that they are doing, they are not very interested in it • *She was studying law, but her heart wasn't in it and she gave up after a year.*

sb's **heart misses/skips a beat**

if someone's heart misses a beat, they suddenly feel so excited or frightened that their heart beats faster • *Ben walked into the room and her heart skipped a beat.*

sb's **heart sinks**

if someone's heart sinks, they start to feel sad or worried • *He looked at the huge pile of work on his desk and his heart sank.*

in your **heart of hearts**

if you know something in your heart of hearts, you are certain of it although you might not want to admit it • ***I knew in my heart of hearts*** *that something was wrong, but I just wasn't ready to deal with it.* • *Do you believe in your heart of hearts that things will get better?*

know/learn sth **(off) by heart**

if you know or learn something, especially a piece of writing, by heart, you know or learn it so that you can remember it perfectly • *He's my favourite poet. I know several of his poems by heart.*

lose heart

to stop believing that you can succeed • *Don't lose heart, there'll be plenty more chances for promotion.*

a man/woman after your **own heart**

if someone is a man or woman after your own heart, you admire them because they do or believe the same things as you • *He likes a good curry – a man after my own heart.*

put your **heart and soul into** sth/doing sth

to do something with a lot of energy and interest • *He put his heart and soul into running that café.*

heart and soul • *She loves him heart and soul.* (= completely)

take heart

to start to feel more hopeful and more confident • (often + **from**) *House owners can take heart from the news that property prices are starting to rise again.*

take sth **to heart**

if you take criticism or advice to heart, you think about it seriously, often because it upsets you • *Don't take it to heart – he was only joking about your hair.*

to your **heart's content**

if you do something enjoyable to your heart's content, you do it as much as you want to • *The pool is open all day so you can swim to your heart's content.*

▶ See also: **bare** your heart/soul
break sb's heart
It's/You're **breaking** my heart!
cross my heart (and hope to die).
sb, **eat** your heart out!
harden your heart
let your heart rule your head
lose your heart to sb
open your heart
pour your heart out
set your heart on sth/doing sth
strike at the heart of sth
wear your heart on your sleeve

hearth

hearth and home *literary*

your family and home • *His first loyalties are to hearth and home.*

heartstrings

tear/tug at your **heartstrings**
tear/tug at the heartstrings

if something or someone tugs at your heartstrings, they make you feel strong love or sympathy • *It's the story of a lost child – guaranteed to tug at the heart-strings.*

heart-to-heart

a heart-to-heart

a serious conversation between two people in which they talk honestly about their feelings • *We had a real heart-to-heart and we're getting on much better now.*

heart-to-heart • (always before noun) *Have you tried having a heart-to-heart talk with him?*

heat

the heat is on

if the heat is on, you are very busy or in a difficult situation • *There are only 3 weeks left before the deadline, so the heat is on.*

in the heat of the moment

if you say or do something in the heat of

the moment, you say or do it without thinking because you are angry or excited • *Frank doesn't hate you. He just said that in the heat of the moment.*

put the heat on sb

1 *British, American & Australian* to try to force or persuade someone to do something • (usually + to do sth) *Environmental groups are putting the heat on the government to stop pollution from power stations.*

2 *American & Australian* if you put the heat on someone who is competing with you, you start to do well so they have to work harder or play better • *The Dodgers have won three games in a row and are starting to put the heat on the Mets.*

take the heat off sb

to stop people criticizing or attacking someone • *If your deputy admitted responsibility and resigned, it would take a lot of the heat off you.*

▶ See also: If you can't **stand** the heat, get out of the kitchen.
turn up the heat

Heath Robinson

Heath Robinson *British*

if a machine or system is Heath Robinson, it is very complicated in a way that is funny, but not practical or effective ✍Heath Robinson was an English artist who drew strange, complicated machines that could do simple jobs. • *My granny's got this great Heath Robinson device for slicing eggs.*

heave

give sb **the (old) heave ho** *informal*

to make someone leave a job, or to end your relationship with someone • (usually passive) *When sales fell, most of the staff were given the old heave ho.*

heaven

a marriage/match made in heaven

1 a marriage which is likely to be happy and successful because the two people are very well suited to each other • *Jane and Pete had exactly the same likes and interests – it was a marriage made in heaven.*

2 a combination of two things or two people which is very successful • *Strawberries and cream are a marriage made in heaven.*

▶ See also: God/Heaven **help** sb
move heaven and earth

heavens

the heavens opened *literary*

something that you say which means it started to rain a lot • *Suddenly, the heavens opened and we all had to run indoors.*

heavy

be heavy going

1 if something, especially something you read, is heavy going, it is not easy or enjoyable • *The first half of the novel is rather heavy going, but don't give up.*

2 if someone is heavy going, they are boring • *Please don't make me sit next to Dennis at the party. I find him really heavy going.*

have a heavy foot *American informal*

to drive a car too fast • *She has a heavy foot – does the trip in half the time it takes me!*

be heavy-footed *American informal* • *I don't think he's heard of speed limits. He's pretty heavy-footed.*

a heavy date *American & Australian humorous*

a planned meeting between two people who are very interested in having a romantic or sexual relationship • *I think Carol has a heavy date – she's been in the bathroom for over an hour.*

a heavy hitter *American*

someone who is powerful and has achieved a lot • *Have you seen his resumé? He's a real heavy hitter.*

heavy petting

the activity of kissing and touching someone sexually • *That baby couldn't be mine. We never got further than some heavy petting.*

make heavy weather of sth/doing sth *British & Australian*

to take a longer time than necessary to do something • *He's making heavy weather of writing his report – Ingrid finished hers days ago.*

heavy-duty

heavy-duty *American & Australian informal*
complicated and very serious • (always before noun) *Studies show that the homeless develop some heavy-duty health problems living on the streets.*

heavy-handed

heavy-handed
1 if you try to control someone or something in a heavy-handed way, you use more force than is necessary or suitable • *His heavy-handed style of management is extremely unpopular.*
2 if an attempt to tell or teach someone something is heavy-handed, it is too obvious • *The theme of drug abuse is treated in a way that is convincing without being heavy-handed.*

heck

(just) for the heck of it *American & Australian*
if you do something for the heck of it, you do it only because you want to or because you think it is funny • *They spent the afternoon phoning different numbers and talking to strangers – just for the heck of it.*

hedge

hedge your **bets**
to try to avoid giving an opinion or choosing only one thing, so that whatever happens in the future you will not have problems or seem stupid • (sometimes + **on**) *Journalists are hedging their bets on the likely outcome of the election.* • *I decided to hedge my bets by buying shares in several different companies.*

heebie-jeebies

give sb **the heebie-jeebies** *informal*
to make someone feel anxious or frightened • *Walking across the park after dark gives me the heebie-jeebies.*

heel

bring/call sb **to heel**
to force someone to obey you • *He decided that threatening to sue the publishers was the easiest way of bringing them to heel.*

come to heel
to stop behaving in a way that annoys someone in authority and to start obeying their orders • *A few government rebels refused to come to heel and had to be expelled from the party.*

under sb's **heel** *formal*
if you are under someone's heel, they have complete control over you • *For nine years this isolated community lived under the heel of China.*

heels

at sb's **heels**
1 if you are at someone's heels, you are following very close behind them • *Dr Grange walked through the ward with a group of student doctors at his heels.*
2 if you are at the heels of someone that you are competing with, you are very close to defeating them • *With so many promising young contenders at his heels, Roper can't afford to make any mistakes.* • *There are many younger women **snapping at her heels**, eager to replace her as company director.*

hard/hot on sb's **heels**
1 if you are hard on someone's heels, you are following very close behind them, especially because you are trying to catch them • *She ran down the steps with a group of journalists hard on her heels.*
2 if you are hard on the heels of someone that you are competing with, you are very close to defeating them • *They know we're hard on their heels and they've got to win their next three games to retain the championship.*

hard/hot on the heels of sth
if something comes hard on the heels of something else, it happens very soon after it • *A film contract **came hard on the heels of** the success of their first album.*

take to your **heels**
to run away quickly • *As soon as they saw the soldiers coming, they took to their heels.*

► See also: **cool** your heels
dig your heels in
drag your feet/heels
kick your heels
kick up your heels

hell

(a) hell on earth
a living hell
if a place or a situation is hell on earth, it is extremely unpleasant • *Soldiers who survived the war in the jungle described it as hell on earth.*

(just) for the hell of it *informal*
if you do something for the hell of it, you do it only because you want to, or because you think it is funny • *I decided to dye my hair bright green, just for the hell of it.*

the [child/house/mother etc.] from hell *humorous*
the worst or most unpleasant person or thing of that type that anyone can imagine • *His mother's awful. She really is the mother-in-law from hell.*

[fight/run/work etc.] like hell
if you fight, run or work like hell, you do it a lot or very quickly • *We heard the alarm and ran like hell.*

all hell breaks loose *informal*
if all hell breaks loose, a situation suddenly becomes noisy and violent, usually with a lot of people arguing or fighting • *This big guy walked up to the bar and hit Freddie and suddenly all hell broke loose.*

be hell on wheels *American informal*
to behave in an angry or difficult way • *When he was drinking, Ken was hell on wheels.*

catch/get hell *American & Australian informal*
if you are going to catch hell, someone will be very angry with you • *We're going to catch hell when she finds out we used her car.*

come hell or high water
if you say you will do something come hell or high water, you mean you are determined to do it even if it is difficult • *I'll get you to the airport by 12 o'clock, come hell or high water.*

frighten/scare the hell out of sb *informal*
to make someone feel very frightened • *He drives like a madman – frightens the hell out of me.*

get the hell out *very informal*
to leave a place very quickly • (usually + **of**) *We didn't stop to argue, we just got the hell out of there.* • (often an order) *Get the hell out of my house, before I call the cops.*

give sb **hell** *informal*
1 to speak to someone in a very angry way, because they have done something which has annoyed or upset you • *Did your Dad give you hell about the dent in the car?*
2 to make someone suffer • (usually in continuous tenses) *The children have been giving me hell all afternoon, so I'm not in a very good mood.* • *His new shoes are giving him hell.*

Give them hell!
something that you say in order to tell someone who is going to take part in a competition to try as hard as they can to win • *Remember, you're the best. Now go out there and give them hell!*

go hell for leather *informal*
to go somewhere or do something very quickly • *He was going hell for leather to get to the supermarket before it closed.*

go through hell
to have a very unpleasant experience, especially one that lasts for a long period of time • *The poor woman's been going through hell over the last few months, not knowing whether her son was alive or dead.*

go to hell in a handbasket/handcart *American informal*
if a person or system is going to hell in a handbasket, they are in an extremely bad state and becoming worse • *He believes the welfare system in this country is going to hell in a handcart.*

Go to hell! *very informal*
an impolite way of telling someone that what they do or say is not important to you • *'I don't think it's a good idea to shout at him.' 'Oh, go to hell!'*

not **have a chance/hope in hell**
to have no chance at all of achieving something • (usually + **of** + doing sth) *She hasn't a hope in hell of passing these exams.*

Hell hath no fury (like a woman scorned).
something that you say which means a

woman will make someone suffer if they treat her badly • *Don't be so sure she'll forgive you. Hell hath no fury like a woman scorned.*

Hell's bells! *old-fashioned*
something that you say when you are very surprised or annoyed • *Hell's bells, the washing machine's overflowing again!*

put sb **through hell**
to make someone suffer • *Our coach put us through hell trying to get us fit for the big race.*

there'll be hell to pay *informal*
something that you say which means someone will be very angry if something happens • *There'll be hell to pay if she doesn't get the money in time.*

to hell with sb/sth *very informal*
an impolite way of saying that someone or something is not important to you any more • *To hell with saving money! I'm going shopping.*

until hell freezes over *informal*
if you say that someone can do something until hell freezes over, you mean they will not get the result they want • *They can talk until hell freezes over – they won't make me change my mind.*
when hell freezes over if you say that something will happen when hell freezes over, you mean that it will never happen • *Taxes will be abolished when hell freezes over.*

what the hell *informal*
something that you say when you suddenly change your plans to show that you will not worry about any problems this might cause • *I was going to work this evening, but what the hell – let's go to a movie instead.*

▸ See also: **play** (merry) hell
play (merry) hell with sth
raise hell
would **see** sb in hell before you would do sth
be **shot** to hell/pieces

hell-bent

be hell-bent on sth/doing sth
to be determined to do something, usually something that people think is wrong • *Local fans seemed hell-bent on causing as much trouble as possible during the match.*

help

God/Heaven help sb
1 something that you say in order to warn someone that they may be hurt or punished • *Heaven help you if your father catches you wearing his best jacket!*
2 something that you say when you are worried about someone who is in a very dangerous or unpleasant situation • *God help anyone who has to be outdoors on a dreadful night like this!*

helter-skelter

helter-skelter
if you do something helter-skelter, you do it very quickly and without organization • *We all ran helter-skelter down the stairs as soon as the alarm sounded.*
helter-skelter • (always before noun) *Police have been unable to control the helter-skelter growth of the drugs trade.*

hem

▸ See: hem and **haw**

hen

a hen night/party *British & Australian*
a party for women only, especially one that is organized for a woman who is soon going to get married • *Barbara's having her hen night a week before the wedding.*

herd

▸ See: **ride** herd on sb/sth

here

▸ See: here **today**, gone tomorrow

hidden

a hidden agenda
a reason for doing something that you are hiding by pretending that you have a different reason • *He stressed that the review was to identify staffing needs and there was no hidden agenda to cut jobs.*

hide

hide your **light under a bushel**
to avoid letting people know that you are good at something, usually because you are shy • (often in continuous tenses) *I didn't realize you could play the piano –*

you've been hiding your light under a bushel.

▶ See also: cover/hide a **multitude** of sins
haven't **seen** hide nor hair of sb/sth
tan sb's hide

hiding

be on a hiding to nothing *British informal*
to be in a situation where it is impossible to succeed • *We were on a hiding to nothing trying to get more money out of the government.*

high

be as high as a kite

1 *informal* to behave in a silly and excited way because you have taken drugs or drunk a lot of alcohol • *I tried to talk to her, but she was as high as a kite.*

2 *informal* to feel very happy and excited • *Winning the prize gave my self-confidence a tremendous boost; I felt as high as a kite for several days afterwards.*

be for the high jump *British & Australian*
if someone is for the high jump, they will be punished or severely criticized for something they have done wrong • *She'll be for the high jump when her mother finds out she's been smoking.*

climb/get on your **high horse**
if someone gets on their high horse about a subject, they become angry about it and start criticizing other people as if they are better or more clever than them • (often + **about**) *It's no good getting on your high horse about single parents. You can't force people to get married.*
come/get (down) off your high horse to stop talking as if you were better or more clever than other people • *It's time you came down off your high horse and admitted you might have made a mistake.*

from on high
from someone in a position of authority • *All the rules are imposed from on high.*

high and mighty
someone who is high and mighty behaves as if they are more important than other people • *Ellie's started acting all high and mighty since she got her promotion.*
the high and mighty *humorous* important people • *The prince was only allowed to socialize with the high and mighty and had no contact with ordinary people.*

the high ground

1 if a person or an organization has the high ground, they are in the best and most successful situation • *His company holds the high ground in the area of multi-media disks.* • *Both parties could be seen trying to* ***take the high ground*** *on issues such as education.*

2 if something has the high ground, it is thought to be of good quality, serious, and honest • *Our programmes hold the high ground of British broadcast journalism.* • *We have lost* ***the moral high ground*** *by backing regimes with poor human rights records.*

high jinks
excited and often silly behaviour when people are enjoying themselves • *They were dancing on the tables and getting up to all sorts of high jinks.*

a high roller *American & Australian*
someone who spends a lot of money in a careless way, especially risking money in games • *He became known as a high roller, and was invited to the biggest gambling tables in town.*

hunt/search high and low
to search everywhere for something • (usually + **for**) *I've been hunting high and low for the certificate, but I still haven't found it.*

in high dudgeon *humorous*
if you do something in high dudgeon, you do it because you are very angry • *Slamming the door in Meg's face, she drove off in high dudgeon.*

it's high time
if you say it's high time that something happened, you mean that it should already have been done • *Her parents decided it was high time she started paying some rent.* • (often + **that**) *It's high time that nurses were given better pay and conditions.*

on high
something or someone on high is in heaven • *The angels on high sang His praises.*

smell/stink to high heaven
to smell very bad • *That chicken farm stinks to high heaven.*

▶ See also: high on the/sb's **agenda**
leave sb high and dry
live high off/on the hog
pile it/them high and sell it/them cheap

high-flier

a high-flier
a high-flyer
someone who is very successful at their job and soon becomes powerful or rich • *A high-flier in the eighties, he was earning over £200 000 a year.*

highly-strung

highly-strung *British & Australian*
high-strung *American*
nervous and easily upset • *Anna has always been highly-strung, whereas her brother is one of the most relaxed people you could meet.*

highways

the highways and byways *literary*
the highways and byways of a place are its roads and paths • (usually + **of**) *They travelled the highways and byways of Britain to find people who could still sing the old traditional folksongs.*

hike

▶ See: **Take** a hike/walk!

hill

be over the hill *informal*
someone who is over the hill is too old to do things well • *In the world of pop music, people think you're over the hill at the age of twenty-five.*

up hill and down dale *literary*
if you travel up hill and down dale, you travel all over an area • *The man carried his basket of goods up hill and down dale.*

▶ See also: not be **worth** a hill of beans

hilt

(up) to the hilt
1 if you do something to the hilt, you do it in the strongest and most complete way that you can • *All through the trial, he has backed his wife up to the hilt.* • *They took the new aircraft and tested it to the hilt.*
2 if you borrow to the hilt, you borrow as much money as you can, often so much that it is difficult to pay it back • *We can't raise any more money – we're mortgaged up to the hilt as it is.* • *With the government borrowing up to the hilt we can expect tax rises.*

hind

▶ See: can **talk** the hind leg(s) off a donkey

hip

▶ See: be **joined** at the hip
shoot from the hip

hit

hit sb **(right) between the eyes** *informal*
if something hits someone between the eyes, it shocks them • *I remember when I read that article. It hit me right between the eyes.*

hit a/the (brick) wall *informal*
if you hit the wall when you are trying to achieve something, you reach a situation where you cannot make any more progress • *We've just about hit the wall in terms of what we can do to balance the budget.* • *The enquiry hit a brick wall of banking security.*

hit and/or miss
if something is hit and miss, you cannot be certain of its quality because it is sometimes good and sometimes bad • *We used a cheap printer, but the quality was a bit hit or miss.* • *Weather forecasting used to be a very hit-and-miss affair.*

hit sth **hard**
to cause something to be much less successful • (usually passive) *The tourist trade has been hit hard following the recent spate of bombings.*

hit sb **like a ton of bricks** *American informal*
to surprise or shock someone very much • *The truth hit him like a ton of bricks. The woman in the video was his own sister.*

a hit list
1 a list of people that someone is planning to kill • *His name was on a terrorist hit list.*
2 a list of people or organizations that someone plans to do bad things to,

especially to get rid of • *There are a hundred schools on the department's hit list, which are threatened with closure if their standards do not improve.*

a hit man
a criminal who is paid to kill people • *A professional hit man can be hired for around £10,000.*

hit the books

hit the books *American & Australian informal*
to study • *I can't go out tonight. I've got to hit the books.*

hit the bottle
to start drinking too much alcohol regularly, usually in order to forget your problems • *He lost his job and hit the bottle.*
be on the bottle • *She wasn't making much sense when I talked to her. I think she's on the bottle again.*

hit the buffers *British*
if a plan or activity hits the buffers, it fails to develop or is stopped ✍The buffers are two pieces of metal at the end of a railway line that a train will hit if it does not stop. • *The talks hit the buffers after only 4 hours.*

hit the ceiling/roof *informal*
to become very angry and start shouting • *If I'm late again he'll hit the roof.*

hit the deck/dirt *American & Australian informal*
to fall to the ground, or to quickly lie on the ground, especially to avoid danger • *The shooting started, and I heard someone shout 'Hit the deck!'*

hit the ground running *mainly American*
to immediately work very hard and successfully at a new activity • *If elected, they promise to hit the ground running in their first few weeks of office.*

hit the jackpot
to be very successful, often in a way which means you make a lot of money • *When my second book was published I thought I'd really hit the jackpot.*

hit the mark
to be correct, suitable, or successful • *If you're looking for a word to describe Dave, 'urbane' would probably hit the mark.* • *She had a good voice, but her songs never quite hit the mark.*

hit the sth **mark**
to reach a certain point or level • *Did the temperature really hit the -32 degrees centigrade mark last winter?* • *His debts have hit the $3 million mark.*

hit the nail on the head
to describe exactly what is causing a situation or problem • *I think Mick hit the nail on the head when he said that what's lacking in this company is a feeling of confidence.*

hit the road
to start a journey • *It's getting late – I'd better hit the road.*

hit the sack *British, American & Australian informal*
hit the hay *American informal*
to go to bed • *I'm going to hit the sack – I'm exhausted.*

hit the skids
1 *Australian informal* to leave a place quickly • *When his ex-girlfriend arrived at the party Ben really hit the skids.*
2 *Australian informal* to make a vehicle stop very suddenly • *A car suddenly pulled out in front of us and Jake hit the skids.*
3 *Australian informal* to get into a very bad situation, especially by losing your money, home, or job • *Poor old Dennis has really hit the skids since he split up with his wife.*

hit the spot
if food hits the spot, it tastes good and

makes you feel satisfied • *Mmm, that pecan pie hit the spot.*

hit sb **where it hurts (most)**
to do something which will upset someone as much as possible • *She hit him where it hurt most – in his bank account.* • *If you want to hit her where it really hurts, tell her she's putting on weight again.*

not **know what hit** you
to feel very shocked and confused because something, usually something bad, happens to you suddenly when you were not expecting it • *The poor man stood there not knowing what had hit him, while the police arrested his wife and son.*
before sb **knows what hit** them
• *We'll break down the door and have the handcuffs on them before they know what's hit them.*

▶ See also: hit/make the **headlines**
hit/strike **home**
hit/touch a (raw) **nerve**
hit/press/push the **panic** button
hit/strike **pay** dirt
hit/strike the **right** note
hit your **stride**

hitch

hitch your **wagon to** sb/sth
hitch your **wagon to a star**
to try to become successful by becoming involved with someone or something that is already successful or has a good chance of becoming successful • *He wisely decided to hitch his wagon to the environmentalist movement, which was then gaining support throughout the country.* • *She hitched her wagon to a rising young star on the music scene.*

hitting

▶ See: be banging/hitting your **head** against a brick wall

hobbyhorse

on your **hobbyhorse**
if someone is on their hobbyhorse, they are talking about a subject which they think is interesting and important, and which they talk about at any time that they can, even if other people are not interested • *Don't mention tax, or Bernard'll **get on his hobbyhorse** again.*

Hobson

Hobson's choice
a situation in which it seems that you can choose between different things or actions, but there is really only one thing that you can take or do ✍Thomas Hobson was a man who kept horses and did not give people a choice about which horse they could have. • *It's Hobson's choice, because if I don't agree to do what they want, I'll lose my job.*

hog

go hog wild *American informal*
to become too excited and eager about something, often so that you do too much • *There's no need to go hog wild just because it's Sarah's birthday – she won't want such a fuss.*

ho-hum

ho-hum *American informal*
disappointing or not very interesting • *It was a ho-hum speech, no big deal really.* • *He still thinks soccer is kind of ho-hum and not worth watching.*

hoist

be hoist by/with your **own petard** *formal*
if you are hoist by your own petard, something that you did in order to bring you advantages or to harm someone else is now causing serious problems for you • *The government, who have made such a point of criticizing the opposition's morals now find themselves hoist by their own petard as yet another minister is revealed as having an illicit affair.*

hoist a few *American informal*
to drink several glasses of beer or other alcoholic drink • *We stopped at Donovan's on the way home and hoisted a few.*

hold

can't hold a candle to sb/sth
if someone or something cannot hold a candle to someone or something else, they are not as good as that other person or thing • *These pop bands that you hear nowadays can't hold a candle to the groups we used to listen to in the sixties.*

can't hold their **drink/liquor**
if someone can't hold their drink, they get drunk after drinking very little alcohol • *You can't hold your drink, that's your problem. Two beers and you're under the table.*

Don't hold your breath.
something that you say in order to tell someone that an event is not likely to happen • *She said she'd phone but don't hold your breath.*

hold court *humorous*
to get a lot of attention from a group of people by talking in a way that is entertaining, especially on social occasions ✍In the past, a king or queen held court when they talked to the people who gave them advice. • *You'll find Mick holding court in the kitchen.*

hold good
if a statement holds good for something or someone, it is true of that thing or person • (often + **for**) *The saying 'good things come in small packages' holds good for this excellent miniature TV set.* • *It looks as though my predictions for snow at Christmas are holding good.*

hold sb's **hand**
to support someone when they are doing something difficult or frightening by being with them • *'I'm dreading giving that talk.' 'You'll be all right. I'll be there to hold your hand.'*

hold your **head up high**
to show that you are proud of something • *When this country has full employment and an education system for all, then we can hold our head up high.*

Hold your **horses!** *informal*
something that you say in order to tell someone to stop doing or saying something because they are going too fast • *Just hold your horses, Bill. Let's think about this for a moment.*

hold your **own**
to be as successful as other people or things in a situation • *She can hold her own in any debate on religion.* • (often + **against**) *The French franc held its own against the D-mark.*

hold the fort *British, American & Australian*
hold down the fort *American*
to be left in charge of a situation or place while someone is away • *Someone had to stay at home and hold the fort while my mother was out.*

hold the key
to provide the explanation for something that you could not previously understand • *Fiennes, who had been looking for the place for twenty years, became convinced that this road held the key.*

hold sb **to ransom**
to force someone to do something by putting them in a situation where something bad will happen to them if they do not • *Some people regarded the miners' strike as the union holding the nation to ransom.*

hold your **tongue** *old-fashioned*
to stop talking • *George had learned to accept these little insults. He held his tongue.*

not **hold water**
if an opinion or a statement does not hold water, it can be shown to be wrong • *Most of the arguments put forward by our opponents simply do not hold water.*
hold water • *If his theory holds water, it could be a breakthrough in cancer research.*

on hold
if you are on hold when you are using the telephone, you are waiting to speak to someone • *Ms Evans is on the other line at the moment – shall I **put** you **on hold**?*

put sth **on hold**
to decide that you will leave an activity until a later time • (usually passive) *The project has been put on hold until our financial position improves.*
be on hold • *Everything's on hold again because of the bad weather.*

► See also: have/hold all the **aces**
hold/keep sb at **arm**'s length
have/hold all the **cards**
hold/keep sth/sb in **check**
hang/hold on (to sth/sb) for **dear** life
hold/keep your **end** up
hang/hold **fire**
hang/hold on like **grim** death

hold/stand your **ground**
hold/put a **gun** to sb's head
hold out/offer an **olive** branch
hold the **purse** strings

holding

▶ See: be **left** holding the baby

holds

no holds barred
without limits or controls • *His new show may offend some viewers. This is comedy with no holds barred.*
no-holds-barred • (always before noun) *In a no-holds-barred campaign, the nice guys are always the losers.*

hole

be in a hole *British & Australian informal*
to be in a difficult or embarrassing situation • *We're in a bit of a hole here, because we've lost the letter they sent telling us what we were supposed to do.*
dig yourself **into a hole** *British & Australian informal* to do something which makes you embarrassed or causes you problems which will be difficult to solve • *The government is digging itself into an even deeper hole by refusing to admit it made a mistake.*
OPPOSITE **dig/get** sb **out of a hole** *British & Australian informal* to help someone who is in a difficult situation • *She dug me out of a hole by lending me the money for the flight back to New York.* • (often reflexive) *I managed to dig myself out of a hole by pretending I had only been joking.*

be in the hole *American informal*
if someone is an amount of money in the hole, they owe that amount of money • *He's $500 in the hole after buying his car.*
go into the hole *American informal* • *The campaign has run out of money and is going into the hole.*

blow/make a hole in sth
if something makes a hole in an amount of money, it takes a lot of that money to pay for it • *The trip made a hole in our savings, but it was worth it.* • *The new tax is likely to blow an enormous hole in our profits.*

a hole card *American*
a secret advantage that is ready to use when you need it • *She still had one hole card to get out of police custody – a phone call to an influential friend.*

a hole in the wall *American*
a small, dark shop or restaurant • *It's just a hole in the wall, but the food is good.*
hole-in-the-wall • (always before noun) *We spent the day going around hole-in-the-wall antique shops looking for bargains.*

▶ See also: **blow** a hole in sth
have sth **burning** a hole in your pocket
need sth like (you **need**) a hole in the head

hole-and-corner

hole-and-corner *British*
hole-in-the-corner *British*
hole-and-corner activities are kept secret, usually because they are dishonest • (always before noun) *I don't want any more hole-in-the-corner deals, from now all our business will be done in the open.*

holes

▶ See: **pick** holes in sth

holier-than-thou

holier-than-thou
someone who is holier-than-thou behaves as if they have better morals than other people • *I can't stand that holier-than-thou attitude that some vegetarians have.*

hollow

ring/sound hollow
if something someone says rings hollow, it does not sound true or sincere • *The claims they made two years ago that peace was just around the corner ring very hollow now.*
have a hollow ring • *In view of the government's financial problems, these promises have a hollow ring.*

▶ See also: **beat** sb hollow

holy

the holy of holies *humorous*
a very special place ✍The holy of holies is the most special part of a religious building. • *This football stadium is the holy of holies to many fans.*

home

be at home
1 if someone is at home in a situation, they

feel confident and happy because it is familiar to them and they know how to deal with it • (often + **in**) *By the end of the week she was beginning to feel more at home in her new job.* • *He is equally at home in a symphony orchestra or playing jazz with friends.*

2 if something or someone is at home somewhere, they are suitable for that place and look right in it • *This painting would be more at home in an art gallery than hanging on someone's living room wall.*

be home and dry *mainly British*
be home and hosed *Australian*
to have completed something successfully • *I've just got one more report to write and I'll be home and dry.*

be home free *American & Australian*
to be certain to succeed at something because you have finished the most difficult part of it • *Once you leave the expressway and cross the bridge, you're home free – we're the third house after the bridge.*

drive/hammer sth **home**
to say something very clearly and with a lot of force, often repeating it several times, so that you are sure that people understand it • *She used charts and statistics to drive home her message that we need to economize.*

hit/strike home
1 if something that someone says hits home, it has a strong effect on you because it forces you to understand something unpleasant • *I could see that the criticism was beginning to hit home.*
2 if an action or a situation hits home, it has a strong negative effect • *Consumer spending has decreased as tax rises have begun to hit home.*

a home from home *British*
a home away from home *American & Australian*
a place where you feel as comfortable as you do in your own home • *I visit Australia so often, it's become a home from home for me.*

Home is where the heart is.
something that you say which means that your true home is with the person or in the place that you love most • *I don't mind moving round the world with Chris. Home is where the heart is.*

the home straight *British & Australian*
the last part of a long or difficult activity • *We can't give up now we're* ***on the home straight****.*

the home stretch
the last part of a long or difficult activity • *We've been working on the project for six months, but we're* ***in the home stretch*** *now.*

a home truth
if you tell someone a home truth, you tell them an unpleasant fact, usually something bad about themselves • (usually plural) *It's time someone told that boy a few home truths about his behaviour.*

make yourself **at home**
to behave in a relaxed way in a place, as if it was your own home • (often an order) *Sit down and make yourself at home while I make some coffee.* • *We made ourselves at home, using the bathroom and drinking all their beer.*

What's sth **when it's at home?** *British & Australian informal*
Who's sb **when he's/she's at home?** *British & Australian informal*
something that you say when you want to know what something is or who someone is • *Feng shui?* ***What's that when it's at home?*** • *Who's Mariella Frostrup when she's at home?*

► See also: **bring** home the bacon
bring sth home to sb
keep the home fires burning
play away from home
be nothing much to **write** home about

homework

do your **homework**
to make careful preparations so that you know all you need to know about something and are able to deal with it successfully • *They hadn't done their homework, or they'd have known it was a waste of time asking her that question.*

honest

be as honest as the day (is long)
to be completely honest • *You can be as honest as the day is long and still get into*

trouble if you fill in your tax form incorrectly.

honest to God *informal*
something you say in order to emphasize that you are telling the truth • *I didn't mean to hurt him, honest to God I didn't!*

make an honest woman of sb *humorous*
if a man makes an honest woman of someone that he is having a relationship with, he marries her • *You've been living with Jean for five years, isn't it time you made an honest woman of her?*

honest-to-goodness

honest-to-goodness
an honest-to-goodness thing or person is plain, simple, and exactly what they appear to be • (always before noun) *I'd much rather have an honest-to-goodness steak than any of the fancy stuff he cooks.*

honesty

Honesty is the best policy.
something that you say which means that it is best to be honest • *With relationships, as with so many aspects of life, honesty is undoubtedly the best policy.*

honeymoon

a honeymoon period
a short period at the beginning of a new job or a new government, when no one criticizes you • *Labour's brief honeymoon period only lasted until the first budget.*

honour-bound

be/feel honour-bound to do sth *British & Australian*
be/feel honor-bound to do sth *American & Australian*
to feel that you must do something because it is morally right, even if you do not want to do it • *I'd rather go to Andrew's party but I feel honour-bound to go to Caroline's because she asked me first.*

honours

do the honours *British & Australian humorous*
do the honors *American & Australian*
to pour drinks or serve food • *'Let's eat. Shall I do the honours?'*

hoof

on the hoof
1 *British & Australian* if you make a decision on the hoof, you make it quickly to react to a situation which is happening, and do not have time to think about it carefully • *I don't want to make a decision on the hoof – I need to give this some thought.*
2 *British & Australian* if you do something on the hoof, you do it while you are walking around doing other things • *He's so busy, he usually has lunch on the hoof.*

hook

be off the hook
if a telephone is off the hook, the part that you speak into is not lying in the part that holds it so the telephone will not ring • *He left the telephone off the hook because he didn't want to be disturbed.*

by hook or by crook
if you intend to do something by hook or by crook, you are determined not to let anything stop you doing it and are ready to use any methods • *I decided that I was going to get that job by hook or by crook.*

get/let sb **off the hook**
to allow someone to escape from a difficult situation or to avoid doing something that they do not want to do • *John's agreed to go to the meeting in my place, so that lets me off the hook.*
be off the hook • *You're off the hook – someone else has volunteered to do the job.* • *If Lucy picks the children up from school, that will get me off the hook.*

► See also: **fall** for sth hook, line and sinker
off the hook
fall for sb hook, line and sinker
ring off the hook
Sling your hook!

hooks

get your **hooks into** sth/sb
to get control or influence over something or someone • *We'll all be seeing a lot less of Robert if Joanna gets her hooks into him.*

hooky

► See: **play** hooky

hoops

go/jump through hoops
to do a lot of difficult things before you are allowed to have or do something you want • *They really make you jump through hoops before they allow you to adopt a baby.*
put sb **through hoops** • *She was put through far more hoops than a man would have been before the studio allowed her to direct her first film.*

hoot

not **care/give a hoot** *informal*
not **care/give two hoots** *informal*
if you do not give a hoot about something or someone, you do not care about them at all • (often + **about**) *I don't give a hoot about keeping the house tidy.* • (often + question word) *They don't care two hoots who wins as long as it's a good game.*

hop

▶ See: climb/get/hop into **bed** with sb
catch sb on the hop

hope

hope against hope
to hope very strongly that something will happen, although you know it is not very likely • (usually in continuous tenses; usually + **that**) *We were just hoping against hope that she would be rescued.*

a hope chest *American*
the things a young woman collects to use in her home after she is married • *Gloria spent the next few months embroidering sheets for her hope chest.*

▶ See also: not have a chance/hope in **hell**
live in hope

hopes

▶ See: **pin** your hopes on sth/sb

hopping

be hopping mad

be hopping mad *old-fashioned*
to be very angry • *My Dad was hopping mad when I told him I'd crashed his car.*

horizon

on the horizon
something that is on the horizon is likely to happen soon • *There is no new drug on the horizon that will make this disease easier to treat.*

horizons

broaden/widen sb's **horizons**
to increase the range of things that someone knows about, has experienced, or is able to do • *This trip to the Far East has certainly broadened our family's horizons.*

hornet

a hornet's nest
a situation or subject which causes a lot of people to become angry and upset ✍A hornet is a large insect that stings people badly. • *His remarks on the role of women have* ***stirred up a hornet's nest*** *amongst feminists.* • *Animal cloning is a real hornet's nest.*

horns

be on the horns of a dilemma
to be unable to decide which of two things to do because either could have bad results • *How can we decide which hospital to close? We are on the horns of a dilemma.*

draw/pull in your **horns**
to act in a more careful way than you did

before, especially by spending less money • *He'll have to draw in his horns, now that he's lost his job.*

▶ See also: **lock** horns

horse

(straight) from the horse's mouth
if you get information about something from the horse's mouth, you get it from someone who is involved in it and knows a lot about it • *'Are you sure she's leaving?' 'Definitely, I heard it straight from the horse's mouth.'*

a horse of another/a different color *American*
a situation or a subject that is different from what you had first thought it was • *You said you didn't like going to the movies, but if you don't want to go because you're broke, that's a horse of another color.*

horse sense *old-fashioned*
ordinary practical knowledge of the best way to deal with people and situations • *Has he got enough horse sense not to get into debt?*

▶ See also: **eat** like a horse
I could **eat** a horse.
You can **lead** a horse to water (but you can't make him/it drink).

horses

Horses for courses. *British & Australian*
something that you say which means that it is important to choose suitable people for particular activities because everyone has different skills • *Ah well, horses for courses. Just because a plumber can mend your washing machine, it doesn't follow that he can mend your car as well.*

▶ See also: **Hold** your horses!
Don't **spare** the horses.

hostage

a hostage to fortune *formal*
if something is a hostage to fortune, it could be harmed by things that happen in the future • *Inviting terrorists to take part in the talks has created a hostage to fortune.*
give a hostage to fortune *formal* if something gives a hostage to fortune, it may cause problems in the future • *She could never be president because her journalistic work gives too many hostages to fortune.*

hot

(all) hot and bothered *informal*
worried or angry, and sometimes physically hot • *Dad gets all hot and bothered if someone parks in his parking space.*

be hot off the press
news that is hot off the press has just been printed and often contains the most recent information about something • *This is the latest news from Bosnia, hot off the press.*

be hot stuff *very informal*
if someone is hot stuff, they are sexually attractive • *There's a new girl in our class. She's hot stuff.*

be in hot water
if someone is in hot water, people are angry with them and they are likely to be punished • *He found himself in hot water over his speech about immigration.*
get (sb) **into hot water** • *You'll get into hot water if your teacher finds out.*

be too hot to handle *informal*
if something or someone is too hot to handle, people cannot deal with them, because they are dangerous or difficult • *The book was so sexually explicit, it was considered too hot to handle by most publishers.*

feel/go hot and cold (all over) *British & Australian informal*
to feel that your body is hot and cold at the same time, because you have had a shock • *When I suddenly saw him again in the street after all these years, I went hot and cold all over.*

go/sell like hot cakes
if things are going like hot cakes, people are buying a lot of them very fast • (often in continuous tenses) *The book has only just been published and copies are already selling like hot cakes in both Britain and America.*

have [done/seen/had etc.] more sth **than** sb **has had hot dinners** *British & Australian*
to have done, seen, had etc. something many times, so that you have had more experience of it than the person you are

talking to • *Young man, I've been to more football matches than you've had hot dinners, so you don't have to explain the rules of the game to me.*

hot air *informal*
if something that someone says is just hot air, it is not sincere and will have no practical results • *Their promises turned out to be just so much hot air.*

hot and heavy *American informal*
if something or someone is hot and heavy, they are full of strong emotions or sexual feelings • *Guess who I saw getting hot and heavy on the dance floor?* • *Television news coverage of the fighting has been hot and heavy.*

a hot button *American informal*
a subject that is important to people and which they feel very strongly about • *Gender issues have become something of a hot button of late.*
hot-button *American* • (always before noun) *Sex discrimination in employment is a* ***hot-button*** *political* ***issue*** *now.*

Hot dog! *American old-fashioned*
something that you say when you are very pleased about something • *You won the race? Hot dog!*

hot dog *American informal*
to perform actions in a sport so that people notice you because of your skill or speed • (always + *adv/prep*) *They spent the day hot dogging down the slopes at Aspen.*
a hot dog *American informal* someone who tries to make people notice them by performing especially fast or well in a sport • *Mike's just one hot dog! – it's amazing what he does in front of a big crowd.*

a hot potato *informal*
something that is difficult or dangerous to deal with • *The abortion issue is a political hot potato in the United States.*

a hot spot
a place where people go for exciting entertainment like dancing • *The club is one of the city's premiere hot spots.*
a dangerous place where there may be a war or other violent events • *I spent my career reporting from the world's hot spots.*

the hot ticket *American*
someone or something that is very popular at the present time • *Fashion writers predict that ankle-strap shoes will be the hot ticket this fall.* • *Keira Knightley's become one of the hotist tickets in Hollywood since she starred in 'Pride and Prejudice'.*
hot-ticket *American* • (always before noun) *Star Wars Lego® is a hot-ticket item in the stores right now.*

hot under the collar *informal*
if someone is hot under the collar, they are angry • *He* ***got*** *very* ***hot under the collar*** *when I suggested that he might be mistaken.* • *The issue of waste disposal is getting a lot of people hot under the collar.* • *Don't get all hot under the collar – I'm only suggesting some minor changes to our plans!*

in hot pursuit
if you are in hot pursuit of someone or something, you are following closely behind them and trying hard to catch them • *The gang fled from the scene of the crime with the police in hot pursuit.* • (often + **of**) *Jean immediately jumped into her car and set off in hot pursuit of the truck.* • *Owen Good raced round the final bend in the track, with Mark Bishop in hot pursuit.*

in the hot seat *British, American & Australian*
on the hot seat *American*
in a position where you are responsible for important or difficult things • *He suddenly found himself in the hot seat, facing a hundred angry residents at a protest meeting.* • *She has been the woman in the hot seat at this company during the last five difficult years.* • *Give me a break – I've been sitting on the hot seat all morning, fielding phone calls from angry customers!*

▶ See also: **blow** hot and cold
drop sb/sth like a hot brick/potato
hard/hot on sb's **heels**
hard/hot on the **heels** of sth

hotfoot

hotfoot it

hotfoot it *informal*
to walk or run quickly • *You'd better hotfoot it down to the video shop before it closes.*

hots

to have the hots for sb *very informal*
to be strongly sexually attracted to someone • *He's had the hots for Sue ever since he first met her.*

hot-to-trot

hot-to-trot *American very informal*
sexually exciting or sexually excited • *He used to buy her hot-to-trot underwear and little red lycra numbers with plunging necklines.*

hour

in sb's **hour of need**
at a time when someone needs help very much • *I shall never forget that they were the people who helped me in my hour of need.*

hours

at all hours (of the day and night)
at any time of the day or night • *They keep calling me on the phone at all hours to ask questions I've already answered.*

at all hours (of the night)
very late at night • *How do you expect me to sleep when you're playing loud music at all hours?*
till all hours (of the night) until very late at night • *They sit up till all hours of the night drinking beer and playing cards.*

house

get on like a house on fire *informal*
if two people get on like a house on fire, they like each other very much and become friends very quickly • *I was worried that they wouldn't like each other, but in fact they're getting on like a house on fire.*

get/put your **own house in order**
to solve your own problems • *You should put your own house in order before you start giving me advice.*

not **give** sth/sb **house room**
to refuse to become involved with someone or something, because you do not like them or approve of them • *A respectable organization shouldn't be giving house room to a bunch of bigoted fanatics.*

a house of cards
an organization or a plan that is very weak and can easily be destroyed • *The organization that looked so solid and dependable turned out to be a house of cards.*

on the house
if food or drink is on the house in a bar or restaurant, it is provided free by the owner • *We had to wait for a table so they gave us all gin and tonics on the house.*

▶ See also: **bring** the house down
eat sb out of house and home

houses

go (all) round the houses *British*
to waste time saying a lot of things that are not important before you get to the subject you want to talk about • *There's no need to go all round the houses, just tell me straight out what's wrong.*

how

And how! *American & Australian*
something that you say in order to emphasize that you agree with what someone has just said • *'It was a great game last night.' 'And how!'*

How strange/stupid/cool etc. is that? *informal*
used to emphasize that something is strange/stupid etc.

huddle

get/go into a huddle
to form a group away from other people to discuss something secretly • *They went into a huddle for a minute, then accepted the offer.*

hue

a hue and cry
when there is a hue and cry about something, a lot of people complain noisily about it • *Local people* ***raised a*** *terrible* ***hue and cry*** *about the plan to close the village school.*

huff

huff and puff
1 to breathe noisily, usually because you have been doing physical exercise • *They're so unfit they start huffing and puffing if they have to run further than twenty yards.*
2 *informal* to complain noisily about something but not be able to do anything about it • *They huffed and puffed about the price, but eventually they paid up.*

in a huff *informal*
feeling angry with someone because they have done or said something to upset you • *She's in a huff because I forgot to call her last night.* • *He walked off in a huff because I hadn't saved him a space at the table.*

hum

▶ See: hum and **haw**

human

▶ See: To **err** is human, (to forgive, divine).

humble

▶ See: **eat** humble pie

hump

be over the hump *American informal*
to be past the most difficult or dangerous part of an activity or period of time • *We're over the hump now. I'm back at work and we've repaid our debts.*

get the hump *British informal*
to get annoyed or upset with someone because you think they have done something bad to you • *Tony got the hump because he thought we hadn't invited him to the party.*
have got the hump *British informal* • *She's got the hump because I forgot her birthday.*

hung

▶ See: I might as well be hanged/hung for a **sheep** as a lamb.

hunky-dory

be hunky-dory *informal*
if a situation is hunky-dory, there are no problems and people are happy • *It's no good pretending everything is hunky-dory. I heard you two arguing last night.*

hunt

▶ See: hunt/search **high** and low

hurt

▶ See: wouldn't harm/hurt a **fly**

hush

hush money
money that you pay someone to stop them telling anyone else about something that you want to keep secret • *His assistant had been paid hush money to stop him from speaking to the press.*

hustle

hustle and bustle
busy and noisy activity • (usually + **of**) *He wanted a little cottage far away from the hustle and bustle of city life.*

ice

be on ice

if plans are on ice, they are not going to be dealt with until some point in the future • *Both projects are on ice until the question of funding is resolved.*

put sth **on ice** • *Plans for a women-only film screening have been put on ice following threats of legal action.*

▶ See also: **break** the ice
cut no ice with sb

icing

the icing on the cake *British, American & Australian*
the frosting on the cake *American*

something which makes a good situation even better • *I was just content to see my daughter in such a stable relationship but a grandchild, that was really the icing on the cake.*

ideas

put ideas into sb's **head**

to make someone want to do something they had not thought about doing before, especially something stupid • (often in continuous tenses) *Don't **go putting ideas into** his **head**. We haven't got the money for a car.* • *Who put all these ideas into her head about becoming an actress?*

ifs

no ifs and buts *British & Australian*
no ifs, ands or buts *American*

something that you say to a child to stop them arguing with you when you want them to do something • *I **want no ifs and buts**, just tidy your room like I told you to!* • *No ifs, ands or buts, you're going up to bed now!*

ignorance

Ignorance is bliss.

something that you say which means if you do not know about a problem or an unpleasant fact, you do not worry about it • *I wish the newspapers would stop telling us about the dangers of eating meat. It seems to me ignorance is bliss.*

ill

be ill at ease

to feel anxious or embarrassed • (often + **with**) *He always felt a little ill at ease with strangers.* • (sometimes + **in**) *The girl behind the bar looked ill at ease in her uniform.*

It's an ill wind (that blows nobody any good).

something that you say which means most bad things that happen have a good result for someone • *But it's an ill wind. The wettest June in history has replenished the reservoirs.*

in

You're in there! *British informal*

something that you say in order to tell someone that another person is sexually attracted to them • *Did you see how that girl was looking at you? You're in there, mate!*

in absentia

in absentia *formal*

if something happens to someone in absentia, they are not present when it happens to them • *The court convicted her in absentia and fined her $500.*

inch

be every inch sth

to be a particular kind of person in every way • *He looked every inch the slick, city businessman.*

not **budge/give an inch**

to refuse to change your opinion or agree to even very small changes that another person wants • *I keep asking her to think again, but she won't budge an inch.* • (sometimes + **on**) *He refuses to give an inch on health and safety issues.*

come within an inch of doing sth

to very nearly do something, especially something dangerous or exciting • *I came within an inch of losing my life on the rocks below.*

Give sb **an inch and** they'll **take a mile.**

something that you say which means that if you allow someone to behave badly at all, they will start to behave very badly • *I'm always wary about making concessions to these people. Give them an inch and they'll take a mile.*

▶ See also: not **trust** sb an inch

Indian

an Indian summer

1 a period of warm weather which sometimes happens in early autumn • *Both the UK and Ireland have been enjoying an Indian summer over the past few weeks.*

2 a successful or pleasant period in someone's life, especially towards the end of their life • *The book describes the last 20 years of Churchill's life, including his Indian summer as prime minister between 1951 and 1955.*

infinite

▶ See: in his/her/their (infinite) **wisdom**

in flagrante delicto

in flagrante (delicto) *humorous*

if someone is discovered in flagrante delicto, they are discovered doing something wrong, especially having sex with someone who is not their husband or wife • *She came home to catch her husband in flagrante delicto with the next-door neighbour.*

influence

under the influence

if someone is under the influence, they are drunk • *Were you serious last night about wanting a baby or was it just because you were under the influence?* • *Driving under the influence is a very serious offence.*

information

Too much information! *humorous*

used when you want to tell someone that what they have said should be kept private or is embarrassing • *'His kisses were really wet.' 'Ugh – too much information!'*

in loco parentis

in loco parentis *formal*

to be responsible for a child while the child's parents are absent • *Teachers are in loco parentis while children are at school.*

ins

the ins and outs *informal*

the details or facts about something • (usually + **of**) *I don't know all the ins and outs of the situation but I gather Roger and Mark haven't been getting on too well.*

inside

an inside job

a crime committed by someone against the organization that they work for • (not used with *the*) *The computers were taken from a locked room, which makes it look like an inside job.*

have the inside track *mainly American*

to have a special position within an organization or a special relationship with a person that gives you advantages that other people do not have • (often + **with**) *He thinks I have the inside track with the director so he keeps hassling me for information.*

▶ See also: **know** sth inside out

insignificance

fade/pale into insignificance

if something pales into insignificance, it does not seem at all important when compared to something else • *When your child's ill, everything else pales into insignificance.* • *With the outbreak of war all else fades into insignificance.*

in situ

in situ *formal*

if something is in situ, it is in its original place • *The cave paintings must be viewed in situ because they are considered too delicate to be moved to a museum.*

insult

▶ See: **add** insult to injury

intents

to all intents and purposes

in all the most important ways • *We've got a few odd things to finish, but to all intents and purposes the job is done.* • *They redesigned the old model and created something which was to all intents and purposes a brand new car.*

interesting

► See: be as interesting as **watching** grass grow
be as interesting as **watching** paint dry

interference

► See: **run** interference

invent

► See: invent sth out of **whole** cloth

inverted

in inverted commas *British & Australian*
something that you say when a phrase you are using to describe something is the phrase that people usually use but it does not really show the truth ✍Inverted commas are a pair of printed marks put at the beginning and end of a word or phrase to show that someone else has written or said it. • *They were the kind of well-meaning people that wanted to 'do good' in inverted commas.*

iron

an iron fist/hand in a velvet glove
something that you say when you are describing someone who seems to be gentle but is in fact severe and firm • *To enforce each new law the president uses persuasion first, and then force – the iron hand in the velvet glove.*

an iron man *American & Australian*
a man who is physically very strong and can work hard for a long time • *He likes to think of himself as some sort of iron man who doesn't need sleep like the rest of us.*

iron out the kinks *mainly American*
to get rid of any problems that you are having with the way that you are doing something • *The team was still trying to iron out the kinks in their game in the last quarter.*

► See also: **pump** iron
rule (sb) with a rod of iron
strike while the iron is hot

irons

have [a few/a lot etc.] irons in the fire
to have several jobs at the same time or to have several possibilities of work • *If that job application doesn't work out I've got a couple more irons in the fire.*

itchy

have itchy feet *British & Australian informal*
to want to travel or to do something different • *Why've you got all these travel brochures? Do you have itchy feet?*
get itchy feet *British & Australian informal* • *He's been in the same job for too long and he's getting itchy feet.*

ivories

tickle/tinkle the ivories *humorous*
to play the piano ✍The parts of a piano that you press to play it used to be made of a hard white substance called ivory. • *Grandma could tickle the ivories like a professional.*

ivory

an ivory tower
if you are in an ivory tower, you are in a place or situation where you are separated from ordinary life and its problems • *How much of the research done by academics in their ivory towers is ever read or published?*

ivy

the Ivy League *American*
a group of old and very good colleges in the north-east of the US • *The company thinks the best management trainees come from the Ivy League.*
Ivy League *American* • *He doesn't have the Ivy League education of some of his opponents.* • *He hated the Ivy League conformity of the college.*

jack

a jack of all trades
someone who has many skills or who does many different jobs • *Bill can do plumbing, carpentry, or a bit of gardening – he's a jack of all trades, really.*

a Jack the Lad *British informal, old-fashioned*
a confident and not very serious young man who behaves as he wants to without thinking about other people • *Three children with three different women? Well, he always was a bit of a Jack the Lad.*

► See also: before you can **say** Jack Robinson

jackpot

► See: **hit** the jackpot

Jack Robinson

► See: before you can **say** Jack Robinson

jam

be in (a bit of) a jam *old-fashioned*
to be in a difficult situation • *I'm in bit of a jam. Could you possibly lend me some money till next week?*

jam tomorrow *British*
something that you want which you are told you will get soon but which never appears • *Nobody will accept a pay cut, and it's not enough to* ***promise jam tomorrow****.*

What more do you want – jam on it? *British informal*
used to say that someone should be grateful for what they have or have been offered, and not demand something better • *They've given him a holiday in Italy. What more does he want – jam on it?*

Jane Doe

Jane Doe *American*
a woman or girl whose name must be kept secret or is not known, especially in a court of law • *A former employee, referred to only as Jane Doe, is suing the company for unfair discrimination.*

jazz

and all that jazz *informal*
and other similar things • *They sell televisions and all that jazz.*

Jekyll

a Jekyll and Hyde
someone whose personality has two different parts, one very nice and the other very unpleasant ✍This phrase comes from the main character in the book *The Strange Case of Dr Jekyll and Mr Hyde* by Robert Louis Stevenson. • *You can't depend on him to be friendly – he's a Jekyll and Hyde.*
Jekyll and Hyde • *Many alcoholics develop Jekyll and Hyde personalities.*

jelly

► See: like **nailing** jelly to the wall

je ne sais quoi

a je ne sais quoi
a pleasant quality which you cannot describe or name • *He's not particularly attractive but he has* ***a certain je ne sais quoi*** *which women find irresistible.*

jewel

the jewel in the crown
the best or most valuable thing in a group of things • (often + **of**) *The island of Tresco, with its beautiful tropical gardens, is the jewel in the crown of the Scilly Isles.*

jiggery-pokery

jiggery-pokery *old-fashioned*
secret activities that are not honest • *We suspect there's been some financial jiggery-pokery going on in the accounts department.*

Jim Crow

Jim Crow *American*
a situation that existed until the 1960's in the south of the US, when black people were treated badly, especially by being separated from white people in public

places ✍Jim Crow was the name of a black character in a 19th century song and dance act. • *Jim Crow meant there were no black kids in white schools.*

Jim Crow *American* • (always before noun) *Jim Crow laws*

jitters

get the jitters

get the jitters *informal*

to feel anxious, especially before an important event • *I always get the jitters before an interview.*

give sb **the jitters** *informal* • *Don't drive so fast. You're giving me the jitters.*

job

do a job on sb/sth *mainly American informal*

to hurt or damage someone or something • *He really did a job on her, telling her how much he loved her and then leaving her.* • *Someone sure did a job on this table – there are scratches all over it.*

do the job *informal*

if something does the job, it is suitable for a particular purpose • *Here, this knife should do the job.* • *I needed to tie the two parts together and an old stocking did the job perfectly.*

It's more than my job's worth. *British & Australian informal*

something that you say in order to tell someone that you cannot do what they want you to do because you would lose your job if you did • *I'm sorry, but it'd be more than my job's worth to take any money from you.*

a job lot *British & Australian*

a collection of objects that are bought or sold together as a group • *I bought a job lot of furniture at an auction.*

a Job's comforter *old-fashioned*

someone who tries to make you feel happier but makes you feel worse instead ✍Job was a character in the Bible who had a lot of bad things happen to him. • *She's a real Job's comforter. She keeps telling me I'm going to die soon anyway so I shouldn't worry about anything.*

▶ See also: **fall** down on the job
be **just** the job
lie down on the job

jobs

jobs for the boys *British & Australian*

work that is given by someone who is in an important position to their friends or members of their family • *They operated a system of jobs for the boys.*

Joe Bloggs

Joe Bloggs *British & Australian*

an ordinary person • *There's no point asking your average Joe Bloggs what he thinks about opera.*

Joe Blow

Joe Blow *American & Australian*

an ordinary person • *Television today is geared to your average Joe Blow.*

Joe Public

Joe Public *British informal*

the public • *The test of any new product is will Joe Public buy it?*

jog

jog your **memory**

to cause you to remember something • *Police are hoping to jog people's memory by showing them pictures of a car that was used in a robbery.*

John Bull

John Bull *old-fashioned*

a character who represents a typical English man or the English people ✍This phrase comes from a book called *The History of John Bull* written by John Arbuthnot in 1712. • *In the cartoon, John Bull appears as a short, stocky figure wearing a waistcoat with the British flag on.*

John Doe

John Doe *American*

a man or boy whose real name must be kept secret or is not known, especially in a court of law • *The patient was referred to in court documents as John Doe.*

John Hancock

your **John Hancock** *American humorous*

your signature ✍John Hancock's signature was the biggest signature on the American Declaration of Independence in 1776 • *If you put your John Hancock on the last page we'll be finished with the formalities.*

Johnny-come-lately

a Johnny-come-lately *old-fashioned*

someone who has only recently started a job or activity and has suddenly become very successful • *She denies suggestions that she's a Johnny-come-lately, saying that she has worked for years to get her own show.*

Johnny-on-the-spot

Johnny-on-the-spot *American informal*

someone who is immediately ready to do something, especially to help someone • *This guy had just gotten a flat tire, and there I was, Johnny-on-the-spot with my tools in the back of the car.*

John Q Public

John Q Public *American humorous*

the public • *You have to ask yourself what John Q Public will think when he hears about the government overspending.*

joie de vivre

joie de vivre

a feeling of happiness and enjoyment of life • *She will be remembered above all for her kindness and her great joie de vivre.*

join

join the ranks of sth

to become part of a large group • *Thousands of young people join the ranks of the unemployed each summer when they leave school.*

▶ See also: Join the **club**!
enter/join the **fray**

joined

be joined at the hip

if you say that two people are joined at the hip, you mean that they are very friendly with each other and spend more time together than is usual • *I can go to London without Mike. We're not joined at the hip, you know.*

joke

be no joke

if a situation is no joke, it is very serious or very difficult • *There are two of us here, trying to do the work of four people – it's no joke.*

get/go beyond a joke

if a situation gets beyond a joke, it becomes extremely serious and worrying • *He's drunk more nights than he's sober these days – this has gone beyond a joke.*

the joke's on sb

something that you say which means someone who tried to make other people seem silly has made themselves seem silly instead • *The burglars managed to lock themselves into the house until the police arrived, so the joke's on them!*

joker

the joker in the pack

someone or something that could change a situation in a way that you do not expect • *The independent candidate is the joker in the pack in this election.*

joking

You must be joking! *informal*

something that you say in order to tell someone you do not think something they have said is serious because it is not likely to be true or to happen • *'Did Alex get you a present, then?' 'You must be joking! He didn't even remember it was my birthday.'*

You're joking! *informal*

something that you say when you are very surprised by what someone has just told you • *'They're getting married, you know' 'You're joking! They've only known each other a month.'*

jolly

be jolly hockey sticks *British humorous*

if a woman or situation is jolly hockey

sticks, the woman or the people involved in that situation belong to a high social class, and often talk in a very happy way that seems false • *Well, she's okay, but a little jolly hockey sticks, if you know what I mean.*

Joneses

▶ See: **keep** up with the Joneses

joy

▶ See: **jump** for joy

judge

You can't judge a book by its cover.
something that you say which means you cannot judge the quality or character of someone or something just by looking at them • *She doesn't look very intelligent, but you can't judge a book by its cover.*

judgement

▶ See: **sit** in judgment on/over sb

judgment

a judgment call *American*
a decision someone has to make using their own ideas and opinions ✍In sport, a judgment call is a decision made by an official in a competition using their own opinion of what they have seen. • *It's a judgment call – do we go by plane or risk taking the car to the conference.*

juggling

▶ See: a balancing/juggling **act**

jugular

go for the jugular *informal*
to criticize someone very cruelly by talking about what you know will hurt them most ✍The jugular is a large vein that carries blood to the heart. • *Cunningham, who usually* ***goes straight for the jugular****, seemed strangely reluctant to say anything.*

juice

▶ See: **stew** in your own juice/juices

jump

get a/the jump on sb/sth *mainly American informal*
to start doing something before other people start, or before something happens, in order to get an advantage for yourself • *If I leave work early on Fridays I can get a jump on the traffic.*

Go jump in a/the lake! *informal*
an impolite way of telling someone to go away and stop annoying you • *This guy just wouldn't leave us alone, so finally I told him to go jump in the lake.*

jump down sb's **throat**
to react angrily to something that someone says or does • *She's been very irritable recently, jumping down my throat every time I open my mouth.*

jump for joy
to be very happy about something good that has happened • *Tina jumped for joy when she found out she'd be in the team.*

jump in with both feet
jump in feet first
to become involved in something very quickly, often without thinking carefully about it first • *Take time to think things over before you make a decision, don't jump straight in with both feet.*

jump out of the frying pan (and) into the fire
to go from a bad situation to an even worse one • *Many kids who run away from unhappy homes discover they've jumped out of the frying pan and into the fire.*

jump ship
if you jump ship, you leave a job or activity suddenly before it is finished, especially to go and work for someone else • *Another advertising agency offered him $1000 to jump ship.*

jump the gun
to do something too soon, especially without thinking carefully about it ✍If someone running in a race jumps the gun, they start running before the gun has been fired to start the race. • *He shouted at me before I had time to explain, but later he apologised for jumping the gun.*

jump the queue *British & Australian*
to move in front of people who have been waiting longer for something than you • *If you try to jump the queue at a bus stop you'll get shouted at by old ladies.* • *There's a long waiting list for hip operations, but you can jump the queue if you pay.*

queue-jump *British & Australian* • *Sorry, I didn't mean to queue-jump.*
a queue-jumper *British & Australian* • *People who had waited all night to get a ticket were very upset by queue-jumpers.*

jump to conclusions
to guess the facts about a situation without having enough information • *I might be jumping to conclusions but I've seen them together twice in town.*

nearly jump out of your **skin**
if you nearly jump out of your skin when something happens, it makes you feel very surprised or shocked • *I heard a loud bang and nearly jumped out of my skin.*

▶ See also: get/jump/leap on the **bandwagon**
jump in at the **deep** end
go/jump through **hoops**

jury

the jury is (still) out
if the jury is still out on a subject, no decision has been made or the answer is not yet certain • (usually + **on**) *The jury's still out on whether animal experiments are really necessary.* • *We asked people to comment on the latest male fashions, but it seems the jury's out.*

just

be just the job *British & Australian*
be just the ticket *British old-fashioned*
to be perfect for a particular purpose • *He needed a car to pick her up in and Will's sports car seemed just the job.*

get your **just deserts**
if you get your just deserts, something bad happens to you that you deserve because of something bad you have done • *Did you read about the burglar whose own house was broken into? He really got his just deserts.*

▶ See also: be just what the **doctor** ordered
just **gay** enough
Just my **luck**!
Half/Just a **mo**.
not be just a **pretty** face

kangaroo

a kangaroo court

a court of law which is not official and which judges someone in an unfair way • *A kangaroo court was set up by the strikers to deal with people who had refused to stop working.*

keen

be as keen as mustard *British & Australian old-fashioned*

to be very eager • *Why don't we ask Tom to captain the cricket team? He's as keen as mustard.*

keep

keep your/**an eye on** sth/sb

to watch or look after something or someone • *Could you keep an eye on the baby for me a while?* • *I kept my eye on him all the time as I felt sure he was about to do something stupid.*

keep your/**both feet on the ground**

to not have your character spoilt by becoming famous or successful • *Friends say she's kept her feet firmly on the ground – fame hasn't changed her.*

have your/**both feet on the ground** • *Acting is a tough profession and you need to have both feet on the ground if you're going to survive.*

keep a civil tongue in your **head** *slightly formal*

if you tell someone to keep a civil tongue in their head, you are telling them to be polite, especially after they have said something rude • (often an order) *Try to keep a civil tongue in your head. We want him on our side.*

keep a lid on sth

to control the level of something in order to stop it increasing • *Economic difficulties continued and the government intervened to keep a lid on inflation.*

keep a straight face

to look serious and not laugh, although you are in a funny situation or are saying something funny or stupid • *I can never play jokes on people because I can't keep a straight face.*

with a straight face • *I don't know how you can stand there and repeat all that nonsense with a straight face.*

straight-faced • *She remained rigidly straight-faced while everyone else was falling about with laughter.*

keep a tight rein on sb/sth
keep sb/sth **on a tight rein**

to have a lot of control over someone or something • *He made ends meet by keeping a tight rein on his budget.* • *Our parents always kept us on a pretty tight rein.*

keep a weather eye on sth/sb *British & Australian*

to watch something or someone carefully, because they may cause trouble or they may need help • *I'd like you to keep a weather eye on the situation and report any major developments to me at once.*

keep an eye out for sb/sth

to watch carefully for someone or something to appear • *Keep an eye out for signposts for Yosemite.*

keep an/your **ear to the ground**

to watch and listen carefully to what is happening around you so that you know about everything ✍American Indians used to put their ear against the ground to help them discover where animals or other people were. • *I'll keep an ear to the ground and tell you if I hear of any vacancies.*

keep sth/sb **at bay**

to prevent something or someone unpleasant from coming too near you or harming you • *If we can keep the rabbits at bay, we should have a good crop of vegetables in the garden.* • *For me, overeating is a way of keeping my feelings at bay.*

keep body and soul together

to just be able to pay for the things that you need in order to live • *We can barely keep body and soul together on what he earns.*

keep your **cool**
to remain calm, especially in a difficult situation • *If you see a difficult question in the exam, don't panic. Just keep your cool.*

keep your **eyes peeled/skinned** *informal*
to watch very carefully for something • (often + **for**) *Keep your eyes peeled for a signpost.*

keep faith with sth/sb *formal*
to continue to support an idea or person, especially by doing what you promised to do • *Has the company kept faith with its promise to invest in training?*

keep sb **guessing**
if you keep someone guessing, you do not tell them what you are going to do or what will happen next • *The clever and complex plot kept the audience guessing right up to the superb final twist.*

keep your **hand in**
to practise a skill often enough so that you do not lose the skill • *I do a bit of teaching now and then just to keep my hand in.*

keep your **hands clean**
to avoid becoming involved in any activities which are bad or illegal • *Politicians can leave the lies and smear campaigns to journalists and keep their own hands clean.*
have clean hands • *The country's leaders must be seen to have clean hands.*

keep your **head**
to stay calm, especially in difficult or dangerous situations • *Can you keep your head at times of pressure and stress?*

keep your **head above water**
to have just enough money to live or to continue a business • *With extra income from private sponsorship, the club is just about managing to keep its head above water.*

keep your **head down**
to do or say as little as possible in order to avoid problems or arguments • *The best we can do is keep our heads down and hope that people will soon get used to the new system.*

keep your **mouth shut** *informal*
to keep something secret • *You can trust Sarah – she knows how to keep her mouth shut.* • (sometimes + **about**) *Do you think I should keep my mouth shut about seeing Jim with another woman?*

keep your **nose clean**
to avoid getting into trouble or doing anything illegal • *I'd only been out of prison three months so I was trying to keep my nose clean.*

keep your **nose out of** sth *informal*
to not become involved in other people's activities or relationships • *What goes on between me and Pete is none of her business so she can keep her big nose out of it!*

keep your **nose to the grindstone**
to continue to work very hard, without stopping • *I've only got six weeks before my exams start so I'm trying to keep my nose to the grindstone.*

keep sb **on** their **toes**
to force someone to continue giving all their attention and energy to what they are doing • *He gave me a couple of extra things to do just to keep me on my toes.*

keep your **own counsel** *slightly formal*
to not tell other people about your opinions or plans • *He was a quiet man who kept his own counsel.*

Keep your **pecker up!** *British informal*
something that you say to someone in order to tell them to be happy when something unpleasant is happening to them • *I know things are hard, love, but keep your pecker up.*

keep sb **posted**
to make sure that someone always knows what is happening • (sometimes + **on**) *Keep me posted on anything that happens while I'm away.*

keep your **powder dry**
to be ready to take action if necessary • *All you have to do is keep your powder dry and await orders.*

Keep your **shirt on!** *British, American & Australian informal*
Keep your **hair on!** *British & Australian informal*
a slightly impolite way of telling someone who is angry to try to be calm and patient • *Keep your shirt on! I'll be with you in a second.*

keep sb **sweet**
to do things to please someone so that they help you or treat you well in the future • *I like to keep the neighbours sweet in case we have to borrow a ladder or something from them.*

keep tabs on sth/sb
to watch a person or a situation carefully so that you always know what they are doing or what is happening • *I like to keep tabs on my bank balance so that I don't get overdrawn.* • *I get the feeling he's keeping tabs on me and watching my every move.*

keep the home fires burning
to keep your home pleasant and in good order while people who usually live with you are away, especially at war • *They relied on their wives and sweethearts to keep the home fires burning when they marched off to war.*

keep the wolf from the door
to have enough money to be able to eat and live • *Forty percent of the country's population receive part-time wages that barely keep the wolf from the door.*

keep yourself **to** yourself
if you keep yourself to yourself, you live a quiet life and avoid doing things with or talking to other people • *We don't know anything about her, she keeps herself to herself.*

keep track
to continue to know what is happening to something or someone • *I don't know what he's doing now, he's had so many different jobs that it's difficult to keep track.* • (often + **of**) *I've never been very good at keeping track of what I spend my money on.*

OPPOSITE **lose track** to no longer know what is happening to something or someone • *I can't remember what her husband's called, she's been married so many times I've lost track.* • *We were chatting away and we just* ***lost track of time.*** (= did not know what the time was)

keep sth **under** your **hat**
to keep something secret • *I've got some interesting news, but you must promise to keep it under your hat for the moment.*

keep up appearances
to hide your personal or financial problems from other people by continuing to live and behave in the same way that you did in the past • *Simply keeping up appearances was stretching their resources to the limit.*

keep up with the Joneses
to try to own all the same things as people you know in order to seem as good as them • *Her only concern in life was keeping up with the Joneses.*

Why keep a dog and bark yourself?
British & Australian
something that you say which means there is no purpose in doing something yourself when there is someone else who will do it for you • *Just leave the glasses on the table – the bar staff will collect them. After all, why keep a dog and bark yourself?*

You can't keep a good man/woman down. *humorous*
something that you say which means that a person with a strong character will always succeed, even if they have a lot of problems • *When they sacked her, she simply set up a rival company of her own. You can't keep a good woman down.*

► See also: hold/keep sb at **arm**'s length
keep the **ball** rolling
keep/play your **cards** close to your chest
hold/keep sth/sb in **check**
keep sb on the **edge** of their seat
hold/keep your **end** up
keep your **eye** on the ball
can't take/keep your **eyes** off sb/sth
have/keep a **foot** in both camps
have/keep **half** an eye on sth/sb
can't keep your **hands** off sb
keep a **low** profile
have/keep an **open** mind
change/keep up/move with the **times**
have/keep your **wits** about you

keeper

not **be** your **brother's keeper**
not **be** sb's **keeper**
to not be responsible for what someone does or for what happens to them • *It's all too easy for us not to intervene in another country's problems, telling ourselves that we're not our brother's keeper.* • *You shouldn't blame yourself for what's happened to Simon. You're not his keeper, you know.*

keeping

in keeping with sth

in a way that is suitable or right for a particular situation, style, or tradition • *In keeping with tradition, we always have turkey on Christmas Day.* • *Her millionaire lifestyle is very much in keeping with her celebrity status.*

OPPOSITE **out of keeping with** sth • *The antique desk seems out of keeping with the modern furniture in the rest of the house.*

keeps

for keeps *informal*

for ever • *'Do you want your tennis racket back?' 'No, it's yours for keeps.'* • *She said she's left him for keeps this time.*

▶ See also: **play** for keeps

ken

be beyond sb's **ken**

if a particular subject is beyond your ken, you do not understand it or know much about it • *Don't talk to me about finance – it's beyond my ken.* • *Most of Derrida's work is beyond the ken of the average student.*

kept

a kept man/woman *humorous*

someone who does not work and who is given money and a place to live by the person who they are having a sexual relationship with • *She was determined to find work and not become a kept woman like her sister.*

kerb-crawler

a kerb-crawler *British & Australian*
a curb-crawler *American*

someone who drives slowly along a road looking for someone to have sex with • *I don't like walking down this road at night – it's full of prostitutes and kerb-crawlers.*

kerb-crawling *British & Australian* • *There was a big scandal after the judge was prosecuted for kerb-crawling.*

kettle

be another/a different kettle of fish

if you say that something or someone is a different kettle of fish, you mean that they are completely different from something or someone else that has been talked about • *Andy was never very interested in school, but Anna, now she was a completely different kettle of fish.* • *I'd driven an automatic for years but learning to handle a car with gears was another kettle of fish altogether.*

a fine/pretty kettle of fish *mainly American*

a difficult situation • *That's a fine kettle of fish – the car won't start and I have to leave in five minutes.*

key

▶ See: **hold** the key

kibosh

put the kibosh on sth *old-fashioned, informal*

to prevent something that is planned from happening • *The rain put the kibosh on our plans for a picnic.*

kick

get a kick out of sth/doing sth *informal*

to enjoy doing something very much • *Anyone who gets a kick out of horror movies will love this show.* • *I get a real kick out of shopping for new shoes.*

kick yourself

if you say that you'll kick yourself when or if something happens, you mean that you will feel angry with yourself because you have done something stupid or missed an opportunity • *You'll kick yourself when I tell you who came in just after you left.* • *If I don't get one now and they've sold out by next week, I'll kick myself.*

kick against the pricks *British & Australian literary*

to fight against people in authority • *People in this country tend to follow rather than lead. It takes courage to kick against the pricks.*

kick (sb's) **ass** *mainly American very informal*

to punish someone or to defeat someone with a lot of force • *The General saw the conflict as a chance for the Marines to go in and kick ass.* • *We want to go into the game and* ***kick some ass****.*

kick (sb's) **butt** *American & Australian very informal*

to punish someone or to defeat someone

with a lot of force • *The officer told his men to move in on the protestors and kick butt – show them who's boss!* • *We went out with the gang to* ***kick some butt****.*

kick your **heels** *British*
to be forced to wait for a period of time • (usually in continuous tenses) *I'm fed up kicking my heels at home while all my friends are out enjoying themselves.*

a kick in the teeth
if you describe the way someone treats you as a kick in the teeth, you mean that they treat you badly and unfairly, especially at a time when you need their support • *She was refused promotion which was a real kick in the teeth after all the extra work she'd done.*
kick sb **in the teeth** • *She'd only been trying to help him and she felt that she'd been kicked in the teeth.*

kick over the traces *British & Australian*
to do what you want and not show any respect for authority ✍Traces are long pieces of leather which join a vehicle to the horse which is pulling it. If a horse kicks over the traces, it kicks its legs over these pieces of leather and goes out of control. • *Some kids go straight to university and spend the first year kicking over the traces.*

kick the bucket *informal*
to die • *Didn't you hear? He kicked the bucket. Had a heart attack, I think.*

kick the habit *informal*
to stop doing something that is difficult to stop doing, especially taking drugs, smoking, or drinking alcohol • *No coffee for me, thanks. I'm trying to kick the habit.* • *'Does she still smoke?' 'No, she kicked the habit a couple of years ago.'*

kick up a fuss/row/stink
to complain loudly in order to show that you are very annoyed about something • *Our food was cold so my father kicked up a fuss and refused to pay the service charge.*

kick up your **heels** *American & Australian*
to do things that you enjoy • *After the exams, we kicked up our heels and had a really good party.*

a kick up the arse/backside *British & Australian very informal*
if you give someone a kick up the backside, you do or say something to try to stop them being lazy • *He does nothing but watch TV all day. His mother should give him a kick up the backside.* • *The threat of losing my job was the kick in the pants I needed.*

kick sb **upstairs**
to give someone a new job which seems more powerful but is really less powerful, usually in order to stop them causing trouble for you • *Brown is being kicked upstairs to become chairman of the new company.*

kick sb **when** they're **down**
to do something bad to someone when you know they already have a lot of problems • *His wife left him last month and I don't want to* ***kick a man when he's down****, but we simply don't have any more work for him.*

► See also: kick up a **stink**

kick-off

for a kick-off *informal*
something that you say which means that what you are going to say next is the first of a list of things you could say • *'What's wrong with it?' 'Well, for a kick off, it hasn't been cooked properly.'*

kicks

for kicks *informal*
if you do something for kicks, especially something dangerous, you do it because you think it is exciting • *Local kids steal cars and race them up and down the street, just for kicks.*

kid

be like a kid in a candy store *American & Australian*
to be very happy and excited about the things around you, and often to react to them in a way which is silly and not controlled • *You should have seen him when they arrived. He was like a kid in a candy store.*

handle/treat sb **with kid gloves**
to be very polite or kind to someone who is important or easily upset because you do not want to make them angry or upset

✍Kid gloves are gloves made from very soft leather which would feel very soft if someone touched you with them. • *Linda can be a very difficult woman – you've really got to handle her with kid gloves.*

kids

kids' stuff *British & Australian*
kid stuff *American*
an activity or piece of work that is very easy • *A five-mile bike ride? That's kids' stuff.*

kill

kill or cure *British & Australian*
a way of solving a problem which will either fail completely or be very successful • *Having a baby can be kill or cure for a troubled marriage.*

kill the fatted calf
to celebrate in order to welcome a friend or relative that you have not seen for a long time ✍This phrase comes from a story in the Bible when a father killed a young cow in order to celebrate the return of his son who he thought was dead. • *Annie's coming home, let's kill the fatted calf!*

kill the goose that lays the golden egg
to destroy something that makes a lot of money • *If you sell your shares now, you could be killing the goose that lays the golden egg.*

kill time
to do something which is not very useful or interesting while you are waiting for time to pass • *We usually play guessing games to kill time at airports.*

kill two birds with one stone
to manage to do two things at the same time instead of just one, because it is convenient to do both • *I killed two birds with one stone and saw some old friends while I was in Leeds visiting my parents.*

kill sb **with kindness**
to be too kind to someone • *Rob's killing me with kindness – he phones me all the time to see if I'm alright when really I just need to be left alone.*

move in for the kill
go (in) for the kill
to prepare to defeat someone completely in an argument or competition when they are already in a weak position • *After two days of constant media coverage, journalists sensed the minister was weakening and they moved in for the kill.* • *At 6-3 6-2 up, Sampras went in for the kill and won the final set 6-0.*

▶ See also: kill the **clock**

killing

make a killing *informal*
to earn a lot of money very easily • (often + **on**) *She made a killing on the house so she can't be short of money.*

kilter

out of kilter
1 if something is out of kilter, it is not operating or working as it should • *Even one sleepless night can throw your body out of kilter.*
2 if two things are out of kilter, or if one thing is out of kilter with another, they are not similar any more • (often + **with**) *A further tax increase on cigarettes would put Britain out of kilter with the rest of Europe.*

kind

▶ See: be **one** of a kind
be **two** of a kind

kindly

not **take kindly to** sth
to not like something that someone says or does • *Be careful what you say to Mike – he doesn't take kindly to criticism.* • *I didn't take kindly to being thrown out of the team.*

kindness

▶ See: **kill** sb with kindness

king

king of the castle *British*
king of the hill *American*
the most successful or most powerful person in a group of people • *Jamie Spence was king of the castle yesterday when he beat the defending champion in the third round.* • *Our team is sure to be king of the hill this year.*

a king's ransom
a very large amount of money • (not used with *the*) *She was wearing a diamond*

necklace which must have been worth a king's ransom.

▶ See also: **live** like a king
turn king's/queen's evidence

kingdom

blast/blow sb/sth **to kingdom come** *informal*
to kill someone or destroy something by using a gun or bomb • *Fifteen soldiers were blown to kingdom come in the attack.* • *Police discovered a bomb which was large enough to blast the whole town to kingdom come.*

till/until kingdom come
for a very long time ✍'Until Kingdom come' is a phrase from a prayer in the Bible and means 'until the world ends'. • *I don't want to wait until kingdom come for you to decide what you're doing.*

kinks

▶ See: **iron** out the kinks

kiss

give sb **the kiss of life** *British & Australian*
to help someone who has stopped breathing to breathe again by blowing into their mouth and pressing their chest • *A doctor who had witnessed the accident gave the victim the kiss of life but failed to revive him.*

kiss and make up *humorous*
if two people kiss and make up, they stop being angry with each other and become friendly again • *Ian and I used to fight a lot, but we always kissed and made up afterwards.*

kiss and tell
to talk on television, in a newspaper etc. about a sexual relationship you have had with a famous person, especially in order to get a lot of money • *The singer's ex-girlfriend was paid £20,000 by a tabloid newspaper to kiss and tell.*
kiss-and-tell • (always before noun) *Her kiss-and-tell revelations scandalized Hollywood.*

kiss (sb's) **ass** *American very informal*
to try too hard to please someone and to agree with everything they say, in a way which other people find unpleasant • *If you want promotion around here, you're going to have to kiss ass.*
ass-kisser *American taboo* • *They're just a load of ass-kissers*

Kiss my arse! *British & Australian taboo*
Kiss my ass! *American taboo*
something that you say in order to tell someone that you will not do what they want you to • *He asked for money, and I told him he could kiss my arse.*

the kiss of death *informal*
an event or action that causes something to fail or be spoiled • (often + **for**) *Asking Jenny to cook is the kiss of death for any dinner party.*

▶ See also: kiss/lick sb's **arse**
kiss/say/wave **goodbye** to sth

kissing

a kissing cousin *old-fashioned*
someone you are related to but not very closely • *I didn't realize she knew Tony, but in fact, they're kissing cousins.*

kitchen

everything but the kitchen sink *humorous*
a lot of different things, many of which you do not need • *We were only going away for the weekend, but Jack insisted on taking everything but the kitchen sink.*

kitchen-sink

kitchen-sink *British & Australian*
a kitchen-sink play, film, or style of painting is one which shows ordinary people's lives • (always before noun) ***Kitchen-sink drama** came into fashion in the 1950s.* • *In his latest work, he is moving away from kitchen-sink realism towards a more experimental style of painting.*

kite

kite-flying *British & Australian*
the act of telling people about an idea or plan so that you can find out what they think about it • *Mr Baker's hint about US intervention in the war was undoubtedly an exercise in kite-flying.*

▶ See also: **fly** a kite
Go **fly** a kite!

kith

kith and kin *old-fashioned*
friends and relatives ✍Kith is an old-fashioned word which means friends.

• *They wanted to keep alive the memory of their kith and kin who had died in the war.*

kittens

have kittens *informal*
to become very worried or upset about something • *She nearly had kittens when I said I was going to buy a motorbike.*

kitty-corner

kitty-corner *American*
kitty-cornered *American*
in a direction from one corner of a square to the opposite, far corner • (often + **to**) *You know the building – it's kitty-corner to my office.*

knee

put sb **over** your **knee** *old-fashioned*
to punish a child by hitting them on the bottom • *Her father threatened to put her over his knee if she missed school again.*

knee-deep

be knee-deep in sth
to have too much of something • *I'm knee-deep in work at the moment, so I'm not stopping for lunch.*

knee-high

be knee-high to a grasshopper *humorous*
to be very young ✍A grasshopper is an extremely small insect. • *The last time I came here I was knee-high to a grasshopper.*

knees

► See: **bring** sb/sth to their knees

knickers

get your **knickers in a twist** *British & Australian informal*
get your **knickers in a knot** *Australian informal*
to become very upset about something, usually something that is not important • *Now, before you get your knickers in a twist, let me explain the situation.*

knife

cut/go through sth **like a (hot) knife through butter**
to cut something very easily • *A laser beam can cut through metal like a hot knife through butter.*

go under the knife
to have a medical operation • *More and more women are choosing to go under the knife just to improve their appearance.*
under the knife *humorous* • *The hospital is worried about the number of patients who have died under the knife.*

have your **knife into** sb *British & Australian informal*
to try to cause problems for someone because you do not like them • *Mike's had his knife into me ever since he found out I was seeing his ex-girlfriend.*

put/stick the knife in *British & Australian informal*
to do or say something unpleasant to someone in an unkind way • *'No one in the office likes you, you know, Tim', she said, putting the knife in.* • *The reviewer from The Times really stuck the knife in, calling it the worst play he'd seen in years.*

turn/twist the knife
to do or say something unpleasant which makes someone who is already upset feel worse • *Having made the poor girl cry, he twisted the knife by saying she was weak and unable to cope with pressure.*
a turn/twist of the knife • *'I never loved you', she said, with a final twist of the knife.*

knife-edge

on a knife-edge
if a person or organization is on a knife-edge, they are in a difficult situation and are worried about what will happen in the future • *She's been living on a knife-edge since her ex-husband was released from prison last month.* • *The theatre is on a financial knife-edge and must sell 75% of its seats every night to survive.*

knight

a knight in shining armour *British & Australian*
a knight in shining armor *American & Australian*
someone who helps you when you are in a difficult situation ✍In stories about medieval times (= the time between 500 and 1500 AD), knights were soldiers who rode on horses and helped women in difficult or dangerous situations. • *She looked around the bar to see if there was a*

knight in shining armour who might come and save her from this awful man.

knit

knit your **brows** *literary*
to move your eyebrows (= the hair above your eyes) closer together when you are worried or thinking carefully • *Sasha knitted her brows as she listened to the storm forecast.*

knitting

▶ See: **stick** to your knitting

knives

the knives are out *British & Australian*
something that you say which means that a group of people are angry with someone and want to criticize them or cause problems for them • (often + **for**) *The knives are out for Danvers following his team's poor performance in six successive games.*

knobs

with (brass) knobs on *British & Australian humorous*
if you describe something as a particular thing with knobs on, you mean it has similar qualities to that thing but they are more extreme • *Disney World was like an ordinary amusement park with knobs on.*

knock

knock (some) sense into sb *informal*
to use strong methods in order to teach someone to stop behaving stupidly • *A month in prison should knock some sense into him.*

knock sb's **block off** *informal*
if you say you will knock someone's block off, you mean you will hit them very hard • *Say that again and I'll knock your block off!*

knock sb **for six** *British & Australian informal*
to surprise and upset someone a lot • *It really knocked me for six when my ex-boyfriend announced he was getting married.*

Knock it off! *informal*
something that you say in order to tell someone to stop doing something that is annoying you • *Knock it off, will you? I can't work with all that noise.*

knock sb **off** their **perch** *British & Australian*
to make someone fail or lose their leading position • *Will Rovers win the European Cup and knock United off their perch?*

knock sth **on the head** *British informal*
to stop doing something • *'Do you still play football?' 'No, I knocked that on the head a while ago.'*

knock sb **sideways** *British & Australian*
to surprise, confuse or upset someone very much • *The news of her brother's death knocked her sideways.*

knock spots off sb/sth *British & Australian informal*
to be very much better than someone or something else • *There's a vegetarian restaurant in Brighton that knocks spots off any round here.*

knock the bottom out of sth *informal*
to harm something and make it weaker, especially by taking away the thing it needs in order to continue or be successful • *Ben losing his job has knocked the bottom out of our plans to buy a house.*

knock the stuffing out of sb
to make someone feel less confident or physically weaker • *An operation like that is bound to knock the stuffing out of you.* • *It was their third defeat in a row and it really knocked the stuffing out of them.*

knock them/'em dead *informal*
to perform so well or to look so attractive that other people admire you a lot • *You'll knock them dead at the party tonight in your new black dress!* • (often an order) *Just go out there tonight and knock 'em dead!*

take a knock
to be badly affected by something • *His reputation has taken quite a knock following the revelations published in his recent biography.*

▶ See also: beat/knock the (living) **daylights** out of sb
knock/throw sb for a **loop**
knock/lick sth/sb into **shape**
blow/knock your **socks** off
beat/knock the **tar** out of sb
knock (on) **wood**

knock-down-drag-out

knock-down-drag-out *American*
a knock-down-drag-out fight or argument is very serious and continues for a long time • (always before noun) *Look, I don't want to get into a knock-down-drag-out fight with you over this so let's forget it.*

knocked

You could have knocked me down/ over with a feather! *humorous*
something that you say in order to emphasize how surprised you were when something happened • *I only entered for a joke and I won first prize. You could have knocked me down with a feather.*

knocking

a knocking shop *British very informal*
a knock-shop *Australian very informal*
a place where men pay to have sex with women • *People say it's a knocking shop but I've never seen anything going on.*

knot

► See: **tie** the knot

knots

► See: **tie** yourself (up) in knots

knotted

Get knotted! *British & Australian informal, old-fashioned*
an impolite way of telling someone who is annoying you to go away • *Oh, get knotted, will you, I'm trying to work!*

know

be in the know *informal*
to know about something which most people do not know about • *The resort is considered by those who are in the know to have the best downhill skiing in Europe.*

know a thing or two *informal*
to have a lot of practical skills and knowledge learnt through experience • (usually + **about**) *My uncle grew up on a farm and knows a thing or two about looking after animals.*
[show/teach/tell etc.] sb **a thing or two** • (usually + **about**) *Julie – now she could teach you a thing or two about dealing with men.*

know sth **backwards** *British & Australian*
know sth **backwards and forwards** *American*
if you know a subject or a piece of writing backwards, you know it very well • *Ed knows the play backwards – he's seen it eight or nine times.* • *After 30 years in the business she knows it backwards and forwards.*

not **know beans about** sth *American & Australian informal*
to know nothing about something • *I don't know beans about computers – I've never even used one.*

not **know** sb **from Adam**
to have never met someone and not know anything about them • *Why should I lend him money? I don't know him from Adam.*

not **know if/whether** you **are coming or going**
to be unable to think clearly and decide what to do because you have so many things to deal with • *I had so much to do yesterday that I didn't know whether I was coming or going.* • *The recent changes in the school curriculum mean that most teachers don't know if they're coming or going.*

know sth **inside out** *informal*
to know everything about a subject • *Why don't you ask Mike? He knows the system inside out.*

know sth **like the back of** your **hand** *informal*
to know a place very well • *He knew East London like the back of his hand.*

know no bounds *formal*
if an emotion or quality knows no bounds, it is not limited • *Tom's loyalty to the company knows no bounds.*

know your **onions** *British & Australian humorous*
to know a lot about a particular subject • *That car salesman certainly knew his onions, didn't he?*

know your **place** *humorous*
to accept your low position in society or in a group without trying to improve it • *I just get on with my job and do as I'm told. I know my place.*

know your **stuff** *informal*

to know a lot about a subject, or to be very good at doing something • *When it comes to restoring grand pianos, Mr Morley really knows his stuff.*

not **know the first thing about** sth

to not know anything about a particular subject • *I don't know why you're asking Rob, he doesn't know the first thing about classical music.*

not **know the meaning of the word**

if you are talking about a quality or an activity and you say that someone does not know the meaning of the word, you mean they do not have that quality or they have no experience of that activity • *Work? He doesn't know the meaning of the word!* • *And the irony of Phil talking about ethics. He doesn't know the meaning of the word.*

know the score *informal*

to know all the important facts in a situation, especially the unpleasant ones • *You know the score – no payment until after the article is published.*

know sb **through and through**

to know someone very well and know everything about them • *She tried to hide her disappointment, but I know her through and through and I could tell she was upset.*

know what's what

if you know what's what, you have a lot of experience and can judge people and situations well • *Harry's been in the business for 40 years – he knows what's what.*

know where you **stand**

to know what someone thinks about you, how they expect you to behave, and how they are likely to behave themselves • *She's quite a strict boss, but at least you know where you stand with her.* • *Peter didn't even send me a birthday card, so I know where I stand now.*

not **know where to put** yourself *informal*

to feel very embarrassed • *And then he started to sing. Well, I didn't know where to put myself!*

not **know whether to laugh or cry**

to be extremely upset by something bad that has happened • *Then they announced that my flight was delayed for ten hours. I didn't know whether to laugh or cry.*

know which side your **bread is buttered (on)**

to be careful not to upset people who you know can help you • *Ollie won't refuse to come with us. He knows which side his bread is buttered.*

not **know which way to turn**

to not know what to do or who to ask for help in a difficult situation • *I had no home, no money, and I didn't know which way to turn.*

What you **don't know won't hurt** you.

something that you say which means that if you do not know about a fact or a problem, you do not worry about it • *'Tell me how much you spent on the car, then.' 'No, what you don't know won't hurt you.'*

wouldn't know sth **if it hit** you **in the face**
wouldn't know sth **if** you **fell over one**

to not notice something although it is very obvious • *Julie wouldn't know a good deal if it hit her in the face!*

► See also: not know your **arse** from your elbow
not know the **half** of it
know/learn sth (off) by **heart**
know the **ropes**

know-all

a know-all *British & Australian*
a know-it-all *American & Australian*

someone who seems to know everything and annoys other people by showing how clever they are • *No one likes him because he's such a know-all.*

knows

for all sb **knows** *informal*

if you say that a situation could be true for all you know, you are emphasizing that you do not know anything about it • *Heidi could be married with ten children for all I know! We haven't spoken for years.*

if sb **knows what's good for** them

if you say that someone will do something if they know what's good for them, you mean that they should do that thing or else something bad might happen to them • *You'll obey my orders if you know what's good for you.*

knuckle

a knuckle sandwich *humorous*

if you give someone a knuckle sandwich, you hit them • *You'll get a knuckle sandwich if you don't shut up.*

labour

a labour of love *British & Australian*
a labor of love *American & Australian*
an activity that is hard work but that you do because you enjoy it • *He prefers to paint the house himself – it's a real labour of love.*

ladder

▶ See: at the **top** of the ladder

lady

Lady Bountiful
a woman who enjoys showing people how rich and kind she is by giving things to poor people ✍Bountiful means generous. • *I've got a lot of clothes that they might make use of but I'm worried they they might see me as some sort of Lady Bountiful.*

Lady Muck *British & Australian humorous*
a woman who thinks she is very important and should be treated better than everyone else • *Look at Lady Muck over there, expecting everyone to wait on her!*

lady-killer

a lady-killer *old-fashioned*
a man who has sexual relationships with a lot of women • *With his good looks and charm, he was often cast as the lady-killer in films.*

lager

a lager lout *British*
a young man who drinks too much alcohol and is then noisy, rude, or violent • (often plural) *They'd ended up in some cheap holiday resort that was full of British lager louts.*

lah-di-dah

lah-di-dah *old-fashioned*
la-di-da *old-fashioned*
a woman who is lah-di-dah thinks she is better than other people and tries to speak as if she is from a high social class • *No one really liked her in the village. They all thought she was a bit lah-di-dah.*

laid-back

laid-back
a person who is laid-back is very relaxed and does not get anxious or angry very often • *I can imagine he's good to work for – he seems very laid-back.* • *He comes across as your typical laid-back Californian.*

laissez-faire

laissez-faire
1 the principle that businesses should not be controlled by the government • *The previous government had a policy of laissez-faire, whereas this government wants a closer partnership with industry.*
laissez-faire • (always before noun) *They have adopted a laissez-faire approach to business.*
2 the wish not to control people or not to become involved in their actions • *There are no effective laws to protect women from abusive husbands. An attitude of laissez-faire prevails.*
laissez-faire • (always before noun) *The problems in our education system, she said, would not be solved by a laissez-faire approach.*

lake

▶ See: Go **jump** in a/the lake!

lam

on the lam *mainly American informal*
running away from the police or someone in authority in order to escape going to prison • *He finally gave himself up to the police after 12 years on the lam.*

lamb

like a lamb
if you go somewhere that you are being forced to go like a lamb, you go there calmly and without complaining • *I thought I was going to have to drag her screaming to school but when the time*

came she went like a lamb.

like a lamb to the slaughter
something that you say about someone who does something or goes somewhere calmly and happily, not knowing that something unpleasant is going to happen to them ✍This phrase comes from the Bible. The slaughter is the time when animals are killed for their meat. • *Here comes the bride, like a lamb to the slaughter.*

lame

a lame duck

1 a person or company that is in trouble and needs help • *In under two years, it was transformed from a state-owned lame duck into a successful company.*

2 someone, especially an elected official, who cannot influence events any more, often because their job is going to end soon • *The Mayor intends to run for re-election to avoid being thought of as a lame duck.*

lame-duck *mainly American* • (always before noun) *Having lost control of Congress, he was in danger of becoming a* ***lame-duck president****.*

land

be in the land of nod *old-fashioned*
to be sleeping • *Joe's in the land of nod at last.*

be in the land of the living *humorous*
to be awake • *She was partying till the early hours so I don't imagine she'll be in the land of the living before lunchtime.*

find out/see how the land lies
to get information about a situation before making decisions or taking action • *I thought I'd better call my mother and see how the land lies before inviting myself home for the weekend.*

the lie of the land *British & Australian*
• *It's always a good idea to find out the lie of the land before applying to a company.*

the land of milk and honey
a country where people from other countries would like to live because they imagine that the living conditions are excellent and it is easy to make money • *People in poorer parts of the world still look on the States as the land of milk and honey.*

▶ See also: land on your **feet**
land/sock sb **one**

land-office

do a land-office business *American old-fashioned*
if a company does a land-office business, they are very successful in selling their product • *They only set up the company eight months ago and they're doing a land-office business.*

lap

be in the lap of the gods
if the result of a situation is in the lap of the gods, you cannot control what will happen • *I've sent in my application form and I've sorted out my references so it's in the lap of the gods now.*

drop/fall into your **lap**
if something good falls into your lap, you get it without making any effort • *You can't expect the ideal job to just fall into your lap – you've got to go out there and look for it.*

in the lap of luxury
if you are in the lap of luxury, you live in conditions of much comfort because you have a lot of money • *I have to earn enough to keep my wife in the lap of luxury.* • *They* ***live in the lap of luxury*** *in a huge great house in the south of France.*

lard-arse

a lard-arse *British very informal*
someone who is fat • *You could do with a bit of exercise yourself, lard-arse!* • *Your brother's a bit of a lard-arse, isn't he?*

large

by and large
generally or mostly • *The films they show are, by and large, American imports.*

loom large
if a subject looms large, it causes people to think or worry a lot • *The threat of unemployment looms large in these people's lives.*

▶ See also: as large as **life**

larger

▶ See: be larger than **life**

lark

▶ See: be **up** with the lark

last

be on its last legs

be on its last legs *informal*
if a machine is on its last legs, it is in bad condition because it is old and it will probably stop working soon • *We've had the same vacuum cleaner for twenty years now and it's on its last legs.*

be on your **last legs**
1 *informal* to be going to die soon • *It looks as if her grandfather's on his last legs now.*
2 *informal* to be very tired, especially after a lot of physical activity or work • *I'd just done fifteen miles and I was on my last legs.*

be the last word in sth
to be the best or most modern example of something • *It's a nice enough restaurant and it's very reasonably priced but it's not exactly the last word in style.*

have heard/seen the last of sb/sth
if you have heard the last of someone or something unpleasant, they will not cause you any more problems in the future • (often negative) *It's a worrying problem and I dare say we haven't heard the last of it.* • *He's a very unpleasant man. I sincerely hope we've seen the last of him.*

have the last laugh
to make someone who has criticized or defeated you look stupid by succeeding at something more important or by seeing them fail • *They fired her last year but she had the last laugh because she was taken on by their main rivals at twice the salary.*

last but not least
something that you say before introducing the last person or thing on a list, meaning that they are equally important • *This is Jeremy, this is Kath, and, last but not least, this is Artie.* • *Right, I've got my money, my sunglasses and, last but not least, my lipstick.*

the last gasp of sth *literary*
the end of a particular period or process • *This period witnessed the decline and last gasp of the British Empire.*

a last hurrah *mainly American*
a final action or performance before someone finishes a job or activity • *At 31, he knows this tournament may be his last hurrah.*

the last of the big spenders *humorous*
something that you say when you are spending very little money or when someone else is spending very little money • *Just an orange juice and some peanuts, please. The last of the big spenders!*

▶ See also: the final/last **straw**
have the final/last **word**

last-ditch

last-ditch
a last-ditch attempt to solve a problem is the final attempt that you make after you have failed several times to solve it • (always before noun) *The gesture has been seen by many as a* ***last-ditch attempt*** *to win voters.* • *The UN is trying to secure talks between the two sides in a* ***last-ditch effort*** *to avert war.*

last-gasp

last-gasp
achieved at the last possible moment • (always before noun) *And with only a minute left, Brinkworth scored a last-gasp equaliser bringing the score to 2-2.*

latchkey

a latchkey child/kid *mainly American*
a child who is often in the house alone because both parents are at work • *My dad came home at seven in the evening and my mom only an hour earlier so I was a latchkey kid.*

late

late in the day
too late to be useful • (often + **for**) *The new gun laws came a little late in the day for those whose friends or families were killed in the massacre.* • (often + to do sth) *It seems rather late in the day to announce that diet drinks might cause cancer.*

▶ See also: **better** late than never.

lather

be in a lather *informal*
to be very anxious about something • *She was in a real lather when I left this morning because she couldn't find the tickets.*
get (yourself) **in/into a lather** *informal* • *It's really not worth getting yourself into a lather over it.*

laugh

be a laugh a minute *informal*
to be very funny and entertaining ✍This phrase is often used humorously to mean the opposite. • *You know what Mark's like – he's not exactly a laugh a minute.* • *'A two-hour meeting with Nigel Owen? I bet that was fun.' 'Oh, it was a laugh a minute.'*

Don't make me laugh. *informal*
something that you say when someone has suggested something that you think is not at all likely to happen • *'You never know, Pete might help out.' 'Pete? Help out? Don't make me laugh!'*

laugh in sb's **face**
to show someone that you do not respect them and do not think their ideas are important • *He asked them to put out their cigarettes but they just laughed in his face.*

laugh like a drain *British & Australian*
to laugh very loudly • *I told her what had happened and she laughed like a drain.*

laugh sth/sb **out of court**
to refuse to think seriously about an idea, belief or a possibility • (usually passive) *At the meeting, her proposal was laughed out of court.* • *Anyone who had made such a ludicrous suggestion would have been laughed out of court*

laughing

be laughing all the way to the bank *informal*
if someone is laughing all the way to the bank, they have made a lot of money very easily, often because someone else has been stupid • *If we don't take this opportunity, you can be sure our competitors will and they'll be laughing all the way to the bank.*

be laughing on the other side of your **face** *British, American & Australian informal*
be laughing out of the other side of your **mouth** *American & Australian informal*
if you say someone who is happy will be laughing on the other side of their face, you are angry about the thing that is making them happy and think that something will soon happen to upset them • *You'll be laughing out of the other side of your face if you fail your exams.*

be laughing up your **sleeve**
to laugh at someone secretly, often in an unkind way • (often + **at**) *He persuaded people to believe in him and all the time he was laughing up his sleeve at them.*

be no laughing matter
if a subject is no laughing matter, it is serious and not something that people should make jokes about • *Haemorrhoids are all very funny when other people have them, but if you get them yourself, it's no laughing matter.*

a laughing stock
someone who does something very stupid which makes other people laugh at them • (usually + **of**) *I can't cycle around on that old thing! I'll be the laughing stock of the neighbourhood.*

laughter

Laughter is the best medicine.
something that you say which means that it is good for your physical and mental health to laugh • *A visit from Camille always makes me feel better – she's so hilarious. It's like they say, laughter's the best medicine.*

laundry

a laundry list *mainly American*
a long list of subjects • (usually + **of**) *It*

wasn't much of a speech – just a laundry list of accusations against the government.

laurels

▶ See: **look** to your laurels
rest on your laurels

law

be a law unto yourself
if you are a law unto yourself, you do things differently to other people and ignore the usual rules • *Charles certainly doesn't stick to the standard company procedures, but then, he's a law unto himself.*

the law of averages
the probability that you will get one result about the same number of times as another if you do something often enough • ***By the law of averages** we can't give a good performance every night of the tour.*

the law of the jungle
the way in which only the strongest and cleverest people in a society stay alive or succeed • *I was brought up on the streets where the law of the jungle applies, so I soon learnt how to look after myself.*

take the law into your **own hands**
to do something illegal in order to punish someone because you know that the law will not punish that person • *One day, after years of violent abuse from her husband, she decided to take the law into her own hands.*

there's no law against sth/doing sth *informal*
something that you say in order to tell someone who is criticizing you that you are not doing anything wrong • *'You were in the pub at lunchtime, weren't you?' 'Well, **there's no law against it**.'* • *'Have you been shopping again?' 'What if I have? There's no law against spending money.'*

▶ See also: **lay** down the law

lay

lay a finger on sb/sth
to touch or harm someone or something • (usually negative) *Honestly, I never laid a finger on him, he just fell over.* • *If you so much as lay a finger on my sister, I'll break your arm!*

lay a hand on sb
to hurt someone • *If you lay a hand on her I'll report you to the police.* • (often negative) *I never laid a hand on her.*

lay an egg *American informal*
to fail to make people enjoy or be interested in something • *Our first two sketches got big laughs, but the next two laid an egg.*

lay sth **at** sb's **door**
to blame someone for something bad that has happened • *The blame for their deaths was laid firmly at the government's door.*

lay bare sth
to discover or tell people about something that was not previously known or was previously kept secret • *It's been promoted as the biography that lays bare the truth behind the legend.*

lay down the law
to tell people what they should do, without caring about how they feel • *I'm not going to have someone come into this office and start laying down the law.*

lay it on the line *informal*
to tell someone the truth although it will upset them • *You're just going to have to lay it on the line and tell her her work's not good enough.*

lay it on thick *informal*
lay it on with a trowel *informal*
to make an emotion or experience seem more important or serious than it really is • *He'd injured his hand slightly but he was laying it on a bit thick about how painful it was.* • *They must have told us ten times how wonderful their daughter was – they were really laying it on with a trowel.*

lay sb **low**
if an illness lays someone low, they are unable to do what they usually do for a period of time • (usually passive) *He was at home at the time, laid low with the flu.*

lay the ghost of sth/sb **(to rest)**
to finally stop being worried or upset by something or someone that has worried or upset you for a long time • *With one stunning performance, Chelsea have laid to rest the ghost of their humiliating defeat at Old Trafford last season.*

▶ See also: lay/put your **cards** on the table
lay/set **eyes** on sb/sth
lay/put a **guilt** trip on sb
get/lay your **hands** on sth
lay down your **life**

lead

go down like a lead balloon *humorous*
if something that you say or show to people goes down like a lead balloon, they do not like it at all • *My joke about the alcoholic went down like a lead balloon.*

lead sb **a (merry) dance** *old-fashioned*
to confuse someone or to cause problems for them by deceiving them or behaving in a way that they cannot understand • *She's led us a merry dance over the plans for the party.*

lead sb **astray**
1 to influence someone so that they do bad things • *Parents always worry about their children being led astray by unsuitable friends.*
2 to cause someone to make a mistake • *The police were led astray by false information from one of the witnesses.*

lead sb **by the nose**
to control someone and make them do exactly what you want them to do ✍Cows are often led by a ring which has been put through their nose. • (usually passive) *They simply didn't know what they were doing and they were led by the nose by a manipulative government.*

lead the field
1 if you lead the field in a race or a sports event, you are better than all the people competing against you and are likely to win • *At the end of the second day's play, Ballasteros is leading the field.*
2 if you lead the field in an activity or business, you are more successful than anyone else • *There are some areas of medical research where Russian scientists still lead the field.*

lead sb **up the garden path** *British, American & Australian informal*
lead sb **down the garden path** *American informal*
to deceive someone • *We were led up the garden path about the cost of the building work – it turned out really expensive.*

put lead in your **pencil** *British humorous*
to increase a man's sexual ability • *You should eat a few oysters – that'll put some lead in your pencil.*
have lead in your **pencil** *British humorous* • *'My uncle's 65 and he's getting remarried.' 'He still has a bit of lead in his pencil then!'*

You can lead a horse to water (but you can't make him/it drink).
something that you say which means you can give someone the opportunity to do something, but you cannot force them to do it if they do not want to • *I made all the arrangements, bought the ticket, and even took him to the airport, but he just wouldn't get on the plane. Well, you can lead a horse to water, but you cannot make him drink.*

▶ See also: have/lead/live a **charmed** life
lead/live the **life** of Riley
swing the lead

leading

a leading light
an important and respected person in a group or organization • (often + **in**) *A leading light in the art and ballet world, he was a close friend of Princess Diana.* • (often + **of**) *Jeffries, at 23 a leading light of the campaign, was the first to speak.*

leaf

take a leaf out of sb's **book**
to copy something that someone else does because it will bring you advantages • *Maybe I should take a leaf out of Robert's book and start coming in at ten every morning.*

▶ See also: **shake** like a leaf

league

be out of sb's **league**
to be too good or too expensive for you • *He was so good-looking and so popular that I felt he was out of my league.*

leak

take a leak *very informal*
to pass liquid waste out of the body • *I'll be back in a moment – I've gotta take a leak.*

lean

▶ See: bend/lean over **backwards** to do sth

leap

a leap in the dark
something you do without being certain

what will happen as a result • *I had very little information about the company, so writing to them was a bit of a leap in the dark.*

leaps

by/in leaps and bounds
if progress or growth happens in leaps and bounds, it happens very quickly • *Ashley's reading has* ***come on in leaps and bounds*** *since she's been at her new school.* • *Leaders of the organization say their membership is growing by leaps and bounds.*

learn

learn your **lesson**
to learn something useful about life from an unpleasant experience • *I'm never going to mix my drinks again – I've learnt my lesson.*

learn sth **off pat** *British, American & Australian*
learn sth **down pat** *American*
to learn something so well that you do not have to think about how to do or say it • *All the answers he'd learned off pat for the interview sounded unconvincing now.* **have** sth **off pat** *British, American & Australian* • *I've given the same speech so many times I have* (= know) *it down pat now.*

► See also: know/learn sth (off) by **heart**

leash

have/keep sb **on a short/tight leash**
to have a lot of control over someone's behaviour and allow them very little freedom to do what they want • *He doesn't go out with the lads so much these days. Michelle keeps him on a tight leash.*

least

Least said, soonest mended. *British & Australian old-fashioned*
something that you say which means a bad event or situation can be forgotten more easily if you do not talk about it • *I've always thought it best not to dwell on grievances too long. Least said, soonest mended.*

take the line/path of least resistance
to act in the way which will be easiest because you will not have to argue with other people about it • *You could always take the line of least resistance and go with the majority vote.*

leave

leave a bad taste in your **mouth**
if an experience leaves a bad taste in your mouth, you have an unpleasant memory of it • *I think we all felt that he'd been treated unfairly and it left a bad taste in people's mouths.*

leave sb **cold**
if something leaves you cold, it does not cause you to feel any emotion • *Mary said the book had her in tears, but it left me cold.*

leave sb **high and dry**
to put someone in a very difficult situation which they have no way of making better • *The stock market crash left us high and dry with debts of over £200 000.*

leave sb **in the lurch**
to leave someone at a time when they need you to stay and help them • *I hope they can find someone to replace me at work. I don't want to leave them in the lurch.*

leave your/**its mark on** sb/sth
to have an effect that changes someone or something • *Her unhappy childhood left its mark on her all through her life.*

leave no stone unturned
to do everything that you can in order to achieve something or to find someone or something • *Both organizations have vowed to leave no stone unturned in the search for peace.*

leave sb **out in the cold**
to not allow someone to become part of a group or an activity • *The government's transport policy leaves people who do not own cars out in the cold.* • *Women's football teams feel they are left out in the cold as far as media coverage is concerned.*

leave sb/sth **standing** *British & Australian*
to be much better than everyone or everything else • *Stella's singing was so good, she left the others standing.* • *This is the best hoover I've ever had. It leaves the rest standing.*

leave the field clear for sb
to stop competing with someone, which

gives them a better chance of achieving success • *John decided not to apply for the job, which left the field clear for Emma.*

leave sb **to** their **own devices**
to let someone do what they want without helping them or trying to control them • (usually passive) *There are four hours of lessons each morning, and in the afternoon students are left to their own devices.* • *Left to my own devices I wouldn't bother cooking in the evenings.*

leave sb **to** sb's **tender mercies** *humorous*
to let someone be dealt with by another person who is not likely to show them any kindness or sympathy • *Should I have a word with her myself or leave her to Mick's tender mercies?*

leave sb **to twist in the wind** *American*
if someone is left to twist in the wind, they are left in a very difficult situation by the actions of another person • *The director resigned and left the rest of the department twisting in the wind, waiting to see if the project would continue.*

leave well alone *British & Australian*
leave well enough alone *American*
to not change or try to improve something that is not causing any problems • *So long as the machine still does what you want it to, my advice is to leave well alone.* • *Surgeons are aware that every operation carries some risk, and sometimes decide to leave well enough alone.*

▶ See also: keep/leave sb/in the **dark**
leave/let well **alone**
fly/leave the **nest**
leave sb to **stew**
leave sb to the **wolves**

left

be left hanging (in the air/in midair)
if a problem or question is left hanging in the air, it is not dealt with or answered • *We failed to resolve the issue at the last meeting and it was left hanging in the air.*

be left holding the baby *British*
be left holding the bag *American*
to suddenly have to deal with a difficult problem or responsibility because someone else has decided they do not want to deal with it • *He abandoned the project after a year because he felt that it was going to fail and I was left holding the baby.*

be out in left field
1 *American informal* to be completely wrong • *They're out in left field, blaming you for this fiasco.*
2 *American informal* to be very strange or very different from other people or things • *She's kind of out in left field but she's fun.*

the left hand doesn't know what the right hand is doing
something that you say which means that communication in an organization is bad so that one part does not know what is happening in another part • *I was sent the same letter from two different departments. I get the feeling the left hand doesn't know what the right hand is doing.*

left, right and centre *British informal*
right and left *American informal*
left and right *American informal*
if something bad is happening left, right and centre, it is happening in a lot of places or to a lot of people • *They were firing at people left, right and centre.* • *The Postal Service has been losing customers left and right these past couple of years.*

▶ See also: have **two** left feet

left-handed

▶ See: a left-handed **compliment**

leg

get your **leg over** *British & Australian very informal*
if a man gets his leg over, he succeeds in having sex with someone • *How was the party, then? Did you get your leg over?*

give sb **a leg up** *informal*
to help someone to be more successful • *It must give you a leg up if you want to be an actor and your parents are both in the profession.*
get a leg up *informal* • *If you know people in the company you can sometimes get a leg up.*

not **have a leg to stand on**
to be in a situation where you cannot prove something • *The problem is, if you don't have a witness, you don't have a leg*

to stand on. • *I haven't even got the receipt to prove where I bought it, so I don't have a leg to stand on.*

have a leg up on sb *American*
to have an advantage over someone else • *She probably has a leg up on the other applicants for the job because she has more experience.*

▶ See also: **Break** a leg!
get a leg in the **door**
pull sb's leg
Shake a leg!
Show a leg!

legs

have legs *mainly American*
if a story in the news has legs, it will continue for a long time • *This latest scandal has legs – you'll probably still be reading about it in a year's time.*

▶ See also: can **talk** the legs off an iron pot

lend

lend sb **a hand**

lend (sb) **a hand**
to help someone do something, especially something that involves physical effort • *Could you lend me a hand with these books?* • *He's always willing to lend a hand in the kitchen.*

lend an ear
to listen carefully and in a friendly way to someone, especially someone who is telling you about a problem • *If you have any problems, go to Claire. She'll always lend a sympathetic ear.*

lengths

▶ See: go to **great** lengths to do sth

leopard

A leopard can't/doesn't change its spots.
something that you say which means that a person's character, especially if it is bad, will not change, even if they pretend it has • *I doubt very much that marriage will change Chris for the better. A leopard doesn't change its spots.*

lesser

the lesser of two evils
a lesser evil
the less unpleasant of two choices, neither of which are good • *I suppose I regard the Democratic candidate as the lesser of two evils.*

lesson

▶ See: **learn** your lesson
teach sb a lesson

let

Let bygones be bygones. *slightly formal*
something that you say in order to tell someone to forget about unpleasant things that have happened in the past • *Why can't you put all that bad feeling behind you and let bygones be bygones?*

let fly (sth)
to start shouting angrily • (sometimes + **at**) *I was so angry I let fly at them as soon as they came in.* • *Gripping the arms of his chair, he let fly a barrage of offensive comments.*

let yourself **go**
1 to relax completely and enjoy yourself • *It's a party – let yourself go!* • *I think she finds it difficult to let herself go.*
2 to take less care of your appearance • *She's really let herself go since she split up with her husband.*

let your **hair down**
to relax and enjoy yourself without worrying what other people will think • *It's nice to let your hair down once in a while and go a bit wild.*

let your **heart rule** your **head**
to do something because you want to rather than for practical reasons • *Don't*

let your heart rule your head. If you lend him that money you'll never see it again.

the heart rules the head • *I can't make her understand how stupid she's being. It's a case of the heart ruling the head.*

let it all hang out *informal*
to relax and do or say exactly what you want to • *When I'm on holiday I like to let it all hang out.*

let it/things slide
to allow a situation to become slowly worse • *We've really let things slide over the past few months. The accounts are in a terrible state.*

let sth **ride**
to not take action to change something wrong or unpleasant • *Don't panic about low sales. Let it ride for a while till we see if business picks up.*

let it/her **rip** *mainly American informal*
if someone lets a vehicle rip, they make it move very fast • *She put her foot on the car's accelerator, and he said, 'OK, let her rip'.*

let slip sth
to say something that you did not intend to say because you wanted to keep it secret • *Pam let slip an interesting bit of gossip yesterday.* • (often + **that**) *Stupidly, I* ***let it slip*** *that they'd decided not to give him the job.*

let the cat out of the bag

let the cat out of the bag
to tell people secret information, often without intending to • *I was trying to keep the party a secret, but Jim went and let the cat out of the bag.*

let the chips fall where they may *American*
to do something without worrying about the effects of your actions • *She promised to ask a series of questions in her interview and let the chips fall where they may.*

let the genie out of the bottle *mainly American*
to allow something bad to happen which cannot then be stopped ✍In old Arabian stories, a genie was a magic spirit that would do whatever the person who controlled it wanted. • *With the Internet, we really let the genie out of the bottle. People now have unlimited access to all manner of material.*
OPPOSITE **put the genie back in the bottle** *mainly American* • *Now that these sorts of drugs are so widely available, it may be too late to put the genie back in the bottle.*

not **let the grass grow under** your **feet**
to not waste time by delaying doing something • *We can't let the grass grow under our feet – we've really got to get going with this project.*

let the side down *British & Australian*
to behave in a way that embarrasses or causes problems for a group of people that you are part of • *The general feeling is that cleaners who ignore the union's ban on overtime are letting the side down.*

▶ See also: leave/let well **alone**
get/let sb off the **hook**
let off **steam**
let sb **stew**

letter

the letter of the law *formal*
the exact words of a law and not its more important general meaning • *There is always the danger that a judge may follow the letter of the law rather than its spirit.*

to the letter *slightly formal*
if you follow instructions or obey rules to the letter, you do exactly what you are told to do • *I followed the instructions to the letter but I still couldn't get it to work.*

level

be level pegging *British & Australian*
if two people or groups who are

competing in a race or election are level pegging, they are equal and it is not certain who will win • *With three weeks to go to the election, Labour and the Alliance are still level pegging.*

be on the level *old-fashioned*
to be honest or true • *The offer seems too good to be true. Are you quite sure the man's on the level?*

do your **level best**
to try very hard to do something • (often + to do sth) *Tickets are quite hard to come by but I'll do my level best to get you one.*

a level playing field
a fair situation • *There are calls for less restrictive laws in order to allow them to compete* ***on a level playing field*** (= in a way that is fair) *with other financial institutions.*

liberties

take liberties
1 to change something, especially a piece of writing, in a way that people disagree with • (usually + **with**) *Whoever wrote the screenplay for the film took great liberties with the original text of the novel.*
2 *old-fashioned* to be too friendly to someone in a way that shows a lack of respect, especially in a sexual way • (often + **with**) *Don't let him take liberties with you.*

liberty

take the liberty of doing sth *formal*
to do something that will have an effect on someone else without asking their permission • (usually in past tenses) *I took the liberty of reserving us two seats at the conference. I hope that's all right by you.*

licence

be a licence to print money *British & Australian*
be a license to print money *American*
if a company or activity is a licence to print money, it causes people to become very rich without having to make any effort • *These shopping channels are just a licence to print money.*

lick

give sth **a lick and a promise**
1 *British & Australian old-fashioned* to clean something quickly and not carefully • *I put on my new suit, gave my shoes a lick and a promise, and left the house.*
2 *American & Australian old-fashioned* to do a job or piece of work quickly and not carefully • *We didn't have time to do much clearing up in the yard – just gave the grass a lick and a promise.*

lick sb's **boots** *informal*
to try too hard to please someone important • *I'm not prepared to lick someone's boots to get a promotion.*
boot-licking • *Far too much boot-licking goes on in this office.*

lick your **lips**
to feel pleased and excited about something that is going to happen, usually because you think you will get something good from it • *Meanwhile, the property developers are licking their lips at the prospect of all the money they're going to make.*

Lick my arse! *British & Australian taboo*
something that you say in order to tell someone that you will not do what they want you to do • *'I think you'd better leave now.' 'Lick my arse!'*

lick your **wounds**
to feel unhappy after a defeat or an unpleasant experience ✍When dogs and other animals are injured, they lick their wounds (= injuries) in order to help them get better. • *After retiring to lick its wounds, the party is regaining its confidence.*

► See also: kiss/lick sb's **arse**
knock/lick sth/sb into **shape**

lickety-split

lickety-split *mainly American informal*
very quickly • *He drove off lickety-split down the highway.*

licking

take a licking *American & Australian informal*
to be defeated or very strongly criticized • *Their latest album took a licking from the critics, but it's selling well.*

lid

blow/take the lid off sth
lift the lid on sth
to cause something bad that was previously kept secret to be known by the public • *In 1989 they started an investigation that was to blow the lid off corruption in the police force.*

▶ See also: **flip** your lid
keep a lid on sth
Put a lid on it!
put the lid on sth

lie

couldn't lie straight in bed *Australian informal*
if you say someone couldn't lie straight in bed, you mean they are very dishonest • *Nothing you could say about Pete would surprise me. The man couldn't even lie straight in bed.*

give the lie to sth *formal*
to show that something is not true • *The high incidence of cancer in the region surely gives the lie to official assurances that the factory is safe.*

lie doggo *British & Australian old-fashioned*
to hide, especially in order to avoid doing something that someone wants you to do • *'Where's Mike?' 'Probably lying doggo till the washing up's done.'*

lie down on the job
to not work as hard at something as you should • *The new Police Chief fired two officers he accused of lying down on the job.*

lie low
to remain hidden so that you will not be found • *We thought someone might have seen us leaving the building, so we figured we'd better lie low for a while.*

lie through your **teeth**
to tell someone something that you know is completely false • *The man's lying through his teeth. He never said anything of the sort.*

▶ See also: be/lie at the **bottom** of sth
live a lie

lies

a pack of lies
a tissue of lies *formal*
a story that someone has invented in order to deceive people • *He dismissed recent rumours that he'd had affairs with a number of women as 'a pack of lies'.* • *The entire account of where she'd been and who she'd been with that night was a tissue of lies.*

life

as large as life *British, American & Australian*
as big as life *American*
if you say that someone was somewhere as large as life, you mean that you were surprised to see them there • *I looked up from my paper and there he was, as large as life, Tim Taylor!*

be another/one of life's great mysteries *humorous*
to be something that it is impossible for you to understand • *Why people write their names on the walls of public toilets is one of life's great mysteries.*

be larger than life *British, American & Australian*
be bigger than life *American*
if someone is larger than life, they attract a lot of attention because they are more exciting and interesting than most people • *Most characters in his films are somewhat larger than life.*

be the life and soul of the party *British, American & Australian*
be the life of the party *American & Australian*
to be the type of person who enjoys social occasions and makes them more enjoyable for other people • *He's a very sweet man but he's not exactly the life and soul of the party.* • *Give him a few drinks and he's the life of the party!*

can't for the life of me
if you say you can't for the life of you remember something, you mean that you cannot remember it at all • *I know I filed it somewhere but I can't for the life of me remember where.*

frighten/scare the life out of sb
to make someone feel very frightened • *She frightened the life out of me,*

shouting like that.

Get a life! *informal*
something that you say which means someone is boring and they should find more exciting things to do • (often an order) *You're surely not going to stay in and clean the house on a Saturday night – oh, come on, get a life!* • *I hear him talking about his stamp collection and I feel like saying, 'You sad man, get a life!'*

give your **life**
lay down your **life** *slightly formal*
to die in order to save other people or in order to defend a belief that you support • *Millions of soldiers laid down their lives for their country in the Great War.*

lead/live the life of Riley *informal*
to have a happy life without hard work, problems or worries • *He lived the life of Riley, having inherited a huge amount of money.*

life in the fast lane
a way of living which is full of excitement and activity and often danger ✍The fast lane is the part of a motorway (= a large road) where drivers go the fastest. • *His was a life in the fast lane – parties, drugs, and a constant stream of glamorous women.*

life in the raw
life at its most difficult, without money or the comforts that money brings • *Travelling on the cheap exposes you to local life in the raw.*

life is cheap
if life is cheap somewhere, people's lives have little value so if they die it is not important • *In the city, gunmen rule the streets and life is cheap.*

your **life is in** sb's **hands**
if your life is in someone's hands, that person is completely responsible for what happens to you, often for whether you live or die • *When you fly, your life is in the hands of complete strangers.*
place/put your **life in** sb's **hands** • *Every time you drive a car, you put your life in the hands of other motorists.*

Life is just a bowl of cherries.
something that you say which means that life is very pleasant ✍This phrase is sometimes used humorously to mean the opposite • *The hotel is wonderful and the weather too. Life's just a bowl of cherries.* • *So as well as cleaning up the apartment and getting the paperwork done, I have three children to look after. Yes, life's just a bowl of cherries!*

life's too short
something that you say which means you should not waste time doing or worrying about things that are not important • (often + to do sth) *Life's too short to iron your underwear.* • *I can't get worried over an amount of money as small as that. Life's too short.*

Not on your life! *informal*
something that you say in order to tell someone with a lot of force that you will not do something • *'Would you kiss him?' 'Not on your life!'*

put your **life on the line**
to risk death in order to try to achieve something • *Politicians aren't the ones putting their lives on the line fighting wars.*

Such is life.
That's life.
something that you say when you are talking about bad things that happen or exist which you cannot prevent and must therefore accept • *In an ideal world, I'd rather have the child and the career but it's not possible. That's life.*

take your **life in/into** your **hands**
to do something dangerous • *I'm sure this elevator isn't properly maintained. I feel as though I'm taking my life into my hands every time I go in it.*

There's life in the old dog yet. *humorous*
something that you say which means that although someone is old, they still have enough energy to do things • *I may be 90 but there's life in the old dog yet.*

This is the life!
something that you say when you are relaxing and very much enjoying the fact that you are not at work • *Sun, sand and cocktails – this is the life!*

▶ See also: you can **bet** your life/your bottom dollar
breathe (new) life into sth
depart this life
risk life and limb

can't do sth to **save** your life
see life
set sb up for life

life-saver

a life-saver
someone or something that gives you a lot of help when you are in a very difficult situation • *When you're stuck in traffic like this, a mobile phone's an absolute life-saver.*

lifetime

once in a lifetime
only likely to happen once in someone's life • *Opportunities to play in the Cup Final only come once in a lifetime so we've got to make the most of it.*
once-in-a-lifetime • (always before noun) *Enter this competition to win a once-in-a-lifetime trip to the Caribbean.*

lift

not **lift a finger**
to not help someone to do something, usually because you are lazy • (usually + to do sth) *He spends all day stretched out on the sofa and never lifts a finger to help.*

▶ See also: lift the **lid** on sth

light

be as light as a feather
to be very light in weight • *I could easily pick you up – you're as light as a feather.*

be light years away
to be a very long time in the future • *A cure for all kinds of cancer is still light years away.* • (often + **from** + doing sth) *Scientists are light years away from understanding* (= it will be a very long time before scientists understand) *the human brain.*

be light years away from sth
if something is light years away from something else, it has made so much progress that the two things are now very different • *Modern computers are light years away from the huge machines we used in the seventies.*

be the light of sb's **life**
to be the person you love most • *My daughter is the light of my life.*

be/go out like a light *informal*
to go to sleep very quickly • *I was out like a light after all that fresh air.*

in the light of sth *British & Australian*
in light of sth *American & Australian*
if something is done or happens in the light of facts, it is done or happens because of those facts • *In the light of new evidence he has been allowed to appeal against his prison sentence.* • *In light of what you've just told me, I can understand why you and David were fighting.*

light a fire under sb *mainly American*
to make someone work better or harder • *It's time you lit a fire under those guys or they'll never finish painting the house.*

light at the end of the tunnel
something which makes you believe that a difficult or unpleasant situation will end • *We're halfway through our exams now, so we can **see light at the end of the tunnel**.* • *Unemployment is still rising but analysts assure us there is light at the end of the tunnel.*

light dawns
if light dawns on you, you suddenly understand something • *He was lying to me, but it was months before the light dawned.* • (often + **on**) *Light dawned on me when I heard she knew my mother.*

light your **fire** *informal*
to make someone excited, especially sexually • *I've met some decent men but none that light my fire.*

light relief
something that is entertaining or relaxing after something that is serious or boring • *A lively argument between the two main speakers provided a bit of light relief in an otherwise dull conference.*

make light of sth
to suggest by the way that you talk or behave that you do not think a problem is serious • *You shouldn't make light of other people's fears.*

make light work of sth/doing sth
to do something quickly and easily • *Heather made light work of painting the walls.* • *You made light work of that chocolate cake!* (= you ate it quickly)

see the light (of day)
1 if an object sees the light of day, it is

brought out so that people can see it • *The archives contain vintage recordings, some of which have never seen the light of day.*

2 if something, especially an idea or a plan, sees the light of day, it starts to exist • *It was the year when the equal opportunities bill first saw the light of day.*

shed/throw light on sth

to help people understand a situation • *Thank you for shedding some light on what is really a very complicated subject.*

► See also: **bring** sth to light
hide your light under a bushel
see the light
trip the light fantastic

lighten

lighten sb's/**the load**

to make a difficult or upsetting situation easier to deal with • *Anyway, we'll be getting a temp in next month to do some of this work so that should lighten your load.*

light-headed

be/feel light-headed

to feel weak and as if you might fall over • *I feel a bit light-headed. I shouldn't have drunk that second glass of wine.*

lightning

Lightning does not strike twice.

something that you say which means that a bad thing will not happen to the same person twice • *I know the crash has scared you, but lightning doesn't strike twice.*

a lightning rod *American*

someone or something that takes all the blame for a situation, although other people or things are responsible too • (often + **for**) *In a harsh economic climate, raises for teachers have become a lightning rod for criticism.*

lights

The lights are on but nobody's/no-one's home. *humorous*

something that you say when you think someone is stupid, or when someone does not react because they are thinking about something else • *It's no good expecting John to say anything. The lights are on but no-one's home.*

► See also: **punch** sb's lights out

like

How do you like them apples!

1 *American & Australian informal* something that you say when you want someone to know how clever or successful you are, especially when you have done something better than they have • *You know that girl we were talking to last night – with the long blond hair? Well, I got her number. How do you like them apples!*

2 *American & Australian informal* something that you say to show you are surprised or disappointed by something that has happened • *So Marilyn has moved to Florida? Well, how do you like them apples!*

like it or lump it *informal*

if you tell someone to like it or lump it, you mean they must accept a situation they do not like, because they cannot change it • *The fact remains, that's all we're going to pay him and he can like it or lump it.* • *Like it or lump it, romantic fiction is read regularly by thousands.*

► See also: be of like/one **mind**

likely

A likely story.

something that you say when you do not believe that an explanation is true • *He claims he thought he was drinking low alcohol lager. A likely story.* • *So he was just giving her a friendly hug because she was upset, was he? That's a likely story if ever I heard one.*

lily

► See: **gild** the lily

lily-livered

lily-livered *literary*

not brave • *I've never seen such a lily-livered bunch of wimps in my life!*

lily-white

lily-white

1 *British, American & Australian* completely white in colour • *He marvelled at her lily-white hands.*

2 *American & Australian* completely honest • (often negative) *He's not exactly lily-white himself, so he has some nerve calling her a cheat!*

3 *American & Australian* having only

white people near, often because of a wish to keep black people away • *The black family found it difficult to feel comfortable in this lily-white, prosperous suburb.*

limb

be out on a limb
alone and lacking support from other people • *Because we're geographically so far removed from the main office, we do sometimes feel as if we're out on a limb.*

go out on a limb
if you go out on a limb, you state an opinion or you do something which is very different to most other people • *I don't think we're going out on a limb in claiming that global warming is a problem that must be addressed.* • *Rob Thompson, the producer, admits the series is going out on a limb in that it is quite different to anything else currently on television.*

▶ See also: **tear** sb limb from limb

limelight

be in the limelight

be in the limelight
to receive attention and interest from the public ✍Limelight was a type of lighting used in the past in theatres to light the stage. • *He's been in the limelight recently, following the publication of a controversial novel.*
steal the limelight • *The whole team played well, but Rooney stole the limelight* (= got most attention) *with two stunning goals.*

limits

off limits
1 if an area is off limits, you are not allowed to enter it • *When we were kids, our parents' bedroom was definitely off limits.*
2 not allowed • *Today's magazines tackle the sort of subjects that would once have been considered off limits.* • *What he does make very clear is that questions about his private life are off limits.*

limp-wristed

limp-wristed *informal*
a man who is limp-wristed seems weak and lacks the qualities that people usually admire in a man • *My mother liked him though I suspect my father thought he was a bit limp-wristed.*

line

all along the line
all the way down the line
at every stage in a process • *The project's been plagued with financial problems all along the line.* • *Managerial mistakes were made all the way down the line.*

be in sb's **line** *old-fashioned*
to be a subject or activity that you are interested in or good at • *I wouldn't have thought gardening was in your line, Ben.*

be in line for sth
to be likely to get something good • *If anyone's in line for promotion, I should think it's Helen.* • *After his performance last season, it's reckoned that Taylor is* ***next in line for*** *the captaincy.*

be on the line
if something is on the line, it is in a situation in which it could be lost or harmed • *I didn't know his job was on the line.*
lay/put sth **on the line** • *I feel pretty strongly about the matter, but I'm not going to lay my career on the line for it.*

be out of line
1 if someone's actions or words are out of line, they are not suitable and they should not have been done or said • *And the way he spoke to her in the meeting – that was completely out of line.* • *Her remarks to the papers were* ***way out of line.***
2 if the amount or cost of something is out of line it is not what is expected or usual

• (usually + **with**) *His salary is* ***way out of line*** *with what other people in the company get.*

down the line
if an event is a particular period of time down the line, it will not happen until that period of time has passed • *We'll probably want kids too but that's a few years down the line.*

a fine/thin line
if there is a fine line between one thing and another, they are very similar although the second thing is bad • (often + **between**) *There's a thin line between courage and foolishness.*

tread a fine/thin line between sth if someone treads a fine line between a good quality and a bad quality, they succeed in having only the good quality • *Somehow he manages to tread that fine line between honesty and tactlessness.*

get a line on sb/sth *American*
to get special information that will help you find someone or do something • *Detectives hope to get a line on the suspect from the fingerprints he left.*
have a line on sb/sth • *She talked like she has a line on what it will take to win.*

in the line of duty
if you do something in the line of duty, or if something happens to you in the line of duty, you do it or it happens as a part of your job • *He was killed in the line of duty.*

in the line of fire
likely to be criticized, attacked, or got rid of • *Lawyers often find themselves in the line of fire.*

line your **(own) pockets**
to make a lot of money in a way that is not fair or honest • *Sharp resigned after allegations that he had been lining his pockets during his time as company director.*

line sb's **pockets**
if money or a system is lining someone's pockets, that person is receiving too much money or is receiving money that is not intended for them • *There's to be an investigation following allegations that the money raised is lining the pockets of officials.*

somewhere along the line *informal*
at some point during a period or an activity • *I don't know what went wrong with our relationship but somewhere along the line we stopped loving each other.*

toe/tow the line
to do what you are ordered or expected to do • *He might not like the rules but he'll toe the line just to avoid trouble.* • *Ministers who refused to toe the Party line were swiftly got rid of.*

► See also: **cross** the line
draw a line under sth
draw the line
draw the line at sth
drop sb a line
fall in/into line
feed sb a line
lay it on the line
take the line/path of **least** resistance
step out of line

lines

along the lines of sth
along those lines
similar in type • *I can't remember exactly what words he used but it was something along those lines.* • *I was thinking of doing a dinner party along the lines of that meal I cooked for Annie and Dave.*
along/on the same lines in a similar way • *We've been thinking along the same lines for a while now.*

► See also: get your lines/wires **crossed**
read between the lines
be on the **right** lines

lingua franca

a lingua franca
a language that is used for communication between people whose main languages are different • (often + **of**) *English is the undisputed lingua franca of the business world.*

lion

the lion's share
the biggest part of something • *The lion's share of the museum's budget goes on special exhibitions.*

► See also: **beard** the lion in their den

lions

feed/throw sb **to the lions**
to cause someone to be in a situation where they are criticized strongly or treated badly and to not try to protect them • *No one prepared me for the audience's hostility – I really felt I'd been fed to the lions.*

the lions' den
an unpleasant situation in which a person or group of people criticizes you or your ideas • *It's your turn for the lions' den. Gordon wants to see you in his office now.*

lip

give/pay lip service to sth
to say that you agree with and support an idea or plan but not do anything to help it to succeed • *The company pays lip service to the notion of racial equality but you look around you and all you see are white faces.*

▶ See also: **curl** your lip

lips

be on everyone's lips
if a word or question is on everyone's lips, a lot of people are talking about it and interested in it • *And the question that's on everyone's lips at the moment is, will he have to resign over the scandal?*

My lips are sealed. *humorous*
something you say to let someone know that you will not tell anyone else what they have just told you • *'I'd prefer you not to mention this to anyone else.' 'My lips are sealed.'*

▶ See also: **lick** your lips
Read my lips!

liquid

a liquid lunch *humorous*
if someone has a liquid lunch, they drink alcoholic drinks instead of eating food • *I had a two hour liquid lunch and nearly fell asleep at my desk in the afternoon.*

liquid refreshment *humorous*
a drink, usually an alcoholic drink • *After 5 hours in front of a computer I'm in need of some liquid refreshment.*

liquor

▶ See: can't **hold** their drink/liquor

list

a list as long as your **arm**
if you say a list is as long as your arm, you mean that it is very long • *Anyway, I'd better make a start. I've got a list as long as my arm of jobs to do.*

litmus

a litmus test
something that shows clearly what someone's opinions or intentions are ✍Litmus is a substance used in chemical tests because it changes colour. • *His views on abortion are effectively a litmus test of his views on women's rights.*

little

A little bird told me (so).
something that you say in order to let someone know that you are not going to tell them who gave you the information being discussed • *'So who told you she'd got the job?' 'Oh, let's just say a little bird told me so.'*

a little horror *humorous*
a child who behaves very badly • *I had six of the little horrors running round the house all day.*

too little, too late
if the help that is given to a person is described as too little, too late, there is not enough of it and it was given too late to be useful • *The government have finally decided to put some money into research but it's too little, too late.*

twist/wrap sb **around/round** your **little finger**
to be able to persuade someone to do anything you want, usually because they like you so much • *He'd do anything you asked him to. You've got him wrapped around your little finger!*

live

go live
if a new system, especially a computer system, goes live, it starts to operate • *Our new payments system will go live at the beginning of next month.*

live (from) hand to mouth
to have just enough money to live on and nothing extra • *My father earned very little and there were four of us kids so we lived from hand to mouth.*

hand-to-mouth • (always before noun) *Low wages mean a* ***hand-to-mouth existence*** *for many people.*

live a lie
to live a life that is dishonest because you are pretending to be something that you are not, either to yourself or to other people • *Walker, who admitted that he was gay last year, spoke of the relief he felt at no longer having to live a lie.*

live and breathe sth
if you live and breathe an activity or subject, you spend most of your time doing it or thinking about it because you like it so much • *For twenty years I've lived and breathed dance. It's been my whole life.*

live and let live
believing that other people should be allowed to live their lives in the way that they want to • *They seem as a society to have a very live and let live attitude towards issues like gay rights.*

live by/on your **wits**
to earn enough money to live by being clever or cheating people • *A lot of these kids are thrown out onto the streets and they have to live by their wits.*

live high off/on the hog *American & Australian*
to have a lot of money and live in comfort, especially eating and drinking a lot • *He was a millionaire who lived high on the hog at all times.*

live in a fool's paradise
to be happy because you do not know or will not accept how bad a situation really is • *James is living in a fool's paradise if he thinks things are always going to be this good.*

live in cloud-cuckoo land
to believe that things you want will happen, when really they are impossible • *Anyone who thinks this project will be finished within six weeks is living in cloud-cuckoo land.*

live in each other's pockets
if people live in each other's pockets, they spend too much time together • *I don't think it's healthy the way those two live in each other's pockets.*

live in hope
to hope that something you want to happen will happen one day • *None of my poems have been published yet, but I live in hope.*

live in sin *humorous*
to live with someone that you are having a sexual relationship with but are not married to • (usually in continuous tenses) *Last I heard they'd moved in together and were living in sin.*

live it up *informal*
to enjoy yourself by doing things that involve spending a lot of money • *I decided to live it up for a while – at least until the money ran out.*

live like a king
to live in a very comfortable way with all the luxuries you want • *He lived like a king for six months, drinking champagne and driving a Porsche, until the money finally ran out.*

live off the backs of sb
to use what other people produce in order to live, without giving them anything in exchange • *He was one of the wealthiest dictators of all time and he lived off the backs of the people.*

live off the fat of the land
to have enough money to live in a very comfortable way without having to do much work • *Times have changed for the upper classes, many of whom are no longer able to live off the fat of the land.*

live on your **nerves** *British & Australian*
to always be very anxious • *She doesn't sleep or eat well. I get the feeling she's really living on her nerves.*

live to a ripe old age
to live until you are very old • *Both his grandparents lived to a ripe old age.*
at the ripe old age of sth • *He died at the ripe old age of eighty-seven.*

live to fight another day
to lose a fight or competition but not be completely defeated and therefore be able to try again in the future • *The anti-pollution campaigners lost the debate but lived to fight another day.*

live to tell the tale
to still be alive after a dangerous or frightening experience • *I should imagine very few people have fallen from that height and lived to tell the tale.* • *I had*

dinner with her and lived to tell the tale.

a live wire
someone who is very quick and active, both mentally and physically • *I hadn't met Rory before – he's a real live wire.*

never live sth **down**
if you say that you will never live down something bad or embarrassing that you have done, you mean people will not forget it • *Three million people saw the singer fall off the edge of the stage. He'll never live it down.* • *I'll never live down the fact that I spilt champagne down my boss's trousers.*

You live and learn. *British*
Live and learn. *American*
something that you say when you have just discovered something that you did not know • *I had no idea they were related. Oh well, you live and learn.*

▶ See also: be/live on the **breadline**
have/lead/live a **charmed** life
be/live in a **dream** world
lead/live the **life** of Riley

lived

you **haven't lived** *humorous*
if you tell someone they haven't lived if they have not experienced something, you mean that this experience is very pleasant or exciting and they should try it • *You've never been to a Turkish bath? Oh, you haven't lived!*

lively

▶ See: **Look** lively!

living

be the living end
1 *American & Australian old-fashioned* to be extremely good • *We were big fans of their band. We thought it was the living end in those days.*
2 *American & Australian old-fashioned* to be very annoying • *Helen is late again. She really is the living end!*

in/within living memory
events or situations in living memory can be remembered by people who are alive now • *Areas of southern Italy are experiencing some of the worst storms in living memory.* (= the worst storms that people can remember) • *Some of these houses still had outside toilets within living memory.*

a living death
a life that is so full of suffering that it would be better to be dead • *She can't walk, she can't feed herself and she can scarcely speak. It's a living death.* • *For me, marriage to someone like that would be a living death.*

living on borrowed time
if someone is living on borrowed time, they are not expected to live much longer • *I've got cancer – I'm living on borrowed time.*

▶ See also: (a) living **hell**

lo

lo and behold *humorous*
something that you say when you tell someone about something surprising that happened • *I went into a bar just next to our hotel and, lo and behold, who should I see sitting there but Jim Gibson.*

load

Get a load of that! *very informal*
1 something that you say when you are very surprised by something, or to show approval • *Get a load of that! Is that not the most beautiful car you have ever seen?*
2 something that you say when you see someone who is very sexually attractive • *Get a load of that, lads! Very nice.*

▶ See also: **lighten** sb's/the load
be a load/weight off your **mind**
shoot your load

loaded

loaded for bear *American informal*
ready and eager to deal with something that is going to be difficult • *Their team came out onto the field, loaded for bear, but our defense stopped them.*

loaf

▶ See: **Half** a loaf is better than none.
Use your loaf.

lock

lock horns
if two people lock horns, they argue about something • (often + **over**) *The mayor and her deputy locked horns over the plans for the new road.*

lock, stock, and barrel
including all or every part of something • *He's been pressing for the organization to move, lock, stock, and barrel, from Paris to Brussels.*

under lock and key
1 kept safely in a room or container that is locked • *I tend to keep medicines under lock and key because of the kids.*
2 in prison • *I think the feeling from the general public is that people like that should be kept under lock and key for the rest of their lives.*

locker-room

locker-room
locker-room jokes or remarks are the type of rude, sexual jokes and remarks that men are thought to enjoy when they are with other men ✍A locker room is a place where people change their clothes before and after playing sport. • (always before noun) *There's the usual locker-room banter which I try to stay out of.*

log

▶ See: **sleep** like a log/top

loggerheads

be at loggerheads
if two people or groups are at loggerheads, they disagree strongly about something • (often + **with**) *They're constantly at loggerheads with the farmers' union.* • (sometimes + **over**) *The Senate and the House are still at loggerheads over the most crucial parts of the bill.*

loins

▶ See: **gird** (up) your loins

lone

a lone wolf
a person who prefers to do things on their own • *The typical role for Bogart was the Casablanca character, a lone wolf, cynical but heroic.*

▶ See also: **plough** a lone/lonely furrow
a (lone) **voice** in the wilderness

lonely

▶ See: **plough** a lone/lonely furrow

long

not **be long for this world**
to be going to die soon • *Judging by the look of him, he's not long for this world either.*

be long in the tooth *humorous*
to be too old ✍The older a horse is, the longer its teeth are. • *I'd have thought she was a bit long in the tooth to be starring as the romantic heroine.*

go a long way
if you say that someone will go a long way, you mean that they will be successful • *'I like my men older – and richer.' 'You'll go a long way with ideas like that, my girl!'*

go back a long way
if two people go back a long way, they have known each other for a long time • *Justin and I were at college together so we go back a long way.*

have come a long way
to have made a lot of progress • (often + **since**) *We've come a long way since the days when you had to call an operator to phone another country.*

How long is a piece of string? *British & Australian*
something that you say when someone asks you a question that you cannot answer about how big something is or how much time something will take • *'So how long does a project like that take?' 'How long's a piece of string?'*

It's a long story.
something that you say when someone has asked you about something that happened and you do not want to explain it to them because it would take too long • *'So why was Carlo knocking on your door at midnight?' 'It's a long story.'*

the long and the short of it
something that you say when you intend to tell someone something in the quickest and simplest way possible • *Anyway, the long and the short of it is that he's not going to be working for us any more.*

the long arm of the law *humorous*
the police • *You know what they say, you can't escape the long arm of the law.*

a long face
if you have a long face, you look sad • *'Why've you got such a long face?' 'My boyfriend doesn't want to see me any more.'*

a long haul
something that takes a lot of time and energy • *It's been a long haul but we've finally got the house looking the way we want it.*
in/over the long haul *American* for a long period of time • *You have to think how the company will perform over the long haul.*

long on sth **and short on** sth
having too much of one quality and not enough of another • *I've always found his films long on style and short on content.*

a long shot
something that will probably not succeed but is worth trying • *It's a long shot but I could call Tony and see if he knows her address.*

Long time no see.
something that you say in order to greet someone who you have not seen for a long time • *Hi there, Paul. Long time no see.*

not by a long shot *informal*
not by a long chalk *old-fashioned*
something that you say when you think something is not at all true • *'Do you think it's as good as her last movie?' 'No, not by a long shot.'* • *It's not over yet, not by a long chalk, we still have a very good chance of winning.*

So long. *American informal*
a friendly way of saying goodbye to someone • *So long – see you tomorrow.*

take a long, hard look at sth
to examine something very carefully in order to improve it in the future • *We need to take a long, hard look at the way we control gun ownership.*

take the long view
to think about the effects that something will have in the future instead of in the present • *If you take the long view, of course, you can regard staff training as an investment for the company.*

to cut a long story short *British & Australian*
to make a long story short *American*
something that you say when you are about to stop telling someone all the details of something that happened and tell them only the main facts • *Anyway, to cut a long story short, we left at midnight and James left somewhat later.*

▶ See also: in the long/short **run**
in the long/medium/short **term**
think long and hard

long-winded

long-winded
long-winded speech or writing continues for too long in a way that is boring • *She launched into a long-winded explanation of how she'd found the books and I'm afraid I didn't really listen.*

look

not **be much to look at** *informal*
to not be attractive • *She's not much to look at, but she's got a lovely personality.*

get a look in *British & Australian informal*
to get a chance to do something that you would like to do or to succeed in something • (usually negative) *Chris was so popular with the girls that whenever he was around I didn't get a look in.* • *The other team were so much better than us. We didn't get a look in.*

not **look a gift horse in the mouth**
if someone tells you not to look a gift horse in the mouth, they mean that you should not criticize or feel doubt about something good that has been offered to you • *Okay, it's not the job of your dreams but it pays good money. I'd be inclined not to look a gift horse in the mouth if I were you.*

Look before you leap.
something that you say in order to advise someone to think about possible problems before doing something • *If you're thinking of buying a house, my advice is, look before you leap.*

look daggers at sb
to look very angrily at someone • *I suddenly noticed David looking daggers at me and thought I'd better shut up.*

look down your **nose at** sth/sb *informal*
to think that someone is less important than you or that something is not good enough for you • *I always felt that she looked down her nose at us because we*

spoke with strong accents and hadn't been to college.

look sb **in the eye/eyes**
to look directly at someone without fear or shame • *Look me in the eyes and tell me the truth.* • *I felt so embarrassed – I just couldn't look him in the eye.*

look sb **in the face**
to look directly at someone without fear or shame • *I don't know how you can look your sister in the face after what you've done.*

look like a drowned rat
to be very wet, especially because you have been in heavy rain • *I had to cycle home in the rain and came in looking like a drowned rat.*

look like something the cat brought/dragged in *informal*
if someone looks like something the cat brought in, they are very untidy and dirty • *You can't possibly go to school like that – you look like something the cat dragged in!*

Look lively! *British & Australian informal old-fashioned*
something you say to tell someone to hurry • *Look lively – we've got to be there in half an hour!*

look on the bright side
to try to see something good in a bad situation • *Look on the bright side. The accident insurance might pay for a new car.*

look right/straight through sb
to behave as if you do not see someone when you look at them, either because you do not notice them or because you are ignoring them • *I'm sure I was at school with that girl, but she just looked straight through me.*

Look sharp!
1 *old-fashioned* something that you say in order to tell someone to hurry • *Look sharp! We have to leave in five minutes.*
2 *mainly American* something that you say in order to warn someone about something • *Look sharp! That ladder isn't very steady.*

look the other way
to ignore something wrong or unpleasant that you know is happening instead of trying to deal with it • *When one of their own friends or colleagues is involved in wrongdoing, people sometimes prefer to look the other way.*

look the part
to look suitable for a particular situation • *If you want to get a job as a fashion buyer, it helps if you look the part.*

look to your **laurels**
to make an extra effort to succeed because there is more competition • *Nowadays there are a number of rival products on the market and the older, established companies are having to look to their laurels.*

Look what the cat's dragged in! *informal*
an insulting way of saying that someone has just arrived, suggesting that they are ugly and badly dressed • *Well, look what the cat's dragged in. Did you make that dress or borrow it from your mother?*

Look who's talking! *informal*
something that you say when someone criticizes another person for doing something that they do themselves • *'She drinks too much, that's her problem.' 'Look who's talking!'*

▶ See also: look/feel (like) a **million** dollars
look like **thunder**

looking

be like looking for a needle in a haystack
to be difficult or impossible to find • *I don't know how you find anything in your desk, Polly. It's like looking for a needle in a haystack.*

looks

If it looks like a duck and walks/quack/flies etc. like a duck, it is a duck. *humorous*
used to say that something is probably exactly what it seems to be and we should trust our judgment about it • *They're calling it a clinic, not a prison, but if it looks like a duck and swims like a duck, then it is a duck, I think.*

If looks could kill...
something that you say in order to describe the unpleasant or angry way in which someone looked at you • *I'll never forget the expression on her face when she*

saw me with Pete. If looks could kill...

loop

be in the loop *American informal*
to have the special knowledge or power that belongs to a particular group of people • *You can tell she's in the loop. She always knows about policy decisions before the rest of us.*
OPPOSITE **be out of the loop** *American informal* • *I've been out of the loop since I changed jobs. I didn't realize Wendy and Bob had gotten engaged.*

knock/throw sb **for a loop** *American informal*
if something that happens knocks you for a loop, it upsets or confuses you because you do not expect it • *He knocked me for a loop when he said he was quitting his job.*

loose

be at a loose end *British & Australian*
be at loose ends *American*
to have nothing to do • *If you find yourself at a loose end over the weekend, you could always clean out the garden shed.* • *Sarah was at loose ends in a strange city when she first met Bob.*

be on the loose
if a dangerous person or animal is on the loose, they have escaped from prison or a cage and are free • *A killer who preys on attractive women is feared to be on the loose in Moscow.*

a loose cannon
a person who cannot be completely trusted because their behaviour is sometimes strange or violent • *He's seen as a loose cannon by other team members. If anyone's going to get into a fight, it'll be Pete.*

loose ends
the last few details that need to be finished or explained in order for something to be complete • *The job's nearly done. I'm just* ***tying up one or two loose ends*** *at the moment.*

▶ See also: **cut** loose
Hang loose!

loosen

loosen your **tongue**
if alcohol loosens your tongue, it makes you talk a lot without thinking carefully about what you are saying • *Her tongue loosened by drink, she began to say things that she would later regret.*

lord

your **lord and master** *humorous*
someone who you must obey because they have power over you • *I have to go and cook supper for my lord and master.*

lord it over sb
to behave as if you are better than someone else and have the right to tell them what to do • *She likes to lord it over the more junior staff in the office.*

lose

lose your **cool**
to suddenly become very angry and start shouting • *I try to be patient with her but she was so irritating in that meeting, I just lost my cool.*

lose your **edge**
to lose the qualities or skills that made you successful in the past • *She's still competing, but she's two years older now and she's lost her edge.*

lose face
to do something which makes other people stop respecting you • *He refused to admit he made a mistake because he didn't want to lose face.*

lose your **grip**
to lose your ability to control or deal with a situation • *He was losing his grip at work and knew it was time to retire.* • (often + **on**) *It suggests that the ruling party is losing its grip on the middle classes in some of the bigger cities.*

lose your **head**
to suddenly become very angry or upset • *He usually stays quite calm in stressful situations but this time he really lost his head.*

lose your **heart to** sb *literary*
to fall in love with someone • *I think he lost his heart to Mary on the day they met.*

lose your **marbles** *informal*
to start acting in a strange way and forgetting things • *I may be old, but I haven't lost my marbles yet.*
OPPOSITE **have all** your **marbles**

informal • *He's pretty old but he still has all his marbles, if that's what you mean.*

lose your **mind**
to become crazy • *Taking a child on a motorbike without a helmet! Have you completely lost your mind?*

lose your **rag** *British & Australian informal*
to suddenly become very angry and start shouting • *He said one too many stupid things and I just lost my rag.* • *It was the only time I've ever lost my rag with someone in an office situation.*

lose sight of sth
to forget about an important idea or a fact because you are thinking too much about other things • *Some members of the peace force seem to have lost sight of the fact that they are here to help people.*

not **lose sleep over** sth
to not worry about something • *I don't intend to lose any sleep over this problem.*

lose the plot *British & Australian humorous*
to become crazy • *I was waking up in the middle of the night, not knowing who I was or where I was. I really thought I was losing the plot.*

lose the thread
to stop understanding something someone says or something you are reading because it is too complicated or because you cannot concentrate • *When he started quoting Martin Luther King, I completely* ***lost the thread of*** *his argument.*

lose your **touch**
if you lose your touch, you can no longer do something as well as you could before • (usually in continuous tenses) *It's good to see their goalkeeper's not losing his touch.*

▶ See also: what you lose on the **swings**, you gain on the roundabouts

losing

▶ See: **fight** a losing battle

loss

be at a loss
to not know what to do or say • (usually + to do sth) *He won't accept financial help from me so I'm at a loss to know what to do.* • *For once I found myself completely* ***at a loss for words.*** (= I did not know what to say)

losses

▶ See: **cut** your losses

lost

be lost for words
to be unable to speak because you are so surprised • *I was so amazed at what she'd said I found myself completely lost for words.*

Get lost! *very informal*
something that you say when you are annoyed with someone or you want someone to go away • *Oh, get lost! I'm not in the mood for your jokes.*

like a lost soul
if someone is walking around a place like a lost soul, they are walking slowly without direction or purpose in a way that makes them look sad and lost • *I found him wandering aimlessly around the hall like a lost soul.*

a lost cause
something or someone that has no chance of success • *I tried to stop the kids dropping their clothes on the floor, but finally decided it was a lost cause.*

lost in the mists of time
if something is lost in the mists of time, everyone has forgotten it because it happened such a long time ago • *The true significance of these symbols has become lost in the mists of time.*

lost in the shuffle *American & Australian*
if something or someone gets lost in the shuffle, they do not get the attention that they deserve • *Refugee children in the big camps just get lost in the shuffle and are sometimes left without food.*

make up for lost time
to spend a lot of time doing something because you did not have the opportunity to do it previously • *I didn't travel much as a young adult but I'm certainly making up for lost time now.*

lot

have a lot going for you
to have many good qualities or advantages that will make it easier for you to

succeed • *She's bound to find a job. She's got such a lot going for her.*

OPPOSITE not **have much going for** you • *Poor thing, she hasn't got much going for her really. She's neither clever nor attractive.*

have a lot of time for sb/sth

to like and admire someone or something • *I've got a lot of time for Jenny. She always has something interesting to say.* • *I've got a lot of time for his ideas about child psychology.*

OPPOSITE not **have much time for** sb/sth • *I've got no time for negative people.* • *She doesn't have much time for liberal ideas about dealing with criminals.*

have a lot to answer for

to be the main cause of a problem or an unpleasant situation • *People who sell drugs to kids have a lot to answer for.*

leave a lot to be desired

to be much worse than you would like • (never in continuous tenses) *Apparently, Meg's cooking leaves a lot to be desired.*

throw in your **lot with** sb
cast your **lot with** sb

to join a person or group and accept that whatever happens to them will also happen to you • *He's understandably reluctant to throw in his lot with a struggling young company who might not exist in a year's time.*

► See also: be **all** over the lot
have a lot/enough on your **plate**

loud

loud and clear

if an idea is expressed loud and clear, it is expressed very clearly in a way that is easy to understand • *In all this research, one message comes through loud and clear: excessive exposure to sun causes skin cancer.*

loud-mouthed

a loud-mouthed person often says rude or stupid things in a loud voice • *So long as he doesn't bring along those loud-mouthed friends of his.*

lounge

a lounge lizard *mainly American*

a man who spends a lot of time trying to meet rich people, especially women, in bars and at social occasions • *The bar was empty except for the lounge lizard in the corner, who was obviously waiting for someone.*

love

not **for love nor/or money**

if you say that you cannot or will not do something for love nor money, you mean that it is impossible to do or that you will not do it whatever happens • *It's incredibly popular. You can't get tickets for love nor money.* • *He's hopeless and unreliable. I wouldn't give him a job for love nor money.*

I must/I'll love you and leave you. *humorous*

something that you say when you say goodbye to someone that you are leaving • *Well, I'm sure you've got work to be doing so I'll love you and leave you.*

a love child

a child whose parents are not married to each other • *He allegedly has a love child in Australia from an affair with a much younger woman.*

love handles *humorous*

a layer of extra fat around the middle of a person's body • *You wouldn't want me to lose my love handles, would you?*

a love nest

a home where two people who love each other live together, or a home where two people meet secretly in order to have sex • *Apparently, they had a love nest in Soho where they used to meet at lunchtime.*

the love of your **life** *humorous*

the person that you love most in all your life • *And there I was, watching the love of my life board a plane to go to the other side of the world.*

love sb/sth **to bits** *informal*

to like or to love someone or something a lot • *Clive's the nicest person I know. I love him to bits.* • *'Do you like your new bike, then?' 'Oh, I love it to bits!'*

make love

to have sex with someone • *We went back to his apartment and made love.* • (often + **to**) *I was just thinking how nice it would be to make love to you.*

love-making • *It was our conversations more than the love-making* *that I remembered after the affair was over.*

no/little love lost between sb

if there is no love lost between two people, they do not like each other • *There's no love lost between those two. They could never work together.*

love-in

a love-in *informal*

a situation where two or more people praise each other a lot, especially when the praise is more than they deserve • *The awards ceremony, as usual, was a love-in.*

low

keep a low profile

to avoid attracting attention to yourself • *He's been keeping a low profile at work ever since his argument with Peter.*

a low ebb

a bad state • (not used with *the*) *Respect for the police is* ***at a low ebb.*** • *I'd just separated from my wife and was at a fairly low ebb.* (= was feeling sad and without hope) • *Relations between the two countries have reached their lowest ebb* (= are the worst they have been) *since the second world war.*

low-key

not intended to attract a lot of attention • *She had requested that the funeral be a low-key affair.* • *The reception itself was surprisingly low-key.*

low life

the behaviour and activities of people from a low social class, especially criminal activities • *She worked as a prostitute and experienced the harsher side of Parisian low life.*

the low man on the totem pole *American*

someone who has the least important position in an organization • *He started as the low man on the totem pole and worked his way up to be manager.*

▸ See also: **lay** sb low
lie low

low-end

low-end *American informal*

a low-end product is cheaper than, and not as good as the best product of its type • (always before noun) *You can get low-end color printers that still do a good job.*

lower

lower your **sights**

to accept something less good than the thing you were hoping for • *With so few jobs around she's had to lower her sights.*

lower the boom *American informal*

to suddenly stop someone doing something you do not approve of • *Dad lowered the boom. I have to stay in the next two weekends.*

lower the tone

if something lowers the tone of a place, it makes it less suitable for people of a high social class, and if something lowers the tone of a conversation or a piece of writing, it makes it less polite or of a lower quality • (usually + **of**) *The locals don't like students living around here. It lowers the tone of the neighbourhood.* • *Trust you to lower the tone of the evening by telling rude jokes, Ian!*
OPPOSITE **raise the tone** • *A preface from a local clergyman had raised the moral tone of the book.*

▸ See also: drop/lower your **guard**

lowest

the lowest common denominator

the large number of people in society who will accept low-quality products and entertainment • *The problem with so much television is that it aims at the lowest common denominator.*

the lowest of the low

people who have no moral standards and lack any personal qualities • *He regards the police as the lowest of the low. Drug-dealers and pimps come a close second.*

luck

be down on your **luck**

to be suffering because a lot of bad things are happening to you, usually things which cause you to have no money • *He plays the manager of a night-club who's down on his luck and resorts to gambling to pay his debts.*

be in luck

be in luck
to be able to have or do something, especially when you do not expect to • *'Have you got any prawn sandwiches left?' 'You're in luck – this is the last one.'*
OPPOSITE **be out of luck** • *I'm afraid you're out of luck – the concert is fully booked.*

have the luck of the devil *old-fashioned*
to be very lucky • *Then he won £3000 on the lottery – that man has the luck of the devil!*

Just my luck! *humorous*
something that you say when something bad happens to you • *So he left five minutes before I got here, did he? Just my luck.*

the luck of the draw
if something is the luck of the draw, it is the result of chance and you have no control over it ✍A draw is a competition in which you win if the number on your ticket is chosen. • *You can't choose who you play against. It's just the luck of the draw.*

more by luck than judgement
if you achieve something more by luck than judgement, you achieve it by chance and not because of skill • *And somehow I managed to get the ball in the net – more by luck than judgement.*

No such luck!
something that you say in order to express disappointment that you were not able to do something that you wanted to • *I had hoped we'd have time for lunch somewhere. No such luck.*

Your luck's in! *British humorous*
something that you say in order to tell someone that you think another person would like a sexual relationship with them • *Hey, Sal, your luck's in! He's yours for the asking.*

► See also: **push** your luck
try your luck

lucky

get lucky *informal*
to meet someone who you can have sex with • *Why don't you come along? You never know, you might get lucky.*

You should be so lucky! *informal*
something that you say in order to tell someone that what they want is not likely to happen • *A pay increase? You should be so lucky!*

► See also: **strike** it lucky
thank your lucky stars

lull

► See: lull sb into a **false** sense of security

lump

► See: **bring** a lump to your throat

lumps

take your **lumps** *American*
to receive and accept criticism or punishment for something you have done • *Joe blames nobody but himself for his problems. He takes his lumps and doesn't complain.*

lunch

be out to lunch *informal*
to be behaving in a very strange or silly way • *And yet the conversation we had with him this morning suggests that he's not entirely out to lunch.*

lurch

► See: **leave** sb in the lurch

lying

not **take** sth **lying down**
to refuse to be treated badly by someone • *He can't just order you about like that. Surely you're not going to take that lying down!*

lyrical

► See: **wax** lyrical

mad

be as mad as a hatter
to be crazy ✍A long time ago, people who made hats used a substance that gave them an illness which made people think they were crazy. • *Her brother's as mad as a hatter.*

be as mad as a hornet *American*
to be very angry ✍A hornet is a large insect which stings people. • *He was as mad as a hornet when he heard what she said about him.*

be as mad as a March hare *old-fashioned*
to be crazy • *This woman was dancing in the road and singing very loudly – I thought she was mad as a March hare.*

Don't get mad, get even.
something that you say in order to tell someone not to be angry when someone has upset them, but to do something that will upset them as much • *This is my advice to wives whose husbands have left them for a younger woman – don't get mad, get even!*

like mad *informal*
if something hurts like mad it hurts very much, and if you do something like mad you do it very quickly and with a lot of force • *This cut stings like mad.* • *I braked like mad but couldn't stop in time and hit the car in front.*

made

be made for sb/sth
to be exactly suitable for someone or something • *Paul and Ann were **made for each other**.* • *This wallpaper was made for my bedroom.*

have (got) it made
someone who has got it made is certain to be successful and have a good life, often without much effort • *With his father at the head of the firm, he's got it made.*

▶ See also: I'm not made of **money**!
show (sb) what you are made of

magic

a magic moment
a short period of time which is very special, especially because something happens which makes you very happy • *The young eagle was only in view for a few seconds, but for a bird-lover like me it was a magic moment.*

a magic touch
a special ability to do something very well • *The film's great success will no doubt please the 46-year old director who was rumoured to have lost his magic touch.*

a magic wand
an easy way to solve a problem ✍A magic wand is a stick that a person who performs magic tricks waves to make things happen. • (usually negative) *Artiside has warned that he has no magic wand to provide food and work overnight.* • *I wish I could just **wave a magic wand** and make all your troubles go away, but I can't.*

What's the magic word? *British & Australian*
something that you say to a child in order to make them say 'please' or 'thank you' • *'Can I have a chocolate, mummy?' 'What's the magic word?' 'Please.'*

▶ See also: **work** your/its magic
work like magic

main

be sb's **main squeeze** *American informal*
to be the person that someone has a romantic or sexual relationship with • *Didn't you know? Jennifer is Bob's main squeeze.*

in the main
mostly, usually • *Bystanders, middle-aged women in the main, protested loudly.* • *In the main, our students reach exam level after a year.*

the main drag *American & Australian informal*
the biggest and most important road in a town • *We walked up and down the town's main drag looking for a post office.*

make

be on the make *informal*
if a person is on the make, they are trying to get money or power in a way which is not pleasant or honest • *I wouldn't trust him – he's always on the make.*

Do you want to make something of it?
something that you say to someone who disagrees with you in order to threaten them and offer to fight them • *'That's my beer you're drinking.' 'Do you want to make something of it?'*

make a [day/night/weekend etc.] of it
to spend a whole day, night, weekend etc. somewhere, instead of only a short time, so that you can enjoy it more • *We decided to go on to a club after the show and really make a night of it.*

make as if to do sth
to make a movement which makes people think you are going to do a particular thing • *She made as if to reach for the gun.*

make do
to manage to live without things you would like to have or with things of a worse quality than you would like • (often + **with**) *When we got married we didn't have any cupboards. We had to make do with wooden boxes.* • *They didn't have much money, but they made do.*

make do and mend *British old-fashioned*
to manage with less than you would like, by repairing old things instead of buying new ones • *Our family never had any new furniture. We just had to make do and mend.*

make it *informal*

1 to manage to arrive at a place or go to an event • *She made it to the airport just in time to catch her plane.* • *We're having a party on Saturday – can you make it?*

2 to be successful, especially in a job • *Now he's got his own TV show he feels as though he's really made it.* • (sometimes + **as**) *She hasn't got a hope of making it as a dancer.*

3 to stay alive • *She was losing so much blood, I really thought she wasn't going to make it.*

make it up to sb
to do something good for someone who you have done something bad to in the past, or to someone who has done something good for you • *I know I've behaved badly and I've upset you but I'll make it up to you, I promise.*

make it with sb *American informal*
to have sex with someone • *So what happened after the party? Did she make it with him?*

make or break sth
to make something a success or a failure • *TV will either make or break courtroom justice in this country.*
be make or break for sb/sth • *The Milan show will be make or break for his new designs.*
make-or-break • (always before noun) *It's make-or-break time for Britain's tennis players.*

put the make on sb *American very informal*
to try to have sex with someone • *Was that idiot at the party trying to put the make on you?*

▶ See also: make an **ass** of yourself
make it **big**
make no **bones** about sth
You can't make **bricks** without straw.
make (out) a **case** for sth/doing sth
make all the **difference**
make/pull a **face**
make (funny) **faces**
make a **federal** case (out) of sth
make sb's **flesh** crawl/creep
make a **fool** of yourself
make **free** with sth
make **fun** of sb/sth
make a **go** of sth
make a **good** fist of sth/doing sth
make (it) **good**
make **good** on sth
make the **grade**
make (sb's) **hackles** rise
make **hard** work of sth/doing sth
make **hay** while the sun shines
can't make **head** nor/or tail of sth
hit/make the **headlines**
blow/make a **hole** in sth
make yourself at **home**

make a **killing**
make **light** of sth
make up for **lost** time
make a **man** (out) of sb
make your/a **mark**
make a **meal** (out) of sth
make up your **mind**
make a **monkey** (out) of sb
make the **most** of sth
make a **move**
make a **move** on sb
make a **name** for yourself
make a **noise** about sth
make **noises**
make a **pass** at sb
make a **pitch** for sth
make (a) great **play** of sth
make a **play** for sth
make your **presence** felt
make a **production** (out) of sth
make (all) the **right** noises
make a **rod** for your own back
make the **rounds**
do/make (all) the **running**
make yourself **scarce**
make **sheep**'s eyes at sb
make **short** work of sth
make a **spectacle** of yourself
make a **splash**
make a **stand**
make/raise a **stink**
make **tracks**
make **waves**
make **whoopee**

maker

▶ See: **meet** your maker

makes

▶ See: That makes **two** of us.

making

be a [athlete/star/writer etc.] in the making
if someone is an athlete, star, writer etc. in the making, they are likely to develop into that thing • *This young swimmer is an athlete in the making.*

be a [crisis/disaster etc.] in the making
if something is a crisis, disaster etc. in the making, it is likely to develop into that thing • *What we're witnessing here is a disaster in the making.*

be of your **own making**
if an unpleasant situation is of your own making, you have caused it • *The problems she has with that child are all of her own making.*

be the making of sb
if you say that an event or experience was the making of someone, you mean that it made them develop good qualities • (never in present tenses) *A spell in the army will be the making of him!* • *University was the making of her, because she was able to escape the influence of her family at last.*

makings

have (all) the makings of sth
to seem likely to develop into something • *The story has all the makings of a first-class scandal.* • *She has the makings of a great violinist.*

malice

with malice aforethought *humorous*
if you say that someone did something bad with malice aforethought, you mean that they intended to do it and it was not an accident ✍This is a legal phrase, but it is used humorously in general language. • *She has certainly got me in trouble with my boss, but I'm not sure whether she did it with malice aforethought.*

mama

▶ See: a mama's **boy**

man

Are you a man or a mouse?
something that you say in order to encourage someone to be brave when they are frightened to do something • *Just tell your boss that you think she's making the wrong decision: what are you, a man or a mouse?*

be man enough to do sth
to be brave enough to do something • *He was man enough to admit he had made a mistake.*

be no good/use to man or beast *humorous*
to not be useful at all • *This bike has got two flat tyres – it's no use to man or beast.*

It's every man for himself.
something that you say which means that

everyone in a particular situation is trying to do what is best for themselves and no one is trying to help anyone else • *It might be a civilized place to shop at other times but come the January sales, it's every man for himself.*

make a man (out) of sb
to make a young man without much experience develop into a confident and experienced adult • *The army will make a man out of you.*

man and boy *old-fashioned*
all a man's life • *I've worked down this coal mine man and boy.*

Man cannot live by bread alone.
something that you say which means people need things such as art, music and poetry as well as food, in order to live a happy life ✍This phrase comes from the Bible. • *Our cultural heritage is important. Man cannot live by bread alone.*

a man for all seasons *slightly formal*
a man who is very successful in many different types of activity ✍This is the title of a play about Sir Thomas More. • *He's chairman of a large chemicals company as well as a successful painter – really a man for all seasons.*

a man of God *formal*
a male priest, or a very religious man • *I don't expect to hear that kind of language from a man of God.*

a man of letters *formal*
a man, usually a writer, who knows a lot about literature • *A distinguished statesman and man of letters, he was born just before the turn of the century.*

a man of many parts
a man who is able to do many different things • *George is a man of many parts – ruthless businessman, loving father, and accomplished sportsman, to name a few.*

a man of straw *British, American & Australian*
a straw man *American*
a person or an idea that is weak and easy to defeat • *Compared to their illustrious predecessors, the country's leaders seem to be men of straw.*

a man of the cloth *formal*
a priest • *Are you a man of the cloth?*

the man of the moment
a man who is popular or famous now because he has just done something interesting or important • *Mansell is the man of the moment after two marvellous victories in five days on the race track.*

man's best friend

man's best friend
a dog • *This 500 page book is a tribute to man's best friend.*

A man's got to do what a man's got to do. *humorous*
something men say when they are going to do something which may be unpleasant or which they are pretending will be unpleasant as a joke ✍From a similar line in John Steinbeck's book, *Grapes of Wrath* and often used in films. • *I hate catching spiders. Still, a man's got to do what a man's got to do.*

a man's man
a man who likes to have other men as friends and who enjoys activities which men typically enjoy • *Terry's what you'd call a man's man. I don't expect you'd find him at the ballet too many nights a week.*

to a man *slightly formal*
if a group of people do something to a man, they all do it • *They supported him to a man.*

▶ See also: the man/woman on the **Clapham** omnibus
the man/woman/sth of your **dreams**
every man jack (of us/them)
a girl/man/person **Friday**
a man/woman after your own **heart**

a man/woman of **means**
as **one** man
One man's meat is another man's poison.
like a man/woman **possessed**
go to **see** a man about a dog
the man/woman/person in the **street**
the **thinking** man's/woman's crumpet
a man of his **word**
a man/woman of the **world**

man-about-town

a man-about-town
a rich man who usually does not work and enjoys a lot of social activities • *He's a millionaire businessman and man-about-town who is seen in all the best places.*

man-eater

a man-eater *informal*
a woman who attracts men very easily and has many relationships • *She had a reputation as a man-eater.*

manna

manna from heaven
something that you need which you get when you are not expecting to get it ✍In the Bible, manna was a type of bread which God gave to the Israelites when they needed food. • *I had been unemployed for two years, so when somebody phoned me up and offered me a permanent job it was like manna from heaven.*

manner

(as) to the manner born *slightly formal*
if you behave to the manner born, you behave confidently, as if a particular situation is usual and familiar for you • *Although he never lost his lower-class accent, he lived the life of a rich and successful businessman as to the manner born.*

man-to-man

man-to-man
a man-to-man talk is when men talk honestly about subjects which may be difficult or embarrassing • (always before noun) *When I found a packet of condoms in Jamie's bedroom, I decided it was time for a man-to-man chat.*

many

▶ See: many **moons** ago
There's many a **slip** twixt cup and lip.
There's many a **true** word spoken in jest.
in so many **words**

map

[blow/bomb/wipe etc.] sth/swh **off the map**
to destroy something completely, especially with bombs • *At least eight Spanish warships were blown off the map.*

put swh/sth/sb **on the map**
to make a place, thing, or person famous • *The Alaska-Yukon-Pacific Exposition of 1909 put Seattle on the map.* • *If Newcastle United win the championship it will really put them back on the map as far as European football is concerned.*

marbles

▶ See: **lose** your marbles
pick up your marbles (and go home/leave)

march

be on the march
if a dangerous or unpleasant political idea is on the march, it is becoming more popular • *Fascism is on the march again in Europe.*

march to a different drummer *mainly American*
march to a different tune *British*
to behave in a different way or to believe in different things from the people around you • *While most of the country supported military action, Santini was marching to a different drummer.*

▶ See also: **steal** a march on sb/sth

marching

give sb their **marching orders**
to tell someone to leave • *Debbie's finally given her husband his marching orders after ten years of an unhappy marriage.*
get your **marching orders** • *He'd only been in the job a month when he got his marching orders.*

mare

a mare's nest
a very confused situation • *The law on restrictive trade is a mare's nest that scarcely anyone can comprehend.*

margins

on the margins of sth
if someone is on the margins of a group of people, they are part of the group, but are different in important ways • *Homeless people are on the margins of our society.* • *The fact that they held their exhibition in a corridor reflects their position on the margins of the London art scene.*

marines

▶ See: (Go) **tell** it/that to the marines.

mark

(You) mark my words. *old-fashioned*
something that you say when you tell someone about something that you are certain will happen in the future • *That girl's going to cause trouble, you mark my words.*

be close to the mark
be near the mark
if something someone says or writes is close to the mark, it is correct or nearly correct • *He says he can't find a job, but I think it would be closer to the mark to say he doesn't want to work.*

be off the mark
if something someone says or writes is off the mark, it is not correct • *His criticisms are* ***way off the mark.*** • *Bedini and Curzi were probably* ***not far off the mark*** *in their analysis.*

be up to the mark
to be good enough • *I have to watch my staff all the time to keep them up to the mark.* • (often negative) *The efforts of the security services have not been quite up to the mark.*

get off the mark *British & Australian*
to score for the first time in a sports competition • *Liverpool got off the mark with a blinding goal.*

make your/**a mark**
to make people notice you or to have an important effect on something • (sometimes + **as**) *Mr Sorrell first made his mark as finance director at Wimpole and Soames.* • (often + **on**) *Richards made a tremendous mark on Australian cricket during 1985.*

mark time
to do something which is not very interesting while you are waiting to start doing something more important • (usually in continuous tenses) *She's just marking time in her father's shop until it's time to go to university.*

▶ See also: **hit** the sth mark
hit the mark
leave your/its mark on sb/sth
overstep the mark

marked

a marked man
someone who is being watched by someone who wants to harm or kill them • *He is still free to travel the world, but he knows he is a marked man.*

market

be in the market for sth
to be interested in buying something and to have the money to be able to do so • *As lovely as it is, we're really not in the market for a five-bedroomed house.*

a cattle market *British, American & Australian informal*
a meat market *American & Australian informal*
a place where people go to see sexually attractive women or to find sexual partners • *Beauty contests are just cattle markets.* • *That new nightclub called The Venue is awful – it's a real meat market.*

▶ See also: **corner** the market

marriage

▶ See: a marriage/match made in **heaven**

marrow

be chilled/frozen to the marrow *British & Australian*
to be extremely cold ✍Marrow is the soft material in the middle of your bones. • *After an hour on the mountain, we were chilled to the marrow.*

▶ See also: **chill** sb to the bone/marrow
be **chilled** to the bone/marrow

marry

marry beneath your **station** *old-fashioned*
to marry someone who belongs to a lower social class than you • *Her father, who felt that she had married beneath her station, refused to speak to her.*

Marry in haste, repent at leisure. *old-fashioned*
something that you say which means if you marry someone too soon, without knowing for certain that they are the right person for you, you will have an unhappy marriage • *It's true I've only known him for six months and I know you're thinking 'marry in haste, repent at leisure' but I'm telling you, he's the man for me.*

marrying

not **be the marrying kind** *humorous*
if a man is not the marrying kind, he does not want to be married ✍People sometimes use this phrase to mean that the man is homosexual (= sexually attracted to other men). • *George has had several girlfriends, but he's not the marrying kind.*

martyr

make a martyr of sb
to treat someone badly with the result that other people feel sympathy for them • *The government knows that if they stop him standing in the elections they will make a martyr of him from the point of view of the international community.*

make a martyr of yourself
to do things which are difficult or unpleasant for you, often when it is not necessary • *She's made a real martyr of herself, wearing herself out doing everything for her family.*

mask

sb's **mask slips**
if someone's mask slips, they do something which shows people their real personality, when they have been pretending to be a different, usually nicer, type of person ✍A mask is something that covers your face to hide it. • *His mask had suddenly slipped, and she saw him as the angry and cruel man that he really was.*

mat

▶ See: **sweep** sth under the mat/rug

match

be no match for sth/sb
to be less powerful or effective than something or someone else • *Health warnings are no match for the addictive power of cigarettes.*

a shouting match *British, American & Australian*
a slanging match *British & Australian*
an argument where people shout at each other • *If your child says something rude or unpleasant to you, don't* ***get into a shouting match with them****, just leave the room.* • *The debate turned into a slanging match.*

▶ See also: a marriage/match made in **heaven**
meet your match

matter

as a matter of course
if something happens as a matter of course, it happens without people thinking about whether they want it or not • *I don't think the Welsh language should be taught in schools as a matter of course – if students want to learn it, that's their choice.*

be a matter of opinion
1 if something is a matter of opinion, different people have different opinions about it • *I don't think there is a perfect way to teach a child to read – it's a matter of opinion, really.*
2 if you say that something someone has just said is a matter of opinion, you mean that you do not agree • *'She's a wonderful mother.' 'That's a matter of opinion.'*

be a matter of record
if a fact is a matter of record, you know it is true because it has been written down • *His views on immigration are a matter of record.*

be only a matter of time
if you say that it is only a matter of time before something happens, you mean that you are sure it is going to happen, although you do not know when • (usually + **before**) *It is only a matter of time before he is forced to resign.* • *I know she will be a great novelist. It is only a matter of time.*

the matter in hand *British, American & Australian formal*
the matter at hand *American formal*
the subject or situation that is being thought about or talked about • *Do these figures have anything to do with the*

matter in hand?

a matter of life and/or death
a serious situation where people could die • (not used with *the*) *The results of the peace negotiations could be a matter of life or death for people in the war zone.*

no matter *slightly formal*
something that you say which means that a problem is not important • *It's raining, but no matter, I'll take the dog for a walk anyway.*

▶ See also: no matter how you **slice** it

matters

take matters into your **own hands**
to deal with a problem yourself because the people who should have dealt with it have failed to do so • *The police haven't done anything about the vandalism, so local residents have taken matters into their own hands.*

max

to the max *American informal*
as much as possible • *We're stretched to the max – we can't possibly take on any more work.* • *A lot of these guys push their bodies to the max, spending three or more hours a day in the gym.*

may

▶ See: You may well **ask**!
be that as it may

mea culpa

mea culpa *humorous*
something that you say in order to admit that something is your fault • *'Tim, do you know why the back door was unlocked when I came home?' 'Mea culpa. I'm sorry – it won't happen again.'*

meal

make a meal (out) of sth *British & Australian*
to spend more time or energy doing something than is necessary • *I only asked her to write a brief summary of the main points but she made a real meal out of it.*

a meal ticket
someone or something that you use as a way of getting regular amounts of money for the rest of your life • *Gone are the days when a university degree was a meal ticket for life.*

mealy-mouthed

mealy-mouthed
not brave enough to say what you mean directly and honestly • *Strangely enough, although we are getting more mealy-mouthed about mental and physical disabilities, we are increasingly frank about bodily functions.*

mean

mean business
to be serious about achieving something, even if other people disagree with you • *The changes the new government has made show they mean business.*

meaning

▶ See: not **know** the meaning of the word

means

a man/woman of means
someone who has a lot of money • *I could tell from her address that she was a woman of means.*

a means to an end
something that you are not interested in but that you do because it will help you to achieve something else • (not used with *the*) *Mike doesn't have any professional ambitions. For him, work is just a means to an end.*

measure

have the measure of sb/sth *slightly formal*
to understand what someone or something is like and to know how to deal with them • *What was clear was that the president no longer had the measure of his country's problems.* • *I don't think she's under any illusions about her husband – she's got the measure of him.*
get/take the measure of sb/sth
• *We got the measure of the opposition in the first half and set about beating them in the second.*

meat

be meat and drink to sb
if something is meat and drink to someone, they very much enjoy doing it and find it easy, although most people would find it difficult or unpleasant • *He gives*

all these talks to terrifyingly large audiences but it's meat and drink to Peter.

be the meat in the sandwich *British & Australian*
to be in a difficult situation because you are the friend of two people who are arguing • *I grew up with my parents continually yelling at each other so I was the meat in the sandwich.*

the meat and potatoes *American informal*
the most important or basic parts of something • *They stuck to the meat and potatoes of broadcasting – sports and news.*
meat-and-potatoes *American informal* • (always before noun) *The focus was on jobs, health care, and other meat-and-potatoes issues.*

meat and two veg *British informal*
a traditional type of meal, often found in Britain, which is basic and slightly boring, usually a piece of meat and two vegetables • *The food is very much meat and two veg – you won't find any of your fancy French cuisine here.*

your **meat and two veg** *British humorous*
a man's sexual organs • *I tell you what, his trousers were so tight you could see his meat and two veg!*

▶ See also: a meat **market**

medal

▶ See: **deserve** a medal

medallion

a medallion man *British humorous*
a man, usually an older man, who dresses in a way that he thinks women find attractive, often wearing an open shirt in order to show his chest and a lot of gold jewellery ✍A medallion is a circle of metal like a large coin that is worn on a chain around the neck. • *And there he was, a real-live 70's medallion man, just stepped out of a time machine.*

medicine

give sb **a dose/taste of** their **own medicine**
to do the same bad thing to someone that they have often done to you, in order to show them how unpleasant it is • *She's always turning up late for me so I thought I'd give her a taste of her own medicine and see how she likes it.*

medium

▶ See: in the long/medium/short **term**

meet

meet sb **halfway**
to show that you really want to reach an agreement or improve your relationship with someone by doing some of the things that they ask you to • *I really want this relationship, Simon, and I'm prepared to work at it but you have to meet me halfway.*

meet your **maker** *humorous*
to die • *I'm afraid Zoe's rabbit is no more. He's **gone to meet his maker**.*

meet your **match**
to meet someone who is able to defeat you in an argument or a competition • *The world chess champion finally met his match when he was beaten by a computer.*

meet your **Waterloo**
if someone who has been successful in the past meets their Waterloo, they are defeated by someone who is too strong for them or by a problem which is too difficult for them ✍The French leader Napoleon was finally defeated at the battle of Waterloo in 1815. • *She finally met her Waterloo when she tried to take on the club champion.*

▶ See also: meet/see sb in the **flesh**
come to/meet a **sticky** end

meeting

a meeting of minds *slightly formal*
a situation in which two people find that they have the same ideas and opinions and find it easy to agree with each other • *Government officials say there was a meeting of minds between the two leaders during the six-hour talks in Pretoria.*

melt

melt in the/your **mouth**
if food melts in your mouth, it is soft and tastes very pleasant • *This sponge cake just melts in your mouth.*

melting

a melting pot
a place where people of many different

races and from many different countries live together • *Rules of mutual tolerance must be agreed in an area which is a melting pot of such diverse cultures.*

member

be a fully paid-up member of sth *informal*
be a card-carrying member of sth *informal*
to be part of a particular group • *Unlike former leaders, he displays a degree of sensitivity that shows him to be a fully paid-up member of the human race.*

memory

have a memory like an elephant
to be very good at remembering things ✍Elephants are believed to have good memories. • *'I remember where I first saw her – it was at Tim Fisher's party about ten years ago.' 'Yes, you're right – you've got a memory like an elephant!'*

take a stroll/trip down memory lane
to remember some of the happy things that you did in the past • *We were just taking a stroll down memory lane and recalling the days of our youth.*

▶ See also: **commit** sth to memory
jog your memory
have a memory/mind like a **sieve**

men

the men in grey suits
men in business or politics who have a lot of power and influence although the public does not see them or know about them • *As usual, it is the men in grey suits who will decide the future of the industry.*

the men in white coats *humorous*
doctors who look after people who are mentally ill • *The men in white coats will be coming to take me away if I stay in this job much longer.*

separate/sort out the men from the boys
if a difficult situation or activity separates the men from the boys, it shows which people in a group are brave and strong and which are not • *You have to survive outdoors for three days and three nights. That should separate the men from the boys.*

ménage à trois

a ménage à trois
an arrangement in which three people who have a sexual relationship live together • *They married in '73 and then met Russell with whom they entered a brief but idyllic ménage à trois.*

mend

be on the mend
if you are on the mend, your health is improving after an illness • *He's still a bit tired but he's definitely on the mend.*

mend (your) **fences**
to try to become friendly again with someone after an argument • (usually + **with**) *China is trying to mend fences with Russia after the recent border dispute.*

▶ See also: change/mend your **ways**

mental

go mental *informal*
to become very angry • *She'll go mental when she sees what you've done to her car!*

make a mental note
to make an effort to remember something, often something that you want to do later • (often + to do sth) *I made a mental note to call my mother and tell her what he'd said.* • (often + **that**) *Last time we had dinner together I made a mental note that you didn't like fish.*

merchant

a merchant of doom *informal*
someone who is always saying that bad things are going to happen • *With exports rising and unemployment falling, the merchants of doom are having to revise their economic predictions.*

mercy

be at the mercy of sth/sb
to be in a situation in which you cannot do anything to protect yourself from something or someone unpleasant • *Poor people are increasingly at the mercy of money-lenders.* • *Of course, in a tent, you're at the mercy of the elements.*

▶ See also: **throw** yourself on/upon sb's mercy

merry

▶ See: **lead** sb a (merry) dance
play (merry) hell

play (merry) hell with sth

mess

a mess of sth *American informal*
a lot of something • *He picked up a mess of keys and handed me one.*

message

get the message *informal*
to understand what someone is trying to tell you even if they are not expressing themselves directly • *Next time he calls, tell him you're busy for the next three months – he'll soon get the message.* • *Okay, I get the message – you want to be alone.*

messenger

▶ See: **shoot** the messenger

messing

and no messing *British informal*
without any difficulties • *She did the entire job in under an hour and no messing.*

no messing *British informal*
something that you say which means you have done something in a very complete way • *'I ordered a glass of white wine but I see Ian's brought a whole bottle.' 'Yeah, no messing.'*

method

there's method in sb's **madness** *British, American & Australian*
there's a method to sb's **madness** *American*
something that you say which means that although someone seems to be behaving strangely, there is a reason for their behaviour ✍This phrase comes from Shakespeare's play 'Hamlet'. • *When he picked the side I thought he must be crazy but, judging by their performance this season, there's obviously method in his madness.*

mettle

be on your **mettle** *slightly formal*
to be determined to prove that you are good at something, especially in a difficult situation • *It's a tough interview – you'll have to be on your mettle.*

prove/show your **mettle** *slightly formal*
to prove that you are good at doing something by succeeding in a difficult situation • *A relative newcomer to the game, he's certainly proved his mettle in the last two games.*

mick

take the mick/mickey *British & Australian informal*
to make people laugh at someone, usually by copying what they do or say in a way that seems funny • *They used to* ***take the mick out of him*** *because of the way he walked.* • *I thought you were being serious – I didn't realise you were taking the mickey.*

mickey-taking *British & Australian informal* • *I had to put up with a bit of mickey-taking from some of the blokes when I first told them but they've calmed down now.*

Mickey-Mouse

Mickey-Mouse *informal*
not important or not good compared with other things of the same type • (always before noun) *We're talking about a respected organization here – not some Mickey-Mouse outfit.*

microscope

put sth **under the microscope**
to examine or think about a situation very carefully ✍A microscope is a piece of scientific equipment that allows you to see small things very clearly. • *Because they're both public figures, their relationship has been put under the microscope.*

Midas

the Midas touch
the ability to make a lot of money ✍Midas was a king in Greek stories who had the power to turn anything he touched into gold. • *Profits are down – has that 80s entrepreneur lost his Midas touch?*

middle

(out) in the middle of nowhere
in a place that is far away from where most people live • *I'll need a map to find that pub – it's out in the middle of nowhere, apparently.*

the middle ground
something that two people or groups that are arguing can agree about • *The lawyer*

will then attempt to find the middle ground between the two parties.

▶ See also: be **caught** in the middle

middle-aged

a middle-aged spread
the fat area around the waist that a lot of people get as they grow older • *A dark blue shirt worn outside his trousers concealed the middle-aged spread.*

middle-of-the-road

middle-of-the-road
1 not extreme politically • *Neither party is exactly radical – they're both fairly middle-of-the-road.*
2 entertainment that is middle-of-the-road is ordinary and acceptable to most people but it is not exciting or special in any way • *Most of the music they play is pretty middle-of-the-road.*

midnight

▶ See: **burn** the midnight oil

might

(with) might and main *formal*
with all your effort and strength • *War is something we should be working might and main to avoid.*

might is right *British, American & Australian*
might makes right *American*
the belief that you can do what you want because you are the most powerful person or country • *To allow this invasion to happen will give a signal to every petty dictator that might is right.*

▶ See also: I might as well be hanged/hung for a **sheep** as a lamb.

mighty

▶ See: Great/Mighty **oaks** from little acorns grow.

mile

by a mile
by miles
if someone or something wins or is the best by a mile, they win easily or are much better than everyone or everything else • *Of all the strawberry ice-creams we've tasted, this is the best by miles.* • *Everyone expected him to win the championship by a mile.*

a mile a minute *American & Australian*
very quickly • *Mike was very excited and **talking a mile a minute.*** • *My heart beat a mile a minute waiting for his plane to land.*

a mile off *informal*
if you can see or recognize something a mile off, you notice it very easily • *It's obvious he fancies you – you can see that a mile off.*

stand/stick out a mile
to be very obvious • *She sticks out a mile with her red hair.* • *Of course he's unhappy – it stands out a mile.*

▶ See also: **run** a mile

miles

be miles away
to not be listening to what someone is saying because you are thinking about something else • *'Jim, did you hear what I just said?' 'Sorry, I was miles away.'*

milk

the milk of human kindness *literary*
being good and kind to other people ✍This phrase comes from Shakespeare's play 'Macbeth'. • *She's one of those amazing people who's just overflowing with the milk of human kindness.*

mill

go through the mill
to experience a very difficult or unpleasant period in your life • *She really went through the mill with that son of hers.*

put sb **through the mill**
to ask someone a lot of difficult questions in order to test them • *They really put me through the mill in my interview.*

million

look/feel (like) a million dollars *British, American & Australian*
look/feel (like) a million bucks *American*
to look or feel extremely attractive • *You look like a million dollars in that dress!*

▶ See also: be **one** in a million
Thanks a million!

million-dollar

▶ See: the million-dollar **question**

millstone

a millstone around your **neck**

a problem or responsibility that you have all the time which prevents you from doing what you want ✍A millstone is a large stone that is very heavy. • *I'd rather not be in debt – I don't want that millstone around my neck.*

mince

not **mince** (your) **words**

to say what you mean clearly and directly, even if you upset people by doing this • *The report does not mince words about the incompetence of some government officials.* • *Never a woman to mince her words, she described the former minister as self-centred and arrogant.*

mincemeat

make mincemeat of sb *informal*

to defeat someone very easily • *A good lawyer would have made mincemeat of them in court.*

mind

be a load/weight off your **mind**

if something is a weight off your mind, you have been worrying about it and you are pleased that the problem has now been solved • *I'm so relieved I don't have to give a speech – it's a real load off my mind.*

be all in the/your **mind**

if you say that a problem that is worrying someone is all in their mind, you mean that they have imagined the problem and that it does not really exist • *His doctor tried to convince him that he wasn't ill and that it was all in the mind.*

be of like/one mind
be of the same mind

if two or more people are of like mind, they agree with each other about something • (often + **on**) *We're of like mind on most political issues.*

be out of your **mind with [boredom/fear/worry etc.]**

to be extremely bored, frightened, worried etc. • *He was four hours late and I was out of my mind with worry.*

be [bored/scared/worried etc.] out of your **mind** • *I really thought he was going to crash the car and I was scared out of my mind.* • *He was the only young person at the party and he looked bored out of his mind.*

be out of your **mind** *informal*

to be crazy • *You paid three thousand pounds for that heap of junk! Are you out of your mind?*

go out of your mind *informal* • *Did I just imagine all of this – am I going out of my mind?*

bear/keep sth **in mind**

to remember a piece of information when you are making decisions or thinking about a matter • (often + **that**) *Bearing in mind that she's had so little experience, I thought she did very well.* • *Of course, repair work on older buildings is an expensive business and that's always something to be borne in mind.*

come/spring to mind

if someone or something springs to mind, you immediately think of them • *I'm trying to think of someone who might help out with the kids. Yvette comes to mind.* • *'Don't you think sex is funny, Marty?' ''Funny' isn't the word that immediately springs to mind, no.'*

Do you mind!

something that you say when someone does something that annoys you • *Do you mind! There's a queue here and some of us have been waiting half an hour to get to this point!* • *Do you mind! That's my brother you're talking about!*

get your **mind around** sth

to succeed in understanding something difficult or strange • (usually negative) *I still can't get my mind around the strange things she said that night.*

have a mind like a steel trap

to be able to think very quickly, clearly and intelligently • *She'll be a brilliant lawyer – she has a mind like a steel trap.*

have a mind of its own *humorous*

if a machine or vehicle has a mind of its own, it does not work or move the way you want it to, as if it is controlling itself • *This computer's got a mind of its own – it just won't do what I ask it to.*

have sth in mind

have sth **in mind**
to be thinking about something as a possibility • (usually used in questions) *'I thought we might eat out tonight.' 'Where did you have in mind?'* • *I think that's probably what he had in mind.*

have your **mind on** sth
to be thinking about something • *It's hard to work when you've got your mind on other things.*
your **mind is on** sth • *I wasn't really listening – my mind was on other matters.*

in your **mind's eye**
in your imagination or memory • *In my mind's eye, she is still the little girl she was the last time I saw her.*

make up your **mind**
1 to decide what to choose • (often + question word) *I can't make up my mind whether to have the salmon or the chicken.*
2 to become very certain that you want to do something • (often + to do sth) *At a very early age she made up her mind to become an actress.* • *My mind's made up. I'm handing in my resignation tomorrow.*

The mind boggles.
something that you say which means that a situation or subject is very difficult to understand or imagine • *A cloned sheep? The mind boggles.* • (often + **at**) *The mind boggles at the thought of what you could do with all that money.*
mind-boggling • *His latest book is a mixture of physics, astronomy and philosophy – all mind-boggling stuff.*

your **mind goes blank**
if you are asked a question and your mind goes blank, you cannot think of anything to say • *I was so nervous during the interview that when I was asked about my experience, my mind went blank.*
your **mind is a blank** • *I can't even tell you what his name was – my mind's a complete blank.*

mind over matter
the power of the mind to control and influence the body and the physical world generally • *I'm sure you can talk yourself into believing that you're well. It's a case of mind over matter.*

Mind your **own business!** *informal*
something that you say in order to tell someone not to ask questions or show too much interest in other people's lives • *'How much did that dress cost you?' 'Mind your own business!'* • *I wish he'd mind his own business and stop telling me how to do my job!*

mind the store *American*
to be responsible for dealing with arrangements at work or at home while the person who is usually responsible is not there • *So who's going to be minding the store while your manager's away?*

on sb's **mind**
if something is on someone's mind, they are thinking about it a lot or worrying about it • *Something's worrying you, isn't it? What's on your mind?* • *I wanted to talk about men but Helen obviously* ***had other things on her mind***. • *I'm sorry if I've been a bit irritable recently but I've* ***got a lot on my mind*** (= I'm worrying a lot) *at the moment.*

put sb **in mind of** sb/sth *old-fashioned*
to cause someone to think of someone or something, usually because of a similarity • *Something about the way he spoke put me in mind of Ben.*

put your **mind to it**
to put all your attention and efforts into doing something • *If you put your mind to it, you could have the job finished in an afternoon.*

put/set sb's **mind at rest**
to make someone stop worrying • *If it'll*

put your mind at rest, I can drive you home and you can make sure the door's locked.

take sb's **mind off** sth/sb
if an activity takes someone's mind off their problems, it stops them from thinking about them • *That's the good thing about helping other people – it takes your mind off your own problems.*

to my mind
in my opinion • *He's got red walls and a green carpet which, to my mind, looks all wrong.*

▶ See also: at the **back** of your mind
blow your mind
bring sth/sb to mind
eye/mind **candy**
cast your mind back
cross your mind
lose your mind
mind/watch your **p**'s and q's
prey on sb's mind
read sb's mind
have a memory/mind like a **sieve**
slip your mind
speak your mind
Mind/Watch your **step**.
sticks in the/your mind

minds

▶ See: be in/of **two** minds

mine

a mine of information
a person or a book with a lot of information • (often + **about**) *He's a mine of information about the cinema.*

mint

be in mint condition
if something is in mint condition, it looks as if it is new ✍The mint is a place where new coins are made. • *There's an ad here for a 1974 Volkswagen Beetle. It's dark blue and in mint condition, apparently.*

minting

be minting it *British & Australian informal*
be minting money *American & Australian*
to be earning a lot of money quickly • *Ice cream sellers are minting it as the unseasonal heatwave continues.*

minute

not **have a minute to call** your **own**
to be extremely busy • *With a full-time job and a family to look after, I don't have a minute to call my own.*

miracles

perform/work miracles
to be extremely effective in improving a situation • *Di's worked miracles in the kitchen – I've never seen it look so clean.* • *These days plastic surgeons can perform miracles.*
a miracle-worker • *You've managed to fix the car! You're a miracle-worker!*

mischief

do yourself **a mischief** *British & Australian humorous*
if you tell someone they will do themselves a mischief if they do something, you mean they will hurt themselves • *You want to be careful jumping over spikes like that – you might do yourself a mischief!*

misery

a misery guts *informal*
someone who complains all the time and is never happy • *Of course, your father, old misery guts, wanted to come home after half an hour because he was bored.*

Misery loves company.
something that you say which means that people who are feeling sad usually want the people they are with to also feel sad • *On a bad day, she isn't satisfied till the entire family is in tears. Misery loves company.*

put sb **out of** their **misery**
to stop someone worrying, usually by giving them information that they have been waiting for • *I thought I'd call her with the results today and put her out of her misery.*

put sth/sb **out of** their **misery**
to kill an animal or person because they are in a lot of pain and you want to end their suffering • *Both of its back legs were shattered and I figured the kindest thing would be to put it out of its misery with a bullet.*

miss

give sth **a miss** *informal*
to not take part in an activity • *I think I'll give the barbecue a miss. I'm on a diet.*

not **miss a trick**
to not fail to notice and use a good opportunity • *You can rely on Sarah to get what she wants, she never misses a trick.*

A miss is as good as a mile.
something that you say which means that failing to do something when you almost succeeded is no better than failing very badly • *I've tried to reassure him that he only failed by three percent but the way he sees it, a miss is as good as a mile.*

miss the boat
to be too late to get something that you want • *Anyone still hoping for concert tickets will discover they have missed the boat.* • *I sent off my university application at the last minute and nearly missed the boat.*

miss the point
to fail to understand what is important about something • *I think you've missed the point. It's not the money that's the problem, it's the fact that she's not consulting him when she spends it.*

missing

without missing a beat *American*
if you do or say something without missing a beat, you continue confidently with what you are saying or doing • *She was asked what single achievement she was most proud of. 'My son,' she replied, without missing a beat.*

mission

mission accomplished
something that you say when you have finished doing something that you were told to do ✍This was a military phrase in World War II. • *Mission accomplished. I've got everything you asked for on the list.*

missionary

the missionary position
a sexual position in which the woman lies on her back with the man on top and facing her • *And for the less adventurous, there's always the good old missionary position.*

mists

▶ See: **lost** in the mists of time

mix

mix business with pleasure
to combine work with social activities or enjoyment • (usually negative) *Let's keep this relationship strictly professional. I prefer not to mix business with pleasure.*

mix it *American & Australian informal*
mix it up *American informal*
to fight or argue • *Don't take any notice of Sally. She just likes to mix it.* • *He was seen mixing it up in a brawl after the game.*

mixed

be a mixed blessing
something that has bad effects as well as advantages • *Beauty can be a mixed blessing. It gets you a lot of attention but people are less likely to take you seriously.*

have mixed feelings about sth
to be both pleased and not pleased about something at the same time • (often + **about**) *I had mixed feelings about leaving home. I was looking forward to going to university but I would miss my family.*
with mixed feelings • *News of the takeover was received with mixed feelings.*

a mixed bag
a combination of different things or different types of people • *The group is quite a mixed bag – we have members with all levels of experience.*

mo

Hang on a mo. *informal*
Half/Just a mo. *informal*
something that you say when you want someone to wait a short time • *If you hang on a mo, I'll just check whether Barbara's in her office.*

mockers

put the mockers on sth *British informal*
to spoil something or to prevent it happening • *Carol's parents decided to stay in on Saturday night, which put the mockers on her plans for a party.*

mockery

make a mockery of sth
to make something seem stupid or without value • *The fact that he sent his children to private school makes a mockery of his socialist principles.*

model

be a/the model of sth
to be an excellent example of something • *Claudia, always the model of good taste, looked elegant in a black silk gown.*

moderation

Moderation in all things.
something that you say which means you should not do or have too much of anything • *The latest thinking is that eating a little of the food you like won't harm you. Moderation in all things, as they say.*

modesty

in all modesty *humorous*
something that you say when you are going to talk about your own achievements • *I have to say, in all modesty, that we wouldn't have won the game if I hadn't been playing.*

Mohammed

If Mohammed will not go to the mountain, the mountain must come to Mohammed.
something that you say which means that if someone will not come to you, you have to go to them ✍This phrase comes from a story about Mohammed who was asked to show how powerful he was by making a mountain come to him. • *They never visit me now they have a family. Well, if Mohammed won't go to the mountain, the mountain must come to Mohammed.*

moment

have a senior/blond etc. moment *humorous*
to behave for a short time as though you are old/silly etc. • *I posted the letters without putting stamps on them – I must have been having a senior moment.*

the moment of truth
the time when someone has to make an important decision or when you can see if something has been successful or not • *The moment of truth came when I had to decide whether to move in with Jim or get a flat on my own.*

▶ See also: from **one** moment to the next

moments

have your/**its moments**
to be sometimes very successful • *This album's not as good as their last one, but it has its moments.*

Monday

a Monday morning quarterback *American*
someone who says how an event or problem should have been dealt with, after other people have already dealt with it • *It's easy to be a Monday morning quarterback when you see the kids' low test scores, but there are no easy answers to improving education.*

that Monday morning feeling *informal*
if you have that Monday morning feeling, you are unhappy that the weekend has finished and you have to go back to work • *'You look fed up. What's wrong?' 'Oh, it's just that Monday morning feeling.'*

money

be (right) on the money *American & Australian informal*
if something someone says or does is on the money, it is correct • *When you said he'd do the job well, you were right on the money.*

be in the money
to suddenly have a lot of money, especially when you did not expect it • *If I can get a commission for a royal portrait, I'll be in the money.*

be money for old rope *British informal*
be money for jam *British informal*
if a job is money for old rope, it is an easy way of earning money • *Babysitting is money for old rope if the children go to sleep early.* • *Most people think being a professional footballer is money for jam.*

for my money
in my opinion • *For my money, the northwest of Scotland is the most beautiful part of Britain.*

have money to burn
to have a lot of money and spend large

amounts on things that are not necessary • *Christine's new boyfriend seems to have money to burn. He's always buying her extravagant gifts.*

with money to burn • *The only people who can afford to stay at this hotel are rich people with money to burn.*

I'm not made of money!
something that you say in order to tell someone who asks you for money that you do not have very much • *No, I can't lend you twenty pounds. I'm not made of money, you know.*

Money (is) no object.
something that you say which means it does not matter how much something costs because there is a lot of money available • *If money was no object, what sort of a house would you live in?*

Money doesn't grow on trees.
something that you say which means you should be careful how much money you spend because there is only a limited amount • *'Dad, can I have a new bike?' 'We can't afford one. Money doesn't grow on trees, you know.'*

Money talks.
something that you say which means people who are rich have a lot of power and influence • *'He can't act so how did he get the part in the first place?' 'His father's a millionaire. Money talks.'*

put your **money on** sb/sth
to believe that someone will do something or something will happen • *'Who do you reckon will get the job, then?' 'I'd put my money on Val.'* • *I'd put my money on Zola leaving Chelsea within the next two years.*

put your **money where** your **mouth is**
to support something that you believe in, especially by giving money • *If people are really interested in helping the homeless they should put their money where their mouth is.*

▶ See also: You **pays** your money (and you takes your chances).
You **pays** your money (and you takes your choice).
spend money like water
throw (your) money around
throw money at sth

money-spinner

a money-spinner *British & Australian*
a business or product that makes a lot of money for someone • *Cookery books are becoming a real money-spinner for the publishing industry.*

monkey

not **give a monkey's** *British & Australian informal*
if you do not give a monkey's about something, you do not care about it at all • *She couldn't give a monkey's if everyone's talking about her.* • (often + question word) *I don't give a monkey's how much he earns, I just don't like him.*

I'll be a monkey's uncle! *old-fashioned*
something that you say when you are very surprised • *Well, I'll be a monkey's uncle. I never thought Bill would remarry.*

make a monkey (out) of sb *old-fashioned*
to make someone seem stupid • *That's enough of your silly tricks. Nobody makes a monkey out of me!*

monkey business *slightly informal*
silly behaviour or dishonest behaviour • *So what kind of monkey business have you kids been up to while I was out?* • *The tax inspectors discovered that there had been some monkey business with the accounts.*

a monkey on sb's **back** *American & Australian*
a serious problem that will not go away • *The divorce proceedings are a monkey on her back.*

▶ See also: put/throw a (monkey) wrench in the **works**

monopoly

not **have a monopoly on** sth
if someone does not have a monopoly on something, they are not the only person who has that thing • *You don't have a monopoly on suffering, you know. Other people have problems too.*

monopoly money
money that seems to have little or no value ✍Monopoly is the trademark for a game in which you buy property with pretend money • *Win or lose this contract,*

it's all monopoly money to him.

month

not **in a month of Sundays**

if you say that something will not happen in a month of Sundays, you mean that it is not likely to happen • *He'll never run the marathon, not in a month of Sundays.*

moon

ask/cry for the moon

to want something that is not possible • (usually in continuous tenses) *There's no point hoping for a permanent peace in the area. It's like asking for the moon.*

be over the moon

be over the moon *informal*

to be extremely pleased about something • *Marie got the job. She's over the moon.*

▶ See also: **promise** (sb) the moon
reach for the moon/stars

moonlight

not **be all moonlight and roses**

if a situation is not all moonlight and roses, it is not always pleasant • *Marriage isn't all moonlight and roses. It can be hard work keeping a relationship together.*

do a moonlight flit *British informal*

to leave somewhere secretly at night, usually to avoid paying money that you owe • *We could always do a moonlight flit – that way we wouldn't have to explain about the money.*

moons

many moons ago *old-fashioned*

a long time ago • *I only have the faintest memory of that time. It all happened many moons ago.*

mop

▶ See: mop the **floor** with sb

more

The more the merrier.

something that you say which means you are happy for other people to join your group in an activity • *'Do you mind if Ann comes to the cinema with us?' 'Not at all. The more the merrier.'*

That's more like it. *informal*

something that you say when someone improves an offer or an attempt • *'I can raise my offer to $500.' 'That's more like it.'*

▶ See also: more by **accident** than (by) design
bite off more than you can chew
There is more to sth/sb than meets the **eye**.
More **fool** you!
have [done/seen/had etc.] more sth than sb has had **hot** dinners
What more do you want – **jam** on it?
It's more than my **job**'s worth.
more by **luck** than judgement
More **power** to your elbow!

morning

the morning after (the night before) *informal*

the morning after a party, when you feel ill because you were drunk • *Frank's got a bad case of the morning after.*

morning, noon, and night

if you do something morning, noon, and night, you do it most of the time • *They've been working morning, noon, and night to finish the decorating before the baby's born.*

mortal

▶ See: **shuffle** off this mortal coil

most

make the most of sth

to take full advantage of something because it may not last long • *Make the most of the good weather because rain is forecast for tomorrow.* • *There'll be a lot* *of travelling involved in my new job and I plan to **make the most of it**.*

mother

at your **mother's knee**
if you learned to do something at your mother's knee, you learned it when you were a young child • *I learned to sew at my mother's knee.*

a mother lode of sth *American*
a large collection of a particular type of thing • *His collection of letters and papers is a mother lode of information for writers and journalists.*

Mother Nature
the force that controls the natural world • *Look at those trees blown down in the storm. Just shows you what Mother Nature can do when she gets angry.*

the mother of all sth *informal*
an extreme example of something • *Mike's suffering from the mother of all hangovers after the party last night.*

Shall I be mother? *British & Australian humorous*
something that you say in order to ask whether you should serve food or drink to someone • *Here comes the tea. Shall I be mother?*

▶ See also: a mummy's/mother's **boy**
be **tied** to your mother's apron strings

moths

like moths to a flame *literary*
if people gather round someone like moths to a flame, they try to be near someone who seems very attractive or very interesting ✍Moths are small flying insects that are attracted to bright light. • *I never understood why people flocked around him like moths to a flame.*

motion

put/set sth **in motion**
if you set something in motion, you start it happening • *The government have set in motion plans to reform the justice system.*

motions

go through the motions
to do something because you are expected to do it and not because you want to • (often in continuous tenses) *These days when we go out, cook a meal together or even make love, I get the feeling that he's just going through the motions.*

mot juste

the mot juste *formal*
the word or phrase that exactly describes what you want to say • *I'm searching for the mot juste to describe him. Unusual, I think, is the best way of saying it.*

mould

▶ See: **break** the mould
They **broke** the mould when they made sb/sth.
be **cast** in the same mould

mountain

make a mountain out of a molehill
to make a slight difficulty seem like a serious problem • (usually in continuous tenses) *You're making a mountain out of a molehill. You wrote one bad essay – it doesn't mean you're going to fail your degree.*

a mountain to climb *British & Australian*
something that is very difficult to do • *After a bad start to the season, the team has a mountain to climb if they want to win the league.*

mountains

▶ See: **move** mountains

mouth

be all mouth *British, American & Australian informal*
be all mouth and (no) trousers *British informal*
if someone is all mouth, they talk a lot about doing something but they never do it • *She says she'll complain to the manager but I think she's all mouth.* • *You're all mouth and no trousers. Why don't you just go over there and ask her out?*

be down in the mouth *informal*
to be sad • *Jake looks a bit down in the mouth. Shall we try to find out what's wrong?*

make sb's **mouth water**
if the smell or the sight of food makes your mouth water, it makes you want to eat it • *The smell of fish and chips made my mouth water.*

mouth-watering • *The restaurant had a selection of mouth-watering desserts.*

a mouth to feed
someone, especially a new-born baby for whom you must provide food • *With three small children and hardly any money, the last thing they needed was **another mouth to feed**.*

▶ See also: **keep** your mouth shut
melt in the/your mouth
run off at the mouth
shoot your mouth off
Shut your face/gob/mouth/trap!
Wash your mouth out!

mouths

Out of the mouths of babes (and sucklings). *literary*
something that you say when a small child says something that surprises you because it shows an adult's wisdom and understanding of a situation • *I was so stunned that a child of six could be so adult in her perceptions. Out of the mouths of babes...*

movable

a movable feast
something that happens often but at different times so that you are not certain when it will next happen • *They usually have a party at some point in the summer but it's something of a movable feast.*

move

get a move on *informal*
to hurry • (often an order) *Get a move on, man! We don't have all day.* • *Simon realised he'd have to get a move on if he was to finish by 4 o'clock.*

make a move
1 to do something in order to achieve a particular result • *Who will make the first move towards resolving the dispute?* • (often + to do sth) *There were plenty of witnesses to the attack, but nobody made a move to stop it.*
2 to leave a place • *It's getting late – perhaps we ought to make a move.*

make a move on sb *informal*
to try to start a romantic or sexual relationship with someone • *As soon as Ellen left the room, her boyfriend made a move on me.*

not **move a muscle**
to stay completely still • *She sat without moving a muscle as the nurse injected the anaesthetic.*

move heaven and earth
to do everything you can to achieve something • (usually + to do sth) *I moved heaven and earth to get you that interview, and you didn't even bother to show up for it!*

move mountains
1 if someone or someone's beliefs or feelings can move mountains, they can achieve something that is very difficult • *If faith can move mountains, we'll win the Cup.*
2 if you would move mountains for someone, they are so important to you that you would do anything to please them • *He'd move mountains for her but she treats him like dirt.*

move the goalposts *British, American & Australian*
move the goal *American*
to change the rules in a situation in a way that is not fair, usually in order to make it more difficult for someone to achieve something • *My boss is never satisfied. Whenever I think I've done what he wants, he moves the goalposts.*

▶ See also: Move/Shift your **arse**!
move/step up a **gear**
move in for the **kill**
change/keep up/move with the **times**
move down in the **world**

movers

the movers and shakers
people who have a lot of power and influence • *This play has attracted the attention of the Broadway movers and shakers.*

moving

the moving spirit *literary*
someone who starts an important organization or course of action • (often + **behind**) *Born in Nkroful, Ghana, he was the moving spirit behind the Charter of African States.*

Mr

Mr Big *informal*
the most important man in a group of people, especially a group involved in

criminal activities • *Police have arrested a man they believe is the Mr Big of Brighton's drug scene.*

Mr Right
a man who would be the perfect husband for a particular woman because he has all the qualities that she wants • *I'm sure she'll settle down with a nice man one day soon. She just hasn't found Mr Right yet.*

No more Mr Nice Guy.
something that you say when you have decided to behave in a less pleasant way • *I'm fed up with people taking advantage of me. From now on, it's no more Mr Nice Guy.*

much

be much of a muchness *informal*
to be very similar • *Pop music these days is all much of a muchness as far as I'm concerned.*

not **be up to much** *British & Australian*
to not be of a very high quality • *It's a very beautiful-looking town but the shopping's not up to much.*

▶ See also: much **ado** about nothing
not be much **cop**
be nothing much to **write** home about

muck

Where there's muck, there's brass. *British*
something that you say which means you can make a lot of money from work that most people do not want to do because they think it is dirty or unpleasant • *Decorating's a messy job, but where there's muck, there's brass.*

▶ See also: **treat** sb like muck

muck-raking

muck-raking *informal*
the activity of trying to discover unpleasant information about people so that you can tell the public • *These reports are nothing but muck-raking – journalists should not be allowed to investigate ministers' private business dealings.*

mud

Here's mud in your eye! *old-fashioned*
something that you say in order to wish success or happiness to someone who is drinking with you • *Well, here's mud in your eye! I hope you'll both be very happy together.*

Mud sticks. *British & Australian*
something that you say which means it is difficult to make people change their bad opinion of someone • *The court cleared him of fraud, but mud sticks.*

sling/throw mud at sb
if someone slings mud at another person, they try to make other people have a low opinion of them by saying unpleasant things about them • *Companies should think carefully before slinging mud at someone who may respond with a libel action costing millions of dollars.*

mud-slinging • *I left Hollywood because I was fed up with all the mud-slinging that goes on there.*

muddy

muddy the waters
to make a situation more confused and less easy to understand or deal with • *The statistics you quoted didn't prove anything, they simply muddied the waters.*

mug

a mug's game *British informal*
an activity that will not make you happy or successful ✍A mug is a person who is easily deceived. • *Working for a big company is a mug's game – if you want to make money you need to start your own business.*

multitude

cover/hide a multitude of sins *humorous*
if something hides a multitude of sins, it prevents people from seeing or discovering something bad • *Big sweaters are warm and practical and they hide a multitude of sins.*

mum

Mum's the word. *informal*
something that you say which means something should be kept secret • *I think I'm pregnant, but mum's the word until I know for sure.*

mumbo

mumbo jumbo
speech or writing that is nonsense or

very complicated and cannot be understood • *There's so much legal mumbo jumbo in these documents that it's hard to make sense of them.*

mummy

▶ See: a mummy's/mother's **boy**

munchies

get the munchies *informal*
to feel a bit hungry • *Do you ever get the munchies late at night and find there's absolutely nothing in the house you want to eat?*

murder

get away with murder *informal*
to be allowed to do things that other people would be punished or criticized for • *Dave gets away with murder because he's so charming.*

I could murder sth. *British informal*
something that you say when you want a particular kind of food or drink very much • *I'm starving. I could murder a curry.*

murmur

without a murmur
if you do something without a murmur, you do it without complaining • *Louise was so tired that she went to bed without a murmur for once.*

Murphy

Murphy's law *humorous*
the way in which plans always fail and bad things always happen where there is any possibility of them doing so • *I'm a great believer in Murphy's law – what can go wrong will go wrong.*

muscle

▶ See: not **move** a muscle

muscles

▶ See: **flex** your muscles

music

be music to sb's **ears**
if something you hear is music to your ears, it makes you very happy • *The news of his resignation was music to my ears.*

▶ See also: **face** the music

must

▶ See: You must be **joking!**

mustard

▶ See: can't **cut** the mustard

muster

▶ See: **pass** the muster

mutton

mutton dressed (up) as lamb *British informal*
an offensive way of saying that a woman is dressed in a style that is more suitable for a much younger woman • *Do you think this skirt is too short? I don't want to look like mutton dressed as lamb.*

mutual

a mutual admiration society *humorous*
a situation in which two people express a lot of admiration for each other • *'You haven't aged at all.' 'Neither have you and look how slim you are!' 'Hey, you two, why don't you form a mutual admiration society!'*

nail

another nail in the coffin
the final nail in the coffin
an event which causes the failure of something that had already started to fail • (usually + **of**) *I think that argument was the final nail in the coffin of our friendship.*

nail sb **to the wall** *informal*
to punish or hurt someone severely because you are very angry with them • *I didn't care about why they did it, I just wanted to nail the guys that robbed me to the wall.*

on the nail *British & Australian*
if you pay an amount of money on the nail, you pay all of it immediately • *He always paid cash, on the nail.*

▶ See also: nail your **colours** to the mast
hit the nail on the head

nail-biting

nail-biting
a nail-biting event or period of time makes you feel very nervous, usually because you are waiting for something important to happen • (always before noun) *The teams were very evenly matched and played a close game right up to the nail-biting finish.*

nailing

like nailing jelly to the wall
if something is like nailing jelly to the wall, it is impossible to understand or describe it exactly • *Writing a history of the period is like nailing jelly to the wall.*

nails

▶ See: **spit** nails

name

have sb's **name on it** *informal*
if something has your name on it, it is the type of thing that you like very much and so you have to buy, eat, or drink it • *Come on, Paul, there's one piece of chocolate cake left and it's got your name on it.*

have sb's **name written all over it** *informal*
if a job has someone's name written all over it, they have all the qualifications that are needed for that job • *You've got to apply for this job. It's got your name written all over it.*

have/see your **name in lights** *informal*
to be famous for your work in film, theatre, music etc. • *She accepted the few badly-paid roles she was offered and continued to dream of seeing her name in lights.*

I can't put a name to her/him.
something that you say when you cannot remember someone's name • *I can picture his face exactly but I can't put a name to him.*

in all but name
if a situation exists in all but name, it exists although it is not officially described that way • *They'd been living together for over ten years. It was a marriage in all but name.*

in name only
if something exists in name only, it is officially described in a particular way, although that description is not really true • *Two-thirds of the population are Catholic, though many are so in name only.*

in the name of sth
if bad things are done in the name of something, they are done in order to help that thing succeed • *When you think about the atrocities that have been committed in the name of religion, you start to wonder what it's all about.*

make a name for yourself
make your **name**
to become famous or respected by a lot of people • *It was with his third novel, 'The Darkest Hours', that he made a name for himself.*

sb's **name is mud** *informal*
if someone's name is mud, other people are angry with that person because of something they have done or said • *Well*

he'd better turn up tonight or his name will be mud.

name names

to tell people who is involved in a secret or illegal activity • *He wouldn't name names but has promised that the accusations will be fully investigated.*

the name of the game

the most important part of an activity, or the quality that you most need for that activity • *You have to know the right people in acting. That's the name of the game.*

name the day

to announce when you plan to do something important, especially get married • *Have you and Chris named the day yet?*

a name to conjure with

1 a very important and famous name • *There are some names to conjure with on the programme – Poland's Polanski and India's Satyajit Ray to name but two.*
2 an interesting or strange name • *Arnold Spunkmeyer – now that's a name to conjure with!*

take sb's **name in vain** *humorous*

to say someone's name when they are not there, usually when you are criticizing them • *Did I hear someone taking my name in vain?*

you name it

something that you say which means anything you say or choose • *I've tried just about every diet there is going, you name it and I've done it.* • *What would you like? Gin, vodka, lager, wine? You name it, we've got it.*

▶ See also: **clear** sb's name
drag sb's name through the mire/mud

names

▶ See: **call** sb names
name names

narrow

a narrow escape

a situation in which you were lucky because you just managed to avoid danger or trouble • *He only just got out of the vehicle before the whole thing blew up. It was a narrow escape.*

nasty

be a nasty piece of work *British & Australian informal*

to be a very unpleasant person • *He's a nasty piece of work, is Carl. I'd avoid him if I were you.*

native

go native *humorous*

if you say that someone living in a foreign country has gone native, you mean that they have lost some of their own character because they have started to behave like the people in that country • *After a month in Egypt he went native, swapping his linen suit for a pair of wide trousers and a loose tunic.*

natural

▶ See: **die** a natural death

natural-born

natural-born *informal*

having the qualities and abilities which you need in order to be good at doing a particular thing • (always before noun) *Carl was a natural-born salesman, and quickly expanded the company's world-wide sales.*

nature

be (in) the nature of the beast

if something unpleasant is in the nature of the beast, it cannot be avoided because it is part of the character of something • *Relationships always involve some degree of dependence. It's in the nature of the beast.*

let nature take its course

to allow someone or something to live or die naturally • *By this stage, her illness was so severe that the doctors agreed to let nature take its course rather than prolong her suffering.* • *We plant the seeds in springtime and then just let nature take its course.*

navel

gaze at/contemplate your **navel** *humorous*

to spend too much time thinking about yourself and your own problems ✍Your navel is the small round piece of skin in the middle of your stomach. • *I read his novel, and thought the man's obviously spent far too long contemplating his own navel.*

navel-gazing • *He's a man of action and navel-gazing has never been his style.*

near

be near the knuckle *British informal*

if a joke or a remark is near the knuckle, it is about sex in a way that some people find offensive • *Some of his jokes were a bit near the knuckle and, unfortunately, I was watching the show with my parents.*

a near miss

a situation in which an accident or unpleasant situation almost happened and was only just avoided • *I managed to brake just in time but it was a near miss.*

so near and yet so far

something that you say which means that you have almost achieved something but that what you still have to do in order to achieve it is very difficult or impossible • *I've only got the last chapter to write but it's taking forever. So near, yet so agonisingly far.*

► See also: be near the **bone**
close/near at **hand**
be near the **mark**

nearest

your **nearest and dearest** *humorous*

your family • *When people are stressed at work, they tend to go home and take it out on their nearest and dearest.*

nearly

► See: nearly **fall** off your chair

necessary

a necessary evil

something that you do not like but which you know must exist or happen • *He considers taxes a necessary evil.*

necessity

Necessity is the mother of invention.

something that you say which means that if you want to do something very much you will think of a way to do it • *We can't afford expensive paper to paint on so we use old envelopes and newspaper. They do say necessity is the mother of invention.*

neck

be up to your **neck in** sth

1 to be very busy • *Right now I'm up to my neck in work.*

2 to be in a difficult or unpleasant situation • *He's paid practically nothing and he's up to his neck in debt.*

get it in the neck *British & Australian informal*

to be punished or criticized for something that you have done • *It always seems to be the chairman of these football clubs who gets it in the neck when the team does badly.*

neck and neck

if two people who are competing are neck and neck, they are very close and either of them could win • (often + **with**) *Recent polls show the Republicans almost neck and neck with the Democratic Party.*

neck of the woods *informal*

area of the country • *I'm surprised to see you in this neck of the woods. What brings you here?* • *There's no scenery like this in your neck of the woods, is there?*

put your **neck on the line**

to do something that you know might fail and spoil other people's opinion of you or cause you to lose money • *There's a lot of money at stake here and none of the directors wants to put his neck on the line.* • *No one wants to put their neck on the line and predict an outcome.*

► See also: put your head/neck on the **block**
breathe down sb's neck
risk your neck
save sb's neck
stick your neck out
I'll **wring** your neck!

need

I don't need this! *informal*

something that you say when you are annoyed because something is causing you a lot of trouble • *And the next thing that happens is the printer stops working and I'm thinking, I don't need this!*

need your **head examined/examining** *British, American & Australian humorous*

need your **head testing** *British humorous*

if you tell someone they need their head

testing, you think that they are crazy because they have done something stupid or strange • *You need your head examined if you're willing to spend £120 on a pair of jeans.*

need sth **like (**you **need) a hole in the head** *humorous*
if you say you need something like a hole in the head, you mean you do not need it and do not want it • *We need a new shopping centre in our neighbourhood like we need a hole in the head!*

That's all you **need!**
something that you say to show your anger when something happens which will cause you problems when you already have other problems • *A train strike. That's all I need!* • *Her son was arrested yesterday? Poor Brenda, that's all she needs at the moment!*

needle

▶ See: be like **looking** for a needle in a haystack

needs

needs must
something that you say which means that you will do something only because it is necessary • *I really don't feel like cooking for all these people tonight but needs must.*

Who needs it/them? *informal*
something that you say which means that you think something causes trouble • *Stress, who needs it?* • *Men, who needs them anyway?*

neither

be neither one thing nor the other
if you say that something is neither one thing nor the other, you think it is bad because it is a mixture of two different things that do not combine well together • *I prefer a book to be either fact or fiction – this one's neither one thing nor the other.*

neither here nor there
if a fact is neither here nor there, it is not important • *Whether they go or not is neither here nor there as far as I'm concerned.*

▶ See also: be neither **fish** nor fowl

nelly

Not on your nelly! *British & Australian old-fashioned*
something that you say in order to tell someone that you will not do something • *'Perhaps you could take Phil with you to the party.' 'Not on your nelly!'*

nerve

hit/touch a (raw) nerve
to upset someone by talking about a particular subject • *I think I hit a nerve with my comments about divorce.* • *She suddenly looked distressed and I knew I'd touched a raw nerve.*

▶ See also: **strain** every nerve

nerves

a battle/war of nerves
a situation in which two competing groups of people try to defeat each other by frightening and threatening each other without taking action • *This has become a battle of nerves with neither side seeming willing to back down.*

be a bundle of nerves *British, American & Australian informal*
be a bag of nerves *British informal*
to be very nervous • *You should have seen me before the interview. I was a bundle of nerves.*

get/grate on sb's **nerves** *informal*
to annoy someone, especially by doing something again and again • *If we spend too much time together, we end up getting on each other's nerves.* • *The telephone hadn't stopped ringing all morning and it was starting to grate on my nerves.*

nerves of steel
if someone has nerves of steel, they are very brave • *You'd have to have nerves of steel to play in front of a crowd this size.*

▶ See also: **live** on your nerves

nest

fly/leave the nest

fly/leave the nest
to leave your parents' home for the first time in order to live somewhere else • *Once the kids have all flown the nest we might sell this house and move somewhere smaller.*

a nest egg
an amount of money that you have saved • *Regular investment of small amounts of money is an excellent way of building a nest egg.*

net

▶ See: **cast** your net wide/wider
slip through the net

nettle

▶ See: **grasp** the nettle

never

Never say die.
something that you say which means that you should not accept that you have failed while there is still a chance that you may succeed • *There are still a couple of job agencies that you haven't tried. Never say die.*

▶ See also: You'll never hear the **end** of it.
It'll never **fly**.
It never **rains** but it pours.
Never the **twain** shall meet.

never-never

a never-never land
an imaginary place where everything is perfect in a way that it is not in the real world • *The film is set in a pre-war English never-never land of roses and sunny days.*

on the never-never *British humorous*
if you buy something on the never-never, you pay for it in regular, small amounts over a period of time • *Buy something on the never-never and you end up paying twice as much.*

new

be new to the game
to lack any experience of a particular activity • *I'd never interviewed anyone on television before. I was new to the game and needed all the advice I could get.*

give sb **a new lease of life** *British & Australian*
give sb **a new lease on life** *American*
if something gives someone a new lease of life, it makes them happy or healthy and gives them new energy after a period of illness or sadness • *The operation was such a success – it really has given her a new lease of life.*

give sth **a new lease of life**
to improve something that was old or old-fashioned so that it works better or looks better • *I've had that blue sofa re-covered and it's really given it a new lease of life.*

the new black
used to say that something is the most popular or fashionable colour or thing at the moment • *Designers say that brown is the new black.*

new blood
new people in an organization who will provide new ideas and energy • *It's time we injected some new blood into this organization.*

a new broom
a new leader of an organization who makes a lot of changes and improvements • *There was a feeling that White had been in charge long enough and that what was needed was a new broom.*

the new kid on the block *American & Australian informal*
someone who is new in a place or organization and has many things to learn about it • *Realizing I was the new kid on the block in this job, I was*

determined to prove myself.

a New Man *British & Australian*
a man who shows his belief in the equality of the sexes by helping his partner with the care of the children and by sharing the work that needs to be done in the house • *I bet you Chris does at least half of the cooking and the housework. He's very much a New Man.*

That's a new one on me! *informal*
something that you say when someone has just told you about a surprising fact or idea that you have never heard before • *And you eat cheese and peanut butter together? That's a new one on me!*

▶ See also: a whole new **ball** game
break new ground
breathe (new) life into sth
turn over a new leaf

news

No news is good news.
something that you say when you have not spoken to someone or heard any information about them and you are hoping that this is because nothing bad has happened to them • *I haven't heard from Johnny for over a week now but I suppose no news is good news.*

That's news to me.
something that you say to someone when they have just told you a piece of information that surprises you • *And he told you he did a lot of cooking, did he? Well, that's news to me.*

next

the boy/girl next door
used to describe someone who is completely ordinary, not rich, famous, etc • *We couldn't believe it when he got a record deal. To us, he was just the boy next door.*

▶ See also: in next to no **time**

nice

be as nice as pie *informal*
if someone is nice as pie, they are friendly to you when you are expecting them not to be • *I came in this morning expecting him to be furious with me and he was nice as pie.*

a nice little earner *British & Australian informal*
something such as a job or a business that allows you to earn a lot of money • *His picture-framing business is a nice little earner.*

Nice one! *British & Australian informal*
something that you say when you have just heard that someone has done something which you think is good • *'Graham's brought some champagne along to mark the occasion.' 'Oh, nice one, Graham!'*

Nice work if you can get it!
something that you say when you are talking about a way of earning money easily that you would do if you had the opportunity • *Top soap opera stars are paid around £2,000 an episode. Nice work if you can get it!*

nick

in the nick of time
at the last possible moment ✍A nick was a mark on a stick which was used in the past to measure time. • *We got there just in the nick of time. A minute later and she'd have left.*

nickel

nickel-and-dime *American informal*
very ordinary and not important ✍Nickels and dimes are American coins which are very low in value. • (always before noun) *We drove along past deserted gas stations and nickel-and-dime diners.*

nickel and dime sb *American informal*
to charge someone small amounts of money for something, often as an extra payment • *I hate being nickeled and dimed by hotels for local telephone calls – they already charge you so much for the room.*

nickels

▶ See: not have **two** nickels to rub together

night

a night owl
someone who often goes to bed late because they prefer to do things at night • *A night owl from his youth, he is rarely in bed before 4 o'clock.*

nightmare

▶ See: the nightmare/worst-case **scenario**

nine

go the whole nine yards *American informal*
to continue doing something dangerous or difficult until it is finished • *The weather was terrible but I wanted to go the whole nine yards and get to the top of the mountain.*

nine times out of ten
almost always • *Nine times out of ten when you're dreading an occasion it turns out to be perfectly all right.*

the whole nine yards *American informal*
the whole of something, including everything that is connected with it • *When I eat Mexican food, I like to have fajitas, bean dip, guacamole – the whole nine yards.*

nine-day

▶ See: a nine/one/seven-day **wonder**

ninepins

go down/fall like ninepins *British old-fashioned*
to be injured, or to fail in large numbers ✍Ninepins is a game in which you try to make bottle-shaped objects fall by rolling a ball at them. • (usually in continuous tenses) *I've never seen so many players injured. They were going down like ninepins.*

nineteen

▶ See: nineteen/ten to the **dozen**

nip

be nip and tuck *American informal*
if two people who are competing are nip and tuck, they have almost the same number of points and either of them could win • *There's no saying who's going to win this game. It's been nip and tuck all the way.*

a nip and (a) tuck
1 a medical operation to improve the appearance of your face • *I don't think you could look like that at her age without a little nip and tuck.*
2 *American* small changes or reductions made in order to improve something • *A nip and a tuck in their household budget would give them the extra money they need.*

a nip in the air
if there is a nip in the air, the air is cold • *There's quite a nip in the air. I think you'll need your jacket on.*

nip sth **in the bud**
to prevent a small problem from getting worse by stopping it soon after it starts • *The strike was nipped in the bud by some clever negotiation.*

nitty-gritty

the nitty-gritty
the most basic and important facts of something • *We didn't actually* ***get down to the nitty-gritty*** (= start to talk about the most important facts) *until half way through the meeting.*

no

no dice *American & Australian informal*
no soap *American informal*
something that you say in order to refuse a request or to make clear that something is not possible • *'Can you lend me ten dollars?' 'Sorry, no dice – I don't have any money with me.'* • *We were looking for a house to rent on the island but it was no soap.*

no end *informal*
very much • *Jack's visit cheered me up no end.*
no end of sth *informal* a lot of something • *We've had no end of problems with the washing machine.*

No fear! *British & Australian informal*
something that you say in order to emphasize that you do not want to do something • *'So are you coming camping with us this weekend?' 'No fear! I hate camping!'*

no go *informal*
something that you say when something is not going to happen • *We were supposed to be going to Ann's for the weekend but* ***it's no go*** *because of the weather.*

▶ See also: not take no for an **answer**
be no/nobody's **fool**
no **ifs** and buts
be no **joke**
No such **luck**!

no **matter**
and no **messing**
no **messing**
No more **Mr** Nice Guy.
No **news** is good **news**.
be no **oil** painting
be no **picnic**
no **prizes** for guessing sth
There's no **smoke** without fire.
be no **spring** chicken
no **strings** (attached)
No **sweat**!
There's no such **thing** as a free lunch.
in next to no **time**
like there's no **tomorrow**
in no **uncertain** terms
No **way**!

no-win

▶ See: a no-win **situation**

nobody

like nobody's business *informal*
very quickly or very well • *We get through butter in our house like nobody's business.* • *She cooks like nobody's business.* (= she cooks very well)

▶ See also: be no/nobody's **fool**

nod

give sb **the nod** *British & Australian informal*
to give someone permission to do something • *We're just waiting for the council to give us the nod then we'll start building.*
get the nod *British & Australian informal* to get permission to do something • *It remains to be seen which scheme will get the nod.*

A nod's as good as a wink. *British & Australian humorous*
something that you say when you have understood what was meant by something although it was not expressed in a direct way • *I know when I'm not wanted, so don't try to say anything more – a nod's as good as a wink.*

on the nod *British & Australian informal*
if a suggestion is agreed to on the nod, it is accepted without discussion • *The Stock Exchange clearly hopes these proposals will go through on the nod.*

noise

make a noise about sth
to complain a lot about something • *If you don't make a noise about things, nothing gets changed.*

noises

make noises
to talk about something that you might do, but not in a detailed or certain way • *She's been making noises about going back to college.*

none

▶ See: none of your **beeswax**
be none the **wiser**

no-no

be a no-no
if something that someone does is a no-no, people do not think it is an acceptable way of behaving • *Spanking children is a no-no these days.*

non sequitur

a non sequitur
a statement which does not seem to be connected with what has just been said • *'Have you arranged for us to visit Eileen?' I asked. 'But I thought you were coming by train', said Gwen, in what seemed a complete non sequitur.*

nook

every nook and cranny
every part of a place • *This house is where I grew up. I know every nook and cranny of it.*
nooks and crannies • *I dusted the living room really thoroughly, making sure I got into all the nooks and crannies.*

nose

by a nose
if a person or animal wins a race or competition by a nose, they win it by only very little • *My horse won but only by a nose. In fact it was a very exciting finish.*

get up sb's **nose** *British & Australian informal*
to annoy someone • *It's the way he follows me around everywhere – it gets right up my nose.* • *To be honest, I prefer not to have to deal with her. She gets up my nose.*

have a nose (round) *British & Australian informal*
to look around a place • *He left the room for a few minutes so I thought I'd have a nose round.*

have a nose for sth *informal*
to be good at finding a particular kind of thing • *Like any good newspaper journalist, she has a nose for a good story.* • *He's always finding things in the sales. He seems to have a nose for a bargain.*

have your **nose in a book**
to be reading • *My daughter reads all the time. She's always got her nose in a book.*

nose to tail *British*
if cars that are moving are nose to tail, they are very close to each other, one behind the other • *Traffic is nose to tail on the east-bound section of the M62.*

on the nose *mainly American*
exactly right, often an exact amount of money or time • *We arrived at three o'clock on the nose.* • *Her description of the play really **hit it on the nose**.*

poke/stick your **nose into** sth *informal*
to show too much interest in a situation that does not involve you • *That'll teach him to go poking his nose into other people's business!*

put sb's **nose out of joint** *informal*
to upset or annoy someone • *Martin refused to let her chair the meeting which rather put her nose out of joint.*

under sb's **nose**
if something bad happens under your nose, it happens very close to you but you do not notice it • *I'm amazed that it was going on right under his nose all that while and he didn't realize.*

with your **nose in the air**
behaving as if you think you are better than other people and do not want to speak to them • *I quite often see him in the street and he always walks past with his nose in the air.*
have your **nose in the air** • *Every inch the aristocrat, he always has his nose in the air.*

▶ See also: **cut** off your nose to spite your face
follow your nose
keep your nose clean
keep your nose out of sth
keep your nose to the grindstone
lead sb by the nose
look down your nose at sth/sb
pay through the nose
powder your nose
rub sb's nose in it
thumb your nose at sth/sb
turn your nose up

no-show

a no-show
1 someone who does not arrive at a place where they are expected • *The disgraced Senator was a no-show at both events.*
2 the action of not arriving somewhere where you are expected • *The concert was called off because of a no-show by the band.*

nosy

a nosy/nosey parker *British & Australian informal*
someone who is too interested in finding out information about other people • *Tell him to mind his own business, the nosy parker!*

not

be not on
if you say that behaving in a particular way is not on, you mean that it is not right and people should not do it • *I've told her that bringing crowds of friends home every evening isn't on.* • *It's not on to expect other people to clear up your mess.*

▶ See also: It's/That's (just) not **cricket**!
Not **half**!
Not on your **life**!
Not on your **nelly**!
(And) not before **time**!

notes

▶ See: **compare** notes

nothing

be nothing short of [astonishing/miraculous etc.]
to be totally astonishing, miraculous etc. • *His achievements as a political reformer have been nothing short of miraculous.*

here goes nothing *American & Australian informal*
something that you say just before you do something that you think will not be

successful • *Well, here goes nothing – let's see if I can pass the driving test.*

like nothing on earth
very strange • *I don't know what instruments they play but it sounds like nothing on earth.*

nothing daunted *British & Australian formal*
if you continue to do something, nothing daunted, you are not worried about problems you have with it • *I've had three letters of refusal but, nothing daunted, I'm writing a fourth application.*

Nothing doing. *informal*
something that you say in order to tell someone that you refuse to do something • *'Will you take us, then?' 'I've told you, nothing doing.'*

Nothing ventured, nothing gained.
something that you say which means that it is necessary to take risks in order to achieve something • *We tried to make television programmes that were new and different, and we weren't always successful, but nothing ventured, nothing gained.*

There's nothing to it. *informal*
something that you say in order to tell someone that something is very easy to do • *'I heard rollerblading was really difficult.' 'Nah, there's nothing to it.'*

▶ See also: have nothing between the/your **ears**
be nothing to **shout** about
stop at nothing
think nothing of doing sth

notice

▶ See: make sb **sit** up and take notice

nouveau riche

the nouveau riche
people who have become rich recently and who buy expensive things in order to show people how much money they have • *He is one of the country's nouveau riche who have made fortunes in shipping, hotels, and real estate.*
nouveau riche • *She refused to live in Beverly Hills which she considered far too nouveau riche.*

now

It's now or never.
something that you say which means that you must do something immediately because you will not get another opportunity • *As she was leaving I thought, it's now or never. So I just went up to her and asked her out.*

▶ See also: Now you're **talking**!

nth

to the nth degree
as much or as far as possible • *What I find is that you can follow instructions to the nth degree and still get it wrong.*

number

do a number on sb
to treat someone very badly or unfairly • *I'm not surprised Caroline doesn't like him. He really did a number on her at work.*

have sb's **number** *informal*
to know that someone is trying to do something bad and therefore be able to deal with them • *I'm not worried about Taylor. I've got his number and I know what to expect.*

a number cruncher *humorous*
1 someone whose job is to work with numbers and mathematics • *She may not look like a number cruncher but she's with a big firm of accountants.*
number crunching • *She's useless with figures – it's her assistant who does all the number crunching for her.*
2 a computer that is able to solve complicated problems of mathematics • *The television broadcasters will use their number crunchers on election night to try and forecast the result.*

sb's **number is up** *informal*
if someone's number is up, they are going to die or to suffer • *This car came hurtling towards me and I thought my number was up.*

number one *informal*
the most important person, especially when you think this is yourself and you do not care about anyone else • *Half of me thinks I should just* ***look out for number one*** *and not give a damn about anyone else.*

numbers

a numbers game
the use of numbers to represent facts in an argument, especially when it makes people believe things that are not true • *It's just a numbers game and everyone does it. You manipulate the statistics till they suit your argument.*

nut

be off your **nut** *informal*
to be crazy • *You can't do that! Are you off your nut or what?*

do your **nut** *British & Australian informal*
to become extremely angry • *If she has to walk from the station again she'll do her nut.*

a hard/tough nut
someone who is difficult to deal with because they are unpleasant or very determined to get what they want • *People don't tend to mess with Sue. She's a tough nut.*

a hard/tough nut to crack
a difficult problem to solve • *A company whose product has sold well in the States may find the European market a tougher nut to crack.*

nuts

can't do sth **for nuts** *British & Australian informal*
if someone cannot do something for nuts, they cannot do it at all • *So Roger had prepared a beautiful meal? I thought you said he couldn't cook for nuts.*

the nuts and bolts
the basic, practical details of a job or other activity • (often + **of**) *Law school teaches wonderful theory but it doesn't teach the nuts and bolts of actually practising law.*

nutshell

in a nutshell
something that you say when you are describing something using as few words as possible • *Karen wants them to get married and buy a house and Mike wants them to carry on as they are and that, in a nutshell, is the problem.* • *Well, to* ***put it in a nutshell****, we're going to have to start again.*

nutty

be as nutty as a fruitcake *British & Australian informal*
to be crazy • *'Isn't she slightly strange, your aunt? 'Oh, she's as nutty as a fruitcake.'*

oaks

Great/Mighty oaks from little acorns grow.
something that you say in order to emphasize that a large, successful organization or plan was very small or simple when it began • *Microsoft, which is now the biggest independent software company in the world, was founded in 1975 by just two men. It goes to show that great oaks from little acorns grow.*

oar

put/stick your **oar in** *British & Australian informal*
to involve yourself in a discussion or a situation when other people do not want you to • *I don't want Janet coming to the meeting and sticking her oar in – she knows nothing about the situation.*

oats

get your **oats** *British very informal*
to have sex regularly • (usually in continuous tenses) *Dan seems a lot happier these days – I think he must be getting his oats.*

occasion

▶ See: **rise** to the occasion

odd

the odd man/one out
someone or something that is different from the other people or things in a group • *She was always the odd one out at school – she didn't really mix with the other children.* • *I felt like the odd man out yesterday. Everyone was watching football except me.*

the odd man/one out

▶ See also: make odd/strange **bedfellows**

odds

against (all) the odds
against all odds
if you do or achieve something against all the odds, you do or achieve it although there were a lot of problems and you were not likely to succeed • *Against all the odds, she conceived her first child at the age of 56.* • *He struggled against the odds to keep his business going during the recession.*

be at odds
to disagree • (often + **with**) *She's at odds with the mayor over cuts in the department's budget.* • (often + **over**) *They're at odds over the funding for the project.*
put sb **at odds with** sb • *His views on Europe put him at odds with the rest of the party.*

be at odds with sth
if one statement or description is at odds with another, it is different when it should be the same • *Blake's version of events was at odds with the official police report.*

odds and ends *British, American & Australian*
odds and sods *British & Australian informal*
a group of small objects of different types which are not very valuable or important • *I eventually found my keys buried beneath the odds and ends in the bottom of my bag.*

▶ See also: **pay** over the odds

off

off the peg *British*
off the hook *American & Australian*
if you buy clothes off the peg, you buy them in a standard size from a shop rather than having them made specially for you • *If I buy trousers off the peg, they're always too short.*

▶ See also: have sth off to a **fine** art
off sb's **hands**
be off your **head**

off-chance

on the off-chance
if you do something on the off-chance, you do it because you hope you will get or find something or someone, even if it is not very likely • *I don't think he works in the shop on Saturdays, but you could stop by on the off-chance.* • (often + **that**) *Journalists often investigate film stars' private lives on the off-chance that they might find something scandalous.* • (often + **of** + doing sth) *She flew in from New York on the off-chance of getting tickets to see Becker play his last match at Wimbledon.*

off-colour

be off-colour *British & Australian*
be off-color *American & Australian*
to not be feeling as well as usual • *He had flu a couple of months ago and he's been a bit off-colour ever since.*

off-colour *British & Australian*
off-color *American & Australian*
off-colour jokes or remarks are about sex in a way that some people find offensive • *Some of his jokes were a little off-colour and I don't think my grandparents particularly appreciated them.*

offer

▶ See: hold out/offer an **olive** branch

off-the-cuff

off-the-cuff
an off-the-cuff remark is one that is not planned • (always before noun) *He made several off-the-cuff remarks which he later denied.*

off the cuff
if you speak off the cuff, you do it without having planned what you will say • *She wasn't expecting to give a speech and just said a few things off the cuff.*

oil

be no oil painting *British & Australian humorous*
if someone is no oil painting, they are not attractive • *She has an interesting face but she's no oil painting.*

oil the wheels
to make it easier for something to happen • (usually + **of**) *An aid programme was established to oil the wheels of economic reform in the region.*

▶ See also: **pour** oil on troubled waters

old

an old chestnut *informal*
a subject, idea, or joke which has been discussed or repeated so many times that it is not interesting or funny any more • *I wondered whether there might, after all, be some truth in the old chestnut that one's school days are the happiest of one's life.* • *Play allows us to rediscover the child in ourselves – that old chestnut.*

an old flame
a person who you had a romantic relationship with in the past • *I bumped into an old flame of yours in Oxford on Saturday.*

an old hand
someone who has done a particular job or activity for a long time and who can do it very well • (often + **at**) *She's an old hand at magazines, having trained on Cosmopolitan before editing Company.*

an old maid *old-fashioned*
an impolite way of referring to a woman who has never married ✍In the past, young women who were not married were called maids. • *Terrified of becoming an old maid, she married the first man who made her an offer.*

an old wives' tale
a piece of advice or an idea which a lot of people believed in the past but which we now know is wrong • *It's an old wives' tale that drinking alcohol before you go to bed helps you sleep.*

be as old as Methuselah
if someone is as old as Methuselah, they are very old ✍Methuselah was a character from the Bible who lived until he was 969. • *I was a young boy at the time so to me he looked as old as Methuselah but he was probably only in his sixties.*

be as old as the hills
if something is as old as the hills, it has existed for a very long time • *Difficult relationships between parents and children are nothing new: the problem's as old as the hills.*

for old times' sake
if you do something for old times' sake, you do it in order to remember a happy time in the past • *Do you want to have lunch together sometime, just for old times' sake?*

of the old school
if someone is of the old school, they have traditional ideas about how to do something and they do not accept new ways of doing it • *She was a teacher of the old school and believed in strict discipline.*

the Old Bill *British informal, old-fashioned*
the police • *The Old Bill was round here yesterday, asking where you were.*

the old country *American & Australian*
the country or place where you or your parents were born but do not now live, especially Europe • *They spent the summer touring the old country.*

the old guard
a group of people who have worked in an organization for a long time and do not want it to change • *She has tried to resist attempts by the old guard to halt the reform process.*
old-guard • (always before noun) *Most people in the party want to see the old-guard leadership replaced.*

old hat
if something is old hat, it is not new or modern any more • *A 24-hour banking service may seem old hat in the United States, but it's still innovative in Europe.*

Old Nick *British & Australian old-fashioned, humorous*
the Devil (= the enemy of God in the Christian religion) • *In his latest film, he plays a gambler who sells his soul to Old Nick in return for winning a fortune.*

the old school tie
the way in which men who have been to the same expensive private school help each other to find good jobs • *The old school tie still has enormous power in many City companies.*

open/reopen old wounds
to make someone remember an unpleasant event or situation that happened in the past • *For many soldiers who served in Vietnam, the current conflict has reopened old wounds.*

▶ See also: an old **head** on young shoulders
You can't **teach** an old dog new tricks.

old-boy

the old-boy network
the way in which men who have been to the same expensive school or university help each other to find good jobs • *He admitted the old boy network had once existed in the company but said that things had changed now.*

oldest

the oldest profession (in the world) *humorous*
prostitution (= being paid to have sex) • *I believe she made a living in the oldest profession in the world.*

the oldest trick in the book
a way of tricking someone which is still effective although it has been used a lot before • *It was the oldest trick in the book – one man distracted me while another stole my wallet.*

olde-worlde

olde-worlde *British & Australian*
a place that is olde-worlde looks very old or has been made to look old in a way that seems false • *It's a sweet little village, full of olde-worlde charm.* • *They own a dreadful olde-worlde tea-shop with fake wooden beams and lace everywhere.*

olive

hold out/offer an olive branch
to do or say something in order to show that you want to end a disagreement with someone ✍An olive branch is traditionally a symbol of peace. • (often + **to**) *He held out an olive branch to the opposition by releasing 42 political prisoners.*

an olive branch • *I've invited them around to dinner by way of an olive branch.*

omelette

You can't make an omelette without breaking eggs.
something that you say which means it is difficult to achieve something important without causing any unpleasant effects • *Twenty jobs will have to be cut if the company's going to be made more efficient. But you can't make an omelette without breaking eggs.*

on

be on about *informal*
if you ask what a person or a piece of writing is on about, you want to know what they mean • (always negative or used in questions) *I read her book, but I couldn't understand what it was on about.* • *What are you on about? I've paid you everything I owed!*

be/go on at sb *informal*
to speak to someone again and again to complain about their behaviour or to ask them to do something • (often + to do sth) *She's been on at me to get my hair cut.*

on and off
off and on
if something happens on and off during a long period of time, it happens sometimes but not regularly or continuously • (often + **for**) *I've had toothache on and off for the past three months.* • (often + **since**) *They've been seeing each other on and off since Christmas.*

▶ See also: be on the **go**
have sth on the **go**
be on the **up** and **up**

once

once and for all
if you do something once and for all, you finish doing it so that it does not have to be dealt with again • *I'm fed up with arguing about this – let's just settle this argument once and for all.* • *He claims his photographs prove once and for all that UFOs do exist.*

Once bitten, twice shy.
something that you say which means when you have had an unpleasant experience you are much more careful to avoid similar experiences in the future • *After he left her she refused to go out with anyone else for a long time – once bitten, twice shy, I suppose.*

once in a blue moon
very rarely • *My sister lives in Alaska, so I only get to see her once in a blue moon.* • *I don't know why I bought that CD-ROM for my computer – I only ever use it once in a blue moon.*

▶ See also: once in a **lifetime**
once upon a **time**

once-over

give sth **a once-over** *informal*
to clean something quickly • (often + **with**) *I'll just give the carpet a once-over with the vacuum cleaner before we go.*

give sb/sth **the once-over** *informal*
to quickly look at someone or examine something in order to see what they are like • *The security guard gave me the once-over but didn't bother checking my pass.* • *Can you give my essay the once-over before I hand it in?*

one

and one (more) for luck
something that you say when you add one more of something for no reason • *I want you to swim ten lengths, and one for luck.*

as one man
if a group of people do something as one man, they all do it together in exactly the same way • *The crowd rose to its feet as one man.*

at/in one sitting
if you do something at one sitting, you do it during one period of time without stopping • *I read the whole book in one sitting.*

be at one *slightly formal*
if people are at one, they agree with each other • (often + **with**) *I am completely at one with Michael on this issue.*

be one in a million
if you say that someone is one in a million, you mean that they are very special because they have such good qualities • *She's the sweetest, most generous person I know – she's one in a million.*

be one in the eye for sb *British & Australian informal*
if something that someone does is one in the eye for someone else, it will annoy that person because they did not want it to happen or did not think it could happen • *When I got my degree, I thought, 'That's one in the eye for my old head teacher, who said I would never get anywhere.'*

be one of a kind
to be the only one of a particular type of thing or person • *As a female engineer who began her career in the 1940s, she was one of a kind.*

be one step ahead
to be slightly better prepared or more successful than someone else • (usually + **of**) *Throughout the incident, the hijackers were always one step ahead of the police.*
keep/stay one step ahead • (usually + **of**) *Crop breeders are continuously developing pesticides to keep one step ahead of the pests.*

be one up on sb/sth
to have an advantage which someone or something else does not have • *We're one up on the other bars in the area because we've got live music.* • *Mario's just spent a year in the States, so he'll be one up on the rest of his English class.*

come one, come all *formal*
something that you say which means that everyone or everything can join or be included • *We can't just invite some people and not others, so I guess it's a case of come one, come all.*

from one moment to the next
if things change from one moment to the next, they change quickly or frequently • *The plans are being changed from one moment to the next.* • ***You never know from one moment to the next** what kind of mood he'll be in.*

get/put one over on sb *informal*
to prove that you are better or more clever than someone else by winning an argument or defeating them • *He's always trying to get one over on the other members of the sales team.*

go in one ear and out the other
if information goes in one ear and out the other, the person who is told it forgets it immediately because they do not listen carefully enough • *You know what it's like when you're told a whole list of names – they just go in one ear and out the other.*

go off on one *British informal*
to suddenly become very angry and start shouting or behaving violently • *He went off on one because he thought I was threatening his dog.*

go one better
to do something better than it has been done before • *The company has decided to go one better than its rivals by offering free drinks with every burger.* • *He set the world record last year. This year he would like to go one better by beating his own record.*

Got it in one!
something that you say when someone has guessed something correctly • *'Don't tell me – is Anna pregnant again?' 'Got it in one!'*

have one foot in the grave *humorous*
to be very old and likely to die soon • *He's been telling everyone he's got one foot in the grave for years now.*

have/keep one eye on sb/sth

have/keep one eye on sth/sb
to give part of your attention to one thing or person while also giving your attention to something or someone else • *As he listened to the speaker he kept one eye on the crowd to gauge their response.*
with one eye on sth/sb • *She sat writing her letter with one eye on the clock.*

It's (just) one thing after another!
If it's not one thing it's another!
something that you say when bad things keep happening to you • *We had our car stolen last week. It's one thing after another at the moment.*

It's just one of those things.
something that you say when you are talking about a bad event or situation that you cannot prevent or change • *Everyone gets ill in the winter. It's just one of those things.*

land/sock sb **one** *informal*
to hit someone hard • *She just walked up and landed him one.*

on the one hand...on the other hand
something that you say when you are speaking about two different facts or two opposite ways of thinking about a situation • *On the one hand, I'd like more money, but on the other hand, I'm not prepared to work the extra hours in order to get it.* • *On the one hand, you complain that you're lonely, and on the other hand you won't come to parties with me.*

one and all *old-fashioned*
everyone • *And a very good evening to one and all.*

one for the road
if you have one for the road, you have a drink, usually an alcoholic drink, before you start a journey • *Come on, there's just time for one for the road.*

One good turn deserves another.
something that you say which means if someone does something to help you, you should do something to help them • *He fixed my bike so I let him use my computer. One good turn deserves another.*

One man's meat is another man's poison.
something that you say which means that something one person likes very much can be something that another person does not like at all • *I wouldn't want to do her job, but she seems to love it. Oh well, one man's meat is another man's poison.*

one of the lads *British & Australian informal*
one of the boys *American informal*
someone who is accepted as part of a group of male friends who all have similar ideas and interests • *Greene, although not one of the lads, is popular with most of them.*

One step forward, two steps back.
something that you say which means every time you make progress, something bad happens which causes you to be in a worse situation than you were to begin with • *Every solution we come up with seems to create more problems than it solves, so it's one step forward, two steps back.*

one swallow doesn't make a summer *British & Australian*
something that you say which means because one good thing has happened, you cannot therefore be certain that more good things will happen and the whole situation will improve • *Okay, they won their last game but one swallow doesn't make a summer. They're still bottom of the league.*

one thing leads to another
if one things leads to another, a series of events happen, each one caused by the previous one • (never in continuous tenses) *I only asked him in for a coffee, but one thing led to another and we ended up in bed together.* • *People don't usually decide to become spies. They agree to do someone a favour and one thing leads to another.*

one way or the other
one way or another
if you say that you will do something or that something will happen one way or the other, you are determined to do it or that it will happen, although you do not know exactly how • *One way or the other, I'm going to finish this job next week.*

one way or the other
if you have to decide one way or the other, you must choose between two possibilities • *They've had a week to think about it and now they must decide one way or the other.* • *It doesn't really matter to me one way or the other.* (= it is not important to me which possibility is chosen)

put one over on sb *informal*
to trick someone • *You're not really sick – you're just trying to put one over on me!*

There's more than one way to skin a cat. *humorous*
something that you say which means that there are several possible ways of achieving something • *It may be illegal for them to organise a strike, but they can still show the management how they feel. There's more than one way to skin a cat, you know.*

There's one born every minute. *humorous*
something that you say about someone who you think has been very stupid • *'He left a window open and then wondered why he'd been burgled!' 'There's one born every minute, isn't there?'*

▶ See also: That's/There's one for the **books**.
take it one **day** at a time
be of like/one **mind**
be one **sandwich** short of a picnic
six of one and half a dozen of the other

one-day

▶ See: a nine/one/seven-day **wonder**

one-hit

a one-hit wonder
someone who performs popular music who makes one successful record and then no others • *The seventies saw a succession of one-hit wonders who were famous overnight and then never heard of again.*

one-horse

a one-horse race
a competition which one particular person or team is very likely to win because they seem much better than the other people competing • *This election has been a one-horse race right from the start.*

a one-horse town *American & Australian*
a small town where very little happens • *Grafton's a real one-horse town with only one grocery store and nothing to do in the evening.*

one-man

a one-man band
an organization in which one person does all the work or has all the power ✍A one-man band is a musician who performs alone and plays several instruments at the same time. • *It's basically a one-man band. He designs, prints and sells the T-shirts himself.* • *Its critics say that the company has become a one-man band in recent years.*

one-night

a one-night stand
1 a sexual relationship which only lasts for one night, or a person who you have had this type of relationship with • *I'd rather have a long-term relationship than a series of one-night stands.* • *It's you I love, Karen – Debbie was just a one-night stand.*
2 a performance which happens only once in a particular place • *We're doing a one-night stand in Durham on Monday followed by a couple of nights in Newcastle.*

one-shot

one-shot *American*
happening only once • (always before noun) *The new current affairs show will be given a one-shot trial on TV next Saturday.* • *The company's offer is a* ***one-shot deal****.*

one-to-one

one-to-one *British, American & Australian*
one-on-one *mainly American*
a one-to-one relationship or activity is when someone works with only one other person • *The school caters for children with special needs who require one-to-one attention.* • *You can choose whether you want to be taught in a class or one-on-one with your own tutor.*

one-track

have a one-track mind
if someone has a one-track mind, they seem to talk and think about one particular subject all the time, especially sex • *'I bet I know what you two were doing last night.' 'Oh, shut up, Sean, you've got a one-track mind.'* • *You've got to have a one-track mind if you want to succeed in business.*

one-two

a one-two punch *American*
two unpleasant things which happen together • *The weather delivered a one-two punch to gardeners with unseasonal*

freezing temperatures and strong winds.

one-upmanship

one-upmanship

if something someone does is one-upmanship, they are trying to make other people admire them by doing it in a better or more clever way than someone else • *There is a great deal of one-upmanship among children anxious to wear the most fashionable clothes.*

one-way

a one-way ticket to sth

if something is a one-way ticket to an unpleasant situation, it will cause that situation to happen • *A rejection of the peace deal would be a one-way ticket to disaster for the country.* • *Experimenting with drugs is a one-way ticket to addiction and misery, as far as I'm concerned.*

onions

▶ See: **know** your onions

only

▶ See: only have **eyes** for sb
not be the only **pebble** on the beach

onwards

onwards and upwards
onward and upward

if someone moves onwards and upwards, they continue being successful or making progress • *The team are moving onwards and upwards after their third win this season.* • *She started her publishing career as an editorial assistant and it was onward and upward from there.*

Onwards and upwards!
Onward and upward!

something that you say in order to encourage someone to forget an unpleasant experience or failure and to think about the future instead • *I know you were disappointed about failing that Spanish exam, but it's not the end of the world. Onwards and upwards!*

open

an open marriage

a marriage in which the partners are free to have sexual relationships with other people • *We have an open marriage, but I never tell my husband about my other lovers.*

an open sesame

a very successful way of achieving something ✍'Open Sesame' are the magic words used by Ali Baba in the story *Tales of the Arabian Nights* to open the door of the place where the thieves are hiding. • (usually + **to**) *A science degree can be an open sesame to a job in almost any field.*

be (wide) open to [abuse/criticism etc.]

to be likely to be abused, criticized etc. • *The system is wide open to abuse.* • *It's a position which **leaves** them **wide open to** criticism.* • *You don't want to **lay** yourself **open to attack**.*

be an open book

1 if a person's life is an open book, you can discover everything about it because none of the details are kept secret • *Like many film stars, he wants to keep his private life private – he doesn't want it becoming an open book.*

2 if someone is an open book, it is easy to know what they are thinking and feeling • *Sarah's an open book, so you'll know right away if she doesn't like the present you've bought her.*

greet/welcome sb/sth with open arms

to be very pleased to see someone, or to be very pleased with something new • *I was rather nervous about meeting my boyfriend's parents, but they welcomed me with open arms.* • *Our company greeted the arrival of the Internet with open arms.*

have/keep an open mind

to wait until you know all the facts before forming an opinion or making a judgement • *Mike might not be guilty – you should keep an open mind until after his case is heard in court.* • (often + **about**) *I like to keep an open mind about what happens to us after we die.*

open-minded willing to think about other people's ideas and suggestions • (often + **about**) *Many doctors have become more open-minded about alternative medicine in the past few years.*

open-mindedness • *She will be remembered by her colleagues for her enthusiasm and open-mindedness.*

open (new) doors

to give someone new opportunities •

(sometimes + **for**) *The success of that film opened new doors for him.* • (sometimes + **to**) *Early results show that the new system would open doors to disadvantaged people.*

open a Pandora's box
to do something that causes a lot of new problems that you did not expect ✍In old Greek stories, Zeus (= the king of the gods) gave Pandora a box that he told her not to open, but she did open it and all the troubles in the world escaped from it. • (often + **of**) *Sadly, his reforms opened a Pandora's box of domestic problems.*

open and shut
if a legal case or problem is open and shut, the facts are very clear and it is easy to make a decision or find a solution • *The police think the case is open and shut: five witnesses saw the man stealing the car.* • *It's going to take a lot of work to deal with this problem. It certainly isn't an open-and-shut matter.*

open sb's **eyes to** sth
to make someone understand something for the first time and know how difficult or unpleasant it is • *Having children of my own opened my eyes to the hurt I had caused my parents.*

an eye-opener
a surprising experience that you learn something new from • *Living in an Indian village was a real eye-opener for all of us.*

open your **heart**
to tell someone your secret thoughts and feelings • (often + **to**) *That night, she opened her heart to me and I think that's when I fell in love with her.*

open season
a period of time when people criticize or unfairly treat a particular person or group of people • (often + **on**) *With the publication of these two reports, it seems to be open season again on single mothers.* • *Newspaper editors have declared open season on the royal family.*

open the door to sth
to allow something new to start • *The ceasefire opens the door to talks between the two sides.* • *A new kind of fat-free fat could open the door to a revolution in snack foods.*

open the floodgates
if an action or a decision opens the floodgates, it allows something to happen a lot or allows many people to do something that was not previously allowed • (often + **to**) *If they win their case it could open the floodgates to others with similar compensation claims.*

open the way for/to sth
to make it possible for something to happen • *Removing customs controls could open the way to an increase in drug smuggling.*

▶ See also: open/reopen **old** wounds
push at an open door

open-ended

open-ended
an open-ended activity or situation does not have a planned ending, so it may develop in several ways • *We are not willing to enter into open-ended discussions.* • *The police investigation was too open-ended. We needed clear responses to our complaints.*

operative

the operative word
the most important word in a phrase, which explains the truth of a situation • *He wants more time for his private life, private being the operative word. Photographers are not allowed anywhere near his family.*

opposite

▶ See: be different/opposite **sides** of the same coin

order

be out of order *informal*
if something that someone says or does is out of order, it is unpleasant or not suitable and it is likely to upset or offend people • *Her behaviour in the meeting was completely out of order.*

be the order of the day
if something is the order of the day, it is thought to be necessary or it is used by everyone in a particular situation • *For countries undergoing a recession, large cuts in public spending seem to be the order of the day.* • *Champagne was the order of the day as we all congratulated Tim on his success.*

organize

couldn't organize a piss-up in a brewery *British & Australian very informal*
if someone couldn't organize a piss-up in a brewery, they are very bad at organizing things ✍A piss-up is a social occasion where everyone drinks a lot of alcohol, and a brewery is a place where beer is made. • *For god's sake don't ask Martin to make the arrangements. He couldn't organize a piss-up in a brewery.*

other

▶ See: **bat** for the other side
have bigger/other **fish** to fry
sb's better/other **half**
how the other **half** lives
look the other way
pass by on the other side
pull the other leg/one (it's got bells on)!
the other **side** of the coin
the other/wrong **side** of the tracks
(all) other **things** being equal
be at each other's **throats**
turn the other cheek
wait for the other shoe to drop

ounce

▶ See: An ounce of **prevention** is worth a pound of cure.

out

be out of it

1 *informal* to be very confused because you are very tired or because of drugs or alcohol • *I didn't feel anything at the moment my baby was born. I was completely out of it by then.*

2 *informal* to feel lonely because you are not included in the activities of people around you • *They were all keen on sports, so I felt really out of it.*

Out with it!
something that you say in order to tell someone to say something they are frightened to say • *Come on, out with it! Tell us all what we're doing wrong!*

▶ See also: get out of **hand**
out of **hand**
be out of your **head**
out of **kilter**
be out on a **limb**
go out on a **limb**
out of **whack**
not be out of the **wood**/woods
be out of this **world**

out-and-out

out-and-out
having all the qualities of a particular thing or person, especially something or someone unpleasant • (always before noun) *The trip was an out-and-out disaster: the airline lost our luggage, the hotel was dirty, and it rained every day.* • *I didn't smash that window – that's an out-and-out lie!*

out-of-date

out-of-date

1 old and therefore not useful or correct any more • *I do have a road map but I suspect it's out-of-date.* • *He claimed the report was inaccurate and based on out-of-date information.* • *Some of her ideas are hopelessly out-of-date.*

2 if a document is out-of-date, it cannot be used any more because the period of time when it could be used has ended • *I found out my passport was out-of-date the day before I was due to travel.* • *No one noticed that he was using an out-of-date permit.*

outstay

▶ See: outstay/overstay your **welcome**

over

get sth **over and done with**
get sth **over with**
to do something difficult or unpleasant as soon as you can so that you do not have to worry about it any more • *I've made an appointment to have my wisdom tooth out tomorrow morning. I just want to get it over and done with.*
be over and done with • *I usually do my homework as soon as I get back from school so that at least it's over and done with.*

over and above
in addition to a particular amount or thing • *Pensioners will receive an increase of £5 per week over and above inflation.* • *The average family pays 40% of their income in taxes, and that's over and above their mortgage, bills, and food.*

▶ See also: That's sb **all** over!

over my **dead** body
It's not over until the **fat** lady sings.
be in over your **head**
be over the **hill**
be over the **hump**
be over the **moon**
be over the **top**

over-egg

over-egg the pudding *British*
to spoil something by trying too hard to improve it • *As a director, I think he has a tendency to over-egg the pudding, with a few too many gorgeous shots of the countryside.*

overboard

go overboard
to do something too much, or to be too excited and eager about something • (often + **on**) *The car's makers seem to have gone overboard on design and sacrificed speed.* • *He went completely overboard on her birthday and bought her a diamond ring.*

overdrive

go into overdrive
to start working very hard, or to start doing something in an excited way • *With her exams only two weeks away, she's gone into overdrive and is studying ten hours a day.* • *The tabloid press went into overdrive at the news that the princess was getting married again.*
be in overdrive • *The whole cast of the show was in overdrive, rehearsing for the first performance the next day.*

overplay

overplay your **hand** *mainly American*
to try to get more advantages from a situation than you are likely to get • *I'm going to ask for promotion but I think it might be overplaying my hand to ask to work fewer hours as well.*

overstay

▶ See: outstay/overstay your **welcome**

overstep

overstep the mark
to upset someone by doing or saying more than you should • *You overstepped the mark when you shouted at your mother.*

own

(all) on your **own**
1 alone • *She's been living on her own for the past ten years.*
2 if you do something on your own, you do it without any help from other people • *Since her husband died two years ago, she's had to look after her children on her own.* • *Dave didn't have time to help so I decorated the house on my own.*

an own goal *British*
something that someone does to try to get an advantage, but which makes a situation worse for them ✍In sport, an own goal is when someone scores a point for the opposite team by mistake. • *The publishing industry believes that new regulations on recycling paper will be an environmental own goal.* • *The government has* ***scored an own goal*** *with its harsh treatment of single parents.*

as if you **own the place**
if someone behaves as if they own the place, they behave in an unpleasantly confident way • *He walked into the office on his first day as if he owned the place.*

be your **own man/woman/person**
to behave in the way that you want and to not let other people influence you • *Despite being the daughter of two Hollywood stars, she's very much her own woman with her own acting style.*

be your **own master**
to be able to live or work in the way that you want to, without anyone else controlling your actions • *The big advantage of working for yourself is that you can be your own master.*

be your **own worst enemy**
if you are your own worst enemy, you do or believe things that prevent you from becoming successful • *Unless he learns to be more confident, he'll never get a decent job. He's his own worst enemy.*

blow your **own trumpet** *British & Australian*
blow/toot your **own horn** *American & Australian*
to tell other people how good and successful you are • *Anyone will tell you she's one of the best journalists we've got, although she'd never blow her own horn.*

come into your/**its own**

to be very useful or successful in a particular situation • *Cars are banned from the city centre so a bicycle really comes into its own here.* • *Ferragamo came into his own in last Sunday's match, scoring three goals in the first half.*

do your **own thing** *informal*

to do exactly what you want without following what other people do or worrying about what they think • *You have to give your children a certain amount of freedom to do their own thing.*

get your **own back**

to do something unpleasant to someone because they have done something unpleasant to you • *Fiona had deliberately stopped me getting that job and I was determined to get my own back.* • (often + **on**) *She got her own back on her unfaithful husband by throwing a pot of red paint over his brand new car.*

get your **own way**

to succeed in persuading other people to let you do what you want • *She sulks every time she doesn't get her own way.* • *I wanted to watch a movie, but Chris got his own way and we spent the afternoon watching the football.*

on your **own hook** *American*

if you do something on your own hook, you do it without anyone else telling you or asking you to do it • *Barbara took up painting on her own hook and developed into a talented artist.*

▶ See also: of your own **accord**
on your own **account**
off your own **bat**
cut your own throat
dig your own grave
with your own **fair** hands
feather your own nest
on sb's (own) **head** be it
hold your own
leave sb to their own devices
be of your own **making**
Mind your own business!
pay sb back in their own coin
play sb at their own game
save your own skin
stand on your own two feet
under your own **steam**
tell its own tale

p

mind/watch your **p's and q's** *old-fashioned*
to make an effort to be polite • *You always felt as if you had to mind your p's and q's with Auntie Lil.*

pace

can't stand/take the pace
to be unable to do things well when you are under a lot of pressure • *If he can't stand the pace he shouldn't be doing the job – it's as simple as that.*

▶ See also: **set** the pace

paces

put sb **through** their **paces**
to test someone's skills or knowledge • *This fitness contest will really put the guys through their paces.*

pack

be ahead of the pack
to be more successful than other people who are trying to achieve the same things as you • *At this stage in the campaign, the Democratic candidate is way ahead of the pack.*

pack a punch *informal*
if someone can pack a punch, they can hit very hard when they are fighting • *He's a big guy – I should imagine he can pack a fair punch.*

pack your **bags**
to leave a place or a job and not return • *The Chief of Police has defied the order to pack his bags.*

a pack rat *American*
someone who collects things that they do not need • *For me there could be nothing worse than living with a pack rat.*

▶ See also: a pack of **lies**

packed

be packed like sardines
if people are packed like sardines, there are a large number of them in a small space • *There were twenty people packed like sardines into a van.*

packing

▶ See: **send** sb packing

paddle

paddle your **own canoe** *informal*
to be independent and not need help from anyone else • *We hoped that after he left college he'd paddle his own canoe.*

page

▶ See: **turn** the page

paid

put paid to sth *British & Australian*
to suddenly stop someone from being able to do what they want or hope to do • *A serious back injury put paid to her tennis career.*

pain

be a pain in the arse/backside *British & Australian very informal*
be a pain in the ass/butt *American & Australian very informal*
to be very annoying • *I can't stand my brother-in-law. He's a real pain in the arse.* • *Getting up for work at 5 a.m. is a pain in the ass.*

be a pain in the neck *informal*
to be very annoying • *My little sister won't leave me alone. She's a real pain in the neck.*

on/under pain of death *formal*
if you are told to do something on pain of death, you will be killed if you do not do it • *They had been told to leave their homes by noon on pain of death.*

pains

be at pains to do sth
to try very hard to make sure that you tell someone the correct information about something and that they understand it • *The management was* ***at great pains*** *to stress that there are no plans for closing down the factory.*

go to/take great pains to do sth
to try very hard to do something • *I went*

to great pains to get this record for you.

paint

paint a [bleak/rosy etc.] picture of sth
to describe a situation in a particular way • *The article paints a bleak* (= hopeless) *picture of the future.* • *He painted a rosy* (= happy) *picture of family life.*

paint yourself **into a corner**
to do something which puts you in a very difficult situation and limits the way that you can act • *I've painted myself into a corner here. Having said I won't take less than £20 an hour, I can't then be seen to accept a job that pays less.*

paint the town red *informal*
to go out and enjoy yourself in the evening, often drinking a lot of alcohol and dancing • *Jack finished his exams today so he's gone out to paint the town red.*

▶ See also: be like **watching** paint dry

painting

be like painting the Forth Bridge *British*
if repairing or improving something is like painting the Forth Bridge, it takes such a long time that by the time you have finished doing it, you have to start again ✍The Forth Bridge is a very large bridge in Edinburgh. • *Home improvements are a bit like painting the Forth Bridge. By the time you've finished the kitchen, the bathroom needs decorating and so it goes on.*

pair

have a [fine/good etc.] pair of lungs *humorous*
if you say that a baby has a good pair of lungs, you mean that they can cry very loudly • *Well she's got a fine pair of lungs, I'll say that for her!*

pale

be beyond the pale
if someone's behaviour is beyond the pale, it is not acceptable • *Her recent conduct is beyond the pale.*
go beyond the pale • *His behaviour at the meeting was going beyond the pale.*

pale by/in comparison
to seem less serious or less important when compared with something else • (often + **with**) *I thought I was badly treated but my experiences pale in comparison with yours.*

▶ See also: fade/pale into **insignificance**

pall

▶ See: **cast** a pall on/over sth

palm

have sb **in the palm of** your **hand**
have sb **eating out of the palm of** your **hand**
to have so much control over someone that they will do whatever you want them to do • *She's got her boyfriend eating out of the palm of her hand.* • *It was such an amazing performance – he had the audience in the palm of his hand.*

▶ See also: **grease** sb's palm

palsy-walsy

palsy-walsy *British & Australian informal*
if two people are palsy-walsy, they seem very friendly, usually in a way that is not sincere • *Those two have been getting very palsy-walsy lately.* • (sometimes + **with**) *She's all palsy-walsy with the boss these days.*

pandora

▶ See: **open** a Pandora's box

panic

hit/press/push the panic button
to do something quickly without thinking about it in order to deal with a difficult or worrying situation • (often negative) *We may have lost the last three games but we're not pushing the panic button yet.*

panic stations *British & Australian informal*
a time when you feel extremely anxious and you must act quickly because something needs to be done urgently • *No matter how organized you think you are, one hour before the show starts* ***it's panic stations.***

pants

[beat/bore/scare etc.] the pants off sb *informal*
if someone or something beats, bores, scares etc. the pants off someone, they beat, bore, or scare them completely • *I hate sunbathing. It bores the pants off me.* • *Horror films scare the pants off me.*

▶ See also: be **caught** with your pants/ trousers down

paper

not **be worth the paper it's/they're printed/written on**
if an agreement or decision is not worth the paper it is written on, it has no value or importance • *A qualification like that isn't worth the paper it's written on.*

on paper
if something seems good or true on paper, it seems to be good or true when you read or think about it but it might not be good or true in a real situation • *She looked good on paper but was one of the weakest interviewees we saw today.* • *On paper it could work, but I won't be convinced until I see it for myself.*

a paper chase *American & Australian*
the activity of dealing with many different documents in order to achieve something • *To receive even the smallest amount of financial aid from a college, it's a real paper chase.*

a paper tiger
a country or organization that seems powerful but is not • *Will the United Nations be able to make any difference, or is it just a paper tiger?*

a paper trail *American & Australian*
documents which show what someone has been doing • *He was easy to find, he left a paper trail a mile wide.*

paper/smooth over the cracks
to hide problems or faults, especially arguments between people, in order to make a situation seem better than it really is • *The two-party coalition has so far been successful in papering over the cracks.* • (sometimes + **in**) *I'm tired of smoothing over the cracks in our marriage – I want a divorce!*

par

be below par
not **be up to par**
1 to be below the usual or expected standard • *His performance yesterday was definitely below par.* • *For some reason her work this week hasn't been up to par.*
2 to be slightly ill • *Do you mind if we put our meeting off till tomorrow? I'm feeling a bit below par today.* • *After a sleepless night, I wasn't quite up to par.*

be par for the course
if the way something happens or is done is par for the course, it happens or is done as you would expect, especially when you do not think this is very good ✍ In golf, par is the number of times you would expect to hit the ball in order to get it in the hole. • *'Gareth was half an hour late.' 'That's just par for the course, isn't it?'*

parade

▶ See: **rain** on sb's parade

pardon

Pardon me for breathing/living! *informal*
something that you say when you are angry with someone because they are always criticizing you or getting annoyed with you • *'If you're just going to get in my way, James, can you leave the kitchen?' 'Oh, pardon me for breathing, I'm sure!'*

Pardon my French! *British humorous*
something that you say which means you are sorry because you have said an impolite word • *The silly sod never turned up, pardon my French.*

par excellence

sb/sth **par excellence**
someone or something par excellence is the best or most extreme example of its type • *China is the destination par excellence for the young and trendy these days.*

Parkinson

Parkinson's law
the idea that the work you have to do will increase to fill all of the time you have to do it in • *If you tell him you want the work done by tomorrow, he'll get it done this afternoon, if you tell him next Thursday,*

he'll spend a week on it. It's Parkinson's law.

parrot-fashion

parrot-fashion *British & Australian*
if you learn something parrot-fashion, you are able to repeat the words, but you do not understand their meaning ✍A parrot is a bird that can repeat words and noises it has just heard. • *When I went to Sunday school, we had to recite passages from the Bible parrot-fashion.*

part

be (all) part of life's rich pageant/ tapestry *literary*
if you say that a bad or difficult experience is all part of life's rich tapestry, you mean that you must accept it because it is a part of life that cannot be avoided ✍A tapestry is a piece of cloth with a picture in it that usually represents a story. • *Having kids certainly causes problems, but that's all part of life's rich tapestry.*

be part of the furniture *informal*
if someone or something is part of the furniture in a place, they have been there for so long that they seem to be a natural part of that place • *I've been working in this office for so long I'm part of the furniture now.* • (sometimes + **of**) *He had become part of the furniture of British politics.*

part and parcel
if something is part and parcel of an experience, it is a necessary part of that experience which cannot be avoided • *Being recognised in the street is all part and parcel of being famous.*

take sb's **part** *old-fashioned*
to support someone in an argument or disagreement • *For once, my brother took my part in the argument.*

▶ See also: **look** the part

parting

the parting of the ways
the point at which two people or organizations separate • *The parting of the ways came after a series of disagreements between the manager and the group's Singer.*

a parting shot
a remark that you say as you are leaving somewhere so that it has a strong effect • *Her parting shot was 'I'm going to spend the evening with people who appreciate my company!'*

partner

sleeping partner *British*
silent partner *American & Australian*
someone who is closely involved with a company, and often provides money for it, but is not a manager of it • *He was an extremely wealthy man, and she was hoping he might become a sleeping partner in their new vineyards.*

partners

partners in crime *humorous*
if two people are partners in crime, they have done something bad together • *She'd kept watch and made sure no one saw us while I actually took the bike so we were partners in crime.*

party

a party animal *informal*
someone who likes going to parties a lot and goes to as many as possible • *She was a real party animal at college. I don't remember her ever staying in in the evening.*

sb's **party piece** *British*
something funny or strange that someone often does to entertain other people in social situations • *Chris can wiggle his ears – it's his party piece.*

a party pooper *humorous*
someone who spoils other people's enjoyment of social activities by being unhappy or by refusing to become involved • *Tim called me a party pooper because I left the party just after midnight.*

▶ See also: **bring** sth to the party
piss on sb's party

pass

make a pass at sb
to speak to or touch someone in a way that shows you would like to start a sexual relationship with them • *He made a pass at her at Simon's party.*

pass by on the other side *British & Australian*
to ignore a person who needs help

✍This phrase comes from a story in the Bible in which two people ignore an injured person and walk past him without offering him any help. • *We cannot just pass by on the other side when we know people are suffering like this.*

pass muster
to be of an acceptable standard for a particular purpose • *Well, how did I do in the test? Do I pass muster?*

pass the buck
to blame someone or to make them responsible for a problem that you should deal with yourself ✍In the card game poker, the buck is an object passed to the person who wins in order to remind them that they must be the first person to give money for the prize in the next game. • (sometimes + **to**) *Parents often try to pass the buck to teachers when children misbehave in school.* • *Bus companies are just passing the buck by saying their drivers are responsible for delays.*

pass the hat around/round
to collect money from a group of people • *We're passing the hat round for Simon's leaving present.*

pass the time of day
to have a short conversation with someone about things which are not important • (often + **with**) *The old man liked to pass the time of day with his neighbours.*

► See also: hand over/pass the **baton**
come through/pass with **flying** colours

past

be past it *informal*
to be too old for a particular activity • *He was a great footballer in his day, but he's past it now.*

be past your **sell-by date**
if someone is past their sell-by date, they are not wanted or useful any more because they are too old ✍A sell-by date is a date put on food products to show the latest date that they can be sold. • *There's plenty of time to have a baby, I'm not past my sell-by date yet.*

I wouldn't put it past sb
something that you say when you think that it is possible that someone might do something wrong or unpleasant • *'Do you really think he'd go off with another woman?' 'I wouldn't put it past him.'* • (often + to do sth) *I wouldn't put it past Lorna to deny all knowledge of this plan.*

pasture

put sb **out to pasture**
to make someone stop working at their job because they are too old to be useful • *He felt he was still too young to be put out to pasture.*

pastures

pastures new *British*
new pastures *American & Australian*
if someone goes to pastures new, they leave their job or home in order to go to a new one • *Tom's off to pastures new. He's got a transfer to Australia.*

pat

a pat on the back
if you give someone a pat on the back, you praise them for something good that they have done • (often + **for**) *She deserves a pat on the back for keeping things going while you were away.*
pat sb **on the back** • *Too many people are patting the players on the back and telling them how great they are.*

stand pat *American informal*
sit pat *Australian informal*
to refuse to make any changes • *Our advice to investors is, stand pat – the recession will soon be over.*

► See also: **learn** sth off pat

patch

not **be a patch on** sb/sth *British & Australian*
to not be as good as someone or something else • *It's a reasonably entertaining film but it's not a patch on 'Bladerunner'.*

path

► See: **beat** a path to sb's door
cross sb's path
take the line/path of **least** resistance

paths

sb's **paths cross**
if two people's paths cross, they meet by chance • *It was a pleasure to meet you. I hope our paths cross again soon.*

patience

the patience of Job/a saint
a lot of patience ✍Job was a character in the bible who still trusted God even though a lot of bad things happened to him. • *You need the patience of a saint to be a teacher.*

patter

the patter of tiny feet *humorous*
something that you say which means that someone is going to have a baby • *I bet it won't be long till we hear the patter of tiny feet.*

pause

give sb **pause (for thought)** *formal*
if something gives you pause, it is surprising or worrying and it makes you think more carefully about something • *It was a tragedy which gave us all pause for thought.*

pave

pave the way for sth
to be a preparation which will make it possible for something to happen in the future • *Scientists hope that data from this expedition will pave the way for a more detailed exploration of Mars.*

pay

hit/strike pay dirt *American & Australian*
to achieve or discover something important or valuable • *She finally hit pay dirt with her third novel which quickly became a best seller.*

If you pay peanuts, you get monkeys.
something that you say which means that only stupid people will work for you if you do not pay very much • *'This company is full of incompetents!' 'Well, if you pay peanuts, you get monkeys.'*

pay sb **back in** their **own coin** *British & Australian old-fashioned*
to treat someone in the same bad way that they have treated you • *I decided to pay her back in her own coin and refuse to help her.*

pay dividends
if something you do pays dividends, it causes good results at a time in the future ✍In the financial world a dividend is part of the profit of a company that is paid to the people who own shares in it. • *Plenty of practice early in the season will pay dividends later on.*

pay your **dues**
to work hard or do something unpleasant over a long period in order to achieve something • *I've looked after four kids for sixteen years, I've paid my dues, and now I want some time to enjoy myself.*

pay its way
if a machine or a piece of equipment pays its way, using it saves you more money than it costs to buy or keep • *Our new combine harvester should be paying its way by next year.*

pay over the odds *British & Australian*
to pay more for something than it is really worth • (often + **for**) *It's a nice enough car but I'm sure she paid over the odds for it.*

pay the price
to accept the unpleasant results of what you have done • *She dropped all her friends when she met Steve and now that he's gone, she's paying the price. She has no one to turn to.* • (often + **for**) *I have paid the price for working nonstop – my health has suffered.*

pay through the nose *informal*
to pay too much for something • (usually + **for**) *If you want a decent wine in a restaurant, you have to pay through the nose for it.*

pay top dollar *American*
to pay a lot of money for something • *Investors can expect to pay top dollar for the stock.*

pay your **way**
if someone pays their way, they pay for all the things they have or use • *We've always paid our own way and never taken a penny from the state.*

▶ See also: give/pay **lip** service to sth

pays

He who pays the piper calls the tune.
something that you say which means that the person who provides the money for something can decide how it should be done • *You may not agree with Mr Brown*

but he funded this venture, and he who pays the piper calls the tune.

You pays your money (and you takes your chances). *informal*
something that you say which means if you do something that involves risk you must accept that you cannot control the result • *The hotels are supposed to have star ratings, but in fact it's a case of you pays your money and you takes your chances.*

You pays your money (and you takes your choice). *informal*
something that you say which means each person has to make their own decisions in a situation, because no decision is more correct than any other • *You can go by motorway, which is quicker, or take the coast road, which is prettier. You pays your money and you takes your choice.*

pea-brained

pea-brained *informal*
a pea-brained person is very stupid • (always before noun) *Take no notice – he's just a pea-brained idiot.*

peace

be at peace with the world
to be feeling calm and happy because you are satisfied with your life • *Sitting on the terrace, looking out over the olive groves, she felt at peace with the world.*

a peace offering
something that you give to someone to show that you are sorry or that you want to be friendly, especially after you have argued with them • *I took Beth some flowers as a peace offering.*

▶ See also: There's no peace/rest for the **wicked**!

peanuts

▶ See: If you **pay** peanuts, you get monkeys.

pearl

a pearl of wisdom
an important piece of advice ✍This phrase is usually used humorously to mean the opposite. • *Thank you for that pearl of wisdom, Jerry. Now do you think you could suggest something more useful?*

pearls

cast pearls before swine *literary*
to offer something valuable to someone who does not understand that it is valuable • *Giving him advice is just casting pearls before swine. He doesn't listen.*

pearly

the pearly gates *humorous*
the entrance to heaven, where some people believe you go when you die • *I'll meet you at the pearly gates and we can compare notes.*

pear-shaped

go pear-shaped *British & Australian informal*
if a plan goes pear-shaped, it fails • *We'd arranged to be in France that weekend but it all went pear-shaped.*

peas

▶ See: like **shelling** peas
be like **two** peas in a pod

pebble

not **be the only pebble on the beach**
to not be the only person who is important in a situation or in a group • *Laura always expects to get her own way. It's time she learned that she's not the only pebble on the beach.*

pecker

▶ See: **keep** your pecker up!

pecking

a pecking order
the order of importance of the people in a group or an organization • *There's a clearly established pecking order in this office.*

pedestal

put sb **on a pedestal**
to believe that someone is perfect • *The way her father put her on a pedestal just made her want to behave badly.*
knock sb **off** their **pedestal** • *This recent scandal has really knocked the President off his pedestal.* (= shown people that he is not perfect)

peeping

a peeping Tom

a man who secretly watches women while they are taking their clothes off or having sex • *I always close the curtains in case there are any peeping Toms across the road.*

peg

▶ See: **bring** sb down a peg or two
off the peg

pegged

have sb pegged *mainly American*

to know exactly what kind of person someone is • *He thinks we're all taken in by his charm, but I've got him pegged.*

pell-mell

pell-mell

very quickly and without control • *She ran pell-mell down the stairs and out of the house.*

pell-mell • *Local residents have banded together to protest about the pell-mell pace of development in the area.*

pen

The pen is mightier than the sword. *formal*

something that you say which means thinking and writing have more influence on people and events than the use of force or violence • *Reason is our greatest weapon against such tyrants. The pen is mightier than the sword.*

put pen to paper

to start to write something • *I keep meaning to write to her but I haven't yet managed to put pen to paper.*

pennies

▶ See: not have **two** pennies to rub together

penny

be ten/two a penny *British & Australian*

to be very common • *TV cookery shows seem to be ten a penny these days.*

In for a penny, (in for a pound). *British & Australian*

something that you say when you have decided to become very involved in an activity, and to put a lot of money or effort into it • *I've put all my savings into this new venture. In for a penny, in for a pound.*

penny ante *American*

of little value or importance • *He was proposing some penny ante increase in child-care that amounted to an extra ten dollars a week.* • *We were burgled but they didn't take much – just penny ante stuff in the front office.*

the penny drops *British & Australian*

if you say the penny drops, you mean that you have finally understood something • *It was only when I saw Ron's car outside Penny's house that the penny finally dropped and I realised they were having an affair.*

A penny for your thoughts.
A penny for them.

something that you say in order to ask someone who is being very quiet what they are thinking about • *'A penny for your thoughts.' 'Oh, I was just thinking about how to tell him I'm leaving.'*

A penny saved is a penny earned.

something that you say which means it is wise to save money • *I'd advise anyone to put aside a proportion of their earnings – a penny saved is a penny earned.*

▶ See also: **spend** a penny

penny-wise

be penny-wise and pound-foolish *old-fashioned*

to be extremely careful about small amounts of money and not careful enough about larger amounts of money • *Saving a little bit of money on repairs can lead to long-term damage. You don't want to be penny-wise and pound-foolish, now do you?*

people

People who live in glass houses (shouldn't throw stones).

something that you say which means people should not criticize other people for faults that they have themselves • *He's always criticizing Rick for the way he treats his wife and I feel like saying, people who live in glass houses shouldn't throw stones.*

pep

a pep talk

a pep talk
a speech that you give to people in order to encourage them to work harder or win a competition • *I thought I'd give the lads a pep talk before the match.*

per capita

per capita
for each person in a country or area • *France and Germany both invest more per capita in public transport than Britain.*

perch

▶ See: **fall** off your perch
knock sb off their perch

perform

▶ See: perform/work **miracles**

perish

Perish the thought!
something that you say which means you hope very much that something does not happen • *If his father came to live with us, perish the thought, I can't imagine what strain that would put on our relationship.*

person

about/on your **person** *formal*
if you have something about your person, you are carrying it with you, often hidden in your clothing • *She had a small tape recorder concealed about her person.*

▶ See also: a girl/man/person **Friday**
the man/woman/person in the **street**

persona non grata

persona non grata *formal*
someone who is not acceptable or not welcome • *He published a book criticizing the war and was instantly **declared persona non grata** by the authorities.*

pet

sb's **pet hate** *British & Australian*
sb's **pet peeve** *American*
something that you do not like at all • *A pet hate of ours is telephone salesmen who phone just as we're sitting down to watch TV.* • *Cleaning the bathroom is my pet peeve.*

petard

▶ See: be **hoist** by/with your own petard

peter

▶ See: **rob** Peter to pay Paul

pew

Take a pew. *British & Australian humorous*
if you tell someone to take a pew, you are asking them to sit down • *Come in and take a pew.*

phrase

▶ See: to **coin** a phrase

pick

have your **pick of** sth
if you can have your pick of a group of things, you can have the one you want • *The plane was fairly empty, so we had our pick of the seats.*

pick and mix *British*
to combine things that are not similar, especially things that do not go well together ✍Pick'n'mix is a system in shops where people can choose a few of several different types of sweets. • *Increasingly, students are being given total freedom to pick and mix different modules on their courses.*

pick-and-mix • (always before noun) *People no longer give their loyalty to just one band. The pick-and-mix approach to music is much more common these days.*

pick sb's **brains**
to ask for information or advice from someone who knows more about a subject than you do • *I'd love to pick your*

brains about computers – you seem to be the expert around here.

pick holes in sth
to find mistakes in something someone has done or said, to show that it is not good or not correct • *The lawyer did her best to pick holes in the witness's statement.*

the pick of sth
the best of a group of things or people • *Send in your poems and we will print* ***the pick of the bunch.***

pick sb's **pocket**
to steal money from someone's pocket or bag • *You'd think you'd feel something if someone tried to pick your pocket.*

pick up your **marbles (and go home/leave)** *American*
to suddenly leave an activity you have been involved in with other people, because you do not like what is happening • *If you don't like the way we do things around here, well, you can pick up your marbles and leave.*

pick up steam *American*
to start to be much more effective or successful • *In the third month the campaign really started to pick up steam.* • *There are signs that the economy is picking up steam.*

pick up the bill/tab *informal*
to pay for something, often something that is not your responsibility • *When we go out for dinner it's always Jack who picks up the bill.* • (often + **for**) *It's the taxpayer who picks up the tab for all these crazy government schemes.*

pick up the pieces
to try to get back to an ordinary way of life after a difficult experience • *After Ruth's death, Joe found it hard to pick up the pieces and carry on with his life.*

pick up the threads of sth
to try to start something again, especially after problems prevented you from continuing it • *In '97, I came out of prison and tried to pick up the threads of my life.*

take your pick
to choose what you want • *We've got tea, coffee, or hot chocolate – take your pick.*

▶ See also: pick up/take the **ball** and run (with it)
pick up the **baton**
pick/pull sb/sth to **pieces**
pick/take up the **slack**
pick up **sticks**

pickle

be in a (pretty/right) pickle
old-fashioned, informal
to be in a difficult situation • *If you run out of money in the middle of your stay you'll be in a right pickle.*

pick-me-up

a pick-me-up *informal*
something that makes you feel better, especially a drink or medicine • *I needed a pick-me-up so I stopped at a bar on my way home.*

picnic

be no picnic
if a situation or activity is no picnic, it is unpleasant or difficult • *Bringing up four children on your own is no picnic, I can tell you.*

make sth **seem like a picnic**
if a difficult experience makes another experience seem like a picnic, it makes it seem very easy because it is much more difficult • *University makes school seem like a picnic.*

picture

be out of the picture
to not be involved in a particular situation • *Withers is out of the picture with a leg injury, so Jackson is in goal today.*
OPPOSITE **be in the picture** • *Although Derek has handed over control of the company to his son, he's still very much in the picture.*

be the picture of [health/innocence etc.]
to look very healthy, innocent etc. • *I can't believe there's anything seriously wrong with him – he's the picture of health.*

get the picture *informal*
to understand a situation • *'He doesn't want her but he doesn't want anyone else to have her, you know?' 'I get the picture.'*

put sb **in the picture**
to explain to someone what is happening • *Jim had no idea what was going on until*

I put him in the picture.

keep sb **in the picture** • *I'll be counting on you to keep me in the picture while I'm away.*

▶ See also: **paint** a [bleak/rosy etc.] picture of sth

picture-perfect

picture-perfect *American*

perfect in appearance or quality • *He built a dream house in a picture-perfect neighborhood.* • *Cloudless sky, brilliant sunshine – the weather was picture-perfect.*

pie

pie in the sky

if an idea or plan is pie in the sky, it seems good but is not likely to be achieved • *Those plans of his to set up his own business are just pie in the sky.*

piece

be (all) of a piece

if one thing is all of a piece with another thing, it is suitable or right for that thing • (often + **with**) *These prices are all of a piece with the quality of the goods.*

be a piece of cake *British, American & Australian*

be a piece of piss *British very informal*

to be very easy • *'How was the test?' 'A piece of cake!'* • *The interview was a piece of piss.*

give sb **a piece of** your **mind** *informal*

to speak angrily to someone because they have done something wrong • *I've had enough of him coming home late. I'm going to give him a piece of my mind when he gets in tonight.*

take a piece out of sb *Australian informal*

to speak angrily to someone because they have done something wrong • *Jill just took a piece out of Ben for being late again.*

▶ See also: a piece/slice of the **action**
say your piece

pièce de résistance

the pièce de résistance

the best or most important thing in a group or series • *The pièce de résistance of his act was to make a car vanish on stage.*

pieces

go/fall to pieces

1 if someone goes to pieces, they become so upset that they are unable to control their feelings or think clearly • *I kept my composure throughout the funeral, but I went to pieces after everyone had gone home.*

2 to suddenly fail completely • *After winning the British Open last year, his game has really gone to pieces.*

pick/pull sb/sth **to pieces**

to criticize someone or something very severely, often in a way that is not fair • *It's discouraging because every time I show him a bit of work I've done he picks it to pieces.*

▶ See also: **pick** up the pieces
be **shot** to hell/pieces

pied-à-terre

a pied-à-terre

a small apartment or house in a city which belongs to someone whose main home is somewhere else and which they have so that they can visit the city whenever they want • *He has a pied-à-terre in Mayfair and a five-bedroom house in Dorset.*

pie-eyed

be pie-eyed *old-fashioned*

to be drunk • *After only two bottles of cider they were completely pie-eyed.*

pig

in a pig's eye *American informal*

something that you say which means you think there is no chance that something is true or that something will happen • *Me, in love with Sandra? In a pig's eye I am.*

make a pig of yourself *informal*

to eat too much • *I made a real pig of myself at Christmas so I'm on a diet again.*

make a pig's ear of sth/doing sth *British informal*

to do something very badly • *Tim made a right pig's ear of putting those shelves up.*

a pig in a poke

something that you buy or accept without first seeing it or knowing what it is like, with the result that it might not be what you want • *Clothes from a catalogue are a pig in a poke. You can't feel the quality of the fabric or know if the clothes will fit.*

Pig's arse! *Australian very informal*
something that you say when you do not believe what someone has just told you • *She told you she was pregnant? Pig's arse! – don't believe a word she says.*

▶ See also: **eat** like a pig
sweat like a pig

pigeon

be sb's **pigeon** *British & Australian old-fashioned*
if something is someone's pigeon, they are responsible for it • *Finance isn't my pigeon. Ask Brian about that.*

piggy

piggy in the middle *British & Australian*
someone who is between two people or groups who are arguing but who does not want to agree with either of them • *It's awful. They argue the whole time and I always end up as piggy in the middle.*

pigs

Pigs might fly. *British, American & Australian informal*
Pigs can fly. *American informal*
something that you say which means you think there is no chance at all of something happening • *'I'll pay you back on Friday, I promise.' 'Yeah, and pigs might fly.'*

pike

come down the pike *American*
to happen or appear ✍Pike is short for 'turnpike' in American English and means a large, main road. • *Malnourished children are liable to catch any disease that comes down the pike.*

down the pike *American*
if an event is a particular period of time down the pike, it will not happen until that period of time has passed • *Five years down the pike, they'll probably have a kid or two.*

pile

pile it/them high and sell it/them cheap *mainly British*
to sell large amounts of something at cheap prices • *The shops at the lower end of the clothing market have survived by piling it high and selling it cheap.*

pile on the agony *British & Australian informal*
to try to get sympathy from other people by making your problems seem worse than they really are • (usually in continuous tenses) *He was really piling on the agony, saying he was heart-broken and hadn't got anything left to live for.*

pill

sugar/sweeten the pill *British, American & Australian*
sugar-coat the pill *American*
to make something bad seem less unpleasant • *The government have cut income tax to sweeten the pill of a tough budget.*

pillar

from pillar to post *British & Australian*
if someone goes from pillar to post, they are forced to keep moving from one place to another • *After his mother died, Billy was passed from pillar to post and ended up in a children's home.*

▶ See also: a pillar/tower of **strength**

pillow

pillow talk *informal*
conversations that people who are in love have when they are in bed together • *She enjoyed most the quiet time they spent together after they had made love, the pillow talk, the shared embraces.*

pills

▶ See: **pop** pills

pin

pin back your **ears** *British*
to listen carefully to something • (often an order) *Pin back your ears – she could be about to say something important.*

pin your **hopes on** sth/sb
to hope that something or someone will help you achieve what you want • *The party is pinning its hopes on its new leader who is young, good-looking, and very popular with ordinary people.*

pin money
a small amount of money that you earn and spend on things for yourself • *She has a part-time job that gives her pin*

money for extra treats for herself and the kids.

pin sth **on** sb
to blame someone for something, especially something they did not do • *The police tried to pin the murder on the dead woman's husband.*

▶ See also: You could have **heard** a pin drop.

pinch

at a pinch *British & Australian*
in a pinch *American*
if something can be done at a pinch, it is possible in an urgent situation but it is difficult • *Will's car can take four people comfortably, five at a pinch.*

▶ See also: **feel** the pinch
take sth with a pinch of **salt**

pinch-hit

pinch-hit *American*
to do something for someone because they are suddenly unable to do it • (often + **for**) *He was pinch-hitting for one of the regular TV sportscasters, and was a great success.*

pink

be in the pink *old-fashioned*
to be very healthy • *I wasn't well last week, but I'm back in the pink, I'm pleased to say.*

the pink pound *British*
the pink dollar *American*
the money that is spent by people who are homosexual (= attracted to people of their own sex) • *Further proof of the strength of the pink pound can be seen in Brighton, where there are numerous successful gay clubs.*

a pink slip *American*
a letter from your employer which tells you that you do not have a job any more • *It was Christmas time when Miller got his pink slip from the company.*

pink-collar

pink-collar *American*
pink-collar jobs are jobs that women usually do, often in offices and for little money • *Most women returning to work after raising children, head for pink-collar jobs in sales and service.*

pins

be on pins and needles *American & Australian*
to be nervously waiting to see what is going to happen • *We're on pins and needles waiting to hear whether she got the job.*

have pins and needles
to feel slight, sharp pains in a part of your body when you move it after it has been kept still for a period of time • (often + **in**) *I've been sitting on my leg for the last hour and now I've got pins and needles in my foot.*

pipe

a pipe dream
an idea that could never happen because it is impossible • *The classless society is just a pipe dream.*

Put/stick that in your pipe and smoke it! *informal*
an impolite way of telling someone that they must accept what you have just said even if they do not like it • *Well, I'm going anyway, so put that in your pipe and smoke it!*

pipeline

be in the pipeline
if a plan is in the pipeline, it is being developed and will happen in the future • *We have several major property deals in the pipeline.*

piper

▶ See: He who **pays** the piper calls the tune.

pipped

be pipped at/to the post *British & Australian*
to be beaten in a competition or race by a very small amount • *I'd have won quite a lot of money but my horse was pipped to the post.*

piss

be (out) on the piss *British & Australian very informal*
to be in bars, drinking a lot of alcohol • *I haven't seen Phil this morning. I think he was out on the piss again last night.*
go (out) on the piss *British & Australian very informal* • *We're going out on the piss tonight – you coming?*

Go piss up a rope! *American taboo*
a very impolite way of telling someone to go away • *Oh go piss up a rope! I'm sick of your complaining.*

piss on sb's **party** *British & Australian very informal*
to do something that spoils someone's plans • *I don't want to piss on your party but next week Malc and I won't be here.*

Piss or get off the can/pot! *American taboo*
something that you say to someone when you want them to make a decision and take action without any more delay • *Make your mind up. It's time to piss or get off the pot!*

take the piss
1 *British & Australian very informal* to make a joke about someone or to make someone look silly • (often + **out of**) *They're always taking the piss out of her because she's a Barry Manilow fan.* • *'You should wear miniskirts more often – you've got the legs for them.' 'Are you taking the piss?'*
a piss-take *British & Australian very informal* • *Have I really won or is this a piss-take?*
2 *British & Australian very informal* to treat someone badly in order to get what you want • *Four pounds an hour is taking the piss.* • *£50 for that old thing? That's just taking the piss.*

piss-artist

a piss-artist
1 *British & Australian informal* someone who tries to make people believe they have knowledge about a subject, but who really does not know much about it • *Those so-called multi-media consultants were just a bunch of piss-artists.*
2 *British & Australian informal* someone who is often drunk • *He's a nice enough bloke but he's a real piss-artist.*

pissed

as pissed as a fart *British & Australian very informal*
as pissed as a newt *British very informal*
very drunk • *Peter came home from the pub pissed as a fart.*

pissed out of your **head/mind/skull** *very informal*
very drunk • *Anna was pissed out of her mind – she couldn't even walk.*

pissing

▶ See: be pissing in/into the **wind**

piss-up

a piss-up *very informal*
a social occasion where everyone drinks a lot of alcohol • *The party was a complete piss-up.*
▶ See also: couldn't **organize** a piss-up in a brewery

pit

a pit stop *mainly American informal*
a short stop that you make on a long car journey in order to rest, eat and go to the toilet • *Clean toilets and a nice place to eat are what drivers are looking for when they* ***make a pit stop***.

pit your **wits against** sb/sth
to compete against someone or something using your intelligence • *That's the pleasure of fishing – pitting your wits against these clever little fish that are trying desperately not to get caught.*

pitch

make a pitch for sth
to try to persuade people to support you or give you something • *The union made a pitch for a reduction in working hours.*
▶ See also: **queer** sb's pitch

pitched

a pitched battle
an angry fight or argument • *There was a pitched battle between police and rioters.*

place

a/sb's **place in the sun**
a job or situation that makes you happy and that provides you with all the money and things that you want • *After struggling for years to make a name for himself, he's certainly earned his place in the sun.*

all over the place
in or to many different places • *There was blood all over the place.* • *I ran all over the place looking for them.*

be out of place
if something or someone is out of place,

they are not right or suitable for the situation they are in • *A modern building can look out of place amongst Victorian architecture.* • *I felt out of place in my office clothes, with everyone else wearing jeans.*

put sb **in** their **place**
to let someone know that they are not as important as they think they are • *She didn't like my suggestions at all. I was put firmly in my place, like a naughty schoolgirl.*

▶ See also: **fall** into place
know your place
as if you **own** the place
scream the place down

places

go places
to become very successful • (never in simple past tenses) *He was such a gifted musician, I always knew he would go places.*

plague

▶ See: **avoid** sb/sth like the plague

plain

a plain Jane
a woman or girl who is not attractive • *If she'd been a plain Jane, she wouldn't have had all the attention.*

be as plain as the nose on your face *old-fashioned*
to be very obvious • *There's no doubt that he's interested in her. It's as plain as the nose on your face.*

be plain sailing
to be very easy • *The roads were busy as we drove out of town but after that it was plain sailing all the way to the coast.*

▶ See also: be as clear/plain as **day**

planet

be (living) on another planet *informal*
if you say that someone is on another planet, you mean they do not notice what is happening around them and behave differently from other people • *He doesn't always make much sense. It's like he's on another planet half the time.*
What planet is sb **on?** *informal* • *Of course we can't afford any more staff. What planet is she on?*

plank

▶ See: **walk** the plank

plate

give/hand sth **to** sb **on a plate**
to let someone get something very easily, without having to work for it • *You can't expect everything to be handed to you on a plate – you've got to make a bit of effort.*

have a lot/enough on your **plate**
have your **plate full**
to have a lot of work to do or a lot of problems to deal with • *I don't want to burden my daughter with my problems; she's got enough on her plate with her husband in prison.* • *Simon can't take on any more work. He's got his plate full as it is.*

platter

give/hand sth **to** sb **on a (silver) platter**
to let someone get something very easily, without having to work for it • *If you sell your share in the company now, you're handing the ownership to him on a silver platter.*

play

(if you) play your **cards right** *informal*
something that you say to someone which means that if they behave in the right way, they might succeed at something • *Play your cards right and you could be managing this place in a year or so.*

make (a) great play of sth
make a big play of sth
to do something in a way that makes people notice what you are doing, often in order to make it seem more important than it really is • *She made great play of ignoring me when I spoke to her.*

make a play for sb
to try to start a romantic relationship with someone • *If I wasn't happily married, I might make a play for him myself.*

make a play for sth
to try to get something • *It was rumoured that he would make a play for the director's post.*

play (it) safe *informal*
to be careful and not take risks • *We decided to play safe and paint the walls a fairly neutral colour.* • *They're playing it*

safe by not investing too much money until they've seen the first year's accounts.

play (merry) hell *informal*
to complain a lot or to behave very badly • *She played merry hell about coming on this trip, but I think she enjoyed it in the end.*

play (merry) hell with sth *informal*
to stop something from working as it should • *The power cuts played merry hell with our computer systems.*

play a blinder *British informal*
to perform with a lot of skill, especially when you are playing sport • *He's played a blinder in every game so far this season.*

play a straight bat
1 *British* to avoid answering someone's questions or giving them the information they want • *When asked about the affair, he plays a straight bat.*
2 *British old-fashioned* someone who plays a straight bat is honest and has traditional ideas and beliefs • *Wilf has played a straight bat all his life – I can't believe he'd get mixed up in anything illegal.*

play a/the waiting game
to delay doing something so that you can see what happens or what other people do first • *Those investors who are willing to play the waiting game may find it to their advantage.*

play sb **at** their **own game** *British & Australian*
to try to get an advantage over someone by using the same methods as them • *If women want to succeed in business, they have to play men at their own game.*
beat sb **at** their **own game** *British, American & Australian* • *He's always playing practical jokes on other people so just for once, I felt I'd beaten him at his own game.*

play away from home *British & Australian informal*
to have sex with someone who is not your usual partner • (usually in continuous tenses) *How did you discover that your husband was playing away from home?*

play ball *informal*
to agree to do what someone asks you to do, or to agree to work with someone in order to achieve something together • (usually negative) *Fourteen out of the fifteen nations have agreed to the new restrictions but one country still refuses to play ball.*

play cat and mouse
to try to defeat someone by tricking them into making a mistake so that you have an advantage over them • (often + **with**) *The 32-year-old actress spent a large proportion of the week playing cat and mouse with the press.*
a cat and mouse game • *It's just the latest manoeuvre in the eternal cat and mouse game between the police and drug runners.*

play devil's advocate
to pretend to be against an idea or plan which a lot of people support in order to make people discuss it in more detail and think about it more carefully ✍The 'Advocatus Diaboli' was a person employed by the Roman Catholic church to argue against someone being made a saint (= someone given the honour of being called Saint by the Roman Catholic church). • *I don't think he was really in favour of getting rid of the scheme, he was just playing devil's advocate.* • *I know that most people here support the project, but let me play devil's advocate for a moment and ask if anyone has considered the cost?*

play dirty

play dirty *informal*
to behave dishonestly, especially by cheating in a game • *He loses his temper from time to time, but he never plays dirty.*

play footsie *informal*
to secretly touch someone's feet under a table with your feet, in order to show that you are sexually attracted to them • (usually in continuous tenses) *I think they were playing footsie in the meeting!*

play footsie with sb *mainly American*
to be involved with a person or an organization secretly, because you know that other people will not approve • *The government never forgave him for playing footsie with the terrorists.*

play sb **for a fool** *American & Australian*
to treat someone as if they are stupid, especially by trying to get something from them in a way that is not fair • *He's playing you for a fool. Just don't lend him any more money.*

play sb **for a sucker** *American & Australian very informal*
to treat someone as if they are stupid • *Don't try to play me for a sucker. I want to know where the rest of the money went.*

play for keeps *American & Australian informal*
to do something very seriously and not just for enjoyment • *These arms dealers play for keeps – they want the best weapons available and will do anything to get them.*

play for time
to try to delay something so that you have more time to prepare for it • *We can't sign the agreement yet – we'll have to play for time.*

play games
to deceive someone about what you intend to do • (often + **with**) *I don't think they ever really intended to buy the software. They were just playing games with us.*

play God
to behave as if you have the right to make very important decisions that seriously affect other people's lives • *Genetic engineers claim that most countries have already put legislation in place that will stop them from playing God.*

play gooseberry *British humorous*
to be with two people who are having a romantic relationship and who would prefer to be alone • *Yes, thank you, I'd love to go to the cinema, if you two are sure you don't mind me playing gooseberry.*

play hard to get *informal*
to pretend that you are less interested in someone than you really are as a way of making them more interested in you, especially at the start of a romantic relationship • (often in continuous tenses) *Why don't you return any of his calls? Are you playing hard to get?*

play hardball *American & Australian*
to be so determined to get what you want, especially in business, that you use methods that are unfair or harm other people • (often + **with**) *The company is playing hardball with the bank, holding back on payments it owes them to force an agreement.*

play hooky *American & Australian informal*
to stay away from school without permission • *Any kid who's not in school at this time of day must be playing hooky.*

play into sb's **hands**
to do something that gives someone else an advantage over you, although this was not your intention • *If we allow terrorists to disrupt our lives to that extent we're just playing into their hands.*

play it by ear
to decide how to deal with a situation as it develops rather than planning how you are going to react • *I'm not sure how long I'll stay at the party. I'll just play it by ear.*

play it cool *informal*
to pretend to be calmer, or to be less interested in something or someone, than you really are • *Sometimes if you play it cool with a guy he gets more interested.* • (often an order) *Play it cool. Don't let them know how much you need the money.*

a play on words
a type of joke using a word or phrase that has two meanings • *It's a play on words – I suppose by calling a hairdresser's 'A Cut Above' they were hoping to give themselves a more sophisticated image.*

play possum
to pretend to be dead or sleeping so that someone will not annoy or attack you • *I*

don't think he's really asleep. He's playing possum.

play Russian roulette
to take big risks, in a way which is very dangerous ✍Russian roulette is a very dangerous game where players aim a gun containing one bullet at their own heads. • (often + **with**) *I'm not willing to play Russian roulette with people's lives by drinking and driving.*

play second fiddle
if you play second fiddle to someone, they are in a stronger position or are more important than you • (usually + **to**) *You'll have to choose between your wife and me. I won't play second fiddle to anyone.*

play silly buggers *British & Australian very informal*
to behave in a stupid or annoying way • (often in continuous tenses) *Stop playing silly buggers and come down off the roof.*

play the field
to have many romantic or sexual relationships • *She's not interested in marriage at this stage, so she's quite happy to play the field.*

play the game
to behave in a way that is accepted or demanded by those in authority • *You have to learn to play the game if you want to be successful at work.*

play to the gallery
to spend time doing or saying things that will make people admire or support you, instead of dealing with more important matters • *Politicians these days are more interested in playing to the gallery than exercising real influence on world events.*

play with fire
to be involved in an activity that could be dangerous • (usually in continuous tenses) *We're playing with fire if we continue with genetic modification of our food.*

► See also: play your **ace**
bring sth into play
keep/play your **cards** close to your chest
play both **ends** against the middle
act/play the **fool**
act/play the **goat**
play/run out of your **skin**

plea

► See: **cop** a plea

plead

► See: I take/plead the **fifth** (Amendment)

pleased

be as pleased as Punch *old-fashioned*
to be very happy about something ✍Punch is a character in a traditional children's entertainment who is always happy and excited. • *'How does Stella feel about becoming a granny?' 'She's as pleased as Punch.'*

pledge

sign/take the pledge *humorous*
to decide that you are never going to drink alcohol again • *Why are you drinking Coke? Have you signed the pledge or something?*

plenty

There are plenty more where they/that came from.
something that you say in order to tell someone they will easily find another person or thing similar to the one they have lost • *'Roger and I split up last month.' 'Oh, never mind, There are plenty more where he came from.'*

► See also: there are plenty more **fish** in the sea

plot

The plot thickens. *humorous*
something that you say when something happens which makes a strange situation even more difficult to understand • *I had assumed the Irishman who keeps phoning June was her husband, but it seems her husband is American. The plot thickens.*

► See also: **lose** the plot

plough

plough a lone/lonely furrow *mainly British literary*
to do something alone and without help from other people • *He'd always been happier working in isolation, ploughing a lone furrow.*

pluck

pluck sth **out of the air**
if you pluck a number out of the air, you say any number and not one that is the

result of careful calculation • *That figure of eighty thousand pounds isn't something we've just plucked out of the air. We've done a detailed costing of the project.*

plug

▶ See: **pull** the plug

plughole

go down the plughole *British & Australian informal*
if a plan or work goes down the plughole, it fails or is wasted • *I'll be so annoyed if all my hard work goes down the plughole just because he's too lazy to finish his bit in time.*

plum

▶ See: **speak** with a plum in your mouth

plumb

plumb the depths

1 to experience extreme sadness • (usually + **of**) *His wife left him in May and during the following months he plumbed the depths of despair.*

2 to understand something in detail, especially something that is difficult to understand • (usually + **of**) *In hypnosis we plumb the depths of the unconscious.*

3 if something that someone does or says plumbs the depths, it is very bad • (often + **of**) *I read one review which said the show plumbed the depths of tastelessness.*
plumb new depths to become even worse than before • *Man's inhumanity to man has plumbed new depths in this conflict.* • *Industrial relations had plumbed new depths, even for Hackney, with a series of disputes and strikes.*

plunge

take the plunge
to do something important or difficult that you have been thinking about doing for a long time • *I've decided to take the plunge and start up my own business.*

plus ça change

plus ça change (plus c'est la même chose) *mainly British*
something that you say which means that a situation or problem is the same even when the people or things involved in it have changed • *Despite the change in government, single mothers are still the target of spending cuts. Plus ça change, it would seem.*

ply

ply your **trade** *literary*
to do your usual work or business • *Fishermen in small boats ply their trade up and down the coast.*

poacher

a poacher turned gamekeeper *British*
someone whose job seems to involve working against the person who is now doing the job which they did before ✍A poacher illegally kills and steals animals on someone else's land, and a gamekeeper's job is to stop this from happening. • *He used to be the the union rep but now he's in management – a case of poacher turned gamekeeper.*

pocket

be in sb's **pocket**
if you are in someone's pocket, you do everything that they want you to do • *The school governors are completely in the head teacher's pocket.*

be out of pocket
to have less money than you should have • *I'll give you the money for my ticket now, so you won't be out of pocket.*

dig/dip into your **pocket**
to use your own money to pay for something • *Parents of young children have to* ***dig deep into their pockets*** *at Christmas-time.*

▶ See also: **pick** sb's pocket

pockets

▶ See: **line** your (own) pockets
line sb's pockets

poetic

poetic justice
if something that happens is poetic justice, someone who has done something bad is made to suffer in a way that seems fair • *There is a kind of poetic justice in the fact that the country responsible for the worst ecological disaster this century is the one suffering most from its effects.*

poetic license
the way in which writers and other artists are allowed to ignore rules or change facts in their work • *It's obvious the*

writer was using a certain amount of poetic licence because the route she mentions has been closed for 50 years.

po-faced

po-faced *British & Australian informal*
if someone is po-faced, they look very serious and unfriendly • *The po-faced librarian refused to let me in without my card.* • *Why does she always look so po-faced?*

point

be beside the point
to be in no way connected to the subject that is being discussed • *Ian's a nice guy but that's beside the point. He doesn't have the right experience for the job.*

point blank
1 if you refuse point blank, you refuse completely and will not change your decision • *He locked himself in the bathroom and refused point blank to come out.*
point-blank • (always before noun) *Journalists were infuriated by her point-blank refusal to discuss their divorce.*
2 if you ask or tell someone point blank about something that could upset or embarrass them, you ask or tell them directly • *You'll have to ask him point blank whether he took the money or not.*

the point of no return
the time in an activity when you cannot stop doing it but must continue to the end • *And although I was bored, I'd already spent so much time doing the research for the novel that I felt I'd* ***reached the point of no return****.*

point the finger at sb
to accuse someone of being responsible for something bad that has happened • *Critics were quick to point the finger at the board of directors when the theatre started losing money.*

point the way
to show what can or should be done in the future • *Their recent work on developing an AIDS vaccine points the way forward.* • (often + **to**) *Her speeches pointed the way to several important social reforms.*

▶ See also: **miss** the point

point-blank

at point-blank range
if someone is shot at point-blank range, they are shot from a very short distance away • *The killers walked into the bar and shot him at point-blank range.*

poison

What's your poison? *humorous*
something that you say in order to ask someone what they would like to drink • *It's my round. What's your poison?*

poisoned

a poisoned chalice *British*
something that harms the person it is given to although it seemed very good when they first got it • *The leadership of the party turned out to be a poisoned chalice.*

poison-pen

a poison-pen letter
a letter that has no signature and says unpleasant things about the person it is sent to • *After he was convicted, his family received a number of poison-pen letters.*

poke

▶ See: poke **fun** at sb/sth
poke/stick your **nose** into sth

pole

be in pole position *British & Australian*
to be in the best position to win a competition ✍In motor racing, pole position is the best place a car can start from. • (often + to do sth) *United are in pole position to win the championship this year.*

poles

be poles apart
if two people or things are poles apart, they are complete opposites • *My sister and I are poles apart in personality.* • *Our political views are poles apart.*

political

a political football
a problem that politicians from different parties argue about and try to use in order to get an advantage for themselves • *We don't want the immigration issue to* ***become a political football****.*

politically

politically correct
avoiding language or statements that could be offensive to women, people of other races, or people who are disabled (= who cannot use part of their body) • *I noticed that he never referred to her as his 'girlfriend', preferring the politically correct term 'partner'.*

polls

go to the polls
to vote in an election • *The country will go to the polls on 6th June.*

pomp

pomp and circumstance
formal ceremony • *The royal visit was accompanied by all the usual pomp and circumstance.*

poor

be as poor as church mice *old-fashioned*
to be very poor • *When we first got married, we were as poor as church mice.*

a poor man's sb/sth
someone or something that is similar to a well-known person or thing but is not as good • *He was only ever a mediocre singer – they used to call him 'the poor man's Frank Sinatra'.* • *'So what did you think of the film?' 'It was just a poor man's 'Pulp Fiction'.'*

a poor relation
someone or something that is believed to be less important than another similar person or thing • *Video, once seen as* ***the poor relation of*** *cinema, is now a major source of revenue for film companies.*

pop

pop your **clogs** *British humorous*
to die • *This place hasn't been the same since poor old Harry popped his clogs.*

pop pills
to take too many pills • (usually in continuous tenses) *Soon she was popping pills again in an effort to cope with the increasing pressure of her job.*
pill-popping • *As their relationship fell apart, his pill-popping started to get seriously out of control.*

pop the question

pop the question *informal*
to ask someone to marry you • *So we were having dinner in this Italian restaurant and that's when he popped the question.* • *Do you think he's going to pop the question then, Kath?*

pope

Is the pope a Catholic? *humorous*
used to say that the answer to a question you have just been asked is obviously 'yes' • *Do I like chocolate? Is the pope a Catholic?*

pork

pork barrel *American informal*
the action by a government of spending money in an area in order to make themselves more popular with the people there • *He was critical of these new, expensive job programs as just a form of pork barrel.*
pork-barrel *American informal* • (always before noun) *The President needs to find a way to block these wasteful pork-barrel projects coming from Congress.*

port

Any port in a storm.
something that you say which means you must accept any help you are offered when you are in a difficult situation, although you may not want to do this • *I don't even like him very much, but I had to move out of my flat and he offered me a place to stay. Any port in a storm, as they say.*

a port of call
a place where you stop for a short time, especially on a journey • *Our **first port of call** was the delightful town of Bruges.*

possessed

like a man/woman possessed
if you do something like a man possessed, you do it with a lot of energy in a way that is not controlled • *He'd lost the tickets and was running round the house like a man possessed.*

possession

Possession is nine-tenths of the law.
something that you say which means that if you have something, it is difficult for other people to take it away from you • *It would be hard to ask for the piano back after they've had it for so long. Possession is nine-tenths of the law and all that.*

possum

▶ See: **play** possum

post

▶ See: be **pipped** at/to the post

postal

go postal *American very informal*
to become very angry, or to suddenly behave in a violent and angry way, especially in the place where you work ✍This idiom started when a post office worker in America shot several of the people he worked with. • *My Mom will go postal if I get home late.* • *When she heard she'd been fired she went postal and started throwing things around the office.*

posted

▶ See: **keep** sb posted

post-haste

post-haste *formal*
as quickly as possible • *A letter was dispatched post-haste to their offices.*

pot

go to pot
to be damaged or spoilt because of a lack of care or effort • *My diet has gone to pot since the holidays.*

not **have a pot to piss in** *very informal*
to be very poor • *Any help we can offer them will be appreciated. They don't have a pot to piss in.*

the pot calling the kettle black
something that you say which means someone should not criticize another person for a fault that they have themselves • *Elliot accused me of being selfish. Talk about the pot calling the kettle black!*

take a pot shot
to criticize someone suddenly • (often + **at**) *As the director was finishing his speech he took a pot shot at their rival's lack of principles.*

take pot luck
to accept or choose from whatever is available, without knowing whether it will be good or not • *I took pot luck at the airport and just got on the first available flight.*

▶ See also: **piss** or get off the can/pot!
throw sth into the pot
A **watched** pot never boils.

pots

pots of money
a lot of money • *They've got pots of money but they never spend any of it.*

pound

your **pound of flesh**
if someone demands their pound of flesh, they make someone give them something that they owe them, although they do not need it and it will cause problems for the other person ✍This phrase comes from Shakespeare's play, *The Merchant of Venice.* • *His boss, demanding his pound of flesh, made him come into work even though his daughter was seriously ill.*

pour

pour your **heart out**
to tell someone your secret feelings and worries, usually because you feel a strong need to talk about them • (often + **to**) *I'd only met him once, and here he was, pouring out his heart to me.*

pour oil on troubled waters
to do or say something in order to make people stop arguing and become calmer • *She was furious with Dave for forgetting her birthday so I tried to pour oil on troubled waters by offering to take them*

both out for a meal.

▶ See also: pour/throw **cold** water on sth

powder

a powder keg

a situation that could suddenly become extremely dangerous ✍A powder keg was a wooden container for gunpowder (= a substance used for making explosions). • *We left just before the revolution, realizing that we were* ***sitting on a powder keg****.*

powder your **nose** *humorous*

if a woman says she is going to powder her nose, she means she is going to go to the toilet • *Well, if you'll excuse me a moment, I'm going to powder my nose.*

take a powder *American informal*

to leave a place suddenly, especially in order to avoid an unpleasant situation • *He saw the police coming and took a powder.*

▶ See also: **keep** your powder dry

power

do sb **a power of good** *informal*

to make someone feel much better • *That walk in the fresh air did me a power of good.*

More power to your elbow! *British & Australian*

More power to you! *American & Australian*

something that you say to praise someone and to say that you hope they continue to have success • *'I've decided to set up my own business.' 'Good for you. More power to your elbow!'*

the power behind the throne

someone who does not have an official position in a government or organization but who secretly controls it • *In his later years, the chairman's daughter was the power behind the throne.*

powers

the powers that be

the people who control things but who are not known • *It's up to the powers that be to decide what should be done next.*

practice

Practice makes perfect.

something that you say which means if you do something many times you will learn to do it very well • *You can't expect to become a brilliant dancer overnight, but practice makes perfect.*

practise

practise what you **preach** *British & Australian*

practice what you **preach** *American*

to do what you advise other people to do • *I would have more respect for him if he practised what he preaches.*

praise

praise sb/sth **to the skies**

to praise someone or something very much • *At first she would praise him to the skies for every minor achievement.*

praises

▶ See: **sing** sb's/sth's praises

prayer

not **have a prayer**

to be not at all likely to succeed • (often + **of**) *She hasn't a prayer of winning the competition.*

preach

preach to the converted

to try to persuade people to believe things they already believe • (usually in continuous tenses) *There's no need to tell us about the benefits of recycling. You're preaching to the converted.*

prepare

prepare the ground

if you prepare the ground for an activity or a situation, you do something that will help it to happen • (usually + **for**) *The leaders of both countries are preparing the ground for negotiations which may lead to peace.*

presence

make your **presence felt**

to have a strong effect on other people or on a situation • *The new police chief has really made his presence felt.*

present

present company excepted *British, American & Australian humorous*

present company excluded *American humorous*

something that you say which means that

the criticism you have just made does not describe the people who are listening to you now • *People just don't know how to dress in this country, present company excepted, of course.*

press

press the flesh *mainly American humorous*
if politicians or famous people press the flesh, they shake hands with the public • *Even after 12 hours on the campaign trail, he was still meeting his supporters and pressing the flesh.*

▶ See also: hit/press/push the **panic** button
press/push the **right** button/buttons

pretend

▶ See: pretend/say that **black** is white

pretty

not **be a pretty sight** *humorous*
to not be pleasant to look at • *First thing in the morning, he's not a pretty sight.*

not **be just a pretty face** *humorous*
if someone is not just a pretty face, they are not only attractive but also intelligent • *'How did you know that?' 'Well, I'm not just a pretty face, you know.'*

Pretty is as pretty does. *old-fashioned*
something that you say which means that you should judge people by the way they behave, not by their appearance • *'She's very pretty.' 'Yes, but pretty is as pretty does. I haven't been terribly impressed by her manners.'*

▶ See also: **cost** (sb) a pretty penny
a fine/pretty **kettle** of fish

prevention

Prevention is better than cure. *British & Australian*
An ounce of prevention is worth a pound of cure. *American*
something that you say which means it is better to stop something bad happening than it is to deal with it after it has happened • *More advice is needed on how to stay healthy because, as we all know, prevention is better than cure.*

prey

prey on sb's **mind**
if something preys on someone's mind, they worry about it for a long time • *I lost my temper with her the other day and it's been preying on my mind ever since.*

price

at a price
1 if you can get something at a price, you have to pay a lot of money for it • *Forged passports are available, at a price.*
2 if you can get something at a price, you have to accept something unpleasant in order to get it • *Progress has been achieved, but at a price. Many who worked on farms and in factories are now without jobs.*

at any price
if you want something at any price, you will do whatever you have to do in order to get it • *We want peace at any price.*

What price [fame/success/victory etc.]?
something that you say which means it is possible that the fame, success etc. that has been achieved was not worth all the suffering it has caused • *What price victory when so many people have died to make it possible?*

▶ See also: **pay** the price

prick

prick sb's **conscience**
to make someone feel guilty • *Seeing pictures of starving children pricks my conscience, but I rarely give money to charity.*

prick your **ears up** *informal*
to start to listen carefully to what someone is saying, often because you think you may find out something interesting ✍Many animals prick up (= raise) their ears when they hear something. • *Eve pricked her ears up when she heard her name being mentioned.*

pricks

▶ See: **kick** against the pricks

pride

have/take pride of place
if something takes pride of place, it is in the best position to be seen by a lot of people • *Bella's show-jumping trophies take pride of place in the display cabinet.*

give sth **pride of place** • (usually passive) *Works by contemporary artists are given pride of place in the exhibition.*

Pride comes before a fall. *British & Australian*
Pride goes before a fall. *American*
something that you say which means if you are too confident about yourself, something bad will happen to show you that you are not as good as you think you are • *Just because you did well in your exams doesn't mean you can stop working. Pride comes before a fall.*

► See also: **swallow** your pride

prim

prim and proper
someone who is prim and proper behaves in a very formal and correct way and is easily shocked by anything rude • *I can't quite imagine Ellen drinking pints of beer – she's very prim and proper.*

prima donna

a prima donna
someone who demands to be treated in a special way and is very difficult to please • *It was my job to take visiting authors out to dinner before they gave their talks and some of them were real prima donnas.*

prime

a prime mover
someone who has a lot of influence in starting something important • *He was a prime mover in developing a new style of customer-friendly bookshops in the UK.*

prime the pump *mainly American*
to do something in order to make something succeed, especially to spend money • *European governments and banks are priming the pump world-wide looking for alternative energy.*

primrose

the primrose path *literary*
if you lead someone down the primrose path, you encourage them to live an easy life that is full of pleasure but bad for them • *Unable to enjoy his newly acquired wealth, he felt he was being* ***led down the primrose path*** *that leads to destruction.*

Prince Charming

Prince Charming *humorous*
a woman's Prince Charming is her perfect partner • *How much time have you wasted sitting around waiting for Prince Charming to appear?*

print

the fine/small print
the part of a printed agreement that is printed smaller than the rest but which contains very important information • *Never sign a contract until you have read the small print.*

prisoners

take no prisoners
if someone takes no prisoners, when they try to achieve something they are very determined and do not care about other people's feelings • *When Eric's anger is aroused, he takes no prisoners.*

prizes

no prizes for guessing sth *British & Australian*
something that you say when it is very easy to guess something • (usually + question word) *No prizes for guessing who Neil wants to ask to the party.*

prodigal

the prodigal son
a man or boy who left a family or organization in order to do something they did not approve of and who has now returned to them feeling sorry for what he did ✍This phrase comes from the Bible. • *Manchester City football club sees the return of the prodigal son tonight with Black once again in the team after a season away.*

production

make a production (out) of sth
to make something seem more complicated or difficult to do than it is • *If you ask Tom to do anything, he always makes such a production of it that you wish you'd just done it yourself.*

program

get with the program *American informal*
to accept new ideas and give more attention to what is happening now • *They've been playing the same old music for ten years or so – it's time to get with the program.*

promise

promise (sb) the moon *British, American & Australian*
promise (sb) the earth *British & Australian*
to promise something impossible • *He had promised her the earth but five years later they were still living in the same small house.*

promised

the promised land
a place that offers a lot of good opportunities ✍This phrase comes from the Bible. • *America was the promised land for many immigrant families.*

promises

Promises, promises! *informal*
something that you say when someone says they will do something and you do not believe them • *'Honestly, I will call you back this time.' 'Promises, promises!'*

proof

The proof of the pudding (is in the eating).
something that you say which means that you cannot judge the value of something until you have tried it • *I've read the proposal and it looks promising, but the proof of the pudding is in the eating.*

proper

good/right and proper
socially and morally acceptable • *There is a long-held assumption that motherhood is the right and proper path for a woman to take.*

prophet

a prophet of doom
someone who always expects bad things to happen • *My father is convinced that this venture will fail, but then he's always been a prophet of doom.*

proportion

▶ See: **blow** sth out of (all) proportion

pros

the pros and cons
the good and bad parts of a situation, or the reasons why you should or should not do something ✍This phrase comes from the Latin words 'pro', which means 'for' and 'contra' which means 'against'. • (often + **of**) *We've been discussing the pros and cons of buying a house.*

protest

protest too much *literary*
if someone protests too much, they tell you more often than is necessary what they feel about a situation so that you start to doubt they are sincere ✍This phrase comes from Shakespeare's play *Hamlet*. • *He constantly denies there is any autobiographical input in his novels, but does he protest too much?*

proud

do sb proud
1 *informal* to treat someone who is visiting you very well, especially by giving them lots of good food • *We had a lovely lunch. Rosemary did us proud.*
2 *informal* to make someone proud of you by doing something very well • *Once again, the armed forces have done us proud.*

prove

▶ See: prove/show your **mettle**

providence

▶ See: **tempt** fate/providence

pub

a pub crawl *British & Australian informal*
an occasion on which you go to several different pubs (= type of bar found in Britain) in order to drink alcohol • *I thought we might* ***go on a pub crawl*** *tonight.*

public

be in the public eye
if someone is in the public eye, they are famous and are written about in newspapers and magazines and seen on television • *It's not always easy being in the public eye.*

public enemy number one
someone or something that many people do not like or approve of • *Inflation has been public enemy number one for this government.*

pudding

be in the pudding club *British old-fashioned*
to be pregnant • *Tina says Karen's in the pudding club.*

▶ See also: **over-egg** the pudding

pull

pull a rabbit out of the hat
to surprise everyone by suddenly doing something that shows a lot of skill, often in order to solve a problem ✍Pulling a rabbit out of a hat is something that is often done by a person who performs magic tricks. • *He's one of those players who, just when you think the game's over, can pull a rabbit out of the hat.*

not **pull any punches**
to speak in an honest way without trying to be kind • *This man doesn't pull any punches. I wouldn't like to get into an argument with him*

pull sb's **leg** *informal*
to tell someone something that is not true as a way of joking with them • (usually in continuous tenses) *Is he really angry with me or do you think he's just pulling my leg?*

pull out all the stops
to do everything you can to make something successful ✍The stops are handles on an organ (= a large instrument used in churches), which you pull out when you want to play as loudly as possible. • *They pulled out all the stops for their daughter's wedding.* • (often + to do sth) *The airline certainly pulled out all the stops to impress us.*

pull rank
to use the power that your position gives you over someone in order to make them do what you want • (often + **on**) *He doesn't have the authority to pull rank on me any more.* • *She was boss of forty or more people but, to her credit, she never once pulled rank.*

pull your **socks up**
to make an effort to improve your work or behaviour because it is not good enough • *He's going to have to pull his socks up if he wants to stay in the team.*

pull something out of the bag
to suddenly do something which solves a problem or improves a bad situation • *They're really going to have to pull something out of the bag tonight if they want to qualify for the championship.*

pull strings
to secretly use the influence that you have over important people in order to get something or to help someone • *I may be able to pull a few strings for you if you need the document urgently.*

Pull the other leg/one (it's got bells on)!
something that you say in order to tell someone that you do not believe what they have just said • *Helen, going rock climbing? Pull the other one – she can't even climb a ladder without feeling sick!*

pull the plug
to do something which prevents an activity from continuing, especially to stop giving money • (often + **on**) *If the viewing figures drop much further, the TV company will pull the plug on the whole series.*

pull the rug from under sb/sth
pull the rug from under sb's **feet**
to suddenly take away help or support from someone, or to suddenly do something which causes many problems for them • *The school pulled the rug from under the basketball team by making them pay to practise in the school gymnasium.*

pull the strings
to be in control of an organization, often secretly • *I'd really like to know who's pulling the strings in that organization, because it's not the elected committee.*

pull the wool over sb's **eyes**
to deceive someone in order to prevent them from knowing what you are really doing • *Don't let insurance companies pull the wool over your eyes – ask for a list of all the hidden charges.*

pull sb **up short**
if something pulls someone up short, they suddenly stop what they are doing, especially because they are very surprised • *Seeing her picture in the paper pulled me up short.*
pull up short *American* • *Carol pulled up short when she realized Jack could hear what she was saying.*

pull up stakes *American & Australian*
to leave the place where you have been living • *He pulled up stakes in Indiana and moved, permanently.*

pull your weight

to work as hard as other people in a group • *The rest of the team complained that Sarah wasn't pulling her weight.*

▶ See also: haul/pull yourself up by your **bootstraps**
pull/yank sb's **chain**
make/pull a **face**
get/pull your **finger** out
pull/tear your **hair** out
draw/pull in your **horns**
pick/pull sb/sth to **pieces**
bring/pull sb up with a **start**

pulling

like pulling teeth
If you say that making someone do something was like pulling teeth, it was very difficult and they did not want to do it • *Getting her to tell me about her childhood was like pulling teeth.*

pulp

▶ See: **beat** sb to a pulp

pulse

▶ See: **quicken** your/the pulse

pump

pump iron

pump iron *informal*
to lift heavy objects for exercise in order to increase your strength or to improve your appearance • *These days, both men and women pump iron for fitness.*

▶ See also: **prime** the pump

punch

punch sb's **lights out** *informal*
to hit someone hard again and again • *He wouldn't shut up so I punched his lights out.*

▶ See also: **beat** sb to the punch
pack a punch

punch-drunk

be punch-drunk
to feel very tired and confused, especially after dealing with a difficult situation ✍If a boxer (= man who fights as a sport) is punch-drunk, his brain is damaged because he has been hit on the head too much or too hard. • *Social workers are punch-drunk from the criticism they have received in recent months.*

punches

▶ See: not **pull** any punches
roll with the punches

pup

▶ See: be **sold** a pup

puppy

puppy fat *British & Australian*
fat that a child has but which they lose when they become older • *He's a little overweight but that's just puppy fat.*

puppy love

puppy love
romantic love which a young person feels for someone and which usually disappears as they become older • *At the*

time I was sure I would marry him when I grew up but of course it was just puppy love.

pure

be as pure as the driven snow
to be morally good • *How dare he criticize me for having an affair? He's not exactly as pure as the driven snow himself.*

purely

purely and simply
for only one reason or purpose • *They closed the museum purely and simply because it cost too much to run.*
pure and simple • *They built their cabin at the lake for enjoyment, pure and simple.*

purple

purple prose
writing that is more complicated and formal than necessary • *Despite occasional passages of purple prose, her latest novel is still very readable.*
purple passages • *There are long purple passages which distract the reader from the real point of the argument.*

purse

hold the purse strings
to control the spending of a family's or an organization's money • *In our house it was my mother who held the purse strings.*
loosen the purse strings to allow more money to be spent • *We shouldn't expect the Chancellor to loosen the purse strings too much in the Budget.*
tighten the purse strings to reduce the amount of money that can be spent • *If the economy gets any weaker, it will be necessary for the government to tighten the national purse strings still further.*

push

at a push *British & Australian*
if you can do something at a push, you can do it but it will be difficult • *I could finish the job by Friday – at a push, Thursday afternoon.*

give sb **the push**
1 *British & Australian informal* to end someone's employment • *After twenty years' loyal service, they gave her the push.*
get the push *British & Australian informal* • *I hear Nick got the push from the brickworks last week.*
2 *British & Australian informal* to end a relationship with someone • *They'd only been seeing each other for two weeks when he gave her the push.*
get the push *British & Australian informal* • *Mandy's a bit upset – she got the push from Martin last night.*

if/when push comes to shove
if you say that something can be done if push comes to shove, you mean that it can be done if the situation becomes so bad that you have to do it • *Look, if push comes to shove we'll just have to sell the car.*

push at an open door
to achieve what you want easily because a lot of people agree with you or help you • (usually in continuous tenses) *The campaigners are pushing at an open door because most local residents support their campaign against the new road.*

push your **luck**
to try too hard to get a particular result and risk losing what you have achieved • (usually negative) *Don't push your luck – they've agreed to pay your travel expenses, I don't think it would be wise to ask for more money.*

push the boat out *British*
to spend a lot of money or more money than you usually do, especially when you are celebrating • *As it's your birthday, I think we can push the boat out and have a bottle of champagne.* • (sometimes + **for**) *They really pushed the boat out for Jane's wedding.*

► See also: push/drive sb over the **edge**
hit/press/push the **panic** button
press/push the **right** button/buttons

pusher

a pen pusher *British & Australian*
a pencil pusher *American*
someone who has a boring job in an office • *He's a frustrated desk-bound pen pusher who dreams of trekking through jungles.*
pen pushing *British & Australian* • *Who does all the pen pushing for the golf club?*

pushing

be pushing up (the) daisies *humorous*
to be dead • *It won't affect me anyway. I'll be pushing up the daisies long before it happens.*

put

Put a lid on it! *mainly American informal*
something that you say in order to tell someone to stop talking • *Put a lid on it, you two! You've been shouting all afternoon.*

put it about
1 *British very informal* to have sexual relationships with a lot of different people • (usually in continuous tenses) *She's been putting it about a bit recently, hasn't she?*
2 to tell a lot of people news or information that may not be true • (usually + **that**) *Her rivals put it about that she was responsible for the crisis.*

put sb **off** their **stride** *British, American & Australian*
put sb **off** their **stroke** *British & Australian*
to take someone's attention away from what they are doing so they are not able to do it well • *She was making funny faces at me, trying to put me off my stroke.* • *When I'm playing chess, the slightest noise can put me off my stride.*

put on the dog *American & Australian informal*
to try to seem richer or more important than you really are • *They really put on the dog in front of their guests.*

put the lid on sth *British old-fashioned*
if something that happens puts the lid on a plan, it causes the plan to fail • *When James resigned that put the lid on the whole project.*

put up or shut up *informal*
if you say someone should put up or shut up, you mean they should either take action in order to do what they have been talking about or stop talking about it • *You keep saying you're going to ask her out. Well, put up or shut up.*

► See also: put the **arm** on sb
get/put sb's **back** up
put your **back** into sth
put the **ball** in sb's court
put sth to **bed**
put the **bite** on sb
put a **bomb** under sth/sb
put the **boot** in
put the **brakes** on
lay/put your **cards** on the table
put the **cart** before the horse
put/set the **cat** among the pigeons
put/turn the **clock** back
put sb on **edge**
put the **fear** of God into sb
put out **feelers**
put your **feet** up
put your **finger** on sth
put the **finger** on sb
Put the **flags** out!
put **flesh** on (the bones of) sth
not put a **foot** wrong
put your **foot** down
put your **foot** in it
put your **foot** to the floor
put the **frighteners** on sb
put on/up a **front**
put in a **good** word for sb
lay/put a **guilt** trip on sb
hold/put a **gun** to sb's head
put **hair**(s) on your chest
put your **hand** in your pocket
put your **hand** on your heart
get/put your **head** down
put/stick your **head** above the parapet
put their **heads** together
put your **heart** and soul into sth/doing sth
put the **heat** on sb
put sb through **hell**
put sth on **hold**
get/put your own **house** in order
put **ideas** into sb's head
put the **kibosh** on sth
put sb over your **knee**
put/stick the **knife** in
put your **life** on the line
put the **make** on sb
put swh/sth/sb on the **map**
put sth under the **microscope**
put sb through the **mill**
put sb in **mind** of sb/sth
put your **mind** to it
put/set sb's **mind** at rest
put sth/sb out of their **misery**
put the **mockers** on sth
put your **money** on sb/sth
put your **money** where your mouth is
put/set sth in **motion**

put your **neck** on the line
put sb's **nose** out of joint
put/stick your **oar** in
get/put **one** over on sb
put **one** over on sb
put sb through their **paces**
put **paid** to sth
I wouldn't put it **past** sb
put sb out to **pasture**
put sb on a **pedestal**
put **pen** to paper
put sb in the **picture**
Put/stick that in your **pipe** and smoke it!
put sb in their **place**
put/set the **record** straight
put a **rocket** under sb
put down **roots**
put/throw sb off the **scent**
put the **screws** on sb
put/set the **seal** on sth
put sb/sth in the **shade**
put your **shirt** on sth
put the **skids** under sb/sth
Put a **sock** in it!
put a **spoke** in sb's wheel
put sb on the **spot**
put your **thinking** cap on
put in/stick in your **two** penn'orth
put **two** and **two** together
put your **two** cents (worth) in
put/stick **two** fingers up at sb/sth
get/put the **wind** up sb
put **words** in/into sb's mouth
put/throw a spanner in the **works**
put sb through the **wringer**
put **years** on sb

putty

be putty in your **hands**

if someone is putty in your hands, they will do anything you want them to do, usually because they like you so much • *He can't say no to her – he's putty in her hands.*

put-up

a put-up job *informal*

an attempt to trick or deceive someone • *At the time he seemed honest enough, but later, after I'd given him the money, I realized it was a put-up job.*

Pyrrhic

a Pyrrhic victory

a victory that is not worth winning because you have suffered so much to achieve it • *Winning the case may well prove to be a Pyrrhic victory as the award will not even cover their legal fees.*

qed

QED *formal*
something that you say in order to emphasize that a fact proves what you have just said is true ✍QED is a short form of the latin phrase 'quod erat demonstrandum' which means 'which was to have been proven'. • *People are getting taller all the time – apparently it's progress and has to do with quality of life (cavemen were short QED).*

q.t.

on the q.t. *old-fashioned*
secretly, without anyone knowing ✍q.t. is a short way of writing 'quiet'. • *All this time she'd been making plans on the q.t. to change her job.*

quaking

be quaking in your **boots**
to be very frightened or anxious • *My first teacher had one of those deep, booming voices that had you quaking in your boots.*
make sb **quake in** their **boots** • *Just the sound of her voice made me quake in my boots.*

quantum

a quantum leap *British & American*
a quantum jump *American*
a very important improvement or development in something • (often + **forward**) *The election of a female president is a quantum leap forward for sexual equality.* • (often + **from**) *The food at Rockresorts is a quantum jump from the meals served at most Caribbean resorts.*

quart

get/put a quart into a pint pot *British*
to try to put too much of something into a small space ✍A quart is a unit for measuring liquids. It is equal to two pints. • *I'm trying to get this huge pile of clothes crammed into these two drawers. Talk about trying to get a quart into a pint pot!*

queen

▸ See: **turn** king's/queen's evidence

queer

be in Queer Street *British old-fashioned, humorous*
to owe a lot of money to other people • *Now don't you go doing anything that'll land you in Queer Street!*

a queer fish *British old-fashioned*
a strange person • *I knew his father and he was a queer fish too.*

queer sb's **pitch** *British & Australian*
to spoil someone's chances of doing something • *She queered my pitch by asking for promotion before I did.*

question

be out of the question
if something is out of the question, it is not possible or not allowed • *A trip to New Zealand is out of the question this year.*

a question mark over sth
1 if there is a question mark over something, no one knows whether it will continue to exist in the future or what will happen to it • *Neither company has performed well over the last year and there's a question mark over their long-term survival.* • *A* ***question mark hangs over*** *the future of the whole project.*
2 a feeling of doubt about the ability or quality of something • *The recent spate of government scandals has left a question mark over their ability to govern.*

the sixty-four-thousand-dollar question *informal*
the million-dollar question *informal*
an important or difficult question which people do not know the answer to • *So will she marry him or not? – that's the sixty-four-thousand-dollar question.*

▸ See also: **beg** the question
call sth into question
pop the question

queue

▶ See: **jump** the queue

quick

as quick as a flash/wink
as quick as lightning
if you do something as quick as a flash, you do it very quickly • *Quick as a flash, he snatched the book and ran out of the room.*

be quick off the mark
to be quick to act or to react to an event or situation • *The police were quick off the mark reaching the scene of the accident.*
be first/quickest off the mark • *Do you know which company was first off the mark to sell computers for home use?*

a quick fix *informal*
a quick solution to a problem, especially one which is only temporary • *The truth about dieting is that there is no quick fix. Weight must be lost gradually, over a period of time.*
quick-fix • (always before noun) *It's a system of medicine that doesn't promote the quick-fix approach to the treatment of illness.*

a quick one *informal*
a quick, usually alcoholic drink • *Have you got time for a quick one before you go?*

a quick study *American informal*
someone who is able to learn things quickly • *He's a quick study and easily grasps all the details of a discussion.*

▶ See also: make a fast/quick **buck**
cut sb to the quick
be quick on the **draw**

quicken

quicken your/**the pulse**
to make someone excited or interested • *There's nothing in this book to quicken the pulse.*

quid pro quo

a quid pro quo *formal*
something that you do for someone or give to someone when they have agreed to do something for you ✍This is a Latin phrase which means 'something for something'. • (often + **for**) *The government's commitment to release political prisoners is a quid pro quo for the suspension of armed struggle by the rebels.*

quids

be quids in *British informal*
to be making a profit • *If this deal goes ahead we'll be quids in.*

not **for quids** *Australian informal*
if you say that you would not do something for quids, you mean that you would hate to do that thing • *I wouldn't do your job for quids.*

quiet

be as quiet as a mouse
to be very quiet • *She was as quiet as a mouse. I didn't even know she'd come in.*

on the quiet *informal*
secretly • *His marriage broke up when his wife found out he'd been seeing someone else on the quiet.*

quits

▶ See: **call** it quits

quote

quote, unquote *British, American & Australian*
quote, end quote *American*
something that you say when you want to show that you are using someone else's phrase, especially when you do not think that phrase is true • *And to think he chose to practise law because it's a quote, unquote 'respected' profession!*

▶ See also: give/quote (sb) **chapter** and verse

Rr

rabbit

▶ See: be like a deer/rabbit caught in the **headlights**
pull a rabbit out of the hat

rabbits

▶ See: **breed** like rabbits

race

race against the clock
in sport, if people race against the clock, they try to race faster than a particular time instead of racing against other people • *In time trials, cyclists race against the clock.*

a race against time/the clock
an attempt to do something very quickly because there is only a short time in which it can be done • *It's a race against time to get the building finished before the rainy season sets in.*
race against time/the clock • *Rescuers were racing against time last night to reach the four divers, trapped 200 feet down on the seabed.*

rack

on the rack
anxious, often because you are waiting for something or because people are asking you difficult questions • *You're left on the rack for three days waiting for the results from the hospital.* • *Here was a respected politician being* **put on the rack** (= asked a lot of difficult questions) *by aggressive junior politicians.*

rack your **brain/brains**
to think very hard, usually in order to remember something or to find a solution to a problem • *I've been racking my brains but I still can't remember who wrote that play.*

▶ See also: go to rack/wrack and **ruin**

radar

fall off/drop off the radar
drop beneath the/sb's **radar**
to be forgotten or ignored, often because someone's attention is on something more important • *I was so busy at work, organising a summer holiday just dropped off the radar.*
be on the/sb's **radar** • *The needs of the country's unemployed aren't even on his radar.*

rag

▶ See: **chew** the rag
lose your rag

rage

be all the rage *old-fashioned, informal*
to be very fashionable • *Fake leopard print, so fashionable in the seventies, is all the rage again now.*

ragged

be on the ragged edge *American*
to be so tired or upset that you feel you cannot deal with a situation • *Top professional coaches are on the ragged edge of exhaustion and frustration.*

▶ See also: **run** sb ragged

rags

go from rags to riches
to start your life very poor and then later in life become very rich • *People who go from rags to riches are often afraid the good life will be snatched away from them.*
rags-to-riches • (always before noun) *Raised in poverty by an uncle in Oklahoma, his was a real rags-to-riches story.*

rails

be back on the rails *British*
to be making progress once more • *The minister emerged from three hours of discussions, confident that the talks are now back on the rails.*
put sth **back on the rails** *British* • *With this new album, he hopes to put his career back on the rails.*

go off the rails *informal*
to start behaving strangely or in a way that is not acceptable to society • *He went off the rails in his twenties and started living on the streets.* • *By the law of probabilities if you have five kids, one of*

them's going to go off the rails.

rain

(come) rain or shine

1 whatever the weather is • *He runs every morning, rain or shine.*

2 if you say you will do something come rain or shine, you mean you will do it whatever happens • *Come rain or shine, I'll be there, I promise.*

I'll take a rain check *American, British & Australian informal*
I'll get a rain check *American informal*
something that you say when you cannot accept someone's invitation to do something but you would like to do it another time • (often + **on**) *I'll take a rain check on that drink tonight, if that's all right.* • *I won't play tennis this afternoon but can I get a rain check?*

ask (sb) **for a rain check** *American informal* • *I was supposed to see Marge on Saturday – I'll have to ask her for a rain check.*

rain on sb's **parade**
to do something that spoils someone's plans • *I'm sorry to rain on your parade, but you're not allowed to have alcohol on the premises.*

rainbows

▶ See: **chase** rainbows

raining

It's raining cats and dogs! *old-fashioned*
something that you say when it is raining very heavily • *It's raining cats and dogs out there! It's a wonder any of the men can see what they're doing!*

rains

It never rains but it pours.
something that you say which means that when one bad thing happens, a lot of other bad things also happen, making the situation even worse • *First of all it was the car breaking down, then the fire in the kitchen and now Mike's accident. It never rains but it pours!*

rainy

▶ See: **save** (sth) for a rainy day

raise

raise (a few) eyebrows
to shock or surprise people • *Anna's miniskirt raised eyebrows at the board meeting.* • *The player's huge transfer fee raised a few eyebrows in the football world.*

raised eyebrows • *There were raised eyebrows and coughs of disapproval when the speaker turned up drunk for the lecture.*

raise Cain *old-fashioned*
to complain angrily about something and to cause a lot of trouble for the people who are responsible for it • *They know that the children's parents will raise Cain if they're excluded from classes.*

raise your **game**
to make an effort to improve the way that you play a game • *They're going to have to raise their game if they want to stay in the Premier Division this season.*

raise your **hand against/to** sb
to hit someone, or to threaten to hit them • *I would never raise my hand against a child.*

raise hell

1 to complain in a loud and angry way about something • *She raised hell when she realized her office had no windows.*

2 *mainly American* to behave in a noisy or wild way that upsets other people • *A group of kids were raising hell in the street.*

a hell-raiser someone who behaves in a noisy or wild way that upsets other people • *When he was younger he was a real hell-raiser.*

raise the roof
to make a loud noise by shouting, clapping or singing • *They finished the set with their current hit and the audience raised the roof.*

▶ See also: raise/up the **ante**
raise (sb's) **hackles**
raise/rear its (ugly) **head**
make/raise a **stink**

raison d'être

sb's/sth's **raison d'être** *formal*
the most important reason why something exists, or the most important thing in someone's life • *She's never going to*

retire – work is her raison d'être. • *Serious, experimental drama was once the raison d'être of the festival but it has now been replaced by comedy and cabaret shows.*

rake

rake over the ashes
to think about or to talk about unpleasant events from the past ✍Ashes are what is left of something after it has been destroyed by fire. • *There is no point in raking over the ashes now, you did what you thought was right at the time.*

rake over the coals
to talk about unpleasant things from the past that other people would prefer not to talk about • (usually in continuous tenses) *There's no point in raking over the coals – all that happened twenty years ago, and there's nothing we can do about it now.*

rake-off

a rake-off *informal*
a share of the profits of something, often taken in a way that is not honest • *Corrupt customs officers were taking a rake-off from import taxes.*

ram

ram sth **down** sb's **throat** *informal*
if someone rams their opinions or ideas down your throat, they force you to listen to them and try to make you accept them • *And although he's got very strong views on such subjects, he doesn't try to ram them down your throat.* • *He's a committed Christian but he doesn't ram it down your throat.*

ramrod

be as stiff/straight as a ramrod *old-fashioned*
if someone is as stiff as a ramrod, they stand or sit with their back very straight and stiff • *At eighty-three, he's still as straight as a ramrod.*

ranch

▶ See: **bet** the farm/ranch

rank

the rank and file
the ordinary members of an organization and not its leaders • *The party leadership seems to be losing the support of the rank and file.*
rank-and-file • (always before noun) *Nearly two-thirds of the vote went to union leaders and rank-and-file party activists.*

▶ See also: **pull** rank

ranks

▶ See: **break** ranks
close ranks
join the ranks of sth

ransom

▶ See: **hold** sb to ransom

rap

a rap across/on/over the knuckles
a punishment which is not very severe but which warns you not to behave that way again • *The company received a rap over the knuckles from the Food and Drug Administration.* • *Her remarks earned her a sharp rap across the knuckles from the Prime Minister.*
rap sb's **knuckles** • *She rapped my knuckles and sent me on my way.*

a rap sheet *American informal*
information kept by the police about someone's criminal activities • *The gunman's rap sheet had a long list of weapons and narcotics offenses.*

take the rap
to be blamed or punished for something bad that has happened, especially when it is not your fault • (often + **for**) *I'm not going to take the rap for someone else's mistakes.*

▶ See also: **beat** the rap

raptures

go into raptures
to talk about something in a very pleased and excited way • (often + **about**) *She went into raptures about the chocolate cake.*

raring

be raring to go
to be full of energy and ready to do something • *At three in the morning he was still wide awake and raring to go.*

raspberry

blow a raspberry *British & Australian informal*
give a raspberry *American informal*
to make a rude noise by putting your tongue between your lips and blowing • (often + **at**) *A boy of no more than six appeared, blew a raspberry at me and then ran away.*

rat

a rat fink *American informal*
an extremely unpleasant person, or someone who has given secret information about you to the police • *If I find the rat fink who informed on me, he won't live long enough to do it again.*

a rat race
an unpleasant way in which people compete against each other at work in order to succeed • *I'd love to get out of the rat race and buy a house in some remote part of the countryside.*

▶ See also: **smell** a rat

rat-arsed

rat-arsed *British very informal*
rat-assed *American very informal*
very drunk • *They came home completely rat-arsed.*

rate

at a rate of knots *British & Australian*
if someone does something at a rate of knots, they do it very quickly ✍The speed a boat travels is measured in knots. • *She did her homework at a rate of knots so that she could go out with her friends.*

rattle

rattle sb's **cage**
to make someone angry on purpose, often in order to make them seem silly • *She tried to rattle his cage with questions about his failed army career.*

raw

come the raw prawn *Australian informal*
to pretend that you have no knowledge of what someone is talking about • (usually + **with**) *Oh, don't come the raw prawn with me, Scott, I saw you writing down her telephone number as I walked into the room!*

get a raw deal
to not be treated as well as other people • *The fact is that kids who are taught in classes of over thirty get a raw deal.*

in the raw *informal*
naked • *She often swims in the raw.*

▶ See also: hit/touch a (raw) **nerve**

ray

a ray of sunshine
someone or something that makes you feel happy, especially in a difficult situation • *Amid all the gloom, their grandchild has been a real ray of sunshine.*

rays

▶ See: **catch** some rays

razzle

be/go (out) on the razzle *British informal, old-fashioned*
to enjoy yourself by doing things like going to parties or dances • *We're going out on the razzle on New Year's Eve – do you fancy coming?*
a night (out) on the razzle *informal, old-fashioned* • *We've had a night on the razzle, so I've got a bit of a hangover.*

razzle-dazzle

razzle-dazzle
activity that is intended to attract people's attention by being noisy or exciting • *Amid all the razzle-dazzle of the party convention, it is easy to forget about the real political issues.*
razzle-dazzle • (always before noun) *It was their razzle-dazzle style that caught people's eye.*

reach

reach boiling point
if a situation or an emotion reaches boiling point, it becomes impossible to control because the emotions involved are so strong • *Public anger reached boiling point when troops were called in to control protesters.*

reach for the moon/stars
to try to achieve something that is very difficult • *If you want success, you have to reach for the moon.*

▶ See also: reach a **crossroads**

read

read between the lines
to try to understand someone's real feelings or intentions from what they say or write • *Reading between the lines, I'd say that Martin isn't very happy with the situation.*

read sb's **mind** *humorous*
to know what someone is thinking without being told • *'How about a drink, then?' 'You read my mind, Kev.'*
mind-reader • *If something's bothering you, then tell me. I'm not a mind-reader, you know!*

Read my lips! *informal*
a slightly impolite way of telling someone to listen to what you are saying • *Read my lips. You're not having any more ice-cream.*

read (sb) **the riot act**
to speak angrily to someone about something they have done and warn them that they will be punished if they do it again ✍The riot act was a law made in 1715 which said how to deal with groups of twelve or more people who were causing trouble. • *He'd put up with a lot of bad behaviour from his son and thought it was time to read him the riot act.*

read the runes *British formal*
to try to guess what is going to happen in the future by examining what is happening now ✍Runes are letters of an ancient alphabet with secret or magic meaning. • *He was the first Eastern European leader to read the runes and make political changes to stay in power.*

take it as read *British & Australian*
to accept that something is true without making sure that it is • (often + **that**) *We just took it as read that we were invited.*

ready

be ready to roll
1 *mainly American* to be going to start soon • *The new TV series from the Hill Street Blues creator, Steve Bochco, is ready to roll.*
2 *American* to be going to leave soon • *Give me a call when you're ready to roll, and I'll meet you outside.*

ready cash/money
money that is immediately available to spend • *They need investors with ready money if they're going to get the project started.*

▶ See also: fit/ready to **drop**

real

Get real! *informal*
something that you say in order to tell someone that they should try to understand the true facts of a situation instead of hoping for something impossible • *Oh, get real! You're not tall enough to be a model.*

the real McCoy
the real thing and not a copy or something similar ✍Kid McCoy, an American boxer (= a man who fights as a sport), was called 'the real McCoy' to show that he was not another boxer who had the same name. • *Cheap sparkling wines cannot be labelled 'champagne'. It has to be the real McCoy.*

reap

reap a/the harvest of sth
to receive the good or bad results of past actions • *Homelessness is rising. We are reaping the harvest of a lack of investment in housing and social services.*

reap the whirlwind *American*
to have serious problems because you did something stupid in the past • *Having fired some of his best reporters, he's now reaping the whirlwind with rapidly declining newspaper sales.*

You reap what you sow.
As you sow, so shall you reap. *formal*
something that you say which means everything that happens to you is a result of your own actions • *If you treat your friends like that, of course they drop you. You reap what you sow in this life.*

rear

▶ See: **bring** up the rear
raise/rear its (ugly) **head**

rear-end

rear-end sth *American*
to cause an accident by hitting the back of the car in front of you • *His car was*

rear-ended while he was stopped at the light.

rearguard

▶ See: **fight** a rearguard action

rearranging

be like rearranging the deckchairs on the Titanic *British & Australian humorous*

if an activity is like rearranging the deckchairs on the Titanic, it it will have no effect ✍The Titanic was a large ship that sank suddenly in 1912 with most of its passengers. • *With unemployment at record levels, plans for better advertising of job vacancies are a bit like rearranging the deckchairs on the Titanic.*

reason

▶ See: it **stands** to reason

rebound

on the rebound

unhappy and confused because a close, romantic relationship of yours has recently finished • *She was on the rebound when she met Jack.* • *Six months after Julia left him, he married someone else on the rebound.*

received

▶ See: the conventional/received **wisdom**

receiving

be at/on the receiving end

if you are on the receiving end of something unpleasant that someone does, you suffer because of it • (usually + **of**) *Sales assistants are often at the receiving end of verbal abuse from customers.*

recharge

recharge your **batteries**

to rest in order to get back your strength and energy • *A week away would give you time to rest and recharge your batteries.*

recipe

be a recipe for [disaster/happiness/ success etc.]

if something is a recipe for disaster, happiness, success etc., it is very likely to cause this • *Living with your husband's family is a recipe for disaster.*

record

for the record

something that you say when you are about to tell someone something important that you want them to remember • *Just for the record, I've never been to his house and I've only met him a few times, whatever the media is saying.*

go on record

to publicly and officially tell people your opinion about something • (often + **as** + doing sth) *Are you prepared to go on record as supporting the council on this issue?*

be on record • (often + **as** + doing sth) *Both doctors are on record as saying the drug trials were an unqualified success.*

off the record

if you say something off the record, you do not want it to be publicly reported • *She made it clear that her comments were strictly off the record and should not be included in the article.*

off-the-record • (always before noun) *It's not a good idea to make these off-the-record remarks too often.*

on the record • *None of the company directors were prepared to comment on the record yesterday.*

put/set the record straight

to tell the true facts about a situation in order to show people that what they believed previously was not correct • *She is writing her memoirs to set the record straight once and for all.*

red

be in the red

to owe money to a bank ✍Accountants (= people who keep records of money) often write amounts of money that are owed in red ink. • *Many of the students were in the red at the end of their first year.*

be like a red rag to a bull

if a statement or an action is like a red rag to a bull, it makes someone very angry ✍Some people believe that bulls become very angry when they see the colour red. • *For Claire, the suggestion of a women-only committee was like a red rag to a bull.*

not a red cent *American informal*
no money at all ✍A cent is the smallest coin in value in American money and is worth very little. • *I did all that work for them and they didn't pay me a red cent!* • *It turns out his paintings* ***aren't worth a red cent.***

red eye *American very informal*
cheap whiskey (= strong alcoholic drink) • *The man was leaning against the wall, swigging from a bottle of red eye.*

a red eye *American informal*
a flight that leaves late at night and arrives early the next morning • *We took the red eye from Seattle to New York.*
red-eye • (always before noun) *There's a red-eye flight to Los Angeles leaving at 10pm.*

a red herring
something that takes people's attention away from the main subject being talked or written about • *About halfway through the book it looked as though the butler was the murderer, but that turned out to be a red herring.*

red tape
official rules which do not seem necessary and make things happen very slowly • *My passport application has been held up by red tape.*

▶ See also: be on full/red **alert**
go **beet** red
go **beetroot** (red)
roll out the red carpet
see red

red-blooded

red-blooded
a red-blooded man has a lot of energy and enjoys sex very much • *He's a normal, red-blooded male – of course he wants to sleep with you!*

red-handed

▶ See: **catch** sb red-handed

red-hot

red-hot *informal*
very exciting or successful • *British athletes are red-hot at the moment.* • *Their divorce is the red-hot story in this morning's press.*

red-letter

a red-letter day
a day that is very important or very special • *The day our daughter was born was a real red-letter day for us.*

red-light

the red-light district
the part of a city where many people offer sex for money • *A prostitute was found murdered in the city's red-light district last night.*

reduce

reduce sb **to tears**
to make someone cry • *His classmates jeered, reducing him to tears.*

reduced

in reduced circumstances *slightly formal*
if someone, especially someone from a high social class, is in reduced circumstances, they have a lot less money than they did before • *They found him living in reduced circumstances in a flat off Fulham Road.*

regular

be as regular as clockwork
if something is as regular as clockwork, it happens at exactly regular times • *Her letters arrived every week, regular as clockwork.*

reign

a reign of terror
a period of time when a ruler controls people in a violent and cruel way • *My father's generation, who lived through the reign of terror, will never forget it.*

reins

take over/up the reins
to take control of something, especially an organization or a country • (often + **of**) *He took up the reins of government immediately after the coup.*

▶ See also: **hand** over the reins
tighten the reins

reinvent

reinvent the wheel
to waste time trying to develop products or systems that you think are original when in fact they have already been done

before • *Why reinvent the wheel when there are drugs already on the market that are effective?*

religion

get religion

1 *humorous* to become very religious • *He suddenly got religion when he went to college.*

2 *American humorous* to start doing something in a serious and careful way • *I get religion each time I do my income tax – I always wonder why I didn't keep better records.*

Renaissance

a Renaissance man *formal*

an intelligent and well-educated man who knows a lot about many different subjects • *He's a poet, astronomer, musician – an all-round Renaissance man.*

rent

a rent boy *British*

a boy or a young man who has sex with other men for money • *He spent a year in London working as a rent boy.*

reopen

▶ See: open/reopen **old** wounds

rest

Give it a rest! *informal*

something that you say when you want someone to stop talking about something • *'When are you going to wash the car?' 'Oh, give it a rest! I'll do it in a minute.'*

I rest my case.

something that you say when someone says or does something that proves the truth of something you have just said • *'It's time Nigel left home, or he'll never learn to be independent.' 'He doesn't even know how to boil an egg.' 'I rest my case.'*

the rest is history

something that you say when you do not need to finish a story because everyone knows what happened • *The Beatles signed a recording contract in 1962 and the rest is history.*

rest on your laurels

to be so satisfied with your own achievements that you make no effort to improve • *Just because you passed all your exams, that's no reason to rest on your laurels.*

▶ See also: There's no peace/rest for the **wicked**!

retreat

▶ See: **beat** a retreat

return

return the compliment

to do something for someone because they have done something for you • *Thanks for looking after the house while we were away. I hope I'll be able to return the compliment some time.*

revert

revert to type

if someone reverts to type, they return to their usual behaviour after a period of behaving in a different, usually better, way • *After several weeks without saying a rude word to anyone, he seems to have reverted to type.*

revolving

a revolving door *mainly American*

the movement of people from one organization or activity to another, especially from government jobs to private companies • (often + **between**) *Congress has tightened regulations to slow down the revolving door between government and industry.*

rhyme

no rhyme or reason

if there is no rhyme or reason why something happens, there is no obvious explanation for it • *I don't know what makes her behave like that. There's no rhyme or reason to it.*

without rhyme or reason • *Changes have been made to the text without rhyme or reason.*

ribs

▶ See: **stick** to your ribs

rich

filthy/stinking rich *informal*

extremely rich • *Most of us are stinking rich compared to the average citizen in the Third World.* • *Palm Beach has the highest concentration of filthy rich folk in the world.*

a rich seam *formal*

a subject which provides a lot of opportunities for people to discuss, write about or make jokes about • (often + **of**) *Both wars have provided a rich seam of drama for playwrights and novelists alike.* • *His second novel* ***mines*** *the same* ***rich seam*** *of mother-son relations.*

That's (a bit) rich!

something that you say when someone criticizes you to show that you do not think they are being fair because they are as bad as you • *I'm greedy?* ***That's a bit rich, coming from you!***

▶ See also: **strike** it rich

riddles

▶ See: **talk** in riddles

ride

a bumpy/rough ride

a difficult time • *Government plans to cut sick pay had a rough ride in the House of Commons.* • *The construction industry is in for a bumpy ride next year.*

OPPOSITE **an easy/smooth ride** • *It has taken years to set up a support network without adequate funding. It hasn't been an easy ride.*

come/go along for the ride

to join in an activity without playing an important part in it • *My husband is speaking at the dinner and I'm just going along for the ride.*

ride (on) a/the wave

to become involved with and get advantages from opinions or activities which have become very common or popular • (often + **of**) *She came to power riding on a wave of personal popularity.*

ride herd on sb/sth *American*

to be responsible for controlling a group of people and their actions • *The new editor will ride herd on the staff, checking on the overall policy and tone of the paper.*

ride on the back of sth

to use something successful which already exists or has already happened in order to achieve something else • *Poetry performances are riding on the back of the popularity of stand-up comedy.*

ride roughshod over sth/sb

to act in the way you want to, ignoring rules, traditions, or other people's wishes • *They accused the government of riding roughshod over parliamentary procedure.* • *He cannot be allowed to ride roughshod over his colleagues with his ambitious plans.*

take sb **for a ride**

to cheat or deceive someone • *I trusted him but he took me for a ride.*

▶ See also: **let** sth ride
ride out/weather the **storm**

riding

be riding high

to be very successful • *With 3 hit singles in the charts, the band are riding high.* • (often + **on**) *Shops are riding high on the latest consumer spending boom.*

▶ See also: be heading/riding for a **fall**

riff-raff

riff-raff

an impolite way of describing people from a low social class, especially people who behave badly • *We don't want drug addicts and other riff-raff living near us.*

right

be as right as rain

to feel well • *I'll be as right as rain as soon as I take my pills.*

be in the right place at the right time

to be in the place where an opportunity is being offered • *The secret of success is being in the right place at the right time.*

be on the right lines

if you are on the right lines, you are doing something in a way that will bring good results • *Do you think we're on the right lines with this project?*

be on the right track

to be doing something in a way that will bring good results • *Our success in the opinion polls proves we're on the right track.*

put sb **on the right track** • *When things went wrong I had a chat with Phil and he put me* ***back on the right track.***

not **be right in the head** *informal*

to be mentally ill • *His aunt's not right in the head, poor soul – you sometimes see her wandering up the street in her nightie.*

hit/strike the right note
if something you say or do hits the right note, it is suitable and has a good effect • *He saw his remarks had struck the right note – his friend was smiling now.* • (sometimes + **of**) *The General's calm manner hit the right note of moderation, to reassure his audience.*

make (all) the right noises
to seem to be enthusiastic about something • *I think she liked my presentation. She certainly made all the right noises.*

press/push the right button/buttons
to do exactly what is necessary to get the result that you want • *You have to know how to* ***push all the right buttons*** *if you want to be a successful diplomat.* • *Sometimes you're interviewing someone really shy and then you press the right button and they just don't stop talking.*

Right on! *American & Australian*
something that you say when you agree completely with what someone has just said • *He said he didn't think I really wanted him to be here and I thought, 'Right on!'*

We've got a right one here! *British & Australian informal*
something that you say when you think someone is silly or stupid • *We've got a right one here! This guy has forgotten to sign his letter.*

would give their **right arm**
if someone would give their right arm for something, they would like it very much • (often + to do sth) *I'd give my right arm to meet Sean Connery.* • (often + **for**) *Lots of people would give their right arm for a job like yours.*

▶ See also: give sb (the right of/to) **first** refusal
good/right and **proper**
see sb right
serve sb right

right-hand

sb's **right-hand man/woman**
someone who helps you with your work and who you depend upon • *How will the Director cope without his right-hand man, who resigned yesterday due to ill health?*

right-on

right-on *British*
if people or their opinions are right-on, they believe everyone should be treated in a fair way and they are careful not to offend anyone because of their sex, colour, age, etc. • *She wrote a very right-on book about attitudes to fat people.*

rights

catch/have sb **dead to rights** *British, American & Australian*
catch/have sb **bang to rights** *British*
to have enough proof to show that someone has done something wrong • *I was driving way above the speed limit and the police radar caught me dead to rights.*

ring

have a ring to it
if a word or idea has a ring to it, it sounds interesting or attractive • (never in continuous tenses) *I suppose 'Cathy's Country Cooking' has a certain ring to it.*

ring a bell
ring any bells
if a phrase or a word, especially a name, rings a bell, you think you have heard it before • *Does the name 'Fitzpatrick' ring a bell?* • (often + **with**) *No, I'm sorry, that description doesn't ring any bells with me.*

ring off the hook *American informal*
if your telephone rings off the hook, it rings a lot • *The box office phones were ringing off the hook all day.*

ring the changes *British & Australian*
to make something more interesting by changing it in some way • *Bored with your old look? Ring the changes with our new-look hairstyles and make-up!*

ring true
if something someone has said or written rings true, it seems to be true • (often negative) *Something about the story didn't quite ring true.*

▶ See also: ring/sound **hollow**

rings

▶ See: **run** rings around/round sb

ringside

a ringside seat/view
if you have a ringside seat, you are in a good position to watch what is happening

at an event • *If there's going to be a confrontation between management and the unions, I'd like a ringside seat.*

rinky-dink

rinky-dink *American informal*
not important or of bad quality • (always before noun) *We drove into a rinky-dink town in rural Pennsylvania.* • *This isn't rinky-dink stuff – it's high quality furniture.*

riot

run riot

1 if people run riot, they behave in a way that is not controlled, running in all directions or being noisy or violent • *I dread them coming round because they let their kids run riot.*

2 if your imagination runs riot, you have a lot of strange, exciting, or surprising thoughts • *My imagination was running riot, thinking of all the ways that I could spend the money.*

► See also: **read** (sb) the riot act

rip

let rip

1 to suddenly express your emotions without control • *This time I was furious and I let rip.* • *He's a very restrained sort of person – you can't imagine him ever really letting rip.*

2 *British & Australian very informal* to allow gas to escape from your bottom loudly • *You can't just let rip when you're in a smart restaurant.*

► See also: **let** it/her rip

ripe

► See: **live** to a ripe old age

rip-off

a rip-off *informal*
something that is not worth as much money as you have to pay for it • *Mobile phones can be a real rip-off if you're not careful.*

ripple

a ripple effect
if something has a ripple effect, it affects something else, which then affects other things • *Court rulings often have a ripple effect, spreading into areas of law that weren't part of the original cases.*

rip-roaring

rip-roaring
very exciting and successful • (always before noun) *The show was* ***a rip-roaring success.*** • *The car was launched with a rip-roaring publicity campaign.*

rise

get a rise out of sb
to succeed in annoying someone • *Ignore him – he's just trying to get a rise out of you.*

Rise and shine! *old-fashioned*
something that you say to tell someone to get out of bed and start their day • *Rise and shine, sleepy head – you have to leave for school in twenty minutes.*

rise to the bait
to react to something that someone has said in exactly the way that they wanted you to react, usually by becoming angry • (often negative) *Anthony keeps saying that women make bad drivers but I refuse to rise to the bait.*

rise to the occasion
to succeed in dealing with a difficult situation • *It's not easy to play your first match in front of a crowd that size but he certainly rose to the occasion.*

► See also: rise from the **dead**

risk

risk life and limb
to do something very dangerous where you might get hurt • *These skiers risk life and limb every day for the thrill of speed.*

risk your **neck**
to do something very dangerous • *I'm not going to risk my neck climbing over a twenty-foot wall!*

rite

a rite of passage
an activity or ceremony that shows that someone has reached an important new stage in their life, especially the start of their adult life • *There's an element of danger to most adolescent rites of passage, whether they be driving, sex, alcohol or drugs.*
rite-of-passage • *This is not merely another dreary rite-of-passage novel.*

river

▶ See: **sell** sb down the river

road

down the road

1 if an event is a particular period of time down the road, it will not happen until that period has passed • *This is a wonderful invention, but a marketable product is several years down the road yet.*

2 *American* if you say that something will happen down the road, you mean it will happen in the future • *We may at some point buy a house but that's down the road.*

go down that road

to decide to do something in a particular way • *We're thinking of automating our finances, but if we do go down that road we'll need specialist advice.*

a road hog *old-fashioned*

a bad driver who does not allow other drivers to pass them on the road • *Come on, let me past, road hog!*

your **road to Damascus** *British & Australian formal*

a very important experience which changes your whole life • *It was this chance meeting in a bar in Portland that he would later describe as his road to Damascus.*

road-to-Damascus *British & Australian formal* • (always before noun) *I used to be a slob, but then I underwent a sort of* ***road-to-Damascus conversion*** *to fitness.*

The road to hell is paved with good intentions.

something that you say which means people often intend to do good things but much of the time, they do not make the effort to do those things • *'I kept meaning to visit her but I didn't get round to it.' 'The road to hell is paved with good intentions.'*

▶ See also: **hit** the road

roaring

do a roaring trade *British & Australian*
do a roaring business *American*

to sell a lot of goods quickly • (usually in continuous tenses) *It was a hot day and the ice-cream sellers were doing a roaring trade.* • (often + **in**) *The toy department was doing a roaring trade in furry dinosaurs.*

rob

rob Peter to pay Paul

to borrow money from someone in order to give to someone else the money that you already owe them • *Then I'd take out another loan to pay my debts, robbing Peter to pay Paul.*

robbery

daylight robbery *British, American & Australian*
highway robbery *American & Australian*

a situation in which you are charged much more for something than you think you should have to pay • *Three pounds for an orange juice? It's daylight robbery!*

rock

between a rock and a hard place

if you are between a rock and a hard place, you have to make a difficult decision between two things that are equally unpleasant • *I'm* ***caught between a rock and a hard place****. If I go with Isobel, it'll be much more expensive and if I go with Julie, Isobel probably won't speak to me again.*

rock bottom

1 the lowest possible level • *The morale of prison officers is at rock bottom.* • *The president's opinion poll ratings have* ***hit rock bottom****.*

rock-bottom • *It says here they're selling off carpet stock at rock-bottom prices.*

2 if you are at rock bottom, you are the most unhappy you have ever been in your life • *I'd never felt so depressed in my life – I was at rock bottom – so I started drinking.* • *After Carly left me I* ***hit rock bottom****.*

rock the boat *informal*

to do or say something that causes problems, especially if you try to change a situation which most people do not want to change • *We certainly don't want anyone rocking the boat just before the election.* • *I tried to suggest a few ways in which we might improve our image and was told very firmly not to rock the boat.*

▶ See also: rock/shake sth to its **foundations**

rocker

be off your **rocker** *informal*
to be crazy • *Spending that much on a car! He must be off his rocker!*
go off your **rocker** *informal* • *I'd go off my rocker if I had to stay at home all day looking after kids.*

rocket

give sb **a rocket** *British & Australian informal*
to speak angrily to someone about something that they have done • (often + **for** + doing sth) *My mum gave me a rocket for tearing my new jeans.*
get a rocket *British & Australian informal* • *He got a rocket from his boss for being late.*

go like a rocket *Australian*
if a machine goes like a rocket, it works very well • *'How's the new computer?' 'Great, goes like a rocket.'*

it doesn't take a rocket scientist
you don't have to be a rocket scientist
if you say that it doesn't take a rocket scientist to understand something, you mean that it is obvious • (usually + to do sth) *Drugs equals crime. It doesn't take a rocket scientist to figure that one out.*
it's not rocket science • *We're talking basic common sense here – it isn't rocket science.*

put a rocket under sb *British & Australian*
to do something to make someone hurry • *We're going to have to put a rocket under Tim if we want to catch that train.*

rocks

be on the rocks
if a marriage or other romantic relationship is on the rocks, it has problems and is likely to end soon • *It was no great surprise when they announced their divorce. The marriage had been on the rocks for some time.*

get your **rocks off** *taboo*
if a man gets his rocks off, he has sex • *I don't think he cares what she looks like so long as he gets his rocks off.*

rod

make a rod for your **own back** *British*
to do something that is likely to cause problems for you in the future • *People say that if you let your baby sleep in your bed with you for the first few months, you're just making a rod for your own back.*

▶ See also: **rule** (sb) with a rod of iron

roll

be on a roll
to be having a successful period • *United are on a roll right now. They've won thirteen games in a row.*

a roll in the hay *humorous*
sexual activity which is quick and enjoyable and does not involve serious feelings • *I wouldn't sacrifice my marriage for a roll in the hay with a waitress.*

roll out the red carpet
to give an important person a special welcome • *The red carpet was rolled out for the President's visit.*
the red-carpet treatment • *She was given the red-carpet treatment in Japan where her books are extremely popular.*

roll your **sleeves up**
to prepare for hard work • *Our local team need to roll their sleeves up and put a bit more effort into their football.*

roll with the punches *American & Australian*
to be able to deal well with difficulties or criticism • *The poor woman has been jeered at and threatened with her life, but she just rolls with the punches.*

▶ See also: roll/trip off the **tongue**

roller

a roller coaster
a situation which changes suddenly and often between being good and being bad ✍A roller coaster is a type of small railway in an amusement park which travels very quickly climbing up and down hills. • *The Norwegian stockmarket has been* ***on a roller coaster*** *during the past 18 months.* • *What the book does describe very well is the* ***emotional roller-coaster*** *of puberty.*
roller-coaster • (always before noun)

His 11-year career has been a ***roller-coaster ride*** *of injury, rehabilitation, and triumph.*

rolling

be rolling in it *informal*
to be very rich • *If they can afford a yacht, they must be rolling in it.*

get rolling
1 *American & Australian* if a business or activity gets rolling, it starts • *The Junior Soccer League got rolling with its first two games last week.* • *He spent six months working for a small, local bank that never got rolling.*
get sth **rolling** *American* • *She made a few light-hearted comments to get the conversation rolling.*
2 *American informal* to leave a place • *Come on, let's get rolling – it's late.*

have sb **rolling in the aisles**
to make an audience (= a group of people watching a performance) laugh a lot • *Considered by many to be one of Britain's best comedians, Izzard has had audiences rolling in the aisles all over the country.*
be rolling in the aisles • *I don't think I laughed once and yet all around me people were rolling in the aisles.*

Rome

Rome wasn't built in a day.
something that you say which means that it takes a long time to do an important job • *'Sometimes it feels like we've spent all our lives decorating this house.' 'Well, Rome wasn't built in a day.'*

When in Rome (do as the Romans do).
something that you say which means when you are visiting another country, you should behave like the people in that country • *I don't drink wine when I'm at home but on holiday, well, when in Rome...*

▶ See also: **fiddle** while Rome burns

roof

go through the roof
if the level of something, especially a price, goes through the roof, it increases very quickly • *As a result of the war, oil prices have gone through the roof.*

the roof caves/falls in *American*
if the roof caves in, something very bad suddenly happens to you • *For the first six years of my life I was happy. Then my father died and the roof caved in.*

a roof over your **head**
somewhere to live • *We didn't have any money, but at least we had a roof over our heads and food in our stomachs.*

▶ See also: **hit** the ceiling/roof
raise the roof

rooftops

▶ See: **shout** sth from the rooftops

room

not room to swing a cat

not **room to swing a cat** *informal*
if there is not room to swing a cat in a place, that place is very small • *There isn't room to swing a cat in the third room, it's so tiny.* • *Get a sofa in the living room? You'll be lucky – there isn't room to swing a cat in there.*

roost

▶ See: **rule** the roost

root

root and branch *formal*
if something is changed or removed root and branch, it is changed or removed completely because it is bad • *Racism must be eliminated, root and branch.*
root-and-branch *formal* • (always before noun) *These proposals amount to a root-and-branch reform of the system.*

take root
if an idea, belief, or system takes root somewhere, it starts to be accepted or established there • *Democracy is now struggling to take root in most of these countries.*

rooted

▶ See: glued/rooted to the **spot**

roots

put down roots
if you put down roots in a place, you do things which show that you want to stay there, for example making friends or buying a home • *It would be hard to leave Brighton after eleven years – he's put down roots there.*

rope

give sb **enough rope (to hang** themselves**)**
to allow someone to do what they want to, knowing that they will probably fail or get into trouble • *I let him speak on, knowing that he would offend the director, and gave him just enough rope.*

▶ See also: Go **piss** up a rope!

ropes

be on the ropes *mainly American*
to be doing badly and likely to fail • *His political career is on the ropes.*

show sb **the ropes**
to explain to someone how to do a job or activity • *The new secretary started today so I spent most of the morning showing her the ropes.*
know the ropes • *She's been in this job long enough to know the ropes.*

rose-coloured

rose-coloured glasses *British & Australian*
rose-colored glasses *American & Australian*
rose-coloured spectacles *British*
if someone thinks about or looks at something with rose-coloured glasses, they think it is more pleasant than it really is • *She's nostalgic for a past that she sees through rose-colored glasses.*

roses

put the roses in sb's **cheeks**
bring the roses to sb's **cheeks**
to make someone look healthy • *A brisk walk will soon put the roses back in your cheeks.*

▶ See also: come out/up **smelling** of roses

rose-tinted

rose-tinted glasses *British, American & Australian*
rose-tinted spectacles *British*
if someone looks at something through rose-tinted glasses, they see only the pleasant parts of it • *She has always looked at life through rose-tinted glasses.*

rot

the rot sets in
if the rot sets in, a situation starts to get worse • *If couples stop communicating, that's when the rot really sets in.*

▶ See also: **stop** the rot

rotten

be rotten to the core
if a person or an organization is rotten to the core, it behaves in a way that is not honest or moral • *The whole legal system is rotten to the core.*

▶ See also: a bad/rotten **apple**
spoil sb rotten

rough

give sb **a rough time**
to treat someone severely or to cause difficulties for them • *The boss gives me a rough time if I make any mistakes.*
have a rough time (of it) • *She's had a rough time of it in prison.*

give sb **the rough side of** your **tongue** *British & Australian old-fashioned*
to speak angrily to someone • *The boss gave me the rough side of her tongue for being late twice this week.*

rough and ready
1 if you do something in a rough and ready way, you do it quickly and without preparing it carefully • *I've done a rough and ready translation of the instructions. I hope it's clear enough.*
2 not very polite or well educated • *Just a warning about the men who work for him,*

they're a bit rough and ready.

the rough and tumble of sth
the part of an activity that involves fighting or competing • *He enjoys the rough and tumble of politics.*
rough-and-tumble • (always before noun) *He is used to life in the rough-and-tumble airline industry.*

a rough diamond *British & Australian*
a diamond in the rough *American & Australian*
a person who does not seem very polite or well educated at first, although they have a good character • *Mitchell may have been a rough diamond, but he was absolutely loyal to his employer.*

rough edges
1 if a piece of work or a performance has rough edges, some parts of it are not of very good quality • *He's a great footballer, but his game still has a few rough edges.*
2 if a person has rough edges, they do not always behave well and politely • *I knew him before he was successful, and he had a lot of rough edges back then.*

rough it
to live in a way that is simple and not very comfortable • *They prefer to rough it on their travels, and sleep in the car or take a tent.*

rough justice
a punishment that is not fair or is too severe • *New evidence suggests that the girls were given rough justice.*

rough trade *very informal*
men who have sex with other men for money and who look as if they come from a low social class • *He went to the docks to pick up a bit of rough trade.*

take the rough with the smooth *British & Australian*
to accept the unpleasant parts of a situation as well as the pleasant parts • *You have to be prepared to take the rough with the smooth in marriage.*

► See also: **cut** up rough
when the **going** gets rough/tough
a bumpy/rough **ride**

roughshod

► See: **ride** roughshod over sth/sb

round

► See: round the **bend**

rounds

do the rounds *British & Australian*
make the rounds *American & Australian*
if you do the rounds of people, organizations, or places, you visit or telephone them all • (usually + **of**) *Tony and I made the rounds of the cheap bars in the city.* • *I've done the rounds of all the agents, but nobody has any tickets left.*

roving

a roving eye *humorous*
if someone has a roving eye, they are sexually attracted to people other than their partner • *She left her husband because she was fed up with his roving eye.*

row

a hard/tough row to hoe *American*
a difficult situation to deal with • *Teachers have a tough row to hoe in today's schools.*

► See also: **kick** up a fuss/row/stink

rub

rub it in *informal*

if someone rubs it in, they keep talking about something that makes you feel embarrassed or upset • *I know I made a mistake, but you don't have to rub it in.*

rub sb's **nose in it** *informal*
rub sb's **nose in the dirt** *informal*
to say or do something which makes someone remember that they have failed • *I didn't tell him I'd started another relationship. I didn't want to rub his nose in it.*

the rub of the green *mainly British*
if you have the rub of the green, you have good luck, especially in a sports competition • *This player hasn't had the rub of the green in the last few tournaments.*

rub salt in/into the wound
to make a difficult situation even worse for someone • *Losing was bad enough, having to watch them receiving the trophy just rubbed salt into the wound.*

rub shoulders with sb *British, American & Australian informal*
rub elbows with sb *American & Australian informal*
to spend time with famous people • *He's Hollywood's most popular hairdresser and regularly rubs shoulders with top movie stars.*

rub sb **up the wrong way** *British & Australian*
rub sb **the wrong way** *American*
to annoy someone without intending to • *It's not her fault – she just rubs me up the wrong way.* • *Whenever they meet, they always manage to rub each other the wrong way.*

There's the rub. *old-fashioned*
Therein lies the rub. *old-fashioned*
something that you say when you are explaining what the difficulty is in a particular situation • *You can't get a job unless you have experience. And there's the rub – how do you get experience if you can't get a job?*

rubber

a rubber check *American humorous*
a cheque (= a piece of paper from someone's bank that they sign and use for money) that is not worth anything because the person does not have enough money in the bank • *The woman was accused of writing more than $100,000 in rubber checks to pay for expensive jewelry.*

rubber-stamp

rubber-stamp sth
if someone rubber-stamps a decision or a plan, they give it official approval, often without thinking about it enough ✍If someone official has examined a document, they often put a special mark on it using a rubber stamp (= a small printing device made of rubber). • *School governors will not simply rubber-stamp what teachers have already decided.* • *The court was asked to rubber-stamp the Department's decision to free the men.*
a rubber stamp • *The committee is just a rubber stamp for the president's policies.*

Rube

Rube Goldberg *American informal*
a Rube Goldberg piece of equipment or plan is very complicated and not very practical ✍Rube Goldberg was an American who drew funny pictures for newspapers showing complicated inventions. • *They use a Rube Goldberg type contraption to open and close the farm gate.* • *The city is not well served by this Rube Goldberg scheme for economic development.*

Rubicon

▶ See: **cross** the Rubicon

rude

a rude awakening
if you have a rude awakening, you have a severe shock when you discover the truth of a situation • *We had a rude awakening when we saw the amount of our phone bill.* • *You've been so spoiled by your parents, you are **in for a rude awakening** when you start to look after yourself.*

ruffle

ruffle sb's **feathers**
to make someone annoyed • *He wasn't asked to speak at the conference, and I know that ruffled his feathers a bit.*

ruffled

▶ See: **smooth** (sb's) ruffled feathers

rug

▶ See: **cut** a rug
pull the rug from under sb/sth
sweep sth under the mat/rug

ruin

go to rack/wrack and ruin *old-fashioned*
if a building goes to rack and ruin, its condition becomes very bad because no one is taking care of it • *She's let that house go to rack and ruin since Clive died.*

rule

a rule of thumb
a way of calculating something which is not exact but which will help you to be correct enough ✍A rule of thumb was originally a way of measuring using the width or length of your thumb. • *A good rule of thumb is to cook two handfuls of rice per person.*

rule the roost
to be the most powerful person who

makes all the decisions in a group • *It was my mother who ruled the roost at home.*

rule (sb) **with a rod of iron** *British, American & Australian*
rule (sb) **with an iron fist/hand** *American & Australian*
to control a group of people very firmly, having complete power over everything that they do • *For 17 years she ruled the country with a rod of iron.* • *My uncle rules the family business with an iron hand.*

rules

bend/stretch the rules
to do something or to allow someone to do something which is not usually allowed • *We don't usually let students take books away, but I'm willing to bend the rules on this occasion.*

rum

a rum do *British old-fashioned*
if a situation is a rum do, it is strange and people often do not approve of it • *All three of his ex-wives still live with him. It's a rum do if you ask me.*

rumpy-pumpy

rumpy-pumpy *British & Australian humorous*
sexual activity • *So I asked her if she fancied* ***a bit of rumpy-pumpy****.*

run

be on the run
to try to avoid being caught, especially by the police • *A serial killer was on the run last night after escaping from a maximum-security prison.* • (sometimes + **from**) *He met his future wife while he was on the run from the police in Germany.*

a dry run *British, American & Australian*
a dummy run *British & Australian*
an occasion when you practise doing something to make sure there will be no problems when you really do it • *We decided to do a dry run at the church the day before the wedding.* • *We'd better have a couple of dummy runs before we do the real thing.*

give sb **a run for** their **money**
to compete very strongly against someone who is expected to win a competition • *I think only Liverpool will be able to give Manchester United a run for their money next season.*

have sb **on the run**
to be in a strong position to defeat someone • *After last night's broadcast debate, he has the opposition candidate on the run.*

have the run of swh
to be allowed to go anywhere in an area • *The children had the run of the farm all week.*

in the long/short run
a long or short time in the future • *It means spending a bit now, but in the long run it'll save us a lot of money.* • *Although prices may rise in the short run, they should begin to fall again by the end of the year.*

make a run for it
to suddenly run fast in order to escape from somewhere or get to somewhere • *When the guard turned away, the two prisoners made a run for it.* • *Let's make a run for it as soon as the rain lets up a bit.*

run a mile *informal*
if you say that someone would run a mile if they had to deal with a particular situation, you mean that they would do anything to avoid it • *He flirts the whole time but it's not serious – he'd run a mile if a woman actually made him an offer.*

run a tight ship
to control a business or other organization firmly and effectively • *Ruth runs a tight ship and has no time for shirkers.*

run and run *mainly British*
if a subject or an argument is going to run and run, people will continue to be interested in it for a long time • *We've had over 500 letters on the subject of human cloning. It looks like* ***this one will run and run****.*

run before you **can walk**
to try to do something complicated and difficult before you have learned the basic skills you need to attempt it • *I think you should stick to a simple menu*

for your dinner party. There's no point ***trying to run before you can walk.***

run in the family

run in the family
if a particular quality or ability runs in the family, a lot of people in that family have it • *Athletic ability runs in the family: his father played basketball in college and his mother was a high school athlete.*

run interference *American*
to help someone achieve something by dealing with the people or problems that might prevent them from doing so • (usually + **for**) *When it comes to finding a hotel room, you'll be glad to have a tourist guide run interference for you.*

run sth **into the ground**
to treat something so badly or use something so much that you destroy it • *I loaned her my car for 6 months and she ran it into the ground.*

run its course
if something runs its course, it continues naturally until it has finished • *Many people believe that feminism has run its course.* • *The doctor insisted I rest for a few days while the infection ran its course.*

run like the wind
to run very fast • *She's very slight in build and she can run like the wind.*

run off at the mouth *American informal*
to talk a lot without saying anything important • *He's just another one of these politicians who run off at the mouth.*

run out of steam *British informal*
run out of gas *American & Australian informal*
to suddenly lose the energy or interest to continue doing what you are doing • *She'd been talking for two hours and was just starting to run out of steam.* • *I worked really well for two months of the project then I suddenly ran out of gas.*

run sb **ragged**
to make someone very tired, usually by making them work too hard • *What with party preparations and having to look after the kids all this week, I've been run ragged.*

run rings around/round sb
to have much more skill, ability, or intelligence than someone else • *Why does he talk to Alison as if she's stupid, when we all know she could run rings around him?*

run scared *mainly American*
to be worried that you are going to be defeated • (usually in continuous tenses) *There are rumours that the Democrats are running scared after recent opinion polls showed their rivals to be way out in front.*

run the gauntlet
to have to deal with a lot of people who are criticizing or attacking you • (usually + **of**) *The minister had to run the gauntlet of anti-nuclear protesters when he arrived at the plant.*

run the show *informal*
to be in charge of an organization or an activity • (often in continuous tenses) *He started off working in the kitchen and now he's running the show.*

run sb **to earth** *British & Australian*
to find someone after searching for them • *The film star was run to earth by reporters in an exclusive golf complex.*

run sb **to ground** *British & Australian*
to find someone after searching for a long time • *Chinese detectives ran him to ground in a Shanghai night club.*

run sth **up the flagpole** *mainly American*
to tell people about an idea in order to see what they think of it • *Run your suggestion up the flagpole and see what the others say.*

run with the hare and hunt with the hounds *old-fashioned*
to support two competing sides in an argument • *You've got to decide where you stand on this issue. You can't run with the hare and hunt with the hounds.*

▶ See also: run out the **clock**
go/run/work like **clockwork**
go/run **deep**
cast/run your/an **eye** over sth
be run/rushed off your **feet**
have a **good** run for your money
drive/run/work yourself into the **ground**
go/run to **seed**

runaround

give sb **the runaround** *informal*
to act in a way which makes it difficult for someone to do something, for example by refusing to tell them things they need to know • *I'm trying to get a visa, but the embassy staff keep giving me the runaround.*
get the runaround *informal* • *Every time I phone to complain, I keep getting the runaround.*

runes

▶ See: **read** the runes

rung

the [first/highest/next etc.] rung on the ladder
the first, highest, next etc. position, especially in society or in a job • *In our society, a nurse is hardly on the same rung of the ladder as a judge.* • *President of the Union at Oxford University was the first rung on the political ladder for him.*

running

(Go) take a running jump! *informal*
an impolite way of telling someone to go away or that you will not give them something they want • *'Jim wants to borrow your new CD.' 'Tell him to take a running jump.'*

be in the running
if you are in the running for something, you are in a good position to win it or achieve it • (often + **for**) *This film must be in the running for a Best Picture Oscar.*
out of the running • *Her poor health has put her out of the running for the election.*

be running on empty *informal*
1 to continue to work and be active when you have no energy left • *I get the impression he's been running on empty for months now. A holiday will do him good.*
2 *American & Australian* if a person or an organization is running on empty, they have no new ideas or are not as effective as they were before • *The fund-raising campaign was running on empty after ten years under the same leader.*

do/make (all) the running *British*
to be the person who causes things to happen and develop • *Men are no longer expected to do all the running at the beginning of a relationship.* • *If we want this campaign to be a success, it's up to us to make the running.*

a running battle
if you have a running battle with someone, you have an argument that continues over a long period of time • (often + **with**) *I've had a running battle with the neighbours over their kids throwing stones over the fence.*

run-of-the-mill

run-of-the-mill
ordinary • *It's just a run-of-the-mill war film.*

rush

a (sudden) rush of blood (to the head)
if you have a rush of blood to the head, you suddenly feel very excited or very angry, and do or say something silly • *Thomson was sent off for head-butting Gray in a rush of blood to the head.*

rushed

▶ See: be run/rushed off your **feet**

Russian

▶ See: **play** Russian roulette

rut

be (stuck) in a rut
to do the same things all the time so that you become bored, or to be in a situation where it is impossible to make progress

• *At forty my life was in a rut, so I gave up work and travelled to India.* • *It's clear the economy is still stuck in a rut.*

get in/into a rut • *When you have to cook dinner every night it's easy to get into a rut.*

[drag/get/lift etc.] sb/sth **out of a/** their **rut** to help someone or something to change their situation and to make progress • *The president has to get his election campaign out of a rut.*

Ss

sabre-rattling

sabre-rattling *British, American & Australian*
saber-rattling *American*
threatening behaviour which is intended to frighten someone • *After months of sabre-rattling, the two sides have agreed to a peaceful resolution of their differences.*

sack

get the sack
to be told to leave your job • *He got the sack when they found out that he'd lied about his qualifications.*
give sb **the sack** • *After only 2 weeks she was given the sack for being rude to a customer.*

▶ See also: **hit** the sack

sackcloth

sackcloth and ashes *slightly formal*
if you wear sackcloth and ashes, you show by your behaviour that you are very sorry for something you did wrong ✍In the past, clothes made of sackcloth (= a rough cloth) were worn by the Jews in religious activities to show that they were sad or sorry for the things they had done wrong. • *I've already apologized. How long must I* ***wear sackcloth and ashes*** *before you'll forgive me?*

sacred

a sacred cow
a belief or system that is treated with much respect and is not usually criticized • *The British legal system remains a sacred cow, despite increasing evidence that serious mistakes have been made.*

sacrificed

be sacrificed on the altar of sth *formal*
to be destroyed by an activity, system or belief that is bad but more important or more powerful • *Service and quality have been sacrificed on the altar of profit.*

sadder

sadder but wiser
if someone is sadder but wiser after a bad experience, they have suffered but they have also learned something from it • *He bought a second-hand car and ended up sadder but wiser after a series of breakdowns and expensive repairs.*

saddle

be in the saddle
to be in control of a situation • *With a new leader firmly in the saddle the party looks set for victory at the next election.*

safe

be as safe as houses *British & Australian*
to be very safe • *Don't worry, I've locked your bicycle in the shed – it's as safe as houses.*

be in safe hands
if someone or something is in safe hands, they are being looked after by someone who can be trusted • *I know my daughter's in safe hands at the nursery.*

safe and sound
if you are safe and sound, you are not harmed in any way, although you were in a dangerous situation • *It was a difficult drive but we all arrived safe and sound.*

a safe pair of hands *British & Australian*
someone who you can trust to do an important job well without making mistakes • *He's what this troubled club needs, a good, solid manager, a safe pair of hands.*

to be on the safe side
if you do something to be on the safe side, you do something that may not be necessary in order to protect yourself against possible problems • *I don't think there are any broken bones, but you should have an X-ray* ***just to be on the safe side****.*

▶ See also: a safe **bet**
better (to be) safe than sorry.
play (it) safe

safety

a safety net
a system or arrangement that helps you if

you have problems, especially financial problems • (often + **for**) *The hardship fund provides a safety net for students who run out of money before they've completed their course.*

a safety valve
a way of allowing someone to express strong or negative emotions without harming other people • (often + **for**) *I often think football acts as a safety valve for a lot of stored-up male aggression.*

There's safety in numbers.
something that you say which means if people do something difficult or unpleasant together, they are less likely to get harmed or blamed • *Working on the principle that there's safety in numbers, we decided we should all go and complain together.*

said

there's [much/a lot etc.] to be said for sth/doing sth
something that you say which means that something has a lot of advantages • *There's a lot to be said for living alone.*

when all is said and done
something that you say when you are about to tell someone the most important fact in a situation • *When all is said and done, a child's moral upbringing is the parents' responsibility.*

sail

sail close to the wind
to do something that is dangerous or only just legal or acceptable • (often in continuous tenses) *I think she realized she was sailing a little too close to the wind and decided to tone down her criticism.*

sail under false colours *British & Australian*
sail under false colors *American & Australian*
to pretend to be something that you are not in order to deceive people ✍If a ship sails under false colours, it uses the flag of another country in order to deceive people. • *Lewis was sailing under false colours – he never told her he was a journalist.*

sails

▶ See: **trim** your sails

salad

your **salad days** *old-fashioned*
the time when you were young and had little experience of life • *But that was **in my salad days**, before I got married and had children.*

salt

any [judge/lawyer/teacher etc.] worth their **salt**
any judge, lawyer, teacher etc. who is good at their job • *Any lawyer worth his salt should be aware of the latest changes in taxation.* • *No judge worth her salt would attempt to influence the jury.*

be the salt of the earth
if someone is the salt of the earth, they are a very good and honest person • *His mother's the salt of the earth. She'd give you her last penny.*

take sth **with a pinch of salt** *British & Australian*
take sth **with a grain of salt** *American & Australian*
if you take what someone says with a pinch of salt, you do not completely believe it • *You have to take everything she says with a pinch of salt. She has a tendency to exaggerate.* • *It's interesting to read the reports in the newspapers, but I tend to take them with a grain of salt.*

▶ See also: **rub** salt in/into the wound

same

be in the same boat
to be in the same unpleasant situation as other people • *She's always complaining that she doesn't have enough money, but we're all in the same boat.* • (often + **as**) *If he loses his job he'll be in the same boat as any other unemployed person.*

by the same token
something that you say which means that the thing you are going to say next is true for the same reasons as the thing you have just said • *When he liked a person, he loved them, and, by the same token, when he didn't like a person, he hated them.*

in the same breath
1 if you say two things in the same breath, you say two things that are so different that if one is true the other must be false • *She said she didn't love him any more*

but in the same breath said how wonderful he was.

2 if you talk about two people or things in the same breath, you think they are very similar • (often + **as**) *He's a relatively new director but his name has been mentioned in the same breath as Hitchcock.*

not **in the same league**
not nearly as good as something or someone else • (often + **as**) *My four-year-old computer's just not in the same league as the latest machines with their super-fast processors.*

It's the same old story.
something that you say when a bad situation has happened many times before • *It's the same old story – the women do all the work and the men just sit around talking.*

Same difference.
something that you say which means that the difference between two things is not important • *They were married for forty years, or was it thirty? Same difference – it was a long time anyway.*

same old same old *informal*
used to say that a situation or someone's behaviour remains the same, especially when it is boring or annoying • *'How's work going?' 'Oh, you know. Same old same old.'*

speak/talk the same language
if two people speak the same language, they have similar beliefs and opinions, and express themselves in similar ways • *There's no use setting up a meeting between the environmentalists and the construction company – they just don't speak the same language.*

▶ See also: It's **all** the same to me.
be **cut** from the same cloth
be of the same **mind**
sing the same tune
tar sb with the same brush
be on the same **wavelength**

sand

▶ See: be **built** on sand

sandwich

be one sandwich short of a picnic *humorous*
be a couple of sandwiches short of a picnic *humorous*
if someone is one sandwich short of a picnic, they are stupid or crazy • *After talking to him for about 10 minutes I decided he was definitely one sandwich short of a picnic.*

sang froid

sang froid
the ability to stay calm in a difficult or dangerous situation • *She showed remarkable sang froid despite a rude and noisy audience.*

sarcasm

Sarcasm is the lowest form of wit.
something that you say which means that using sarcasm (= saying the opposite of what you mean to make a joke) is unpleasant and is not a very clever thing to do • *'We're so grateful to you for arriving only 20 minutes late!' 'Oh really, Matthew, don't you know sarcasm is the lowest form of wit?'*

sardines

▶ See: be **packed** like sardines

sauce

▶ See: What's sauce for the **goose** (is sauce for the gander).

save

can't do sth **to save** your **life** *informal*
if you say that someone can't do something to save their life, you mean that they are extremely bad at that thing • *I can't draw to save my life.*

save sb's **bacon** *mainly British informal*
to save someone from failure or difficulties • *You saved my bacon there. I'd probably have lost my job if you hadn't been ready with an explanation.*

save face
to do something so that people will continue to respect you • *Are the ministers involved more interested in saving face than telling the truth?*
face-saving • (always before noun) *They denied that the decision to sack the director was simply a face-saving exercise.*

save (sth) **for a rainy day**
to keep an amount of money for a time in the future when it might be needed • *She has a couple of thousand pounds kept aside which she's saving for a rainy day.*
a rainy day fund an amount of money that you have saved • *I'm hoping that I can pay for my holiday without dipping into my rainy day fund.*

save sb's **neck**
to prevent something bad from happening to someone • *You really saved my neck. I'd have been in so much trouble if you'd told him the truth.*

save your **own skin**
to protect yourself from danger or difficulties, without worrying about other people • *He saved his own skin by telling them his partner had taken the money.*

save sb's **skin**
to save someone from failure or difficulties • *You saved my skin telling my parents I stayed with you last night.*

save the day
to do something that solves a serious problem • *Schwarzenegger saves the day by arriving just in time to shoot the kidnappers and rescue the hostages.*

► See also: save/spare sb's **blushes**

saved

Saved by the bell.
something that you say when a difficult situation is ended suddenly before you have to do or say something that you do not want to ✍In a boxing match, a bell rings when it is time for the fighting to stop. • *Luckily, my bus arrived before I had time to reply. Saved by the bell.*

saving

a saving grace
a good quality that makes you like something or someone although you do not like anything else about them • *It's a small cinema and the seats are uncomfortable, but the saving grace is that people aren't allowed to eat during the film.*

savoir-faire

savoir-faire
the ability to do or say the right thing in any social situation • *She demonstrates great savoir-faire when dealing with clients.*

say

before you **can say Jack Robinson**
old-fashioned
if you say that something happens before you can say Jack Robinson, it happens very suddenly • *I offered her a chocolate but before you could say Jack Robinson she'd eaten half the box.*

I/You can't say fairer than that.
British & Australian informal
something that you say in order to tell someone that an offer you have made is fair and that you think they should accept it • *I'll wash the dishes if you cook dinner. You can't say fairer than that, can you?*

not **say boo** *American informal*
to say nothing • *She expected the boss to be really angry, but he didn't say boo.*

Say cheese! *informal*
something that someone who is taking a photograph of you tells you to say so that your mouth makes the shape of a smile • *OK everyone, look at the camera and say cheese.*

say your **piece**
to express your opinion about something, especially something that you do not like • *I don't feel there's anything more I can add now – I've said my piece.*

say the word
if you tell someone that they only have to say the word and you will do something for them, you mean that you will do it immediately if they ask you • *You **only have to say the word** and I'll come and help.* • ***Just say the word** and the boys'll make sure he never gives you any more trouble.*

say uncle *American informal*
to admit that you have been defeated ✍In children's fights, a child being held down had to say 'uncle' before being allowed to get up. • *I'm determined to show them I can be a star. I'm not going to say uncle.*

wouldn't say boo to a goose *British informal*
wouldn't say boo *American informal*
wouldn't say boo to a fly *Australian informal*
if someone wouldn't say boo to a goose, they are shy and nervous • *She wouldn't say boo to a goose, so I don't think she's cut out for a career in the police.* • *I remember her as a quiet little girl who wouldn't say boo.*

You can say that again! *informal*
something that you say in order to show you completely agree with something that someone has just said • *'That was an absolutely delicious lunch.' 'You can say that again!'*

► See also: pretend/say that **black** is white
kiss/say/wave **goodbye** to sth

saying

It goes without saying.
something that you say when you believe that what you will say next is generally accepted or understood • *It goes without saying that we're delighted about the new baby.*

says

What sb **says goes.** *informal*
something that you say in order to tell someone which person in a group makes the final decisions about what happens • *Maria's the team leader and what she says goes.*

scales

The scales fall from sb's **eyes.** *literary*
if the scales fall from someone's eyes, they are suddenly able to understand the truth • *When I saw his photograph in the paper, the scales fell from my eyes and I realized I'd been conned.*

► See also: **tip** the scales

scalp

be out for/after sb's **scalp** *mainly American*
to want to punish someone because you blame them for something bad that has happened • *The mayor has made one mistake too many and the voters are out for his scalp.*

scandal

a scandal sheet *American & Australian informal*
a newspaper or magazine that contains many articles about shocking or surprising events • *It's just a scandal sheet – full of murders, beatings, suicides and little else.*

scarce

be as scarce as hen's teeth *American & Australian*
to be very difficult or impossible to find • *It was the President's inauguration and hotel rooms in Washington were as scarce as hen's teeth.*

make yourself **scarce** *informal*
to leave, especially in order to avoid trouble • *I think you'd better make yourself scarce – at least until I've had a chance to talk to your father.*

scare

scare the shit out of sb *taboo*
to make someone feel very frightened • *I wish you wouldn't come in without knocking – you scared the shit out of me.*
be shit scared *taboo* to be very frightened • *But you hate heights! I bet you were shit scared on the big wheel.*

► See also: frighten/scare the (living) **daylights** out of sb
frighten/scare the **hell** out of sb
frighten/scare the **life** out of sb
frighten/scare sb out of their **wits**

scared

be scared shitless *British, American & Australian taboo*
be scared shit *American taboo*
to be very frightened • *I was woken by the sound of someone moving around downstairs – I was scared shitless!*

► See also: **run** scared

scaredy-cat

a scaredy-cat *informal*
someone who is frightened when there is no reason to be ✍This phrase is used especially by children. • *Go on you scaredy-cat, jump in.*

scarlet

a scarlet woman *old-fashioned*
a woman who people think is morally bad

because she has sex with a lot of men • *She was labelled a scarlet woman and excluded from polite society.*

scattered

be scattered to the four winds *literary*
if a group of things or people are scattered to the four winds, they are sent to different places which are far away from each other • *Homes were destroyed and families were scattered to the four winds.*

scenario

the nightmare/worst-case scenario
the worst thing that could possibly happen • *I suppose the worst-case scenario would be if both of us lost our jobs at the same time.*

scene

▶ See: **set** the scene
set the scene for sth

scenes

behind the scenes
if something happens behind the scenes, it happens secretly, especially when something else is happening publicly • *Diplomats have been working hard behind the scenes in preparation for the peace talks.*
behind-the-scenes • (always before noun) *The Government presented a united front to the cameras, showing no sign of the behind-the-scenes discord of the last few days.*

scent

put/throw sb **off the scent**
if you throw someone off the scent, you give them false or confusing information to try to stop them discovering something ✍A scent is a smell produced by an animal which can act as a signal to other animals trying to find or follow it. • *The police were thrown off the scent for a while by false evidence given by two of the witnesses.*

scent blood
to believe that someone you are competing against is having difficulties or problems and to use this to get an advantage for yourself • *The manager has already made some serious errors of judgement and it is clear that other employees scent blood.*

scheme

in the grand/great scheme of things
if you say that in the grand scheme of things something is not important, you mean that it is not important when compared to much more serious things • *In the grand scheme of things, whether another actress has her navel pierced is not really that significant.*

school

the school of hard knocks
learning through difficult experiences • *An early training in the school of hard knocks was good preparation for a career in politics.*

schoolboy

schoolboy humour *British & Australian*
schoolboy humor *American & Australian*
stupid jokes that are rude but not very offensive • *Isn't he a bit old for this type of schoolboy humour?*

science

▶ See: **blind** sb with science

score

▶ See: **know** the score
settle a score

scot-free

get away/off scot-free *informal*
to avoid the punishment that you deserve or expect • *If you don't take out a complaint against him he'll get off scot-free!*

scrap

▶ See: **throw** sb/sth on the scrap heap

scrape

scrape the barrel *informal*
to use something or someone that you do not want to use because nothing or no one else is available • (usually in continuous tenses) *You know you're really scraping the barrel when you have to ask your old mother to come to the cinema with you.*

scratch

not **be up to scratch**
to not be of an acceptable standard or quality • *I'm afraid your last essay wasn't up to scratch.*
not **come up to scratch** *British & Australian* • *Under the new system, we will not continue to employ teachers whose work doesn't come up to scratch.*
bring sb/sth **up to scratch** *British & Australian* • *If you practise hard on this piece you should be able to bring it up to scratch by next week.*

from scratch
if you do something from scratch, you start right at the beginning • *We lost all our work in the fire and had to* ***start from scratch.*** • *George built a garage from scratch.*

scratch the surface
if you scratch the surface of a subject or a problem, you only discover or deal with a very small part of it • (usually + **of**) *Up to now newspaper articles have only scratched the surface of this tremendously complex issue.*

You scratch my back and I'll scratch yours.
I'll scratch your back if you scratch mine.
something that you say to tell someone that you will help them if they will help you • *I do have some information you might be interested in, but what can you offer me in return? You scratch my back and I'll scratch yours.*

scream

scream blue murder *British, American & Australian informal*
scream bloody murder *American & Australian informal*
to shout or to complain very loudly • *Readers screamed blue murder when the price of their daily paper went up.* • *Someone took the child's ice cream away and he started screaming bloody murder.*

scream the place down *informal*
to scream very loudly • *You can scream the place down if you like, but no one will hear you.*

screw

have a screw loose *informal*
to be crazy • *I think that woman has a screw loose – she goes out in her slippers.*

screw up your **courage**
to force yourself to be brave and do something that makes you nervous • *She screwed up her courage and asked to see the manager.*

screws

put the screws on sb *informal*
to use force or threats to make someone do what you want ✍In the past, screws or thumbscrews were devices used to hurt people by crushing their thumbs in order to force them to do something. • *They put the screws on him until eventually he was forced to resign.*
tighten/turn the screws on sb *informal* • *The police are turning the screws on drivers who don't wear their seat belts by fining them.*

scrimp

scrimp and save
to spend very little money, especially because you are saving it to buy something expensive • (often + to do sth) *We had to scrimp and save to buy our first house.*

scum

the scum of the earth *very informal*
if a group of people are the scum of the earth, they are the worst type of people ✍Scum is a layer of unpleasant or dirty substance that has formed on top of a liquid. • *People who abuse children are the scum of the earth.*

sea

be at sea *British, American & Australian*
be all at sea *British & Australian*
if someone is at sea, they are completely confused • *I'm all at sea with this computer manual.*

a sea change *literary*
a complete change • (often + **in**) *The huge increase in the number of people working freelance represents a sea change in patterns of employment over the last 10 years.*

your **sea legs**
the ability to keep your balance when

walking on a moving ship and not feel ill • *It took me a while to* ***get my sea legs****, but I feel fine now.*

seal

put/set the seal on sth *slightly formal*
to make something certain or complete • *The ambassador's visit set the seal on the trade agreement between the two countries.*

seal sb's **fate**
if an event seals someone's fate, they are certain to fail or to have an unpleasant experience in the future • *His father's illness sealed his fate – Sam gave up his hopes of a college education and stayed home to run the family business.*

seams

be bulging/bursting at the seams *informal*
if a place is bursting at the seams, it has a very large number of people or things in it • *All my family came to stay for the wedding and our little house was bursting at the seams.*

be coming/falling apart at the seams
1 if a system or organization is coming apart at the seams, it is in a very bad condition and likely to fail • *For a while it seemed that the whole Asian economy was just coming apart at the seams.*
2 if someone is coming apart at the seams, they are feeling extremely upset and have difficulty continuing to do the things they usually do • *It's no excuse, but we were all working really hard and none of us noticed that Rory was just falling apart at the seams.*

search

Search me! *informal*
something that you say when you do not know the answer to a question • *'Where's Jack gone?' 'Search me!'*

▶ See also: hunt/search **high** and low

seat

be in the driving seat *British*
be in the driver's seat *American & Australian*
to be in control of a situation • *The consumer is in the driving seat due to the huge range of goods on the market.*

▶ See also: **fly** by the seat of your pants

seats

bums on seats *British & Australian informal*
fannies in the seats *American informal*
if a public performance or a sports event puts bums on seats, many people pay to go and see it • *This production needs a big name to* ***put bums on seats****.*

second

be second to none
to be better than anything or anyone else • *The hotel's restaurant facilities are second to none.*

come off second best
to be beaten in a competition or an argument • *I've given up arguing with my big brother because I always come off second best.*

get a/your **second wind** *British, American & Australian*
get a/your **second breath** *American*
to suddenly have new energy to continue doing something after you were feeling tired • *After two hours we could hardly walk another step, but we got a second wind as we neared home.*

have second thoughts
if you have second thoughts about something, you change your opinion or start to have doubts about it • (often + **about**) *You're not having second thoughts about coming to Brighton with me, are you?*

on second thoughts *British & Australian* • *I'll have tea, please – on second thoughts, make that coffee.*

second best
something that is not as good as the thing that you really want • *I know exactly what sort of apartment I'm looking for and I'm not going to settle for second best.*

without a second thought
if you do something without a second thought, you do it without thinking about whether or not you should • *She doesn't worry about money – she'll spend a hundred pounds on a dress without a second thought.*

not **give** sth **a second thought**
• *He'd fire you if he had to – he wouldn't give it a second thought.*

▶ See also: **play** second fiddle

second-class

a second-class citizen
someone who is treated as if they are less important than other people in society • *Although she was married to an Australian, Louise couldn't get a work visa and it made her feel like a second-class citizen.*

second-guess

second-guess sb/sth
1 to try to guess what will happen or what someone will do • *It's not for us to second-guess the court's decision – we'll just have to wait and see.*
2 to criticize someone's actions or an event after it has happened • *It's easy to second-guess the team's coach – but let's face it, he made big mistakes.*

see

be [glad/happy/pleased etc.] to see the back of sb/sth
to be pleased when someone leaves or when something ends because you did not like them • *She was an absolute pain when she stayed with us and we were both really pleased to see the back of her.* • *I'll be glad to see the back of this thesis. It's been going on far too long.*

can't see the wood for the trees *British, American & Australian*
can't see the forest for the trees *American & Australian*
if someone can't see the wood for the trees, they are unable to understand what is important in a situation because they are giving too much attention to details • *After you've spent years researching a single topic you get to a point where you can't see the wood for the trees.*

go to see a man about a dog *humorous*
if you tell someone you are going to see a man about a dog, it is a way of saying that you do not want to tell them where you are really going, especially when you are going to the toilet • *I won't be long. I'm just going to see a man about a dog.*

see eye to eye
if two people see eye to eye, they agree with each other • (often negative; often + **with**) *He's asked for a transfer because he doesn't see eye to eye with the new manager.* • (often + **on**) *We see eye to eye on most important issues.*

not **see** sb **for dust** *British & Australian informal*
if you say that you won't see someone for dust, you mean that they will leave a place very quickly, usually in order to avoid something • *If you tell her that Jim's coming, you won't see her for dust!*

see sb/sth **for what** they **(really) are**
to start to understand the truth about someone or something, especially when the truth is bad • *She suddenly saw him for what he was – a cold-hearted, calculating killer.*

see it coming
to see that something is likely to happen, especially something bad • *I wasn't surprised when the company closed down. You* ***could see it coming.***

see life
if someone wants or needs to see life, they want or need to experience many different things, especially by travelling around the world and meeting interesting people • *Young people should see life before they get jobs and buy houses and do other boring things like that!* • *He's decided to do a round-the-world trip, he wants to see life a bit before he starts university.*

see red
to become very angry • *When he laughed in my face, I just saw red.*

see sb **right**
1 *British informal* to give someone money, especially in payment for work they have done • *Go and talk to Mr Mason when you've finished – he'll see you right.*
2 *British & Australian informal* to help someone • *If you run into a problem, speak to Lucy. She'll see you right.*

see the light
1 to understand something clearly, especially after you have been confused about it for a long time • *Sarah used to have very racist views, but I think she's finally seen the light.*
2 to start believing in a religion, often suddenly • *I hope my book will help others to see the light.*

see which way the cat jumps *Australian informal*
to delay making a decision or doing something until you know what is going to happen or what other people are going to do • *We'd better wait and see which way the cat jumps before we commit ourselves.*

see which way the wind is blowing
see how the wind is blowing
to see how a situation is developing before you make a decision about it • *I think we ought to talk to other members of staff and see which way the wind's blowing before we make any firm decisions.*

see your way (clear) to doing sth *old-fashioned*
to be able to do something and agree to do it • *Do you think you could see your way clear to lending me a bit more money?*

would see sb **in hell before** you **would** do sth
if you say that you would see someone in hell before you would do something, especially something that they have asked you to do, you mean that you would never do that thing • *I'd see her in hell before I'd agree to an arrangement like that.*

▶ See also: see the **error** of your ways
meet/see sb in the **flesh**
find out/see how the **land** lies
see sb in their **true** colours

seed

go/run to seed
to stop taking care of your appearance so that you no longer look attractive • *I almost didn't recognize John. He's really gone to seed since his wife left him.*

seed money *American & Australian*
money that is used to start a business or other activity • *With $250,000 in seed money they started to recruit executives and advisers for their new venture.*

seeds

▶ See: **sow** the seeds of sth

seeing

Seeing is believing.
something that you say which means you can only believe that something surprising or strange is true if you see it yourself • *I'd never have imagined my parents could dance, but seeing is believing.*

seem

▶ See: make sth seem like a **picnic**

seen

have seen better days *humorous*
if something or someone has seen better days, they are not in such a good condition as they used to be • *Our washing machine has seen better days.* • *We were met at the hotel entrance by an ageing porter who had evidently seen better days.*

have to be seen to be believed
if something has to be seen to be believed, it is so surprising or shocking that it is difficult to believe • *The devastation had to be seen to be believed.*

haven't seen hide nor hair of sb/sth *informal*
if you have not seen hide nor hair of someone or something, you have not seen them for a period of time • (often + **since**) *I haven't seen hide nor hair of her since last Sunday, and I'm beginning to get rather worried.*

▶ See also: wouldn't be caught/seen **dead**
have heard/seen the **last** of sb/sth

seize

seize the day *formal*
to use an opportunity to do something that you want and not to worry about the future • *Seize the day, young man. You may never get the chance to embark on such an adventure again.*

self-made

a self-made man
a man who is rich and successful as a result of his own work and not because his family had a lot of money • *Critchley was a self-made man who learned accounting while working in a brush factory.*

sell

sell sb **a bill of goods** *American*
to make someone believe something that is not true • *Politicians have sold all of us a bill of goods, that if we put more people in prison we're going to be safer.* • *The electrician said I'd need the outdoor*

lighting on a different circuit – is he just selling me a bill of goods?

sell sb **down the river**
to do something which harms or disappoints someone who trusted you, in order to get an advantage for yourself • *A lot of people feel they have been sold down the river by a government who have failed to keep their pre-election promises.*

sell sb/sth **short**
to not value someone or something as much as they deserve to be valued • *I'm fed up with people selling this country short.* • (often reflexive) *'Who'd employ me at my age?' 'Don't sell yourself short! You're intelligent and you've got loads of experience.'*

sell your **soul (to the devil)**
to do something bad in order to succeed or get money or power • *As far as Mike was concerned, he badly wanted the job and he'd sell his soul to the devil to get it.*

▶ See also: the **hard** sell
go/sell like **hot** cakes

send

send sb **away with a flea in** their **ear**
British & Australian informal
to angrily tell someone to go away • *A young kid came asking for money but I sent him away with a flea in his ear.*

send sb **packing** *informal*
to tell someone to go away, usually because you are annoyed with them • *There were some kids at the door asking for money, but I sent them packing.*

send shivers down/up sb's **spine**
to make someone feel very frightened or excited • *The way he looked at me sent shivers down my spine.*

send sb **to Coventry** *British informal*
if a group of people send someone to Coventry, they refuse to speak to them, usually in order to punish them • *The other workers sent him to Coventry for not supporting the strike.*

send sb **to the showers** *American*
to stop someone, especially someone on a sports team, from playing or working because they are behaving badly or their work is not good enough • *A fight broke out and both players were sent to the showers.*

▶ See also: drive/send sb round the **bend**
send sb on a **guilt** trip
send/throw sb into a **tizz**/tizzy
drive/send sb round the **twist**

sense

▶ See: **knock** (some) sense into sb

senses

come to your **senses**
to start to understand that you have been behaving in a stupid way • *So you've finally realized what a mistake you're making. I wondered how long it would take you to come to your senses.*
bring sb **to** their **senses** • *It was my father who finally brought me to my senses by telling me that if I didn't go back to college I might regret it for the rest of my life.*

separate

separate the wheat from the chaff
to choose the things or people that are of high quality from a group of mixed quality • *A preliminary look through the applications will help you to separate the wheat from the chaff.*

▶ See also: separate/sort out/the **men** from the boys
separate the **sheep** from the goats

serve

serve sb **right**
if something bad that happens serves someone right, they deserve it • ***It would serve you right** if your children never spoke to you again.* • *And she didn't get the promotion she'd hoped for, which served her right for being so smug.*

set

be set in concrete
if an arrangement, a plan or a rule is set in concrete, it is completely fixed so that it cannot be changed • (usually negative) *We've drawn up some rough guidelines – they're by no means set in concrete.*

set your **face against** sth/doing sth
formal
to be determined not to do something • *Despite fierce competition from rival companies, they've set their face against price cuts.*

set great/much store by sth
to believe that something is very

important or valuable • *I've always set great store by his opinion.* • *What would happen if this relationship that she set so much store by ended?*

set your **heart on** sth/doing sth
to decide to achieve something • *She's set her heart on a big wedding.*
have your **heart set on** sth/doing sth • *John had his heart set on becoming a doctor.*

set in train
if you set in train an activity or an event, you make it begin • *His book set in train the events which eventually led to revolution.*
be in train • *Investigations were in train to identify the person responsible for the theft.*

set out your **stall** *British & Australian*
to show other people that you are determined to do something • *We've set out our stall to win the championship and we'll be disappointed if we don't.*

set your **sights on** sth/doing sth
to decide to achieve something • *She's set her sights on winning.*
have your **sights set on** sth/doing sth • *I hear she has her sights set on becoming a journalist.*

set the agenda
to decide what subjects other people should discuss and deal with, often in a way which shows that you have more authority than them • *Opposition parties have managed to set the agenda during this election by emphasizing the public's fear of crime.*

set the pace
if someone sets the pace in a particular activity, they do it very well or very quickly and other people try to do the same • (often + **for**) *America's reforms have set the pace for European finance ministers.* • *For many years this company has set the pace in the communications industry.*

set the scene
to describe a situation where something is going to happen soon • *First, let's set the scene – it was a cold dark night with a strong wind blowing...*

set the scene for sth
if you set the scene for something, you make it possible or likely to happen • *The recent resignation of two government ministers has set the scene for a pre-election crisis.*
the scene is set for sth • *After a disastrous first half, the scene was set for a humiliating defeat.*

set the stage for sth
if you set the stage for something, you make it possible or likely to happen • *The purpose of that first meeting was to set the stage for future co-operation between Russia and the USA.*
the stage is set for sth • *The stage is now set for a really exciting climax to this year's championship.*

set the tone
if something someone says or does sets the tone for an event or activity, it establishes the way that event or activity will continue, especially the mood of the people involved • (often + **for**) *He was furious when she arrived late, and that set the tone for the whole evening.*

set the wheels in motion
to cause a series of actions to start that will help you achieve what you want • *A phone call to the right person should set the wheels in motion.*

not **set the world on fire**
to not be very exciting or successful • *The restaurant offers a decent menu, but it wouldn't set the world on fire.*

set sb **up for life** *informal*
to provide someone with enough money for the rest of their life • *His father died when he was young and the inheritance set him up for life.*

► See also: set (the) **alarm** bells ringing
set/start the **ball** rolling
put/set the **cat** among the pigeons
lay/set **eyes** on sb/sth
put/set sb's **mind** at rest
put/set sth in **motion**
put/set the **record** straight
put/set the **seal** on sth
be carved/set in **stone**
set/start **tongues** wagging

settle

settle a score
to harm someone who has harmed you in the past • (often + **with**) *Police believe the killer was a gang member settling a score with a rival gang.*
settle old scores • (often + **with**) *She used her farewell speech to settle some old scores with her opponents.*

seven

the seven year itch *humorous*
if someone who is married gets the seven year itch, they become bored with their relationship after about seven years and often want to start a sexual relationship with another person • *He keeps talking about all the women he knew before we were married – I think he's **got the seven-year itch**.*

seven-day

► See: a nine/one/seven-day **wonder**

seventh

be in seventh heaven *humorous*
to be extremely happy • *Since they got married they've been in seventh heaven.*

sex

a sex kitten *old-fashioned*
a young woman who is sexually exciting or attractive ✍Some women think this phrase is offensive. • *All she needs to do is untie her hair and remove her spectacles and she's transformed into a gorgeous sex kitten.*

a sex object
if someone thinks of a person as a sex object, they only think about having sex with them and do not think about their character or abilities • *How on earth can you feel anything for a man who just treats you as a sex object?*

shade

put sb/sth **in the shade**
to be so interesting or so good that other similar people or things seem less important by comparison • *I thought I'd done quite well, but Claire's exam results put mine in the shade.*

shades

Shades of sb/sth**.**
something that you say when someone or something makes you think of another person or thing • *We visited the university campus and had a few drinks in the bar. Shades of my student days.*

shadow

beyond/without a shadow of a doubt
if something is true beyond a shadow of a doubt, there is no doubt that it is true • *This is without a shadow of a doubt the best film I have seen all year.*

in sb's **shadow**
if you are in someone's shadow, you receive less attention and seem less important than them • *For most of his life he lived in the shadow of his more famous brother.*

in/under sth's **shadow**
if you are in the shadow of an unpleasant event, you cannot forget that it has happened or might happen in the future • *The local population were living under the shadow of war.*

a shadow of your **former self**
if you are a shadow of your former self, you are less strong or less powerful than you were in the past • *He came back to work after 3 months, completely cured of the cancer but a shadow of his former self.*

shaft

get the shaft *American informal*
if someone gets the shaft, they are not treated in a fair way • *The tax system is all wrong – the rich just get richer and it's the poor who get the shaft.*
give sb **the shaft** *American informal* • *They gave him the shaft – he lost his job for no reason at all.*

shag

like a shag on a rock *Australian very informal*
completely alone ✍A shag is a large sea bird. • *They walked out and left me like a shag on a rock.*

shaggy

a shaggy dog story
a joke which is a long story with a silly

end • *My grandad insists on telling these shaggy dog stories, which nobody finds funny except him.*

shake

more sth **than** you **can shake a stick at** *old-fashioned*

a very large number of something • *I don't know why she wants more shoes – she's already got more pairs than you can shake a stick at.*

Shake a leg! *old-fashioned, informal*

something that you say in order to tell people to hurry up • *Come on, shake a leg! The film starts in 20 minutes.*

shake like a leaf

to shake a lot because you are nervous or frightened • (usually in continuous tenses) *I saw her just before her talk and she was shaking like a leaf.*

▶ See also: rock/shake sth to its **foundations**

shakes

in two shakes (of a lamb's tail) *old-fashioned*

in a couple of shakes *old-fashioned*

very soon • *I'll be with you in two shakes of a lamb's tail.*

shaking

be shaking in your **boots/shoes**

to be very frightened or anxious • *Damon was shaking in his shoes when he heard all the shouting.*

shall

▶ See: Shall I be **mother**?

shanks

Shanks's pony *British, American & Australian old-fashioned*

Shank's mare *American old-fashioned*

walking as a method of travel • *I missed the last bus and had to get home on Shanks's pony.*

shape

in any shape or form

of any type • *I'm opposed to war in any shape or form.*

knock/lick/whip sth/sb **into shape**

to improve the condition of something or the condition or behaviour of someone • *The prime minister's main aim is to knock the economy into shape.* • *Little Sean is a bit wild but the teachers'll soon lick him into shape when he starts school.*

the shape of things to come

if something is the shape of things to come, it is a sign of what is likely to become popular in the future • *Is shopping on the Internet the shape of things to come?*

Shape up or ship out. *informal*

something that you say in order to tell someone that if their behaviour does not improve, they will have to leave • *This is the third serious mistake you've made this month. It's not good enough – you're going to have to shape up or ship out.*

▶ See also: get **bent** out of shape

shapes

all shapes and sizes

many different types of people or things • *Mortgage deals* ***come in all shapes and sizes*** *these days.*

share

Share and share alike.

something that you say which means that it is good to share things fairly and equally • *Come on now, don't keep them all to yourself – share and share alike.*

sharp

be as sharp as a tack *American*

to be very intelligent • *He may be old, but he's still as sharp as a tack.*

the sharp end *mainly British*

the sharp end of an activity or job is the most difficult part where problems are likely to happen • (usually + **of**) *She enjoys the challenge of being at the sharp end of investment banking.*

▶ See also: **look** sharp!

shebang

the whole shebang *informal*

the whole of something, including everything that is connected with it • *The party's next week but my parents are organizing the whole shebang.*

shed

▶ See: shed/weep **crocodile** tears
shed/throw **light** on sth

sheep

I might as well be hanged/hung for a sheep as a lamb.
something that you say when you are going to be punished for something so you decide to do something worse because your punishment will not be any more severe ✍In the past, people who stole lambs were killed, so it was worth stealing something more because there was no worse punishment. • *I'm going to be late for work anyway, so I think I'll go to the shop for a paper. I might as well be hanged for a sheep as a lamb.*

make sheep's eyes at sb *old-fashioned*
to look at someone in a way that shows that you love them or are attracted to them • *Ken's been making sheep's eyes at his ex-girlfriend all night.*

separate the sheep from the goats *British, American & Australian*
sort (out) the sheep from the goats *British & Australian*
to choose the people or things of high quality from a group of mixed quality • *I'll look through the application forms and separate the sheep from the goats.*

shelf

on the shelf *British & Australian old-fashioned*
if someone, especially a woman, is on the shelf, they are not married and people now believe they are too old to get married • *I was afraid my daughter would never find a husband, that she'd be left on the shelf.*

a shelf life
the length of time that something will last or remain useful ✍The shelf life of a product is the amount of time that it can be offered for sale before it must be thrown away. • *These days many marriages have a fairly short shelf life.*

shell

come out of your **shell**
to become less shy and more friendly • *Tom used to be very withdrawn but he's really come out of his shell since Susan took an interest in him.*
bring sb **out of** their **shell** • *Joining the drama group has brought Ian out of his shell.*

a shell game *American*
a method of deceiving or cheating someone, by moving things from one place to another in order to hide what you are doing ✍A shell game is a game in which someone must guess which of three shells a ball or pea (= a small, round, green vegetable) is placed under when they are moved quickly around. • *The thieves **played a shell game** with the police, constantly shifting the stolen goods.* • *He owns many small businesses in different states as part of a shell game to save on taxes.*

shelling

like shelling peas
If an activity is like shelling peas, it is very easy for you. • *For Adam, learning to ski was like shelling peas.*

shift

shift your **ground**
if you shift your ground in an argument or a discussion, you start to express a different opinion • *He's impossible to argue with because he keeps shifting his ground.*

▶ See also: Move/Shift your **arse**!

shine

take a shine to sb *informal*
to like someone immediately • *I think Andrew has taken a bit of a shine to our new member of staff.*

take the shine off sth *informal*
if something that happens takes the shine off something pleasant, it spoils it or makes it less enjoyable • *Having my purse stolen took the shine off my visit to Dublin.*

shingle

▶ See: **hang** out your shingle

ship

when your **ship comes in**
if you talk about what you will do when your ship comes in, you mean when you are rich and successful • *When my ship comes in, I'll build you a huge house in the country.*

▶ See also: **jump** ship
spoil the ship for a hap'orth of tar

ships

be like ships that pass in the night
if two people are like ships that pass in the night, they meet once or twice by chance for a short time and then do not see each other again • *I only met him once or twice – we were like ships that pass in the night – but I've never met anyone else like him.*

shirt

have/take the shirt off sb's **back**
to take so much of someone's money, for instance as a payment or punishment, that it is not fair and may cause them difficulties • *Watch out for those landlords – they'll have the shirt off your back.*

put your **shirt on** sth *British & Australian*
to risk all your money on something because you are sure you will win • *I put my shirt on the last race and lost everything.*
lose your **shirt** *British, American & Australian* • (usually + **on**) *He said he'd lost his shirt on that race.*

would give you the shirt off their **back** *informal*
if someone would give you the shirt off their back, they are extremely generous • *Karen's not well off, but she'd give you the shirt off her back.*

▶ See also: **keep** your shirt on!

shirt-lifter

a shirt-lifter *British & Australian informal*
an offensive way of referring to a man who is homosexual (= sexually attracted to other men) • *He was taunted by a chorus of adolescent gay haters shouting 'shirt-lifter!'*

shit

be in deep/the shit *British & Australian taboo*
if someone is in deep shit, they are in a lot of trouble • *When I crashed my uncle's car, I knew I was in deep shit.*

be on sb's **shit list** *American taboo*
if you are on someone's shit list, they do not like you • *She blames a lot of people for what happened, and you're on her shit list.*

get your **shit together** *taboo*
to become more organized and effective • *He's really got his shit together since he left college.*

not **give a shit** *taboo*
to not be interested in or worried about something or someone • *You can do what you like. I don't give a shit!* • (often + **about**) *My parents don't give a shit about my problems. They're totally selfish.*

have shit for brains *American & Australian taboo*
to be very stupid • *What are you talking about, Martha? You've got shit for brains.*

shit a brick *taboo*
to be very frightened or worried • *My niece took me on the rollercoaster and I nearly shit a brick.*

the shit hits the fan *taboo*
if the shit hits the fan, a person or an organization gets into serious trouble • *If Dad finds out how much money you spent, the shit will really hit the fan.*

Shit or get off the can/pot! *mainly American taboo*
something that you say when you want someone to make a decision and take action without any more delay • *It's time for management to shit or get off the pot. If they aren't going to meet the striker's demands they should say so.*

▶ See also: be up shit **creek** (without a paddle)
scare the shit out of sb

shit-eating

a shit-eating grin *American taboo*
a look of extreme satisfaction on someone's face that is annoying to other people who are less happy • *Ever since she heard they'd won she's been sitting there with that shit-eating grin on her face.*

shits

give sb **the shits** *Australian taboo*
to make someone angry • *She really gives me the shits when she makes up these stories about why she's late.*

shit-stirrer

a shit-stirrer *mainly British taboo*
someone who makes trouble for another person, especially by saying unpleasant things about them • *What a shit-stirrer –*

she's gone and told his wife that she saw him with another woman at the party.

shitting

be shitting bricks *taboo*
to be very frightened or worried • *The bull was following us across the field. Tony was shitting bricks.*

shivers

give sb **the shivers** *informal*
to frighten someone or make them nervous • *That man who hangs about in the lane gives me the shivers.*

▶ See also: **send** shivers down/up sb's spine

shoe

▶ See: If the hat/shoe **fits** (wear it).
the shoe is on the other **foot**

shoes

be in sb's **shoes** *informal*
to be in the same situation as someone else, especially an unpleasant situation • *If I were in your shoes, I'd speak to the boy's parents.* • *Poor Matthew.* ***I wouldn't like to be in his shoes*** *when the results are announced.*

step into sb's **shoes**
fill sb's **shoes**
to take the job or position that someone else had before you • *When his father retires, Victor will be ready to step into his shoes.* • *It will take a very special person to fill Barbara's shoes.*

▶ See also: be **shaking** in your boots/shoes

shoestring

on a shoestring *informal*
if you do something on a shoestring, you do it using very little money • *The restaurant is run on a shoestring, so we can't afford to take on any more staff.*

shoo-in

a shoo-in *American & Australian*
if someone is a shoo-in for a competition, or a competition is a shoo-in for them, they will win it easily • *She's a shoo-in for re-election to the Senate.* • *The election looks like a shoo-in for our man.*

shoot

shoot your **bolt**
to use all your energy trying to do something, so that you do not have enough energy left to finish it • (never in continuous tenses) *By the end of the third lap it was obvious that she had shot her bolt, and the Canadian runner took the lead.*

shoot sth/sb **down in flames** *informal*
to strongly criticize an idea or plan, or to refuse to accept it • *Several months ago this highly impractical idea would have been shot down in flames.* • *I thought I'd made a sensible suggestion, but they just shot me down in flames.*

shoot from the hip
to react to a situation very quickly and with a lot of force, without thinking about the possible effects of your actions • *His critics accuse him of shooting from the hip when challenged.*

shoot yourself **in the foot**
to do or say something stupid which causes problems for you • *He shot himself in the foot by suggesting that women politicians were incompetent.*

shoot your **load** *very informal*
if a man shoots his load, semen (= thick liquid containing a man's seed) comes out of his penis • *Man, I was so hot, I was ready to shoot my load!*

shoot your **mouth off** *very informal*
to talk too much, especially about something you should not talk about • (often + **about**) *Don't go shooting your mouth off about how much money you're earning.*

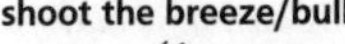
shoot the breeze/bull

shoot the breeze/bull *American informal*
to talk in a relaxed way about things that are not important • *We sat out on the porch until late, just shooting the breeze.*

shoot the messenger *humorous*
to blame or punish the person who tells you about something bad that has happened instead of the person who is responsible for it • *And now for tomorrow's weather – it's going to be cold, wet and stormy, but don't shoot the messenger!*

shoot the works *American informal*
to spend all your money or to use as much effort as possible to do something • (usually + **on**) *I could shoot the works on a round the world trip.* • *They shot the works on their daughter's wedding.*

shoot your **wad**
1 *American informal* to spend or use everything that you have • *He's going to shoot his wad on his night out – whatever it costs for a good time.*
2 *American informal* to say everything that you want to say about a particular subject • *Our opponents shot their wad at the meeting and left everyone in no doubt that they would oppose our plans.*
3 *British, American & Australian taboo* if a man shoots his wad, semen (= thick liquid containing a man's seed) comes out of his penis • *He shot his wad as soon as she took her blouse off.*

▶ See also: fire/shoot **blanks**

shooting

the whole shooting match *informal*
the whole of something, including everything that is connected with it • *There are four projects at present and Gerry's in charge of the whole shooting match.*

shop

shut up shop *British & Australian*
close up shop *mainly American*
to stop doing business, either temporarily or permanently • *They were forced to shut up shop because they weren't getting enough customers.*

▶ See also: be **all** over the shop
talk shop

short

not **be short of a bob or two** *British & Australian old-fashioned*
to have a lot of money • *This guy Lester that she's engaged to, he's not short of a bob or two you know.*

get the short end of the stick *American & Australian*
to suffer the bad effects of a situation • *The people who get the short end of the stick are those whose income is just too high to qualify for help from the government.*

give sb/sth **short shrift**
to give very little attention to someone or something, either because you are not interested in them or because you are annoyed with them • (usually passive) *A planning application for a new nightclub in the town centre was given short shrift by the council.* • *Sue gave Robert short shrift when he turned up drunk for her party.*
get short shrift from sb • *The proposal got short shrift from state officials.*

have sb **by the short and curlies** *very informal*
have sb **by the short hairs** *very informal*
to have complete power over someone • *They've got us by the short and curlies. We have no choice but to agree.*

make short work of sth
to deal with or finish something quickly

• *We made short work of the food that was put in front of us.*

short and sweet *humorous*
pleasantly short • *This morning's lecture was short and sweet.*

a short fuse
if someone has a short fuse, they become angry quickly and often • *Charlie has a sharp tongue and a short fuse.*

a short sharp shock *British & Australian*
a type of punishment that is quick and severe • *What young offenders need is a short sharp shock that will frighten them into behaving more responsibly.*

► See also: **draw** the short straw
fall short of sth
have/keep sb on a short/tight **leash**
be **nothing** short of [astonishing/miraculous etc.]
pull sb up short
in the long/short **run**
sell sb/sth short
stop short
stop short of sth/doing sth
in the long/medium/short **term**

short-arse

a short-arse *British & Australian very informal*
an offensive way of referring to someone who is very short • *Yeah, well, I might be fat but at least I'm not a short-arse!* • *Come here and say that, short-arse!*

short-change

short-change sb *informal*
to cheat someone by giving them less than they expected • (usually passive) *No one told me the film was only an hour long – I was short-changed!*

shot

be shot to hell/pieces *informal*
to be destroyed or in a very bad condition • *His nerves were shot to hell after only 2 years in that job.*

get shot of sb/sth *British informal*
to get rid of someone or something • *She got shot of her no-good husband and went back to university.*
be shot of sb/sth • *This boy has caused so much trouble that the school just want to be shot of him.*

have a shot at sb *Australian informal*
to criticize someone • *It's clear the film's director was having a shot at the government.*

have a shot at sth *British, American & Australian informal*
take a shot at sth *American informal*
to try to do something, often for the first time • *He's proven himself to be a talented actor and now he's having a shot at directing his first play.*
give sth **a shot** *informal* • *I've never been ice skating but I'll give it a shot.*

like a shot
if someone does something like a shot, they do it quickly and eagerly • *If I had the chance to go to Paris, I'd be there like a shot.*

a shot in the arm *informal*
if something gives you a shot in the arm, it gives you encouragement or energy • *The opening of a new research centre will give a much-needed shot in the arm for science in Britain.*

a shot in the dark
an attempt to guess something when you have no information or knowledge about it • *The whole theory is a shot in the dark – no-one will ever take us seriously.*

► See also: **fire** a shot across sb's/the bows
give it a shot/whirl

shotgun

a shotgun wedding *British, American & Australian old-fashioned*
a shotgun marriage *American old-fashioned*
a marriage that is arranged very quickly because the woman is going to have a baby • *After a shotgun wedding at 20, she had 3 children before divorcing from her husband.*

shots

► See: **call** the shots/tune

shoulder

put your **shoulder to the wheel**
to work hard and make an effort • *If everyone puts their shoulder to the wheel, the job will be finished in no time.*

a shoulder to cry on
someone who gives you sympathy when you are upset • *My father had just died*

and I needed a shoulder to cry on.

shoulder to shoulder
if you stand shoulder to shoulder with a person or a group of people, you support them during a difficult time • *The chairman stood shoulder to shoulder with the managing director throughout the investigation.*

shoulders

▶ See: **rub** shoulders with sb

shout

be nothing to shout about
not **be much to shout about**
to not be especially good or exciting • *The pay rise wasn't much to shout about, but I suppose it's better than nothing.*

shout sth **from the rooftops**
if you say you want to shout some news from the rooftops, you mean that you want to tell everyone about it because you are so excited • *When I discovered I was pregnant, I wanted to* ***shout it from the rooftops****.*

shouting

It's all over bar the shouting. *British & Australian*
something that you say when the result of an event or situation is certain • *The Italian team played superbly, and by half-time it was all over bar the shouting* (= it was certain they would win).

▶ See also: a shouting **match**

shove

▶ See: Shove/Stick sth up your **arse**!

show

go to show (sth)
if an event or situation goes to show something, it proves that it is true • (never in continuous tenses; usually + **that**) *There are more women in parliament now than ever before.* ***It just goes to show*** *that things are changing.* • (often + question word) *The painting was gone for a week before anyone noticed, which only goes to show how unobservant people are.*

Let's get the/this show on the road. *informal*
something that you say in order to tell people you want to start an activity or a journey • *We've got less than 2 hours to get this room ready for the party so let's get this show on the road.*

Show a leg! *British old-fashioned, informal*
something that you say in order to tell someone to get out of bed • *Show a leg! It's past 11 o'clock.*

show your **face**
if you show your face in a place, you go there, even when you feel embarrassed about something that you have done • (always + *adv/prep*) *I don't know how he dares show his face in this pub after how he behaved the other night!* • *If he ever shows his face in this town again, I'll get the police.*

show your **hand**
to tell people your plans or ideas, especially if you were keeping them secret before ✍When card players show their hand in a game of cards, they show the other players the cards they are holding, usually because they cannot continue to play the game. • *I'm a bit reluctant to show my hand at this stage in the proceedings.*

The show must go on.
something that you say which means that an event or activity must continue even if there are problems or difficulties • *There may be a war on, but here at the industrial design fair, the show must go on.*

show your **teeth**
to show that you are angry and prepared to defend yourself • *Come on, let him know you're angry – show your teeth!*

show sb **the door**
to make it clear that someone must leave • *I told her that I wasn't interested in her scheme and she showed me the door in no uncertain terms.*

show (sb) **what** you **are made of**
to prove how strong or clever or brave you are • *Next week's race will give her a chance to show what she's really made of.*
see what sb **is made of** • *Tomorrow it's the twelve-mile run. Then we'll see what you're made of.*

▶ See also: fly/show/wave the **flag**
prove/show your **mettle**
show sb the **ropes**
run the show

steal the show
show sb in their **true** colours

showers

▶ See: **send** sb to the showers

show-stopper

a show-stopper
a performance or part of a performance that is extremely good • *Her conference speech was a real show-stopper.*
show-stopping • (always before noun) *She gave a show-stopping performance in La Traviata.*

shrinking

a shrinking violet
a very shy person • (usually negative) *She's **no shrinking violet**.* • *I wouldn't exactly describe him as a shrinking violet.*

shudder

▶ See: I dread/shudder to **think**

shuffle

shuffle off this mortal coil *humorous*
to die ✍This phrase comes from the play *Hamlet* by William Shakespeare. • *I really want to see the Coliseum before I shuffle off this mortal coil.*

▶ See also: **lost** in the shuffle

shufti

have a shufti *British old-fashioned*
to have a quick look at something • *She'd brought her wedding photos in so I thought I might have a quick shufti.*

shut

Shut your **face/gob/mouth/trap!** *very informal*
an impolite way of telling someone to stop talking • *'That was a really stupid thing to do.' 'Oh, shut your trap!'* • *'Shut your face, will you? I'm trying to watch TV.'*

shut up like a clam
to suddenly stop talking and to refuse to say any more ✍A clam is a fish with a shell which closes up very quickly if something attacks it. • *When I asked him about his trip to Korea, he shut up like a clam.*

▶ See also: close/shut the **door** on sth
close/shut your **eyes** to sth
shut up **shop**

shutting

▶ See: closing/shutting the **stable** door after the horse has bolted

shuttle

shuttle diplomacy
an attempt to make peace between two groups of people who refuse to meet and talk to each other by meeting both groups separately and travelling between them • *The shuttle diplomacy continues this week as ambassadors fly to Paris for more talks with the French.*

shy

▶ See: **fight** shy of sth/doing sth

sick

be as sick as a dog *informal*
to be very sick • *She was as sick as a dog after that curry.*

be as sick as a parrot *British humorous*
to be very disappointed • *Tim was sick as a parrot when he heard Manchester had lost the match.*

be sick and tired of sth/doing sth *informal*
be sick to death of sth/doing sth *informal*
to be angry and bored because something unpleasant has been happening for too long • *You've been giving me the same old excuses for months and I'm sick and tired of hearing them!* • *I've been treated like dirt for two years now and I'm sick to death of it!*

feel sick to your **stomach** *American & Australian*
if something makes you feel sick to your stomach, it is so unpleasant that it makes you feel ill • *Looking at those pieces of raw meat I felt sick to my stomach.*

sick at heart *literary*
very sad • *The thought of her home so far away made her sick at heart.*

▶ See also: be fed up/sick to the **back** teeth

side

be on the [expensive/heavy/large etc.] side
to be a little too expensive, heavy, large etc. • *It's a really good restaurant – it's on the expensive side, mind.* • *I really like the*

table but I think it's a bit on the large side for our room.

be on the side of the angels
someone who is on the side of the angels is doing something good or kind • *The aid agencies are the only people firmly on the side of the angels in this conflict.*

on the side
in addition to your usual job • *He makes a little money on the side by fixing people's cars.*

the other side of the coin
a different and usually opposite view of a situation that you have previously talked about • *The other side of the coin is that fewer working hours means less pay.*

the other/wrong side of the tracks *American & Australian*
the poor area of a town • *She grew up on the wrong side of the tracks in a small southern town.*

this side of the grave *literary*
while you are alive • *My mother's generation were taught to expect only suffering this side of the grave.*

▶ See also: **err** on the side of caution
know which side your bread is buttered (on)
be **laughing** on the other side of your face
let the side down
be (on) the **wrong** side of 30/40 etc.

sidelines

▶ See: **stay** on the sidelines

sides

be speaking/talking out of both sides of your **mouth** *American*
to say different things about the same subject when you are with different people in order to always please the people you are with • *How can we trust any politicians when we know they're speaking out of both sides of their mouths?*

be two sides of the same coin
be different/opposite sides of the same coin
if two things are two sides of the same coin, they are very closely related although they seem different • *Violent behaviour and deep insecurity are often two sides of the same coin.* • *Higher living standards and an increase in the general level of dissatisfaction are opposite sides of the same coin.*

▶ See also: **split** your sides (laughing)

sideways

▶ See: **knock** sb sideways

siege

a siege mentality
the belief that you must protect yourself because other people are going to attack you • *Many designers develop a siege mentality because they're terrified someone will steal their ideas.*

sieve

have a memory/mind like a sieve
to be very bad at remembering things • *I've never known anyone so forgetful – she's got a memory like a sieve.*

sight

be a sight for sore eyes *informal*
if someone or something is a sight for sore eyes, you feel happy to see them • *A cup of coffee – that's a sight for sore eyes.* • *You're a sight for sore eyes, all dressed up in your new outfit.*

out of sight *American*
if the amount of something, especially money, is out of sight, it is very large • *The cost of health care in this country is going out of sight.* • *These executives in big corporations get salaries that are out of sight.*

Out of sight, out of mind.
something that you say which means if you do not hear about or see someone or something for a period of time, you stop thinking about them • *You'll soon forget about him after he leaves – out of sight, out of mind.*

▶ See also: **lose** sight of sth

sights

have sb **in** your **sights**
to intend to attack or defeat someone • *He's trying to build up his media empire and he has the owners of rival newspapers in his sights.*

have sth **in** your **sights**
to be trying to achieve something, especially when you are very likely to succeed • *After months of training, Hilary now has*

the gold medal firmly in her sights.

▶ See also: **lower** your sights
set your sights on sth/doing sth

sign

be a sign of the times
to be something that shows that society is worse now than it was in the past • *Young people are so rude these days. It's a sign of the times.*

sign on the dotted line
to formally agree to something by signing a legal document • *According to promoter Andrew James, the band has signed on the dotted line and will be playing at the Coliseum on November 2, 3 and 4.*

sign your **own death warrant**
to do something which will stop you from being successful ✍A death warrant is an official document which orders someone to be killed as a punishment. • *The company signed its own death warrant by choosing to remain independent rather than going into partnership.*
sign sth's **death warrant** to cause an organization or an activity to fail or end • *The cancellation of the multi-million dollar order signed the company's death warrant.*

▶ See also: sign/take the **pledge**

signed

signed, sealed and delivered *informal*
signed and sealed *informal*
if a document or an agreement is signed, sealed and delivered, it has been officially signed and completed • *A copy of the will, signed, sealed and delivered, arrived at our house the next morning.* • *There was a signed and sealed statement from the prime minister to confirm the treaty had been accepted.*

significant

a significant other *mainly American*
a person that someone is married to or who they have a serious sexual or romantic relationship with • (not used with *the*) *The ad read, 'Take your significant other to the Café Carlyle for a romantic night out.'*

silent

be as silent as the grave *literary*
to be completely silent • *It was four o'clock in the morning and London was as silent as the grave.*

the silent majority
the large numbers of people in a country or group who do not express their opinions publicly • *What does the silent majority expect from a new Labour government?*

▶ See also: silent **partner**

silk

You can't make a silk purse out of a sow's ear. *old-fashioned*
something that you say which means you cannot make a good quality product using bad quality materials • *To make chairs that'll last, you need good strong pieces of wood. You can't make a silk purse out of a sow's ear.*

silly

the silly season *British & Australian informal*
a period of time in the summer when there is not much news, especially political news, so the newspapers have articles about events that are not important • *It's the silly season again, and as usual, the papers are full of stories about the Loch Ness Monster.*

▶ See also: **play** silly buggers

silver

the silver screen *old-fashioned*
the cinema • *All the stars of the silver screen are here tonight to celebrate this great occasion.*

▶ See also: give/hand sth to sb on a (silver) **platter**

silver-tongued

silver-tongued *literary*
a silver-tongued person speaks to someone in a pleasant way and praises them in order to persuade them to do what they want • (always before noun) *He was a silver-tongued orator who convinced many people to support him.*

sin

a sin tax *American informal*
a tax on things that are bad for you, like cigarettes and alcohol • (not used with *the*) *Politicians like a sin tax as it brings*

in lots of revenue and not too many complaints.

▶ See also: **live** in sin

sine qua non

a sine qua non *formal*
something that is necessary, especially if you are going to achieve a particular thing • (often + **of**) *The company sees training as the sine qua non of success.*

sing

sing for your **supper** *old-fashioned*
to do something for someone else in order to receive something in return, especially food • *Dan's upstairs fixing my computer – I'm making him sing for his supper.*

sing sb's/sth's **praises**
to praise someone or something very much • *You've obviously made a good impression on Paul – he was singing your praises last night.* • *Mat seems happy enough in Brighton – he's always singing its praises.*

sing the same tune *British, American & Australian*
sing from the same hymnsheet/songsheet *British*
if a group of people sing the same tune, they say the same things about a subject in public • (usually in continuous tenses) *I want to make sure we're all singing the same tune before we give any interviews to the newspapers.*

sink

sink like a stone
to fail completely • *He had published two novels, both of which sank like a stone.*

sink or swim
to fail or succeed • *Newcomers are given no training – they are simply left to sink or swim.*

sink to such depths
to behave very badly • *I find it hard to believe that human beings could sink to such depths.*

sink without trace
to be forgotten about completely, after being popular for a while • *They enjoyed brief success with their second album and then sank without trace.*

▶ See also: get/sink your **teeth** into sth

sinking

a sinking feeling *informal*
a feeling that something bad is going to happen • *I had **that sinking feeling** you get going into an exam you haven't studied for.*

a sinking ship
a company or other organization that is failing • *He'd seen the company's accounts, realized he was on a sinking ship, and decided to get off.*

sins

for my sins *British & Australian humorous*
something that you say in order to make a joke that something you have to do or something that you are is a punishment for being bad • *I'm organizing the office Christmas party this year for my sins.* • *I'm an Arsenal supporter for my sins.*

sit

make sb **sit up and take notice**
to make someone suddenly notice something and become interested in it • (often + **of**) *That was the record that made me sit up and take notice of Neil Hannon.*

sit in judgment on/over sb
to say that what someone has done is morally wrong, believing yourself to be better • *We none of us have the right to sit in judgment on our fellow man.*

sit on your **arse** *British & Australian very informal*
sit on your ass *American very informal*
to do nothing, especially when other people are busy or need your help • *It's time you stopped sitting on your arse and found yourself a job.*

sit on your **hands**
to do nothing about a problem or a situation that needs dealing with • *Every day the crisis worsens and yet the government seems content to sit on its hands.*

sit on the fence
to delay making a decision when you have to choose between two sides in an argument or a competition • *She criticized members of the committee for sitting on the fence and failing to make a useful contribution to the debate.*

sit tight *informal*
1 to remain in a place, usually sitting down • *Just sit tight while I go and phone for help.* • *Sit tight and don't move that leg.*
2 to not take any action while you wait for something to happen • *Shareholders are advised to sit tight and see how the situation develops.*

not **sit well with** sb *mainly American*
if a situation or an idea does not sit well with someone, they do not like it or accept it • *The idea of people other than police combating crime does not sit well with many of the public.*

▶ See also: sit **pat**

sitting

be sitting on a goldmine
to have or own something that is very valuable • *When property prices doubled in our area, we suddenly realised we were sitting on a goldmine.*

be sitting pretty
to be in a good situation, usually because you have a lot of money • *They bought their house when prices were much lower so they're sitting pretty.*

a sitting duck
something or someone that is easy to attack or criticize • *Unarmed policemen walking the streets late at night are sitting ducks.*

▶ See also: be (sitting) in the **catbird** seat
at/in **one** sitting
be (sitting) on your **tail**

situation

a no-win situation
a difficult situation in which whatever happens the result will be bad for the people involved • *I'm in a no-win situation here. Whatever I do, I'm going to annoy someone.*
OPPOSITE **a no-lose situation** *American*
a situation in which whatever happens the result will be good • *He's in a no-lose situation. If he wins the tournament he gets a big bonus, and if he doesn't he's had valuable experience.*

six

be six feet under *informal*
to be dead • *You're just waiting until he's six feet under so you can get your hands on his money.*

six of one and half a dozen of the other
if you say that a bad situation is six of one and half a dozen of the other, you mean that two people or groups are equally responsible • *Harriet's always accusing Donald of starting arguments, but if you ask me, it's six of one and half a dozen of the other.*

six of the best *British & Australian old-fashioned*
if you give someone six of the best, you punish them by hitting them, usually on their bottom with a long, thin stick • *Many teachers are faced with finding an alternative to six of the best for pupils who regularly break the rules.*

▶ See also: **knock** sb for six

sixes

be at sixes and sevens *informal*
to be confused or badly organized • *We were at sixes and sevens for about a week after we moved in.*

sixty-four-thousand-dollar

▶ See: the sixty-four-thousand-dollar **question**

size

That's about the size of it. *informal*
used to agree that someone's opinion or description of a situation is correct • *'So she just ignored all the warnings and went up the mountain anyway?' 'That's about the size of it.'*

▶ See also: **cut** sb down to size
try sth for size

skates

Get your **skates on!** *British & Australian informal*
something that you say in order to tell someone to hurry • (usually an order) *Get your skates on! We're going to miss the train.* • *House buyers should get their skates on if they want to buy while prices are low.*

skating

▶ See: be (skating/walking) on **thin** ice

skeleton

a skeleton in the/your **cupboard** *British & Australian*
a skeleton in the/your **closet** *American*
an embarrassing secret • *If you want to be a successful politician, you can't afford to have too many skeletons in your cupboard.*

skid

skid row *mainly American informal*
a poor area in a city where people who have no jobs and homes live in cheap rooms or sleep outdoors • *She works as a social worker with alcoholics* ***on skid row.***
skid-row *mainly American informal* • (always before noun) *He ended up back in a skid-row hotel.*

skids

be on the skids *informal*
to be having a lot of problems and be likely to fail • *I hear their space programme is on the skids.*

put the skids under sb/sth *British & Australian informal*
to make something likely to fail • *Opposition from local residents has put the skids under plans for a new nightclub.*

▶ See also: **hit** the skids

skies

▶ See: **praise** sb/sth to the skies

skin

be skin and bone/bones
to be extremely thin • *We saw a few stray dogs that were nothing but skin and bones.*

by the skin of your **teeth** *informal*
if you do something by the skin of your teeth, you only just succeed in doing it • *We escaped by the skin of our teeth.* • *England held on by the skin of their teeth to win 1-0.*

get under sb's **skin**
1 to annoy someone • *It really got under my skin when he said women were bad drivers.*
2 to affect someone very strongly in a way that is difficult to forget • *Something about the haunting beauty of the place really got under my skin.*

It's no skin off my nose. *British, American & Australian informal*
It's no skin off my (back) teeth. *American informal*
something that you say which means you do not care about something because it will not affect you • *We can go in his car if he prefers. It's no skin off my nose.*

make sb's **skin crawl**
if something or someone makes your skin crawl, you think they are very unpleasant or frightening • *Just thinking about the way he had touched her made her skin crawl.*

play/run out of your skin *informal*
to play/run very well and with as much energy as you possibly can • *All those young lads were playing out of their skin last night.*

skin sb **alive**
to punish someone very severely • *Sharon will skin me alive if I'm late.*

▶ See also: nearly **jump** out of your skin
save sb's skin

sky

The sky's the limit.
something that you say which means there is no limit to what something or someone can achieve • *With two important film roles and a major award, it seems like the sky's the limit for this talented young actress.*

sky-high

▶ See: **blow** sth sky-high

slack

pick/take up the slack *American & Australian informal*
to do the work which someone else has stopped doing, but which still needs to be done • *When Sue starts going out to work each day, Bob and the kids will have to take up the slack and help more at home.*

▶ See also: **cut** sb some slack

slanging

▶ See: a slanging **match**

slap

slap and tickle *mainly British old-fashioned, humorous*
sexual activity that is not serious • *They were having a bit of slap and tickle on the*

sofa when I walked in.

a slap in the face
an action that insults or upsets someone • (often + **for**) *The decision to close the sports hall was a slap in the face for all those who had campaigned to keep it open.*

a slap on the back
praise or approval • *We **gave** her **a** big **slap on the back** for helping to organize the concert.*

a slap on the wrist
a warning or punishment that is not severe • *I got a slap on the wrist for arriving late again.*
get your **wrist slapped** • *We got our wrists slapped for leaving the door unlocked all night.*

sledgehammer

use a sledgehammer to crack a nut
British & Australian
to do something with more force than is necessary to achieve the result you want ✍A sledgehammer is a large, heavy tool with a wooden handle and a metal head that is used for hitting things. • *Sending ten men to arrest one small boy was a clear case of using a sledgehammer to crack a nut.*

sleep

could do sth **in** their **sleep**
if someone could do something in their sleep, they can do it very easily, usually because they have done it so often • *I've done the same recipe so many times I could do it in my sleep now.*

sleep like a log/top

sleep like a log/top
to sleep very well • *I don't know if it had anything to do with the wine we drank but I slept like a log.*

sleep on it
to not make an immediate decision about a plan or idea, but to wait until the next day in order to have more time to think about it • *You don't have to give me your decision now. Sleep on it, and let me know tomorrow.*

▶ See also: not **lose** sleep over sth
not sleep a **wink**

sleeping

let sleeping dogs lie
to not talk about things which have caused problems in the past, or to not try to change a situation because you might cause problems • *His parents never referred to the shoplifting incident again. I suppose they thought it best to let sleeping dogs lie.* • *It wasn't that we didn't want to improve the school – it was more a case of letting sleeping dogs lie.*

▶ See also: sleeping **partner**

sleeve

have sth **up** your **sleeve**
to have a secret idea or plan • *If this trip doesn't work out I've still got a few ideas up my sleeve.*

sleeves

▶ See: **roll** your sleeves up

sleight

sleight of hand
1 ways of deceiving people which you need skill to do • *Some mathematical sleight of hand was required to make the figures add up.*
2 quick, clever movements of your hands, especially when performing magic tricks • *With impressive sleight of hand he produced two pigeons out of his top hat.*

slice

any way you slice it *mainly American informal*
no matter how you slice it *mainly American informal*
something that you say which means you will not change your opinion about something, whatever anyone says about

the matter • *He shouldn't have hit her, any way you slice it.*

a slice of life
if a film, a play, or a piece of writing shows a slice of life, it shows life as it really is • *The drama, a slice of life about a group of unmarried mothers, starts tonight.*

a slice of the cake *British, American & Australian*
a slice of the pie *American*
a part of the money that is to be shared by everyone • *The government has less money to spend on education this year, so primary schools will get a smaller slice of the cake than last year.*

▶ See also: a piece/slice of the **action**

slime

a slime ball *informal*
an unpleasant man who is friendly in a way which is not sincere • *I don't know what she sees in him – he's such a slime ball!*

sling

Sling your **hook!** *British informal, old-fashioned*
an impolite way of telling someone to go away • *When he couldn't pay the rent, she told him to sling his hook.*

▶ See also: sling/throw **mud** at sb

slings

the slings and arrows (of outrageous fortune) *literary*
unpleasant things that happen to you that you cannot prevent ✍This phrase comes from Shakespeare's play, *Hamlet*. Slings and arrows are weapons used to attack people, and fortune means things that happen to you. • *We all have to suffer the slings and arrows, so there's no point getting depressed when things go wrong.*

slip

give sb **the slip** *informal*
to escape from someone who is with you, following you, or watching you • *There was a man following me when I left the office, but I gave him the slip on the crowded main street.*

slip your **mind**
if something slips your mind, you forget about it • *I meant to tell her Nigel had phoned, but it completely slipped my mind.*

a slip of the tongue
a mistake you make when speaking, such as using the wrong word • *Did I say she was forty? I meant fourteen – just a slip of the tongue.*

slip through your **fingers**
1 if something you hope to achieve slips through your fingers, you do not manage to achieve it • *He has seen the world championship slip through his fingers twice.* • *This is my big chance to make a career in journalism. I can't* ***let*** *it* ***slip through my fingers****.*
2 if someone slips through your fingers they manage to escape from you • *We've got men guarding all the exits and more men on the roof. He won't slip through our fingers this time.*

slip through the net
to not be caught or dealt with by the system that should be catching or dealing with you • *The system is failing and mental patients who badly need help are still slipping through the net.* • *Innocent people have been falsely convicted while the guilty ones may be slipping through the net.*

There's many a slip twixt cup and lip. *literary*
something that you say in order to warn someone not to be too confident about the result of a plan, because many things can go wrong before it is completed • *We still might finish in time for the deadline, but there's many a slip twixt cup and lip.*

▶ See also: fall/slip through the **cracks**
let slip sth

slippery

be as slippery as an eel
someone who is as slippery as an eel cannot be trusted ✍An eel is a long fish which has a body like a snake. • *You'd be mad to go into business with him. He's as slippery as an eel.*

a slippery slope
a situation or habit that is likely to lead to a worse situation or habit • *If you let kids stay up late a few nights you're* ***on a slippery slope****.* • *My advice is to keep away from all drugs. It's a slippery slope.*

slog

▶ See: slog/sweat/work your **guts** out

slow

be slow off the mark
to be slow to act or to react to an event or situation • *The federal government was criticized for being slow off the mark in helping towns hit by the recent hurricane.*

OPPOSITE **be quick off the mark** • *You'll have to be quick off the mark if you want to get tickets for her show.*

be slow on the uptake
to be slow to understand new ideas • *I tried to explain the new database, but they were remarkably slow on the uptake.*

OPPOSITE **be quick on the uptake** • *Some of the games were quite complex but the children were very quick on the uptake.*

do a slow burn *American & Australian informal*
to have a feeling of anger that gradually increases • *As he heard more about the plan to develop the area for industrial use he started doing a slow burn.*

smack-bang

smack-bang *British, American & Australian informal*
smack-dab *American informal*
exactly in a particular place, especially in the middle of somewhere • (always + *adv/prep*) *She lives* ***smack-bang in the middle*** *of London.*

small

be grateful/thankful for small mercies
if someone should be grateful for small mercies, they should feel grateful that something good has happened, although it is not everything that they wanted • *They've agreed to end the meeting half an hour early. I suppose we should be thankful for small mercies.*

in small doses
if you like someone or something in small doses, you only like them for short periods • *She's all right in small doses but I wouldn't want to spend a whole lot of time with her.*

It's a small world.
something that you say when you discover that someone knows a person that you know • *Imagine you knowing Erik! It's a small world, isn't it?*

small beer *British, American & Australian informal*
small potatoes *American & Australian informal*
something that is not important, especially when compared to something else • *A loan of that size is small beer – these banks are lending millions of pounds a day.* • *And we are not talking small potatoes – building the airport means many people in the area will lose their homes.*

a small fortune
a lot of money • *Her hair ought to look good – she spends a small fortune on it.*

small fry *informal*
1 people, organizations, or activities that are not large or important • *The small fry are soon going to be pushed out of business by all these multinationals.* • *This investigation is small fry for a police force used to massive inquiries.*
2 *American humorous* very young children • *These computer games will really intrigue the small fry in your house – kids love them.*

the small hours
the early hours of the morning • (often + **of**) *I was up till the small hours of Wednesday morning finishing off that report.* • *She was born* ***in the small hours*** *of Saturday morning.*

▶ See also: make sb **feel** small
the fine/small **print**
Don't **sweat** the small stuff.

smart

a/your **smart mouth** *American informal*
if someone has a smart mouth, they speak in a way that is too clever and does not show enough respect for other people • *If you aren't more careful, your smart mouth could lose you your job.*

a smart alec/aleck *informal*
someone who is always trying to seem more clever than everyone else in a way that is annoying • *Some smart alec in the audience kept making witty remarks during my talk.*

smart-alec/-aleck • (always before

noun) *He's just some smart-alec journalist.*

a smart bomb
a bomb that guides itself by receiving signals from the ground • *Laser-guided smart bombs were hitting targets only about 60 per cent of the time.*

a smart cookie *American*
someone who is clever and good at dealing with difficult situations • *If anyone can make this company succeed, it's Kathy – she's one smart cookie.*

smart drugs *British & Australian*
drugs which make you more intelligent or make you think more clearly • *I have my exams in two weeks – I could use some smart drugs.*

the smart money
1 if the smart money is on something happening, or on someone or something being successful, people with a good knowledge about it believe that is what will happen • *Hurt's best-actor award surprised even Hollywood insiders – **the smart money was on** Jack Nicholson.* • *The smart money says that the industry will end up drastically reduced.*
2 money which is spent by people who are very successful in business • *The smart money is coming back into mortgages as the best investment right now.*

smart-arse

a smart-arse *British very informal*
a smart-ass *American very informal*
someone who is always trying to seem more clever than everyone else in a way that is annoying • *OK, smart-arse, do you have a better idea?*
smart-arse *British very informal* • (always before noun) *That's all I need – some smart-arse kid telling me what to do!*

smarty

a smarty pants *informal*
someone who is always trying to seem more clever than everyone else in a way that is annoying • *Cindy, the little smarty pants, will be the first to tell us where we went wrong.*

smell

smell a rat
to start to believe that something is wrong about a situation, especially that someone is being dishonest • *She smelled a rat when she phoned him at the office where he was supposed to be working late and he wasn't there.*

smell fishy *informal*
if a situation or an explanation smells fishy, it causes you to think that someone is being dishonest • *Webbers's account of what he was doing that evening smells a bit fishy to me.*

▶ See also: smell/taste **blood**
smell/stink to **high** heaven
wake up and smell the coffee!

smelling

come out/up smelling of roses *British & Australian*
come out/up smelling like roses *American*
if you come out smelling of roses, people believe you are good and honest after a difficult situation which could have made you seem bad or dishonest • *There was a major fraud investigation, but Smith still came out smelling of roses.*

smile

▶ See: **crack** a smile
grin/smile from **ear** to **ear**
wipe the smile off sb's face

smiles

be all smiles
to look very happy and friendly, especially when other people are not expecting you to • *She spent the whole of yesterday shouting at people and yet this morning she's all smiles.*

smoke

the (big) smoke *British & Australian*
a big city, especially London, Sydney or Melbourne • *So when were you last in the smoke, then?*

go up in smoke
if a plan or some work goes up in smoke, it is spoiled or wasted • *Then his business went bankrupt and 20 years of hard work went up in smoke.*

smoke and mirrors *American & Australian*
something which is intended to confuse or deceive people, especially by making them believe that a situation is better than it really is • *Smoke and mirrors*

made the company seem bigger and healthier than it really was. It was just clever marketing.

smoke-and-mirrors • (always before noun) *City Hall has saved taxpayers little with its smoke-and-mirrors trick of using money set aside for building renovations.*

smoke signals

a sign that something is probably going to happen • *All the smoke signals from Downing Street indicate that the taxpayer will have to pay up again.* • *Conflicting smoke signals are coming from the peace talks, and it is impossible to say how they are going.*

There's no smoke without fire.
Where there's smoke, there's fire.

something that you say which means that if people are saying that someone has done something bad but no one knows whether it is true, it probably is true • *He claims that they were just good friends and that they never slept together but there's no smoke without fire, that's what I say.*

► See also: **blow** smoke

smoking

a smoking gun

information which proves without doubt that someone committed a crime • *A smoking gun was found in the form of an incriminating memorandum and Walker was convicted of theft.*

smooth

smooth (sb's) **ruffled feathers**

to try to make someone feel less angry or upset, especially after an argument • *I spent the afternoon smoothing ruffled feathers and trying to convince people to give the talks another chance.*

smooth the way for sb/sth
smooth sb's/sth's **way**

to make it easier for someone to do something or for something to happen • *Parents can do a lot to smooth the way for their children when they start school.* • *To smooth the bill's way through Congress, the President met with Republican leaders to hear their views.*

► See also: **paper**/smooth over the cracks

snail

at a snail's pace

very slowly ✍A snail is a small animal with a shell that moves very slowly. • *The roads were full of traffic and we were travelling at a snail's pace.*

snail mail *humorous*

the system of sending letters through the post • *What's your preferred means of communication? Fax, email or snail mail?*

snake

a snake in the grass

someone who pretends to be your friend while secretly doing things to harm you • *It's upsetting to learn that someone you once viewed as a good colleague is in fact a snake in the grass.*

snake oil *American informal*

advice or solutions to problems which are of no use ✍People used to sell substances called snake oil in the US which they said would cure illnesses but which were of no use. • *In my opinion, government measures for balancing the budget are just so much snake oil.*

a snake-oil salesman *American informal* someone who tries to sell you something of no value • *The American people are too easily deceived – the perfect target for any passing snake-oil salesman.*

snap

Snap to it! *British, American & Australian informal*
Snap it up! *American informal*

something that you say to someone when you want them to hurry • *We're leaving in five minutes so you'd better snap to it.* • *Snap it up, can't you? Surely you've had enough time to write that letter!*

► See also: bite/snap sb's **head** off

snappy

Make it snappy! *informal*

an impolite way of telling someone to hurry • *We'd like four coffees please, and make it snappy!*

sneezed

not **to be sneezed/sniffed at** *informal*

1 if something, especially an amount of money, is not to be sneezed at, it is large enough to be worth having • *And there's*

the increase in salary to be considered. £3000 extra a year is not to be sneezed at.

2 if something or someone is not to be sneezed at, they are important or dangerous enough to deserve serious attention • *Goodman is not a man to be sniffed at.*

be nothing to sneeze/sniff at *American & Australian informal* • *Blizzards with a foot of snow are nothing to sneeze at even in the mid-West.*

sneezes

▶ See: when sb/sth sneezes, sb/sth catches a **cold**

snook

▶ See: **cock** a snook

snow

a snow job *American & Australian informal*

an attempt to persuade or deceive someone by praising them or not telling the truth • *Danny'll need to* ***do a snow job on*** *his Dad if he's going to borrow the car again.*

snowball

not **have a snowball's chance in hell**

to have no chance at all of achieving something • (usually + **of** + doing sth) *With those grades she hasn't a snowball's chance in hell of getting into college.*

a snowball effect

a situation in which something increases in size or importance at a faster and faster rate • *The more successful you become, the more publicity you get and that publicity generates sales. It's a sort of snowball effect.*

snowed

be snowed under

to have so much work that you have problems dealing with it all • (often + **with**) *She wants me to take some time off but I'm snowed under with work at the moment.*

snuff

a snuff movie

a film that is intended to be sexually exciting which shows a person being murdered • *In May '92 he was arrested and charged with importing snuff movies into the country.*

up to snuff

if someone or something is up to snuff, they are of an acceptable standard or quality • (often negative) *Their wine-list is very good but I'm afraid the food isn't really up to snuff.* • *The police force is replacing its older patrol cars to make sure they all* ***come up to snuff***. • *We have spent a tremendous amount of money* ***bringing*** *the department* ***up to snuff***.

snug

be as snug as a bug in a rug *humorous*

to feel very comfortable and warm because you are in bed or under a cover • *You get in your nice warm bed with your teddy and you'll be as snug as a bug in a rug!*

so

▶ See: So **long**.

soaked

be soaked to the skin

to be extremely wet • *The rain was so heavy we were soaked to the skin after only ten minutes.*

get soaked to the skin • *I had no umbrella so I got soaked to the skin.*

soap

▶ See: **no** soap

soapbox

get on your **soapbox**

to start expressing strong opinions, especially about a subject that people are bored of hearing you speak about ✍A soapbox is a wooden box that people stood on in the past when they were making a speech in public. • *It was that point in the evening when my father got on his soapbox and started lecturing us on the evils of the modern world.*

sob

a sob story

a sad story that someone tells you about themselves in order to make you feel sympathy for them • *She told me some sob story about not having enough money to go and see her father who was ill.*

▶ See also: cry/sob your **heart** out

sober

be as sober as a judge
to not be at all drunk • *It's awful when everyone else around you has been drinking and you're as sober as a judge.*

social

a social climber
someone who tries to join a higher social class, especially by becoming friends with people from that class • *He was a dedicated social climber and was at all the best parties.*

sock

Put a sock in it! *informal*
an impolite way of telling someone to be quiet • *Put a sock in it! Some of us are trying to work around here.*

▶ See also: land/sock sb **one**

socks

[beat/bore/charm etc.] the socks off sb
if someone beats, bores, charms etc. the socks off someone, they beat, bore, or charm them completely • *He was one of those teachers who bored the socks off his students with his classes.*

blow/knock your **socks off** *informal*
if something knocks your socks off, you find it extremely exciting or good • *I'm going to take you to a restaurant that'll knock your socks off.*

▶ See also: **pull** your socks up
work your socks off

sod

Sod's Law *British humorous*
the way in which plans fail and bad things happen where there is any possibility of them doing so • *It's Sod's Law that on the one occasion when the train arrives on time, I'm late!*

soft

be soft on sb *old-fashioned*
to be in love with someone • *I think Conor must be soft on Julie – he keeps sending her cards.*

have a soft spot for sb/sth
to feel a lot of affection for someone or something, often without knowing why • *I've got a real soft spot for Thomas – I just find something about him very appealing.*

soft in the head *informal*
stupid or crazy • *I can't change my mind now, she'll think I've* ***gone soft in the head****.*

▶ See also: be an easy/soft **touch**

soften

▶ See: cushion/soften the **blow**

softly

a softly, softly approach *British & Australian*
a gradual way of solving a problem that shows patience and does not involve immediate action or force • *The recent unrest in the capital suggests that the government's softly, softly approach to reform is not working.*

sold

be sold a pup *British informal*
to be tricked into buying something that is not worth anything • *I'm afraid you've been sold a pup there. You should always get an expert to look over a second-hand car before you buy it.*

soldier

a soldier of fortune *literary*
someone who fights for any country or group that will pay him • *A soldier of fortune in the service of both Christian and Muslim kings, he was constantly fighting from 1065.*

solid

be as solid as a rock
to be very solid • *So much furniture these days is so flimsy – this table here was made a hundred years ago and it's solid as a rock.*

some

and then some *American & Australian*
and even more • *It looked like 20,000 people and then some at the demonstration.* • *'Did Joe give you a hard time?' 'Yeah, and then some!'*

something

▶ See: **look** like something the cat brought/dragged in

son

a son of a bitch

1 *American & Australian very informal* a man who is unpleasant or who has made you angry • *He's a lazy, drunken son of a bitch and she's better off without him.*

2 *American very informal* a way of referring to an object, an activity, or a situation which causes difficulties for you • *Cleaning up after the robbery was a son of a bitch.*

Son of a bitch! *mainly American very informal*

something that you say in order to show that you are very angry or upset • *Son of a bitch! Have you seen what he wrote in this letter?*

a son of a gun

1 *American informal* a man who is unpleasant or who has made you angry • *He's one mean son of gun – so be careful around him.*

2 *American & Australian informal* if you call a man or a boy a son of a gun, it is a way of showing affection for them • *The little son of a gun has done it again – he's won all his races.*

3 *American informal* a way of referring to an object which is causing problems for you or making you angry • *The computer's crashed and I don't know how to get the son of a gun working again.*

Son of a gun! *American & Australian informal*

something that you say in order to show that you are very surprised and shocked • *Son of a gun! I can't believe they put her in jail for that!*

song

be on song *British*

to be playing or performing well • *Ravanelli looked a bit tired in last Saturday's match but he's certainly on song tonight.*

for a song

very cheaply • *This is one of my favourite pieces of furniture and I got it for a song in a market.* • *Property prices have come right down – houses are* ***going for a song*** (= being sold very cheaply) *at the moment.*

make a song and dance about sth/doing sth *British & Australian*

to make something seem more important than it really is so that everyone notices it • *I only asked her to move her car but she made such a song and dance about it.* • *He made a real song and dance about giving up meat.*

a song and dance *American*

a long and complicated statement or story, especially one that is not true • (usually + **about**) *She gave me some song and dance about her kids always being sick and not being able to get to the meetings.*

sooner

No sooner said than done.

something that you say when something is done as soon as someone asks for it or suggests it • *'Would you mind closing the window for a while?' 'No sooner said than done.'*

sore

a sore point/spot

a subject which someone would prefer not to talk about because it makes them angry or embarrassed • (often + **with**) *I tried not to make any reference to Mike's drinking habits – I know it's a sore point with Kay at the moment.*

stand/stick out like a sore thumb

if someone or something sticks out like a sore thumb, everyone notices them because they are very different from the other people or things around them • *Everyone else was in jeans and casual gear and I had my office clothes on – I stuck out like a sore thumb.*

sorrows

▶ See: **drown** your sorrows

sort

▶ See: separate/sort out the **men** from the boys
sort (out) the **sheep** from the goats

sorts

be out of sorts

to feel slightly ill or slightly unhappy • *I'd been feeling tired and headachy and generally out of sorts for some time.*

It takes all sorts (to make a world).
something that you say which means that all people are different and even strange people should be accepted • *Now the couple next door, they go swimming in the sea in the middle of winter. Well, it takes all sorts, as they say.*

soul

be the soul of discretion
to be good at not talking about things that other people want to keep secret • *As regards Nigel, he's the soul of discretion. I'm quite sure he won't mention this to anyone.*

▶ See also: **bare** your heart/soul
sell your soul (to the devil)

sound

be as sound as a bell
to be very healthy or in very good condition • *Her constitution is as sound as a bell.*

be as sound as a dollar *American old-fashioned*
if a machine or an object is as sound as a dollar, it works well and is in very good condition • *The engine has been as sound as a dollar since it was overhauled.*

sound/toll the death knell
to cause an organization, system, or activity to fail or end ✍A knell is the sound of a bell being rung slowly to tell people that someone has died. • (often + **for**) *The new superstore will sound the death knell for hundreds of small independent shops.* • (sometimes + **of**) *The closure of the local car factory tolled the death knell of the town.*
the death knell the reason why something fails and ends • (often + **for**) *Computer-operated machinery has been seen as the death knell for traditional skills.*

▶ See also: ring/sound **hollow**

soup

be in the soup *old-fashioned*
to be in trouble • *This team know that if they lose on Saturday, they'll really be in the soup.*

from soup to nuts *American informal*
from the beginning to the end • *She told us everything about the trip, from soup to nuts.*

sour

sour grapes
if you say that something someone says is sour grapes, you mean that they said it because they are jealous • *I don't think it's such a great job – and that's not just sour grapes because I didn't get it.*

south

go south *American informal*
to lose value or quality • *When oil prices went south, it caused problems right across the economy.* • *She played well in the tennis championships, except her serve seemed to have gone south.*

sow

sow the seeds of sth
to do something that will cause an unpleasant situation in the future • *He may be sowing the seeds of his own destruction by using violence against his people.*

sow your **wild oats**
if a young man sows his wild oats, he has a period of his life when he does a lot of exciting things and has a lot of sexual relationships • *He'd spent his twenties sowing his wild oats but felt that it was time to settle down.*

▶ See also: You **reap** what you sow.

space

a space cadet *humorous*
a strange or crazy person • *I wouldn't trust him with the children – he's a real space cadet.*

▶ See also: **watch** this space.

spade

▶ See: **call** a spade a spade

spades

in spades *mainly American*
in large amounts or to a very great degree • *The thing that you absolutely must have for this job is confidence – and Adam has it in spades.* • *I don't get colds often, but when I do I get them in spades.*

spanner

▶ See: put/throw a spanner in the **works**

spare

be going spare *British & Australian*
if something is going spare, you can have

it because no one else wants it • *'Do you want some more cheesecake?' 'Yes, if it's going spare.'*

be like a spare prick at a wedding *British taboo, humorous*
to feel silly because you are present at an event but no one needs you and no one is talking to you • *Everyone else there had come with their partners and I was left feeling like a spare prick at a wedding.*

Don't spare the horses. *Australian informal*
something that you say to someone in order to tell them to hurry • *Go and buy some milk and don't spare the horses.*

go spare *British & Australian informal*
to become very angry • *She'd go spare if she found out he was spending all that money.*

▶ See also: save/spare sb's **blushes**

spark

a spark plug *American informal*
a person with a lot of energy and ideas who encourages the other people in a group • *The school's new principal is the spark plug in a team that includes parents, teachers and community.*

sparks

sparks fly
if sparks fly between two or more people, they argue angrily • *They don't have the easiest of relationships and when they get together in a meeting sparks fly.*

speak

speak for itself/themselves
if something speaks for itself, it does not need any explanation • *I'm not going to talk about our business successes. I think the report speaks for itself.*
let sth **speak for itself/themselves**
• *The book offers no analysis of Bonnard's work, it just lets the paintings speak for themselves.*

speak your **mind**
to be honest to people about your opinions • *She's not afraid to speak her mind, even if it upsets people.*

speak volumes
if something speaks volumes, it makes a situation very clear without the use of words • (never in continuous tenses) *He refused to comment on reports of his dismissal, but his furious expression spoke volumes.* • (often + **about**) *What we wear speaks volumes about our personality.*

speak with (a) forked tongue
to make false promises or to speak in a way which is not honest • *The minister is speaking with a forked tongue, promising support he will never deliver.*

speak with a plum in your **mouth** *British & Australian*
if someone speaks with a plum in their mouth, they speak in a way that shows they are from a very high social group • *All I can remember is that he was overweight and spoke with a plum in his mouth.*

▶ See also: speak/talk of the **devil**
speak/talk the **same** language
speak/talk out of **turn**

speaking

not **be on speaking terms**
to be refusing to talk to someone because you have had an argument and are still angry with them • (often + **with**) *She's not on speaking terms with her ex-husband.* • *Jeanette and her mother haven't been on speaking terms since the wedding.*

▶ See also: be speaking/talking out of both **sides** of your mouth

spec

on spec
if you do something on spec, you do it without being sure that you will get what you want • *You could always turn up at the airport on spec and see what's available on the day.* • *I sent in an article on spec and they published it.*

spectacle

make a spectacle of yourself
to do something that makes you look stupid and attracts other people's attention • *I wasn't going to make a spectacle of myself by dancing with my grandma!*

spectre

raise the spectre of sth *British, American & Australian*
raise the specter of sth *American*
to make people worry that something unpleasant will happen • *Drought and*

war have raised the spectre of food shortages for millions of people. • *Napoli's 1-0 defeat at Bologna raised the spectre of relegation for the Italian champions.*

▶ See also: the ghost/spectre at the **feast**

speed

up to speed

if you are up to speed with a subject or an activity, you have all the latest information about it and are able to do it well • (often + **with**) *We arranged for some home tutoring to **get** him **up to speed** with the other children in his class.* • (often + **on**) *Before we start the meeting, I'm just going to **bring** you **up to speed** on the latest developments.*

spell

spell trouble

to be the cause of possible problems in the future • (often + **for**) *The continuing dry weather could spell trouble for farmers.*

spend

spend a penny *British & Australian informal*

if you say you are going to spend a penny, you mean you are going to go to the toilet • *Excuse me, I must go and spend a penny.*

spend money like water

of someone spends money like water, they spend too much • *Carol spends money like water – no wonder she's always broke.*

spick

be spick and span

a place that is spick and span is very tidy and clean • *The kitchen was spick and span as ever, every surface wiped down and everything in its place.*

spike

spike sb's **guns**

to spoil someone's plans ✍In the past, soldiers put spikes (= thin, pointed pieces of metal) into their enemies' guns in order to stop them working. • *The African runner spiked her guns, overtaking her in the final minute.*

spill

spill your **guts** *American & Australian informal*

to tell someone all about yourself, especially your problems • *Why do people take part in these shows and spill their guts on camera in front of a studio audience?*

spill the beans

to tell people secret information • *It was then that she threatened to spill the beans about her affair with the president.*

spin

be in a spin

to be very anxious and confused • *She's in a spin over the arrangements for the party.*

send/throw sb **into a spin** • *News of the director's resignation had sent management into a spin.*

spin sb **a line** *British*

to try to make someone believe that something is true, often so that they will do what you want or not be angry with you • *He spun her a line about having to work late at the office.*

a spin doctor

someone whose job is to make sure that the information the public receives about a particular event makes them approve of the organization they work for, usually a political party • *In politics, this is the age of the spin doctor and image maker.*

spin your **wheels** *American informal*

to waste time doing things that achieve nothing • (often in continuous tenses) *If we're just spinning our wheels, let us know and we'll quit.*

spirit

as/when the spirit moves you *humorous*

if you do something when the spirit moves you, you only do it when you want to • *He'll cook now and again, when the spirit moves him.*

enter/get into the spirit of sth

to show that you are happy to be at a social event by talking to a lot of people, dancing, or wearing special clothes • *'Hey, I like your hat!' 'Well, I thought I'd better **enter into the spirit of things**.'*

• I'm afraid I was feeling too ill to really get into the spirit of the evening.

spit

I could (just) spit! *informal*
something that you say when you are very angry, usually because of something someone has done • *When I think of all the hours I put into that company and that's how they treat me. I could just spit!*

spit and polish
cleaning and rubbing • *All it needed was a bit of spit and polish and we got it looking as good as new.*

spit blood
to speak or behave in a way that shows you are very angry • *After her speech, people who she had criticized were spitting blood.*

spit nails *American & Australian informal*
spit chips/tacks *Australian informal*
to speak or behave in a way that shows you are very angry • *He was spitting nails when he saw what had happened to his car.*

spit-and-sawdust

spit-and-sawdust *British*
a spit-and-sawdust pub (= type of bar that is found in Britain) is dirty and untidy and is not modern or attractive • (always before noun) *There are one or two spit-and-sawdust pubs in the town centre but nothing remotely trendy.*

spitting

be the spitting image of sb
to look very much the same as someone else • *He's the spitting image of his father.*

► See also: in/within spitting **distance**
be spitting in/into the **wind**

splash

make a splash
to get a lot of public attention • *It wasn't a best-seller but it did make quite a splash in American literary circles.*

spleen

► See: **vent** your spleen

split

split hairs
to argue about whether details that are not important are exactly correct • *'She earns three time what I earn.' 'Actually, it's more like two and a half.' 'Oh stop splitting hairs!'*
hair-splitting • *I don't have very much patience with all this legal hair-splitting.*

split your **sides (laughing)**
to laugh a lot at something • *We nearly split our sides laughing watching Paul trying to give the rabbit a bath.*
side-splitting • (always before noun) *He was a great comic who could give side-splitting imitations of famous people.*

spoil

spoil sb **rotten**
to do whatever someone wants you to do or to give them anything they want • *My husband spoils me rotten. Look at all this jewellery he's given me.* • *Those children are spoiled rotten by their grandparents.*

spoil the ship for a hap'orth of tar
to spoil something big or important by refusing to spend a small amount of money or make a small amount of effort • *They spent millions on a wonderful architect-designed building, but they've bought really cheap furniture. It's just spoiling the ship for a hap'orth of tar.*

spoiled

► See: be spoiled for **choice**

spoiling

be spoiling for a fight
to be very eager to fight or argue about something • *The trouble was caused by a group of demonstrators who were obviously spoiling for a fight.*

spoilt

► See: be spoilt for **choice**

spoke

put a spoke in sb's **wheel** *British & Australian*
to spoil someone else's plans and stop them from doing something • *Tell him you're using the car that weekend – that should put a spoke in his wheel.*

sponge

► See: **throw** in the sponge/towel

spoon-fed

be spoon-fed
to be given too much help or information

• *When I was at school we weren't spoon-fed, we had to work things out for ourselves.*

sporting

a sporting chance
a good chance that something will happen, although it is not certain • *It's by no means definite but there's a sporting chance he'll get the job.*

spot

glued/rooted to the spot
if you are glued to the spot, you cannot move, usually because you are very shocked or frightened • *I stood there rooted to the spot as he came nearer and nearer.*

on the spot
1 immediately • *If you're caught without a ticket, you're fined on the spot.* • *We asked for the money and he paid us on the spot.*

2 in the place where something is happening or has just happened • *The police were called and they were on the spot within three minutes.*
on-the-spot • (always before noun) *Her on-the-spot reports from war zones around the world won her several awards.*
3 if you run or turn on the spot, you do it without moving away from the place where you are • *I ran on the spot for ten minutes to warm myself up.*

put sb **on the spot**
to cause someone difficulty or make them embarrassed by forcing them at that moment to make a difficult decision or answer an embarrassing question • *Steve rather put him on the spot by asking when we were going to get a pay-rise.*

▶ See also: **hit** the spot

spotlight

be in the spotlight *mainly American*
to get attention and interest from the public • *I always assumed she liked being in the spotlight.*
steal the spotlight *mainly American* • *It was said that he was jealous of his wife because she stole the spotlight from him.*

spots

▶ See: **knock** spots off sb/sth

spout

be up the spout *British informal*
to be pregnant • *His sister's only just turned sixteen and she's up the spout.*

up the spout *British & Australian informal*
wasted or spoiled • *Pete lost his job so that meant our holiday plans* ***went up the spout****.* • *And they refused to give me a refund so that was two hundred pounds up the spout.*

spread

spread like wildfire
if disease or news spreads like wildfire, it quickly affects or becomes known by more and more people • *Once one child in the school has become infected, the disease spreads like wildfire.* • *Scandal spreads like wildfire round here.*

spread the word
to tell other people, often a lot of other people, about something • *A meeting has been arranged for next Thursday, so if you see anyone, do spread the word.* • (often + **that**) *We need to start spreading the word that recycling is important.*

spread yourself **too thin**
to try to do too many things at the same time, so that you cannot give enough time or attention to any of them • *I realised I'd been spreading myself too thin so I resigned as secretary of the golf club.*

spread your **wings**
to start to do new and exciting things for the first time in your life • *The kids had all grown up and left home and I thought it was time to spread my wings and live a little.*

spring

be no spring chicken *humorous*
to not be young any more • *He must be ten years older than Grace, and she's no spring chicken.*

▶ See also: come/spring to **mind**

spur

on the spur of the moment
if you do something on the spur of the moment, you do it suddenly, without planning it • *It was something I bought on the spur of the moment, and I've regretted it ever since.*

spur-of-the-moment • (always before noun) *We hadn't planned to get married – it was a spur-of-the-moment thing.*

spurs

earn/win your **spurs**
to do something to show that you deserve a particular position and have the skills needed for it • *He won his political spurs fighting hospital closures during his time as a local councillor in Bristol.*

square

back to square one
if you are back to square one, you have to start working on a plan from the beginning because your previous attempt failed and the progress you made is now wasted • *We thought everything was settled, but now they say they're not happy with the deal, so we're back to square one again.* • *If this guy rejects our offer we'll have to* ***go back to square one*** *and start the whole recruitment process again.*

be on the square *mainly American*
to be completely honest in what you say and do • *So this guy you're buying the car from – how do you know he's on the square?*

a square meal
a big meal that provides your body with all the different types of food it needs to stay healthy • *Most of these supermodels don't look like they've had a square meal in their life.* • *If you're only eating a chocolate bar for lunch you need a good square meal in the evening.*

a square peg (in a round hole)
someone whose character makes them completely wrong for the type of work they are doing or for the situation they are in • *I never did understand what Paddy was doing in accounts – he was a square peg in a round hole.*

square the circle
to find a good solution to a problem when that seems impossible, especially because the people involved have very different needs or opinions about it • *Few poor countries can afford to look after their works of art properly, but neglect is unwise if you want to attract tourists. Thailand is attempting to square the circle.*

squeaky

squeaky clean
1 someone who is squeaky clean is completely good and honest and never does anything bad • *Journalists have been trying to discover whether the Senator really is as squeaky clean as he claims to be.*
2 completely clean • *I love the squeaky clean feel of my hair after I've washed it.*

squeal

squeal like a stuck pig *informal*
to make a long, high sound, usually because you are hurt • *It was only a scratch, but he started squealing like a stuck pig.*

squeeze

put the squeeze on sb/sth
1 to try to influence a person or organization to make them act in the way you want • *Human rights activists hope the US president will put the squeeze on the island's rulers.*
2 to cause problems for someone, especially by making it difficult for them to achieve something • *The recession has put the squeeze on many small businesses.*

stab

have/make a stab at sth/doing sth
to try to do something, or to try an activity that you have not done before • *I'd never tried water skiing before, but I had a stab at it while I was in Greece.* • *She made a reasonable stab at solving the problem.*

stab sb **in the back**
to do something harmful to someone who trusted you • *He had been lied to, stabbed in the back, by people he thought were his friends.*
a stab in the back • *To have your brother tell the press about your private life. That must feel like a real stab in the back.*

stable

closing/shutting the stable door after the horse has bolted
trying to stop something bad happening when it has already happened and the situation cannot be changed • *Improving security after a major theft would seem to be a bit like closing the stable door after*

the horse has bolted.

stack

stack the deck *mainly American*
to arrange something in a way that is not fair in order to achieve what you want ✍This phrase comes from the idea of arranging a set of cards in a card game so that you will win. • *The manager stacked the deck in Joe's favor so he got the promotion.*

▶ See also: **blow** your stack/top

staff

the staff of life *literary*
a food such as bread that is eaten in large amounts by a lot of people • *Bread is the staff of life, which is why we only use the finest organic flour to make ours.*

stag

go stag *American*
if a man goes stag to a social event, he goes without a woman • *He usually prefers to go stag to parties.*

a stag night/party
a party for a man who is going to get married, to which only his male friends are invited • *On Keith's stag night, his friends left him tied to a lamp-post in Trafalgar Square, wearing only his underpants.*

stage

▶ See: **set** the stage for sth

stake

go to the stake *mainly British*
if you say you would go to the stake for a belief or principle, you mean you would risk anything in order to defend it ✍In the past, the stake was the wooden post to which people were tied before being burned to death as a punishment. • *She believed passionately that the government were wrong on this issue and was prepared to go to the stake for her views.*

stake a/your **claim**
to make it clear that you want something, and that you think you deserve to get it • (often + **to**) *Descendants of the original settlers are going to court to stake their claim to the land.* • *In order to stake a claim for world prominence in astronomy, the university is building a huge new optical telescope.*

stakes

▶ See: **pull** up stakes

stalking

a stalking horse
1 a politician who tests the strength of a party's support for its leader by competing for the job of leading the party although they do not really intend to be elected • *He was a stalking horse, intended to undermine what was regarded at the time as a weak leadership.*
2 something that is used to hide someone's real purpose • *It's feared that the talks are just a stalking horse for a much wider deal between the two parties.*

stall

▶ See: **set** out your stall

stamping

▶ See: sb's stamping/stomping **ground**

stand

If you **can't stand the heat, get out of the kitchen.**
something that you say which means if you are not able to deal with a difficult or unpleasant situation, you should leave • *He says he didn't realize banking was such a stressful job. Well, if you can't stand the heat, get out of the kitchen.*

make a stand
to make a determined effort to defend something or to stop something from happening • *I felt the situation had existed for far too long and it was time to make a stand.*

stand a chance
to have a chance of success • (usually negative) *If government funding is withdrawn, small, independent theatres don't stand a chance.* • (often + **of** + doing sth) *We might stand a chance of winning if we continue to play as well as we did today.*

stand sb **in good stead**
if an experience, a skill, or a qualification will stand you in good stead, it will be useful in the future • *She hoped that being editor of the school magazine would stand her in good stead for a career in journalism later on.*

stand on your **dignity**

to demand to be treated with more respect than other people because you think you are more important • *And although he held a senior position in the company he would never stand on his dignity.*

stand on your **own two feet**

to be independent and provide yourself with all the things that you need to live without having to ask anyone else to help you • *I've supported those children long enough – it's time they learned to stand on their own two feet.*

stand or fall by sth

if you stand or fall by something, that thing alone causes you to succeed or fail • *The new television channel will stand or fall by its ability to attract younger viewers.*

stand the test of time

if something stands the test of time, it remains popular or respected for a long time • *Very little of the drama from this period has stood the test of time.*

stand up and be counted

to let people know your opinions, although it might cause trouble for you • *Those who did have the courage to stand up and be counted were arrested and imprisoned.*

take a stand

to publicly express an opinion about something, especially to say whether you support or are against something • (usually + **on**) *Many politicians fail to take a stand on equal rights for women.*

▶ See also: hold/stand your **ground**
stand by your **guns**
stand/turn sth on its **head**
stand/stick out a **mile**
can't stand/take the **pace**
stand **pat**
stand/stick out like a **sore** thumb
stand/walk **tall**

standard-bearer

a standard-bearer

someone or something that represents a particular group of people or set of ideas • (often + **of**) *He's the standard-bearer of the party's right.* • (often + **for**) *The Centre Party has long been the standard-bearer for environmental ideas.*

standing

could do sth **standing on** your **head**

informal

if you could do something standing on your head, you can do it very easily, usually because you have done it many times before • *I've done this job for so long I could do it standing on my head.*

▶ See also: **leave** sb/sth standing

stands

as it stands

as something is now, without changes to it • *The law as it stands is very unclear.* • *As it stands, the Panel's decisions can be reviewed by the courts.*

it stands to reason

if it stands to reason that something happens or is true, it is what you would expect • (often + **that**) *It stands to reason that a child that is constantly criticised will grow up to have no self-confidence.*

standstill

▶ See: **grind** to a halt/standstill

staring

be staring sb **in the face**

1 if a solution to a problem is staring you in the face, it is very obvious • *We spent ages wondering how we could make more space in the shop and the answer was staring us in the face all the time.*

2 if an unpleasant experience is staring you in the face, it is very likely to happen to you • *With only one day's supply of water left, death was staring him in the face.*

stark

be stark raving mad *British, American & Australian*

be stark staring mad *British*

to be completely crazy • *She looked at me as though she thought I was stark raving mad.*

stark naked

completely naked • *He walked into the room stark naked.*

starry-eyed

starry-eyed

happy and hopeful about something, in a

way which prevents you from thinking about the bad things about it • *Starry-eyed youngsters may dream of running away to the circus but life on the road is far from romantic.* • *Her accounts of small town America are far less starry-eyed than many writers.*

stars

stars in your **eyes**

someone who has stars in their eyes is very excited and hopeful about the future and imagines they are going to be very successful and famous • *She was a girl with stars in her eyes and dreams of becoming famous.*

▶ See also: **reach** for the moon/stars

start

bring/pull sb **up with a start**

if something that someone says brings you up with a start, it surprises you and often causes you to suddenly stop what you were doing • *The sound of his voice pulled me up with a start.*

▶ See also: set/start the **ball** rolling
set/start **tongues** wagging

starting

▶ See: be off the (starting) **blocks**

state

the state of play *British & Australian*

the present situation • (often + **in**) *The article provides a useful summary of the current state of play in the negotiations.*

state-of-the-art

state-of-the-art

state-of-the-art equipment and machines are the most modern and of the best quality available • *State-of-the-art computer graphics show how your kitchen could be transformed.*

station

▶ See: **marry** beneath your station

status quo

the status quo

the situation as it is at present, without any changes • *The army, having* ***maintained the status quo*** *for so long, is embarking on a series of reforms.*

stay

stay on the sidelines

to not be actively involved in something ✍The sidelines are the lines that mark the edges of a sports field. • *The majority of western countries decided to stay on the sidelines during the crisis in the Middle East.*

be left on the sidelines • *Telephone companies which do not offer competitive rates will be left on the sidelines.*

stay the course

to continue to do something that is difficult or takes a long time until it is finished • *Giving up smoking won't be easy – you must be prepared to stay the course.*

steady

▶ See: a firm/steady **hand** on the tiller

steal

steal a march on sb/sth

to spoil someone's plans and get an advantage over them by doing something sooner or better than them • *The company plans to steal a march on its competitors by offering the same computer at a lower price.*

steal the show

to get all the attention and praise at an event or performance • *All the singers were good, but 16-year-old Karine stole the show.*

steal sb's **thunder**

to do something that takes attention away from what someone else has done ✍In the 17th century the writer John Dennis built a machine which made sounds like thunder for one of his plays, but the idea was copied by someone else and used in another play. • *I kept quiet about my pregnancy because Cathy was getting married, and I didn't want to steal her thunder.*

steam

let off steam *British, American & Australian*

blow off steam *American & Australian*

to do or say something that helps you to get rid of strong feelings or energy • *Meetings give people the chance to let off steam if something has been bothering them for a long time.* • *After a long journey, the kids need to run around a bit and let off steam.* • *I've told her she can call me and talk any time she wants to blow off steam.*

under your **own steam**
without help from anyone else • *Don't bother sending a car for us – we can get there under our own steam.*

▶ See also: **pick** up steam
run out of steam

steep

▶ See: It's/That's a **bit** steep!

steer

steer clear of sth/sb
to avoid something or someone because they are dangerous or bad for you • *I'd steer clear of Joe if I were you – he'll only cause trouble.* • *I try to steer clear of heavy meals these days.*

stem

from stem to stern *American*
from one end of something to the other • *We overhauled the car from stem to stern.*

stem the tide
to stop something bad which is happening a lot • (often + **of**) *We have to stem the tide of emigration if our economy is to recover.* • *Ohio State were losing 24-48 when Jackson stepped in to stem the tide.*

step

be out of step (with sb**)**
to have different opinions from someone or to act in a way that is not suitable for a particular situation • *On the issue of immigration, the party is out of step with voters.* • *The child care available is often out of step with modern family life.*

Mind/Watch your **step.**
something that you say in order to tell someone to walk carefully • *Watch your step, the floor's wet and it's a bit slippery.*

step into the breach *formal*
to do someone's work when they are suddenly not able to do it • *Professor Collier stepped into the breach when the guest lecturer failed to turn up.*

Step on it! *British, American & Australian informal*
Step on the gas! *American & Australian informal*
something that you say to someone when you want them to drive more quickly • *Step on the gas, will you, we have to be there in five minutes!*

step out of line
to not behave as you are ordered or expected to • *It was made quite clear to me that if I stepped out of line again I'd be out of a job.*

▶ See also: move/step up a **gear**
be **one** step ahead
one step forward, two steps back.
step into sb's **shoes**
step/tread on sb's **toes**
watch your step

stew

be in a stew *old-fashioned*
to be worried and confused about something • *She was in a stew over the party arrangements.*

leave sb **to stew**
let sb **stew**
if you leave someone to stew, you leave them to worry about something bad that has happened or something stupid they have done • *I could have said a few comforting words and made him feel better but I thought I'd let him stew a while instead.*

stew in your **own juice/juices** *informal*
if you leave someone to stew in their own juice, you leave them to worry about something bad that has happened or something stupid they have done • *She'll calm down – just leave her to stew in her own juices for a bit.*

stick

get on the stick *American*
to force yourself to hurry or to start working • *If I get on the stick I'll finish the report by this evening.*

get/take [a lot of/some etc.] stick *British informal*
come in for [a lot of/some etc.] stick *British informal*
to be criticized or laughed at because of something that you do • (often + **from**) *I get a lot of stick from people at work over*

the way I dress. • *The government has come in for a lot of stick from the press over its handling of the crisis.*

give sb **[a lot of/some etc.] stick** *British informal* • (often + **about**) *I got your name wrong when I first met you. I recall you gave me a lot of stick about that.*

stick in your **craw**

1 *old-fashioned* if a situation or someone's behaviour sticks in your craw, it annoys you, usually because you think it is wrong • *I do lots of jobs in the house but my brother says I'm lazy, and that really sticks in my craw.*

2 *Australian* if someone sticks in your craw, they annoy you • *She sticks in my craw every time I have to deal with her.*

stick in your **gullet/throat** *informal*

if a situation or someone's behaviour sticks in your gullet, it annoys you, usually because you think it is wrong • *What really sticks in my gullet is the way he treats the women in the office.*

stick your **neck out**

to give an opinion which other people may not like or which other people are frightened to give • *I'm going to stick my neck out and predict a Republican victory.* • *He's never been afraid of sticking his neck out.*

a stick to beat sb/sth **with** *British*

something that gives you an excuse for criticizing someone or something that you do not like or approve of • *As far as the opposition are concerned, the slightest hint of scandal is yet another stick to beat the government with.*

stick to your **knitting**

if a person or company sticks to their knitting, they continue to do what they have always done instead of trying to do something they know very little about • *He believes the key to a company's success is to stick to its knitting rather than trying to diversify.*

stick to your **ribs**

if something that you eat sticks to your ribs, it makes you feel you have eaten a lot • *That chocolate pudding really sticks to your ribs.*

► See also: Shove/Stick sth up your **arse**!
stick to your **guns**
put/stick your **head** above the parapet
put/stick the **knife** in
stand/stick out a **mile**
poke/stick your **nose** into sth
put/stick your **oar** in
Put/stick that in your **pipe** and smoke it!
more sth than you can **shake** a stick at
stand/stick out like a **sore** thumb
put in/stick in your **two** penn'orth
put/stick **two** fingers up at sb/sth

sticking

a sticking point

a subject that people who are involved in a discussion cannot agree about • *The role of the army was the main sticking point at Thursday's abortive talks.* • *Pay has been a major sticking point in negotiations.*

stick-in-the-mud

a stick-in-the-mud

someone who has old-fashioned ideas and does not want to try new activities • *'Anyway, I'm not interested in married men.' 'Oh, don't be such a stick-in-the-mud.'*

sticks

Sticks and stones may break my bones (but words will never hurt me).

something that you say which means that people cannot hurt you with bad things they say or write about you • *Criticism has never bothered me. Sticks and stones may break my bones, and all that.*

sticks in the/your **mind**

if something sticks in the mind, you remember it easily, often because it was exciting or strange • *Of all the things that we did in Crete, that boat trip really sticks in my mind.* • *She had one of those faces that sticks in the mind.*

up sticks *British & Australian*
pick up sticks *Australian*

to leave the place where you have been living • *I was even thinking I might up sticks and move to somewhere completely new.*

sticky

be (batting) on a sticky wicket *British & Australian*

to be in a difficult situation because you

have not behaved in the correct way • *You know you're batting on a sticky wicket there, not paying tax.*

come to a sticky end *British & Australian humorous*
meet a sticky end *British & Australian humorous*
to die in an unpleasant way • *Of course the villain comes to a sticky end in the last act of the play.*

have sticky fingers
someone who has sticky fingers often steals things • *Another wallet has been stolen, so it looks as though someone in the office has sticky fingers.*

stiff

be as stiff as a board

be as stiff as a board
1 to be very stiff • *It's so cold out there – the washing was as stiff as a board when I brought it in off the line.*
2 if you are as stiff as a board, your body feels stiff and hurts when you try to move it, usually after a lot of physical exercise • *I cycled fifty miles yesterday and this morning I was as stiff as a board.*

a stiff upper lip
an ability to stay calm and not show feelings of sadness or fear • *You weren't allowed to show emotion in those days. You had to* ***keep a stiff upper lip*** *at all times.* • *I never once saw my father cry or show any sign of vulnerability – it's that old British stiff upper lip.*

▶ See also: Stiff **cheddar**!
Stiff **cheese**!
be as stiff/straight as a **ramrod**

still

still waters run deep
something that you say which means people who say very little often have very interesting and complicated personalities • *He's quiet and shy, it's true, but still waters run deep.*

sting

a sting in the tail *British & Australian*
an unpleasant end to something that began pleasantly, especially a story or suggestion • *At the start, it's humorous and light but like most of her short stories, there's a sting in the tail.*

take the sting out of sth
to make something that is unpleasant a little less unpleasant • *Humour, of course, can take the sting out of almost any unpleasant situation.*

stink

kick up a stink *British informal*
make/raise a stink *American informal*
to complain angrily about something that you are not satisfied with • *He kicked up a stink at the restaurant because the meal was late.*

▶ See also: smell/stink to **high** heaven
kick up a fuss/row/stink

stinking

▶ See: filthy/stinking **rich**

stir

cause/create a stir
to cause a lot of interest and excitement • *Emma caused quite a stir in her little black dress last night.*

stir-crazy

stir-crazy *mainly American informal*
upset and nervous because you have been in one place for too long ✍Stir is a word used in American English for a prison. • *It's no wonder she's* ***going stir-crazy****, shut in that tiny house all day with three young children.*

stitch

A stitch in time (saves nine).
something that you say which means it is better to deal with a problem early before

it gets too bad • *If you don't repair the oil leak now, you might damage the whole engine. It's a case of a stitch in time.*

stitches

have sb **in stitches** *informal*

to make someone laugh a lot • *She told a couple of jokes that had us all in stitches.*

stocking

▶ See: in (your) stocking/stockinged **feet**

stockinged

▶ See: in (your) stocking/stockinged **feet**

stomach

not **have the stomach for** sth
have no stomach for sth

to not feel brave or determined enough to do something unpleasant • *Demoralised and exhausted, the soldiers did not have the stomach for another fight.*

▶ See also: **turn** your stomach

stomping

▶ See: sb's stamping/stomping **ground**

stone

be carved/set in stone

if an arrangement, a plan, or a rule is set in stone, it is completely fixed so that it cannot be changed • (usually negative) *The rules aren't set in stone; they can be altered to suit changing circumstances.* • *These are just a few ideas to be discussed – nothing is carved in stone.*

Stone the crows! *British & Australian informal, old-fashioned*

something that you say in order to show that you are very surprised • *So she's a film director now. Well, stone the crows!*

a stone's throw

a very short distance • (usually + **from**) *We were staying in a small apartment just a stone's throw from the beach.* • (sometimes + **away**) *The city centre is only a stone's throw away.*

▶ See also: **leave** no stone unturned
sink like a stone

stony

▶ See: **fall** on stony ground

stool

a stool pigeon

a person, especially a criminal, who secretly gives information to the police in order to help them catch other criminals • *Once they discovered he was a stool pigeon, it was only a matter of time before they had him killed.*

stools

▶ See: fall between **two** stools

stop

stop at nothing

to be willing to do anything in order to achieve something, even if it is dangerous or harms other people • (often + to do sth) *She's one of these people who sets herself a goal and then she'll stop at nothing to achieve it.*

stop (sb) **in** their **tracks**

if something stops someone in their tracks, or if they stop in their tracks, they suddenly stop what they are doing because they are so surprised • *A loud scream* ***stopped me dead in my tracks.*** • *He opened the door and stopped in his tracks. A complete stranger was sitting in his office.*

stop short

to stop walking suddenly • *Lucy stopped short in amazement.*

stop short of sth/doing sth

to decide not to do something • *I stopped short of telling him what I really felt about him.*

stop the rot

to do something to prevent a situation from continuing to get worse • *The team had been suffering low morale before Smith was brought in to stop the rot.*

stops

▶ See: **pull** out all the stops

store

▶ See: **mind** the store
set great/much store by sth

storm

[dance/sing/talk etc.] up a storm *American informal*

to do something with a lot of energy • *Her dog barks up a storm every time the phone rings.* • *They were sitting in a corner, talking up a storm.*

ride out/weather the storm

to continue to exist and not be harmed

during a very difficult period • *When smaller companies were going bankrupt, the big companies with wider interests managed to ride out the storm.* • *It remains to be seen if the President will weather the political storm caused by his remarks.*

a storm in a teacup *British & Australian*
a situation where people get very angry or worried about something that is not important • (not used with *the*) *I think it's all a storm in a teacup – there's probably no danger to public health at all.*

take sb/sth **by storm**
to suddenly be very successful in a particular place or with a particular group of people • *Today we're interviewing the 20-year-old fashion designer who has taken Paris by storm.*

story

but that's another story
something that you say when you have spoken about something, but do not want to say anything more about it at that time • *Alex, meanwhile, was falling madly in love with Nicky, but that's another story.* • *Funnily enough, we bumped into each other again in Amsterdam, but that's another story.*

It's/That's the story of my life. *humorous*
something that you say when something bad happens to you that has happened to you many times before • *She said she just wanted us to be friends. That's the story of my life.*

That's my story and I'm sticking to it. *humorous*
something that you say when you have given an explanation about yourself which is not completely true • *I'm not fat, I've just got big bones. Well, that's my story and I'm sticking to it!*

straight

as straight as a die *British & Australian*
as straight as a pin *American*
completely straight • *The road runs straight as a die for fifty miles.*

be as straight as a die
to be completely honest • *You can trust Penny to tell you the truth – she's as straight as a die*

can't think straight
not **be thinking straight**
if you can't think straight, you are not thinking calmly and clearly about something • *I was so tired I wasn't thinking straight any more.* • *There are so many people talking, I just can't think straight.*

Give it to me straight. *informal*
something that you say when you want someone to tell you something unpleasant directly and honestly • *Just give it to me straight. How badly hurt is he?*

the straight and narrow *humorous*
if you keep on the straight and narrow, you behave in a way that is honest and moral • *The threat of a good beating should* ***keep him on the straight and narrow****.* • *Have you ever been tempted to stray from the straight and narrow?*

a straight arrow *American*
someone who is very honest and careful to behave in a socially acceptable way • *Friends describe Menendez as a straight arrow who rarely drank and was close to his family.*
straight-arrow • (always before noun) *In most of his films he plays the straight-arrow, all-American guy.*

straight from the shoulder *American*
if you speak straight from the shoulder, you speak directly and honestly • ***I gave it to him straight from the shoulder****. 'You're talking garbage,' I said.*
straight-from-the-shoulder *American* • *Then he spoke and it was his usual straight-from-the-shoulder performance.*

a straight shooter *American & Australian*
someone who you can trust because they are very honest • *He'll mean what he says – he's a straight shooter.*
shoot straight *American* • *Marvin will shoot straight* (= be honest) *with you. He's a good guy to do business with.*

straight up *British & Australian informal*
something that you say in order to emphasize that you are being honest or to ask someone whether they are being honest • *Straight up, John, I never laid a finger on her.* • *You're not telling me she's sixty! Straight up?*

► See also: (straight) from the **horse**'s mouth
keep a straight face
couldn't **lie** straight in bed
play a straight bat
be as stiff/straight as a **ramrod**

strain

strain every nerve

to try extremely hard to do something • *I was straining every nerve to catch what they were saying but they were sitting just a bit too far away from me.*

straining

be straining at the leash

to be very eager to do something that you are being prevented from doing at the present time • *Meanwhile we hear that our soldiers have reached a peak of fitness and are straining at the leash.*

strange

► See: make odd/strange **bedfellows**

strangle

strangle sth at birth

to stop something at an early stage of its development • *Plans to provide better nursery care are being strangled at birth by lack of funding.*

straw

the final/last straw

the last in a series of unpleasant events which finally makes you feel that you cannot continue to accept a bad situation • *One night he came home drunk at 5 o'clock in the morning and that was the last straw.* • *He'd been unhappy at work for a long time but **the last straw came** when he was refused promotion.* • (often + **for**) *Lucy leaving was the last straw for him and he pretty much gave up the will to live.*

a straw in the wind

something that shows you what might happen in the future • (usually plural) *There were one or two straws in the wind yesterday that suggested an offensive was imminent.*

the straw that breaks the camel's back

the last in a series of unpleasant events which finally makes you feel that you cannot continue to accept a bad situation • *Losing my job was bad enough but having the relationship end like that was the straw that broke the camel's back.*

straws

clutch/grasp at straws

1 to try any method, even those that are not likely to succeed, because you are in such a bad situation • (usually in continuous tenses) *He's hoping that this new treatment will help him but I think he's clutching at straws.*

2 to try to find reasons to feel hopeful about a situation when there is no real cause for hope • (usually in continuous tenses) *She thinks he might still be interested because he calls her now and then but I think she's clutching at straws.*

street

be (just/right) up sb's street

if something is right up someone's street, it is exactly the type of thing that they know about or like to do • *I've got a little job here which should be right up your street.*

the man/woman/person in the street

a typical, ordinary person • *Do the plans for celebrating the millennium take into account the views of the man in the street?*

street smarts *American*

the knowledge and experience you need in order to deal with difficult and dangerous situations in a city • *The kids around here may not be much good at reading or writing, but they sure have a lot of street smarts.*

streets

be streets ahead *British & Australian*

to be much better or more advanced than someone or something else • (usually + **of**) *In terms of profitability, the company is streets ahead of its nearest rival.* • *He's fairly average at English but his maths is streets ahead of any other kid in the class.*

strength

go from strength to strength

to become better and better or more and more successful • *The firm has gone from strength to strength since he took over as manager.*

on the strength of sth

1 if you do something on the strength of facts or advice, you do it because you are influenced by them • *On the strength of the projected sales figures, we decided to expand our business.*

2 if you get a job or an opportunity on the strength of something you have done, you get it because what you did was good enough to persuade someone you deserve it • *He was accepted for the writing course on the strength of a few articles in his local paper.*

a pillar/tower of strength

someone who gives a lot of support to someone else who is in a difficult situation • *Roger was a tower of strength when my parents died.*

stretch

not **by any stretch of the imagination**

by no stretch of the imagination

if you say that by no stretch of the imagination can you describe something or someone in a particular way, you mean that this way of describing them is certainly not correct • *She was never a great player, not by any stretch of the imagination.* • *He's pleasant looking but by no stretch of the imagination could you describe him as handsome.*

▶ See also: bend/stretch the **rules**

strictly

▶ See: be (strictly) for the **birds**

stride

get into your **stride** *British & Australian*

hit your **stride** *American & Australian*

to start to do something well and confidently because you have been doing it for enough time to become familiar with it • *Once I get into my stride, I'm sure I'll work much faster.* • *She began writing novels in the 1930's but really only hit her stride after the war.*

take sth **in** your **stride** *British, American & Australian*

take sth **in stride** *American*

to calmly and easily deal with something unpleasant or difficult and not let it affect what you are doing • *There's a lot of pressure at work but she seems to take it all in her stride.* • *A certain amount of criticism comes with the job and you have to learn to take it in stride.*

▶ See also: **put** sb off their stride

strike

strike a blow for sth/sb

to do something to support an idea or to change a situation to something which you believe is good • *He claims to be striking a blow for gender equality by employing an equal number of men and women.* • *This latest agreement will strike a blow for free trade within the EU.*

strike a blow against/at sth/sb • *The court's decision strikes a blow against minority rights.*

strike a chord

if something you hear or see strikes a chord, it seems familiar to you • *Carson? That name strikes a chord.*

strike at the heart of sth

to damage something severely by attacking the most important part of it • *The recent recession has struck at the heart of industrial development.*

strike gold *informal*

1 to become rich • *Some investors have struck gold investing in airlines.*

2 to win a gold medal (= a round piece of metal given as a prize) in a sports competition • *Not since the 1964 Olympics, when Ann Packer and Mary Rand struck gold have women's expectations been so high.*

strike it lucky *British, American & Australian*

strike lucky *British & Australian*

to suddenly have some good luck • *They struck it lucky with their second album which became an immediate best-seller.*

strike it rich

to suddenly become rich • *He struck it rich in the oil business.*

strike while the iron is hot

to do something immediately while you have a good chance of achieving success • *You may not get a better offer – I'd strike while the iron's hot, if I were you.*

▶ See also: strike/touch a **chord**
hit/strike **home**
hit/strike **pay** dirt

hit/strike the **right** note

striking

▶ See: in/within striking **distance**

string

another string to your **bow** *British & Australian*
an extra skill or qualification which you can use if you cannot use your main one • *If you can teach English as well as yoga, it's another string to your bow.*
have [a lot of/a few/several etc.] strings to your **bow** *British & Australian* • *She's a trained counsellor and she does pottery classes in the evenings – she has several strings to her bow.*

have sb **on a string**
to completely control someone's behaviour • *She can get him to do anything she wants – she's got him on a string.*

strings

no strings (attached)
if there are no strings attached to an offer or arrangement, there is nothing that is unpleasant or not convenient that you have to accept in order to get the advantage from the offer • *It's very rare that you get a loan that size with no strings attached.* • *The donation has no strings attached, so the charity is free to use it for whatever purpose it chooses.*
OPPOSITE **with strings (attached)** • *Most of their so-called 'special offers' come with strings attached, so beware.*

▶ See also: **pull** strings
pull the strings

strip

▶ See: **tear** sb off a strip

stripes

▶ See: **earn** your stripes

stroke

a stroke of luck
something good that happens to you by chance • *Phil was driving up to Manchester that evening and gave me a lift so that was a stroke of luck.* • ***By a stroke of luck**, someone at work happened to be selling very cheaply exactly the piece of equipment that I needed.*

▶ See also: **put** sb off their stroke

stroll

▶ See: take a stroll/trip down **memory** lane

strong

be as strong as an ox
a person who is as strong as an ox is very strong • *Get Carl to lift it – he's as strong as an ox.*

be sb's **strong point/suit**
if an ability or quality is your strong suit, you have a lot of it • (usually negative) *It has to be said, logic isn't Katherine's strong point.* • *Charm is not his strong suit but at least he knows it.*

come on strong
1 *informal* to speak to someone in a way that shows you have a strong sexual interest in them • *Towards the end of the evening he was coming on strong and I knew it was time to leave.*
2 *mainly American* to speak to someone in a very angry or threatening way • *I have to come on strong with some of the guys to get them to cooperate.*

a strong stomach
the ability to watch very unpleasant things without getting upset or feeling ill • (often + to do sth) *Some of the war scenes are fairly horrific – you need to **have a strong stomach** to watch them.*

strut

strut your **stuff** *informal, humorous*
to show your skill at doing something that involves movement, especially dancing • *I thought you'd be up there on the dance floor, strutting your stuff!*

stubborn

be as stubborn as a mule
to be very determined not to change your decision or opinion about something, even when it is wrong • *You won't get him to change his mind – he's as stubborn as a mule.*

stuck

▶ See: be (stuck) in a **groove**
be (stuck) in a **rut**
squeal like a stuck pig

stud-muffin

a stud-muffin *American informal*
a sexually attractive and sexually active young man • *She met her latest stud-muffin in the gym.*

stuff

do your **stuff** *informal*
to do something that people know you are good at or are expecting you to do • *Well, here's the make-up kit. Do your stuff!* • *She came on stage, did her stuff, and was out of the theatre within an hour.*

Stuff and nonsense! *old-fashioned*
something that you say when you think something is not true or is stupid • *Stuff and nonsense! I never said anything of the sort!*

stuff your **face** *very informal*
to eat a lot of food • (usually in continuous tenses) *We've been stuffing our faces with Susannah's delicious chocolate cake.*

▶ See also: **know** your stuff
strut your stuff

stuffed

Get stuffed! *very informal*
something that you say when you are annoyed with someone or you want someone to go away • *Oh, get stuffed, Jordan! You're not so perfect yourself.*

a stuffed shirt
someone, especially a man, who behaves in a formal, old-fashioned way and thinks they are very important • *I knew he was a banker and expensively educated so I was expecting him to be a stuffed shirt.*

stuffing

▶ See: **knock** the stuffing out of sb

stumbling

a stumbling block
a problem which prevents someone from achieving something • (often + **to**) *Lack of willingness to compromise is the main stumbling block to reaching a settlement.* • *Money, obviously, is a major stumbling block in any project of this size.*

stump

on the stump *mainly American*
a politician who is on the stump is travelling to different places in order to make speeches and get support, especially before an election • *On the stump in North Dakota, Anderson took time out to give this interview to our reporter.*

style

▶ See: **cramp** sb's style

sublime

from the sublime to the ridiculous
from something that is very good or very serious to something that is very bad or silly • *The evening **went from the sublime to the ridiculous**, an hour-long piano recital followed by two hours of karaoke.*

such

▶ See: Such is **life**.
There's no such **thing** as a free lunch.

suck

suck it and see *British & Australian informal*
to try something that you have not done before to discover what it is like or whether it will be successful • *I'm not sure at this stage whether it's the right job for me – I've just got to suck it and see.*

sucker

▶ See: **play** sb for a sucker

suffer

not **suffer fools gladly**
to become angry with people you think are stupid • *Jim's a fair boss, but he doesn't suffer fools gladly.*

sugar

▶ See: sugar/sweeten the **pill**

sugar-coat

▶ See: sugar-coat the **pill**

suit

suit sb **down to the ground** *informal*
if something suits someone down to the ground, it suits them perfectly, usually because it is convenient for them • *She has a young child so working from home suits her down to the ground.*

▶ See also: **follow** suit

sun

think the sun shines out (of) sb's **arse/backside** *British & Australian very informal*
to love or admire someone so much that you do not think they have any faults • *You're never going to hear Maggie criticizing Jim – she thinks the sun shines out his backside!*

under the sun
everything under the sun is everything that exists or is possible • *We talked about everything under the sun.* • *She seems to have an opinion on every subject under the sun.*

supper

▶ See: **sing** for your supper

sure

(as) sure as eggs (are/is eggs) *British & Australian old-fashioned*
something that you say when you are certain about what is going to happen or what someone will do • *He'll be back again next week asking for more money, sure as eggs is eggs.*

be a sure thing *American & Australian informal*
to be certain to happen or to succeed • *It's a sure thing she'll buy the most expensive jacket in the store.* • *His re-election is hardly a sure thing.*

sure as hell *very informal*
something that you say to emphasize that you are very angry or determined about something • *I sure as hell wish I'd never asked him to my house.*

sure thing *American informal*
something that you say in order to agree to someone's request • *'Can you give me a ride tomorrow morning?' 'Sure thing – no problem.'*

▶ See also: a sure **bet**

surface

▶ See: **scratch** the surface

swallow

swallow your **pride**
to accept that you have to do something that you think is embarrassing or that you think you are too good to do • *Swallow your pride and call your daughter to tell her you're sorry.*

▶ See also: swallow/take the **bait**
one swallow doesn't make a summer

swath

▶ See: **cut** a swath/swathe through sth

swathe

▶ See: **cut** a swath/swathe through sth

swear

swear blind *British & Australian*
swear up and down *American & Australian*
swear black and blue *Australian*
to say that something is completely true, especially when someone does not believe you • *He swore up and down that he'd never seen the letter.* • *If I ask her, I know she'll swear blind she locked the door.* • *He swore black and blue he had nothing to do with the missing money.*

swear like a trooper
to swear a lot ✍A trooper is a soldier with a low rank. • *He came in drunk and swearing like a trooper.*

sweat

by the sweat of your **brow** *literary*
if you earn the money that you use to live on by the sweat of your brow, you earn it yourself, by doing hard, often physical work • *A decent, hard-working man, he supported his family by the sweat of his brow.*

Don't sweat it! *American informal*
something that you say in order to tell someone not to worry • *Don't sweat it! We've got plenty of time to get there before the show starts.*

Don't sweat the small stuff. *American informal*
something that you say in order to tell someone not to worry about things that are not important • *Don't sweat the small stuff, Sam. It's just office gossip – no one takes it seriously.*

in a (cold) sweat
very frightened or anxious • *I dreamed I'd left the tickets at home and woke up in a cold sweat.* • *Just the thought of addressing all those people is enough to **bring** me **out in a cold sweat**.* (= make me feel very anxious)

No sweat! *informal*
something that you say which means that you can do something easily • *'Do you think you'll be able to manage all those boxes yourself?' 'Yeah, no sweat!'*

sweat blood
1 to work very hard • *He says that writing does not come naturally to him and he sweats blood over every sentence.* • *I sweat blood every week just to earn enough money to feed my family.*
2 to feel very worried or anxious • *We sweated blood as we waited for the police to phone, not knowing if Charlie was alive or dead.*

sweat buckets *informal*
to sweat (= lose water through your skin) a lot • *I was sweating buckets under my plastic rain jacket.*

sweat bullets *American informal*
to be very worried or frightened • *He was sweating bullets by the time the police had finished questioning him.*

sweat like a pig *informal*
to sweat (= have liquid coming out of your skin) a lot • *I was so nervous, I was sweating like a pig.*

▶ See also: slog/sweat/work your **guts** out

sweep

sweep sb **off** their **feet**
if someone sweeps you off your feet, you fall suddenly and completely in love with them • *She was hoping that some glamorous young Frenchman would come along and sweep her off her feet.*

sweep the board *British*
to win all the prizes or votes in a competition or an election • *Her latest film swept the boards at last night's cinema awards.* • *The liberals look set to sweep the board in the local elections.*

sweep sth **under the carpet** *British, American & Australian*
sweep sth **under the mat/rug** *American & Australian*
to try to hide a problem or keep a problem secret instead of dealing with it • *The incident has forced into the open an issue that the government would rather have swept under the carpet.* • *The evidence was on film and the police couldn't just sweep it under the rug.*

sweet

a sweet deal *American & Australian informal*
a very good business agreement or arrangement • *It's a sweet deal for the companies who get these franchises.*

sweet Fanny Adams *informal*
sweet FA *very informal*
nothing ✍*Fanny Adams* and *FA* are used in this expression to avoid saying *fuck-all.* • *Why's Mark dispensing advice? He knows sweet Fanny Adams about computers!* • *And what did we get for all our hard work? Sweet FA!*

sweet nothings
romantic things that people who are in love say to each other • *He kept leaning across the table, whispering sweet nothings in her ear.*

a sweet tooth
if you have a sweet tooth, you like eating food with sugar in it • *It's things like chocolate and cake that I can't resist – **I've got a** real **sweet tooth**.*

▶ See also: You **bet** your (sweet) ass!
cop it sweet
keep sb sweet

sweeten

▶ See: sugar/sweeten the **pill**

sweetness

be all sweetness and light
to be very pleasant and friendly, especially when other people are not expecting you to be • *I was expecting her to be in a foul mood but she was all sweetness and light.*
all is sweetness and light if all is sweetness and light, everyone is being friendly and pleasant with each other, especially when this was not expected • *They had a furious argument last night but this morning all was sweetness and light.*

sweet-talk

sweet-talk sb **into** doing sth
to persuade someone to do something by saying nice things to them • *Don't let him sweet-talk you into staying the night.*

swim

be in the swim (of things)
to know about and be involved in an

activity, especially something that is new or changing • *When the children were little I still did a day's work a week, just to keep me in the swim of things.*

▶ See also: go/swim against the **tide**

swing

get into the swing of it/things
to become familiar with an activity or situation so that you can start doing it well or enjoying it • *I was just getting into the swing of things when they transferred me to another department.* • *I hadn't worked in an office for a few years and it took me a while to* ***get back into the swing of it****.*

go with a swing *British old-fashioned*
if an event, especially a party, goes with a swing, it is very exciting and successful • *A traditional jazz band – now that would help your party go with a swing.*

swing both ways *informal*
to be sexually attracted to both men and women • *I've seen her out with men as well. She swings both ways, you know.*

swing the lead *British & Australian old-fashioned*
to pretend to be ill so that you do not have to work • (usually in continuous tenses) *And is she genuinely ill or is she just swinging the lead?*

▶ See also: swing/tip the **balance**

swinging

▶ See: **come** out swinging

swings

it's swings and roundabouts
British & Australian
what you **lose on the swings,** you **gain on the roundabouts** *British & Australian*
something that you say to describe a situation in which there are as many advantages as there are problems • *If you make more money, you have to pay more tax, so what we gain on the swings, we lose on the roundabouts.* • *It's swings and roundabouts, really. If you save money by buying a house out of town, you pay more to travel to work.*

sword

a sword of Damocles hangs over sb's **head** *literary*
a sword of Damocles hangs over sb *literary*
if a sword of Damocles hangs over someone, they are in a situation where something bad is likely to happen to them very soon ✍This phrase comes from a story about Damocles who had to eat his food with a sword hanging over him which was tied up by a single hair. • *You live with this sword of Damocles hanging over your head, knowing that you carry the virus for a deadly disease.*

swords

beat/turn swords into ploughshares *formal*
to stop preparing for war and to start using the money you previously spent on weapons to improve people's lives • *It would have been unrealistic to expect a country like the United States to turn swords into ploughshares the moment the Cold War ended.*

▶ See also: **cross** swords with sb

system

get it out of your **system**
to get rid of a bad feeling or a need to do something, often by expressing that feeling or by doing whatever it is that you want to do • *If she wants to see the world, it's best that she does it now, while she's young, and gets it out of her system.* • *There's a lot of anger in me and I have to do something to get it out of my system.*

systems

all systems go
something that you say which means everything is ready for a piece of work or period of activity to start • *We've just got to get the software put in place and then it's all systems go.*

T

to a T
perfectly • *That hat suits you to a T.*

tab

▶ See: **pick** up the bill/tab

table

on the table
1 if a plan or offer is on the table, it has been officially suggested and is now being discussed or thought about • *The offer on the table is an 8% increase on last year's wages.* • *At 6 p.m. on Thursday 29 April, a new deal was **put on the table**.*
2 *American* if a plan is on the table, no one is dealing with it at present but it has not been completely forgotten • *The committee agreed to leave the option to build a stadium in the city on the table.*

under the table *American & Australian*
money that is paid under the table is paid secretly, usually because it is illegal • *A lot of these people work 80-hour weeks with all or half of their salaries paid under the table.*
under-the-table *American* • *There have been allegations of under-the-table payments to football players.*

▶ See also: **bring** sb to the [bargaining/peace etc.] table
drink sb under the table

tables

▶ See: **turn** the tables on sb

tabs

▶ See: **keep** tabs on sth/sb

tack

change tack
try a different tack
to start using a different method for dealing with a situation, especially in the way that you communicate • *I've been very pleasant with them so far but if they don't cooperate, I may have to change tack.* • *Instead of always asking him what he wants, why don't you try a different tack and tell him what you want?*

tacks

▶ See: **spit** chips/tacks

tail

be (sitting) on your **tail**
to be driving too close behind you • *That Volvo's been sitting on my tail for the past ten minutes and it's starting to really annoy me.*

get off your **tail** *American very informal*
to stop being lazy and start doing something • (often an order) *You've just got to get off your tail and start looking for a job.*

the tail end of sth
the last part of something • *I just **caught the tail end of** the news.* • *Despite being at the tail end of an exhausting tour, she delivered a sparkling performance.*

the tail wagging the dog
if you describe a situation as the tail wagging the dog, you mean that the least important part of a situation has too much influence over the most important part • *Steve thinks we should buy an orange carpet to match the lampshade but I think that would be a case of the tail wagging the dog.*

with your **tail between** your **legs**
if you leave somewhere with your tail between your legs, you leave feeling ashamed and embarrassed because you have failed or made a mistake ✍Dogs often put their tail between their legs when someone has spoken angrily to them. • *The losing team walked off with their tails between their legs.*

▶ See also: be **chasing** your tail
turn tail

tailor-made

be tailor-made
to be completely suitable for someone or something • (usually + **for**) *The role of Emma was tailor-made for her.*
tailor-made
specially made for a particular purpose • (often + **for**) *Business schools are offering courses tailor-made for a firm's executives.*

take

I can take it or leave it.

something that you say which means that you do not hate something but you do not like it very much • *My sister's absolutely crazy about chocolate whereas I can take it or leave it.*

take-it-or-leave-it • *He's pretty take-it-or-leave-it about opera – I wouldn't waste the ticket on him.*

Take a hike/walk! *American informal*

an impolite way of telling someone to go away • *The guy kept pestering her, and finally she told him to take a hike.*

take sth **as it comes**

to deal with something as it happens and not plan for it • *At my age you take every day as it comes.*

Take it from me.

something that you say in order to emphasize that you have experience of something, and therefore what you say about it is true • *Take it from me – if you start ironing a man's shirts, you'll be doing it for the rest of your life.*

Take it or leave it.

something that you say when you have made an offer to someone and you want them to know that you are not going to change that offer in any way • *That's my final offer. Take it or leave it.*

take-it-or-leave-it • (always before noun) *It was a firm take-it-or-leave-it proposition.*

take the cake *British, American & Australian*

take the biscuit *British & Australian*

if you say that something someone has said or done takes the cake, you mean that it was very bad, and even worse than things they have said or done before • *She's been opening my letters – that really takes the cake!*

► See also: take sth/sb into **account**
not take no for an **answer**
take a **back** seat
take the **bad** with the good
swallow/take the **bait**
pick up/take the **ball** and run (with it)
draw/take a **bead** on sb/sth
bear/take the brunt of sth
get/take the **bit** between your teeth
not take a **blind** bit of notice
take on **board** sth
be/take **centre** stage
take it on the **chin**
take sb to the **cleaner**'s
take the **cloth**
carry/take **coals** to Newcastle
take it **easy**
Take it **easy**!
can't take/keep your **eyes** off sb/sth
take sth at **face** value
take the **fall** for sb/sth
take/tickle sb's **fancy**
I take/plead the **fifth** (Amendment)
Take **five**!
take sth in **good** part
accept/take sth as **gospel** (truth)
take sth for **granted**
take it for **granted**
catch/take sb off **guard**
I take my **hat** off to sb
take it into your **head** to do sth
take **heart**
take sth to **heart**
take the **heat** off sb
take to your **heels**
not take **kindly** to sth
take a **knock**
take the **law** into your own hands
take a **leaf** out of sb's book
take a **leak**
take **liberties**
take the **liberty** of doing sth
blow/take the **lid** off sth
take your **life** in/into your hands
take your **lumps**
not take sth **lying** down
take **matters** into your own hands
take the **mick**/mickey
take sb's **mind** off sth/sb
take sb's **name** in vain
can't stand/take the **pace**
take sb's **part**
Take a **pew**.
take your **pick**
take a **piece** out of sb
take the **piss**
sign/take the **pledge**
take the **plunge**
take **pot** luck
take a **powder**
take no **prisoners**
I'll take a **rain** check
take the **rap**
take it as **read**

take over/up the **reins**
take sb for a **ride**
take **root**
(Go) take a **running** jump!
take sth with a pinch of **salt**
take a **shine** to sb
take the **shine** off sth
pick/take up the **slack**
take a **stand**
take the **sting** out of sth
take sb/sth by **storm**
take sth in your **stride**
take sb to **task**
take sth by the **throat**
take a **turn** for the worse
take **umbrage**
take the **wind** out of sb's sails
take sb under your **wing**
take sb at their **word**
take sb's **word** for it
take the **words** out of sb's mouth
take the **wraps** off sth
take sth the **wrong** way

taken

have taken leave of your **senses** *old-fashioned*
if you have taken leave of your senses, you are behaving in a strange or silly way • (often used in questions) *You're leaving your family and your job to travel round the world, at your age? Have you taken leave of your senses?*

takes

▶ See: It takes all **sorts** (to make a world).
It takes **two** to tango.

taking

be yours **for the taking**
be there for the taking
if something good is yours for the taking, it would be very easy for you to get or achieve • *She fell on the third lap, just as the gold medal was hers for the taking.* • *If you're interested in the job, it's there for the taking.*

be like taking candy from a baby *American informal*
be as easy as taking candy from a baby *American informal*
to be very easy • *Beating them was the easiest thing in the world – it was like taking candy from a baby.*

tale

▶ See: Thereby/therein **hangs** a tales
live to tell the tale

tales

▶ See: **tell** tales

talk

be all talk (and no action)
if someone is all talk, they often talk about doing something brave or exciting but never do it • *He's always saying that he's going to leave and get another job but he'll never do it. He's all talk.*

be the talk of the town *old-fashioned*
to be the person or subject that everyone is talking about and interested in • *'I didn't realise anyone knew I was seeing Pete at the time.' 'It was the talk of the town, Kath!'*

can talk the hind leg(s) off a donkey *British humorous*
if you say that someone can talk the hind leg off a donkey, you mean that they talk a lot • *His father could talk the hind leg off a donkey.*

can talk the legs off an iron pot
Australian if someone can talk the legs off an iron pot, they talk a lot • *I dread getting into a conversation with Gillian – she can talk the legs off an iron pot.*

could talk under water *Australian informal*
could talk under wet cement *Australian informal*
someone who could talk under water has a lot to say in any situation • *Most of our guests were very quiet, but Harry could talk under water, so he kept the conversation going.*

talk a blue streak *American*
to say a lot very fast • *She talked a blue streak and we just had to listen.*

talk dirty *informal*
to talk rudely about sex, usually in order to make someone sexually excited • *I love it when you talk dirty to me.*

talk in riddles
to talk in a way that is difficult to understand ✍A riddle is a difficult and confusing description of something. • *She keeps talking in riddles, instead of just coming out and saying what she means.*

talk out of/through your **arse** *British & Australian very informal*
talk out of/through your **ass** *American very informal*
to say things which are stupid or wrong • *She says she'll sue us, but she's talking out of her arse.*

talk out of the back of your **head** *British & Australian informal*
to talk nonsense • (usually in continuous tenses) *He's talking out of the back of his head – you can't get a flight to Australia for less than £500 these days.*

talk shop
if people who work together talk shop, they talk about their work when they are not at work • *Even when they go out in the evening, they just talk shop all the time.*
shop talk • *Let's change the subject. That's enough shop talk for one evening.*

talk the talk ... walk the walk
If you say that someone talks the talk but does not walk the walk, you mean that they do not act in a way that agrees with the things they say. • *When it comes to recycling he talks the talk but he doesn't walk the walk.*

talk turkey *mainly American*
to discuss a problem in a serious way with a real intention to solve it • *If the two sides in the dispute are to meet, they must be prepared to talk turkey.*

You can talk! *British, American & Australian informal*
You should talk! *American informal*
something that you say when someone criticizes another person for doing something that they do themselves • *'He's a terrible driver.' 'You can talk!'* • *And you're telling me I'm lazy? You should talk!*

► See also: speak/talk of the **devil**
speak/talk the **same** language
speak/talk out of **turn**

talking

be like talking to a brick wall
if talking to someone is like talking to a brick wall, the person you are speaking to does not listen • *I've tried to discuss my feelings with her, but it's like talking to a brick wall.*

be talking through your **hat** *old-fashioned, informal*
to be talking about a subject as if you know a lot about it when in fact you know very little • *The man's talking through his hat. He doesn't know the first thing about banking.*

Now you're talking!
something that you say when someone makes a better suggestion or offer than one that they made before • *'Or we could go out for dinner if you prefer.' 'Now you're talking!'*

► See also: **look** who's talking!
be speaking/talking out of both **sides** of your mouth

tall

be a tall order
if a piece of work or request is a tall order, it is very difficult to do • *'They've given us three weeks to get the project finished.' 'That's a tall order.'*

stand/walk tall
to be proud of yourself and confident of your abilities • *For the first time in living memory, we have a leader who can stand tall in international gatherings.*

a tall story/tale
a story or a statement that is difficult to believe because it is too exciting or interesting • *He told me a tall story about having met some top models in a nightclub.*

tan

tan sb's **hide** *old-fashioned*
to hit someone, usually a child, many times as a punishment • *I'll tan that boy's hide if he touches my toolbox again.*

tandem

in tandem
if two things happen or are used in tandem, they happen or are used at the same time, and if two people do something in tandem, they do it together • (often + **with**) *The new system is designed to be used in tandem with the existing communications network.* • *She often works in tandem with a psychologist, one writing the software and the other advising on likely user reaction.*

tangent

go off on a tangent *British, American & Australian*
go off at a tangent *British*
to suddenly start talking about a different subject • *We were talking about property prices and you went off on a tangent.*

tangled

a tangled web
a situation that is very complicated and where many people are behaving dishonestly • (usually + **of**) *The inquiry revealed a tangled web of fraud and deception among the agents.*

tank

▶ See: be **built** like a tank

tanked

be tanked up *informal*
to be drunk • (sometimes + **on**) *We were tanked up on gin and orange juice.*

tap

on tap
available and ready to use • *Working in a library, I have all this information on tap.*

taped

have sb **taped** *British & Australian informal*
to know that someone is doing something bad and therefore be able to deal with them • *Spencer doesn't worry me – I've got him taped.*

tar

beat/knock the tar out of sb *American informal*
to keep hitting someone hard, or to completely defeat someone • *We used to fight a lot as kids and he always beat the tar out of me.* • *He was tired of her knocking the tar out of him when they played checkers.*

tar sb **with the same brush**
to believe wrongly that someone or something has the same bad qualities as someone or something that is similar • (usually passive) *I admit that some football supporters do cause trouble but it's not fair that we're all being tarred with the same brush.*

task

take sb **to task**
to criticize someone angrily for something that they have done • (often + **for**) *She took my father to task for getting drunk at my cousin's wedding.*

taste

▶ See: There's no **accounting** for taste!
smell/taste **blood**
give sb a dose/taste of their own **medicine**

tea

tea and sympathy *old-fashioned*
kindness and sympathy that you show to someone who is upset • *Sometimes people want practical advice and sometimes they just want tea and sympathy.*

would not do sth **for all the tea in China** *old-fashioned*
if you say that you would not do something for all the tea in China, you mean that nothing could persuade you to do it • *I wouldn't be a teacher for all the tea in China.*

teach

teach sb **a lesson**
to punish someone so that they will not behave badly again • *The next time she's late, go without her. That should teach her a lesson.*

teach your **grandmother to suck eggs** *British & Australian*
to give advice to someone about a subject that they already know more about than you • *You're teaching your grandmother to suck eggs, Ted. I've been playing this game since before you were born!*

You can't teach an old dog new tricks.
something that you say which means it is difficult to make someone change the way they do something when they have been doing it the same way for a long time • *You're never going to teach your father at the age of 79 to use a computer. You can't teach an old dog new tricks, you know.*

tear

tear sb **limb from limb**
to attack someone violently • *I'm sure if*

she got hold of the guy she'd tear him limb from limb.

tear sb **off a strip** *British informal*
tear a strip off sb *British & Australian informal*
to speak angrily to someone because they have done something wrong • *He tore her off a strip for being late.*

► See also: pull/tear your **hair** out
tear/tug at your **heartstrings**

tears

► See: It'll (all) **end** in tears.
reduce sb to tears

tee

to a tee
perfectly • *The beef was cooked to a tee.*

teeth

get/sink your **teeth into** sth
to start to do something with a lot of energy and enthusiasm • *Up till then she'd only had small parts in films and nothing she could get her teeth into.* • *It's a really exciting project – I can't wait to sink my teeth into it.*

have teeth
if a law or organization has teeth, it has the power to make people obey it • *The committee can make recommendations but it has no real teeth.*

in the teeth of sth
if something happens or is done in the teeth of difficulties, the difficulties cause problems but do not stop it • *The road was built in the teeth of fierce opposition from environmentalists.*

► See also: **cut** your teeth
grit your teeth
lie through your teeth
like **pulling** teeth
show your teeth

teething

teething problems/troubles
problems that you experience in the early stages of an activity ✍When babies are teething (= getting their first set of teeth) they are often in pain and cry a lot. • *There were the usual teething troubles at the start of the project, but that's to be expected.* • *Many marriages go through teething problems in the first few months.*

tell

(Go) tell it/that to the marines. *American*
something that you say in order to tell someone that you do not believe what they have just said ✍A marine is a soldier who works on a ship. Marines were thought to be less likely to believe things that people told them because they had travelled the world and knew a lot. • *You were here all day? Sure, you were – tell it to the marines.*

tell it like it is
to describe a situation honestly, not avoiding any of the unpleasant details • *There's no point pretending to young women that having a baby doesn't hurt. You've got to tell it like it is.* • *She's a straight talker, is Karen. She tells it like it is.*

tell its own tale *British & Australian*
if something tells its own tale, it shows the truth about a situation • *She may smile in public, but the expression in her eyes tells its own tale.*

Tell me about it! *informal*
something that you say in order to show sympathy to someone who has the same problem or bad experience as you • *'I've got so much work to do.' 'Tell me about it!'*

Tell me another (one)! *informal*
something that you say when you do not believe what someone has just said • *'I never drive over the speed limit.' 'Oh, yeah? Tell me another one.'*

tell tales
to tell someone in authority about something bad that someone has done because you want to cause trouble for them • (often + **about**) *She wasn't very popular at school – she was the sort of kid who was always telling tales about other kids.* • *I had half a mind to tell my boss about him but I didn't want her to think I was telling tales.*
a tell-tale • *Bullying often goes unreported because children don't want to be seen as tell-tales.*

tell sb **where to get off** *informal*
to angrily refuse to do what someone wants you to do, usually using direct or rude language • *She wanted to borrow money again so I told her where to get off.*

▶ See also: can't tell your **arse** from your elbow
live to tell the tale

telling

You're telling me! *informal*
something that you say to emphasize that you agree with something someone has just complained about because you have experienced it yourself • *'Brenda's really bad-tempered these days.' 'You're telling me!'*

tempers

tempers fray
tempers become frayed
if tempers fray among a group of people, they all become angry • *Tempers frayed when, after waiting for hours, we were told there were no tickets left.*
frayed tempers • *Traffic jams inevitably lead to frayed tempers.*

tempest

a tempest in a teapot *American*
a situation where people get very angry or worried about something that is not important • (not used with *the*) *The whole affair is just a tempest in a teapot. In a couple of months everyone will have forgotten about it.*

tempt

tempt fate/providence
1 to do something which involves a risk and may cause something unpleasant to happen • *I always feel it's tempting fate to leave the house without an umbrella.*
2 to cause bad luck for yourself by talking too confidently about a situation • *It's probably tempting fate to say so, but I haven't had a cold all year.*

ten

▶ See: nineteen/ten to the **dozen**
be ten/two a **penny**

ten-foot

▶ See: I wouldn't **touch** sb/sth with a ten-foot pole.

tender

▶ See: **leave** sb to sb's tender mercies

tenterhooks

on tenterhooks
nervously waiting to find out what is going to happen • *She waited on tenterhooks for James to call.* • *We were kept on tenterhooks all morning waiting for his decision.*

term

in the long/medium/short term
a long, medium, or short time in the future • *Cuts in company spending now should lead to profits in the long term.* • *In the short term, temporary housing will be provided for all of the flood victims.*
long-/short-/medium-term • (always before noun) *Have you made any long-term plans?* • *Medium-term funding may be offered to help start new projects in developing countries.*

terms

come to terms with sth
to start to accept and deal with a difficult situation • *She's never really come to terms with her son's death.* • *It's very hard coming to terms with the fact that you'll never have children.*

▶ See also: be on **good** terms with sb

territory

come/go with the territory
if you say that something comes with the territory, you mean that you have to accept it as a necessary part or result of a particular situation • *If you're a goalkeeper, you've got to expect injuries – it comes with the territory.* • *He's a public figure, and so a certain amount of media intrusion goes with the territory.*

test

test the water/waters
to try to discover what people think about an idea before you do anything about it, or to try to discover what a situation is really like before you become very involved in it • *I mentioned my idea to a couple of friends as a way of testing the water and they were very enthusiastic about it.* • *Perhaps you should go to a couple of meetings to test the waters before you decide whether to join the club.*

▶ See also: **stand** the test of time

testimony

▶ See: **bear** testimony/witness to sth

tête à tête

a tête à tête
a private conversation between two people • *They were obviously having a romantic tête à tête so I didn't disturb them.*
tête à tête • *We dined tête à tête* (= in private) *in a cosy little French restaurant near the river.*

thank

thank your **lucky stars**
to feel lucky or grateful that you have avoided an unpleasant situation • *I'm just thanking my lucky stars that I wasn't there when she was looking for someone to give the talk.* • *And you can thank your lucky stars* (= you should be grateful to me) *that I didn't tell him when he asked.*

thankful

▶ See: be grateful/thankful for **small** mercies

thanks

no thanks to sb
if you have done something no thanks to a particular person, you have done it although they did not help you or tried to prevent you • *Well, we've finished the painting, no thanks to Sandra who suddenly decided she had to go away for the weekend!*

Thanks a million! *informal*
something that you say to thank someone for something they have done for you ✍This phrase is often used humorously or angrily to mean the opposite. • *It was a really good piece of advice – thanks a million.* • *So you didn't bother to call me and tell me you'd be late? Thanks a million!*

that

and that's that!
something that you say which means you will not change your decision, although other people want you to • *Anyway, I'm not going to the wedding, and that's that!* • *You're not having any more chocolate, Joe, and that's that!*

▶ See also: That'll be the **day**!

them

them and us
in a them and us situation, two groups of people believe they are very different from each other and do not like each other, often because one group has more power than the other • *Separate restaurants for managers and staff have reinforced the them and us divide.*

there

there and then
then and there
if you do something there and then, you do it immediately • *She booked me in to see the consultant there and then.*

There, there. *old-fashioned*
something that you say to comfort someone, especially a child • *There, there. You'll feel better in a minute.*

You've got me there. *informal*
something that you say when you do not know the answer to a question • *'How many miles is five kilometres?' 'You've got me there.'*

▶ See also: There's the **rub**.

thereby

▶ See: Thereby/Therein **hangs** a tale.

therein

▶ See: Thereby/Therein **hangs** a tale.
Therein lies the **rub**.

thick

be as thick as thieves *old-fashioned*
if two people are thick as thieves, they are close friends • *I'm sure she tells Ruth what's going on – they're as thick as thieves, those two.*

be as thick as two short planks *British informal*
be as thick as shit *British taboo*
to be very stupid • *He might be good-looking but he's as thick as two short planks.* • *Most of the people who read these papers are as thick as shit anyway.*

be in the thick of sth
to be very involved at the busiest or most active stage of a situation or activity • *A fierce debate ensued and he found himself* ***in the thick of it.*** • *I can't talk right now – I'm* ***in the thick of things.*** • *When you're in the thick of the action, you don't always have time to think.*

give sb **a thick ear** *British informal*
to hit someone (usually a child) as a

punishment • *If I was cheeky at mealtimes my Dad would give me a thick ear.*

through thick and thin
if you stay with or support someone through thick and thin, you always stay with or support them, even in difficult situations • *That's what relationships are about – you **stick** with someone **through thick and thin**.* • *She remained loyal to the party through thick and thin.*

▶ See also: **lay** it on thick

thick-skinned

thick-skinned
if you are thick-skinned, you do not notice or get upset when people criticize you • *You have to be a bit harsher than that with Caroline to offend her – she's pretty thick-skinned.*
a thick skin • *As a politician, you get so much criticism levelled at you that you eventually develop a thick skin.*

thin

be (skating/walking) on thin ice
to be taking a big risk • *They knew that by publishing the article they were skating on thin ice.*

be as thin as a rake *British, American & Australian*
be as thin as a rail *mainly American*
to be very thin • *He eats like a horse and yet he's as thin as a rake.* • *She's as thin as a rail from all that running.*

be as thin as a stick
to be very thin • *She used to be as thin as a stick.*
stick-thin • *I remember her as a stick-thin teenager dressed all in black.*

be thin on top
if a man is thin on top, there is not much hair on the top of his head • *He hasn't gone grey but he's a bit thin on top.*
go thin on top • *He had really nice hair when he was younger but he's going a bit thin on top now.*

have a thin time (of it) *British & Australian*
to experience a difficult period, often because you do not have enough money • *Rob lost his job last year and they've been having a thin time of it.*

out of thin air
from thin air
if something appears or is made out of thin air, it suddenly and mysteriously appears or is made • *Using volunteers from the audience, he makes cards appear out of thin air.* • *You can't just create wealth from thin air.*
disappear/vanish into thin air • *He ran away eight years ago and it was as though he vanished into thin air.* • *Have you seen my calculator? It seems to have disappeared into thin air.*

the thin end of the wedge *British & Australian*
the start of a harmful development • *There are those who see the closure of the hospital as the thin end of the wedge.*

▶ See also: be thin on the **ground**
a fine/thin **line**
spread yourself too thin
wear thin

thing

be a thing of the past
to be something that does not exist or happen any more • *When video recorders were introduced, people said that the cinema would be a thing of the past.* • *Job security is a thing of the past.*

the best/greatest thing since sliced bread *humorous*
if someone or something is described as the best thing since sliced bread, people think they are extremely good, often better than they really are • *Portable phones are marketed as the best thing since sliced bread, but to me they're just another expensive gadget.* • *The way he goes on about her – you'd think she was the greatest thing since sliced bread.*

the done thing *British, American & Australian*
the thing to do *American*
the correct way to behave in a particular social situation • (usually negative) *Wearing jeans in an office environment isn't really the done thing.* • *You can't smoke during the meal. It's not the thing to do.*

have a thing about sth/sb
1 *informal* to like something or someone very much or to be very interested in

them • *I've got a thing about jackets – I must have twenty or so in my wardrobe.* • *He's got a thing about blondes.*

2 *informal* to hate something or someone, or to be frightened of them • *Andrew's got a thing about children's TV presenters – he absolutely can't stand them.*

There's no such thing as a free lunch.
something that you say which means that if someone gives you something, they always expect you to give them something or to do something for them • *He offered me a room in his house, but he seems to expect me to do all the housework. I should have known there's no such thing as a free lunch.*

▶ See also: **know** a thing or two
It's (just) **one** thing after another!
one thing leads to another

things

(all) other things being equal
all things being equal
if everything happens as you expect it to happen • *All things being equal, I should be home by Thursday.*

be all things to all men
to try to please everyone, even when it is impossible to do this • *You can't possibly keep everyone happy and you've just got to realize that you can't be all things to all men.*

things have come to/reached a pretty pass
something that you say which means a situation is very bad • (often + **when**) *Things have come to a pretty pass when old people are dying of hypothermia because they can't afford to heat their homes.*

think

I dread/shudder to think
something that you say when you do not want to think about something because it is too worrying or too unpleasant • (usually + question word) *He was going so fast – I dread to think what would have happened if my brakes hadn't worked.*

think you **are God's gift to women** *humorous*
if a man thinks he is God's gift to women, he thinks he is extremely attractive and that all women love him • *He's the most arrogant man I've ever met and he thinks he's God's gift to women.* • *Oh for goodness sake, you really think you're God's gift to women, don't you!*

think better of sth
to decide not to do something you had intended to do • *I nearly told him I was leaving, but then I thought better of it.*

think big
to have big plans and ideas and be keen to achieve a lot • *When it comes to starting your own business, it can pay to think big.*

think long and hard
to think very carefully about something before making a decision • *I thought long and hard before deciding to leave my husband.* • (often + **about**) *He thought long and hard about how to tell the children.*

think nothing of doing sth
if you think nothing of doing something that other people find difficult, you do it very easily • *He's so fit. He'd think nothing of running ten miles before breakfast.*

think on your **feet**
to think and react quickly, especially in a situation where things are happening very fast • *An ability to think on your feet is a definite advantage when you're doing live comedy shows.*

think outside the box
to think imaginatively using new ideas instead of traditional or expected ideas • *We try to encourage our researchers to think outside the box.*

think the world of sb
to like or admire someone very much • *He's an excellent doctor. His patients all think the world of him.*

▶ See also: can't think **straight**

thinking

put your **thinking cap on**
to start to think seriously about how to solve a problem • *Let me put my thinking cap on and see if I can come up with an answer.*

the thinking man's/woman's crumpet *British humorous*
a man or woman who is popular with the opposite sex because they are both intelligent and sexually attractive

• *Paxman has apparently grown weary of being labelled the thinking woman's crumpet.*

▶ See also: not be thinking **straight**

thinks

If sb **thinks** sth, they**'ve got another thing/think coming!** *informal*

something that you say when you are angry with someone because they are expecting you to do something for them that you do not want to do • *If he thinks I'm going to do the work for free, he's got another think coming!*

think-tank

a think-tank

a group of people established by a government or organization in order to advise them on particular subjects and to suggest ideas • *The pamphlet was published by the Adam Smith Institute, a right-wing think-tank.* • *Loren Thompson is a military analyst at the Alexis de Tocqueville Institute, a new Washington think-tank.*

thin-skinned

thin-skinned

if you are thin-skinned, you are too easily upset when other people criticize you • *You can't be too thin-skinned if you're in the public eye.*

a thin skin • *For someone who's always saying unpleasant things to other people, he's got a remarkably thin skin.*

third

the third degree *informal*

a situation in which someone tries to find out information by asking you a lot of questions • *Where have I been, who have I been with! What's this? The third degree?* • *If I'm even half an hour late she **gives me the third degree**.* • *I **got the third degree** from my dad when I got in last night.*

▶ See also: a fifth/third **wheel**

this

▶ See: This is the **life**!

thorn

be a thorn in sb's **flesh/side**

someone or something that keeps annoying you or causing you trouble • *A relentless campaigner, he was a thorn in the government's side for years.*

those

▶ See: Those were the **days**!

thought

I thought as much!

something that you say when you discover that something you thought was true is really true • *So they are having an affair? I thought as much!*

▶ See also: **perish** the thought!

thousand

▶ See: be **batting** a thousand

thread

▶ See: **hang** by a thread
lose the thread

threads

▶ See: **pick** up the threads of sth

three

be three sheets to the wind *old-fashioned*

to be drunk • *Bobby was already three sheets to the wind when we arrived.*

the three R's

reading, writing, and arithmetic (= mathematics) • *By the age of 6, all our pupils have a firm grasp of the three R's.*

three-ring

a three-ring circus *American & Australian*

a lot of noisy or confused activity • *It's a three-ring circus in that classroom – the kids can't possibly be learning anything.*

threshold

be on the threshold of doing sth

to be likely to do something soon • *Finland's Conservatives were on the threshold of joining a coalition government.*

be on the threshold of sth

if someone or something is on the threshold of a situation, that situation is likely to happen soon • *He was on the threshold of a great career.*

stand on the threshold of sth • *We are standing on the threshold of environmental collapse.*

thrilled

be thrilled to bits *British, American & Australian informal*
be thrilled to pieces *American informal*
to be extremely pleased • *'So what did your parents say when they heard you were pregnant?' 'Oh, they were thrilled to bits.'*

throat

take sth **by the throat**
to make a determined attempt to deal with something • *The Rockets took this game by the throat in the first quarter and never let go till the final minutes.*

▶ See also: **jump** down sb's throat
ram sth down sb's throat
stick in your gullet/throat

throats

be at each other's throats
if two people are at each other's throats, they are arguing angrily • *When we lived together, we were always at each other's throats.*

throes

be in the throes of sth/doing sth
to be experiencing a very difficult or unpleasant period • *The country is presently in the throes of the worst recession since the second world war.* • *We're in the throes of moving house at the moment.*

through

be a [Londoner/patriot/politician etc.] through and through
be [French/good/honest etc.] through and through
if someone is a Londoner etc. or is French etc. through and through, they behave in a way that is typical of such a person and that is the most important part of their character • *He always managed to say the right thing. He was a politician through and through.* • *She never really settled in England. She was French through and through.*

▶ See also: **know** sb through and through

throw

throw (sb) **a curve (ball)** *American & Australian informal*
to surprise someone with something that is difficult or unpleasant to deal with • *The weather threw a curve at their barbecue and they had to eat indoors.*

throw a wobbler/wobbly *British & Australian informal*
to suddenly become very angry • *She saw Peter talking to an attractive blonde and threw a wobbly.*

throw sth **back in** sb's **face**
to refuse to accept someone's advice or help in an angry or unpleasant way • *Each time I make a suggestion she just throws it back in my face and says I don't understand.*

throw caution to the wind(s)
to take a risk • *You could always throw caution to the wind and have another glass of wine.*

throw down the gauntlet
to invite someone to argue, fight, or compete with you • *A price war could break out in the High Street after a leading supermarket threw down the gauntlet to its competitors.*
OPPOSITE **pick/take up the gauntlet** • *He challenged me to a game of squash last week and I'm thinking I might just take up the gauntlet.*

throw good money after bad
to spend more and more money on something that will never be successful • *Investors in the project began to pull out as they realised they were simply throwing good money after bad.*

throw in your **hand** *British*
to stop doing something because you know you cannot succeed or win ✍When card players throw in their hand, they put all their cards onto the table because they know that they will not be able to win the game. • *I know it's unlikely that I'll get the job but I'm not going to throw in my hand just yet.*

throw in the sponge/towel *informal*
to stop trying to do something because you know that you cannot succeed ✍If a boxer (= man who fights as a sport) throws a towel into the ring, he is showing that the other boxer has won. • *Three of the original five candidates have now thrown in the towel.*

throw sth **into the pot**
if you throw an idea or a subject into the

pot, you suggest it for discussion • *Right, I think we've had enough talk of education. Does anyone have anything else they want to throw into the pot?*

throw (your) **money around**
to often spend money on things that are not necessary • *I'm not surprised she hasn't got any savings. I've never seen anyone throw money around like Polly.*

throw money at sth
to try to solve a problem by spending a lot of money on it, instead of trying to solve it by other methods • *It's no good just throwing money at the problem. We need to change the way the prison system is run.*

throw sb **off balance**
to confuse or upset someone for a short time by saying or doing something that they are not expecting • (usually passive) *I wasn't expecting any interaction with the audience and was thrown off balance by his question.*

throw sb/sth **on the scrap heap** *informal*
to get rid of someone or something that is not wanted or needed any more • (usually passive) *Many people over forty who can't find a job feel they've been thrown on the scrap heap.*
be on the scrap heap • *These kids are on the scrap heap as soon as they leave school.*

throw yourself **on/upon** sb's **mercy**
to ask someone to help you or to forgive you when you are in a difficult situation • *If all else fails, I might throw myself on Sandra's mercy and see if she'll drive me there.*

throw the baby out with the bath water
to get rid of the good parts as well as the bad parts of something when you are trying to improve it • *I don't think we should throw the baby out with the bath water. There are some good features of the present system that I think we should retain.*

throw the book at sb *informal*
to punish or criticize someone as severely as possible • *It was the fifth time Frank had been arrested for drink-driving, so the judge threw the book at him.*

throw sb **to the dogs**
to allow someone to be criticized or attacked, often in order to protect yourself from being criticized or attacked • *I really felt as if I'd been thrown to the dogs just to save other people's reputations.*

throw your **weight around**
to behave in a way which shows that you are more important or powerful than other people • *He tries to impress the rest of us by throwing his weight around at committee meetings.*

throw your weight behind sth/sb
to use your power and influence to support something or someone • *If we could persuade the chairman to throw his weight behind the plan, it would have a much better chance of success.*

▶ See also: pour/throw **cold** water on sth
throw sb in at the **deep** end
have/throw a **fit**
throw/toss your **hat** in the ring
shed/throw **light** on sth
feed/throw sb to the **lions**
knock/throw sb for a **loop**
throw in your **lot** with sb
sling/throw **mud** at sb
put/throw sb off the **scent**
send/throw sb into a **tizz**/tizzy
throw sb to the **wolves**
put/throw a spanner in the **works**

thumb

be under sb's **thumb**
if you are under someone's thumb, they control you completely • *The committee is firmly under his thumb and will agree to whatever he asks.*
be under the thumb *British & Australian informal* if a man is under the thumb, he is completely controlled by his wife • *He won't be able to do any of this without his wife's permission. He's under the thumb these days.*

thumb your **nose at** sth/sb
to show that you do not respect rules, laws, or powerful people or organizations • *The actor, in a further attempt to thumb his nose at Hollywood, declined to accept the award.*

thumbs

be all fingers and thumbs *British & Australian*
be all thumbs *American*
to be awkward with your hands and keep making mistakes • *Can you thread this needle for me? I'm all thumbs today.* • *You know when you get nervous and you're all fingers and thumbs.*

give sth **the thumbs down**
to show that you do not like or approve of something, or that you will not allow something to happen • *The committee gave my suggestion the thumbs down.*
get the thumbs down • (often + **from**) *My new hairstyle got the thumbs down from my family.*

give sth **the thumbs up**
to show that you like or approve of something or that you are happy for something to happen • *We all gave Mary's cake the thumbs up.* • *A new injectable treatment has been given the thumbs up by the authority.*
get the thumbs up • (often + **from**) *We got the thumbs up from the council to hold a fireworks party on the village green.*

▶ See also: **twiddle** your thumbs

thunder

have a face like thunder

have a face like thunder
look like thunder
to have a very angry expression • *I don't know what had happened but he had a face like thunder.* • *She didn't say anything but she looked like thunder.*
with a face like thunder • *He sat there with a face like thunder all evening.*

▶ See also: **steal** sb's thunder

tick

what makes sb **tick**
if you know what makes someone tick, you understand the reasons for their behaviour and personality • *A good salesperson knows what makes a customer tick.*

ticket

▶ See: be **just** the ticket

tickle

▶ See: take/tickle sb's **fancy**
tickle/tinkle the **ivories**

tickled

be tickled pink/to death *old-fashioned*
to be extremely pleased about something • *Val was tickled pink when Susan asked her to be bridesmaid at her wedding.*

tide

go/swim against the tide
to do the opposite of what most other people are doing • *It's not easy to go against the tide in defence of your principles.* • (sometimes + **of**) *He always seemed to be swimming against the tide of public opinion.*
OPPOSITE **go/swim with the tide** • *If you don't feel strongly about an issue, you may as well just swim with the tide.*

▶ See also: **drift** with the tide
stem the tide
turn the tide

tie

tie yourself **(up) in knots**
1 to become very confused or worried when you are trying to make a decision or solve a problem • (often + **over**) *They tied themselves in knots over the seating arrangements.*
2 *British & Australian* to become very confused when you are trying to explain something • *She tied herself up in knots trying to tell me how to operate the video recorder.*

tie the knot

tie the knot *informal*
to get married • *When are you two going to tie the knot?* • (often + **with**) *She's planning to tie the knot with her German boyfriend next June.*

tied

be tied to your **mother's apron strings**
if someone, usually a man, is tied to their mother's apron strings, they still need their mother and cannot think or act independently • *He's 30 but he's still tied to his mother's apron strings.*

tight

be in a tight corner/spot
to be in a difficult situation • *She had been in tight corners before and had always managed to get out of them.*

▶ See also: **keep** a tight rein on sb/sth
have/keep sb on a short/tight **leash**
run a tight ship
sit tight

tight-arse

a tight-arse *British & Australian very informal*
a tight-ass *American very informal*
a person who does not like to spend money or give it to other people • *You won't get a drink out of her, she's a real tight-arse.*

tight-arsed

be tight-arsed *British & Australian very informal*
be tight-assed *American very informal*
to be worried about small details that are not important • *Don't ask Jack to get involved, he's so tight-assed and really irritating.*

tighten

tighten your **belt**
to spend less than you did before because you have less money • *I've had to tighten my belt since I stopped working full-time.*

tighten the reins
to start to control something or someone more carefully • (often + **on**) *She has tightened the reins on her younger sons in an effort to curb their wild behaviour before it's too late.*
OPPOSITE **loosen/relax the reins** • (often + **on**) *The Government has relaxed the reins on wage control to boost consumer spending.*

tight-lipped

be tight-lipped
1 to have an angry expression • *Dad was harassed and tight-lipped and I thought he was going to lose his temper.*
2 to not give any information about something • (usually + **about**) *Army spokesmen are tight-lipped about planned operations.*

tightrope

▶ See: **walk** a tightrope

tiles

be/go out on the tiles *British & Australian informal*
to enjoy yourself by going to things like parties or dances • *'My head is thumping.' 'Oh yes? Were you out on the tiles last night?'*
a night (out) on the tiles *informal* • *Do you fancy going out to a club? It's ages since we had a night on the tiles.*

till

have your **fingers/hand in the till**
to steal money from the place where you work, usually from a shop • *He had his fingers in the till, that's why he lost his job.*
catch sb **with** their **fingers/hand in**

the till • (usually passive) *Senior officials who get caught with their fingers in the till must expect to be punished very severely.*

tilt

tilt at windmills *literary*
to waste time trying to deal with enemies or problems that do not exist • *We're not tilting at windmills here. If we don't do something about these problems, our environment may be in serious danger.*

time

About time too!
(And) not before time!
something that you say when someone tells you about something which has happened, in order to show that you think it should have happened a long time ago • *'They're widening the road outside the school.' 'About time too!'*

be before your **time**
if something was before your time, it happened before you were born or before you were involved with a person or thing • *'Do you remember the Watergate scandal?' 'No, that was before my time.'*

do time *informal*
to spend time in prison • *We did time together in Broadmoor.* • (often + **for**) *He did time for tax evasion in 1976.*

every time sb **turns around/round** *informal*
something that you say when you think something happens very often or too often • *Every time I turn around she's giving me some new rule about recycling the trash.*

for the time being
if you describe how a situation will be for the time being, you mean it will be like that for a period of time, but may change in the future • *You can stay with us for the time being.* • *We've decided to do without a car for the time being.*

from time to time
if something happens or is done from time to time, it happens or is done sometimes, but not regularly • *From time to time we heard a rumble of thunder.* • *We cycle into town from time to time.*

from/since time immemorial *literary*
for longer than anyone can remember • *Her family had farmed that land from time immemorial.*

not **give** sb **the time of day** *informal*
to refuse to speak to someone because you do not like them or because you think you are better than them • *He's so arrogant, he won't even give you the time of day.*

have the time of your **life** *informal*
to enjoy yourself very much • *He had the time of his life working on the ranch.*

have time on your **hands**
to have time when you have nothing to do • *Now that her children are all at school, she has a lot of time on her hands.*

have time on your **side**
time is on your **side**
to have enough time to do something without having to hurry • *There is plenty of time for you to have a baby. At twenty-five you still have time on your side.*

in next to no time *informal*
in no time (at all) *informal*
if something happens or is done in no time, it happens or is done extremely quickly • *It's only another mile or so. We'll be there in next to no time.* • *He had the food ready in no time.*

once upon a time *literary*
1 a long time ago ✍This phrase is often used as a way of beginning children's stories. • *Once upon a time there lived a young girl called Cinderella.*
2 if you say that something happened once upon a time, you mean that it happened in the past and you wish that it still happened now • *Once upon a time, everyone knew each other in this town and nobody bothered locking their doors.*

There's a time and a place.
something that you say when someone is behaving in a way which you do not think is suitable for the situation they are in • *How could she wear a dress like that to a funeral? Honestly, there's a time and a place.* • (often + **for**) *I don't like to see people kissing in the street. There's a time and a place for that sort of thing.*

There's no time like the present.
something that you say in order to show

that you think it is a good idea to do something immediately • *'When do you think I should phone Mr Hughes about that job?' 'Well, there's no time like the present.'*

There's no time to lose.
something that you say when it is important to do something immediately • *Her plane gets in at 3 o'clock so there's no time to lose.*
have no time to lose • *Come on, we've no time to lose if we want to catch the ferry.*

time after time
time and time again
if something happens or is done time after time, it happens or is done many times • *Time after time we were left without electricity.* • *I've told him time and time again not to bring those mice indoors.*

Time flies.
How time flies!
something that you say which means that time passes very quickly, often so quickly that you are surprised • *I can't believe your son is at university already. How time flies!* • *I never seem to manage to finish my work. The time just flies.*

Time flies when you're having fun.
something that you say which means that time passes quickly when you are enjoying yourself ✍Often used humorously when you are talking about an activity which was not enjoyable. • *'I can't believe we've spent four hours cleaning this carpet.' 'Well, time flies when you're having fun.'*

time hangs/lies heavy (on sb's **hands)**
if time hangs heavy, it seems to pass slowly because you do not have enough to do • *Time hangs heavy on your hands in prison.*

the time is ripe
if the time is ripe for something, it is a good time to do it or for it to happen • (often + **for**) *British socialists were convinced that the time was ripe for fundamental social change.* • (often + to do sth) *Many employers feel the time is ripe to give workforces a bigger share of the profits they have helped to create.*

Time will tell.
something that you say which means that the result of something will be clear after a period of time • *I don't know if this marriage will work, but time will tell.* • ***Only time will tell** if the business will be successful.*

▶ See also: **bide** your time
kill time
have a **lot** of time for sb/sth
mark time
pass the time of day
play for time

time-out

time-out *mainly American*
something that you say when you want people to stop what they are doing for a short time, especially when they are having an argument • *OK, time-out. We can calm down over a cup of coffee.*

times

be behind the times
to be old-fashioned and not know much about modern life • *I'd never even heard of half the groups he listens to. I'm a bit behind the times, I'm afraid.* • *Educationally, these schools are 20 years behind the times.*

change/keep up/move with the times
to change your way of living or working to make it modern • *I don't really like using a computer, but you have to move with the times, I suppose.*

tin

a (little) tin god *literary*
someone who behaves as if they are more important or powerful than they really are • *Have you seen him over there, acting like a little tin god?*

a tin ear *informal*
if someone has a tin ear, they do not have a natural ability to understand or enjoy music • *Even to someone with a tin ear like mine, their singing sounded pretty awful.*

tinker

not **give a tinker's cuss** *British & Australian old-fashioned*
not **give a tinker's damn** *American old-fashioned*
to not be interested in or worried about something or someone • (often +

question word) *I don't give a tinker's cuss what she thinks, I'll do what I want!* • *He's never given a tinker's damn for me, or for any of the family.*

tinkle

give sb **a tinkle** *old-fashioned, informal*
to telephone someone • *Okay then, I'll give you a tinkle when I get home.*

▶ See also: tickle/tinkle the **ivories**

tip

be on the tip of your **tongue**
if something you want to say is on the tip of your tongue, you think you know it and that you will be able to remember it very soon • *Now what's her name again? Hang on, it's on the tip of my tongue.*

the tip of the iceberg
a small part of a problem or a difficult situation which is really much larger than it seems ✍An iceberg is a very large mass of ice that floats in the sea and often it is only possible to see a small part of it. • *What you saw last night was* ***just the tip of the iceberg.*** • *The difficulties we've discussed are* ***only the tip of the iceberg.***

tip your **hand** *American*
to let other people know what you are planning to do • (often negative) *Rumours still abound about Saling's next project but the actress has so far refused to tip her hand.*

tip the scales
1 to make something more or less likely to happen, or to make someone more or less likely to succeed • (often + **against**) *Recent environmental disasters have tipped the scales against oil producers.* • *The sudden economic growth in the area should* ***tip the scales in favour of*** *new investment.*
2 to weigh a certain amount • (usually + **at**) *He tips the scales at just over 250 pounds.*

tip sb **the wink** *British & Australian old-fashioned*
to secretly give someone a piece of information that will help them • *So if you hear of any jobs going in your department, just tip me the wink, would you?*

▶ See also: swing/tip the **balance**
I tip my **hat** to sb

tired

be tired and emotional *British & Australian humorous*
to be drunk • *Professor Davis looked a bit tired and emotional, to say the least.*

tissue

▶ See: a tissue of **lies**

tit-for-tat

tit-for-tat *informal*
a tit-for-tat action is something bad that you do to someone because they have done something bad to you • (always before noun) *Six of the victims died in tit-for-tat attacks.*
tit for tat *informal* • *I forgot her birthday and so she didn't send me a card either. It was just tit for tat.*

tits

get on sb's **tits** *British very informal*
to annoy someone • *You just expect me to clean up after you the whole time and I tell you it's really getting on my tits.* • *This woman I work with has been getting on my tits recently.*

tittle-tattle

tittle-tattle *informal*
talk about other people's lives that is usually unkind or not true • *They know that tittle-tattle about the royal family helps to sell newspapers.*

tizz

send/throw sb **into a tizz/tizzy** *informal*
to make someone very upset, excited, or confused • *The idea of producing a meal for fifty people threw her into a tizzy.*
be in a tizz/tizzy *informal* • *The local press is in a complete tizzy about the murders.*

to

▶ See: to my **mind**

toast

be the toast of sb
to be liked and admired by a group of people • *His charm and wit made him the toast of Paris.* • *After rave reviews of her*

*play, she is **the toast of the town**.*

tod

on your **tod** *British informal*
alone ✍Tod is the short form of the Cockney rhyming slang (= an informal kind of language used in parts of London) 'Tod Sloan' which means alone. • *Poor old Reg was there on his tod, trying to get the job finished.*

today

here today, gone tomorrow
if something or someone is here today, gone tomorrow, they only exist or stay in one place for a short time • *He had a string of girlfriends, but they were always here today, gone tomorrow.*

toe

▶ See: toe/tow the **line**

toes

make sb's **toes curl** *American*
curl sb's **toes** *American*
to frighten or shock someone • *A loud scream from the next room made her toes curl.*

make sb's **toes curl** *British & Australian*
if an experience makes your toes curl, it makes you feel extremely embarrassed and ashamed for someone else • *The very thought of what she said makes my toes curl.*
toe-curling *British & Australian* • (always before noun) *She gave a toe-curling performance on the guitar.*

step/tread on sb's **toes**
to say or do something which upsets someone, especially by becoming involved in something which is their responsibility • *I'd like to make some changes to the working procedures, but I don't want to tread on anyone's toes.*

▶ See also: **keep** sb on their toes

toffee

can't do sth **for toffee** *British informal*
if you say that someone can't do something for toffee, you mean that they are extremely bad at doing that thing • *Annie couldn't act for toffee, but she still got a part in the school play.*

toffee-nosed

toffee-nosed *British & Australian informal*
toffee-nosed people think that they are better than other people, especially people of a lower social class • *She's much nicer than that toffee-nosed sister of hers.*

together

get it together
1 *informal* to manage to organize an activity • *We were planning a trip to India, but we never got it together.* • (sometimes + to do sth) *I wonder if he'll ever get it together to set up his own diving school.*
2 *informal* if two people get it together, they start a sexual relationship with each other • *We'd met a few times before, but we didn't really get it together till Rachel's party.*

toing

toing and froing
1 going backwards and forwards between places • (often + **between**) *The job involves a lot of toing and froing between London and New York.*
2 going from one method, idea, or plan to another in a way that wastes time when you are trying to achieve something • *The legal toing and froing will delay payment to Horden of the £10 million due on the contract.*

toll

take a/its/their toll
to have a bad effect on someone or something • (often + **on**) *Bringing up nine children had taken its toll on my mother.* • *The disease has taken a horrendous toll in parts of western Africa.*

▶ See also: **sound**/toll the death knell

Tom

Tom, Dick and/or Harry
anyone, especially people that you do not know or do not think are important • *Draw the curtains or we'll have **every Tom, Dick and Harry** peering through the window.* • *I want a qualified plumber to do the job, not just **any Tom, Dick or Harry**.*

tomorrow

like there's no tomorrow
as if there was/were no tomorrow
very quickly and eagerly • *She's spending money like there's no tomorrow and I don't know how to stop her.* • *Hungry and exhausted, he gobbled down the bread as if there were no tomorrow.*

Tomorrow's another day.
something that you say in order to encourage someone by showing them that there will be another opportunity to do something at a later time • *We've not made much progress today, but don't worry, tomorrow's another day.*

ton

be/come down on sb **like a ton of bricks** *informal*
to punish someone very quickly and severely • *If you miss any more classes, your teachers will be down on you like a ton of bricks.* • *When he failed to supply his accounts, tax inspectors came down on him like a ton of bricks.*
have sb **down on** you **like a ton of bricks** *informal* • *If she starts drinking again she'll have the family down on her like a ton of bricks.*

▶ See also: **hit** sb like a ton of bricks
weigh a ton

tone

▶ See: **lower** the tone
set the tone

tongue

get your **tongue around/round** sth
to pronounce a difficult word or phrase • *I just can't get my tongue around some of those Welsh place names.*

roll/trip off the tongue
if a word or phrase trips off the tongue, it is very easy to say • *The band is called 'Acquired Echoes'. **It doesn't exactly trip off the tongue**, does it?*

tongue in cheek
with your **tongue in** your **cheek**
if you say something tongue in cheek, what you have said is a joke, although it might seem to be serious • *'And we all know what a passionate love life I have!' he said, tongue in cheek.*
tongue-in-cheek • *She writes a very engaging and at times tongue-in-cheek account of her first meeting with the royal family.*

▶ See also: **bite** your tongue
find your tongue
hold your tongue
loosen your tongue

tongue-lashing

a tongue-lashing *informal*
if you give someone a tongue-lashing, you speak to them angrily because they have done something wrong • *The manager gave his team a tongue-lashing after they'd lost the game.*

tongues

set/start tongues wagging *informal*
if something that someone says or does sets tongues wagging, it causes people to talk about them • *His late-night visit to her home has set tongues wagging.*

too

▶ See: too **big** for your boots
too many **chiefs** (and not enough Indians)
Too many **cooks** (spoil the broth).
too much of a **good** thing
Too much **information**!
too **little**, too late

tools

the tools of the/your **trade**
the things that you need to use in order to do a job • *For the modern sales executive, a car phone is one of the tools of the trade.*

▶ See also: **down** tools

toot

▶ See: blow/toot your **own** horn

tooth

▶ See: **fight** tooth and claw/nail

top

at the top of the ladder
in the highest position in an organization • *He's at the top of the ladder after a long and successful career.*
OPPOSITE **at the bottom of the ladder** • *She started at the bottom of the ladder, but was rapidly promoted.*

at the top of your **voice**
if someone says something at the top of their voice, they say it as loudly as they

can • *'Stop it Nathan!' she shouted at the top of her voice.*

be on top of the world
to feel very happy • *She'd just discovered she was pregnant and she felt on top of the world.*

be over the top *informal*
if someone's behaviour or something that has been used or provided is over the top, it is more extreme than is necessary or suitable ✍In British and Australian English, this phrase is often made into the abbreviation OTT. • *I think pink champagne and caviar was a bit over the top for a twelve-year-old's birthday party.* • *I know he was angry, but attacking the waiter was way over the top.*
go over the top
• *They've gone a bit over the top with the Christmas decorations this year.*

from top to bottom
in every part • *We searched the house from top to bottom but we couldn't find the letter.* • *They bought an old hotel and restyled it from top to bottom.*

from top to toe
on every part of a person's body • *He gazed at her across the room, dressed in black leather from top to toe.*

from/out of the top drawer
from a very high social class • *Caroline liked to pretend that she came from the very top drawer of society.*
top-drawer • *His designs are stocked by all the top-drawer retailers in London and New York.*

get on top of you
if a difficult situation gets on top of you, it makes you feel so upset that you cannot deal with it • *She's had a few financial problems and I think things have just been getting on top of her.*

off the top of your **head** *informal*
if you say something off the top of your head, you say it without thinking about it for very long or looking at something that has been written about it • *'What was the name of that plumber you used?' 'I couldn't tell you off the top of my head.'* • *Off the top of my head I could probably only name about three women artists.*

on top of sth
if you are on top of a situation, you are dealing with it successfully • *We had a lot of work to do, but I think we're on top of it now.*

to top it all *British, American & Australian*
to top it all off *American & Australian*
if you have been describing bad things which happened, and then say that to top it all something else happened, you mean that the final thing was even worse • *The washing machine flooded, my car broke down, then to top it all I locked myself out of the house.*

the top brass
the people with the highest rank in an organization, especially an army • *All the top brass turned out for the funeral.*

the top dog *informal*
the most important and powerful person in a group • *Jackson was top dog and he made sure he got what he wanted.*

the top flight
the highest level in a job or a sport • *The Sheffield Eagles move down to the second division after two seasons* ***in the top flight****.*
top-flight • (always before noun) *He was the absolute stereotype of a top-flight executive.*

the top of the tree *British & Australian*
if someone is at the top of the tree, they are at the highest position in their job or in an organization • *Who would have guessed that she would get to the top of the tree before her clever and talented brother?*

▶ See also: at the top of the/sb's **agenda**
to cap/crown/top it **all**
blow your stack/top
pay top dollar
sleep like a log/top

top-notch

top-notch
of the highest possible quality • *We need to offer high salaries to attract top-notch staff.* • *People will pay a fortune for really top-notch wines.*

Topsy

▶ See: **grow** like Topsy

topsy-turvy

topsy-turvy

1 *informal* if a situation is topsy-turvy, it is confused and not well organized because things happen in the wrong order or people believe things are important when they are not • *The government's topsy-turvy priorities mean that spending on education remains low.* • *We're living in topsy-turvy times.*

turn (sth) **topsy-turvy** to completely change something, or to completely change • *The steel industry is about to be turned topsy-turvy by a technological revolution.* • *My life has turned topsy-turvy.*

2 *informal* if a room or a place is topsy-turvy, it is very untidy • *He went out leaving the house all topsy-turvy.*

torch

▶ See: **carry** a torch for sb

toss

not **care/give a toss** *British informal*

to not be worried about or interested in someone or something • (often + question word) *She can say what she likes, I don't give a toss what she thinks.* • (often + **about**) *He's only interested in himself, he doesn't care a toss about his family.*

▶ See also: **argue** the toss
throw/toss your **hat** in the ring

toss-up

a toss-up *informal*

a situation where two or more possibilities are equally likely • (often + **between**) *It's a toss-up between Angela and Moira for the editor's job.* • (often + **whether**) *It was a toss-up whether prices would go up or down.*

touch

be an easy/soft touch

if someone is an easy touch, it is easy to persuade them to do what you want them to do • *Her Dad's an easy touch – he's always giving her money.*

be in touch

to have regular communication with someone by telephone, letter etc. • (usually + **with**) *Are you still in touch with Caroline?*

keep/stay in touch to continue to communicate with someone • (often + **with**) *Her family have kept in touch with me since her death.* • *Do stay in touch after you've moved, won't you?*

OPPOSITE **lose touch** to stop having regular communication with someone • (often + **with**) *I've lost touch with all my old college friends.*

get in touch to communicate with someone, especially for the first time or after a long period of not communicating with them • (usually + **with**) *Anyone who knew the victim should get in touch with the police.*

be out of touch

to not know much about modern life • *Some of these judges are so out of touch, they've never even heard of Ecstasy.*

be out of touch with sth

to not have recent knowledge about a subject, a situation, or people's opinions • *His statement shows he's completely out of touch with reality.* • *Too often, politicians are out of touch with the electorate.*

OPPOSITE **in touch with** sth • *I try to stay in touch with what's going on in the arts world.*

I wouldn't touch sb/sth **with a barge pole.** *British & Australian informal*

I wouldn't touch sb/sth **with a ten-foot pole** *American & Australian informal*

something that you say which means that you think someone or something is so bad that you do not want to be involved with them in any way • *If I were you, I wouldn't touch that property with a barge pole.*

touch base

to talk to someone in order to find out how they are or what they think about something • (usually + **with**) *I had a really good time in Paris. I touched base with some old friends and made a few new ones.*

▶ See also: touch all the **bases**
strike/touch a **chord**
lose your touch
hit/touch a (raw) **nerve**
touch **wood**

touch-and-go

be touch-and-go

to not be at all certain • (often + **whether**) *After the accident it was touch-and-go whether she would survive.*

touchy-feely

touchy-feely *informal*

expressing a lot of emotion easily, often by touching people with your hands, in a way that some people think is embarrassing • *He's one of those touchy-feely people who are always putting their arms round you.* • *They run a support group for people who've recently been divorced – it's very touchy-feely.*

tough

be as tough as old boots
be as tough as nails

if someone is as tough as old boots, they are very strong and not easily injured • *'Do you think Grandad will ever recover?' 'Of course, he's as tough as old boots.'*

be as tough as old boots *British, American & Australian*
be as tough as shoe leather *American*

if food is as tough as old boots, it is difficult to cut or to eat • *That steak I had was as tough as old boots.*

a tough cookie *American & Australian informal*

someone who is very determined to do what they want and who usually succeeds even in difficult situations • *We're talking about a woman who brought up six children on her own – she's one tough cookie.*

tough love *mainly American*

a method of helping someone to change their behaviour by treating them in a very severe way • *Tough love is the only approach to take towards a relative hooked on drugs.*

Tough shit! *taboo*

something that you say in order to show that you have no sympathy for someone • *I know you don't want to go, but tough shit!*

▶ See also: be a hard/tough **act** to follow
Hard/Tough **cheddar**!
Hard/Tough **cheese**!
when the **going** gets rough/tough
hang tough
a hard/tough **nut**
a hard/tough **nut** to crack
a hard/tough **row** to hoe

tour de force

a tour de force

a performance or achievement which shows a lot of skill and which is admired by a lot of people • *His performance as Richard III was a brilliant tour de force.*

tow

in tow

in tow

if you have someone in tow, you have them with you • *She arrived with six small children in tow.*

▶ See also: toe/tow the **line**

towel

▶ See: **throw** in the sponge/towel

tower

▶ See: a pillar/tower of **strength**

town

be/go out on the town

to go out and enjoy yourself at bars, restaurants etc. in the evening • *She stayed in while the others went out on the town.*

a night (out) on the town • *At the end of the conference the girls had a night on the town.*

go to town on sth

to do something in a very eager way and as completely as possible, especially by spending a lot of money • *Angie and Phil have really gone to town on their wedding.*

▶ See also: **paint** the town red

toy

a toy boy *British, American & Australian informal*
a boy toy *American informal*
a young man who is having a sexual relationship with a woman who is much older than him • *Sheila's gone out rowing with Dieter, her new toy boy.* • *These movie stars seem to have a new boy toy every week.*

trace

▶ See: **sink** without trace

traces

▶ See: **kick** over the traces

track

on track
if an activity or a situation is on track, it is making progress and is likely to achieve something • (often + to do sth) *A fighter from Edinburgh is on track to become the world heavyweight boxing champion.* • *If the peace talks remain on track, an agreement can be expected by the end of the month.*
put/get sb/sth **back on track** • *Victory in New Hampshire put the President's failing election campaign back on track.*

a track record
all of the past achievements or failures of a person or organization • *We like to recruit managers with a strong track record.* • (often + **in**) *They have a strong track record in rescuing ailing companies.*

▶ See also: **keep** track

tracks

make tracks *informal*
to leave a place in order to go somewhere • *Jean, it's getting late – we'd better be making tracks.*

▶ See also: **cover** your tracks
stop (sb) in their tracks

trade

▶ See: **ply** your trade

trail

▶ See: **blaze** a trail

train

a train of thought
a series of connected thoughts • *You interrupted my train of thought – Now I can't remember what I was going to say.*

▶ See also: **set** in train

transport

be in a transport of delight/joy *literary*
to feel extremely happy or pleased • *I looked up to the heavens and praised God, in a transport of delight.*

trap

▶ See: **fall** into the trap of doing sth
shut your face/gob/mouth/trap!

travel

Have sth **will travel!** *humorous*
something that you say which means you have the skills or equipment that are necessary to do a particular activity and you are ready to do it anywhere • *Have teaching qualification will travel!*

tread

tread the boards
to act in the theatre • *So you're treading the boards these days, Emma. Earning any money?*

tread water
someone who is treading water is not doing anything to make progress • (often in continuous tenses) *I'm just treading water until I get an opportunity to try for a job with more responsibility.*

▶ See also: step/tread on sb's **toes**

treading

▶ See: be walking/treading on **eggshells**

treat

go down a treat *British & Australian*
if something goes down a treat, people enjoy it very much • *His animal impressions went down a treat with the children.* • *A cup of tea would go down a treat.*

treat sb **like dirt**
to behave badly towards someone in a way that shows that you do not respect them • *I don't know why she stays with him. He treats her like dirt.*

treat sb **like muck** *informal*

to treat someone without respect or kindness • *Mick treats his girlfriend like muck, but she's crazy about him.*

▶ See also: handle/treat sb with **kid** gloves
work a treat

tree

be out of your **tree** *informal*

to be crazy or behaving in a strange way, sometimes because of drugs or alcohol • *Is he going to build the extension himself? He's out of his tree!*

be up a gum tree *British & Australian old-fashioned*

be up a tree *American old-fashioned*

to be in a very difficult situation ✍A small animal in Australia called a possum climbs up a gum tree when it is being chased. • *If the insurance company won't pay for the damage, I'll be up a gum tree.*

trees

▶ See: can't **see** the wood for the trees

trend

▶ See: **buck** the trend

trick

do the trick *informal*

if something does the trick, it achieves what you want or need • *If the sauce tastes a bit sour, add a teaspoon of sugar – that should do the trick.*

every trick in the book

every clever or dishonest way that you know to achieve something that you want • (often + to do sth) *He used every trick in the book to get her to sign the contract.*

▶ See also: not **miss** a trick
turn a trick

tricks

tricks of the trade

clever methods that help you to do a job better or faster • *As a journalist, you* ***learn the tricks of the trade*** *pretty quickly or you don't survive.*

tried

tried and tested/trusted *British, American & Australian*

tried and true *American*

used by many people and proved to be effective • *They ran a highly successful advertising campaign using a tried and tested formula.* • *Most people would prefer to stick to tried and true methods of birth control.*

trigger-happy

trigger-happy

someone who is trigger-happy uses their gun too often and without thinking carefully • *The book's main character is a trigger-happy New York detective.*

trim

trim your **sails**

to spend less money • *The school is having to trim its sails because of government cutbacks.*

trip

trip the light fantastic *humorous*

to dance • *There I was, tripping the light fantastic in a sequinned ballgown.*

▶ See also: take a stroll/trip down **memory** lane
roll/trip off the **tongue**

Trojan

a Trojan horse

someone or something that attacks the group or organization it belongs to ✍In Greek stories, the Trojan horse was a large wooden horse that the Greeks used to take soldiers secretly into the city of Troy in order to destroy it. • *Traditional Labour supporters have accused the new leadership of being a Trojan horse trying to destroy the party from within.*

▶ See also: **work** like a dog/trojan

trolley

be off your **trolley** *humorous*

to be crazy • *What are you doing eating chocolate and cheese again? You're off your trolley!*

go off your **trolley** • *Has he gone completely off his trolley? He'll never get away with it!*

trooper

▶ See: **swear** like a trooper

trot

on the trot *British & Australian*

1 if you do several things on the trot, you do them one after the other • *It's been a*

good year for Britain's top player, who has won seven matches on the trot.

2 if you do something for a number of days, hours, years etc. on the trot, you do it for that amount of time without stopping • *He'd worked 48 hours on the trot and was totally exhausted.*

trouble

▶ See: be **asking** for trouble
spell trouble

trousers

▶ See: be **caught** with your pants/trousers down

trowel

▶ See: **lay** it on with a trowel

truck

have no truck with sth/sb
to refuse to become involved with something or someone because you do not approve of them • *Our committee will have no truck with racist attitudes.*

true

show sb **in** their **true colours** *British & Australian*
show sb in their true colors *American & Australian*
to show what someone's real character is, especially when it is unpleasant • *By showing the terrorists in their true colours, the government hopes to undermine public support for them.*
show your **true colours** • *When someone is faced with such a terrible ordeal, it shows their true colours.*
see sb **in** their **true colours** • *At last he saw her in her true colours as a liar and a cheat.*
see sb's **true colours** • *It wasn't until we started to live together that I saw her true colours.*

There's many a true word spoken in jest.
something that you say when you think that something someone has said as a joke may really be true or become true • *'At this rate we'll be walking all night.' 'Be careful – there's many a true word spoken in jest.'*

true to form/type
if someone does something true to form, they behave in the bad way that you would expect them to • *True to form, she turned up an hour later than we'd arranged.*

▶ See also: **ring** true

true-blue

true-blue *American & Australian*
if someone is true-blue, they support something or someone completely • *Tom's true-blue – he won't let us down.* • *They want control of the company to remain in true-blue American hands.*

trump

a trump card
an advantage that makes you more likely to succeed than other people, especially something that other people do not know about ✍In card games a trump card is one of a set of cards which have been chosen to have the highest value during the game. • *The fact that I had an Italian parent turned out to be my trump card when I applied for the job.* • *Anthea was about to* ***play*** *her* ***trump card*** *– none of the money could be released without her signature.*

trumps

come up/turn up trumps *British & Australian*
to complete an activity successfully or to produce a good result, especially when you were not expected to ✍In card games, trumps are a set of cards which have been chosen to have the highest value during the game. • *John's uncle came up trumps and found us a place to stay at the last minute.*

trust

I wouldn't trust sb **as far as I could throw** them. *informal*
something that you say which means that you do not trust someone at all • *I'll admit John is very charming, but I wouldn't trust him as far as I could throw him.*

not **trust** sb **an inch** *British & Australian*
to not trust someone at all • *He's charming enough but I wouldn't trust him an inch.*

truth

Truth will out. *slightly formal*
something that you say which means the truth will always be discovered • *They're bound to find out what you've done. Truth will out, you know.*

try

try sth **for size** *British & Australian*
try sth **on for size** *American & Australian*
to test something or to think about an idea in order to decide whether it works or whether you can use it • *Try that for size. It's the new software program I've been working on.* • *The government is still trying some ideas on for size before committing itself to action.*

try your **hand at** sth
to try doing something for the first time • *I might try my hand at a bit of Indian cooking.*

try it on *British & Australian*
to behave badly or to try to deceive people, especially in order to make them do something for you • (often in continuous tenses) *He's not really ill, he's just trying it on.* • (sometimes + **with**) *I'm not giving her any money. If she tries it on with me I'll just refuse.*

try your **luck**
to try to achieve something although you know that you might not succeed • *She had always wanted to act and, in 1959, came to London to try her luck on the stage.*

try your **wings** *American*
to try to do something that you have recently learned to do • *She's just qualified and is looking for a chance to try her wings as a design consultant.*

▶ See also: try a different **tack**

tube

down the tube/tubes

1 *informal* if something goes down the tubes, it fails or disappears • *Our holiday plans* ***went down the tube*** *because of the train strike.*

2 *American informal* if someone goes down the tubes, they fail • *He's in danger of going down the tubes if he doesn't learn to get on with people at work.*

tub-thumping

tub-thumping *British*
speech or behaviour that is intended to force people to support an idea or plan • *Far too much tub-thumping goes on during these debates.*
tub-thumping • (always before noun) *She gave a tub-thumping speech.*

tug

▶ See: tear/tug at your **heartstrings**

tune

▶ See: **call** the shots/tune
change your tune
dance to sb's tune

tuppence

not **care/give tuppence** *British & Australian old-fashioned*
to not care about something or someone in any way • (often + **for**) *She doesn't give tuppence for her family.* • *You can do what you like. I don't care tuppence.*

turf

a turf war *American*
a fight or an argument to decide who controls an area or an activity • *The recent shootings in the city are part of a turf war between two competing gangs.*

turkey

a turkey shoot *mainly American*
if a fight or a war is a turkey shoot, one side is certain to be completely defeated because the other side is much stronger • *Their aircraft destroyed every military camp in a three-day turkey shoot.*

▶ See also: **talk** turkey

turkeys

like turkeys voting for (an early) Christmas *British & Australian humorous*
if people are like turkeys voting for Christmas, they choose to accept a situation which will have very bad results for them ✍Turkeys are large birds which are often eaten on Christmas Day. • *Teachers agreeing to even larger class sizes would be like turkeys voting for Christmas.*

turn

at every turn
if something unpleasant happens at every turn, it happens every time you try to do something • *Throughout his life, he felt himself stifled by his father at every turn.*

be cooked/done to a turn
to be cooked for exactly the right amount of time • *The beef was done to a turn.*

speak/talk out of turn *slightly formal*
to say something that you should not have said or that you did not have the authority to say • *I'm sorry if I spoke out of turn, but somebody had to tell him the facts.*

take a turn for the worse
if a situation or an ill person takes a turn for the worse, they become worse or more ill • *Their relationship took a turn for the worse when he lost his job.*

turn a blind eye
to choose to ignore behaviour that you know is wrong • *I knew Hugo was taking the money but I turned a blind eye because he was my sister's child.* • (often + **to**) *Management often turn a blind eye to bullying in the workplace.*

turn a deaf ear
to ignore someone when they complain or ask for something • (often + **to**) *In the past they've tended to turn a deaf ear to such requests.*

not **turn a hair**
to not show any emotion when you are told something bad or when something bad happens • *I was expecting her to be furious but she didn't turn a hair.*

turn a trick *American very informal*
to have sex with someone for money • *She'd been known to turn a trick when she needed a few dollars.*

turn your **back on** sth
to stop being involved in something • *Spain cannot afford to turn its back on tourism.*

turn your **hand to** sth
if you say that someone could turn their hand to an activity or skill, you mean they could do it well although they have no experience of it • *I'm sure you could turn your hand to a bit of writing if you wanted.* • *Stella's very talented. She could turn her hand to anything.*

turn heads
if something or someone turns heads, people notice them because they look interesting or attractive • *Brigitte Bardot still turned heads even in her 40's.*

turn in your **grave** *British, American & Australian*
turn over/spin in your **grave** *American*
if you say that a dead person would turn in their grave, you mean that they would be very angry or upset about something if they knew • *She'd turn in her grave if she knew what he was spending his inheritance on.*

turn king's/queen's evidence
turn state's evidence
if someone who has been accused of a crime turns king's evidence, they give information in a court of law about other people involved in the crime in order to have their own punishment reduced • *She was given a lenient sentence in exchange for turning king's evidence.*

turn your nose up

turn your **nose up** *informal*
to not accept something because you do not think it is good enough for you • (usually + **at**) *He turned his nose up at my offer of soup and said he wanted a proper meal.*

a turn of phrase
1 a way of saying something • *'Significant other', meaning 'partner', now that's an interesting turn of phrase.*
2 the ability to express yourself well • *She*

has a nice turn of phrase which should serve her well in journalism.

a turn of the screw
an action which makes a bad situation worse, especially in order to force someone to do something • *Each letter from my bank manager is another turn of the screw.*

turn on the waterworks *humorous*
to start crying in order to get what you want • *He always turns on the waterworks if he doesn't get exactly what he wants.*

turn over a new leaf
to start behaving in a better way • *Apparently he's turned over a new leaf and he's not drinking any more.*

turn tail

turn tail *informal*
to run away, usually because you are frightened • *When I saw him my first impulse was to turn tail and flee.*

turn the corner
if something or someone turns the corner, their situation starts to improve after a difficult period • *Certainly, the company's been through difficult times but I think we can safely say that we have now turned the corner.* • *I was really ill on Tuesday and Wednesday but I think I've finally turned the corner.*

turn the other cheek
if you turn the other cheek when someone attacks or insults you, you do not get angry and attack or insult them but stay calm instead • *Neither nation is renowned for turning the other cheek.*

turn the page
to begin to behave in a more positive way after a period of difficulties • *It's time to put this tragedy to rest and turn the page to a new and happier chapter of our lives.*

turn the tables on sb
to change a situation so that you now have an advantage over someone who previously had an advantage over you • *She turned the tables on her rival with allegations of corruption.*
The tables are turned. • *In the past it was always Dan who was having affairs while Lucy stuck by him. Now the tables are turned.*

turn the tide
to change a situation or people's opinions to the opposite of what they were before • *The government had planned cuts in the armed forces, but when war broke out, the military saw a chance to turn the tide.*
the tide turns • *The tide has turned and the cinema is becoming popular again.*

turn to dust *literary*
to become worth nothing • *Every promise they have made has turned to dust.*

turn up like a bad penny *old-fashioned*
to arrive at a place or event where you are not wanted • *She'll turn up again, like a bad penny, just you see.*

turn up the heat
1 to make a situation more serious by trying harder to force someone to do something • (often + **on**) *Lorry drivers are discussing whether to turn up the heat on their bosses by holding a one-day strike.* • *The United States has turned up the heat by threatening military action.*
2 to start to work or play in a more determined and effective way • *Nottingham turned up the heat in the second half and forced their opponents back onto the defensive.*

turn your stomach
to make you feel sick, often because you are angry or upset about something • *The amount of money she spends on designer clothes really turns my stomach.* • *The sight of Joe eating raw fish is enough to turn your stomach.*

▶ See also: put/turn the **clock** back
come/go/turn **full** circle

turn/use sth to **good** account
stand/turn sth on its **head**
turn/twist the **knife**
beat/turn **swords** into ploughshares
come up/turn up **trumps**

turn-up

▶ See: That's/There's a turn-up for the **books**.

turnabout

Turnabout is fair play. *American*
something that you say which means you will do something that someone else has done because this is fair • *You cook dinner tonight, I cooked last night. Turnabout is fair play.*

turtle

turn turtle
if a boat turns turtle, it turns upside down in the water • *We lost all our diving gear when the boat turned turtle just off the shore.*

twain

Never the twain shall meet. *literary*
something that you say when two things or people are so different that they can never exist together or agree with each other • *Psychologists support behavioural therapy, pharmacologists support drugs, and never the twain shall meet.*

twiddle

twiddle your **thumbs**
to have nothing useful to do while you are waiting for something to happen • *Until I get the go-ahead, I'm just sitting around twiddling my thumbs.*

twilight

the twilight zone
the area where one thing ends and another begins, especially when it is not clear exactly where or when this happens • (often + **between**) *She'd been unconscious ever since she fell, trapped in the twilight zone between life and death.*

twinkle

when sb **was a (mere) twinkle in** their **father's eye** *humorous*
at a time before someone was born • *All this happened a very long time ago, when you were a mere twinkle in your father's eye.*

twinkling

in the twinkling of an eye
if something happens in the twinkling of an eye, it happens very quickly • *This machine will do all the calculations in the twinkling of an eye.*

twist

drive/send sb **round the twist** *British & Australian informal*
to make someone very angry, especially by continuing to do something annoying • *This non-stop banging is driving me round the twist.* • *A day with my mother is enough to send anyone round the twist.*

round the twist *British & Australian informal*
crazy • *She's completely round the twist – just sits there all day talking to herself.* • *I put the milk in the cupboard and the sugar in the fridge. I think I'm **going round the twist**.*

twist sb's **arm**
to persuade someone to do something that they do not want to do • *He might help us with the painting if you twist his arm.* • (humorous) *'Have a cream cake?' 'Oh, go on then, if you twist my arm.'*

▶ See also: turn/twist the **knife**
leave sb to twist in the wind
twist/wrap sb around/round your **little** finger

two

(There's) no two ways about it.
something that you say in order to emphasize that something is true • *Patricia was the meanest person I've ever met. No two ways about it.*

be in/of two minds
to be unable to decide about something • (often + **whether**) *I was in two minds whether or not to come this morning.* • (often + **about**) *Residents are of two minds about new traffic restrictions in the area.*

be like two peas in a pod
to be very similar • *You can tell they're brothers at a glance – they're like two peas in a pod.*

be two of a kind
if two people are two of a kind, they have

very similar characters • *Amy and I are two of a kind. That's why we've stayed friends for so long.*

fall between two stools *mainly British*
be caught between two stools *mainly British*
if something falls between two stools, it fails because it is neither one type of thing nor another and if someone falls between two stools, they fail because they try to combine two different types of thing that cannot be combined • *For me, it fell between two stools, being neither romantic fiction nor serious literature.* • *If you try to organize an event that will appeal to both young and old, you can end up caught between two stools.*

for two cents *American & Australian informal*
if you say that for two cents you would do something unpleasant to someone, you mean that you want very much to do it to them ✍A cent is the coin with the smallest value in American money and two cents is worth very little. • *For two cents I'd hit him. He's so darned spoiled and stuck up.*

have two left feet *humorous*
to move in a very awkward way when dancing • *When we danced together I discovered he had two left feet.*

not **have two pennies to rub together** *British, American & Australian*
not **have two nickels to rub together** *American*
to be very poor • *She's been out of work for months and doesn't have two pennies to rub together.*

It takes two to tango.
something that you say which means if two people were involved in a bad situation, both must be responsible ✍A tango is a South American dance for two people. • *'She blames Tracy for stealing her husband.' 'Well, it takes two to tango.'*

put in/stick in your **two penn'orth** *British old-fashioned*
to give your opinion in a conversation, often when it is not wanted • *Whenever the subject of hunting comes up you can rely on Anthony to put his two penn'orth in.*

put two and two together
to guess the truth about a situation from pieces of information which you know about it • *I didn't tell her my husband had left, but she'd noticed his car was missing and put two and two together.*

put two and two together and get/make five to guess something wrong about a situation, usually something more exciting than the truth • *She thought I was pregnant. I was sick a couple of times and she just put two and two together and made five.*

put your **two cents (worth) in** *American & Australian informal*
to give your opinion in a conversation, often when it is not wanted • *She always has to put her two cents worth in! Why can't she just keep quiet?*
your **two cents (worth)** • *Stay out of this – if we want your two cents we'll ask for it!*

put/stick two fingers up at sb/sth *British informal*
to show that you are angry with someone, or that you have no respect for someone or something • *These protest marches are a way of putting two fingers up at politicians.*

That makes two of us.
something that you say in order to tell someone that you are in the same unpleasant situation, or have the same negative feelings as them • *'I found his talk really boring.' 'That makes two of us!'*

two can play at that game *informal*
something that you say when you intend to harm someone in the same way as they have harmed you • *So she's been spreading rumours about me, has she? Well, two can play at that game.*

two's company (three's a crowd)
something that you say when you think two people would prefer to be alone together than be with a third person • *They asked me to go to the cinema with them but two's company if you know what I mean.*

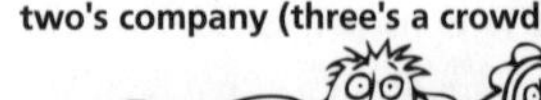
two's company (three's a crowd)

▶ See also: **cut** both/two ways
kill two birds with one stone
be ten/two a **penny**
in two **shakes** (of a lamb's tail)
be two **sides** of the same coin

two-bit

two-bit *American informal*
of very little value or not important • (always before noun) *The man was shot by a two-bit crook who nobody ever heard of.*

two-faced

two-faced
a two-faced person says nice things about people when they are with them, but bad things about them to other people • *Have you seen what he wrote about us? He seemed so nice when we spoke on the phone – what a two-faced creep!*

two-time

two-time sb
to have a sexual or romantic relationship with two people at the same time • *If I ever found out she was two-timing me, I'd kill her.*
two-timing • *You should get rid of that two-timing boyfriend of yours.*
two-timer • *He's just a dirty two-timer.*

two-way

a two-way street *mainly American*
if a situation between two people is a two-way street, both people must make an equal effort in order to achieve good results • *Talks with the nurses have to be a two-way street – if they want to discuss salaries, we want to discuss their performance.*

type

▶ See: **revert** to type
true to form/type

ugly

an ugly duckling
someone or something that is ugly and not successful when they are young or new, but which develops into something beautiful and successful • *The most successful company was last year's ugly duckling.*

be as ugly as sin
to be very ugly • *That dog of his is as ugly as sin.*

um

um and ah
to have difficulty making a decision • (often + **about**) *She's still umming and ahing about telling her mother.* • *He ummed and ahed and finally agreed to let me see the documents.*

umbilical

▶ See: **cut** the (umbilical) cord

umbrage

take umbrage *formal*
to become upset and angry about something someone has said or done • (often + **at**) *He took great umbrage at newspaper reviews of his book.* • *The minister took umbrage when colleagues queried her budget plans.*

uncertain

in no uncertain terms
if someone tells you something in no uncertain terms, they say it in a strong and direct way • *We were told in no uncertain terms that dishonesty would not be tolerated.*

uncle

an Uncle Tom
a black person who is too eager to please white people ✍This phrase is from the book *Uncle Tom's Cabin* by H.B. Stowe, in which the main person in the story is a black slave. (= someone who is legally owned by another person) • *She was seen by other blacks in the neighborhood as an Uncle Tom for not complaining about police harassment.*

Uncle Sam
the government or the country of the United States • *These smaller countries resent being so dependent on Uncle Sam for protection.*

▶ See also: **say** uncle

under

▶ See: under sb's **heel**
under the **influence**
under your own **steam**
under the **sun**
be under sb's **thumb**
under **wraps**

unglued

come unglued
1 *American informal* to lose control of your emotions • *After Dan's death she just came unglued.*
2 *American informal* if a person or something they are trying to achieve comes unglued, they have problems which cause them to fail • *The negotiations are showing signs of coming unglued, with new questions coming up every day.* • *The team played well in the first half but came unglued in the second.*

unknown

an unknown quantity
if someone or something is an unknown quantity, you do not know much about them or what effect they will have in the future • *Turner may do well in the election, though he is an unknown quantity as a campaigner.* • *The new computer system is still an unknown quantity for our department.*

unstuck

come unstuck *British & Australian*
if a person or something they are trying to achieve comes unstuck, they have problems which cause them to fail • *Athletes who don't prepare properly for the humid conditions will certainly come unstuck.* • *The negotiations came unstuck over disagreements about the wording.*

until

▶ See: until you are **blue** in the face

up

be (right) up there with sb/sth

to be as good or as famous as someone or something else • *He's up there with the foremost sculptors of our age.*

be on the up

if someone or something is on the up, they are becoming more successful • *At number 27 in the world tennis rankings he is definitely on the up.* • *It's been a difficult year for our family, but things are on the up again now.*

be on the up and up

1 *informal* if someone or something is on the up and up they are becoming more and more successful • *Since the recession ended, our business has been on the up and up.*

2 *American informal* if a person or an activity is on the up and up, they are honest • *You can trust Mick – he's on the up and up.*

be up yourself *British & Australian very informal*

to think that you are better and more important than other people • *She's so up herself ever since she landed this new job, it's unbearable.*

be up against sth/sb

if you are up against a situation, a person, or a group of people, they make it very difficult for you to achieve what you want to achieve • *When I saw how deeply the racist views were held I began to understand what we were up against.* • *The Welsh rugby team will really* ***be up against it*** (= have a lot of problems) *when they take on France next week.*

be up and about/around

if someone is up and about after an illness, they are well enough to get out of bed and move around • *Trevor's up and about again, but he won't be able to drive for a few weeks.*

be up and down

1 if a person is up and down, they are sometimes happy and sometimes sad, usually after something very bad has happened to them • *She's been very up and down since her husband's death.*

2 if a situation is up and down, it is sometimes good and successful and sometimes bad and not successful • *Things are up and down for dairy farmers at the moment.*

be up and running

if a system, an organization, or a machine is up and running, it is established and working • *Until the new computer system is up and running we will have to work on paper.*

be up for sth *informal*

to want to do something and to be able to do it • *It's a long walk. Are you up for it?* • *After a long day at work I wasn't really up for a party.*

be up to sth

to be doing or planning something, often secretly • *We think those boys are up to something, or they wouldn't be behaving so suspiciously.* • (often used in questions) *What are you up to in there?*

be up to your **ears/eyeballs/eyes in** sth *British, American & Australian*

be up to your **chin in** sth *American*

to have too much of something, especially work • *We're up to our eyeballs in decorating at the moment.*

not **be up to much** *British informal*

if something is not up to much, it is not very good or effective • *This hairdryer's not up to much – it only blows out cold air.*

be up with the lark *British, American & Australian*

be up with the crows *Australian*

to be awake and out of your bed early in the morning ✍Larks and crows are birds that start singing very early in the morning. • *You were up with the lark this morning!*

Up yours! *very informal*

an angry and impolite way of telling someone you do not care about their opinion • *'You're not supposed to be smoking in here.' 'Up yours, mate!'*

▶ See also: raise/up the **ante**

up-and-coming

up-and-coming

becoming more and more successful in a job • (always before noun) *She founded a summer school for up-and-coming musicians.*

uphill

an uphill battle/fight/struggle
an uphill job/task

if something you are trying to do is an uphill struggle, it is very difficult, often because other people are causing problems for you • *Environmentalists* ***face an uphill struggle*** *convincing people to use their cars less.* • *We're trying to expand our business, but it's an uphill battle.*

upper

have the upper hand

if someone has the upper hand, they have a position of power and control over someone else, and if an emotion has the upper hand, it controls what you do • *At half time, the Italian team seem to have the upper hand.*

gain/get the upper hand • (often + **over**) *Government troops are gradually gaining the upper hand over the rebel forces.* • *I shouldn't have read the letter, but curiosity got the upper hand.*

the upper crust

people who have the highest social position and who are usually rich • *Many treasures were brought back to Britain because its upper crust was wealthy and liked travelling abroad.*

upper-crust • *He spoke with an upper-crust accent.*

uppers

be (down) on your **uppers** *British old-fashioned*

to be in a very bad financial situation • *Hungary's once successful film industry is on its uppers.* • *He was always ready to help anyone who was down on their uppers.*

ups

ups and downs

the mixture of good and bad things which happen to people • *Like most married couples we've* ***had our ups and downs.*** • *The book charts the ups and downs of a career in fashion.*

upset

upset the applecart

to cause trouble, especially by spoiling someone's plans • *I don't want to upset the applecart now by asking you to change the date for the meeting.*

upstairs

▶ See: **kick** sb upstairs

uptake

▶ See: be **slow** on the uptake

up-to-the-minute

up-to-the-minute

containing the most modern or recent ideas or information • *For top designer names and up-to-the-minute fashion, shop at Taylors.*

use

Use your **loaf.** *British & Australian old-fashioned*

if you tell someone to use their loaf, you are telling them in a slightly angry way that they should think more carefully about what they are doing ✍In Cockney rhyming slang (= an informal kind of language used in parts of London) 'loaf' is short for 'loaf of bread' which means head. • *You haven't even switched the thing on. Come on, Jamie, use your loaf!*

▶ See also: It's no good/use **crying** over spilt milk.
turn/use sth to **good** account
be no good/use to **man** or beast

usual

the usual suspects *humorous*

the people you would expect to be present somewhere or doing a particular thing • *'Who did you spend the evening with?' 'Oh, Dan, Yuko, Jayne – the usual suspects.'*

vanish

▶ See: disappear/vanish off the **face** of the earth

variety

Variety is the spice of life.
something that you say which means life is more interesting when it changes often and you have many different experiences • *I have to work in the heat of Sudan one week and the cold of Alaska the next, but I suppose variety is the spice of life.*

veil

▶ See: **draw** a veil over sth

vent

vent your **spleen**
to express anger • (often + **on**) *Politicians used the press conference as an opportunity to vent their spleen on reporters.*

ventured

▶ See: **nothing** ventured, nothing gained.

verbal

verbal diarrhoea

verbal diarrhoea *British, American & Australian humorous*
verbal diarrhea *American & Australian humorous*
if someone has verbal diarrhoea, they talk too much • *It was awful – a whole evening with this guy who had verbal diarrhoea.*

vicious

a vicious circle
a difficult situation that cannot be improved because one problem causes another problem that causes the first problem again • *I get depressed so I eat and then I gain weight which depresses me so I eat again – I'm **caught in a vicious circle**.*

villain

the villain of the piece
someone or something that has caused a bad situation ✍This phrase was first used to describe an evil character in a play. • *According to reports of the disaster, the villain of the piece is the mining company who failed to carry out proper safety checks.*

vine

wither on the vine *British, American & Australian literary*
die on the vine *American & Australian literary*
if something withers on the vine, it is destroyed very gradually, usually because no one does anything to help or support it ✍Grapes (= small fruits used to make wine) which are still joined to the vine (= the plant on which grapes grow) die slowly. • *Plans to create cheap housing for the poor seem doomed to wither on the vine.*

virtue

make a virtue of necessity *formal*
to change something you must do into a positive or useful experience • *It's a long way to drive so I thought I'd make a virtue of necessity and stop off at some interesting places along the way.*

virtues

▶ See: **extoll** the virtues of sb/sth

vis-à-vis

vis-à-vis

in relation to • *Can I talk to you vis-à-vis the arrangements for Thursday's meeting?* • *The current strength of the dollar vis-à-vis other currencies makes it hard selling American products overseas.*

voice

a (lone) voice in the wilderness
a voice crying in the wilderness

if you are a voice in the wilderness, you are the only person expressing a particular opinion, although later other people understand that you were right • *With her passionate pleas for peace, she was a lone voice in the wilderness.*

void

fill a/the void

to replace something important that you have lost, or to provide something important that you need • *The country needs a strong leader to help fill the void left by the death of the president.* • *Religion helped me fill a void in my life.*

volte-face

a volte-face *formal*

a sudden change of a belief or plan to the opposite of what it was before • *In the early 90's he made a complete political volte-face, moving from the Republican Party to the Democrats.*

volumes

▶ See: **speak** volumes

vote

vote with your **feet**

to show that you do not support something, especially an organization or a product, by not using or not buying it any more • *Parents are voting with their feet and moving their children to schools where there is better discipline.*

Ww

wad

▶ See: **shoot** your wad

wagon

be on the wagon
someone who is on the wagon has decided not to drink any alcohol for a period of time • *He'd been an alcoholic once, but when I met him he'd been on the wagon for about five years.*
go on the wagon • *The doctor ordered her to go on the wagon, and she hasn't touched a drop since.*

▶ See also: **fall** off the wagon
hitch your wagon to sb/sth

waifs

waifs and strays *British & Australian*
people or animals who have no home and no one to care for them • *Emma was always bringing home waifs and strays and giving them a bed for the night.*

wait

wait for the other shoe to drop
American
to wait for something bad to happen • *Once a company starts laying of employees, those who are still working feel they are waiting for the other shoe to drop.*

wait on sb **hand and foot**
to do everything for someone so that they do not have to do anything for themselves • *He just wants a woman to wait on him hand and foot.*

waiting

be waiting in the wings
to be ready to be used or employed instead of someone or something else ✍In the theatre, the wings are the sides of the stage which cannot be seen by the people watching the play, where actors wait until it is their turn to walk on to the stage. • *The rumour is that Green will be sacked and Brinkworth is waiting in the wings to take over as manager.*

▶ See also: **play** a/the waiting game

wake

Wake up and smell the coffee!
something that you say in order to tell someone that they should try to understand the true facts of a situation or that they should give more attention to what is happening around them • *It's time you woke up and smelled the coffee, Don. We're just not getting enough business any more.*

wake-up

a wake-up call
an event that warns someone that they need to deal with an urgent or dangerous problem • (often + to do sth) *The 1971 earthquake was a wake-up call to strengthen the city's bridges.* • (often + **to**) *The World Trade Center bombing has served as a wake-up call to the FBI on terrorism.*

walk

walk a tightrope
to act very carefully so that you avoid either of two opposite bad situations ✍A tightrope is a tightly stretched wire or rope fixed high above the ground which someone walks across in order to entertain people. • (often + **between**) *Many manufacturers have to walk a tightrope between overpricing their goods and pricing them so low that they make no profit.*

a walk of life
a person's walk of life is the type of job they do or the level of society they belong to • *Volunteers who work at the animal hospital come* ***from all walks of life.*** • *There were people at the meeting from almost every walk of life.*

walk the plank
to be forced to leave your job ✍In the past, people on ships who had committed crimes were forced to walk to the end of a plank (= a long flat piece of wood) and go over the side of the ship into the water. • *Several Cabinet Ministers have been forced to walk the plank following the latest Government scandal.*

▶ See also: **take** a hike/walk!
stand/walk **tall**

walking

give sb their **walking papers** *American*
to tell someone they must leave their job • *The manager gave his old secretary her walking papers and hired his daughter to do the job.*
get your **walking papers** *American* • *Since they got their walking papers from the chemical company, none of them has been able to find another job.*

► See also: be floating/walking on **air**
be walking/treading on **eggshells**
be (skating/walking) on **thin** ice

wall

be off the wall *informal*
to be strange or very different from other people or things • *Even at school he was considered off the wall by most of the students.*
off-the-wall *informal* • (always before noun) *She's got a really off-the-wall sense of humour.*

go to the wall
if a business or other organization goes to the wall, it fails and cannot continue • *After nine months of massive losses, the company finally went to the wall.* • *In theory, good schools will grow and prosper and bad schools will go to the wall.*

the writing is on the wall *British, American & Australian*
the handwriting is on the wall *American*
if the writing is on the wall for a person or an organization, it is clear that they will fail or be unable to continue • (often + **for**) *The team has lost its last six games and the writing is definitely on the wall for the manager.*
read/see the writing on the wall *British, American & Australian* to understand that you are in a dangerous situation and that something unpleasant is likely to happen to you • *They saw the writing on the wall and started to behave better.* • *Those who failed to read the handwriting on the wall lost a lot of money.*

► See also: **drive** sb up the wall
hit a/the (brick) wall
nail sb to the wall

walls

Walls have ears.
something that you say in order to warn someone to be careful what they say because someone may be listening • *Why don't we go and talk about this somewhere quieter? Walls have ears, you know.*

wall-to-wall

wall-to-wall
wall-to-wall things or people exist in a continuous supply or in large amounts • *Independent channels are promising wall-to-wall coverage of the Olympics.* • *It was one of those clubs, you know, with wall-to-wall men and lots of heavy dance music.*

wandering

wandering hands *British & Australian humorous*
a person, usually a man, who has wandering hands often tries to touch other people for sexual excitement • *Joe was notorious for having wandering hands and all the women tried to avoid going into his office.*

want

for want of a better word
if you say that you are using a particular word for want of a better word, you mean that it is not quite exact or suitable but there is no better one • *They have problems, which, for want of a better word, we call psychological.*

How much do you want to bet? *informal*
Do you want a/to bet? *informal*
something that you say when you do not believe that what someone has just said will be true • *'I don't think she'd be stupid enough to lend him any money.' 'How much do you want to bet?'*

want to curl up and die
to feel very embarrassed about something that you have said or done • *I spilt coffee all over their precious new rug and I just wanted to curl up and die.*

war

a war of words
a long argument between two people or groups • (often + **between**) *The war of words between the two rivals for the presi-*

dency continues to dominate the news bulletins. • (often + **over**) *The article describes the war of words over acid rain.*

▶ See also: a battle/war of **nerves**

warm

warm the cockles of your **heart** *old-fashioned*
if something you see or hear warms the cockles of your heart, it makes you feel happy because it shows that people can be good and kind • *It's an old-fashioned romance that will warm the cockles of your heart.*

warpath

be on the warpath *humorous*
to be looking for someone you are angry with in order to speak angrily to them or punish them • *Look out, the boss is on the warpath again!*

wars

have been in the wars *British & Australian humorous*
someone, especially a child, who has been in the wars, has been hurt • *You poor little boy, you have been in the wars!*

warts

warts and all
if you describe or show someone or something warts and all, you do not try to hide the bad things about them ✍A wart is a small hard lump which grows on the skin and looks unpleasant. • *He tried to portray the president as he was, warts and all.*
warts-and-all • (always before noun) *The book is a warts-and-all portrait of the socialist movement.*

wash

come out in the wash *informal*
if something secret or unpleasant comes out in the wash, people discover the truth about it • *They don't want the police to investigate, because they're afraid of what might come out in the wash.*

It'll all come out in the wash. *informal*
something that you say in order to tell someone not to worry because mistakes or problems will not have a serious or permanent effect • *It was the wrong thing to say, but don't get too upset, I'm sure it'll all come out in the wash eventually.*

wash your **hands of** sb/sth
to stop being involved with or responsible for someone or something, usually because they have caused too many problems for you • *I should imagine he couldn't wait to wash his hands of the whole project.*

Wash your mouth out! *old-fashioned*
something that you say to someone who is younger than you when you are angry with them for swearing • *Wash your mouth out, young lady. There's no call for language like that!*

will not wash
if an excuse or an argument will not wash, people will not believe it or accept it • (often + **with**) *That story about missing the last bus won't wash with me, young lady!*

▶ See also: wash your **dirty** laundry/linen in public

waste

be a waste of space *informal*
if you say that someone is a waste of space, you mean that they do not do anything useful and you do not like them • *Her husband's a complete waste of space.*

waste your **breath**
to tell or ask someone something although this will have no effect • (often negative) *Don't waste your breath. I've already asked her to help and she said no.* • *You'd be wasting your breath reporting it to the police – they never look for stolen bikes.*
a waste of breath • *I could try and persuade her to stay, but it would probably be a waste of breath.*

watch

watch your **back** *informal*
to be careful of the people around you, making sure that they do nothing to harm you • *It's a rough neighbourhood so watch your back when you're walking around the streets.*

watch sb **like a hawk**
to watch someone very carefully, especially because you expect them to do something wrong • *I was being watched*

like a hawk by the shop assistant.

watch your **step**

to make sure that you do not say or do anything that causes you to get into trouble • *He'd better watch his step if he wants to carry on working here.*

watch the clock

to keep looking to see what the time is because you are eager to stop what you are doing • *I can tell if a film isn't holding my attention because I find myself watching the clock and changing position a lot.*

clock-watching • *A lot of clock-watching goes on during the general lectures, especially in the second hour.*

Watch this space.

something that you say which means that you think there will soon be exciting changes in a situation • *I have plans for my career. Watch this space.*

▶ See also: watch sb/sth with an **eagle** eye
mind/watch your **p**'s and q's
Mind/Watch your **step**.

watched

A watched pot never boils.

something that you say which means if you wait anxiously for something to happen, it seems to take a very long time • *There's no point sitting by the phone waiting for it to ring. A watched pot never boils.*

watching

be like watching grass grow *humorous*
be as interesting as watching grass grow *humorous*

if you say that watching an activity is like watching grass grow, you mean that it is very boring • *To watch somebody fly-fishing is like watching grass grow.*

be like watching paint dry *humorous*
be as interesting as watching paint dry *humorous*

if you say that watching an activity is like watching paint dry, you mean that it is very boring • *To me, watching golf on television is about as interesting as watching paint dry.*

water

be (like) water off a duck's back

if criticism is water off a duck's back to someone, it has no effect on them at all • (often + **to**) *He's always being told he's lazy and incompetent, but it's just water off a duck's back to him.*

be water under the bridge *British, American & Australian*
be water over the dam *American*

if a problem or an unpleasant situation is water under the bridge, it happened a long time ago and no one is upset about it now • *We certainly had our disagreements in the past, but that's all water under the bridge now.*

▶ See also: **blow** sth/sb out of the water
of the **first** water
not **hold** water
could **talk** under water
test the water/waters
tread water

waterfront

▶ See: **cover** the waterfront

waterloo

▶ See: **meet** your Waterloo

waters

▶ See: **muddy** the waters
test the water/waters

waterworks

▶ See: **turn** on the waterworks

wave

▶ See: **catch** the wave
fly/show/wave the **flag**
kiss/say/wave **goodbye** to sth
ride (on) a/the wave

wavelength

be on the same wavelength

if two people are on the same wavelength, it is easy for them to understand and agree with each other • *To my surprise, I found that we were absolutely on the same wavelength about most of the important issues.* • *I can't discuss anything with her – we're simply not on the same wavelength.*

waves

make waves

to change an existing situation in a way

which causes problems or upsets people • *Some workers felt it was not the time to make waves by organizing a union.* • *Our culture encourages us to fit the norm and not to make waves.*

wax

wax and wane
to grow bigger and stronger and then to become smaller or weaker again • *Their influence waxes and wanes depending on which party is in power.*

wax lyrical
to talk about something with a lot of interest and excitement • *I recall Roz waxing lyrical about the flatness of his stomach.*

way

(in) any way, shape, or form
in any way at all • (often negative) *I have never been involved in any way, shape, or form with criminal activities.*

all the way
if you support something or fight against something all the way, you support it or fight it as much as possible and as long as it continues • *If you want to complain to the boss, I'll support you all the way.* • *If they go ahead with the plan, we'll fight them all the way.*

along the way
during the time that something is happening or that you are doing something • *I've been in this job for thirty years and I've picked up a good deal of expertise along the way.* • *Along the way we'll also be studying French, history and geography.*

be out of the way
if a place is out of the way, it is a long distance from other villages or towns • *It's a lovely village but it's a little out of the way.*
out-of-the-way • *We hired a car and spent a few days visiting some out-of-the-way places.*

be out of sb's **way**
if a place is out of someone's way, it is not in the direction in which they are going • *Are you sure you don't mind taking me home, Ted? It's a bit out of your way.*

couldn't [act/argue/fight] your **way out of a paper bag** *humorous*
if someone couldn't act, argue, fight etc. their way out of a paper bag, they act, argue, fight etc. very badly • *It's no good asking Jim to protect you – he couldn't fight his way out of a paper bag.*

go all the way
1 *informal* to have sex, especially when you have only been kissing and touching before • *I wouldn't go all the way with a boy if I didn't love him.*
2 if you go all the way when you are doing something, you do it completely • *We finally decided to go all the way and redecorate the entire house.* • *The government didn't go all the way; it restricted advertising by tobacco companies, but didn't ban it.*
3 if a person or team goes all the way in a sports competition, they win every part of it • *Do you think she can go all the way at Wimbledon this year?*

go out of your **way** to do sth
to try very hard to do something pleasant for other people • *They really went out of their way to make us feel welcome.*

go the way of all flesh *literary or humorous*
to die or become spoiled or damaged • *Eventually, her uncles went the way of all flesh and she inherited the house.* • *I'm afraid our washing machine has gone the way of all flesh.*

No way!
1 *informal* something that you say in order to make very clear that your answer to a question is 'no' • *'Have you paid for the repair yet?' 'No way! Not until we know for sure that the computer is actually working'.*
2 *informal* something that you say when someone says something that is very surprising • *'Hey, I saw Ellie out with Andrew last night.' 'No way!'*

That's the way the cookie crumbles. *British, American & Australian informal*
That's the way the ball bounces. *American informal*
something that you say which means that bad things sometimes happen and there is nothing you can do to prevent it, so it is

not worth becoming upset about it • *I can't believe they chose Sam for the job and not me. Ah well, that's the way the cookie crumbles.*

▶ See also: **claw** your way back from sth
not **know** which way to turn
be **laughing** all the way to the bank
one way or the other
There's more than **one** way to skin a cat.
open the way for/to sth
pave the way for sth
pay its way
pay your way
point the way
see which way the cat jumps
see your way (clear) to doing sth
see which way the wind is blowing
smooth the way for sb/sth
wing your/its way

way-out

way-out *informal*
new, different and often strange • *He produced some really way-out designs for the opera house.*

ways

change/mend your **ways**
to improve the way in which you behave • *If he wants to carry on living here, he's going to have to change his ways.*

ways and means
methods of achieving something • (often + **of**) *Surely there are ways and means of achieving our objectives which don't involve spending quite so much money.*

▶ See also: (There's) no **two** ways about it.

wayside

▶ See: **fall** by the wayside

weak

have a weak spot for sb/sth *American*
to feel attraction to or affection for someone or something • *Sarah has a weak spot for basketball players.*

weak at the knees
if someone goes weak at the knees, they feel as if they might fall down because they have a sudden strong emotion about something or someone • *The very thought of jumping out of an aircraft with a parachute made him* ***go weak at the knees.*** • *He was so gorgeous, I felt weak at the knees every time he spoke to me.*

a weak link (in the chain)
the weakest part of a system or the weakest member of a group of people that could cause the whole system or group to fail • *It's a strong team, though the goalkeeper may be a weak link because he's rather inexperienced.* • *The weak link in the chain is the computer software that controls the system.*

wear

wear and tear
the damage that happens to an object or a person when they are used or when they do something • *The guarantee covers accidental damage but not ordinary wear and tear.* • (often + **on**) *She made everyone wear slippers inside the house to avoid wear and tear on the carpet.* • *The wear and tear of life in a busy office has taken its toll on our staff.*

wear your **heart on** your **sleeve**
to make your feelings and opinions obvious to other people • *John's always worn his heart on his sleeve, so there's no doubt who he'll be supporting.*

wear the trousers *British, American & Australian humorous*
wear the pants *American & Australian humorous*
to be the person in a relationship who makes all the important decisions • *I don't think there's any doubt about who wears the trousers in their house.*

wear thin

1 if your patience wears thin, you become less and less patient • (often in continuous tenses) *I've warned you several times about being late and my patience is wearing thin.*

2 if a joke, an excuse, or an explanation wears thin, it becomes less effective because it has been used too much • (often in continuous tenses) *This excuse about not having enough staff to run the trains is wearing rather thin, don't you think?*

wear sb **to a frazzle** *informal*
to make someone feel very tired and nervous • (often reflexive) *She's worn herself to a frazzle trying to get that report finished.* • *You've been looking after her*

kids for a month? You must be worn to a frazzle.

▶ See also: wear/work your **fingers** to the bone

wearing

▶ See: be wearing your [teacher's/lawyer's etc.] **hat**

weasel

weasel words *mainly American*
words that you use to avoid answering a question or to deceive someone • *She was too experienced an interviewer to be taken in by the weasel words of crafty politicians.*

weather

be/feel under the weather

be/feel under the weather
to feel ill • *I'm feeling a little under the weather – I think I may have caught a cold.*

▶ See also: **keep** a weather eye on sth/sb
ride out/weather the **storm**

wedding

your **wedding tackle** *British humorous*
a man's sexual organs • *He wears special padding to protect his wedding tackle.*

wedge

▶ See: **drive** a wedge between sb

weep

▶ See: shed/weep **crocodile** tears

weigh

weigh a ton *informal*
to be very heavy • *This suitcase weighs a ton!*

weigh your **words**
weigh each word
to think carefully about something before you say it • *Jake explained the reasons for his decision, weighing each word as he spoke.*

weight

be a weight off your **shoulders**
if something is a weight off your shoulders, you are happy that you do not have to worry about it or feel responsible for it any more • *If you could take over the job of organizing the party, that would be a tremendous weight off my shoulders.*

▶ See also: **carry** weight
be a load/weight off your **mind**
pull your weight
throw your weight around
throw your weight behind sth/sb
have the cares/weight of the **world** on your shoulders

welcome

outstay/overstay your **welcome**
to stay in a place longer than someone wants you to stay • *One more cup of tea and then we'll go. We don't want to outstay our welcome!*

▶ See also: Welcome to the **club**!
greet/welcome sb/sth with **open** arms

well

be well away
1 *British informal* to be completely involved in doing something, especially talking • *They started talking about football and were soon well away.*
2 *British & Australian informal* to be drunk • *Annie was dancing on top of the table, so she must have been well away last night.*
3 *British & Australian informal* to be sleeping • *Her head started to nod and soon she was well away.*

be well in *British & Australian*
be in well *American*
to have a good relationship with a person or group which gives you an advantage • (usually + **with**) *There won't be any*

stopping him now – he's in well with the manager of his company. • *Lunch with her mother? You're well in there, mate!*

be well up on sth

to have a good knowledge of a subject • *I'm not very well up on Ancient Greek history.*

well and truly

completely • *Many people remained in their hiding places until they were sure the war was well and truly over.*

▶ See also: be **all** very well
leave/let well **alone**
leave well alone

well-heeled

well-heeled

rich • *You need to be well-heeled to be able to afford to shop there.*

well-hung

well-hung *very informal*

a well-hung man has a large penis • *A crowd of well-hung young men paraded around in their underwear.*

well-to-do

well-to-do

rich • *In Johannesburg's well-to-do suburbs, residents are hiring security guards to protect their homes.*

west

go west

1 *old-fashioned* if something goes west, it is destroyed or lost • *My watch went west when I accidentally dropped it on a concrete floor.* • *That's my chance of seeing the game gone west!*

2 *British & Australian old-fashioned* if someone goes west, they die • *He went west in a plane crash.*

wet

be all wet *American*

to be completely wrong • *Most doctors agreed that the scientific evidence in the report was simply all wet.*

be wet behind the ears

to be young and not very experienced • *He's fresh out of college, still wet behind the ears.*

a wet blanket *informal*

someone who does or says something that stops other people from enjoying themselves • *I don't want to be a wet blanket, but you really must play your music more quietly or you'll disturb the people next door.*

a wet dream

1 a sexually exciting dream that makes semen (= thick liquid containing a man's seed) come out of a man's penis while he is sleeping • *Most boys start getting wet dreams in their early teens.*

2 *very informal* something that is very pleasant or very exciting for someone • *This new machine is a computer buff's wet dream.*

wet the baby's head

to celebrate the birth of a baby by having an alcoholic drink • *He couldn't wait to get home to wet the baby's head.* • *We bought some champagne to wet the baby's head.*

wet your **whistle** *old-fashioned*

to have a drink, especially an alcoholic drink • *You must be thirsty after all that work – would you care to wet your whistle?*

▶ See also: have a **face** like a wet weekend
could **talk** under wet coment

whack

out of whack

1 *American & Australian informal* if something is out of whack, it is not working as it should • *You can use Carol's old bike – the gears are out of whack, but it still goes.* • *If I don't take any exercise for a while it throws my whole body out of whack.*

2 *American & Australian informal* confused and badly organized • *The state budget is way out of whack and politicians are blaming an influx of immigrants.* • *Our spending priorities are out of whack.*

whale

have a whale of a time

have a whale of a time
to enjoy yourself very much • *'Did Sam enjoy himself at the party?' 'He had a whale of a time.'*

a whale of a [bill/difference/ problem etc.] *American & Australian*
a very large bill, difference, problem etc. • *Another thousand dollars would make a whale of a difference.* • *We ran up a whale of a bill in the restaurant.*

a whale of a [job/party/story etc.] *American & Australian*
a very good job, party, story etc. • *They've done a whale of a job renovating the building.*

what

(Well) what do you know!
something that you say when you are surprised by a piece of information ✍This phrase is often used humorously to mean the opposite. • *And they're getting married? Well, what do you know!* • *(humorous) Well, what do you know! The Raiders lost again.*

and what have you *informal*
and other similar things • *There were a couple of bags full of old records, magazines and what have you.*

what goes around comes around
used to say that if you are bad and not kind, bad things will happen to you, and if you are good and kind, good things will happen to you • *'He ended up with nobody looking after him.' 'Well, what goes around comes around.'*

What's up? *informal*
something that you say in order to ask someone what is wrong • *What's up? Why haven't you left yet?* • *You're quiet – what's up?* • (often + **with**) *What's up with Tom? He hasn't spoken all morning.*

► See also: What's sth in **aid** of?
What's the **big** idea?
What's **biting** sb?
What's the **deal**?
What's sb's **game**?
what the **hell**
What's your **poison**?
What **price** [fame/success/victory etc.]?
What sb **says** goes.
What's the **world** coming to?

whatever

Whatever turns you **on.** *humorous*
something that you say when you are surprised at something that someone likes to do • *So you stuff animals in your spare time? Oh well, whatever turns you on.*

wheat

► See: **separate** the wheat from the chaff

wheel

be at/behind the wheel
if you are at the wheel of a vehicle, you are driving it • *I always feel perfectly safe when Richard's at the wheel.*
get behind the wheel • *When Anna gets behind the wheel of a fast car, she's a danger to the public.*

a fifth/third wheel *American*
someone who is in a situation where they are not really needed or are ignored by other people • *I don't have a role in the office any more – I feel like a fifth wheel.*

► See also: **reinvent** the wheel

wheeling

wheeling and dealing
complicated and sometimes dishonest agreements in business or politics that people try to achieve in order to make profits or get advantages • *It's an article about all the wheeling and dealing that goes on in financial markets.*
wheel and deal • *He's the sort of guy that likes to drive fast cars and wheel and deal on the stock exchange.*

a wheeler-dealer • *He worked in the property business for a number of years, acquiring a reputation as a formidable wheeler-dealer.*

wheels

the wheels are turning
something that you say which means a process is starting to happen • *By the late 1940s the wheels were turning that would make a manned space flight possible by the end of the next decade.*

▶ See also: **oil** the wheels
set the wheels in motion
spin your wheels

when

as and when *British, American & Australian*
if and when *American & Australian*
if you do something as and when, you do it when it is needed or convenient, not in a regular way • *Let's not go to the supermarket this week. We can just pick up some food as and when we need it.*

▶ See also: When in **Rome** (do as the Romans do).
when all is **said** and done

where

where sb **is coming from**
If you know where someone is coming from, you understand their opinions and feelings, especially because you understand things about their past life. • *At the time, I didn't really understand where she was coming from, and her poems just seemed odd.*

▶ See also: Where's the **beef**?
Where there's **smoke**, there's fire.
tell sb where to get off

whet

whet sb's **appetite**
if an experience whets someone's appetite for something, it makes them want more of it • *That first flying lesson whetted her appetite.* • (often + **for**) *I did a short course last year, and it's whetted my appetite for study.*

while

▶ See: When/While the **cat**'s away (the mice will play).
while the **going** is good

whip

have/hold the whip hand
to be the person or group that has the most power in a situation • *So long as we rely on them for money, they have the whip hand.*

▶ See also: **crack** the whip
whip sth/sb into **shape**

whipping

a whipping boy
someone or something that is blamed or punished for problems that are caused by someone or something else • *Television has been the favourite whipping boy of every social reformer in modern America.*

whip-round

a whip-round *British & Australian informal*
a collection of money among a group of people that is used to buy a present for someone • *We had a whip-round for Annie's leaving present.*

whirl

▶ See: **give** it a shot/whirl

whirlwind

▶ See: **reap** the whirlwind

whisker

by a whisker
by a very small amount • *Last time she raced against the Brazilian she won by a whisker.* • *He missed the goal by a whisker.*

come within a whisker of sth/doing sth
if you come within a whisker of doing something, you almost do it or it almost happens to you • *He came within a whisker of beating the world champion.* • *Several times on his trek through the jungle he came within a whisker of death.*

whistle

He/She/They can whistle for it! *old-fashioned*
something that you say which means you are determined that someone will not get what they want • *If they want money, they can whistle for it. They're not getting a penny out of me!*

▶ See also: **blow** the whistle on sb/sth

wet your whistle

whistle-stop

a whistle-stop tour
a very quick visit to several places • (often + **of**) *Coach loads of tourists come for whistle-stop tours of the main European cities.*

whistling

be whistling Dixie *American informal*
to talk in a way that makes things seem better than they really are • (usually negative) *We're really making money these days and I'm not just whistling Dixie.*

be whistling in the dark
to be confident that something good will happen when it is not at all likely • *She seems pretty sure she'll win the title, but she may just be whistling in the dark.*

white

be as white as a sheet
to be very pale, usually because you are frightened or ill • *She was trembling all over and as white as a sheet.*

be as white as snow
to be very white • *His hair and beard were as white as snow.*

a white elephant
something that has cost a lot of money but has no useful purpose • *The town's new leisure centre, recently completed at a cost of ten million pounds, seems likely to prove a white elephant.*

a white knight
someone who gives money to a company in order to prevent it from being bought by another company • *Hope is fading that a white knight will appear to stop the takeover bid.*

a white lie
a lie that you tell in order not to upset someone • *I don't see the harm in telling the occasional white lie if it spares someone's feelings.*

white trash *American very informal*
an offensive way of describing poor white people who are not educated • *These are the poor white trash that the middle class don't want to know about.*

white-bread

white-bread *American*
white-bread people or things are ordinary and boring, and often those that are typical of white, American people • (always before noun) *It's a movie about middle America – white-bread characters living white-bread lives.*

white-collar

white-collar
a white-collar worker is someone who works in an office, doing mental rather than physical work • (always before noun) *The ratio of **white-collar workers** to production workers in the American manufacturing industry was declining.* • *The earnings of women in white-collar jobs are the second highest in Britain.* • *The 1980's saw an explosion in **white-collar crime**.* (= crimes committed by white-collar workers, especially stealing from the organization they work for)

whiter

whiter than white
someone who is whiter than white is completely good and honest and never does anything bad • *I never was convinced by the whiter than white image of her portrayed in the press.*

whizz-kid

a whizz-kid
a young person who is very clever and successful • *They've taken on some financial whizz-kid who's going to sort all their problems out.*

whole

go the whole hog *British, American & Australian*
go whole hog *American*
to do something as completely as possible • *It was going to cost so much to repair my computer, I thought I might as well go the whole hog and buy a new one.* • *I went whole hog and had a huge steak and French fries.*

make sth **up out of whole cloth** *American*
invent sth **out of whole cloth** *American*
if a story or excuse is made up out of whole cloth, it is not true • *Yet the*

explanation was too strange for Joan to have made up out of whole cloth.

the whole ball of wax *American informal*
the whole of something, including everything that is connected with it • *She started working on the project in '96 and within six months was running the whole ball of wax.*

the whole picture
the most important facts about a situation and the effects of that situation on other things • *You're just taking into account Melissa's views of the situation but of course that's not the whole picture.*

▶ See also: a whole new **ball** game
the whole **bit**
the whole (kit and) **caboodle**
the whole **enchilada**
go the whole **nine** yards
the whole **nine** yards
the whole **shebang**
the whole **shooting** match
the (whole) **works**
your whole **world** came crashing down around you

whoopee

make whoopee
1 *old-fashioned, informal* to celebrate and enjoy yourself in a noisy way • (usually in continuous tenses) *It's hard working when everyone else is out there in the streets making whoopee.*
2 *American old-fashioned, informal* to have sex • (usually in continuous tenses) *They spent most of the week in the hotel room making whoopee.*

why

▶ See: Why **break** the habit of a lifetime?

whys

the whys and (the) wherefores
the reasons for something • *I know very little about the whys and the wherefores of the situation.*

wick

get on sb's **wick** *British & Australian informal*
to annoy someone • *She'd been asking me questions all day and it was starting to get on my wick.*

wicked

have your **wicked way with** sb *humorous*
to have sex with someone • *He invited her to France for the weekend, thinking he would have his wicked way with her.*

There's no peace/rest for the wicked! *humorous*
something that you say which means you must continue an activity although you might like to stop • *I can't talk – I've got to finish this essay. There's no rest for the wicked.*

wide

be wide of the mark
1 to be wrong • *Yesterday's weather forecast was rather wide of the mark.*
2 if you are wide of the mark when you aim or shoot at something, you miss what you are trying to hit • *Giggs had another chance early in the second half, but once again his shot was wide of the mark.*

be wide open
if a game or a competition is wide open, any of the people who are competing can win because they are all equally good • *At this stage, with only four points separating the six top teams, the championship is still wide open.*

give sb/sth **a wide berth**
to avoid someone or something • *I try to give the city centre a wide berth on a Saturday.* • *If she's in a bad mood I tend to give her a wide berth.*

a wide boy *British informal*
a man or boy who tries to make a lot of money in ways that are not honest • *He's a bit of a wide boy – I wouldn't get involved in any of his schemes if I were you.*

▶ See also: **blow** sth wide open
into the wide/wild **blue** yonder

widen

▶ See: broaden/widen sb's **horizons**

wild

a wild card
1 someone or something that you do not know much about and whose behaviour in the future you cannot be certain of • *The real wild card is the undecided vote,*

which accounts for 18 to 25 percent of the electorate. • *The company is fast gaining a reputation as the wild card of Wall Street because of violent fluctuations in its profits.*

2 if someone gets a wild card or is a wild card in a sports competition, they are allowed to enter the competition without passing the usual tests • *She was included in the European team as a wild card.*

wild-card • (always before noun) *Connors, the five-times champion, is among eight wild-card entries to the US Open in New York next month.*

wild horses

if you say that wild horses couldn't make you do something, you mean nothing could persuade you to do it • ***Wild horses couldn't drag** me to a party tonight.*

▶ See also: into the wide/wild **blue** yonder
sow your wild oats

wilderness

in the wilderness

someone, especially a politician, who is in the wilderness, does not now have the power or influence that they had before • *He spent several years in the political wilderness after conservatives objected to his attempts to reform the police.*

wildest

beyond your **wildest dreams**

far more than you could have hoped for or imagined • *Twenty years later the company has succeeded beyond his wildest dreams.* • *Her books have brought her riches beyond her wildest dreams.*

not **in my wildest dreams**

if you say that you did not imagine something in your wildest dreams, you mean that something that has happened was so strange that you never thought it would happen • *Never in my wildest dreams did I think she'd actually carry out her threat.* • *Not in my wildest dreams could I have imagined England winning 4-1.*

wildfire

▶ See: **spread** like wildfire

wild-goose

a wild-goose chase

a situation where you waste time looking for something that you are not going to find, either because that thing does not exist or because you have been given wrong information about it • *After two hours spent wandering in the snow, I realised we were **on a wild-goose chase**.* • *When I found out that there was no Anita Hill at the university, I began to suspect that I had been **sent on a wild-goose chase**.*

will

Where there's a will there's a way!

something that you say which means it is possible to do anything if you are very determined to do it • *I don't quite know how I'm going to get to Istanbul with no money, but where there's a will there's a way!*

willies

▶ See: **give** sb the creeps/willies

willy-nilly

willy-nilly

1 *informal* if something happens willy-nilly, it happens whether the people who are involved want it to happen or not • *Both countries are being drawn, willy-nilly, into the conflict.*

2 *informal* without any order • *We threw our bags willy-nilly into the back of the truck.*

win

win (sth) **hands down**

to win easily • *She won the debate hands down.*

beat sb **hands down** • *The last time we played squash he beat me hands down.*

win the day

if you win the day, you persuade people to support your ideas or opinions, or if a particular idea wins the day, it is accepted by a group of people • *By the end of the meeting it became clear that the radicals had won the day.* • *I was pleased to hear that common sense had won the day and the proposal had been accepted.*

You can't win 'em all. *informal*

You win some, you lose some. *informal*

something that you say which means it is not possible to succeed at everything you do • *I'm a bit disappointed I didn't get the job. Oh well, you can't win 'em all.* • *Obviously I would have liked first prize but you win some, you lose some.*

▶ See also: earn/win your **spurs**

wind

be in the wind

to be likely to happen soon • *From my recent conversations with Sara I get the feeling that change is in the wind.*

be spitting in/into the wind
be pissing in/into the wind *very informal*

to waste time trying to achieve something that cannot be achieved • *The government is spitting in the wind if they think a few regulations will stop multinational companies from avoiding tax.* • *Trying to get a pay increase here is like pissing in the wind.*

get wind of sth

to hear a piece of information that someone else was trying to keep secret • *I don't want my boss to get wind of the fact that I'm leaving so I'm not telling many people.*

get/put the wind up sb *British & Australian informal*

to make someone feel anxious about their situation • *Say you'll take him to court if he doesn't pay up – that should put the wind up him.*

take the wind out of sb's **sails**

to make someone feel less confident or less determined to do something, usually by saying or doing something that they are not expecting • *I was going to tell him the relationship was over when he greeted me with a big bunch of flowers and it rather took the wind out of my sails.*

▶ See also: **break** wind
run like the wind
see which way the wind is blowing

windmills

▶ See: **tilt** at windmills

window

go out (of) the window

if a quality, principle, or idea goes out of the window, it does not exist any more • *Then people start drinking and sense goes out of the window.*

wine

wine and dine sb

to entertain someone by giving them an expensive meal and wine • (usually passive) *I'm an old-fashioned girl at heart – I like to be wined and dined on the first few dates.*

wining and dining • *His job involves a lot of wining and dining of potential customers.*

wing

be on the wing *literary*

if a bird or insect is on the wing, it is flying • *Numerous orange-tip butterflies were on the wing in the warm sunshine.*

on a wing and a prayer

if you do something on a wing and a prayer, you do it hoping that you will succeed although you are not prepared enough for it • *With scarcely any funding and a staff of six, they operate on a wing and a prayer.*

take sb **under** your **wing**

to help and protect someone, especially someone who is younger than you or has less experience than you • *One of the older children will usually take a new girl or boy under their wing for the first few weeks.*

under the wing of sth

under the control of an organization • *The newspaper is once again in Scottish hands, under the wing of a newly created company, Caledonian Newspaper Publishing.*

wing your/**its way**

to fly or travel very fast • *Within a few hours the package will be winging its way across the Atlantic.*

wing it *informal*

to do the best that you can in a situation that you are not prepared for • *I hadn't had time to prepare the talk so I just had to wing it.*

wings

▶ See: **clip** sb's wings
spread your wings
try your wings
be **waiting** in the wings

wink

not **sleep a wink**
not **get a wink of sleep**
to not sleep at all • *I was so excited last night – I didn't sleep a wink.* • *I didn't get a wink of sleep on the plane.*

▶ See also: **tip** sb the wink

winner

be onto a winner
to be likely to succeed, usually because what you are selling is very popular • *I think they're onto a winner with their latest product.*

wipe

wipe the smile off sb's **face**
to make someone feel less happy or confident, especially someone who is annoying you because they think they are very clever • *Tell him you saw Helena at the cinema with another guy – that should wipe the smile off his face.*

▶ See also: wipe the **floor** with sb

wire

down to the wire *American & Australian*
until the very last moment that it is possible to do something ✍In a horse race, the wire is a metal thread that marks the finishing line. • *If both teams are playing at their best, the game will **go down to the wire*** (= it will be won at the last moment). • *The Democrats struggled down to the wire to choose their candidate.*

under the wire *American*
if someone does something under the wire, they do it at the last possible moment • *They got in under the wire just before the entry requirements for the training program changed.*

wires

▶ See: get your lines/wires **crossed**

wisdom

the conventional/received wisdom
knowledge or information that people generally believe is true, although in fact it is often false • *The conventional wisdom is that marriage makes a relationship more secure, but as the divorce rates show, this is not necessarily true.*

in his/her/their (infinite) wisdom *humorous*
something that you say when you do not understand why someone has done something and think that it was a stupid action • *The council, in their wisdom, decided to close the library and now the building stands empty.*

wise

a wise guy *American & Australian informal*
a wise-ass *American very informal*
someone who is always trying to seem more clever than everyone else in a way that is annoying • *Okay, wise guy, if you're so damned smart, you can tell everyone how it's done!* • *He's just some wise-ass who thinks he knows all the answers.*
wise-guy *American & Australian informal* • (always before noun) *Hyde's wise-guy humour loses its charm after a few episodes.*

▶ See also: a wise **head** on young shoulders

wiser

be none the wiser
to still be confused about something, even after it has been explained to you • *Isobel must have explained the theory three times to me but I'm afraid I'm still none the wiser.*

no one will be any the wiser
something that you say which means that no one will notice something bad that someone has done • *Take the label off the jar and say you made it yourself. No one will be any the wiser.*

wish

I/You wouldn't wish sth **on my/your worst enemy.**
something that you say in order to emphasize that something is extremely unpleasant • *The effects of this disease are horrible. You wouldn't wish them on your worst enemy.*

a wish list
a list of things that someone wants very much • *Most families with kids have a larger house on their wish list.*

wish the ground would swallow you **up**
to wish that you could disappear because you feel very embarrassed • *Everyone in the room was staring at me and I stood there wishing the ground would swallow me up.*

wishful

wishful thinking
thinking or talking about something that you would very much like to happen although you know it probably will not happen • *'Do you think you might be in line for promotion, then? 'No, it's just wishful thinking.'*

witch-hunt

a witch-hunt
an attempt to find and punish people who have opinions that are believed to be dangerous • *Senator McCarthy led a witch-hunt against suspected communists during the 1950's.*

witching

the witching hour
twelve o'clock at night • *It's time I was in bed – it's already past the witching hour.*

with

be with it *informal*
to be able to think or understand quickly • (usually negative) *I had rather a late night so I'm not very with it this morning, I'm afraid.*

with it *informal, old-fashioned*
knowing a lot about new ideas and fashions • *Jenny's very with it – she'll know what people are wearing this summer.* • *Oh* ***get with it****! They're the band everyone's been talking about for weeks.*

wither

▶ See: wither on the **vine**

within

▶ See: come within an **ace** of sth/doing sth
beat sb to within an inch of their life
come within an **inch** of doing sth

without

▶ See: without further/more **ado**
without a **care** in the world
without a **murmur**
without a **second** thought

witness

▶ See: **bear** testimony/witness to sth

wits

be at your **wits' end**
to be very worried or upset because you have tried every possible way to solve a problem but cannot do it • *I've tried everything I can think of to make her eat and she flatly refuses. I'm really at my wits' end.*

frighten/scare sb **out of** their **wits**
to make someone very frightened • *Don't shout like that – you scared me out of my wits!*

have/keep your **wits about** you
to be ready to think quickly in a situation and react to things that you are not expecting • *Cycling is potentially very dangerous in London – you really need to keep your wits about you.*

▶ See also: **gather** your wits
live by/on your wits
pit your wits against sb/sth

wobbler

▶ See: **throw** a wobbler/wobbly

wobbly

▶ See: **throw** a wobbler/wobbly

woe

woe betide sb *humorous*
if you say woe betide the person who does something, you mean that they will be punished or cause trouble for themselves if they do that thing • *Woe betide anyone who plays Ann's tapes without her permission.*

wolf

a wolf in sheep's clothing
someone who seems to be pleasant and friendly but is in fact dangerous or evil • *My next boss, on the surface very warm and charming, proved to be something of a wolf in sheep's clothing.*

a wolf whistle
a whistle (= high sound that is made by blowing air through the lips) that some men do when they see a woman who is sexually attractive • *She'll get a few wolf*

whistles if she walks through town in those shorts.

wolf-whistle sb *British & Australian* • *I was wolf-whistled by a group of builders as I crossed the street.*

▶ See also: **cry** wolf
keep the wolf from the door

wolves

throw sb **to the wolves** *British, American & Australian*
leave sb **to the wolves** *Australian*
to cause someone to be in a situation where they are criticized strongly or treated badly and to not try to protect them • *No one warned me what sort of people I would be dealing with. I felt I'd been thrown to the wolves.*

woman

▶ See: the man/woman on the **Clapham** omnibus
the man/woman/sth of your **dreams**
a man/woman after your own **heart**
a man/woman of **means**
like a man/woman **possessed**
the man/woman/person in the **street**
the **thinking** man's/woman's crumpet
a man of his **word**
a man/woman of the **world**

won't

▶ See: sb/sth won't **bite**

wonder

a nine/one/seven-day wonder
someone or something that causes interest or excitement for a short period but is then quickly forgotten • *His music was derided by an older generation convinced that he was a nine-day wonder.*

wonders

▶ See: **work** wonders

wood

not **be out of the wood/woods**
to continue having difficulties although a situation has improved • *Financially, things are looking distinctly more hopeful, but we're **not out of the woods yet**.*

touch wood *British, American & Australian*
knock (on) wood *American*
something that you say when you want your luck or a good situation to continue • *It's been fine all week and, touch wood, it'll stay fine for the weekend.* • *We haven't had any problems with the car so far, knock on wood.*

▶ See also: can't **see** the wood for the trees

wooden

Don't take any wooden nickels. *American informal*
something that you say when someone leaves, to tell them to be careful and to take good care of themselves • *Hey guys – have a good trip, and don't take any wooden nickels.*

the wooden spoon *British & Australian*
an imaginary prize given to the person who finishes last in a race or competition • *For the second year running Ireland **took the wooden spoon** in the Rugby tournament.*

woodwork

come/crawl out of the woodwork
to appear after being hidden or not active for a long time, especially in order to do something unpleasant • *After you've been in a relationship for a long while, all sorts of little secrets start to come out of the woodwork.* • *Racists and extreme nationalists are crawling out of the woodwork to protest at the sudden increase in the number of immigrants.*

wool

▶ See: **pull** the wool over sb's eyes

word

by word of mouth
if you hear information by word of mouth, you hear it from other people and not from the radio or television or from reading newspapers • *I think she heard about the job by word of mouth.*

from the word go
from the start of something • *I knew from the word go that she was going to cause problems.*

get a word in edgeways *British, American & Australian informal*
get a word in edgewise *American informal*
if you can't get a word in edgeways, you do not have an opportunity to say anything because someone is talking so

much or so quickly • *Roz was talking so much that nobody else could get a word in edgeways.*

have a word in sb's **ear**

to talk to someone privately, especially in order to give them advice or a warning • *The boss had a word in his ear after the last meeting and I don't think he'll be raising the subject again.*

have the final/last word

1 to say the last statement in a discussion or argument • *Tim can't bear to lose an argument. He always has to have the last word.*

2 to make the final decision about something • (usually + **on**) *Our head chef has the final word on what is served each week.*

in a word

something that you say when you are going to give your opinion about something in a short and direct way • *'So, tell me, do you find him attractive?' 'In a word – no.'*

a man of his word
a woman of her word

someone you can trust because you know they will do what they say they will do • *Rae was a woman of her word – if she said she'd be here on Friday, she'd be here on Friday.*

take sb **at** their **word**

to decide to believe exactly what someone tells you, even if it does not seem likely to be true • *When he said he'd give me a job, I took him at his word and turned up the next day at his office.*

take sb's **word for it**

to believe that something is true because someone tells you it is, without making sure that it really is true • (often in future tenses) *If you say you've checked the money I'll take your word for it.* • *Don't just take her word for it – go and see for yourself.*

word for word

if a written or spoken statement is repeated word for word, it is repeated using exactly the same words • *The article was reprinted word for word in a different newspaper the next day.*

sb's **word is law**

if someone's word is law, everyone must obey them • *There's no use questioning any of his rules – his word is law around here.*

A word to the wise (is sufficient).

something that you say when you are going to give someone some advice • *A word to the wise – if you're going to drive, don't go on a Friday night until after the rush hour traffic.*

▶ See also: not **believe** a word of it
not **breathe** a word
won't **hear** a word (said) against sb/sth
say the word
spread the word

words

have words

to speak to someone angrily • (usually + **with**) *There were several penalties and the referee had words with one of the players after the match.*

in so many words

directly or in a way that makes it very clear what you mean • (usually negative) *'Did he say we could stay with him?' 'Well, not in so many words, but that's definitely what he meant.'* • *He told me, in so many words, to mind my own business.*

in words of one syllable

if you explain something in words of one syllable, you do it in words that are very simple and easy to understand because the person you are speaking to is stupid ✍A syllable is a unit of sound that is made by a combination of letters. Words which only have one syllable are short and simple. • *I was trying to explain to him again, in words of one syllable, why safety regulations must be obeyed at all times.*

put words in/into sb's **mouth**

to tell someone what you think they mean or want to say • *I certainly don't think you should resign, stop putting words in my mouth.*

take the words out of sb's **mouth**

to say exactly what someone else was going to say or what they were thinking • *I was just going to mention that, but you took the words right out of my mouth.*

Words fail me!
something that you say when you are so surprised or shocked by something that you do not know what to say about it • *'So what do you think about that purple outfit Olive's wearing?' 'Words fail me!'*

▶ See also: have to **eat** your words
(You) **mark** my words.
not **mince** (your) words

work

All work and no play (makes Jack a dull boy).
something that you say which means people who work all the time become boring • *You need to get out more in the evenings. You know what they say about all work and no play...*

donkey work *British, American & Australian informal*
grunt work *American informal*
hard, boring work ✍In the past, donkeys were used to carry heavy loads. • *Why do I have to do all the donkey work while you get to do the interesting stuff?*

have your **work cut out (for** you**)**
if you have your work cut out, you have something very difficult to do • *We're training a completely new team, so we've got our work cut out for us.* • (often in future tenses) *Have you seen the state of the garden? She'll have her work cut out to get it looking nice in time for the summer.*

work your/**its magic**
to make a situation improve a lot or to make someone feel happy • *He was a great football player who is now working his magic as manager of Barnet Football Club.* • *The city never failed to work its magic on me.*

work a treat *British & Australian informal*
to be very effective • *If you want to get rid of that wine stain, put some salt on it, it works a treat.*

work against the clock
to work very fast because you know you only have a limited period of time to do something • *Scientists were working against the clock to collect specimens before the volcano erupted again.*

work your **arse/backside off** *British & Australian very informal*
work your **ass/butt off** *American very informal*
to work very hard • *My father worked his backside off to pay for our education.*

work like a charm
if a plan or method works like a charm, it has exactly the effect that you want it to • *I tried that stain remover you gave me on my tablecloth and it worked like a charm.*

work like a dog/trojan
to work very hard • *He worked like a dog all day to finish the wallpapering.*

work like magic
if something works like magic, it is very effective and successful • *That new stain remover worked like magic.*

work your **socks off** *informal*
to work very hard • *The lawyers that I know earn a lot of money but they work their socks off.*

work wonders
to improve something a lot • (often + **for**) *Extra water in the diet is generally beneficial to the health and it works wonders for the skin.* • *He's only been in charge at Arsenal for a couple of months and already he's worked wonders.*

▶ See also: go/run/work like **clockwork**
wear/work your **fingers** to the bone
drive/run/work yourself into the **ground**
slog/sweat/work your **guts** out
build/get/work up a **head** of steam
perform/work **miracles**

works

the (whole) works *informal*
everything that you might want or might expect to find in a particular situation • *The bridegroom was wearing a morning suit, top hat, gloves – the works.*
give sb **the works** *informal* • *It's a celebration dinner – give us the works.*

put/throw a spanner in the works *British & Australian*
put/throw a (monkey) wrench in the works *American*
to do something that prevents a plan or activity from succeeding • *We were hoping to get the project started in June but the funding was withdrawn so that rather threw a spanner in the works.*

• *The sudden withdrawal of the guest speaker really threw a monkey wrench in the works.*

▶ See also: **gum** up the works
shoot the works

world

(all) the world and his wife *British & Australian informal*
a very large number of people • *It's a huge outdoor concert – I imagine the world and his wife will be there.*

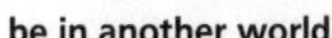

be in another world

be in another world
be in a world of your **own**
to not notice what is happening around you, usually because you are thinking about something else • *She just sat and stared out of the window most of the time – she seemed to be in another world.* • *I don't think you even heard me, did you? You're in a world of your own.*

be out of this world *informal*
to be extremely good or enjoyable • *Their chocolate cake is just out of this world!*

come/go down in the world *British, Australian & American*
move down in the world *American & Australian*
to have less money and a worse social position than you had before • *They used to live in a big house with lots of servants, but they've come down in the world since then.* • *When we had to sell our house and take a small apartment downtown, we felt we'd really moved down in the world.*

OPPOSITE **come/go up in the world** *British, Australian & American* • *Peter and Ann have gone up in the world – they only ever travel first class these days.*

do sb **the world of good**
to make someone feel much healthier or happier • *We had a week away in the sun and it's done us both the world of good.*

have the cares/weight of the world on your **shoulders**
if you look or feel as if you have the cares of the world on your shoulders, you look or feel very worried or sad • *I've never seen such a change in anyone. He looks as if he's got the cares of the world on his shoulders.*

have the world at your **feet**
someone who has the world at their feet is extremely successful and popular • *Only six months after her debut, this young star of the Royal Ballet already has the world at her feet.*

a man/woman of the world
someone who has a lot of experience of life, and is not usually shocked by the way people behave • *You're a man of the world, Roger, I'd appreciate your advice on a rather delicate matter.*

What's the world coming to?
something that you say which means that life is not as pleasant or safe as it was in the past • *What's the world coming to when you can't leave your house for five minutes without someone trying to break in and rob you?*

your **whole world came crashing down around** you
your **whole world (was) turned upside down**
if your whole world comes crashing down around you, something unpleasant happens in your life that suddenly makes you feel very upset or confused • *Suddenly they weren't popular any more, nobody wanted to buy their records, and their whole world came crashing down around them.* • *When I found out he'd had an affair, my whole world turned upside down.*

the world is your **oyster**
if the world is your oyster, you have the ability and the freedom to do anything or go anywhere • *You're young and healthy*

and you've got no commitments, so the world is your oyster.

a world of difference

1 if there is a world of difference between two people or things, they are very different • (usually + **between**) ***There's a world of difference*** *between seeing a film on video and seeing it in the cinema.*

2 if something makes a world of difference, it improves something very much • *A little sympathy* ***makes a world of difference*** *to someone who's been badly treated.*

▶ See also: not **set** the world on fire
think the world of sb

worlds

be worlds apart

if two things or people are worlds apart, they are completely different from each other • *You can't compare a cheap stereo with a top of the range model – they're worlds apart.*

worm

The worm has turned.

something that you say when someone who has always been weak and obedient starts to behave more confidently or take control of a situation • *Yesterday, she just came in and told him to stop bossing her around. The worm has turned!*

a worm's eye view *British & Australian*

if you have a worm's eye view of something, you only know or understand a part of it, usually the worst or least important part • *Set in the Paris underworld, the novel provides us with a worm's eye view of society.*

worried

be worried sick

to be extremely worried • (often + **about**) *Why didn't you call me when you knew you were going to be late? I was worried sick about you!*

worse

be the worse for wear

1 if something is the worse for wear, it is in bad condition or damaged because it has been used a lot • *This sofa is rather the worse for wear, but it will have to do until we can afford a new one.*

2 someone who is the worse for wear is very tired or feeling ill • *I drank far too much and woke up the next morning feeling rather the worse for wear.*

worst

if the worst comes to the worst *British, American & Australian*

if worst comes to worst *American*

something that you say in order to tell someone what you will do if a situation becomes very difficult or serious • *If the worst comes to the worst, we'll have to give them our bed and sleep on the floor.* • *If worst came to worst, could we sell the car to raise some extra cash?*

▶ See also: I/You wouldn't **wish** sth on my/your worst enemy.

worst-case

▶ See: the nightmare/worst-case **scenario**

worth

not **be worth a fig** *old-fashioned*

to not be important or useful • *She's just an ignorant old busybody and her opinions aren't worth a fig.*

not **be worth a hill of beans** *American informal*

to have very little or no value • *None of those guys is worth a hill of beans, so don't worry about what they say.*

be worth its/your **weight in gold**

to be extremely useful or valuable • *A book that could tell me in simple language how to use this computer would be worth its weight in gold.* • *Really good experienced singers are worth their weight in gold to the choir.*

be worth your **while**

if something is worth your while, you will get an advantage if you do it • (often + doing sth) *It's worth your while taking out travel insurance if you are going abroad.*

make sth **worth** your **while** if you tell someone that you will make it worth their while if they do something, you mean you will pay them to do something, especially something bad or illegal • *If you can get us his personal files, we'll make it worth your while.*

▶ See also: not be worth a **dime**
not be worth the **paper** it's/they're printed/written on

any [judge/lawyer/teacher etc.] worth their **salt**

wounds

▶ See: **lick** your wounds

wrack

▶ See: go to rack/wrack and **ruin**

wrap

wrap sb **up in cotton wool** *British & Australian*
to protect someone too much without allowing them to be independent enough • *She wraps that child up in cotton wool as if he's some precious jewel.*

▶ See also: drape/wrap yourself in the **flag**
twist/wrap sb around/round your **little** finger

wraps

take the wraps off sth
to finally let people know about a new product or plan after keeping it secret for a long time • *They have yet to take the wraps off the design for the new opera house.*

under wraps
secret • *The financial details of the case have been **kept** firmly **under wraps**.* • *The identity of the buyer is still under wraps.*

wring

I'll wring your **neck!** *informal*
something that you say when you are very angry with someone • *I'll wring his neck if he does it again.* • *I could wring his neck, I feel so annoyed with him.*

wring your **hands**
to show that you are very sad or anxious about a situation but do nothing to improve it • *It's not enough for us to stand by and wring our hands – we've got to take action.*
hand-wringing • *Until recently, the problem has been a subject for much hand-wringing and little else.*

wringer

put sb **through the wringer**
to make someone have a very difficult or unpleasant experience ✍In the past, a wringer was a machine used for pressing water out of clothes. • *They really put me through the wringer in my interview.*
go through the wringer • *I went through the wringer to get my first film part.*

writ

be writ large *formal*
to be very obvious • *Anger was writ large in his face.*

writ large *formal*
if something is another thing writ large, it is a clearer or stronger form of that thing • *Hollywood is American society writ large.*

write

be nothing much to write home about
not **much to write home about**
to not be especially good or exciting • *The food was OK, but nothing to write home about.*
OPPOSITE **something to write home about** • *If England won the World Cup, that would be something to write home about!*

▶ See also: fit/write sth on the **back** of a postage stamp

writing

▶ See: the writing is on the **wall**

written

be written all over sb's **face**
if an emotion is written all over someone's face, it is clearly shown in their face • *Any fool could see you weren't happy – it was written all over your face.*

It's written in the stars.
something that you say which means something good was was caused by the power that is believed to control what happens to people's lives • *It was written in the stars that we should meet and fall in love.*

wrong

be (on) the wrong side of 30/40 etc.
to be older than 30, 40 etc. • *I don't know his exact age but I should say he's the wrong side of fifty.*
OPPOSITE **be (on) the right side of 30/40 etc.** • *She's not a kid anymore but she's certainly on the right side of (=* younger than*) 30.*

be in the wrong
to have done something which is wrong, for which you should be blamed • *If they failed to notice the damage, they're definitely in the wrong.* • *I fully accept that I was in the wrong and I think I ought to apologize.*

be on the wrong end of sth
to suffer the bad effects of something • *Companies that violate this law can find themselves on the wrong end of big law suits.*

be on the wrong track
to be doing something in a way that will cause you to fail • *I think the government's on the wrong track with this latest policy.*

Don't get me wrong. *informal*
something that you say before you express an opinion about someone or something and you do not want people to think that you are criticizing that person or thing too severely • *Don't get me wrong, I like Carol, I just think she has some irritating habits.*

get (hold of) the wrong end of the stick *informal*
to not understand a situation correctly • *Her friend saw us arrive at the party together and got hold of the wrong end of the stick.* • *I said how nice he was and Julie got the wrong end of the stick and thought I wanted to go out with him.*

get on the wrong side of the law
find yourself **on the wrong side of the law**
to be in trouble with the police because you have done something illegal • *From last Monday, owners of fighting dogs who fail to control them in public could find themselves on the wrong side of the law.*

go down the wrong way
if food or drink goes down the wrong way, it goes down the wrong tube in your throat and makes you cough or stop breathing for a short time • *I'm all right, it's just a piece of chicken that went down the wrong way.*

take sth **the wrong way**
to feel that someone is criticizing you when in fact they are not • ***Don't take this the wrong way**, Jonathan, but at 33 aren't you getting a bit old for this game?* • *If ever I make a suggestion, she always takes it the wrong way and we end up arguing.*

▶ See also: **back** the wrong horse
be **barking** up the wrong tree
get out of **bed** on the wrong side
fall into the wrong hands
rub sb up the wrong way
the other/wrong **side** of the tracks

wrote

That's all she wrote! *American informal*
something that you say when something has come to an end and there is nothing more that you can say about it • *We went out twice – once to the movies and once to a restaurant and that's all she wrote.*

yank

▶ See: pull/yank sb's **chain**

year

from/since the year dot *British & Australian*
from/since the year one *American*
for a very long time • *Children have been fascinated by ghost stories since the year dot.*

▶ See also: the **seven** year itch

years

put years on sb
to make someone look or feel much older • *The breakup of his marriage put years on him.*
OPPOSITE **take years off** sb • *Losing all that weight has taken years off her.*

yellow

yellow journalism *American*
writing in newspapers that tries to get people's attention or influence their opinions by using strong language or false information • *The paper is practising yellow journalism at its worst with its scandalous stories about the Governor and his family.*

yellow-bellied

yellow-bellied *old-fashioned*
a yellow-bellied person is not at all brave • *You're a load of yellow-bellied fools, too frightened to stand up for what you believe in!*

yes

a yes man
someone who agrees with everything their boss or leader says in order to please them • *He denies that he's simply a yes man, and insists he'll be making major changes to the way the club is run.*

you

▶ See: You should be so **lucky**!
You can **talk**!

young

young blood
young people in an organization who will provide new ideas and energy • *These companies are suffering from a lack of young blood.*

your

▶ See: Your **guess** is as good as mine.

Zz

zero-sum

a zero-sum game
a situation where two people compete and if one of them wins anything, exactly the same must be lost by the other • *Radio has become a zero-sum game, with stations gaining listeners only at each other's expense.*

zone

in the zone *mainly American informal*
If you are in the zone, you are happy or excited because you are doing something easily and with skill. • *My legs are feeling strong and my breathing is good – I'm in the zone!*

Topic Pages

Agreeing and disagreeing

Anger

Euphemisms

Everyday life

Explaining and understanding

Friends and family

Happiness and sadness

Health

Idioms in conversation

Idioms in formal writing

Memory

Money

New idioms

Telling stories

Work and business

agreeing and disagreeing

agreeing

• share some of the same opinions and ideas
*There's more **common ground** between the two groups than you'd expect.*
• completely agree
*On this issue, he seems to **be at one with** his French counterpart.*
*All the major political parties **are of the same mind** on this.*
• a way of showing you agree completely with what someone has just said
*'It's really hot out there.' 'Yeah, **you can say that again**!'*

expressing the same opinions

• expressing similar beliefs and opinions, especially in public
*At least the manager and chairman are now **speaking/talking the same language**.*
*We need to ensure that everyone on the board is **singing from the same hymn sheet/ song sheet**.*
• do or say what you have been told to do or say
*Do you think party members will **toe the line** on this issue?*
*Some other board members were reluctant to **fall into line**.*

having and expressing different opinions

• have different opinions
*They **don't see eye to eye** on some key issues.*
*The government and scientists **are at odds** over the possible effects to health.*
• a formal way of disagreeing
*'**I beg to differ/disagree**. I don't think that was his intention at all.'*
• a way of saying that you cannot change your opinion
*'I see your point, but **be that as it may**, I can't agree to a new date now.'*

starting or causing an argument

• say something that causes trouble and makes people angry
*She really **put the cat among the pigeons** by claiming that sexism was widespread in the company.*
• pretend to have an opposite point of view to make people discuss something
*Sometimes an interviewer has to **play devil's advocate** to put the other side of the argument forward.*
• do something that is likely to cause a serious disagreement
*The proposal is bound to **put** the minister **on a collision course** with the unions.*
• something that people argue about
*Human rights remain the main **bone of contention**.*

anger

being in a bad mood

- be in a bad mood

He'd been ***like a bear with a sore head*** *since they left the pub.*

I'd avoid Tom, I think he ***got out of bed the wrong side*** *this morning.*

- be in a bad mood because you've been treated unfairly

We ***felt*** *a bit* ***hard done by*** *because they left us to clear up all the mess.*

- when you say something unpleasant because you are jealous

His criticism is bound to sound like ***sour grapes****.*

being angry

- very angry

I've just seen Anita and she's ***hopping mad.***

Students are ***up in arms*** *over plans to increase their fees.*

- so angry with something that you do not want to continue with it

I've ***had it up to here*** *with her behaviour – something's got to change!*

annoying someone

- annoy someone

Roger was really ***getting on*** *my* ***nerves/getting up*** *my* ***nose*** *with all his silly comments.*

The way she always thinks she knows better really ***gets my goat****.*

- annoy someone without intending to

Jean does have a habit of ***rubbing*** *people* ***up the wrong way****.*

- be very annoying

His brother is only six and ***is a*** *right* ***pain in the neck****.*

making someone angry

- make someone very angry

My neighbours are ***driving*** *me* ***round the bend/up the wall*** *with their loud music.*

When I hear about things like that it ***makes*** *my* ***blood boil*** *– it's just so unfair.*

losing your temper

- suddenly become very angry and start shouting

Then he just ***went off on one*** *– screaming and shouting uncontrollably.*

My boss is going to ***hit the roof/ceiling*** *when he finds out about this.*

My parents would ***go spare*** *if I dropped out of college now.*

He's going to ***blow a fuse*** *if it doesn't work this time.*

I'm sorry, I should not have ***blown*** *my* ***top*** *like that.*

She saw the mess and ***flew off the handle*** *again.*

She was always calm and controlled and never ***lost*** *her* ***rag*** *with the boys.*

euphemisms

Euphemisms are polite or indirect ways of saying things which might seem rude or offend people.

going to the toilet

• a polite way of saying you are going to the toilet

*'Where's Ann?' 'She's just gone to **powder** her **nose**.'*

*I must just go and **spend a penny** before we go out.*

• a very informal way of saying you are going to the toilet

*Hang on a moment, I'm just going to **take a leak**.*

• a polite way of saying that someone needs to go to the toilet

*Eventually he had to nip out to **answer the call of nature**.*

*What do you do if you**'re caught short** when you're out on a hike?*

death

• an informal and humorous way of saying that someone dies

*Two of the main characters **bit the dust** in the first half hour.*

*He inherited a load of cash when his grandmother **popped her clogs**.*

*I like to think that she went to **meet her maker** with a smile on her face.*

• an informal and humorous way of saying that someone is dead

*If it wasn't for her, I'd probably **be six feet under** by now.*

• an informal and humorous way of saying that someone is going to die

*When I saw the gun, I thought my **number was up**.*

*He'll be **pushing up daisies** within six months.*

swearing

• swearing angrily

*No one wants to hear sportsmen **effing and blinding** like that.*

• swear words

*He came out with a stream of **four-letter words**.*

• a humorous way of apologizing for using a swear word

*He's a cheeky little bastard. **Pardon my French**.*

being pregnant

• a polite way of saying a woman is pregnant

*I hear she's **in the family way** again.*

• a humorous way of saying a woman is pregnant

*Did you know that Katie's **got a bun in the oven**?*

• an informal and not very pleasant way of saying a woman is pregnant

*I can't believe she's got herself **up the spout**.*

*And his girlfriend's **up the duff**.*

everyday life

eating

• a big, healthy meal
You need a good balanced diet with three ***square meals*** *a day.*
• a traditional British meal with a piece of meat and two types of vegetable
We were always dished up a diet of ***meat and two veg.***
• while walking around doing other things
I don't have time for a proper lunch, I usually have a sandwich ***on the hoof.***
• feel a bit hungry
Is there anything in the fridge? I've ***got the munchies.***

chatting

• have a short conversation with someone
She always stops to ***pass the time of day*** *with the postman.*
• talk about your work when you're not working
Will you two stop ***talking shop?***
• talk very quickly without stopping
The bus was full of school children ***talking nineteen to the dozen.***
• not have an opportunity to speak because someone is talking so much
She was so excited, the others ***couldn't get a word in edgeways.***

travelling around

• to leave a place
If we're going to see this movie, we'd better ***make a move.***
Come along, George, we ought to be ***making tracks*** *soon.*
Come on, let's pack up and ***hit the road.***
• driving a car
Nobody should be using a mobile phone when they're ***behind the wheel.***
• increase your speed while driving
(*British, informal*) *Once they were on the motorway, Andy* ***put his foot down.***
• traffic in a line one after another moving slowly or stopped
The traffic was ***bumper to bumper*** *all the way into town this morning.*

sleeping and not sleeping

• go to bed
I don't know about you, but I'm ready to ***hit the sack.***
• sleeping deeply
I just checked on Dan and he's ***out for the count/dead to the world.***
• not sleep at all
I had a rotten night; I didn't ***sleep a wink.***
• work late into the night
He's been ***burning the midnight oil*** *lately trying to get ready for the exams.*
• very early in the morning
We had to get up ***at the crack of dawn*** *to set off across the desert.*

explaining and understanding

explaining

• help people to understand a situation
Anything that would ***shed some light on*** *this situation would be welcome.*
• describe exactly what is causing a situation or problem
Yes, he's selfish, exactly – you've ***hit the nail on the head*** *there, Chris.*
• explain in a way that is very simple and easy to understand
Can you just spell it out for me again ***in words of one syllable****?*
• very clear and easy to understand
They've made it ***crystal clear*** *that I'm not their first choice for the job.*
• the detailed reasons or facts
The whys and wherefores *of the procedures need more explanation.*
It's difficult to grasp all ***the ins and outs*** *of a complex situation in a short visit.*
• the basic, practical details
This page is concerned with ***the nuts and bolts*** *of the trip.*

understanding

• succeed in learning how to do something after practising
He's just about ***got the hang of*** *using the software.*
• succeed in understanding and dealing with something, after making an effort
It took a year to really ***get to grips with*** *the language.*
• be able to understand something
It takes some time to ***get your head around*** *his ideas, but the book's worth reading.*
• understand what someone is trying to tell you
I had to threaten legal action before they finally ***got the message*** *I was serious.*
I don't think she quite ***got/caught my drift****.*
• finally understand the truth of the situation
The penny *finally* ***dropped*** *and she realised he'd been lying all along.*

not understanding

• have no knowledge or information
I ***haven't got a clue*** *where this place is. Do you know where we're going?*
• impossible to understand
The instructions that came with the computer were ***as clear as mud****.*
• not be able to understand something at all
I ***couldn't make head nor tail of*** *the instructions, so I rang up the tax office.*
• be something that you know or understand nothing about
At that time, the whole world of investment ***was a closed book*** *to me.*
• fail to understand what is important about something
I think the critics are ***missing the point****. This isn't meant to be high drama.*
• not understand a situation correctly
I think you've ***got the wrong end of the stick****. I'm not his wife.*

friends and family

good friends

- like each other very much and become friends quickly
The two girls ***got on like a house on fire****.*
- have known each other for a long time
Rachel and I ***go back a long way*** *– we first met at college.*
- spend too much time together
We didn't ***live in each other's pockets****, but we were close.*
- always supporting someone, even in difficult situations
My husband stood by me ***through thick and thin****.*
Michael has been ***a tower of strength*** *for her during this difficult time.*

not good friends

- someone who is only your friend when you are happy or successful
She realised that all her ***fair-weather friends*** *were nowhere to be found.*
- refuse to speak to someone because you do not like them
They used to be friends, but now she ***won't give*** *him* ***the time of day****.*
- to be angry with each other and ready to fight or argue
I thought Ben and Alex were still ***at daggers drawn****.*
- something humorous that you say when a friend treats you badly
I couldn't believe what they'd done. ***With friends like these, who needs enemies?***

important friends

- know important people who can help you
She still ***has friends in high places*** *and can get things done.*
- men from the same expensive school or university who help each other
Many top appointments are still made through ***the old-boy network****.*
- to spend time with important or famous people
She socializes in cool places and ***rubs shoulders with*** *celebrities.*
- be listened to by someone important or powerful
He ***has the ear of*** *the prime minister.*

family

- someone's family
I can't believe I've been so let down by ***my own flesh and blood****.*
It's only natural to worry about the safety of ***your nearest and dearest****.*
- be a quality or ability shared by members of the same family
Being stubborn seems to ***run in the family****.*
She's just like her grandmother, ***a real chip off the old block****.*

happiness and sadness

feeling happy

- feeling very happy

Standing there, receiving the gold medal, I felt ***on top of the world****.*

We were ***full of the joys of spring****, excitedly telling everyone about our trip.*

- very happy and excited because of something good that has happened

She was probably ***jumping for joy*** *when she heard the news.*

He went home ***walking/floating on air*** *and couldn't wait to tell Jan the good news.*

- extremely pleased about something

Dave and Kirsty are both ***thrilled to bits*** *with their new daughter.*

Your father will be ***over the moon*** *when he hears you're back.*

They were ***tickled pink*** *to get a telegram from their hero.*

After getting the call, I was ***on cloud nine*** *for a couple of days.*

When she finally said yes, I was ***in seventh heaven****.*

having fun

- relax and enjoy yourself without worrying what people think

It's a chance for us to ***let*** *our* ***hair down*** *at the end of term.*

- enjoy yourself doing something that involves spending lots of money

As I speak, they'll be ***living it up*** *in Paris.*

- the type of person who has fun and makes other people enjoy themselves

He's usually ***the life and soul of the party****.*

feeling sad

- feeling unhappy and with no energy or enthusiasm

We all feel a bit ***down in the dumps*** *sometimes.*

She seems to have been ***in the doldrums*** *lately.*

He has been more than a little ***down in the mouth*** *over the past few days.*

- looking unhappy

Tim greeted her with ***a long face****.*

disappointments

- looking unhappy

My ***heart sank*** *as I opened the curtains and was greeted by pouring rain.*

- a humorous way of saying you are very disappointed

If I couldn't take part in the race after all this training, I'd be ***sick as a parrot****.*

- stop something from being so enjoyable

Mary's illness rather ***put a damper on*** *the Christmas celebrations.*

- something that is not as exciting as expected

Valentine's Day can end up being a bit of ***a damp squib****.*

- not as good as people say it is

*This new version of the game is****n't all it's cracked up to be****.*

health

feeling slightly ill

- slightly unwell; less healthy than usual

George has been feeling a bit ***under the weather/off colour*** *lately.*

I've been rather tired and achy, and I've just generally been feeling ***below par****.*

- look as if you are going to vomit

She found him up on deck, looking distinctly ***green about the gills****.*

- unable to speak clearly until you cough

Excuse me, I've got ***a frog in*** *my* ***throat****.*

feeling very ill

- very sick, especially vomiting a lot

He was up half the night, ***sick as a dog****.*

- very unwell

This morning she looked ***like death warmed up****, so I told her to stay in bed.*

- very ill or badly injured

He was ***in a bad way*** *after the accident.*

- very ill and close to dying

For several days he was ***at death's door*** *and his family gathered around him.*

treatment and recovery

- have a medical operation, especially plastic surgery

Would you consider ***going under the knife*** *to improve your looks?*

- rest in order to get back your strength and energy

I think he needs some time off to ***recharge*** *his* ***batteries****.*

- recovering after an illness

It's good to see that you're ***on the mend****.*

- well enough to get out of bed and move around

The doctor said he would soon be ***up and about*** *again.*

feeling fit and healthy

- telling someone they are healthy

He went back after six months and was given ***a clean bill of health****.*

- feeling well

It's nothing serious, I'm sure you'll be ***as right as rain*** *in a couple of days.*

- very healthy

He's now nearly 83 and still ***as fit as a fiddle/hale and hearty****.*

They're all ***fighting fit*** *and in the best of health.*

idioms in conversation

agreeing

• used to say you completely agree with someone

'I reckon we've been wasting our time.' ***'You can say that again!'***

• used to agree with someone's description of something

'So they get all the credit and we get nothing?' ***'That's about the size of it.'***

• used to show sympathy for someone's experience, situation, etc.

'I'm struggling to keep up with the work.' ***'Tell me about it!'***

• used to say that the answer to a question is obviously 'yes' (*humorous*)

'Are you sure you want to know?' ***'Is the Pope a Catholic?'***

saying no

• informal ways of emphasizing that you don't want something or won't do something

'Are you going to join in?' ***'No fear!*** *It's really not my thing.'*

'Would you try bungee jumping?' ***'No way!*** *I hate heights.'*

'I can just imagine you on stage.' ***'Not on your life!'***

• used to emphasize that you would never do something

'Would you cheat in an exam?' 'I ***wouldn't dream of it****, would you?'*

I ***wouldn't be seen dead*** *in a suit like that.*

not knowing

• used to say you know nothing about something

'What time is his flight due?' 'I ***haven't got a clue****. He sent you the details.'*

'How long will it take?' 'I'm sorry, I ***haven't got the foggiest/the faintest idea****.'*

'Where did she put the insurance stuff?' ***'Search me!/Your guess is as good*** **as** ***mine****.'*

• used to say that you can't remember something

He was a tall bloke, but I ***can't for the life of me*** *remember his name.*

• used to say that you think you know something, but can't remember it

What was that place called? Oh, it's ***on the tip of*** *my* ***tongue****.*

words and gestures

• something you say to emphasize that you are telling the truth

I didn't touch it. ***Cross my heart and hope to die****!*

I can honestly say, ***hand on heart****, I didn't know anything about it.*

• something you say to wish for good luck in the future

Fingers crossed*, all the decorating will be finished by the time we move in.*

• something you say when you want good luck to continue

We haven't had any major problems so far, ***touch wood****.*

idioms in formal writing

now and in the future

- the subject that is being discussed now

Such details are not relevant to ***the matter at hand****.*

- necessary or used by everyone in this situation

Careful negotiation will be ***the order of the day*** *at the forthcoming conference.*

- at a suitable time in the future

Full prices and specifications will be announced ***in due course****.*

The findings of the investigation will be published ***in the fullness of time****.*

being important

- be the most important thing

We are anxious to identify the best candidate soon as speed ***is of the essence****.*

- that must be done whatever happens

These basic rights must be protected ***at all costs****.*

- be very obvious

In such a system, the pressures on students ***are writ large****.*

- be the only thing that causes something to succeed or fail

The business will ***stand or fall by*** *the quality of its products.*

doubting and contradicting

- cause you to doubt something

Rising costs have once again ***called into question*** *the future of such schemes.*

This case ***begs the question*** *of how we can collect such data.*

- be the opposite of what is usual or expected

This new approach ***flies in the face of*** *established practice in the field.*

- confusing because it contains words with meanings that seem opposite

The idea of an eco-friendly insecticide seems like ***a contradiction in terms****.*

producing results

- using influence to change a situation

Pressure should be ***brought to bear*** *on policy-makers to solve this problem.*

- using something to produce good results

The experience gained in this project will be ***turned to good account*** *in future ventures.*

- produce successful results

Their policy of cautious investment has really ***borne fruit****.*

memory

remembering

- remember things for a long time

*A Gemini is traditionally supposed to **have a memory like an elephant**.*

- learn something so you remember it very well

*He knows all their songs **off by heart**.*

*After a bit of practice he had the whole routine **off pat**.*

*He entered the password, which he'd already **committed to memory**.*

- be easily remembered

*It's one of those images that really **sticks in** your **mind**.*

reminding

- to make someone remember something

*Police are still hoping to **jog the memory of** any witnesses.*

- to make someone think of someone or something

*There's something about her that **puts** me **in mind of** Aunt Glenda.*

- to be something you think you have heard before

*'Have you read his book about the girl in India?' 'It does **ring a bell**.'*

*The name does **have a familiar ring** about it. Wasn't he a friend of Alan's?*

*Anderson? Mm, that name **strikes a chord**.*

- something that suddenly makes you remember something from the past

*'I saw Jane Brady last week.' 'Jane Brady. There's **a blast from the past**. I haven't seen her for years.'*

forgetting

- bad at remembering things

*Hang on, I'd better write it down - I've **got a memory like a sieve**.*

- to forget something immediately because you are not listening

*I've told him a hundred times, but it just **goes in one ear and out the other**.*

- to forget something or to do something

*Oh, I'm sorry Mark, it completely **slipped my mind** in all the excitement.*

- to not be able to remember something at all

*When he asked me for an example, my **mind** just **went blank**, I was so nervous.*

*I know who you mean, but I **can't for the life of me remember** his name.*

- to be completely forgotten

*After the success of his debut album, he seemed to **sink without a trace**.*

money

earning money

• earn money to live on
*We rely on James to **bring home the bacon**.*

• the main work which provides someone's income
*Although lawyers hope for exciting cases, it's burglaries and shoplifting that are **their bread and butter**.*

• make a lot of money
*If you're lucky enough to find an original, then you'll **be quids in**.*
*Anyone who bought property there will be **laughing all the way to the bank**.*

• an easy way to earn money
*Getting paid £12,000 for coming sixth in a race seems like **money for old rope**.*

having a lot of money

• be very rich
*Another holiday? She must be **rolling in it**.*
*If you've **got money to burn**, you could stay at the $500 Palace Hotel.*

• spending a lot of money to make something very good
*The trend seems to be for big weddings with **no expense spared**.*

not having much money

• have only just enough money to live on and no extra
*The family were exiled to France, where they **lived from hand to mouth**.*
*Most of the people in the neighbourhood were struggling to **make ends meet**.*

• using very little money
*The whole film was made **on a shoestring**, using unknown actors.*

• spend very little money in order to save to buy something
*Her mother **scrimped and saved** to buy books for the children.*

costing a lot of money

• cost a lot of money
*That outfit must have **cost a small fortune/a pretty penny/a bomb**!*
*This printer produces good quality prints and it won't **cost an arm and a leg**.*

• pay too much, more than it is worth
*Many football fans are prepared to **pay over the odds/pay through the nose** for a ticket to the final.*

costing a little

• isn't too expensive
*The restaurant serves superb food which **won't break the bank**.*

• pleasant or enjoyable, but not expensive
*Just round the corner there's a **cheap and cheerful** pizzeria.*

• very cheaply
*He spotted a fantastic leather armchair at the auction going **for a song**.*

new idioms

There are new idioms coming into the language all the time. Below are some which have started to become popular recently.

new idioms in conversation

• an American idiom used when you tell someone something you think is surprising, stupid or strange
Their music has no guitar, no bass, no funk: basically, everything people usually want from rock music. Yet they're hugely popular. ***Go figure!***
• used to say that you don't want to talk or think about something because it is too difficult or unpleasant
The bedrooms are damp and cold, the kitchen looks like something from 50 years ago and as for the bathroom - ***don't even go there****.*
• a humorous way of telling someone that what they have said should be kept private or is embarrassing
'She'd planned a romantic candlelit meal. She'd had her hair done and apparently, she'd even bought new silk underwear.' 'Oh, ***too much information****!'*

likes and dislikes

• extremely enjoyable
One enthusiastic customer described the food at the top New York restaurant as ***better than sex****.*
• used to describe a man who is not gay, but has enough of the qualities typical of gay men which women often find attractive
Some think his success with women viewers is down to him being ***just gay enough****.*
• the latest fashionable colour or thing
For fans of the i-Pod, white is ***the new black****.*
• not enjoy something or find it fun or interesting (*informal*)
A lot of people enjoy it, but I've found that running just ***doesn't float my boat****.*

thinking and not thinking

• think imaginatively using new ideas instead of traditional ideas
Years of government-funded programmes have failed to solve the problem. It's time to ***think outside the box****.*
• try to give exact details for something that is impossible to know about exactly
Trying to find out who's to blame for this mess is ***like nailing jelly to the wall****.*
• when an older person forgets something obvious
I ***had*** *a bit of* ***a senior moment*** *and couldn't remember the name of the person I was calling.*
• when someone does or says something particularly stupid
She ***has*** *the occasional* ***blonde moment****, but she's actually quite bright.*
• to be forgotten or ignored
She had a really successful debut album, then ***dropped off the radar****.*

telling stories

in the beginning

- from the start

The whole day was a disaster ***from the word go****.*

- how something seems when you first see it

The hotel seemed, ***at first glance****, nothing special, but once we got inside …*

- start a relationship badly

I first met Alice last year and we ***got off on the wrong foot*** *from the start.*

… something surprising happens

- saying you were very surprised by something you heard/saw

The news came like ***a bolt from the blue****.*

I ***nearly fell off my chair*** *when I heard he'd got the job.*

I ***couldn't believe my eyes*** *when I first walked in.*

I ***could hardly believe my ears*** *when he told me he was eighty.*

- you manage to achieve something by chance, not by skill or planning

I came across the bar ***more by luck than judgement****.*

I got into the business ***more by accident than design****.*

… and another thing

- in addition to something else

She stirred in the cream and the chocolate, then added a dash of brandy, just ***for good measure****.*

The room was cold and damp, and overpriced ***into the bargain****.*

…things get worse

- saying that something unlucky happens to you

It'd be ***just my luck*** *if he's not there when I get there.*

- a bad situation becomes even worse

Then, ***to add insult to injury*** *it started raining even harder.*

Things ***went from bad to worse*** *when the car broke down.*

It never rains, it pours! *Helen just rang to say that she can't make it either!*

- one final bad thing happens after several others

I'd had a rotten day, the traffic was terrible, then, ***to top it all****, Alex was late.*

We'd been delayed by hours and ***to cap it all****, we got stopped at the border.*

… the end of the story

- end badly, with people being upset

You should have known it would all ***end in tears****.*

- stop doing something

Finally at about 9 o'clock it was getting dark, so we decided to ***call it a day****.*

work and business

succeeding in business

• sell a lot quickly
The kebab van in the city centre ***does a roaring trade*** *on a Friday night.*
• earn a lot of money very easily
He's already ***made a killing*** *from his investment in a mobile phone company.*
• become so successful selling something that almost no one else sells it
Back in the seventies, the company ***cornered the market*** *in baby clothing.*
• someone who is very successful at their job
She was ***a high-flier*** *at an advertising agency and had a salary to match.*

failing in business

• fail as a business and close down
If this venture ***goes belly up****, they stand to lose a lot of money.*
If things don't improve soon, the smaller hotels will ***go to the wall****.*
• people stop buying something
After the bombings, ***the bottom fell/dropped out of the*** *tourism* ***market****.*
• stop doing business, either temporarily or permanently
The theatre company was forced to ***shut up shop*** *due to funding cuts.*

working life

• the ordinary people working in a factory, not the managers
We've pushed decision-making closer to the people ***on the factory floor****.*
• explain how to do a job
On my first day in the job, it was Janet who ***showed*** *me* ***the ropes****.*
• while doing your job
He paid tribute to the firefighter who was killed ***in the line of duty****.*
• be a usual part of your job
Talking to presidents and prime ministers ***was all in a day's work*** *for her.*
• have more work than you can deal with
We're absolutely ***snowed under*** *with work at the moment.*

leaving work or losing your job

• leave your job, especially to retire
I'll only retire when I stop enjoying my work – I have no plans to ***hang up*** *my* ***hat*** *just yet.*
• a large sum of money given to someone to leave a company
He's expected to receive ***a golden handshake*** *of $5 million to retire early.*
• be told to leave your job
She ***got the sack/push*** *for being rude to a customer.*
The coach was ***given his marching orders*** *after the team lost five games in a row.*

Exercises

exercises

1. numbers

Complete each of these idioms with a number.

1. I don't know who's to blame - it's probably .... of one and half a dozen of another.
2. Don't ask me to dance – I've got .... left feet!
3. We've been getting requests flooding in from all .... corners of the world.
4. She was clearly on cloud .... after winning her first world title.
5. After Nash was ruled out, the police inquiry was back at square ....

2. colours

Complete each of these idioms with a colour from the box.

white	green	blue	gold	black

1. This incident is a .... mark on an otherwise excellent disciplinary record.
2. We can go ahead with the project as soon as we get the .... light from the council.
3. Sometimes you have to tell .... lies to protect people's feelings.
4. She was as good as .... , not making a noise all the way home.
5. No one was expecting his resignation, it came completely out of the ....

3. animals

Complete each of these idioms with an animal from the box.

snail	fish	cat	crow	elephant

1. John let the .... out of the bag about the party.
2. The traffic was moving at a .... 's pace.
3. We don't want the Olympic stadium to become a white ....
4. When I arrived I felt like a .... out of water.
5. It's probably about 50 miles away as the .... flies.

4. names

Complete the idioms below using the names from the box.

Adam	Bob	Jane	Tom	Jack

1. They don't give out awards to just any old .... , Dick or Harry.
2. To do this job you have to be a .... of all trades.
3. She was a plain .... at school who reinvented herself when she went to drama school.
4. She didn't know me from .... , but she was still very helpful.
5. Just add the sounds and special effects and .... 's your uncle.

exercises

5. senses

Complete these idioms with one of the five senses: see, hear, smell, touch and taste.

1. Will you be quiet – I can't .... myself think!
2. Her reaction took him by surprise, although he should have .... it coming.
3. You should report any transactions that .... fishy.
4. It won't do him any harm to get a .... of his own medicine.
5. He knew full well that he had .... a raw nerve.

6. comparisons: as ... as ...

These idioms all contain a comparison using the form 'as (+adj) as (+noun)'. Fill in the missing words.

1. He went as white as a .... then collapsed on the floor.
2. She went up to the actor as .... as brass and asked him for an interview.
3. It hasn't rained for weeks and the ground's as dry as a ....
4. The dress was made from the finest silk and felt as light as a ....
5. She's a great little kid and as .... as a button.

7. comparisons: verb + like + noun

These idioms contain similes using the form 'verb + like + noun'. Fill in the missing words.

1. He spent his summers .... like a dog on the family farm.
2. When he heard about his father's death, he broke down and cried like a ....
3. He used to .... like a fish and smoke 40 a day.
4. I was obviously tired because I slept like a .... last night.
5. The two brothers are very different and .... like cat and dog.

8. collocations 1

Choose the correct verb to complete these sentences.

1. The proposals could **come/fall/ring** foul of European law.
2. Her illness had/moved/took a turn for the worse and she had to be admitted to hospital.
3. Armstrong has now set/put/placed his sights on a third World Title.
4. The company has decided to take/pull/open the plug on its TV sponsorship deal.
5. He was selling it for less than half the usual price, so I should have heard/sensed/smelled a rat.

exercises

9. collocations 2

Choose the correct adjective to complete these sentences.

1. You're a bit of a **quiet/dark/black** horse. I didn't know you could act.
2. She'd always had a bit of a **favourite/soft/tender** spot for her youngest grandson.
3. From her reaction he knew he'd hit a **raw/sharp/tight** nerve.
4. He has kept a **slight/soft/low** profile since taking over the firm last year.
5. She handed me a copy of the latest edition **hot/fresh/wet** off the press.

10. prepositions

Fill in the gaps with the correct preposition.

1. We make regular unannounced inspections, just to keep everyone **at/in/on** their toes.
2. This move seems to fly **at/in/from** the face of recent trends.
3. He saw fatherhood as a chance to turn **in/over/out** a new leaf and give up drugs once and for all.
4. By this time we were all soaked **in/from/to** the skin.
5. Turning back at such a late stage was simply out **down/of/away from** the question.

11. verb forms

Put the verbs in brackets in the correct form to complete the idioms.

1. He doesn't stand a cat in hell's chance of (win) .... the match.
2. She had half a mind (run) .... after him.
3. The manager took a lot of flak for (change) .... the squad.
4. He stopped short of (accuse) .... the minister of lying.
5. Please feel free (try) .... anything on if you like.

12. questions

Match the questions to the contexts in which they might be used.

1. What's eating him?	a. When somebody has said something that is obviously true
2. Is the Pope a Catholic?	b. When somebody doesn't have enough ideas to make a plan work
3. What more do you want – jam on it?	c. When you offer somebody a drink
4. Where's the beef?	d. When you want to know why somebody is angry
5. What's your poison?	e. When you think somebody should be grateful for what they've been offered

exercises

13. pairs of words

Use words from the box to complete these idioms using pairs of words.

dribs	nooks	fingers	hustle	intents
thumbs	crannies	drabs	purposes	bustle

1. Are you looking to get away from the .... and .... of the city?
2. The dust inevitably gets into all the little .... and ....
3. People turn up in .... and .... from the surrounding villages.
4. I can never tie them properly, I'm all .... and ....
5. By last June, the docks had to all .... and .... closed.

14. rhyming pairs

Complete these compounds which contain pairs of rhyming words.

1. His films are often labelled arty-.......... .
2. We need practical ideas, not airy-.......... notions about equality.
3. Try not to get involved in any argy-.......... .
4. He's trying to shake off his fuddy-.......... image.
5. Don't listen to any of the office tittle-.......... .

15. metaphor: life as a journey

Life is often described as a journey. Choose the correct word to complete these idioms.

1. He felt he was at a **turning/crossroads/junction** in his career.
2. After his brother died, he went off the **road/path/rails** and turned to drink.
3. Their **routes/ways/paths** crossed again years later when they worked on a film together.
4. It's a haven for those seeking an escape from life in the fast **lane/road/track**.
5. At 35, as a professional player he's considered over the **way/bridge/hill**.

16. metaphor: cold is unfriendly

People or actions which are unfriendly or have no emotion are often described as being cold. Match these cold idioms to their meanings.

1. a cold fish	a. behave to somebody in an unfriendly way
2. give somebody the cold shoulder	b. not cause somebody to feel emotion
3. in cold blood	c. not include somebody in an activity
4. leave somebody cold	d. an unfriendly person who doesn't show emotions
5. leave somebody out in the cold	e. in a way that is cruel and without emotion

17. British and American idioms

Some idioms have a different form in British and American English. Rewrite these British idioms in American English.

1. It's been a great year and this award is just the icing on the cake.
2. I'd take anything he says with a pinch of salt.
3. Lee's injury has thrown a spanner in the works.
4. The house would be ideal for somebody with green fingers.
5. I wouldn't touch a company like that with a barge pole.

18. idioms including foreign words

Choose a phrase from the box to complete the idioms below.

plus ça change	au fait	compos mentis
ad nauseum	volte face	

1. The minister has done a complete .... over this policy.
2. You could go on almost .... listing her achievements.
3. I don't know how .... you are with the situation.
4. By all accounts she remained .... right up to her death.
5. The first I knew of it was when I read it in the paper – .... !

19. playground language

Match these words and phrases which children might use to describe people with their explanations.

1. goody-goody
2. cry-baby
3. scaredy-cat
4. bossy boots
5. ants in your pants

a. sb who can't keep still
b. sb who cries too easily
c. sb who tells people what to do
d. sb who is easily frightened
e. sb who tries too hard to please the teacher

20. people

Match the idioms to describe people on the left with the explanations on the right.

1. a fat cat
2. a bad egg
3. a pen pusher
4. a live wire
5. a couch potato

a. a quick, active person
b. an inactive person
c. an office worker
d. a rich business person
e. a dishonest person

exercises

21. places

Complete the idioms in these sentences which describe places.

1. I earn just enough to keep a roof over our .... and put food on the table.
2. I grew up in a tiny little village in the back of ....
3. Since their parents divorced, the poor kids have been pushed from pillar to ....
4. The hotel is ideal for those who want to avoid the hoards of tourists and stay somewhere a little off the beaten ....
5. We broke down on a mountain road in the middle of ....

22. problems

Complete the idioms below describing problems using words from the box.

fly	cloud	iceberg	can	stone

1. The only .... in the ointment is that it isn't available at weekends.
2. Next week's safety inspection is the only .... on the horizon.
3. The investigation into election fraud opened up a whole .... of worms.

4. It seems that the current allegations are only the tip of the ....
5. Finding out about her background was like getting blood out of a ....

23. time

Put the idioms in the box into the three groups below.

the year dot	for the time being	the mists of time
down the line	all in good time	

Past:

Present:

Future:

24. age

Which of these people are old and which are young? Mark the sentences O or Y.

1. Jane's a bit long in the tooth for that, isn't she?
2. Some might say he's past it.
3. I've known him since I was knee-high to a grasshopper.
4. He's been around the block a few times.
5. Georgia learnt to cook at her mother's knee.

exercises

25. emotions

These idioms all contain verbs for physical actions but actually describe emotions or reactions. Use the correct form of the verbs in the box to complete the sentences.

jump	lick	grit	swallow	kick

1. The Australian captain must be .... for joy at this news.
2. He must be .... himself now for not accepting her offer.
3. After this embarrassing defeat, they went home to .... their wounds.
4. You'll just have to .... your teeth and carry on for a bit longer.
5. It was a bitter pill to .... after all their hard work.

26. travel

Complete these idioms about travel.

1. I was getting itchy .... and started planning my next trip.
2. It took me some time to find my sea ....
3. We stopped off in Hong Kong en .... to Australia.
4. It's a whistle-stop .... of 11 European cities.
5. We put on our hiking boots and headed off into the wild .... yonder.

27. abilities

Which of these people are clever and which ones are stupid? Mark the sentences C or S.

1. Dan's as thick as two short planks.
2. She's one smart cookie, that sister of yours.
3. Alice always was a bit slow on the uptake.
4. Those guys really know their onions.
5. James has obviously got his head screwed on.

28. idioms using 'dead'

Find an idiom beginning with 'dead' to match the definitions.

1. something very disappointing: a dead ....
2. a situation in which no progress can be made: a dead ....
3. people who are not useful any more: dead ....
4. something that is very likely to happen: a dead ....
5. somebody who is going to be punished severely: dead ....

29. idioms using 'break'

Find an idiom beginning with 'break' to match the definitions.

1. not make money or lose money in business: break ....
2. something you say to wish an actor good luck: break a ....
3. publicly show you disagree with your group: break ....
4. say something to start a conversation: break the ....
5. make somebody feel very sad: break somebody's ....

answers

1. numbers
1. six 2. two 3. four 4. nine 5. one

2. colours
1. black 2. green 3. white 4. gold 5. blue

3. animals
1. cat 2. snail 3. elephant 4. fish 5. crow

4. names
1. Tom 2. Jack 3. Jane 4. Adam 5. Bob

5. senses
1. hear 2. seen 3. smell 4. taste 5. touched

6. comparisons: as ... as ...
1. sheet 2. bold 3. bone 4. feather 5. bright

7. comparisons
1. working 2. baby 3. drink 4. log 5. fight

8. collocations 1
1. fall 2. took 3. set 4. pull 5. smelled

9. collocations 2
1. dark 2. soft 3. raw 4. low 5. hot

10. prepositions
1. on 2. in 3. over 4. to 5. of

11. verb forms
1. winning 2. to run 3. changing 4. accusing 5. to try

12. questions
1. d 2. a 3. e 4. b 5. c

13. pairs of words
1. hustle, bustle 2. nooks, crannies 3. dribs, drabs 4. fingers, thumbs 5. intents, purposes

14. rhyming pairs
1. farty 2. fairy 3. bargy 4. duddy 5. tattle

15. metaphor: life as a journey
1. crossroads 2. rails 3. paths 4. lane 5. hill

16. metaphor: cold is unfriendly
1. d 2. a 3. e 4. b 5. c

17. British and American idioms
1. It's been a great year and this award is just the **frosting** on the cake.
2. I'd take anything he says with a **grain** of salt.
3. Lee's injury has thrown a **wrench** in the works.
4. The house would be ideal for somebody with a green **thumb**.
5. I wouldn't touch a company like that with a **ten-foot** pole.

18. idioms including foreign words
1. volte face 2. ad nauseum 3. au fait 4. compos mentis 5. plus **ç**a change

19. playground language
1. e 2. b 3. d 4. c 5. a

20. people
1. d 2. e 3. c 4. a 5. b

21. places
1. heads 2. beyond 3. post 4. track 5. nowhere

22. problems
1. fly 2. cloud 3. can 4. iceberg 5. stone

23. time
Past: the year dot, the mists of time
Present: for the time being
Future: down the line, all in good time

24. age
1. O 2. O 3. Y 4. O 5. Y

25. emotions
1. jumping 2. kicking 3. lick 4. grit 5. swallow

26. travel
1. feet 2. legs 3. route 4. tour 5. blue

27. abilities
1. S 2. C 3. S 4. C 5. C

28. idioms using 'dead'
1. loss 2. end 3. wood 4. cert 5. meat

29. idioms using 'break'
1. even 2. leg 3. ranks 4. ice 5. heart